THEORY OF SOCIETY, VOLUME I

Cultural Memory
in
the
Present

Mieke Bal and Hent de Vries, Editors

THEORY OF SOCIETY
VOLUME 1

Niklas Luhmann

Translated by Rhodes Barrett

STANFORD UNIVERSITY PRESS
STANFORD, CALIFORNIA

Stanford University Press
Stanford, California

Theory of Society, Volume 1 was originally published in German under the title *Die Gesellschaft der Gesellschaft. Band 1* ©Suhrkamp Verlag Frankfurt am Main 1997.

The translation of this work has been published with the assistance of the Volkswagen Foundation.

Printed in the United States of America on acid-free, archival-quality paper

Library of Congress Cataloging-in-Publication Data

Luhmann, Niklas, 1927–1998, author.
[Gesellschaft der Gesellschaft. English]
Theory of society / Niklas Luhmann ; translated by Rhodes Barrett.
2 volumes cm.--(Cultural memory in the present)
"Originally published in German under the title Die Gesellschaft der Gesellschaft."
Includes bibliographical references and index.
ISBN 978-0-8047-3949-8 (cloth : alk. paper)--ISBN 978-0-8047-3950-4 (pbk. : alk. paper)
1. Sociology. 2. Social systems. 3. Communication. I. Title. II. Series: Cultural memory in the present.
HM590.L84513 2012
301--dc23 2012021883

Typeset by Bruce Lundquist in 11/13.5 Adobe Garamond

Id quod per aliud non potest concipi, per se concipi debet.

SPINOZA, *Ethica* I, Axiomata II

That which cannot be conceived through anything else must be conceived through itself (trans. R.H.M. Elwes [1883]).

Contents

Preface

On my appointment to the Department of Sociology established at the University of Bielefeld in 1969, I was asked what research projects I had running. My project was, and ever since has been, the theory of society; term: thirty years; costs: none. As far as the time frame was concerned, my estimation of the difficulties was realistic. At that time, the literature in sociology gave little cause to consider such a project possible at all, not least because neo-Marxist precepts blocked any ambition of producing a theory of society. My discussion with Jürgen Habermas was published shortly afterward under the title *Theorie der Gesellschaft oder Sozialtechnologie—Was leistet die Systemforschung?* (Theory of Society or Social Technology: What Does Systems Research Accomplish?) [Frankfurt, 1971]. The irony of the title was that neither author wished to stand up for social technology, but we differed on what a theory of society ought to be; and it is symptomatic that the theory of society first came to public attention in the form, not of a theory, but of a controversy.

My initial plan had been to publish the theory of society in three parts: an introductory chapter on systems theory, a treatment of the societal system, and a third part dealing with the most important functional systems of society. The basic concept has remained, but I have had to correct my ideas about the size of the undertaking more than once. In 1984, I brought out the "introductory chapter" in book form under the title *Soziale Systeme: Grundriß einer allgemeinen Theorie* (Social Systems: Outline of a General Theory).[1] In essence, my aim was to apply the concept of self-referential operation to the theory of social systems. This aim has not fundamentally changed, although progress in general systems theory and epistemological constructivism has repeatedly offered opportunities to extend it. Some contributions have been published in collections of essays under the title *Soziologische Aufklärung* (Sociological Enlightenment). Other material is available only in manuscript form or has fed into this book.

Since the early 1980s, it has become increasingly clear how important the *comparability* of functional systems is for the theory of society. This had already been a basic consideration in Talcott Parsons's theory construction. The theoretical importance of comparability is even greater if we concede that society cannot be deduced from a principle or a basic norm, be it the customary justice, solidarity, or reasoned consensus. For even those who do not recognize or who violate such principles contribute to societal operations, and society itself must take account of this possibility. On the other hand, it is not by chance that widely differing functional areas such as science and law, economics and politics, the mass media, and intimate relations can be shown to have comparable structures—not least because their differentiation requires systems to be formed. But can this be shown? Parsons attempted to guarantee it through the analytic of the action concept. If the thought is not convincingly elaborated, we can do no more than formulate theories for individual functional systems and test whether, despite all differences between fields, we can work with the same conceptual apparatus—including autopoiesis and operational closure, first- and second-order observation, self-description, medium and form, coding and, in orthogonal relation thereto, the distinction between self-reference and other-reference as internal structure.

As a result, I gave priority to theories for individual functional systems. The following have already been published: *Die Wirtschaft der Gesellschaft* (The Economy as a Social System) (1988), *Die Wissenschaft der Gesellschaft* (Science as a Social System) (1990), *Das Recht der Gesellschaft* (Law as a Social System) (1993),[2] and *Die Kunst der Gesellschaft* (Art as a Social System) (1995).[3] Further texts of this type are to follow. Meanwhile, however, work on the theory of the societal system had also progressed. I had produced several thousand pages of manuscript, partly to accompany lectures, without having put the material in publishable form. My then secretary retired and the position was frozen for many months. In this situation, the University in Lecce offered me an opportunity to work. So I fled to Italy with the project and the manuscripts. There I wrote a short version of the theory of society, which, translated into Italian, revised several times and adapted for use at an Italian university, has since been published.[4] The manuscript then produced became the basis for a more extensive German edition, on which, once again provided with a secretary, I was able to work in Bielefeld. The present text is the result of this eventful history.

The system under consideration is that of society itself, as opposed to all social systems that develop within society in the performance of societal operations: the functional systems of society, as well as interaction systems, organizational systems, and social movements, all of which presuppose that a system of society has already been constituted. The key issue is therefore what operation produces and reproduces this system whenever it occurs. The answer, discussed in Chapter 2, is communication. It is a circular relationship: society cannot be conceived of without communication, nor can communication be conceived of without society. Questions of genesis and morphogenesis cannot be answered by any hypothesis of origin and are obscured rather than resolved by the thesis that "the human being" is genuinely social in nature. Chapter 3 entrusts these questions to an appropriate evolution theory.

The thesis of self-production by communication postulates clear boundaries between system and environment. The reproduction of communications from communications takes place in society. All further physical, chemical, organic, neurophysiological, and mental conditions are environmental conditions. Society can substitute for them within the limits of its own operational capabilities. No human being is indispensable to society. This naturally does not mean that communication is possible without consciousness, without brains well supplied with blood, without life, without a moderate climate.

All systems formed in society depend in turn on communication; otherwise we would not be able to say that they take place in society. It also means that system formations within society cannot connect with any section of the environment. This is true for segmentary differentiation and even more so, across all intermediate stages, for functional differentiation. In the environment of the societal system there are no families, no nobility, no politics, no economy.

The assumption of reflexive self-reference is built into the concept of communication. Communication always communicates that it communicates. It might correct itself in retrospect or deny that it had meant what it appeared to mean. It can be interpreted by means of communication on a scale from credible to incredible. But it is always accompanied by memory, even though it might be only short-term, which practically excludes any assertion that it has not taken place at all. Retrospectively, norms and excuses, tact requirements and counterfactual disregard arise, with which communication detoxifies itself in the event of the occasional malfunction.

This is probably why all societies appear to ensure that communication can relate to the societal system as the framework condition of its own possibility, as the unity of the coherence of communications that is always connoted. Like Parsons, many have inferred the need for basic consensus, shared values, or unthematic, "life-world" concord. I make do with the slimmed-down concept of self-description, which also allows for the existence of fundamental dissension, and that this dissension is communicated about.

With the concept of a system that describes itself and contains its own descriptions, we venture into logically intractable terrain. A society that describes itself does so internally, but as it were from outside. It observes itself as an object of its own knowledge, but in performing its operations, it cannot itself feed the observation into the object, because this would change this object and require further observation. Whether it observes itself from within or without is a question that society has to leave open. If it also attempts to say so, it opts for a paradoxical identity. The solution sociology found has been styled the "critique" of society. Effectively, this amounts to constantly renewed description of descriptions, the constant introduction of new metaphors or reuse of old metaphors, and thus of "redescriptions" in Mary Hesse's sense.[5] This can very well bring new insights, even though methodologically steeled investigators would not accept them as "explanations."

This text is itself an attempt at communication. It seeks to provide a description of society in full knowledge of the predicament outlined. If the communication of a theory of society succeeds as communication, it changes the description of its object and thus the object receiving this description. To keep this in sight from the outset, the book was titled *Die Gesellschaft der Gesellschaft* (The Society of Society).

Translator's Note

Like Prufrock, the translator does well to point out that he is "not Prince Hamlet, nor was meant to be." Even if no more than an "attendant prince" to the author, he must escape the self-deprecation of Eliot's melancholy figure to cultivate his positive qualities: "Deferential, glad to be of use, / Politic, cautious, and meticulous." Taking on the world according to Niklas Luhmann is certainly not a task not to be assumed without humility, caution, and care ("Do I dare / Disturb the universe? / In a minute there is time / For decisions and revisions which a minute will reverse"). And not without a great deal of informed help.

My first venture in the field appeared in 1993 under the title *Risk: A Sociological Theory.*[1] To my great fortune I was able to discuss my efforts with Luhmann to my and his satisfaction.

Without the invaluable, consistent, and ever ready help and advice of the outstanding Luhmann expert Dirk Baecker, the present translation of Volume 1 of *Die Gesellschaft der Gesellschaft* would not have been possible.

THEORY OF SOCIETY, VOLUME I

1

Society as a Social System

1. The Sociological Theory of Society

The investigations that follow address the social system of modern society. Such a project, it should be said at the outset, engages a circular relationship with its subject matter. What this subject matter is cannot be said in advance. The word "society" does not refer to a clear-cut idea. Even the common term "social" has no incontestably objective reference. Nor can the attempt to describe society be made outside of society. It uses communication. It activates social relations. It exposes itself to observation in society. However we define the subject, its definition is itself already one of the latter's functions. What is described performs the description. In so doing it must therefore also describe itself. It must treat its subject as one that describes itself. Borrowing an expression from logical analysis in linguistics, we could say that every theory of society must have an "autological" component.[1] Whoever feels that the theory of science cannot accommodate this must do without a theory of society, linguistics, and much else.

Classical sociology has sought to establish itself as the science of social facts—facts as opposed to mere opinions, value judgments, or ideological prejudices. Within the context of this distinction, this is not to be disputed. The problem, however, is that the ascertainment of facts can enter the world only as fact. Sociology therefore has to take account of its own factuality. This requirement applies throughout its domain of research and is not to be redeemed by a special interest in a "sociology of sociology." This, as we now know, violates the premises of a bivalent, or two-valued, logic.[2] In choosing limited research topics, this can be disregarded on pragmatic grounds. The investigator sees himself as a subject outside his topic. For the purposes of a theory of society, however, this view is untenable, for the work on such a theory necessarily involves self-referential operations. It can be communicated only within the system of society.

Sociology has hitherto failed to address this problem with the necessary stringency and consistency. It has hence failed to produce anything approaching an adequate theory of society. Toward the end of the nineteenth century, any integration of a description of society into its object tended to be seen as "ideology" and, as such, rejected. On this basis, the raising of sociology to the academic status of a strict science would have been inconceivable. Some even felt they should make do without the concept of society and limit themselves to the strictly formal analysis of social relations.[3] Concepts concerned with difference such as individualization and differentiation seemed sufficient to mark the research interests of sociology. Others, notably Emile Durkheim, considered a strictly positive science of "social facts" and of society as the condition for their possibility to be feasible. Still others were satisfied with the distinction between the natural sciences and the humanities and with the historical relativization of all descriptions of society. Whatever the details, the distinction between subject and object was considered binding for epistemological reasons, leaving a choice only between a scientistically naïve and a transcendental theoretical position.

Many of the peculiarities of what are now classical sociologies must be attributed to the limitations of this selection schema and to efforts to get by nonetheless. This can be said of the strange links between transcendentalism and social psychology we find in Georg Simmel. And of Max Weber's value theoretical concept of action, a loan from Neo-Kantianism. It is also true of Helmut Schelsky's call for a "transcendental theory of society" beyond the reach of normal empirical methods, which, attaching the concept of "transcendental" to the individual subject, made no headway.[4] These positions are now interesting at best for interpreting the classics. In spite of this unquestioned commitment to the subject/object schema and despite the insoluble problem of its subject matter, classical sociology has produced the only description of society to date. This perhaps best explains the lasting fascination the sociological classics continue to exert, which in a strict sense has made seemingly timeless texts of them. Almost all theoretical endeavors today are concerned with retrospection and reconstruction. It is well worth considering what made this success possible.

Without acknowledging a circular relationship with the subject matter! That much can be said. The solution, which hid the problem from the classics, lay in a historical self-location, in the dissolution of the circle by a historical difference in which the theory could define itself historically (and only historically). Nascent sociology had reacted to the structural and semantic problems that had arisen in the nineteenth century, and was aware of having done so. Even where it expressed concepts in abstract terms, they owed their plausibility to the historical situation. The end of confidence in progress had to be accepted; a belief in the positive nature of development at whatever cost was replaced by structural analysis, above all, by analysis of social differentiation, organizational dependencies, and role structures. The economy-focused ("political economy") concept of society that had held sway since the final decades of the eighteenth century could thus be abandoned. This provoked controversy between those who defined society in material (economic) terms and those who adopted a more intellectual (cultural) approach. At the same time, the position of the individual in modern society became the central problem, a referential problem, so to speak, inviting a skeptical view of society as a whole, which could no longer automatically be considered progressive. Concepts such as socialization and role signaled the need for theoretical mediation between the "individual" and "society." Together with the historical difference, this distinction between "individual" and "society" provided a basis for theory formation. But, as in the case of history, this context could not accommodate the question of the distinction's unity. To ask what history is was ruled out methodologically,[5] and what constituted the unity of the difference between individual and society was not even recognized as a problem, because, in keeping with the entire tradition, society was assumed to be composed of individuals. This was then the basis for a "critical" analysis of society, which was not to be "deconstructed" by questions about the unity of the difference between individual and society. In Max Weber, finally, the skepticism such a theoretical approach permitted went so far as to affect assessment of modern Western rationalism. Nor should it be forgotten that a literature arose at the same time that demonstrated that neither within nor outside society does the modern individual find a secure basis for self-observation, self-realization, or, to use the fashionable term, "identity." It suffices here to mention Flaubert, Mallarmé, Henry Adams, and Antonin Artaud.[6]

Since the classics, sociology has made no progress worth mentioning toward a theory of society in the course of the past 100 years or so. Following the unwelcome ideology dispute of the nineteenth century, the paradox of communication *about* society *in* society was addressed in theoretical controversy by such oppositions as structuralist/processualist, domination/conflict, affirmative/critical, and even conservative/progressive.[7] However, since maintaining a position within such "frames" required confrontation with the contrary position and thus the inclusion of exclusion, opting for one side rather than the other was always infected with paradox, and to unfold paradox through controversy was convincing only where it made political sense. Given the inherent dynamism of the political system, this has proved less and less convincing, even though intellectuals have continued to play such games. There is no denying that sociology has achieved much in other fields, both methodologically and theoretically and especially in the collection of empirical knowledge; but it has, so to speak, omitted to describe society as a whole. This presumably has to do with its commitment to the subject/object distinction. There has indeed been specific research into a "sociology of sociology," and a sort of "reflexive" sociology of science has recently emerged.[8] Problems of self-reference arise in such contexts, but they are, as it were, isolated as special phenomena and treated as peculiarities or methodological difficulties. The same can be said of the "self-fulfilling prophecy" trope.

The only systematic sociological theory currently available was elaborated by Talcott Parsons as a general theory of the action system. It provides a codification of classical sociological knowledge and a treatment of the conceptual understanding of action with the aid of cross-tabulation. But it fails to answer the question of cognitive self-implication, because it has nothing to say about the degree of congruence between analytical conceptualization and actual system formation. It merely postulates an "analytical realism," thus reducing the problem of self-implication to a paradoxical formula. What it leaves out of account is that the cognition of social systems depends on social conditions, not only on account of its object, but also as cognition; indeed, the cognition (or definition or analysis) of actions are themselves actions. Parsons consequently does not himself occur in any of the many boxes of his own theory. And this is ultimately why the theory cannot distinguish systematically between social system and society; it only offers impressionistic, more or less feuilletonistic views of modern society.[9]

In the long course of history, the description of human social life (for more ancient times, we can speak of "society" only with reservations) was guided by ideas insufficiently congruent with existing reality. This was true of the old European tradition, with its characteristic sense of the natural perfectibility of humankind and its pursuit of education and the forgiveness of sins. But it still holds true for modern Europe, for the Enlightenment and its double deity Reason and Critique. Even in the present century, this awareness of inadequacy has been kept alive (see Husserl or Habermas) and associated with the notion of modernity. Richard Münch still considers this focus on the tension between reason and reality to be a basic characteristic of modernity and an explanation for its distinctive dynamics.[10] However, the sense of problem has now shifted from ideas to reality itself; *and only now is sociology called upon*. First, we have to understand why society causes itself so many problems, even if we forgo any proposals for improvement (more solidarity, emancipation, reasoned agreement, social integration, etc.). Sociology must understand its relationship with society as one of learning, not instruction. It must analyze the problems it discovers, possibly postpone tackling them, possibly declare them insoluble, albeit without knowing how to proffer "scientifically proven" solutions. All this requires a theoretically grounded description of modern society.

If sociology has to admit to not having produced a theory of society in this format, how can it explain this failure to perform a task so clearly within its purview and of such importance for its standing in society?

It can obviously be argued that society is immensely complex, and that a practicable methodology for dealing with highly complex and differentiated systems (so-called organized complexity) is lacking. This argument is all the more weighty if we point out that the description of the system is part of the system, and that there can be a plurality of such descriptions. The conventional methodology, which operates on a very small scale or under conditions appropriate for statistical analysis, is particularly unsuited for "hypercomplex" systems of this sort. But this argument necessarily prompts renunciation of a theory of society and restricts efforts to develop methods for dealing with highly complex or even hypercomplex systems. But this has been done anyway, although with little success, since the discovery of the methodological problem some fifty years ago.[11]

Another consideration might be headed "epistemological obstacles" ("obstacles épistémologiques," a term coined by Gaston Bachelard),[12] referring to burdens of tradition that prevent adequate scientific analysis and raise expectations that can neither be met nor, despite these evident weaknesses, replaced.[13] Tradition might be said to have responded to natural questions, and therefore to have provided largely convincing answers. As science evolved, however, these natural questions gave way to theory-dependent scientific problems whose solution could be judged only in the scientific context. In retrospect, the guiding principles of these *obstacles épistémologiques* are insufficiently complex; they overestimate themselves and result in a uniformization of the object matter that is finally no longer convincing. Not only have the answers we now require become more difficult (more contingent, more improbable, less convincing); extant questions and answers obstruct further development, which has to detour via implausible evidence.

Such epistemological obstacles are to be found in the prevailing understanding of society in the form of four interconnected, mutually reinforcing assumptions:

(1) that society consists of actual people and relations between people[14]

(2) that society is constituted or at least integrated by consensus among human beings, by concordant opinion and complementary purpose

(3) that societies are regional, territorially defined entities, so that Brazil as a society differs from Thailand, and the United States from Russia, as does Uruguay from Paraguay

(4) that societies, like groups of people and like territories, can be observed from outside

Assumptions 1 to 3 prevent precise conceptual definition of the subject "society." The "human being" (as opposed to animals) was traditionally described on the basis of distinctions (such as reason, intelligence, will, imagination, emotion, morality), received ideas that, although revised, were specified neither empirically nor in their mode of operation. These distinctions seemed to suffice for mutual clarification, but their neurophysiological basis remained unclear.[15] In particular, these "anthropological" concepts offer no possibility for connecting with the psychic/social distinction. The difficulties grow if we abandon these distinctions in favor of scientific and empirical denotability. The problematization of human individuality with regard to the nature of the individual's associations and affective development began in about the mid-eighteenth century, long before the industrial revolution.[16] This exploded the traditional positioning of the human being in an order that gave him status and a way of life. Instead, the relationship between the individual and society became a problem. However traditional concepts, especially "reason" are maintained, it is clear that not everything that individuates the human being (if anything at all about him) belongs to society. Society does not weigh exactly as much as all human beings taken together, nor does its weight change with every birth and death. It is not reproduced, for example, by an exchange of macromolecules in the individual cells of a person or by the exchange of cells in the organisms of individual human beings. It is therefore not alive. Nor would anyone seriously regard neurophysiological processes in the brain inaccessible to consciousness as societal processes, and the same is true of all perceptions and trains of thought occupying the attention of the individual consciousness at a given time. Georg Simmel, who attributed this problem to modern individualism, preferred in the circumstances to sacrifice the concept of society rather than his sociological interest in individuals. Aggregate concepts, as he saw the problem, were questionable and should be replaced by relational theories. After all, he pointed out, astronomy was not a theory of the "starry sky."[17]

If it is no longer obvious that society by its nature comprises actual human beings whose solidarity is prescribed as *ordinata concordia* [well-ordered concord] and in particular as *ordinata caritas* [well-ordered love], a theory of consensus can step in with a substitute concept. In the seventeenth and eighteenth centuries, this led to the resuscitation and radicalization of the theory of social contract.[18] At least in Hobbes, the concept of nature is reduced to the extrasocial domain, in other authors (such as Pufendorf) to an inclination for contract formation. However, this theory soon had to be abandoned. It was a legally circular construction and thus unable to explain the absolute and permanent binding force of the contract; and, in the light of rapidly growing historical knowledge, it could be handled historically only as a fiction without explanatory value. It was superseded in the nineteenth century by consensus theories and by a notion of solidarity and integration on the basis of consensus. Finally, in still weaker dilution, "legitimacy" was demanded for institutions able to impose order even in the absence of consensus, and therefore against resistance. Thus, with Emile Durkheim and Max Weber, sociology begins. Despite all concessions to reality, integration on the basis of consensus has remained the principle by which society is identified as an entity—one might say as an "individual."

However, the whole theoretical system collapses if we inquire more closely into how consensus is to be possible at all in a psychically actualizable sense, and, moreover, how interacting expectations are to be adequately coordinated. Max Weber had taken a first step by reducing the problem to a type-constraint principle as the condition for understanding socially intended meaning. Talcott Parsons, in keeping with Durkheim, sees the solution in a consensus on values that reacts to growing differentiation by growing generalization. Although this built-in abstention from concretization took account of the individuality of actors and the complexity of the societal system, it so diluted what remained of the society concept that the theory could at best function only in sufficiently dense subsections of society. Moreover, against our better judgment, we would then have to deny that social conflicts, dissent, and deviant behavior are part of society, or make do with the assertion that they, too, presuppose some sort of consensus (for example, about the offensive value of certain abuse). John Rawls conversely feels obliged to postulate that the circumstances under which contract-like principles of justice are established are concealed by a "veil of ignorance," which prevents individuals from knowing their position and interests;[19] he thus posits individuals without individuality. This is merely another way of obscuring the paradox of every return to origins.

Another consequence of the assumption that individuals materialize society through their behavior lies in the hypothesis that structural problems of society (e.g., excessive differentiation without sufficient integration, or contradictions in the structures and behavioral expectations of society) manifest themselves in *deviant individual behavior* and can be empirically ascertained in such behavior. The classical monograph on the subject is Durkheim's study on suicide.[20] But family instability, crime, drug taking, or withdrawal from social engagement could also be mentioned.

While people may react to anomie however they choose, we are dealing in essence with functionally equivalent attitudes that serve the sociologist as indicators of problems whose roots he has to seek in society. But even if such correlations could be demonstrated statistically, the question remains of how the individual comes—or fails—to display symptoms of societal pathologies. Particularly important to consider are the structural problems of society in any way liable to translate into deviant individual behavior. This question is imposed not least by ecological problems.

All this should give sociology cause to doubt whether consensual integration is of any *constitutive* importance for a society at all. After all, it would suffice to assume that, as communication proceeds, it generates identities, references, eigenvalues, objects—whatever the individual human being experiences when confronted by it.[21]

This line of reflection converges with a version of systems theory that focuses constitutively (with respect to concept and reality) on the distinction between system and environment. If we accept the system/environment distinction, the human being as a living and consciously sentient being must be assigned either to the system or to the environment (dividing a human into halves or thirds for distribution between the two sides is empirically impossible). If we see the human being as part of the societal system, we are obliged to construct the theory of differentiation as a theory of the distribution of human beings—be it among strata, nations, or ethnic or other groups. This brings us into conspicuous conflict with the concept of human rights, especially the concept of equality. Any "humanism" of this ilk would thus founder on its own conceptions. The only option is to regard human beings in their entirety, body and soul, as part of the environment of the societal system.

If, despite all obvious discrepancies and the well-known philosophical criticism of its anthropological foundations,[22] a human-centric, "humanistic" concept of society is maintained,[23] this is presumably owing to the fear that every standard for judging society and every right to demand that society be "humanely" constructed would have to be abandoned. Even if this were the case, we would still, regardless of such criteria, first have to ascertain what society makes of people and why.

Similarly evident objections can be raised to the territorial concept of society.[24] More than ever before, worldwide interdependencies now intervene in all the details of societal occurrences. Were we to ignore this, we would have to fall back on a concept of society defined in terms of domination or on a culturally nostalgic concept. We would have to make the concept of society dependent on arbitrarily drawn national borders,[25] or, in spite of all concomitant uncertainties, focus on the unity of a regional "culture," on language and the like. All the conditions relevant for further development would be left to another concept, for instance, the "global system."[26] For Anthony Giddens, the concept of society equates with that of nation-state, and it is therefore almost superfluous; we are then left with the "world-embracing" nature of modern institutions.[27] But this would make the concept of global system the successor to what was traditionally called "society" (*societas civilis*). If we tie the concept of society to a premise of centralized power or values, we underestimate not only the diversity and complexity of communicative circumstances at the regional level but also the extent of worldwide, decentralized, and connectionistic communication via networks in the "information society"—a tendency that computerization is likely to intensify still further in the foreseeable future.

Humanistic and regionalistic (national) concepts of society are theoretically no longer acceptable; they survive only in colloquial usage. Current sociological theory leaves a contradictory, Janus-faced impression: it uses concepts that have not yet abandoned tradition, but that enable questions that could explode its framework.[28] To adjust to eventual fundamentals, it treats action as a basic concept, continually recalling that only individual human beings can act. The notion of the global system enables it to acknowledge globalization, while leaving the concept of society at the level of the nation-state.

In the case of the anthropocentric concept of society, too much is included; in that of the territorial concept, too little. In both cases, this insistence on such unserviceable concepts may have to do with the desire to think about society as something that can be observed from outside. However, we must then rely on a long-since obsolete theory of cognition, a theory based on the distinctions between thought/being, knowledge/object, and subject/object that can grasp the real procedure of cognizing on the one side of this distinction only as reflection. This was abandoned at the latest with the linguistic turn in philosophy, notwithstanding all the logical problems that arose with the transition to a "naturalized epistemology" (Willard Van Orman Quine). Why does sociology find it so difficult to emulate this turn?

Perhaps because it knows society too well (or must in any case claim to do so) to take any pleasure in the notion that it is itself part of this reality. Sociology would like to be able to persist in opposition to society, or at least in resolute Frankfurt-style resignation. But this would also be possible if one's own theory were to be recognized as part of its own subject matter; indeed, precisely then. One could copy Perseus's facility and indirect sighting in lopping off the Medusa's head (in sociology, too, only heads are at issue).[29] One could point out that theology had invented the figure of the devil for the purpose of observing God and His creation, and that great sophists of the nineteenth century such as Marx, Nietzsche, and Freud were characterized by their "incongruent perspectives."[30] The problem is therefore more likely to lie in the difficulties of a logical and technical theoretical nature that sociology has to face when dealing with what linguistics calls "autological" concepts, obliging it to discover itself in its own object of study: sociology as the self-description of society. Ultimately, this means that, although the notion that reality is to be recognized by the resistance it exerts can be retained, it has to be admitted that such resistance to communication can be exercised only through communication. If we can accept this, the subject/object distinction would be "deconstructed,"[31] and this would eliminate the secret support for the prevailing epistemological obstacles. And then the humanistic and regionalistic conceptual traditions could be allowed to founder on their own inutility.

In its present understanding of science, sociology can hardly renounce pretensions to explaining the phenomena of social reality. This requires demarcation of the phenomena to be explained and the most precise possible definition of the characteristics that distinguish them from one another. However, even as questions, "What are . . ." questions like "What is an enterprise?" "What is a social movement?" or "What is a city?" require information on essential characteristics, and hence essentialistic concept formation, entrenched no longer in nature but in the methodological requirements of scientific research. *How*, we must therefore ask, is sociology to formulate a theory of society if it cannot say *what* it is after with this concept?

But it should also be noted that sociology puts itself in a state of permanent restlessness with such "What . . . ?" questions, *thus establishing itself as an autopoietic system*. There can be neither any final answers to such questions nor fixed points inaccessible to further research; only observation of what consequences certain conceptual definitions entail. In the mode of second-order (self-)observation, and hence in the mode of constructivist epistemology, all definitions of characteristics therefore dissolve, and we see their necessity for research as well as their contingency. They are, so to speak, self-definitions to be tried out, research programs that are indispensable, but replaceable if there is to be any question of the difference between truth and nontruth.

In the broad field of interdisciplinary research, there are now many approaches that take this into account, for instance, the grounding of every sort of cognition in the operational closure of observing systems; or chaos theory, the mathematics of nonlinear functions and the prediction of unpredictability; or the evolutionary theory of the random induction of structure formation. Where need be, I shall make use of them. Particularly for sociology, these desiderata come together in the endeavor to achieve a theory of society, for in society it has an object that has always itself produced what research needs in the way of object determination (essential characteristics). At issue is therefore only *how* this state of affairs can be taken into account by defining *what* the term "society" means.

The inquiries that follow venture this transition to a radically anti-humanistic, radically anti-regional, and radically constructivist concept of society.[32] They do not, of course, deny that there are human beings, nor do they ignore the glaring differences in living conditions between the various regions of the globe. They merely refrain from making these facts a criterion for defining the concept of society and determining the boundaries of the object under study. And it is precisely this reticence that enables one to recognize normative and evaluative standards in dealing with people—for example, human rights or Habermasian understanding-oriented communication norms—and, ultimately, attitudes toward differences in development between regions, as internal achievements of society, instead of having to posit them as regulative ideas or components of the communication concept. But the preliminary issue remains: How does society bring itself to give currency to this and other matters?

In "On the Uses and Disadvantages of History for Life," Nietzsche rebelled against the dependence of his contemporaries on history, accusing them of adopting an ironic if not cynical attitude along the lines of: Things can go on neither like this nor in any other way. The diagnosis may well still hold true, but instead of irony, we now encounter theoretically helpless embarrassment. It is hence of little use to focus not on history but on life and thus evoke the ability to forget. The recommendation today is therefore to make better use of the theoretical resources available—not least, for reconstructing the relationship with history and its semantic heritage.

2. Preliminary Remarks on Methodology

In keeping with its concept of science, sociology concerns itself with social reality as it actually exists. Normative questions have to be derived from within this reality; they cannot be submitted to society as ideal conceptions of sociology from the outside. As a result, the confrontation between ideal and reality still current in the early nineteenth century has been replaced by the twin questions "What's the case?" and "What's behind it?"[33] Only for the "resolution" of this difference do ideal constructions (such as emancipation or a normative concept of rationality) still play a role. From Marx to Habermas, a "critical" sociology developed along these lines that replaced methodology by evaluation of the views of (what it regarded as) its opponents in terms of its critical ambitions. But this is to give the verdict before the trial.

I shall pursue this line of argument no further. Furthermore, I shall distance myself, too, from what is usually treated as "empirical" research in the discipline.[34] The classical methodology requires researchers to behave as if they were a single "subject," in hope of sustaining the (logical and ontological) tradition of a distinction between thinking and being, which seeks to attain being in thought. Agreement is doubtless a praiseworthy goal, but we must also ask what is lost if research is directed toward this goal. After all, modern society, in which research, too, has to be carried on, is a polycontextural system admitting a plurality of descriptions of its complexity. Research can therefore hardly be expected to impose a monotextural description on society—at any rate, not when a theory of society is at issue.

From a constructivist point of view, the function of methodology cannot be limited to ensuring that reality is correctly (and not incorrectly) described. It is more likely to be concerned with refined forms of intrasystemic information generation and processing. Methods can thus enable scientific research to surprise itself. This requires interruption of the direct continuum of reality and knowledge initially assumed by society.

The confrontation between quantitative and qualitative methods that dominates the debate on sociological methods tends to divert attention from the real problems. Above all, it fails to settle how to transform *distance* from the object into *insight*, and how both to confirm and rise above the street smarts of the socially experienced participants in social communication who will be answering questions. Treating the relevant utterances as "data" is naturally no solution to *this*.

The usual method recommended is formulated in terms of variables, addressing relations between variables, perhaps correlations, and the conditions on which they depend.[35] In research conducted in project form, the few variables that can be handled are treated as a closed area, while, thanks to a methodological fiction, everything else is assumed to be indifferent. What is ignored or left aside for methodological reasons is *that the relationship between inclusion and exclusion is regulated by social systems themselves*; and, moreover, *that the use of meaning in social systems always provides reference to the unknown, the excluded, the indeterminable, to lacking information, and personal ignorance*.[36] This can happen by reference to the future and to the possibilities for determination in prospect (as in Husserl's phenomenology) or in the form of a negative terminology, which only negates what it determines, leaving open what is in its stead. Although the excuse is offered that the "context" has to be taken into account, this remains a paradoxical demand: the "context" would have to be transformed into a "text." Above all, however, if we assign key theoretical importance to the concept of communication, we would always have to note what is not said when something is said;[37] for reactions in social intercourse are very often determined by taking account of what remains unsaid. But if we are to do justice to social reality, we cannot abstract from the circumstance that all the forms of meaning used have another side to them, which they exclude for the moment of their use. I shall attempt to take this into account with the concept of meaning, and with the concept of form, the mathematical concept of the "reentry" of a form into the form, and essentially by adopting a differentialist approach to theory.

The familiar question about relations between variables corresponds very well to action-theoretical notions of the object. Not, however, because action is a particularly suitable object for empirical research. There are good reasons for questioning this. But actions are easy to imagine in interactional contexts if we follow Max Weber and attribute socially intended meaning to action. The motives of actors (and possibly their rationally selective structure) then serve to explain what form interaction takes. But this is the very circumstance that shuts out the other side of the form or at most includes it as rationally nonselectable. The main question for a theory of society, however, is why almost all possible actions and interactions *do not* take place. They are apparently outside the schema of possible motives and rational calculations. How does society manage to sort out what is possible? Why is it part of the meaning of the forms of social life that these vast surplus possibilities are disregarded as unmarked space? It is at least conceivable that societal structures arise not as aggregates of preferred motives for action but much more elementarily as inclusion of this exclusion in the form.

The tendency of methodological individualism (whether of necessity or not) to interrogate the individual about his knowledge or views and then to analyze the resulting data statistically misses the essence of the communication phenomenon, for communication is typically occasioned by ignorance.[38] We must be able to judge which utterances mean information for others, adding something they did not know or did not know for certain. Conversely, every participant has to be ignorant of something if he is to be able to receive information. This role of ignorance cannot be reduced to individual knowledge about the ignorance of others. It is also completely unrealistic to assume that an individual knows what he does not know.[39] Communication itself generates and tests the ignorance necessary for its continued operation. We could say that it lives from the unequal distribution of knowledge and ignorance. It is based on the form of knowledge, which always has a concurrent other side: that which is not yet known. And every participant must be able to judge what cannot be known at all so that he can avoid talking manifest nonsense. This being so, it is hardly surprising that the theoretical premises of the usual methodology address action—and not communication.

Another point concerns the methodological preference for *the simplest possible* explanation—simple in relation to the complexity of the data. At least since Henri Poincaré, we have known that this is a convention with no basis in reality, and hence a convention with which science serves itself.[40] The question of what has thus been excluded (i.e., included as excluded) has never really occupied sociology, not even where it was well aware that science is carried out within society. The problem is not to be resolved with Popper's falsification methodology. It arises in attempts at both falsification and verification. We could assume that the chaos behind all cognizable structures is excluded, but that would divide the world only into cognizable and noncognizable. Another, probably more convincing answer would be that society itself with its other possibilities of communication is excluded and accordingly prevented from interfering in the production of scientific truth. Society can provide for scientific research within itself only if it allows research to try out the easiest possible (e.g., mathematical) explanatory models and to cease further investigation if the explanation satisfies methodological requirements; or otherwise to venture on to more complex data specifications. There is nothing to be said against this. However, where a theory of society is concerned, this permission to certify one's own success or failure with the aid of conventions would have to be included as a particularity of the *object* of research in the investigation. A theory would be needed that disavows the methodological framework of research; Jacques Derrida would perhaps use the word "deconstruct."

After a century of the customary empirical research in sociology, we can say (if I may extrapolate) that although it can capture macrosociological phenomena (such as rising/falling crime rates, migrations, divorce rates), it has failed to produce a theory of society (as the totality of social phenomena), and the prospects of it doing so are not exactly favorable. The ambition of empirical research is rooted in trust of its own tools and in the premise (the "prejudice") that it can arrive at reality by these means, rather than only validating its own constructions. We could object that the coincidence of empirical knowledge and reality cannot be empirically determined, and from an epistemological point of view must accordingly be treated as accidental. This need not mean that the results of empirical research are to be ignored. But they typically provoke stimulating *questions* (Why this? Why so?) and not *answers* in the sense of established knowledge, which could be invalidated only by (albeit typically to be expected) social change.

If we are guided by the alternative between critical and positive (methodologically "empirical") sociology, we shall not get very far. We need not reject it (that would not help). We must complement it. Suggestions can be made in both factual and conceptual respects.

As far as *facts* are concerned, much is obviously known and requires no further empirical study; it is also clear that the known facts often have far more serious consequences than common sense tells us or empirical research ascertains. A great deal could therefore be gained by throwing new light from unusual, incongruent angles on what is known or by placing it in a new context.[41] What we lack at present is an elaborated methodology, which is likely to depend more strongly than generally supposed on the development of theory.

The *conceptualization* of a theory of society needs to enhance its potential for complexity, namely, for interpreting more heterogeneous facts with the same concepts and thus ensuring the comparability of widely differing facts. Functional comparison is a way of treating even the extremely unlike as comparable. Above all, it excludes a purely classificatory method; for classifications assume that, in the case of unlikeness, another class must be considered. I shall not, of course, cease to assign facts to general concepts, but I do not consider classification, hence a sort of naming, to be the form in which methodological efforts to attain cognition can be appeased.

The methodological desideratum of functional comparison reflects peculiarities of modern society, and this is another reason for no longer relying on tradition in either theory or method. For, as I shall show at length, modern society is characterized by the functional autonomization and operational closure of its most important subsystems. Its functional systems are free to organize themselves and reproduce themselves. But this means that the overall system can no longer assert itself through *operational control*, but only through the *structural effects* of its differentiation form on subsystems. This insight has methodological consequences: neither ideals nor norms can offer a basis for methodological guidelines (e.g., measures of approximation); for this would only shift the problem to why society burdens itself with ideas to which it can do no justice, and to how it selects such ideas. Instead, we must establish the societal contingency of findings by demonstrating that, and how, the same basal structures can be found in completely differing functional areas (family and politics, religion and economics, cognitive science and creative art or normative law). The argument is then that such coincidences cannot be accidental; they can and must be attributed to the form of the societal system.

The following inquiries thus depend not only theoretically but also methodologically on very abstract conceptual decisions. The reasons lie in a circular argument. These assumptions about the specificity of modern society and about what can in this connection be considered a sufficiently evident fact naturally depend on the mode of observation and the distinctions with which the theory of society establishes itself. This cannot be avoided, for the theory of society must be formulated in society. "Methodology," too, offers no a priori point of departure that can be introduced from outside.[42] If we wish to take account of this fact, the only possibility is to construct our theory as transparently as possible and to recognize concepts as decisions that can be revised with manifest consequences.

3. Meaning

I have sought to clarify the concept of meaning in a number of publications.[43] In the context of a theory of society, we must at least briefly return to this issue, because it can be assumed that neither theory nor society itself can go beyond what must always be presupposed as meaning. For no societal operation can begin without using meaning.

If we take the general theoretical pattern of "autopoiesis" as the basis, presupposing meaning in no way contradicts generating meaning in the network of the operations that always presuppose it. On the contrary, the specificity of the medium meaning is a necessary correlate to the operational closure of cognitive systems. Meaning exists only as meaning of the operations using it, and hence only at the moment in which it is determined by operations, neither beforehand nor afterward. Meaning is accordingly a *product* of the operations that use meaning and not, for instance, a quality of the world attributable to a creation, a foundation, an origin.[44] There is accordingly no ideality divorced from factual experience and communication. Although Plato was right in thinking that ideas have to do with memory, remembering does not take us back to the real, almost forgotten meaning of that which is, its forms of being, ideas; the memory constructs structures only for momentary use to maintain selectivity and limit connectivity. Meaning-constituting systems delude themselves if they think there have always been and will continue to be enduring identities, and that we can therefore refer to them as extant. All orientation is construction, is difference reactualized from moment to moment.

We reach beyond this statement, which at first sounds like a mere assertion (there is no meaning outside the systems that use and reproduce meaning as a medium), if we call to mind a consequence of operational closure for relations between the system and its operationally unattainable environment. Living systems, that is, organisms, create a special environment for their cells, which protects them and enables them to specialize. They protect themselves by means of *material* boundaries in *space*. Psychic and social systems shape their operations as observational undertakings, which allow the system itself to be distinguished from its environment—even though (and I must add *because*) the operation can take place only within the system. In other words, they distinguish between self-reference and other-reference. For them, boundaries are therefore not material artifacts but forms with two sides.

In abstract terms, this is a "reentry" of a distinction into what it has itself distinguished. The system/environment distinction occurs twice over: as difference *produced through* the system and as difference *observed in* the system. With the concept of "reentry," I cite consequences that George Spencer-Brown has described as constraints of a mathematical calculus restricted to arithmetic and algebra.[45] The system becomes incalculable for itself. It attains a state of indeterminacy that is attributable, not to the unpredictability of external effects (independent variables), but to the system itself. Memory, a "memory function," is therefore needed to make the results of past selections available as a present state (in which forgetting and remembering play a role).[46] And it puts itself in a state of oscillation between positive and negative operations and between self-reference and other-reference.[47] It confronts itself with a future it cannot itself determine, for which, so to speak, adjustment reserves are laid aside for unforeseeable situations.

I shall be referring to the results of these consequences of reentry apparent to the system itself as "meaning."

If we accept this theoretical disposition, we can neither assume that an existing world consists of things, substances, and ideas nor take the concept of world to refer to their totality (*universitas rerum*). For meaning systems, the world is not a gigantic mechanism that produces states from states and thereby determines the systems themselves. The world is an immeasurable potential for surprises; it is virtual information, needing, however, systems to produce information, or, in more precise terms, to give selected irritations the sense of information.[48] All identity must accordingly be understood as the result of information processing or, if relating to the future, as a problem. Identities do not "exist," they merely have the function of ordering recursions so that in processing meaning, we can draw on and anticipate something that can be used recurrently. This requires selective condensation and, at the same time, confirmatory generalization of something that can be called the same as distinguished from other.[49]

That meaningful identities (empirical objects, symbols, signs, figures, sentences, and so on) can be produced only recursively has far-reaching epistemological consequences. While it is clear that the meaning of such entities goes far beyond what can be grasped at the moment of observing, this does not mean that they "exist" when they are not observed. Beneath the premises of the traditional logical-ontological view of reality, a further level, another operational activity, becomes apparent that constitutes objects and the possibilities of indicating them in the first place. Where recursions refer to the past (to tried and tested, known meaning), they refer only to contingent operations whose results are presently available and not to substantiating origins. Where recursions refer to the future, they point to an infinite number of possibilities for observation, hence to the world as virtual reality; and we cannot know whether observational operations will ever feed this reality into systems (and into which ones). Meaning is accordingly a thoroughly historical form of operation and only its use bundles the contingent emergence and indeterminacy of future uses. All determinations must use this medium, in which no registration has any other grounds than its facticity as secured by recursions.

In the communicative production of meaning, this recursivity is provided above all by the vocabulary, which can be used as the same in many situations.[50] There are, however, also objects that as perceivable things can be enriched with social meaning, so that they can perform a coordinating function not dependent on language—such as religious objects or people in trances (prophets, "mediums") purportedly possessed by spirits; or kings, coins, or footballs. The particular way in which "home" is identified can also not be attributed to language alone and can therefore not be adequately expressed in language. This is also true for the structuring of spatial relations through architecture or for the meaning of actions. We are always dealing with the basic function of ordering recursions available at the given moment (and only then).

In the self-constituted medium of meaning, it is indispensable to orient operations on distinctions. This alone can produce the selectivity necessary for recursion.[51] Meaning implies that everything currently indicated connotes and captures reference to other possibilities. Each meaning thus means itself and other things.[52] It would, moreover, run contrary to our experience to assume that a thing disappears if we lose sight of it in turning our attention to other things (for then we would never be able to risk letting it out of our sight). Meaning is co-present as reference to the world in everything that is actualized, and it is "appresented" [*appräsentiert* (Husserl's terminology)] *in actuality*. This includes reference to the conditions of our own ability, our own capacity for achievement and the limits set them *in the world*. Even the distinction between actual and possible can still be rendered meaningful by considering its function in the phenomenology of the world, for example, thus reflecting on functional equivalents, on other possibilities. What this meaning thesis excludes is only the contrary, namely, absolute void, nothingness, chaos in the original sense of the word, and also what Spencer-Brown calls the "unmarked state" of the world. At the same time, however, all meaningful operations always reproduce the presence of what has been excluded,[53] for the world of meaning is a complete world, which can exclude what it excludes only *in itself*. "Non-meaning" ("non-sense"), too, can therefore be thought and communicated only in the medium of meaning, only in the form of meaning.[54] All negation accordingly potentializes what it explicitly negates,[55] and preserves it, hence reestablishing the unmarked space into which every operation, including the negating operation, etches itself through a distinction.

How meaning functions can be discussed with the aid of specific distinctions that define meaning. Meaning can be described phenomenologically as surplus reference accessible from actually given meaning. Meaning is accordingly an infinite and hence indeterminable referential complex that can be made accessible and reproduced in a determined manner—and I attach great importance to the paradoxical formulation.[56] We can describe the form of meaning as the difference between actuality and potentiality, and can therefore also assert that this and no other distinction constitutes meaning. When talking about meaning, we then have something tangible (something we can indicate, distinguish) in mind; and this also means that the meaning thesis limits what we can otherwise make out about society. Society is a meaning-constituting system.

The modalization of actuality by the distinction between actual and possible concerns the meaning actualized in system operations. It is doubly asymmetrical; for actualized meaning is and remains possible, and possible meaning, actualizable. The distinction therefore provides for the "reentry" of the distinction into what it distinguishes. Meaning is hence a form that contains a copy of itself on both sides. This leads to the symmetrization of the initially asymmetrical distinction between actual and possible,[57] and meaning consequently appears to be the same everywhere in the world. Re-asymmetrization is possible, indeed, necessary for observation, but it must be introduced by further distinctions, for example, that between system and environment or signifier and signified.

Systems using meaning are systems that, by their very medium, can observe and describe themselves and their environments only in the form of meaning, in other words with reentry of the form into the form. There are no psychic and social systems that cannot distinguish between themselves and others in the medium of meaning (whatever freedoms may be actualized in matters of causal attribution). More specifically, from moment to moment reentry is used, the treatment of actual meaning is reproduced, and possibilities are thus anticipated. Actuality is, as it were, the track on which ever-new system states are projected and realized. To the system, actuality therefore appears to be a momentary present and, through self-thematization, to be of (however precarious) duration. Such systems cannot avoid the structural consequences of reentry, especially the self-overburdening with possibilities that no observation or description can capture, and that can be observed only as selectivity. A historically much favored way of dealing with such self-overburdening is to measure the system against ideas (e.g., perfection) that it cannot realize.

Systems that operate in the medium of meaning can, indeed, must, distinguish between self-reference and other-reference; and they must do so in such a way that the actualization of self-reference always comprehends other-reference, and that the actualization of other-reference always comprehends self-reference as the other side of the distinction. All forms in the medium of meaning must therefore be constituted relative to the system, regardless of whether the accent is on self-reference or other-reference at the given moment. It is this distinction that makes such processes as learning, system development, and the evolutionary development of complexity possible. And it also makes it possible to set out from two operationally very different meaning-constituting systems that reproduce through consciousness and communication, each producing its own point of departure for the distinction between self-reference and other-reference, while always relating to each another through presupposed or actualized other-reference: psychic systems and social systems.

As the universal medium of all psychic and social systems, all consciously and communicatively operating systems, meaning regenerates effortlessly and as if of its own accord with the autopoiesis of these systems. By contrast, it is difficult to produce nonmeaning, "non-sense," because the effort to do so again produces meaning, "makes sense." This problem can be observed in efforts at nonsense art.[58] Nonmeaning can be produced only if we take a narrower concept of meaningful (e.g., what is usual in everyday life, what can be expected) and then distinguish nonmeaning *from it*. This is also the case where, having made an effort to achieve something particularly "meaningful," we have to accept the futility of the venture.[59] In the generally unnegatable medium of meaning, secondary positive/negative breaks can be introduced; but this inevitably means that such a distinction again has meaning as a distinction and reproduces meaning. Although meaning can therefore be described as a form by distinguishing meaning from nonmeaning (sense from nonsense) and making it possible to cross the boundary, this can happen only where the meaning/nonmeaning difference attains meaning at the moment of its use, hence reproducing meaning as the medium of all form formation.[60]

Meaning arises and is reproduced in certain (consciousness and social) systems as "eigenbehavior,"[61] because these systems produce their ultimate elements as events that arise at a point in time only immediately to disintegrate, can have no duration, and occur for a first and last time. They are temporalized systems, which can gain stability only in the form of dynamic stability, only through the continuous replacement of transient elements by other, new elements. Their structures have to be adapted accordingly. The given actual present is brief and so interpreted that everything that happens in this present happens simultaneously.[62] It is not yet really time. But it becomes time if it is understood as separating a "before" from an "after," a past from a future. Meaning therefore appears in time and can at any moment switch to temporal distinctions; in other words, it can use time to reduce complexity, namely, treat what is past as no longer actual and what is future as not yet actual.[63] If (and only if) we use this distinction can we produce redundancies via the past and variety via the future; and producing means making present in the present.[64] However, temporalizing the present is only one of a number of possibilities for dealing meaningfully with variety (namely, through specific distinctions). The present is primarily the side of the form of meaning that, in contrast to the other side, I have called actuality. The other side of the form is then everything accessible from the first side, whether directly and really or only potentially, in the course of perception, or only in thought or imagination. With loose reference to Spencer-Brown, we could distinguish the inside of the form from its outside as the attractor of the operation.[65] Operating meaningfully then means that all operations on the inside of the form take place (or do not take place) actually; but also that meaning requires another side of the form: the outside as a space of other possibilities reaching to infinity.

That the temporal dimension of meaning can become relevant for differentiation can have a considerable impact on social conditions. The temporal dimension prevents the *material* consolidation of the social dimension. At the next moment, others may observe otherwise; within the factual dimension of meaning, they are temporally mobile. The extent to which societies accept this varies historically with the complexity of the societal system—which is easy to verify if we consider the context of the semantics of thing [*Ding-Semantik*] (*res*), bivalent logic, the treatment of dissenting opinion as error, and the isolation of special views as mere *doxa/opinio* in the old European tradition, whereas the temporal contingency of all attitudes toward the world is now much more strongly assumed.

If every operation is an event dependent on a point in time that vanishes as soon as it is actualized, and that consequently has to be replaced by another event, if a sequence of operations, that is to say, a system is to come about (which need not be the case), continued operation requires the boundaries of the form to be crossed, requires a transition to something on the other side that had previously not been indicated. I shall not go into the logical or mathematical problems of this "crossing" (Spencer-Brown) but simply note that selection is needed to reduce what is and remains possible on the other side to a specific, indicatable actuality. Which in turn requires another side to the form, a surplus of references, a world full of possibilities that cannot simultaneously be actualized. Sequencing operations keeps the totality of potentialities co-present, carrying it along, regenerating it as a world without which no further operations could be selected and the operating system could never be reproduced. In short, meaning can be reproduced only as form. The world itself, as co-occurring other side of all meaning forms, remains unobservable. Its meaning can be symbolized only in self-reflection on the use meaningful operations make of the form.

The problem is that, despite the clarity (or lack of clarity), distinctiveness, and factual indisputability of momentary actualization (Descartes naturally comes to mind), meaning can represent the world of what is accessible from this perspective only as a surplus of reference, thus as a selection constraint. What has actually been appropriated is secure,[66] but unstable; the other side of the meaning form is stable, but insecure, because everything depends on what will be intended in the next moment. The unity of the totality of possibilities and, of course, the unity of the form itself, the unity of actuality and potentiality, cannot be actualized. Instead of giving world, meaning points to selective processing. And this also holds true (as we shall see) if concepts, descriptions of the world, semantics referring to the world are formed; for this, too, must take place in a meaningful operation that distinguishes what it indicates from something else (e.g., *Sein* from *Seiendes*). Without exception, actualized meaning comes about selectively and without exception points to further selection. Its contingency is a necessary element of meaningful operation.

All this presupposes the operationally functioning unity of what is differentiated, comprehensible only as paradox, but not observable.[67] Meaning has to function simultaneously with the two sides of its form; otherwise, it cannot be used operationally to indicate something (and nothing else). Meaning in every sense, too, can be indicated only by actualizing a difference that entails something nonindicated as the other side of the distinction. We can, of course, also indicate the actuality/potentiality distinction itself (I have just done so), but only through a further distinction that distinguishes this from other distinctions and localizes it in the world. Meaningfully processing systems can thus well imagine and communicate that there are other systems for which there is no meaning, for example, stones. But this, too, is possible only with an appropriate distinction, hence only in the form of meaning. Meaningfully operating systems remain bound to the medium of meaning. It alone gives them reality in the form of the sequential actualization of their own operations. They can neither understand nor simulate meaning-free systems. They remain dependent on meaning as the form of complexity reduction specific to them.

Whereas the *use of a distinction* is necessary and cannot be avoided, the *determination of a distinction* takes place explicitly. It presupposes visible selection and may need to be justified. Linguistically, the distinction implied in every phrase is not expressed; when we talk about an apple, for example, it is often not clear what we are distinguishing it from. The determination of a distinction, in contrast, is clearly marked and used to direct further communication;[68] but, of course, in the medium of meaning.

That all observation depends on differences explains the wealth of meaning in the world; for we can identify what we are indicating by exposing it to one difference after another. Various observations by various observers can hence be coordinated, and coordinated in their very diversity. This applies to differences in the temporal dimension and in the social dimension; it holds true for the use of a succession of distinctions and for various observers focusing on the same thing.

Traditional ontological metaphysics had given free rein to this—backed, however, by transcendental critical values. *Seiendes* was understood under the form of thing. Time pointed to an "origin" (*archē*, *origo*, *principium*, source, ground) that, despite changes in currently actualized distinctions, remained the same (and did so in the given present). And this origin was ultimately God as the sole being not defined through distinctions.[69] The radicalization of the meaning concept as a medium for distinction-dependent observation allows these premises to be cancelled. In all the dimensions of meaning, the world can now be understood as the framework (or as Husserl puts it, the horizon) that permits the exchange of distinctions with which we observe the same. However, this presupposes that the world is no longer understood as the totality of things and their relations but as that which cannot be observed, which is reproduced with every change of distinction.

Every distinction represents the world by entailing its other side, what is not indicated at the moment. As Spencer-Brown puts it: "distinction is perfect continence."[70] Distinctions exercise self-control; they spare themselves external references because they already contain them as their other side. They contain continence. For this reason alone the meaning form can never go beyond itself. But in its particular case, it can also itself distinguish only by using itself, in other words "autologically." It is the absolute medium of itself.

This does not exclude taking further steps toward the inquiries into the theory of society that follow. We take recourse to the paradox of differentiation that secures "perfect continence." As an operational unity of distinction and indication, meaning is a form that contains itself, namely, the distinction between distinction and indication. A form is essentially a distinction that recurs in itself as what is distinguished. We can escape this situation only by a leap, by a deparadoxization directive, by concealing the paradox with a further distinction. To this end, Russell and Tarski have proposed distinguishing between types or levels. Despite widespread criticism, this may be useful for the purposes of logic and linguistics. Spencer-Brown manages by ignoring the initial paradox, carrying out his calculus on the basis of a directive ("draw a distinction") to the point where the possibility of an imaginary "reentry" of the form into the form emerges.[71]

With respect to the specific form of meaning, namely, the distinction between actuality and potentiality, meaning therefore becomes operational only by the form reentering the form. The inside of the form must be able to accept this reentry. The difference between momentary actuality and open possibility must itself be actually available for consciousness and/or communication. We must be able to see in actuality how the crossing of this boundary is possible and what subsequent steps come into consideration. This cannot mean that the "unmarked space" of "everything possible" can be accommodated in the "marked space" of what is actually indicated; for it constitutes what is actual precisely by crossing the boundary. Nevertheless, certain possibilities can be captured and indicated in actuality and pre-orient a crossing of the boundary between actual and potential; only, however, where this possibility is realized as an actual operation, hence reconstituting the difference between actuality and potentiality. In this fashion, namely, through reentry of the form into the form, meaning becomes a continually self-regenerating medium for the ongoing selection of particular forms.

The description of this state of affairs verifies it itself, so to speak, and is thus an autological operation. But it also shows that it is possible only in the form of a paradox, for the form reentering the form is the same and is not the same form.

This well-considered audacity in unfolding the meaning paradox can encourage us to look at other distinctions capable of reentry into themselves. In what follows, systems theory is understood as the theory of the distinction between *system* and *environment*, with reentry possible on the side of the system if the system itself, that is to say, in its own operations, distinguishes between self-reference and other-reference. Treatment of communication as the operation that reproduces specific social systems is guided by the distinction between *medium* and *form*. This distinction occurs within itself inasmuch as loosely or strictly coupled elements are presupposed on the two sides that are cognizable only as forms, that is to say, they presuppose a further distinction between medium and form.[72] The final medium that meaning systems cannot transcend is therefore meaning. But in this medium, forms have to be constructed through system operations—whether by directing conscious attention or by communicating. In the case of linguistic communication,[73] words are joined to form sentences complying with the rules of grammar and the requirements of meaning formation. Finally, the theory of societal evolution also uses a distinction that unfolds its paradox. The paradox that something persists that changes is not resolved in the old manner in the distinction between mobile and immobile (mutable/immutable) elements or parts. On the model of Darwinian theory, it is replaced by the distinction between variation and selection, in which variation itself proceeds selectively, since the system cannot be arbitrarily but only highly selectively irritated, in other words, stimulated to variation.

4. The Distinction Between System and Environment

The theoretical resources for a "meaningful" revolutionization of the theory of society paradigm are not taken from sociological tradition. Rather, they are introduced from outside the discipline, based on recent developments in systems theory and developments in fields such as cybernetics, the cognitive sciences, communication theory, and evolution theory. In any case, the discussion runs in interdisciplinary contexts, which have changed radically over the past two to three decades and now have little in common with the systems concepts of the 1950s and 1960s. These are quite new, fascinating intellectual developments, which for the first time make it possible to avoid the old confrontation between the natural sciences and the liberal arts, the hard sciences and the humanities, or between subject matter in natural law form and in text (hermeneutic) form.

The farthest-reaching change, indispensable in understanding what follows, is that we speak no longer of objects but of distinctions. Moreover, we understand distinctions, not as existing facts (differences), but as deriving from directives to draw them, because if we did not we would be unable to indicate anything. We would have nothing to observe and hence nothing to pursue.[74] George Spencer-Brown conceptualizes forms, not as (beautiful or otherwise) shapes, but as boundaries, as markings of differences that oblige us to make clear which side we are indicating, and thus which side of the form we are on, our point of departure for further operations. The other side of the boundary (the "form") is given simultaneously. Each side of the form is the other side to the other side. Neither side is anything on its own. We actualize a side only by indicating it and not the other side. In this sense, form is *unfolded self-reference*, to be more precise *temporally* unfolded self-reference. For we must always set out from the indicated side and need time for a further operation in order to stay on the indicated side or to cross the boundary constituting the form.

Crossing is creative. For whereas repeating an indication merely confirms its identity (and we'll say later: tests and hence condenses its meaning in various situations), crossing back and forth is not repetition and can therefore not be contracted into a single identity.[75] This is merely another way of saying that a distinction cannot identify itself in use. And this, as will be shown in detail with regard to binary coding, is the basis for the productiveness of crossing.

Although this concept of form somewhat resembles Hegel's concept of the concept in that the inclusion of a distinction is constitutive for both, Hegel built in much farther-reaching pretensions, which we cannot accept and do not need. Unlike form in our sense, his concept undertakes to solve the problem of its unity itself. It eliminates the autonomy of what is distinguished (in the concept "human being," for example, the independence of the opposing elements sensibility and reason), doing so through the specific distinction between general and particular upon whose dissolution the concept constitutes itself alone. This can be countered only by recalling that form is the distinction itself, in that it imposes the indication (and thus the observation) of the one side or the other and (quite differently from the concept) can for this very reason not realize its unity on its own. The unity of the form is not its "higher," intellectual meaning. It is rather the excluded middle that cannot be observed as long as we observe with the aid of the form. The concept of form also presupposes that the two sides are determined by reference of the one to the others. This should, however, be regarded as prerequisite, not for a "reconciliation" of opposites, but for drawing a distinction.

Determining, indicating, cognizing, acting are all operations that establish such a form; like the Fall of Man, they cause a break in the world, give rise to a difference, to simultaneity and a need for time, and render inaccessible the indeterminacy ahead.

The form concept no longer differs only from the concept of content but also from that of context.[76] A form may consist in the difference between something and everything else, in the difference between something and its context (for instance, between a building and its urban or rural surroundings), or in the difference between a value and the countervalue to the exclusion of third possibilities. Whenever the form concept marks the one side of a distinction on the condition that there is another side determined by it, there is also a superform, namely, the form of the distinction of the form from something else.[77]

With the help of this concept developed for a calculus of forms, for processing distinctions, we can also interpret the distinction between system and environment.[78] From the point of view of a general calculus of forms, it is a special case, a case of application. From a methodological standpoint, it is therefore not merely a matter of replacing an explanation of society in terms of a principle (be it "mind" or "matter") by one in terms of a distinction. Although we assign key status to the distinction between system and environment, and thus to the form "system," we do so only in the sense that this is the point from which we organize the consistency of the theory, the coherence between a multiplicity of distinctions. This is an inductive procedure, not a deductive one; it tries out what generalizations of a form have to say for others. And consistency in this regard means nothing other than the production of sufficient redundancies, in other words, the parsimonious handling of information.

This form concept helps systems theory make it clear that it is concerned, not with special objects (let alone technical artifacts or analytical constructs), but with a special sort of form, a special form of forms, so to speak, that explicates the general properties of every two-sided form in terms of "system and environment." All the properties of form apply here, too, such as the simultaneity of system and environment, and the time requirement for all operations. Above all, this mode of presentation can show that, although system and environment are separate as two sides of a form, neither can exist without the other.[79] As a difference, the unity of the form remains presupposed; but the difference itself is not a vehicle of operations. It is neither substance nor subject; from a historical point of view, it replaces these classical figures. Operations are possible only as operations of a system, hence only on the inside of the form. But the system can also operate as observer of the form; however, it can observe the unity of the difference, the two-sided form as a form only if it constitutes another form for this purpose, only if the distinction itself can distinguish. Systems, if sufficiently complex, can then apply the distinction between system and environment to themselves; but only if they perform an operation of their own that does this. In other words, they can distinguish themselves from their environment, but only in an operation within the system itself. The form, which they generate blindly by operating recursively, thus differentiating themselves out, is available to them again if they observe themselves as systems in environments. And only thus, only under these conditions, does systems theory provide the basis for a certain practice of distinguishing and indicating. It uses the distinction between system and environment as the form of its observations and descriptions; but in order to do so, it must be able to distinguish this distinction from other distinctions, for example, those of action theory; and if it is to operate in this manner, it must form a system: here, too, it must be science. When applied to systems theory, the concept therefore satisfies the requirement we set, namely, the self-implication of theory. Its relationship with its object obliges it to make "autological" inferences about itself.

If we accept this difference-theoretical point of departure, all developments in recent systems theory can be seen as variations on the theme of "system and environment." The initial concern was to use notions of metabolism or input and output in explaining that there are systems not subject to the law of entropy but able to develop negentropy, and thus to reinforce the distinction between the system and its environment precisely through the system's openness and dependence on the environment. This invited the conclusion that independence of and dependence on the environment were not mutually exclusive characteristics of the system, but could under certain circumstances be enhanced alongside. The question was under what circumstances. Evolution theory pointed the way to an answer.

The next step in development was to include self-referential—that is, circular—relationships. At first, consideration was given to the structures of the system being organized by processes intrinsic to the system, by what was called self-organization. The environment was understood as the source of unspecific (meaningless) "noise," from which the system could nevertheless obtain meaning in the context of its own operations. It was then postulated that the system could organize itself and develop its own order in dependence on the environment, and never without the environment, but without ever being determined by it: order from noise.[80] From the perspective of the system, the environment acts randomly on the system;[81] but this very randomness is indispensable for the emergence of order, and the more complex order becomes, the more this is the case.

At this stage of the discussion, Humberto Maturana introduced a new element with the concept of autopoiesis.[82] Autopoietic systems are systems that themselves produce not only their structures but also the elements of which they consist in the network of these same elements. The elements (which from a temporal point of view are operations) that constitute autopoietic systems have no independent existence. They do not simply come together. They are not simply connected. It is only in the system that they are produced (on whatever energy and material basis) by being *made use of as distinctions.* Elements are information, distinctions that make a difference in the system. They are hence units of use for the production of further units of use for which there is no counterpart in the environment of the system.

In the light of a far-reaching and critical discussion, the low explanatory value of the autopoiesis concept should be pointed out. It requires only that all explanations start with the specific operations that reproduce a system—both the explained and the explaining system. It says nothing about what specific structures develop in such systems owing to structural couplings between system and environment. Nor does it explain the historical states of the system from which further autopoiesis proceeds. The autopoiesis of life is a one-off biochemical invention of evolution; but this does not mean that worms and humans had to be. Similarly for communication. The autopoietic operation of the communication presupposing communication produces society, but this does not yet decide what sort of society. Autopoiesis is accordingly an invariant principle for the system in question, and, once again, for both the explained and the explaining system. This is to abandon the ontological mode of explanation with its invariants of being and hence the distinction between subject and object.

But this does not yet tell us what historical situations set the course for specifying structures via structural couplings. It tells us only that to answer this question, we must examine the system itself.

Autopoiesis is therefore not to be understood as the production of a certain "gestalt." What is decisive is the production of a difference between system and environment.[83] Uncoupling the system from what then remains as environment affords internal latitude, since the system is not determined by its environment. Correctly understood, autopoiesis is in the first place the generation of *indeterminacy within the system*, which can be reduced by the system itself forming structures. This explains not least of all why societal systems have invented the medium of meaning to take account of this openness for further determinations in operations within the system. The only operations of their own they know are therefore communications selecting meaning forms.

This autopoietic reproduction naturally cannot happen without an environment (otherwise, as we know, the other side of the form would not be a system). But we now have to state much more precisely (for the benefit of our theory of society) how autopoietic systems, which themselves produce all the elements they need to continue their autopoiesis, organize their relations with the environment. All the external relations of such a system are therefore *unspecific* (which naturally does not exclude an observer being able to specify what he himself wants to see and can see. Every specification, including that of relations with the environment, presupposes action by the system itself and a historical state of the system as the condition of its action. For specification is itself a *form*, and thus a *distinction*; it consists of selection from a self-constructed selection area (information); and this form can be produced only in the system itself. There is no input of elements into the system and no output of elements from the system. The system is autonomous, not only at the structural level, but also at the operational level. This is what autopoiesis means. The system can constitute operations of its own only further to operations of its own and in anticipation of further operations of the same system. But these are far from all the conditions for existence, and I repeat: How can we now distinguish this recursive dependence of operation on itself from its doubtless continuing dependence on the environment? The answer can be found only by analyzing the specificity of autopoietic operations (in other words, the answer does not lie in the often superficially understood concept of autopoiesis itself). These reflections will lead us to assign key importance to the concept of communication in the theory of society.

To begin with, the concepts as so far defined also clarify the now frequently used concept of operational (or self-referential) closure of the system. This does not, of course, imply that the system is causally isolated, without contact, or self-contained. The insight offered by the theory of open systems that independence and dependence can increase with and through one another remains intact. The wording merely changes: we now say that all openness is based on the closure of the system. In somewhat more detail, this means that only operationally closed systems can develop a high level of inner complexity, which can then serve to specify the respects in which the system reacts to conditions of its environment, while in all other respects, thanks to its autopoiesis, it can remain indifferent.[84]

Nor does this contradict Gödel's insight that no system can close itself off to form a logically consistent order.[85] In effect, it says no more than what we presuppose: that the system concept refers to the environment concept and can therefore be neither logically nor analytically isolated. At the operational level (in our case with regard to communication), Gödel's argument is based on the insight that a statement about numbers implies a statement about a statement about numbers (in other words, communication can function only self-referentially). It should be stressed, however, that this concerns only an observer observing with the aid of the system/environment distinction or with regard to operations, and does not yet settle the question how the unity of the system comes about.

Insight into the circular, self-referential, and hence logically symmetrical structure of these systems has raised the question how this circle can be interrupted and asymmetries produced. Who is then to say what is cause and what effect? Or, putting it more radically, what happens before and what after, what inside and what outside? The authority that decides is now often called the "observer." But we are not thinking only about processes of consciousness, only about psychic systems. The concept is used highly abstractly and independently of the material substratum, the infrastructure, or the specific mode of operation that enable observations to be carried out. Observing means simply distinguishing and indicating, and it is in this sense that I shall be using it in what follows. The concept of observing draws attention to the fact that "distinguishing and indicating" constitute a single operation; we can indicate nothing that we do not, in so doing, distinguish; just as distinguishing makes sense only in that it serves to indicate one side or the other (but not both sides). In the terminology of traditional logic, the distinction is, in relation to the sides it distinguishes, the excluded middle. Observation in the performance of observing is thus also the excluded middle. If, finally, we consider that observing is always an operation that has to be performed by an autopoietic system, and if we term the concept of this system in this function "observer," we can say that the observer is the excluded middle of his observation. He cannot see himself observing. As Michel Serres has put it, the observer is the nonobservable.[86] The distinction he uses to indicate the one side or the other serves as the invisible condition of seeing, as blind spot. And this can be said for all observation, whether the operation be psychic or social, whether it be carried out as actual process of consciousness or as communication.

The system of society is accordingly characterized, not by a specific "nature," let alone a specific morality (spread of happiness, solidarity, the harmonization of living conditions, reasoned-consensual integration, and so on), but solely by the operation that produces and reproduces society:[87] communication.[88] By communication (as by operation), we consequently mean historically concrete and hence context-dependent activity—and not merely the application of rules of correct speech.[89] If communication is to occur, knowledge and ignorance are required of all participants. I noted this as an argument against methodological individualism in my preliminary remarks on methodology. For how can we understand ignorance as a state of consciousness if not in dependence on communicative situations that specify certain requirements or signal certain information opportunities. For this reason alone, communication is an autopoietic operation, because it produces the distribution of knowledge and ignorance only by changing it.

In the practice of meaning, communication, too, is obliged to draw distinctions to indicate one side and to ensure connections on this side. The autopoiesis of the system is thus continued. But what happens with the other side? It remains nonindicated and therefore does not need to be controlled for consistency. No attention is paid to contexts. We thus soon forget what that which was indicated was distinguished from—whether unmarked space or counterconcepts to be left out of account in further operations. Although the other side always co-occurs, because no distinction would otherwise be drawn, it is not used to achieve anything specific.

That the elementary operation of society is an event bound to a point in time that disappears as it occurs is an insight that takes us further. This is true of all components of communication: information, which can surprise only once; utterance, an act tied to a point in time; and understanding, which also cannot be repeated but at best recalled. And it is true of both oral and written communication, with the difference that the dissemination technology of writing can distribute the communication event in time and space to many addressees and can thus be realized at unpredictably many points in time.

With this time-point related concept of communication, we also correct a popular conception of information. Information is a surprising selection from among several possibilities. As a surprise, it can be neither enduring nor able to be transported; and it has to be produced within the system, since it presupposes comparison with expectations. Furthermore, information cannot be gained purely passively as a logical consequence of signals received from the environment. It always contains a volitional component, that is to say, foresight into what can be done with it.[90] Before information can be produced, interest in it must therefore develop.

If we understand communication as an entity comprising the three components information, utterance, and understanding, which are produced only in communicating, this excludes the possibility of assigning ontological primacy to one of these components. It can neither be assumed that there is a factual world that can then be talked about nor does the origin of communication lie in the "subjective" act of communicating that imparts meaning; nor is there a society at the outset that prescribes via cultural institutions how something is to be understood as communication. The unity of communicative events cannot be deduced objectively, subjectively, or socially; and for this very reason communication creates the medium of meaning in which it can decide continuously whether further communication seeks its problem in information, utterance, or understanding. The components of communication presuppose one another; they are circularly connected. They can therefore no longer fix their externalizations ontologically as properties of the world; they have to seek them in the transition from one communication to another.

The time-boundedness of the communication operation relates to the time point of understanding on the basis of observing a difference between information and utterance. It is understanding that then generates communication (we need this to be established to enable us to include written communication, as well as communication by means of money). Communication is thus a certain way of observing the world by means of the specific distinction between information and utterance. It is one of the possibilities for obtaining universality by means of specification. It is not "transmission" of meaning,[91] although at the time point of understanding wide time horizons can be constructed for better understanding communication with regard to the point in time of the utterance. However, communication cannot control what happens simultaneously at the time of understanding, and must therefore always rely on inferences from its own past, on redundancies, on self-constructed recursions.

In communicative contexts, understanding would therefore be quite impossible if it depended on deciphering what was going on psychologically at the same time. Although it must be assumed that consciousness is involved, no one participating in communication can know the details of what happens—either for the others involved or for themselves. Communication (hence society) must rather procure the necessary understanding itself. This is achieved through nonarbitrariness in connecting communicative events, hence through the self-referential structure of communication processes. For each individual event gains meaning (= understandability) only because it refers to others and restricts what they can mean; and this is precisely how it determines itself.[92]

A communication system accordingly exists only at the moment of its operation; but to determine its operations, it uses the medium of meaning, which enables it to relate selectively from each operation to other operations, and to do so within horizons that present the simultaneously existing world to the system.[93] All duration must therefore be produced by transition to other events. Communicative systems are possible only as recursive systems, since their single operations can be produced only by recursion to and anticipation of other operations of the same system.[94] This in turn imposes the double requirement of continuity and discontinuity, raising the question how meaning can be treated in *other* situations as *the same*. It is necessary to install *cognizable repetition*. Only if and insofar as this is the case can the classical conceptuality, which speaks of "elements" and "relations," and that presupposes stable objects, be retained.[95] And the question is how this is possible in the medium of meaning.

In George Spencer-Brown's theory of form, this desideratum is expressed by the double concept of condensation and confirmation,[96] which cannot be reduced to a single concept. Recursions must produce identities suitable for reuse; this can be done only through selective condensation, by leaving out unrepeatable elements of other situations. However, they must also preserve the condensed meaning in new situations, and this requires generalization. If these requirements have to be repeatedly met, for instance, with the aid of language, generalized meaning variants develop whose signification cannot be sufficiently captured in the form of definitions. They arise from experience in use, which depends entirely on the user system. I consider this a cause of the evolution of symbolically generalized communication media.[97]

Jacques Derrida has argued in the same vein under the heading *différance*.[98] Not only in writing but also in speaking, indeed in every type of experience, signs have to be set and transferred to other situations. Distinctions (fractures, ruptures) thus have to be transported in time. This can be done only if what the sign refers to (above all the intention) is absent.[99] In short, the necessity of temporal sequencing imposes differentiation between system and environment and the operational closure of recursions in the system.

The concept of self-referential, operational closure alters the concept of system boundary, complicating it in a way that requires careful analysis. For living systems, for the autopoietic organization of molecules in space, we can still speak of spatial boundaries. Indeed, boundaries in this case are special organs of the system, membranes of cells, the skin of organisms, that perform specific functions in shielding the system and in the selective mediation of exchange processes. This form of boundary (which is of course visible only to the external observer and simply lives in the system) does not occur in the case of systems that operate in the medium of meaning. Such systems are not limited in space at all; they have a quite different, namely, purely internal, form of boundary. This is the case with consciousness, which thus distinguishes itself from the brain and can "externalize" the neurophysiological self-observation of the organism only in this manner.[100] And it applies a fortiori for the communication system society, as has been evident since the invention of writing and at the latest since the advent of telephony. The boundary of this system is produced and reproduced in every single communication in that the communication determines itself as communication in the network of the system's own operations and does not accept any physical, chemical, or neurophysiological components. In other words, every operation contributes to the ongoing differentiation of the system and cannot otherwise attain its own unity. The boundary of the system is nothing other than the type and concretion of its operations, which individualize the system.[101] It is the form of the system whose other side thus becomes the environment.

The same can be formulated with the aid of the distinction between self-reference and other-reference. Meaningfully operating systems reproduce themselves in ongoing implementation of the distinction between self-reference and other-reference. The unity of this distinction cannot be observed; it is carried out only operationally and only internally (otherwise we could not speak of self-reference and other-reference). Like living systems, systems operating with meaning never go beyond their own boundaries with their own operations. But in the medium of meaning, boundaries always have another side, as forms they always exist as two-sided forms (and not as pure facticity of the operational act). This means that the observation accompanying progression from operation to operation always notices the selectivity of the recursive connection and hence something that belongs not to the system but to the environment. In communication, information about something is actualized and changed that is not communication itself. In the network of communication, other-reference always co-occurs in the search for suitable connections. The boundary of the system is therefore nothing other than the self-produced difference between self-reference and other-reference, and as such is present in all communications.

With the continuously reproduced distinction between information and utterance, a social system can observe itself. An observer of this observing, a second-order observer (for example, the social system science) can also distinguish between the *topics* and *functions* of communication and thus observe the conditions for the iterativity of operations (in this case, communications). Topics enable a distinction to be drawn between topics and items, hence between structures and operations, which then attach to the inner side of the boundary to the environment. This allows the sequential ordering of communication, leading to a memory ordered by topic, locally ("topically"), as it were.[102] Functions, by contrast, relate to the autopoiesis of the system and the required reproduction, alteration, or development of structures. In communication about communication, topics and functions of communication can in turn become a topic—a reentry of the distinction into itself. The system closes itself at the reflexive level, thus attaining a state of double closure,[103] which guarantees high internal flexibility but also imposes intransparency for every observer.

As we shall see, this analysis commits us to assuming a single system of world society, which, so to speak, pulsates as it grows or shrinks depending on what is realized in the way of communication. A multiplicity of societies is conceivable only if there are no communicative links between them.

5. Society as a Comprehensive Social System

In the understanding elaborated here, the theory of society is the theory of the comprehensive social system that encompasses all other social systems. This definition is almost a quotation. It recalls the opening sentences of Aristotle's *Politics* defining the political community (*koinōnia politikē*) as the supreme (*kyriōtatē*) community that includes all others within it (*pasas periechousa tas allas*).[104] We thus follow in the old European tradition as far as the concept of society is concerned. However, all components of the definition (including the concept of inclusion = *periechon*, resolvable for the purposes of systems theory with the concept of differentiation) are understood differently, for we are concerned with a theory of modern society for modern society. The link with the old European tradition is hence retained, but a redescription of its key statements is called for.[105]

Society is therefore understood as a system; and the form of the system, as we have seen, is nothing other than the distinction between system and environment. But this does not mean that general systems theory suffices to deduce by logical inference what society is about. We also have to determine the specificity of social systems, and what within the theory of social systems constitutes the specificity of a system of society; in other words, what is implied when we refer to society as the comprehensive social system.

We must therefore distinguish between three levels in analyzing society:

(1) general systems theory and, within it, the general theory of autopoietic systems;

(2) the theory of social systems;

(3) the theory of the societal system as a special instance of social system.

At the level of the general theory of autopoietic, self-referential, operationally closed systems, the theory of society draws on conceptual decisions and findings of empirical research that also apply to other systems of this type (e.g., brains). Far-reaching interdisciplinary exchanges of experience and ideas are possible in this regard. As explained in the previous section, I base the theory of society on innovative developments in this field.

At the level of the theory of social systems, we are concerned with the specificity of autopoietic systems that can be understood as social systems. Here we have to determine the specific operation whose autopoietic process leads to the formation of social systems in corresponding environments. This is communication. The theory of social systems thus brings together all statements that apply to all social systems, even to interaction systems of short duration and little importance (and only such statements).[106] Society at this level (like the classical *societas civilis*) appears to be one social system among many others, and can be compared with other types such as organizational systems and systems of face-to-face interaction.

Only at the third level does the specificity of societal systems come to bear. It needs to be explained at this point what is meant by "comprehensive," an attribute that goes back to the beginning of Aristotle's *Politics*. It is clearly based on a paradox. It states that one social system (*koinōnia*) among others includes all others within it. Aristotle resolved this paradox through emphasis and ultimately through an ethical understanding of politics. It was thus rendered invisible for tradition. This paradox is unfolded by the distinction between levels proposed here for the analysis of society, occasionally permitting recollection of the paradoxical foundations of the overall theory (for the distinction between "levels" in my conceptualization is a "form" that has two sides; the concept of level implies that there are other levels).

Notwithstanding the distinction made between these levels, the subject of the inquiry (its "system reference") remains the system of society. In other words, in the context of distinguishing between the levels to analyze the subject, society, we are not concerned with systems that could also be addressed on the other levels. Methodologically, drawing a distinction between levels invites us to exhaust the possibilities of abstraction, to extend comparisons between systems to systems that are as diverse as possible, and to make any knowledge gained from the analysis of society available in the greatest possible measure for exploitation at more general levels.

This is not, as sociologists so often fear, a matter of analogical inference, nor is it a "merely metaphorical" use of biological ideas. The distinction says nothing about the being or the nature of things in the "analogy of being" (*analogia entis*) sense. It is nothing other than a form for unfolding the paradox of self-inclusive unity, and has the specific function of encouraging the exchange of ideas between disciplines and enhancing the potential for mutual stimulation. Nonetheless, it is not a statement of fact but a construction specific to science.

I shall use systems-theoretical means at all levels in analyzing the system of society to specify the necessary theoretical decisions. The general theory of autopoietic systems requires precise identification of the operation that carries out the autopoiesis of the system and thus demarcates the system from its environment. In the case of social systems, this is done through communication.

Communication has all the required properties: it is a genuinely social operation (and the only genuinely social one). It is genuinely social in that, although it presupposes a multiplicity of participating consciousness systems, it cannot (for this very reason) be attributed to any individual consciousness. Moreover, under the conditions of its own functioning, it excludes consciousness systems' knowing the given inner state of the other or others:[107] in oral communication because interlocutors participate in utterance/understanding *simultaneously*; in written communication because the partners participate *in their absence*. Communication can therefore only assume that adequate understanding also has psychic correlates.[108] In this sense (and "interpenetration" can mean no other), it depends on operational fictions that have to be tested only occasionally and only through communication.

Communication is also genuinely social in that a "common" (collective) consciousness can by no means and in no sense be produced, and that consensus in the full sense of complete agreement is hence also unattainable; communication operates in its place.[109] It is the smallest possible unit of a social system, namely, the unit to which communication can still react through communication.[110] In another version of the same argument, communication may be said to be autopoietic in that it can be produced only in recursive relation to other communications, thus every single communication contributes to reproducing only in a network.[111] A unit of communication is completed with understanding or misunderstanding regardless of the essentially infinite possibilities for clarifying *what* has been understood. But this completion takes the form of a transition to further communication that can pursue this clarification or turn to other topics. The production of elements is autopoiesis. Communicating acceptance or rejection of the proposed meaning of a communication is already *another* communication, and, regardless of all thematic ties, does not arise of itself from the preceding communication. An essential precondition for the autopoiesis of society and its structure formation is that communication does not of itself contain its own acceptance; this has to be decided through further, independent communication.

Since communication requires time to connect communications to communications, this mode of operation results in a temporal uncoupling of system and environment. The system and the environment nonetheless exist simultaneously and this simultaneity underlies all constitution of time.[112] But within the limitations this imposes, the system has to constitute an "eigentime" that adapts the speed of operation and the temporal perspectives of the system to internal possibilities. The system must then renounce one-to-one couplings between environmental events and systemic events and create arrangements within that take into account that other temporal relations obtain in the environment than in the system. The system develops structures (memories and expectations) to enable it in its operations to keep the temporal relations in the system and those in the environment apart and to organize eigentime. To some extent, the system must gain time vis-à-vis the environment, in other words, take precautions; and to some extent, too, it must be able to accept and cope with surprises. It must be able to delay or accelerate reactions while something quite different has begun to happen in the environment. But this becomes a problem only because system and environment inevitably operate simultaneously, and because the system can neither forge ahead into the future of the environment nor lag behind in its past. The system can hence never attain a temporal situation in which it can be sure that nothing is happening in the environment.

This is particularly true for the relationship between communication and consciousness, for processes of consciousness and, above all, for processes of perception that are to be presupposed in the environment of society. This difference, too, requires and permits temporal decoupling in indisputably simultaneous interaction. Since George Herbert Mead's pioneering studies,[113] we have known that communication does not come about only through an organism perceiving how another behaves and adapting accordingly; nor does it come about by imitating the gestures of the other (for instance, threat gestures or play gestures). Such behavior leads only to mutual irritation and stimulation of the (autopoiesis of) organisms, to more or less occasional and possibly relatively frequent coordination. According to Mead, what is decisive is that symbols come into being that enable the individual organism to coordinate *within itself* with the behavior of others, while itself using the appropriate "vocal gestures," to permit the coordination of the coordinations of organisms, as Humberto Maturana puts it.[114] This explanation can be developed in the direction of a social semiotics. However, it does not lead to a theory of society as a social system that differentiates itself from an environment (also of the organisms involved) through communication.[115] All propositions about communication remain propositions about the "behavioral organism," about the nervous system (biological) or consciousness (psychological).

This does not yet take account of the fact that participation in communication requires a high, steady speed in identifying successive particles of meaning. Otherwise, the short-term memory of communication would fail. On the other hand, the consciousness is not prepared for this in its neurophysiological basis and must evolve in a very specific sense if it is to keep up.[116] For this purpose, communication has clearly distinct combinations of sounds at the ready. At any rate, this is where the real problem of the co-evolution of the brain, consciousness, and language lies, and not in the mere treatment of signs.

Nothing about these insights requires to be corrected or withdrawn, but there remains the question of whether and how communication can be an operation that leads to the emergence and operational closure of an autonomous social system with its own environment that cannot be perceived (!), but only denoted. Or, to transfer an argument of Maturana's from cell biology to the theory of social systems: a description of the totality of the states of participating nervous systems or consciousness systems does not suffice to tell us how autopoiesis is possible for social systems.

What is likely to be decisive is that speaking (and gestures imitating it) makes the intention of the speaker apparent, thus imposing a distinction between information and utterance and then a reaction to this distinction that also employs linguistic means.[117] Only thus—as a component of this distinction—can information with informational value arise; in other words, information that changes the state of the system processing it (in the sense of Gregory Bateson's famous dictum "a difference that makes a difference"). Moreover, and this distinguishes communication from biological processes of all types, it is an operation endowed with the capacity for self-observation. Every communication must at the same time communicate that it is a communication and mark who has uttered what so that follow-up communication can be determined and autopoiesis continued. It therefore not only generates a difference through mere implementation as operation (this as well!) but also uses a specific distinction, that between utterance and information, to observe that this happens.

This realization has far-reaching consequences. It means not only that the identification of utterance as "action" is the construct of an observer, that is, the construct of a communication system observing itself. It means above all that social systems (including society) can come about only as self-observing systems. This obliges me, in contrast to Talcott Parsons and everything currently on the market in the action theory sector, to renounce an action-theoretical (and hence "individualistic") foundation for sociology.[118] At the same time, it presents us with a problem, but initially nothing more than that of a system forced to observe itself continuously; observation that, as we have seen, is an operation contingent on a distinction that at the moment of operating itself functions as the excluded middle. All self-observation, too, is conditional on a blind spot. It is possible only because it cannot see its seeing. Communication thus functions operationally as the unity of the difference between information, utterance, and understanding without being able to communicate this unity. But for subsequent self-observation, it uses the distinction between information, utterance, and understanding to determine whether further communication has to react to doubts about information, to presumed intentions of the utterance (e.g., deception), or to difficulties in understanding. No self-observation is therefore in a position to capture the full reality of the system that carries it out. It can only do something instead, only choose substitute solutions; and it does so by selecting distinctions with which the system observes itself. If sufficiently complex, a system can pass from observation of its operations to observation of its observation, and finally to observation of the system itself. In this case, it must take the distinction between "system and environment" as the basis, and thus be able to distinguish between self-reference and other-reference. However, this too takes place through operations of the system in the system—otherwise it would not be *self*-observation. The distinction between self-reference and other-reference is one practiced within the system and thought about as such. One might also call it a construction of the system.

Given the impossibility of capturing the fullness of being or making the system transparent to itself, a complex structure of distinctions develops that guides the observation process of the system, steering it inward or outward depending on which side of the distinction is indicated as "inside" and "outside." If the system has appropriate storage capabilities at its disposal, for example, writing, it can then gather experience, condense situational impressions through repetition, and develop an operational memory without running the risk of constantly confusing itself with the environment. All this takes place following the basal distinction between self-reference and other-reference with other suitable distinctions.

The concept of self-observation does not assume that there is only one such possibility in a system. Many communications can be simultaneously performed and self-observed. This also holds true for observation of the unity of the system in distinction to the environment. A social system—particularly, of course, a society—can observe itself at the same time or successively in quite different, we could say "polycontextural," ways. As far as the object is concerned, there is therefore no obligation to integrate self-observations. The system does what it does.

What has been said so far applies to social systems of widely differing types, for example, to organizations or, as family therapists well know, to families. Turning now to the third level on which the specificity of a societal system is to be treated, the problems posed by the diversity of possible self-observations prove particularly evident and far-reaching. For society as the comprehensive social system knows no social systems outside its bounds. It cannot thus be observed from without.[119] Although psychic systems can observe society from outside, this has no social consequences if it is not communicated, if, that is to say, the observation is not carried out within the social system. In other words, society is the extreme case of polycontextural self-observation, the extreme case of a system obliged to observe itself without functioning as an object about which there can be only one correct opinion, so that all deviation is to be treated as error. Even if society routinely distinguishes itself from its environment, it is by no means clear in advance what is thus being distinguished from its environment. And even where texts, that is to say, descriptions, are prepared to guide and coordinate observations, this does not mean that there is only one correct description in each case. One cannot without further ado claim that South Chinese fishermen regarded Confucian ethics as the basis of the empire as did mandarins and bureaucrats. The Indian caste system as a representation of unity through difference, too, takes widely varying forms incompatible with the unity of a hierarchical order. And it remains an empirical question who in the late Middle Ages outside the clergy, the nobility, and the legally schooled magistrates and administrative officials knew and believed in the three estates theory. From the peasants' point of view, society was rather a one-class affair, with the exception of the lord of the manor and his family.

For in the case of society, there is no external description that allows correction, however much men of letters and sociologists may aspire to such a position. Tradition had externalized interest in an infallible description, naming the relevant position "God." God could do everything except err. It had, however, to be conceded that the judgment of priests about the judgment of God could be fallible, and that the correct description, the true catalogue of sins would be known only when the world came to an end, at the Last Judgment, and then in the form of a surprise.

In the light of this thesis of surplus possibilities for self-observation and self-description, I shall attempt in the final chapter [of Volume 2] to show that self-descriptions are nevertheless not the product of chance. There are structural conditions for the plausibility of descriptions; and there are historical trends in the evolution of semantics that severely restrict the scope for variation. Sociological theory can then recognize interrelationships from the type of correlations between societal structures and semantics; but it can also realize that such theories are their own constructs and should not be confused with the current description of the societal system.

In sum, society has no essence. Its unity cannot be discovered by reduction to the essential, allowing contradictory views to be rejected as erroneous (for this, too, would have to be communicated in society and would thus change what is being spoken about). The unity of the societal system therefore lies only in external demarcation, in the form of the system, in the difference reproduced continuously through its operations.

This is the point any "redescription" of the old European tradition has to emphasize.

When we say that *only* communications and *all* communications contribute to the autopoiesis of society and thereby redefine the attribute "comprehensive," this thesis also contains a far-reaching break with tradition. At issue are neither goals nor good convictions, neither cooperation nor conflict, neither consensus nor dissension, neither acceptance nor rejection of the meaning propounded. Nor does individual happiness play a role, or at best only as a topic of communication.[120] Only autopoiesis itself is conveyed by all these communications; and a fortiori by all communications to be attributed to the subsystems of society. Distinctions like those between economy and society, law and society, school and society are therefore confusing and, in our theory, not allowed. They give the impression that the components of the distinction are mutually exclusive, whereas in truth the economy, law, school, and so on, are not outside society but can be considered only as societal performance. Attempting to distinguish between women and human beings is just as nonsensical; it is merely much more widespread nonsense.

"All communications" means communications have an autopoietic effect in so far as *their difference makes no difference. That* communication takes place is therefore not a surprise in society, and therefore not information (it is naturally different with psychic systems that are addressed unexpectedly). On the other hand, communication is the actualization of information. Thus, society consists of the linkage between operations that make no difference in that they make a difference. This relegates all assumptions about understanding, progress, rationality, or other appealing goals to a secondary theoretical position. But precisely this lends particular weight to the theory of symbolically generalized communication media.

"All communication" even includes paradoxical communication, communication that denies that it says what it says. We can communicate paradoxically and do so without communicating "meaninglessly" (in the sense of ununderstandably = autopoietically ineffectively).[121] As an *operation*, paradoxical communication functions even though it bewilders the *observer*, which is well understood to be its intent. Both classical rhetoric and modern literature, both the Nietzsche-Heidegger tradition of philosophy and the family therapist make use of open paradox; what is more, it has become usual to watch for hidden paradoxes in observing the observation of others. The function of paradoxical communication is not fully clarified and is presumably itself paradoxical, namely, as an attempt to destroy and create in one act, which does not cause difficulty for the autopoietic operation, only for its observation.[122]

6. Operational Closure and Structural Couplings

If we describe society as a system, it follows from the general theory of autopoietic systems that it must be an operationally closed one. At the level of the system's own operations there is no ingress to the environment, and environmental systems are just as little able take part in the autopoietic processes of an operationally closed system.[123] This is the case even, indeed especially, *where such operations are observations or operations whose autopoiesis requires self-observation*—a difficult thought that runs counter to the entire epistemological tradition. Observations can only affect observations, can only transform distinctions into other distinctions, can, in other words, only process information; but they cannot touch things of the environment with the important but narrow exception of everything involved through structural couplings. Observing systems, too, have *no contact with the environment* at the operational level. All observation of the environment must be carried out in the system as an internal activity with the aid of the system's *own* distinctions (for which there is *no correspondence* in the environment. Otherwise, it would make no sense at all to speak of observing the *environment.* All observation of the environment presupposes the distinction between self-reference and other-reference, which can be made only in the system itself (where else?). And this also makes it clear that all observation of the environment stimulates self-observation and every gain in distance from the environment raises the question of self, of one's own identity. Since we can observe only with distinctions, the one side of the distinction makes us, as it were, curious about the other, stimulates us to "cross" the boundary (as Spencer-Brown would say) that is marked by the form "system and environment."

At the level of first-order observation, however, this distinction between contact with the environment and only internally connective other-reference is not taken into account—in either consciousness systems or communication systems. All traces of operational closure are deleted. Consciousness systems know nothing about the operating conditions of their brains, but they think "within their heads." Communication systems do not know that communications contact nothing else but communications. Systems therefore operate under the illusion of having contact with the environment—at least as long as they only observe *what* they observe and do not observe *how* they observe. The experience of the resistance and nonarbitrariness of operational outcomes are registered externally and therefore present a world we have no choice but to accept. Phenomenology is practiced as ontology. This condition is easily understood. It can be revoked in second-order observation, but this happens without the possibility of completely renouncing first-order observation; even second-order observation must still be able to observe an observer. Even the recognized illusion of reality therefore remains a fact in the real world. We see that the sun "comes up" and cannot see it otherwise even though we know we are deceiving ourselves. In other words, at the level of first-order observation, which can never be completely abandoned, no distinction can be drawn between reality and the illusion of reality.

One consequence of operational closure is that the system has to rely on *self-organization*. A system's own structures can be built up and changed only through its own operations; language, for example, only through communication and not directly through fire, earthquakes, radiation from space, or the perceptions of the individual consciousness. All operations (communications) therefore have a double function: they (1) establish the historical state of the system, the point of departure for the system in ensuing operations. They determine that the system is the way it is and not otherwise. And (2) they form structures as selection schemata that make recognition and repetition possible, hence condensing identities (many say with Piaget invariances), which they confirm in ever-new situations and thus generalize. This structure formation that permits remembering and forgetting is not possible through external agency; we therefore speak of self-organization. Closure, self-determination, and self-organization—and this is the evolutionary advantage—make a system highly compatible with disorder in the environment, or more precisely with only fragmentary, only incomplete environments not organized as a unity. Evolution hence leads necessarily to the closure of systems, which in turn contributes to overall disorder, against which operational closure and self-organization hold their own. In precisely this sense, the operational closure of the communication system society is in keeping with the emergence of mobile organisms endowed with nervous systems and finally with consciousness. And society, because it tolerates the uncoordinated multiplicity of perspectives of these endogenously restless individual systems, reinforces this diversity.

Within the tradition of systems theory, the closure of systems must appear an extravagant thesis; for, with the law of entropy in mind, it constitutes itself as a theory of open (and therefore negentropic) systems. This position in relation to the law of entropy is naturally not to be retracted. By "closure," I do not mean thermodynamic closure but only operational closure, which means the recursive enablement of a system's own operations through the outcomes of its own operations. For real operations can be assumed to be possible only in a *simultaneously* existing world. This excludes one operation influencing another. If this is nevertheless to occur, it can do so only in direct connection between one operation and another. However, such recursive relations, in which the conclusion of an operation is the condition for another to take place, leads to differentiation between systems whose closure is often realized in a structurally highly complex manner and their simultaneously existing environment. I call the outcome operational closure.

We can also look at this whole subject in relation to consciousness systems and show why and how the modern distance between the individual and society induces the individual to reflect, to ask about the "I" of I, to search for an identity of his own. What had always been seen and what the world was is now "outside." What, then, is "inside"? An indeterminable void? If we apply the theory of autopoietic systems to the case of society, we come to the same conclusion, naturally with regard to another mode of operation, namely, communication.

Society is a communicatively closed system. It generates communication through communication. Its dynamics consist in the effect of communication on communication in the sense of transforming current distinctions and indications but never in the sense of reshaping the external environment.[124] We can no less talk things into shape than we can think them out of existence or rethink them.

Society is hence a system that is completely and exclusively determined by itself. Everything that is determined as communication has to be determined through communication. Everything that is experienced as reality arises from the resistance of communication to communication,[125] and not from any imposition of an outside world ordered in one way or another. This naturally includes communication about dependence on the environment; but then what is communicated is determined with the aid of the distinction between self-reference and other-reference intrinsic to the system and through recursive recourse to and anticipation of further communication. This self-determination is a precondition for the toleration, indeed, the deliberate placing of indeterminacies, for example, of questions, of ambiguities, of paradoxical utterances, of irony. The communication itself decides, if necessary after checking or disregarding matters, on the degree of determinacy required and on a specific illocutionary meaning of indeterminacies. And the final check on self-determination in the determinacy/indeterminacy dimension is to ask what contributes to the continuation or termination of current communications.

As a communication system, society can communicate only within itself, neither with itself nor with its environment. It produces its unity through the operational performance of communications in recursion to and anticipation of other communications. Operating on the basis of the observation schema "system and environment," it can then communicate *within* itself, *about* itself, or *about* its environment, but never *with* itself and never *with* its environment. For neither it nor its environment can reoccur in society as partner in, as addressee of communication. Any such attempt would be talking into the void, would initiate no autopoiesis and would therefore not take place. For society is possible only as an autopoietic system.

This closure has to do with the specific operational manner in which the system reproduces, namely, communication; it does not have to do with causality as such. The environment is, of course, always involved, and without it nothing, absolutely nothing can happen. The term production (or simply poiesis) always refers to only part of the causes an observer can identify as required, namely, the part obtainable through the internal networking of the system's operations, the part with which the system determines its own state. And reproduction in the old sense of the term means production from products, determination of the state of the system as the point of departure for every further determination of the state of the system. And since this production/reproduction requires a distinction to be drawn between external and internal conditions, the system always reproduces its boundaries in the process, that is to say, its unity. Autopoiesis accordingly means production of the system by itself.

But communication only comes about because a distinction is drawn between utterance and information and the distinction is understood. All further communication can then relate either to the utterance or to the information; but it can do so only by means of follow-up communication, which in turn reproduces the difference between utterance and information. In *operational* performance (by taking place *in fact*) communication reproduces the *closure* of the system. Through the *mode of observation* (*how* it takes place, namely, by distinguishing between utterance and information) it reproduces the *difference between closure and openness*. A system thus arises that, owing to its closure, is open to the environment in its operations, because its basal operation is geared to observation. For the system, the difference in form between utterance and information is therefore an inevitable condition for autopoietic reproduction. In other cases, there would be only cessation of communication, an end to the system's operations.

This necessity relative to the form of communication also means that, as we have seen, the system always reproduces a double reference: the distinction between self-reference and other-reference. Through utterance the system refers to itself. Utterance actualizes the possibility of recursively relating further communication to the system. Through information, in contrast, the system typically refers to its environment.[126] The structure of the communicative operation therefore has precisely the form needed to transfer the difference between system and environment into the system and to treat it there as a distinction between self-reference and other-reference. Merely operating reproduces only the difference between system and environment through always selective recursion. The distinction then "reenters" what is distinguished through the distinction between utterance and information.[127] The difference between system and environment appears in the system in the form of directions of reference—and only thus. The problem of the operationally inaccessible environment is hence transposed from operation to cognition.[128] The system reproduces itself in the imaginary space of reference by renewing the distinction between self-reference and other-reference with every communicative operation as the form of its autopoiesis.

The autopoiesis of the communication system society hence always and necessarily reproduces the distinction that divides reference into self-reference and other reference. It can still refer to this distinction by subsuming it as a distinction in its own right under "self-reference." This would then be the reentry of a distinction into an already completed reentry of the distinction between system and environment into the system. At the operational level, this distinction is always presupposed as an operationally inaccessible condition of reference. All internal transformations, all information processing, all transformations of distinctions into distinctions can therefore have to do only with communicative reference. It cannot intervene directly in the environment. For the system, "objects" are accordingly always references; they are never things that exist in the outside world, but structural entities of the system's autopoiesis, that is to say, conditions for the continuation of communication.[129] Nor can the system intervene in its own unity. If it does so, it merely actualizes self-reference, only the one side of the distinction that permits reference. The other side remains unmentioned. For this reason, all self-descriptions of society are concerned only with the half of the reality that they actualize as a unity of self- and other-reference. As an observer, the system operates blindly, because it can accommodate the unity of the distinction that permits observation on neither side of the distinction. And because everything that happens happens as an operation within the system, neither the unity of the environment nor the unity of the system's autopoiesis is accessible to the system. There are only the abridging indications used in observation.

This account does not yet provide an adequate picture of how the system of society relates to its environment. For the real possibility of communication, as an observer can discover, has many factual preconditions, which the system can neither produce itself nor guarantee. Being closed is always being enclosed in something which, seen from inside, is outside. In other words, the establishment and maintenance of system boundaries—including those of living beings—presuppose a continuum of materiality that neither knows nor respects these boundaries (which is why Ilya Prigogine can speak of "dissipative structures" already in the physical and chemical fields). But this raises the question of how a system, here, the system of society, organizes its relationship with the environment if it maintains no contact with this environment and has only its own referential capacity at its disposition. The entire theory of society depends on the answer to this question—and we now see that, and how, humanistic and regionalistic concepts of society have avoided even posing this question.

The answer to a difficult question is a difficult concept. Following Humberto Maturana, we speak of "structural coupling."[130] Structural couplings limit the scope of the possible structures with which a system can carry out its autopoiesis. They presuppose that every autopoietic system operates as a structurally determined system, in other words, a system that can determine its own operations only through its own structures. Structural couplings hence preclude environmental factors from specifying in accordance with their own structures what happens in the system. Maturana would say that structural coupling is in orthogonal relation to the self-determination of the system.[131] It does not determine what happens in the system, but must be presupposed, because autopoiesis would otherwise come to a standstill and the system would cease to exist. To this extent, every system is adapted to its environment (or else it does not exist); but within the given scope, it has every possibility to behave aberrantly. The result is particularly apparent in the ecological problems facing modern society.

In the terminology of informatics, we could say that structural couplings *digitize analog* relations.[132] Since the environment and the other systems within it always operate simultaneously with the given reference system of observation, we are initially dealing only with analog (parallel) relations. The participating systems cannot extract any information, for this requires digitization. Structural couplings must therefore first convert analog into digital relations if they are to influence a system. In relations between the communication system and consciousness systems, this is a function of language, which converts a continuous "alongside" into a discontinuous succession.

Less attention has been paid to another precondition for structural couplings, which must therefore be particularly stressed. Structural couplings presuppose that the system produces surplus possibilities internally (e.g., possibilities for movement defined in direction neither by space nor the organism). This alone allows the system to accept restrictions on its freedom, and to do so in a way that can vary from situation to situation. For psychic and for social systems, these surplus possibilities are set through the medium of meaning. To resolve these indeterminacies (which has to be done internally), the system requires pointers, which can be supplied by its own memory or by structural couplings (the body remembers the limits to its possibilities for movement and sees them in the terrain).

The concept of structural coupling allows us to take into account that the adaptedness of the system cannot be adequately explained as an outcome of either "natural selection" or the system's cognitive performance. For no system can muster the "requisite variety" (W. Ross Ashby). It can only compensate for the unknownness of the environment by the internal surplus of possibilities, by matching indeterminacy with indeterminacy. This is true a fortiori if, unlike Maturana, we define cognition as an indication on the basis of a distinction, thus presupposing a capacity for distinguishing for which there is no correlate of any sort in the environment of the system. If this is to be achieved, the system must be able, first, to close itself operationally and reproduce autopoietically, and, second, to rely on extremely limited structural couplings with the environment. Eyes and ears and the corresponding connective operations in the brain are prime examples.

Structural couplings must have a basis in reality independent of the coupled autopoietic systems (although this alone naturally does not explain the function of structural coupling).[133] In other words, they presuppose a continuum of materiality (or energy) in which the boundaries of the system are *not* marked, and thus above all a physically functioning world. They are moreover very stable—precisely because they are compatible with all the autopoietically possible structural developments of systems. But of course this also means that their endangerment or destruction must have catastrophic consequences to which systems cannot react, because all possibilities for reacting depend on preliminary filtration by structural couplings. Finally, it should be remembered that structural couplings, too, are two-sided forms that include something by excluding other things. They bundle and intensify certain causalities that affect the coupled system, irritating it and thus stimulating it to self-determination. And they exclude other forms of influence. On the outside, there is also causality that can affect the system (as an observer might be aware), but such causality can be only destructive.

In the sense of this already complicated concept, all communication is structurally coupled with consciousness. Without consciousness, communication is impossible. Communication is *totally* dependent (in *every* operation) on consciousness—if only because only consciousness and not communication itself can perceive sensorily, and neither oral nor written communication could function without perception.[134] Moreover, communication, at least in its primary, oral form depends on reciprocity being established within the perceptual scope of the participating consciousness systems in the form of perception of being perceived.[135] It is thus a special capability of the consciousness, which permits the almost simultaneous processing of utterance and understanding, and that can provide for primary self-correction of communication, for example, in stopping an utterance when the sender sees that the receiver is not paying attention. Nonetheless, consciousness is neither the "subject" of communication nor in any other sense a "vehicle" of communication. It contributes no operations of any sort to communication (e.g., in the sense of a successive thought-speech-thought-speech sequence). Communication functions only because no recursions have to be produced between such heterogeneous modes of operation and because communication has no need to thematize the presupposition of consciousness, but accepts it through structural couplings. We must therefore abandon the classical metaphor that communication is a "transmission" of semantic content by one psychic system that possesses it to another.[136]

If we abandon this notion of communication as transmission, it must have far-reaching consequences for general systems theory and its application to social systems, which are difficult to assess. Classical systems theory (Wiener, von Bertalanffy, Forrester) posited a concept of transfer or flow and had understood systems to be their regulation. This was the case for all types of transfer—for biological and economic systems, for organizations, for consciousness systems, and for machines, and made it possible to compare them. Environmental relations were described either with the aid of an input/output model or a feedback loop, always on the assumption that the system controlled or even generated this process through regulation. If, however, we are unable to see communication as transmission, this eliminates one of the key premises of this systems theory. We must either affirm the old suspicion that social matters are quite unsuitable for systems-theoretical treatment—or we have to rethink systems theory. This could be done by asking how the production and reproduction of a difference between system and environment comes about in the first place. For a specific type of system, namely, the social system, the answer to this question lies in the concept of communication.

If reproduced autopoietically though recursions, communications form an emergent reality sui genesis. Human beings cannot communicate; only communication can communicate. Like communication systems, consciousness systems (and brains, cells, and so on, on their other side) are operationally closed systems that can maintain no contact with one another. There is no nonsocially mediated communication from consciousness to consciousness and there is no communication between the individual and society. Every sufficiently precise understanding of communication excludes such possibilities (as well as the other possibility that society could be conceived of as a collective mind). Only a consciousness can think (but not think its way into another consciousness), and only society can communicate. And in both cases, we are dealing with self-operations of an operationally closed, structurally determined system.

Particular to this instance of structural coupling between consciousness and communication is that autopoietic systems are involved on *both* sides. It is therefore not a matter of coupling an autopoietic system to invariant environmental conditions—as the musculature of self-propelled organisms is adapted to the gravitational force of the Earth. In the relationship between consciousness and communication, too, there are some structural invariants, for example, the limited speed of changes in states of consciousness, which communication must not overtax. More important, or at any rate evolutionarily less probable, is that communication presupposes endogenously restless environmental systems that inevitably and repeatedly change their state. This means that communication has to be prepared to cope with continual irritation by its environment without its vocabulary and rules of grammar being allowed to change from moment to moment. Indeed, language has the peculiar ability to convey irritations to communication without breaking down.

In the case of structural coupling, this works as always incessantly and invisibly, it works also and especially when we are not thinking about it and not talking about it—as when going for a walk, we can take the next step without thinking about the weight that is physically required to do so. And just as our weight narrowly limits our scope for walking (in other words, the gravitational force of the earth must be neither too strong nor too weak), consciousness systems and communication systems are adapted to one another to allow them to function in unobtrusive coordination. The mutual intransparency of the coupled systems has not only to be accepted in practice: it is a necessary condition for structural coupling; for the endogenously determined operations of the systems could otherwise not be synchronized. That such highly improbable conditions are to be expected, and that so very few of the many possibilities are realized on both sides of the coupling, can, like the possibility of going for a walk, be explained only in terms of evolution theory.

This unseen, quiet functioning of the structural coupling between communication and consciousness does not exclude participants in communication from being identified and even addressed in communication. Following an old tradition, I shall refer to them in this context as "persons,"[137] and thus say that the communication process is in a position to "personify" external references. Every communication must be able to distinguish between information and utterance (otherwise it would not itself be distinguishable). But this means that corresponding objective and personal references form. Following Spencer-Brown,[138] we could also say that the reuse of such references *condenses* persons (or things), defining them as identical while *confirming* them, that is to say, as enriched with new charges of meaning from different sorts of utterance. If this happens, a corresponding semantics develops. Persons have names. What personality means and how it is to be handled may be described in greater detail in complicated forms. But all this does not alter the separateness and operational closure of structurally coupled systems. And the modern semantics of life, of subjectivity, of individuality give the impression of being invented to compensate for this irrevocable being-for-itself.[139]

Through structural couplings, a system can be connected to highly complex environmental conditions without having to acquire or reconstruct their complexity. As we can recognize from the physical constraints of eyes and ears, structural couplings always cover a very restricted portion of the environment. Everything that is excluded cannot have an irritating and stimulating effect on the system, but only a destructive impact. This is the only way to safeguard the autonomy of the system's autopoiesis and the development of the system's own complexity. This is already true of the physical environmental couplings of the nervous system and particularly impressively for the coupling of the communication system with individually dispersed consciousness systems. For the system, the complexity of coupled environmental systems remain nontransparent; it is not taken over by the system's own mode of operation because the "requisite variety," as W. Ross Ashby puts it, is lacking.[140] It is mostly reconstructed in the operations of the system only in the form of precondition and malfunction, or of normality and irritation. In communication systems, general indications like names or concepts such as "human being," "person," and "consciousness" serve in the system's processing of reference to environmental complexity. It is always a matter of utilizing ordered (structured but certainly not predictable) complexity in accordance with a system's own operational possibilities—and in society this means using it linguistically. Where such relations develop in mutual co-evolution and none of the systems thus structurally coupled could exist without them, we can also speak of *interpenetration*.[141] The relationship between nerve cells and brains is a good example; the relationship between consciousness systems and society is another, also quantitatively more or less comparable.

Plainly, the regular structural coupling of consciousness systems with communication systems is made possible by language.[142] A topic also much discussed in sociology concerning the relationship between society, culture, language, and psychic "mentalities"[143] is thus expressed in a concept that is necessary for theory construction. In subtle analyses, Wilhelm von Humboldt examined both the subjective and objective character of language. The speaker has to choose an objective form and surrender ownership of the spoken word, with the result that in spoken communication, no participant thinks exactly what another thinks. Language frees itself from its creators [*sic*] as form. But he goes on to say: "The true resolution of this contradiction lies in the unity of human nature."[144] A theory of society that took communication, not language, as its point of departure was lacking, and this gap was initially filled by a philosophical anthropology. Only the postulate of two different types of autopoietic system makes it possible to replace the "unity of human nature" with the concept of structural coupling.

This choice of concept implies that language functions without psychic reflection or social comment, which does not exclude choosing our words when the consciousness sees cause to do so, or talking about ways of expressing oneself if a problem of understanding arises for the social system. But such rather exceptional concerns also presuppose that language works unobtrusively; in other words, that it is in "orthogonal" relation to the autopoietic processes of the systems participating in it.

In the evolutionary context, language is an extremely improbable sort of noise, which, precisely because of its improbability, has high attention value and highly complex possibilities of specification. A consciousness present when speech is proceeding can easily distinguish this noise from other noises and finds it difficult to escape the fascination of current communication (whatever it might be thinking within its own inaudible system). At the same time, the possibilities language offers for specification permit highly complex communication structures to be developed, first, through the complexification and subsequent smoothing out of linguistic rules themselves, and, second, by developing social semantics for the situational reactivation of important possibilities for communication. The same applies mutatis mutandis for language transferred from an acoustic to a visual medium, that is to say, for the written word. Chapter 2 will examine the enormous, often underestimated effects of this visualization of language.

Whereas language as a structure has to be relatively permanently fixed, there is a second coupling mechanism that is both unstable and, as it were, capable of learning, for which we may borrow the concept of "schemata" from cognitive psychology.[145] In a poorly coordinated area of research, it goes by many other names, as well: "frames," "scripts," "prototypes," "cognitive maps," and "implicit theories," to mention only a few. These terms denote meaning combinations that serve society and psychic systems to form a memory that can forget almost all their own operations but can nevertheless retain and reuse something in schematized form. Examples are standardized forms of defining something as something (e.g., a beverage as wine), attribution schemata that link causes and effects, possibly vesting them with demands for action or blame apportionment (where they are called scripts).[146] But time schemata, especially past/future or preference codes such as good/bad, true/false, and property/nonproperty also perform the schematization function. In using schemata, communication presupposes that every participating consciousness understands what is meant, but also that this does not determine how consciousness systems handle the schema, let alone what follow-up communications result from the use of schemata. Schemata can be concretized and adapted to every need. For example, corporal punishment can be deemed educationally beneficial or detrimental. In concrete situations, they help "fill gaps" in the search for supplementation and completion.[147] In any case, as extracts from memory, they cannot be used schematically.[148] They serve as reductions of *structural* complexity in the development of *operational* complexity, and hence in the ongoing adjustment of structural coupling between psychic and social systems to changing conditions. Here, too, the function and mechanisms of coupling do not have to take effect in the operations of the systems; they can be supposed to act noiselessly.

In the context of a theory of the system of society, it is not useful to develop—in the form of a vast excursus, as it were—a theory of language and a theory of schematisms based on this function of structural coupling. I would merely point out that doing so contradicts fundamental principles of Saussurian linguistics: language does not have its own mode of operation, it has to be realized either as thought or as communication; it consequently does not form a system of its own. Language is and remains dependent on the circumstance that consciousness systems, on the one hand, and the communication system of society, on the other, continue their own autopoiesis with completely closed operations of their own. Were this not to happen, speech would immediately cease and thinking in language would no longer be possible.

Loosely following Talcott Parsons, we can also call this form of structural coupling "symbolic generalization."[149] However, the term "symbolic" is used differently in this context than with regard to symbol development within societal communication, when, for example, genealogies are compiled on the principle of descent to explain similarities between persons. As a coupling between consciousness systems and communication systems, the symbol means only that there is a difference that can be treated as the same from both standpoints. In this sense, a symbolic use of linguistic generalizations (= reuses) presupposes the referentiality of language, that is to say, the ability to distinguish signifier (words) from signified (things) in consciousness and in communication. Only the signifier is suitable for symbolic use, not the signified things themselves. In other words, contrary to the assumptions of our tradition, conveying human kind and society cannot depend on "nature."

Just as important as artificiality, condensation, confirmation, and the symbolic use of linguistic signs is an element that often attracts less attention: the binary coding of language. All communication offers two possibilities: acceptance and rejection. All (condensed and confirmed) meaning can be expressed in an affirmative version and in a negative version. This sets the course for the further treatment of the topic.[150] The same arrangement is also important as a form of structural coupling and presumably came about for this reason. For the bifurcation of the communication code language also allows consciousness to opt for one side of the form or the other. With this minimum of freedom, it can elude determination by the course of communication and give itself over to (for itself nontransparent) self-determination. For unascertainable reasons, it says yes or no, accepts or rejects, supports or blocks the further course of communication; and does so in a communicatively comprehensible manner for motives that may remain incomprehensible for itself and for others, and that play no thematic role in communication (except in exceptional circumstances). This state of affairs is imposed universally by the code of language, independently of words, topics, motives, and contexts. It is given always and at every moment. In this form, it is an indispensable condition for the structural coupling of different instances of autopoiesis.

That communication systems are coupled to consciousness systems through language, as are consciousness systems to communication systems, has far-reaching consequences for the structural development of the systems involved, for their morphogenesis, for their evolution. Unlike consciousness systems, which can perceive sensorily, communication can be affected only through consciousness. Everything impacting society from outside that is not communication must therefore have passed through the double filter of consciousness and the possibility of communication. The structural coupling of consciousness and communication is hence a form that includes and excludes: it increases the possibilities of mutual irritation in its channel but can do so only on condition that all influences not covered by it are excluded or limited to destructive effects.

We must literally keep an *eye* on what this means: the entire physical world, including the physical basis of communication itself can affect communication only via *operationally closed* brains, and these brains only through *operationally closed* consciousness systems, and thus only through "individuals." This involves an enormous and, from an evolutionary point of view, very improbable process of selection, which at the same time determines the high degree of freedom in societal development. Physical, chemical, and biological processes have no direct access to communication—if not in the sense of destruction. Noise or the withdrawal of air or spatial distance can exclude oral communication. Books can burn or even be burned. But no fire can write a book or even irritate the author strongly enough to cause him write differently while the manuscript burns than had there been no fire. Consciousness is hence in a privileged position under all the external conditions of autopoiesis. It controls the access of the outside world to communication, but it does so, not as the "subject" of communication, not as an entity "underlying" communication, but thanks to its capability for (highly filtered, self-generated) perception, which, under the conditions of structural coupling, depends in turn on the neurophysiological processes of the brain and through these on further processes of the autopoiesis of life.

That communication systems are coupled directly only with consciousness systems and accordingly profit from their selectivity without being specified by them provides a defense that largely prevents the total reality of the world from affecting communication. No system could be complex enough to endure this and maintain its autopoiesis. Only thanks to this protection has a system been able to develop whose reality consists in the processing of mere "signs." It should be remembered that consciousness systems exist in large numbers, now more than five billion units, all operating at the same time. Even if we take into account that consciousness systems on the other side of the world are asleep at the moment and others are not engaged in any sort of communication for other reasons, the number of simultaneously operating systems is still so great that effective coordination (and hence the formation of consensus in an empirically evident sense) is completely excluded. The communication system is therefore necessarily left to its own resources, it has to direct itself; and it can do so as long as it succeeds in activating the required consciousness material in its environment.

There can thus be no question of any sort of homogeneity between the operations and states of structurally coupled systems. The use of language and cognitive schemata does not change this. There must be other reasons why structural couplings nevertheless come into being. They are likely to lie in the *temporality* of the operations not only of neurophysiological and conscious systems, but of communicative systems.[151] Always with an eye on their structural couplings, we must take a closer look at this temporal structure of autopoietic systems; for, although the world exists simultaneously for every system, brains, consciousness systems, and communication systems form differing sequences of events and thus operate at different speeds. What consciousness perceives as intensity is developed in the nervous system by a sequence of impulses. There are such time differences in the experience of volition and emotion, too.[152] The consciousness has accordingly already been in action when communication produces events. The consciousness, we could say, interprets what has already happened in the brain as a decision, a feeling, or an insight. Communication actualizes and thus captures in consciousness what has already been decided. For its part, this peculiar belatedness in structural couplings remains unnoticed. It is interpreted as simultaneity. It is, as it were, translated into the assumption of a reality that exists independently of cognitive operations. The need to synchronize time to suit the requirements of the given system's own autopoiesis thus explains the emergence of a world that is the way it is independently of cognition. Systems convert temporal relations into reality without specifically anticipating particular meaning forms.

Following this analysis, we can do without the assumption that there is an ontological substratum to the world and at the same time explain this assumption itself. We have to assume that the operations of structurally coupled systems are temporal because the basal elements of these systems are produced in relation to time. As more precise analysis can show, all conditions are quite complex. All operations in coupled systems are only events that are over as soon as they occur. They must therefore produce the difference from the environment through a sequence of matching operations. This requires memories specific to systems. Although the memory participates only in the system's own operations, remembering or forgetting only its own operations, it presents the outcomes (products) of operations on the basis of the distinction between self-reference and other-reference. Every system therefore projects synchronization with other systems and similarity of other-referential matters *into the world*, although there are neither checks nor any meta-guarantees for agreement. At the same time it knows itself to be different and the outside world to be also accessible to others. Therefore, in the field of intentional and thematic other-reference, consciousness, like societal communication, develops the idea of things that exist externally, although a system is nothing other and has nothing else but the history of its own movement.[153] This paradox of supposing similarity despite separateness explains that consciousness systems experience continuous irritation when participating in communication, causing a structural drift, which in turn affects the conditions for further participation in communication. In this sense, communication regenerates conditions for the continuation of communication through the way in which it affects its environment. However, what in communication is registered as consensus or dissension remains completely open.

The sole alternative to the consciousness/communication structural coupling that is emerging—with unpredictable consequences—is the computer. There are already computers in use whose operations are accessible to neither consciousness nor communication, neither simultaneously nor reconstructively. Although they are manufactured and programmed machines, such computers function nontransparently for consciousness and for communication; their operations nevertheless affect consciousness and communication through structural couplings. Strictly speaking, they are invisible machines. If we ask whether computers are machines that work analogously to consciousness and can replace or even outdo consciousness systems, we are putting the problem wrongly and probably playing it down. Nor is it relevant whether the internal operations of the computer can be understood as communications. We must presumably leave aside all analogies of this sort and ask instead what consequences it would have if computers could establish a quite independent structural coupling between a reality they were able to construct and consciousness or communication systems.

This question deserves greater attention; it is impossible to judge at present what consequences it would have for the further evolution of the societal system. At any rate, any theory of society should reserve an indeterminacy position for the issue, and the structural coupling concept offers such a possibility. Although we assume in what follows that communication systems are coupled to consciousness systems through language and only for this reason can afford indifference toward everything else, the computer can also be considered likely to make other forms of structural coupling possible.

Finally, the concept of structural coupling explains that, although systems are completely self-determined, they develop by and large in a direction tolerated by the environment. In structural coupling, the inside of the system can be termed irritation (or disturbance or perturbation). Autopoietic systems react directly to negative and nontypifiable stimuli. At any rate, they are not, as economic theory would suppose, utility maximizers per se.[154] In their irritability, too, both consciousness systems and the communication system society are completely autonomous. Irritations arise from an internal comparison of (initially unspecified) events with the system's own possibilities, especially with established structures, with expectations. There is hence no irritation in the system's environment and there is no transfer of irritation from the environment into the system. It is always a construct of the system itself, always self-irritation—albeit occasioned by environmental effects. The system then has the possibility of discovering the cause of the irritation within itself and learning from this discovery or attributing the irritation to the environment and treating it as "accident" or seeking its source in the environment and exploiting or eliminating it. These various possibilities, too, are provided for in the systemic distinction between self-reference and other-reference, and if the system has the possibility of drawing distinctions, it can shift perspective and combine reactions, for example, learning while identifying environmental causes.

Continual irritations of a certain type, for example, the repeated irritation of an infant by the peculiarities of language or the irritation of an agricultural society by the perception of climatic conditions, steer structural developments in certain directions, because these systems are exposed to very specific sources of irritation and are therefore constantly concerned with similar problems. Of course this does not mean that we could return to the climate and culture theories of the eighteenth century; nor does it mean that we are prepared to accept a purely sociological theory of socialization. In all these questions, a multiplicity of system references have to be taken into account and correspondingly complex theory models applied. In any case, the environment gains influence over the structural development of systems only under the condition of structural couplings and only within the framework of the possibilities of self-irritation they channel and accumulate.

All this also holds true for modern society. What is more, the environment itself is changing more strongly than ever before under the influence of society. This is true of the physical, chemical, and biological conditions of life, in other words for the complex usually termed "ecology," but it is also particularly true for the deformation of psychic systems under modern living conditions, for example, for everything covered by the concept of modern individualism or the theory of a growing entitlement mentality. As in an ecological hypercycle, structural couplings between the system of society and the environment are under pressure to vary at a speed that raises the question of whether and how society thus irritated, which has itself to thank for all this, can learn fast enough.

Finally, operational closure provides the key to the theory of system differentiation. However society differentiates social systems within itself, the occasion is always a bifurcation of its own operations. It is never a matter of reflecting distinctions that already exist in the environment.

Only very primitive societies have experimented on the basis of anthropological parameters like gender and age, but this has proved an evolutionary dead end. Even family formation and segmentary differentiation go beyond this. If discriminatory significance is later lent to structural distinctions (e.g., farmers/nomads, city dwellers/country dwellers, or now on occasion racial differences), this is clearly a matter of social aspects important only insofar as they can be linked to forms of system differentiation. From a genetic point of view, it is always a matter of performance by the communication system: a deviation is proposed, observed, tested, rejected, or intensified and used for more and more connections. Self-referential and other-referential components contribute. The differentiation of a system therefore always brings about its further outdifferentiation in the sense of interrupting the point-by-point coincidence of components of the system and components of its environment. And precisely this interruption makes it inevitable that society has to cope with an interpreted environment.

7. Cognition

When we begin to examine communication systems as sui generis autopoietic systems, traditional ideas about "cognition" have to be reviewed. It is also a question of redescribing the humanistic heritage of the European tradition. It had attributed cognitive abilities to humans and defined the particularity of humankind in function of two distinctions, that between human and animal and that between human and machine. In search of characteristics attributable only to humans and not to animals or machines, theories of cognition provided a sort of reserve conceptuality defined in terms of reason, intellect, and reflective capacity. The faculties of sensory perception that humans share with animals were consequently played down. They were counted among the lower (as opposed to higher) faculties.[155] Machines, in contrast, only supplemented and facilitated the human capacity to act, while action itself could be attributed to free will and the possibility of reasoned control.

Developments within science and technology have invalidated this premise of a specifically human-centric theory of cognition. Modern physics allows cognition to be described at best as a special case of changes in relations between electromagnetic fields. This might give us an answer to the question of how the world makes self-observation possible. But this provides no access to the phenomenology of the world. Neurophysiological research describes the brain as an operationally closed system, and the question of how we nevertheless come by the idea of an outside world arises for both animals and humans. The answer lies only in the concept of sensory perception, which is thus preordinate if not superordinate to all reflective processes. In still unfathomable manner, perception externalizes the results of neurophysiological processes—in higher species of animals and in humans. Electronic data processing technology has changed relations with machines. This technology can no longer be regarded as supplementing bodily activity, hence imposing a redescription of the relationship between man and machine.[156] Research into "artificial intelligence" shows such change—even questioning whether couching the problem in terms of the relationship between man and machine is still appropriate for the purposes of cognition theory.

In the circumstances, we need to restate and come up with new answers to the question of a "reserve category" of specifically human characteristics.[157] Examining the medium of meaning can contribute.[158] However, this medium is used by both psychic and social systems. We can therefore just as well define the specificity of humans as a matter of their participation in meaningful communication.

But this alone does not produce an adequate concept of cognition commensurate with the new conditions. For this purpose, we take the concept of observation as our point of departure, treating observation as an indication in the context of a distinction and requiring memory to be defined as the ability to forget and remember. Meaningful cognition is then only another special case; the only one, however, that comes into question for the theory of society. In other words, cognition is the ability to connect new operations to remembered operations. It presupposes that forgetting releases capacities in the system; but also that new situations can lead to highly selective recourse to condensations of past operations.

These considerations oblige us to abandon a traditionally dominant notion, which many still consider self-evident: that a system can adapt to its environment through cognition, and that evolution is hence made possible by improving cognitive capabilities, through more profound, more exact, premonitory knowledge of the environment. There is of course no denying a link between evolution and changes in the cognitive faculties of highly developed systems, but the thesis of a conditioning relation between cognition, better adaptation, and evolution is untenable in this simple version—not least in biology.[159]

Even older cybernetic systems theory gives cause for doubt—as in W. Ross Ashby's thesis that systems are energetically open but informationally closed, and that they lack the "requisite variety."[160] The cybernetic control loop is also geared to function without knowledge of the environment—so to speak without subject and without object. The theory of operational closure and the thesis that autopoietic systems must always be adapted in advance if they are to realize their evolutionary potential go beyond this. The first question is then always what operations the reproduction of the system carries out and how the system can already be adapted on this precognitive level.[161] Only then can we ask how specific observational operations come about and how cognitive abilities (digitization, memory, learning, distance orientation, anticipation, error correction) can develop on this basis.

From a functional point of view, cognition is not a copying or representation of environmental conditions in the system. Its job is rather to produce redundancies that spare the system repetitive information processing.[162] Redundancies are marked as knowledge, registered as recognizable, and then used "economically" to concentrate and expedite any checking of new information. Cognition can accordingly help the system to adjust *temporarily* to situations, a major advantage in a volatile world. But this very specialization prevents cognition from guaranteeing the structural adaptation of systems to the world.

Whereas organisms primarily secure the metabolic processes for reproducing life and have to be adapted at this level before going on to develop specific cognitive abilities, the only basal operation available for the formation of social systems is communication. And whereas organisms can react only to irritation of their outer surfaces, however they interpret these irritations internally, communication systems intensify their irritability by replacing spatial boundaries by meaningful distinctions. As an operational necessity, communication always requires self-observation of the operation, in other words the possibility of distinguishing between information and utterance; and with this distinction it separates off a domain, namely, information, to which it can attach cognition. Here, too, the basal operation *is* not cognition. But it guarantees that cognition inevitably co-occurs and can be developed. The distinction between utterance and information and the dependence on understanding make it clear that communication *as an operation,* too, must adapt to the environment without being able cognitively to control this dependence. No communication process can monitor step by step (in other words, *communicatively* express) whether participants are still alive, whether there is sufficient air to carry sound waves, whether electronic equipment is still in working order. Such demands would paralyze the efficiency of the evolutionary advance of communication; if they had had to be met, communicative systems would not have developed in the first place.[163] In other words, the sequence of communicative operations requires what constitutes its environment to enable and tolerate its mode of operation. Should failures and disturbances occur, they can still be taken into account as events and processed in the form of the communication relating to them.

Only thus can communication concentrate on itself. Only thus can it perform its operations. Only thus can it digitize the information it produces (and does not, for example, take from the environment). Only thus can it test the connectivity (intelligibility, possibly the consensual capacity) of its operations. Only thus is it able to produce vast amounts of information, to distribute it in complex systems and to process it both simultaneously and sequentially. And only thus can it continually cross the inner boundary of its own distinction and treat the utterance of information as information about what has been uttered or about the utterer, or, vice versa, draw conclusions about the quality of the information on the basis of information about the type or motive of utterance.

Communication thus requires no guarantee of congruence with the environment to allow it to proceed. It uses cognition *instead.* In any case, the environment contains neither "information" nor "topics." Nor does it contain any equivalents of the forms with which communication operates. Instead of a guarantee of congruence, we have only the temporal reference of communication: that it consists of operations (events) that pass as they occur; that it consequently prefaces an uncertain future; that it can reconfirm or change all self-formed structures (including those of "knowledge"); that it always operates recursively, connecting to itself. But for this very reason, it is able to reflect about and correct itself.

These considerations have far-reaching consequences for the theory of society. In continuing its own operations, society has to presuppose its adaptation to the environment without being able to monitor it cognitively. It can recognize disturbances and address them in further communication; but in so doing, it must again presuppose that communication can be achieved through communication and can thus continue to reproduce the system. This cannot in principle be changed by developing cognitive abilities through sign systems (especially language), generalizations (one-to-many rules), and dissemination techniques, through well-assorted semantics that make what is worth preserving available for reuse; and through the differentiation of a functional system of science specialized in cognitive innovation (learning) and reserved for this purpose. Recourse has always to be taken to the same basic prerequisites. This means above all that society has to come to terms with a world that remains unknown. It must accordingly develop specialized systems of symbols, particularly religion, as well as "contingency formulae" in the individual functional systems. Finally, it means that, seen over time, society cannot anticipate and cannot plan its own future. In morphogenesis and in far-reaching structural change, it has to depend on evolution. We can even expect that the development of cognitive abilities, which can be used only self-referentially, will not improve the system's adaptation to the environment but at best intensify its irritability, with ongoing self-irritation a source of stress.

If all cognition has to rely on operations made possible in advance, this has far-reaching epistemological consequences. Kant's question about the conditions for the possibility of cognition remains. But the answer is now operational closure; and research turns from the conditions for possibility to the possibility of conditioning in increasingly complex contexts.[164] The classical idea that reality shows in resistance to cognition or to volition also remains. Now, however, the resistance is within the system itself: in the resistance of operations of the system to operations of the same system, and hence of communications to communications.[165] We can also still say that science has to do with self-generated (and only for this reason absolute) uncertainties.[166] But if we admit this, we have to accept a much farther-reaching premise, namely, that science has to do entirely with self-generated uncertainties. For certainty is a form we can use only if we also accept its other side, uncertainty.

Systems theory does not claim that the certainty of knowledge has its *fundamentum in re* within the system (so to speak as the result of its performance), and that uncertainty is to be found outside as the excessive complexity, if not chaos, of the world. It says rather that the certain/uncertain schema is a contribution of cognition itself, which it can use as long as its autopoiesis functions.

8. Ecological Problems

Classical sociology had treated social systems (social facts, social relations, social orders, or whatever) as particular objects. What is environment for society was considered the object of other disciplines whose province was to be respected. The rapid growth of interest in ecological problems over recent decades has therefore come as a surprise to sociology, finding it unprepared and to this day in a state of theoretical helplessness. In accustomed critical fashion, sociologists were able only to lament that modern society deals so heedlessly with the environment. But what they have had to say is at best literary in nature, lending political support to the ecology movements that rightly and successfully call general attention to this problem.

If, as I have proposed, we regard the system form as the form of the difference between system and environment, we establish a fundamentally different theoretical basis. For the moment, however, confusion reigns. The mass media have merged the terms "ecology" and "environment,"[167] and everyday speech has adopted this confusion, giving expression to perplexity and annoyance without clarifying the concepts.

The term "ecology" is no longer understood in the original sense of establishing a livable world, even though this wishful notion implicitly dominates the discussion. On the other hand, the implication cannot be that all the physical, chemical, and biological circumstances of the world have become a problem. For ecological circumstances are of interest only where they affect society as its environment, either because society causes them to change or because they impact society. But we then need a concept of society to clarify what the environment is from this point of view. Only then can each advance in theory design contribute directly or indirectly to understanding the evident ecological problems that have always accompanied the evolution of society, but that have dramatically intensified over the past century.

Sociology is accordingly responsible for a certain system reference, for the system of society and *its* environment. It can no longer limit its attention to an intrasocial perspective. Its subject matter is society and everything else that is environment from the standpoint of society. Among the basic concerns addressed by systems theory is the maintenance of this difference between system and environment.

The conceptual configuration of operational closure, self-organization, and autopoiesis is particularly important in this connection. As has been noted, an operationally closed system cannot reach the environment with its own operations. It cannot adapt to the environment through cognition. It can operate only within the system, not partly inside and partly outside. All structures and all states of the system that function as a condition for the possibility of further operation are produced, are brought about by the system's own operations.

This obliges us to distinguish between operation and causality (without denying the causality of system operations). Operations, as classical concepts such as poiesis or production indicate, control and vary only part of the causes necessary to reproduce the system. The environment is always involved. Moreover, causal determinations always require specific performance by an observer. Certain causes have to be attributed to certain effects, choosing from infinity of causal factors. Depending on the interests concerned, attribution can vary considerably. This has been such a commonplace of legal and economic attribution research, and for some decades now of social psychology studies, that no further argument is required. If we wish to know what causal relations are assumed (selected), we therefore have to observe observers, and we must know that every attribution is contingent (which does not mean arbitrary or purely fictitious).

There is hence no denying that system operations depend causally on environmental conditions that are either mediated through structural couplings or, where they occur, have a destructive effect. Nor can it be denied that system operations causally change environmental states. In other words, in no direction do system boundaries block causalities. A communication causes air to vibrate or marks paper, changes the electromagnetic states of devices and the states of the consciousness systems involved. This concerns the media used for communication,[168] whose loose coupling is temporarily converted into fixed couplings. There can be no doubt about this, nor can it be disregarded if communication is to take place. The question is only how important such environmental causality is for society. Does it somehow change the conditions for selecting further operations in the system (and if so, within what time horizons)?

We are clearly dealing with minimal effects or defects easy to offset in the system when they cause disturbance. We take a different paper—or a different consciousness. In the communication system that is society, it is easy to communicate about disturbances. The resorption capacity of the system generally suffices. This is at any rate how communicative operation normally sees its own conditionalities. Materials or motives may become scarce if used to excess; scarcity is then the form that communication must and can use to continue taking place in the system. Are there then no serious problems?

With this theoretical approach, we open an explanatory gap. How from this perspective can we explain that modern society has special, acute problems with its environment, even though evolution has been generating disastrous impacts on itself for billions of years and the societal systems of our history have never really been in a position to control the ecological conditions of their reproduction? Has anything changed? In other words, has society changed itself? What forms, what variables vary?

One useful hypothesis is that changes have to do with the form of societal system differentiation and with the increasing complexity it provokes.[169] Functional differentiation means above all the operational closure of functional systems, too. This produces subsystems with capabilities that the overall networking of society—we could also say on the basis of language alone—could not supply. Subsystems assume *universal* competence for their *specific* function. This has vastly increased the capacity for resolution and recombination in functional systems' own operations and in their environment within and outside of society. Moreover, organization takes on an importance of its own. The characteristic inclusion/exclusion mechanism for membership allows members' behavior to be regulated with great precision and directed in very concrete terms, in other words, under the influence of communication—relatively independently of members' other obligations in the environment of the given organizational system and hence independently of their own, other roles.

These structural changes do not affect the principle of operational closure. On the contrary, they are based on this principle, repeating it with the autopoiesis of the functional systems within the system of society. What does change, however, are the causal interfaces between communication and noncommunication, thus between the system of society and its environment; this also changes the observation and thematization of causalities through communication. Since the advent of science, they can be formulated with much greater depth of field, but only with much greater uncertainty. The types and quantities of production that the market can profitably absorb can be calculated and checked against experience; the market can then be allowed to determine within society what raw materials are to be extracted from the environment of society and what wastes are to be discharged into this environment. This communication is converted into causalities that affect the environment essentially through organization, but naturally also through the temptations of proffered consumption.

But precisely because functional systems produce these effects without society as a whole controlling and limiting the process, the outcome is difficult to assess. Integration and controllability are lacking, as well as possibilities for giving expression (be it only normatively) to the order of society within society itself through a morality of measure or the notion of *justum pretium* [just price]. If we pay attention to causalities and communicate about them, we find more possibilities, hence greater choice, but also a complexity that escapes prognosis. We can only experiment, not least of all in the field of technologies that are seemingly so controllable.[170]

This invites two conclusions: systems theory must abandon the cherished idea of inferring the adaptation of the system to the environment from the causal relations between system and environment. Evolution theory, too, will have to abandon this notion. Through operational closure, systems produce their own degrees of freedom, which they exploit as long as possible; in other words, as long as the environment tolerates it. Very few, structurally sufficiently amenable forms of autopoiesis can serve this purpose, above all the extremely robust biochemistry of life. As far as I can see, however, the overall effect is not adaptation but greater deviation.

Second, both the potential for self-endangerment and the capacity for recuperation are, for the reasons stated, increasing in modern society. The unintended or at any rate unpurposed effects on the environment appear to be proliferating, and every thought of entering them under "costs" in evaluating economic efficiency is illusory in view of the extent and time horizons of the problem (and in view of communicable nonknowledge). The widespread inclination to evoke "responsibility" in this situation can be seen only as a gesture of despair. At the same time, a greater degree of freedom in reacting to sufficiently clear situations can be noted. Even normative structures are contingent, are subject to change without any recourse to a "natural" order of things. This is particularly the case with positive law. In the economy, communication about ecological problems produces not only costs but also markets. Above all, the mechanism of organization permits an improbable specification of human behavior under rules that can be changed when needed. From this point of view, organization, like money, is a societal medium for only temporary forms. On the other hand, the possibilities for using organizations are limited by the conditions for reproducing functional systems. Salaries must remain attractive and affordable and this cannot be assured without an efficient economic system, which in turn puts a strain on the environment.

Maladjustment to the environment is accordingly not infrequent.[171] The theoretical explanation lies in the thesis that operationally closed systems can orient themselves internally only on internal problems. What is unusual and needs explaining is the extent to which this particular problem occupies communication in today's system of society.

9. Complexity

The attributes listed so far, namely, meaning, self-reference, autopoietic reproduction, and operational closure with monopolization of a specific type of operation—communication—cause a system of society to develop its own *structural complexity* and hence to organize its own autopoiesis.[172] In this connection, we often speak of "emergent" orders in the sense of phenomena coming into being that cannot be reduced to the properties of their components, for example, the intentions of actors. But "emergence" is more a component of a narrative than an explanatory concept.[173] We shall therefore have to make do with the idea that differentiating a system and cutting links with the environment are required if the complexity of a system is to develop within protective boundaries.

Organized (structural) complexity has long since been a point of intersection for theoretical and methodological considerations.[174] According to Helmut Willke, it is the key issue in systems theory, and a problem whose handling through self-organizational, control, and steering processes gives modern society growing cause for concern.[175] Many aspects of the phenomenon need to be discussed, including system differentiation, medium/form differences and duplication processes, codification, and the ego/alter distinction (see especially Chapter 2). Before proceeding, however, certain matters need to be looked at in brief.

Our point of departure is the link between the operational closure of the system and an evolutionary tendency to develop intrasystem complexity. Only if the system isolates itself sufficiently from the environment, only if it thus renounces developing its own internal equivalents for all environmental states can it be distinguished from the environment through its own internal order of interconnecting elements. Only the production on this basis of a system's own elements by its own elements (autopoiesis) can lead to the development of system complexity. The extent to which this happens and where it stops, how viable even relatively simple systems are in a highly complex environment (i.e., whether they can continue their autopoiesis) are questions I must leave it to evolution theory to answer. For the present, I shall merely note the connection between operational closure and the enablement of system complexity development. It is this link that determines the "direction" of evolution.

But what is complexity? What does this term denote?[176] Complexity is not an operation, something that a system does or that happens within it. Rather, it is an understanding of observation and description (including self-observation and self-description). We must therefore ask what the form of this understanding is, what distinction constitutes it. This question alone produces a cascade of considerations, for the concept of complexity is not simple; it is itself complexly constituted, that is to say, autologically.

It is often said that a system is complex for an observer if it is neither completely ordered nor completely unordered but a mixture of redundancy and variety. This is particularly the case for systems with self-generated indeterminacy. The question why a multiplex state of affairs needs to be subsumed under a concept that presupposes its unity is a more profound one. The distinction that constitutes complexity then takes the form of a *paradox*: complexity is the *unity of a manifold*. A state of affairs is expressed in two versions, as unity and as manifold, and the concept denies that we are dealing with different matters. This blocks the easy way out of treating complexity now as a unity, now as a manifold. But this takes us only to the next question, namely, how this paradox can be creatively implemented, or "unfolded."

The usual answer is to decompose complexity with the aid of the concepts of element and relation, and thus with the aid of a further distinction. The more elements a unity has and the more it interconnects these elements through relations, the more complex it is. We can map this out not only by counting elements but also by taking qualitative differences into consideration; and, furthermore, by including the temporal dimension and allowing for sequential difference, hence for unstable elements. This makes the concept more complex and more realistic; but it also becomes multidimensional, so that we no longer compare complexity in terms of greater or lesser (is a brain more complex than a society because there are more nerve cells in a brain than there are people in a society?).

Another distinction is more important for the theory of society. It presupposes the distinction between element and relation, but stresses that possible relations between elements multiply in geometrical progression with the rise in the number of elements and thus the growth of the system. Since there are drastic limits to the real connectivity of elements, this mathematical law imposes the selective interconnection of elements even at very low magnitudes. From this point of view, the "form" of complexity is the boundary to orders in which it is still possible to connect every element with every other element at any time. Everything that goes beyond this is based on selection, thus generating contingent states (states otherwise possible). All recognizable order is based on a complexity that demonstrates that things could be otherwise.[177]

If for the purposes of societal theory we assume the individual communication to be an element, connectivity is clearly extremely restricted: a sentence can refer to only very few other sentences.[178] Over and above the improbabilities apparent in mathematical abstraction, highly evolved systems have drastically to limit the connectivity of their elements and must therefore invent something to compensate the concomitant losses in relationization.

For evolution evidently does not halt the growth of systems at the point from which it is no longer possible to connect every element with every other element at any time and then to monitor every disturbance from outside throughout the system.[179] It is this analysis that brings us to the problem that makes the unfolding of the complexity paradox productive. The key distinction is now between systems with complete interconnection between elements and those with only selective interconnection; and the real systems of the evolved world are obviously to be found on the latter side of the distinction. In brief, the *form* of complexity is hence the *necessity to sustain an only selective connection between elements*, in other words, the selective organization of the system's autopoiesis.

The concept of complexity can be used as a tool for observing and describing all sorts of things as long as the observer is in a position to distinguish between elements and relations in the state of affairs he calls complex. They need not be systems. The world, too, is complex. Nor does the concept assume that a complex matter is complex in only one way. Various descriptions of complexity are possible depending on how the observer resolves the unity of a manifold into elements and relations. Finally, a system can also describe itself as complex in various ways.[180] This follows alone from the paradoxical nature of the concept; but also from the fact that an observer can describe the complexity descriptions of another observer, so that hypercomplex systems can come into being that also contain a plurality of complexity descriptions; and it should be clear that hypercomplexity is an autological concept. Only if we take formal conceptuality to such lengths can we recognize that, and why, the theory of society needs the concept of complexity.

Finally, there have been recent developments in the conceptuality of complexity, which, limiting attention to systems, emphasize their inevitable intransparency. It is a question of how time is taken into account. Even the classical theory of complex systems had taken the time dimension into consideration, describing complexity as, among other things, the sequential diversity of system states. We reach beyond this if we treat the elements to be connected themselves as point-in-time related entities, as events or operations.[181] The theory of complexity then requires recursive operations, in other words recursion to and anticipation of other, nonactual operations in the same system. It then no longer suffices to represent system development as a decision tree or cascade; recursion itself becomes a form in which the system enables boundaries to be drawn and structures to be formed.[182] Dealing with complexity is therefore often described as a *strategy* without a fixed beginning and without a set goal.[183] This means not least that the system sets in with all its own operations at the point of its own historical state, hence operating one-off in each case and having artificially to build all repetitions into its own mode of operation.[184] Certain redundancies can be inserted in proceedings, and they help the system to cope within itself. But this does not change the principle that what is produced as operation depends on a point in time and is unpredictable.[185] This means not least of all that communication can be registered only in retrospect, while observing that there is a future still to be decided.[186] Resolved into the temporal dimension, complexity appears not only as a temporal sequence of different states but also as a simultaneity of already determined and still to be determined states.

Society is clearly an extreme case in the field covered by the concept of complexity. Extreme not because it is more complex than other systems (such as brains) but because the nature of its elementary operations, namely, communications, places considerable constraints on it. It is indeed astonishing that and how highly complex systems can be formed through operations of this type. For communication is extremely narrow-gauged and must rely on sequencing for interconnection. It hence requires a great deal of time, which always threatens it with deterioration. We shall be continually concerned with the structural consequences of this initial situation, that is, with forms that prove their worth especially in connection with the dissemination media of writing and printing, with the problems of concatenation and ramification, and the advantages of system differentiation. At present, we are considering only the general form that has developed because the system of society has to operate under these constraints if it is to evolve. We see two closely related solutions to the problem: (1) a very high measure of self-reference in operations, and (2) the representation of complexity in the form of meaning.

The recursivity of societal autopoiesis is organized neither through causal results (outputs as inputs) nor in the form of results of mathematical operations but reflexively, that is to say, through the application of communication to communication.[187] Every communication exposes itself to query, to doubt, to acceptance or rejection *and anticipates this. Every* communication! Without exception. If attempts to communicate try to escape this form of reflexive recursivity, they fail as communication; they are not recognized as such. This answer to the complexity problem implies the ineliminable *nonfinality* of communication. No one has the last word (there are, of course, ways to make people stop talking). It also means that the representation of the complexity of the system and its environment within the system can remain open as a phenomenon still to be clarified.[188] Moreover, it means that communication has to claim authority in the sense of an ability to say, explain, and justify more than appears expedient at the given time.

The reflexive solution to the problem of sequential recursivity converges with the most important evolutionary achievement that makes societal communications possible in the first place—we can speak of co-evolution—namely, the representation of complexity in the form of meaning.

Here, too, form means distinguishing two sides. We have already discussed the two sides of the meaning form (§ 3). They are *reality* and *possibility*; or, looking ahead to their operational use, *actuality* and *potentiality*. It is this distinction that makes it possible to represent the selective constraints of complexity (the one side; the other being the complete relationization of elements) in meaning-processing systems. Every actualization of meaning potentializes other possibilities.[189] Whoever experiences something determinate is referred by this determinacy to other matters that he can also either actualize or merely potentialize. This makes the selectivity (or, in modal-theoretical terms, the contingency) of all operations an inevitable necessity, the necessity of this form of autopoiesis.

The whole world is thus present at every moment; not as *plenitudo entis* [fullness of being], however, but as the difference between actualized meaning and the possibilities accessible thence. The world is always present *simultaneously; at the same time* the form in which this occurs is geared to sequential processing. All other forms that can guide observation and description in such systems participate in this meaning form; for, as we have seen, they presuppose the form as a two-sided form in which both sides are simultaneously given, but, as we can now assert, the one in actualized, the other in potentialized mode. Time is needed to pass from one side of the form to the other (to cross the boundary), just as we always need time if we wish to actualize potentialities.

As with distinctions in general, the repetition of an operation also has a double effect in the context of the meaning-imparting distinction between actuality and potentiality. On the one hand, it creates and condenses identity; the repetition recognizes itself as repetition and makes what it has repeated available as knowledge. On the other hand, this takes place in a somewhat different context (at least later in time).[190] Meaning is accordingly enriched through suitability for use in various situations. As a result, meaning gains surplus reference and, strictly speaking, is indefinable. We can only invent new denotations (words, names, "definitions") to ensure operational reuse. Ultimately every meaning refers to the world, making it inevitable that operations are generated as selections.

If we speak of "reducing complexity," following Kenneth Burke or Jerome Bruner,[191] we cannot mean by this a sort of annihilation.[192] It is merely a matter of operating in the context of complexity, of a continuous shift from actual to potential. And even at a more complex level, this can mean that certain complex descriptions (for instance, of the system or its environment) can fail to do justice to the complexity of their object, reducing it to the simplified form of a model, a text, a map.

The conclusion to be drawn from all this for the scientific treatment of complexity is that idealization or the simplification of model building do not suffice. Such proceedings misunderstand complexity as complication. Nor do classical anthropomorphisms based on assumptions about the "human being" suffice, which understand meaning "subjectively." These approaches can, however, be replaced by a methodology of second-order observation. We hence abandon the idea of making complexity transparent and intelligible, while retaining the option of asking how it is observed. The first question is always who the observer is whom we observe (without an observer there is no complexity). The observer is defined by the schema on which he bases his observations, and thus on the distinctions he uses. The concept of observer thus brings together the traditional notions of subject and of ideas or concepts. And the autology on which second-order observation is based, namely, the insight that this, too, is only observation, guarantees the cognitive closure of this treatment of complexity. There is neither recourse to external guarantees nor is it needed.

10. World Society

The consequence of defining society as the comprehensive social system is that there can be only one system of society for all connective communication. In purely factual terms, a number of societal systems may well exist, just as one used to speak of a plurality of worlds; but only in the absence of communicative links between these societies or, from the point of view of the individual society, where communication with others is impossible or without consequence.

In this regard, too, our concept both continues and discontinues the old European tradition. The concept of the inclusion of all other social systems stems from this tradition, as do characteristics such as autarchy, self-sufficiency, and autonomy. However, a closer look soon reveals that the meaning of these concepts in the traditional context differs from that in our present context. City systems in antiquity were considered autarchic in that they offered people everything needed to perfect the conduct of their lives. As one would later say in Italy, the *civitas* had to be in a position to guarantee, no more no less, the *bene e virtuose vivere*. There had been discussion since the Middle Ages about the extent to which larger territories, *regna*, were necessary—be it for reasons of security or the endogamous marriage practices of the nobility.[193] In any case, there was never any suggestion that all communication had to take place within this one *civitas sive societas civilis*; and the old European tradition naturally did not think in terms of economic independence. Indeed, the very concept of economy in the modern sense was unknown.

These societies accordingly had a thing-centered concept of the world, in which things could be classified by name, type, and kind. The world was considered an *aggregatio corporum*, a huge, visible living being embracing all other living beings.[194] There were mortal and immortal living beings, humans and animals, cities and countries; and it was reputed (without any direct communicative checks) that in far-off places fabled creatures and monsters existed outside the typology known to society, which in their strangeness functioned, so to speak, as wild cards for what lay beyond the frontier.

This world order assumed that as spatial distance increased, communication became more difficult and uncertain. Although far-ranging trade relations had existed even before the advent of advanced civilizations, they had little communicative effect. Technology was passed on from society to society (e.g., metalworking) and it was also possible to diffuse knowledge in accordance with the receptive capacity of second and third recipients.[195] Technologies and forms of knowledge often matured only in the process of adjusting to conditions for adoption (e.g., phonetic script). All in all, however, these processes took a long time and, although they finally found a response in the universalization of individual religions, they failed to produce a notion of a regionally unbounded world society. Knowledge about distant parts of the world remained sporadic; it was spread by people and obviously amplified and distorted rumor-like by reports of reports. Armed conflicts—and certainly not communicative coordination—appear to have been primarily responsible for the world beyond the borders being described as a plurality of nations.[196] And until well into the modern age, political empires built as communication improved faced the problem of how to rule over a large territory from the center, in other words, how to control it through communication.[197] This experience is probably at the origin of the tendency we have described to identify societies with political territories and hence in regional terms.

The concept of God was a last chance of saving the thing-centered concept of the world. He was posited, as it were, as a duplicate of the world,[198] defined as a person for the functions of second-order observation. The attempt could then be made to observe God in the world and on the basis of the world, and to observe Him as observer of the world. Although this produced the paradox of *docta ignorantia*, learned ignorance, divine revelation offered an escape; and, incidentally, this absorption of paradox sufficed to form a world free of paradox in an ontologically logical sense, accessible for sin-laden, contracted, finite cognition and action.

As long as the world was understood in terms of things—as the totality of things or as creation—everything that remained unaccountable had to be provided for in the world, as an object of *admiratio*: as a miracle, a secret, a mystery, an occasion for terror and dismay or for helpless piety.[199] This changes when the world has only one horizon, only the other side of every definition. This conception of the world was attained at the latest in the philosophy of transcendental consciousness.[200] The mystery can then be replaced by the distinction between marked and unmarked in the everyday usage of observers without the possibility of summing the totality of what is marked, let alone of equating it with what is unmarked. The world of modern society is a background indeterminacy ("unmarked space") that allows objects to appear and subjects to act.[201] But how did this change of mind come about? How can it be explained sociologically?

Presumably, the full discovery of the globe as a closed sphere of meaningful communication was the decisive factor. Older societies had had to take account of boundaries set by things themselves, while simultaneously indulging in observations and communication that could transcend these boundaries and address *admirabilia* in every sense. Since the sixteenth century, these conditions have changed gradually and finally irreversibly. Starting from Europe, the entire globe was "discovered" and by stages colonized or integrated into regular communicative relations. Since the second half of the nineteenth century, there has also been a uniform world time. This means that anywhere on Earth, regardless of local time, we can establish simultaneity with all other places and communicate worldwide without loss of time. Like the constancy of the speed of light in physics, world time in society guarantees the convertibility of all temporal perspectives: what is earlier or later in one place is also earlier or later elsewhere. Society similarly adapted to differentiation into functional systems. This eliminated the possibility of defining the unity of a societal system in terms of territorial borders or members as opposed to nonmembers (e.g., Christians as opposed to heathens).[202] For functional systems like the economy or science, politics or education, medical care or law have their own requirements in setting their boundaries, which can no longer be concretely integrated with a given space or group of human beings.

The final, irrefutable evidence in favor of world society is the adaptation of time semantics to the past/future schema and, within this schema, the shift in primary orientation from past (identity) to future (contingency).[203] With regard to its origins and traditions, world society still appears to be regionally strongly differentiated. If we look to the future, however, there can be little doubt that world society has to negotiate its fate itself—in ecological and economic respects and as regards technology. The differences between functional systems are of interest for their future consequences.

Where all functional systems agree, where they do not differ, is only in the fact of communicative operation.[204] In abstract terms—to repeat the paradoxical formulation—communication is the difference that makes no difference in the system. As a communication system, society differs from its environment; but the boundary is external, not internal. For all subsystems of society, boundaries of communication (as opposed to noncommunication) constitute the external boundaries of society. In this, and only in this, do these systems coincide. All internal differentiation must and can connect at this external boundary by establishing different codes and programs for individual subsystems. In so far as they communicate, all subsystems participate in society. Insofar as they communicate in different ways, they differ.

If we proceed on the assumption that communication is the elementary operation whose reproduction constitutes society, world society is clearly implied in *every* communication, regardless of the specific topic and spatial distance between participants. More and more possibilities for communication are taken for granted, and symbolic media are used that cannot be contained within regional boundaries.[205] This is also true of the conditions under which territorial boundaries are spoken about.[206] For on the other side of every border, there are countries with borders, which in turn have another side to them. This is naturally "only" a theoretical argument, which would not apply in another conceptual field. But the reality content of such "map awareness" is nevertheless strong, for there is now unlikely to be any successful communication that calls the fact of borders behind borders into doubt. World society is the occurrence of world in communication.

Apart from minimal uncertainties (e.g., doubts about whether perceivable behavior is meant as an utterance or not), the boundaries of the societal system are clearly and unambiguously drawn by the operation of communication. Ambivalence continues to be possible and is cultivated (e.g., in the forms of rhetorical paradoxization, humor, or irony), but it is treated as a discretionary mode of expression liable to be called to account and subject to query. The definiteness of the external boundary (= the distinguishability of communication and noncommunication) enables the operational closure of the world societal system, and thus generates an internal indeterminacy of open communication possibilities no longer decided by the environment, possibilities that can be given shape only through the system's own resources, only through self-organization. Moreover, since the advent of printing, the communication network of society has multiplied and intensified enormously—gradually at first and finally with irreversible effect. In principle, society today does not depend on the increase or decline of the population. At any rate, sufficient capacities are available to continue the autopoiesis of the societal system at the development level achieved. And as soon as we become aware of this, we can start describing demographic growth not as a blessing but as a problem, if not a curse.

Finally, all functional systems were adapted operationally to second-order observation, to the observation of observers relating to the given intrasystemic perspectives of the distinction between system and environment. Society thus loses the possibility of a binding representation of the world. The concomitant acknowledgement of cultural diversity—for which purpose the reflexive concept of culture (culture that reflects culture) was introduced in the late eighteenth century—requires abandonment of the thing-oriented concept of the world.[207] It has been replaced by the assumption of an unobservable world. Everything depends on which observer we observe, and the recursive reuse of observations in observing produces only an unobservable unity—the total world as formula for the unity of all distinctions.

What is more, new communication technologies, especially television, have effects that can scarcely be overestimated. They trivialize, we could say, the place from which we see things. What we see on television takes place *elsewhere* and nonetheless almost simultaneously (at any rate, independently of the time we would require to reach the place where events could be directly experienced). But this trivialization of location provokes no doubt about the reality of events, which is guaranteed in a purely temporal sense by the real-time correspondence of filming and events (nothing can be filmed before it happens or after it has happened), notwithstanding scheduled time lapses between filming and transmission and the selective combination of simultaneous takes. In other respects, too, we can assume that, thanks to greater freedom of movement and higher speeds, there has been a shift in reference from place to movement. Notions about the world as the framework for the accessibility of perception and communication adapt accordingly.

This in turn depends on the convertibility of local time. Since the nineteenth century, the division of the globe into time zones has made it possible to assume the simultaneity of events in the world without them being anchored in the physical setting of day and night time, even when communication about them reaches a place at night while it is day elsewhere. This is followed by the temporalization of the difference between present and absent. Across the globe, we can take part in simultaneous events and produce simultaneity through communication even where what is concerned is out of reach for interaction and perception. In this sense, only the past or the future is absent per se.

These structural shifts change the concept of world. The old world had debated whether the world was finite or infinite and whether it had a beginning and would have an end. This controversy was both inevitable and undecidable, because it is not possible to conceive of a boundary without conceiving of another side to the boundary.[208] The change is not in this dimension. In present-day thinking, the world is neither a beautiful living being nor an *aggregatio corporum*. Nor is it the *universitas rerum*, the totality of visible and invisible objects, things, and ideas. Nor, finally, is it infinity to be filled, absolute space or absolute time. It is not an entity that "contains" everything and therefore "lasts." All these descriptions and many more are provided by the world. The world itself is only the overall horizon of all meaningful experience, whether directed inward or outward and forward in time or backward. It is not closed off by boundaries but by the meaning that can be activated within it. The world is to be understood not as an aggregate but a correlate of the operations taking place in it.[209] Once again drawing on George Spencer-Brown's terminology, it is the correlate to the unity of every form; or the "unmarked state" that is violated by every interruption, by the boundary line of the form, which can then be probed only in relation to difference, only in movement from one side of the distinction to the other.[210] And for a systems-theoretical concept of the world, this means that the world is the totality of what constitutes system and environment for each system.

The old world was full of unfathomable "secrets," indeed, like the nature of things and the will of God, it was itself a mystery and made not, or only to a very limited extent, to be known but rather for astonished admiration. Even naming had to be considered dangerous because it opened up the world to communication; a knowledge of names was accordingly associated with the magic that provokes nature to emerge. This, too, was in keeping with the spatial limitations to an understanding of society for which the unknown and unfamiliar could begin a few yards underground or on the summits of the highest mountains or beyond the horizon at sea. The modern world is no longer to be honored and feared as a mystery. And in this sense, it is no longer sacred. Nevertheless, it remains inaccessible, because, although operationally accessible (e.g., amenable in principle to investigation), every operation of cognizance and communication is inaccessible to itself. Observation is possible in the world. In this operation, however, the observer himself functions as the excluded middle. The unity of the world is therefore not a mystery but a paradox. It is the paradox of the observer of the world who is in the world but who cannot observe himself observing.

This appears to have eliminated a premise that had been rashly accepted in the old world. Namely, that the world was determinable for all observers of the same world, and that it was determinable through observation. The remaining problematic state of affairs was unloaded onto religion, which was expected to explain the transformation of indeterminability into determinability. As soon as we problematize the relation of observation to the world, this meta-unity of unity (sameness for all) and determinability dissolves, and the contrary assumption becomes more plausible. If the world is the same for all observers (for every choice of a distinction), it is indeterminable. If it is determinable, it is not the same for all observers, because determination requires distinctions to be drawn. For this very reason it is essential to ask whether and how the system of society connects observation in such a way that the autopoiesis of communication remains possible even though the world has to be presupposed—be it as indeterminable, be it as variously determinable. Society thus becomes the primordial relation of observation to the world.

As a far-reaching debate on "relativism" and "pluralism" has shown, it is difficult to draw conclusions from this state of affairs for the theory of knowledge. It is even conceded that all societies, cultures, and so on, produce a "world of their own," and that the social sciences have to accept this. But then the location of the observer who accepts pluralism still needs to be clarified. We can hardly describe him, in succession to God, as a worldless observer or "freely floating" intelligence. A theory of cognition must therefore be found that allows him to be localized as the observer of other observers *in the world* although all observers, including him, produce *different* projections of the world. There can therefore be no pluralistic ethics, or, if so, then only as the paradox of a demand that allows no alternatives to itself.[211] We can accordingly not assume that the world is a "whole" that is divided into "parts." It is rather an incomprehensible unity that can be observed in various ways, and only in various ways. Its "decomposition" is not to be found, it can only be constructed, and this requires distinctions to be chosen.[212] Radical constructivism takes this into account by assuming that the world cannot be described and by shifting the business of self-observation of the world to the level of second-order observation.

All this is connoted when we refer to modern society as world society. On the one hand, this means that there can be only one society on earth and even in the entire communicatively accessible world. This is the structural and operational side of the concept. At the same time, however, the expression "world society" means that all societies (including, retrospectively, societies in the traditional view) construct a world, thus resolving the paradox of the world observer. The possible semantics must be plausible and fit the structures of the societal system. The semantics of the world varies with the structural evolution of the societal system; but seeing and saying this belongs to the world of our society, is its theory and its construction of history. And we can only observe that the old societies could not observe themselves and their world in this manner.

With its particular characteristics, the modern world is an exact correlate of modern society. A society describing itself as nature and consisting of human beings was matched by a world consisting of things (in the sense of Latin *res*). A society describing itself as an operationally closed communication system, and that grows or shrinks depending on how much is communicated, is matched by a world with precisely the same characteristics: a world that grows or shrinks depending on what occurs. Older societies were organized hierarchically and in function of the distinction between center and periphery. This was in keeping with their world order, which provided for an order of rank (*series rerum*) and a center. Modern society's form of differentiation requires these structural principles to be abandoned, so that this society has a heterarchical world and an acentric world. Its world is a correlate to the networking of operations and is equally accessible from every operation. Owing to their form of differentiation, older societies provided for the fixed inclusion of human beings in certain social positions. They were therefore obliged to understand the world as a totality of things. Its functional differentiation has obliged modern society to give up this notion of inclusion. The individualism of modern times, and above all the freedom discourses of the nineteenth century, hence gave urgent occasion to develop a notion of world society.[213] Functional differentiation has affected the concept of world even independently of this development. Modern society regulates its own extent, the modern world as well. Modern society can only change itself and is therefore prone to constant self-critique. It is a self-substitutive order; the modern world, likewise. It, too, can change only in the world. The semantics of modernity/modernization is one of the most important indicators of this—not as a convergence thesis, but because it allows the regions of world society to be described as more or less modernized (developed), and through this distinction enables a complete description with possibly changing markings. Nothing is not more or less modern. And if society consists of the totality of communications, the rest of the world is condemned to uncommunicativeness. It withdraws into silence. Not even this is a suitable concept, for to remain silent one must be capable of communicating.

And where does this leave God? In parallel to the development of society, the figure of "communication through or with God" has steadily weakened; today, divine communication is represented only as a historical, textually tangible fact, as revelation given once and for all time. We can only guess at the degree of adaptability religion forfeits with the loss of this figure without any prospect of asking God to comment on modernity.

Despite the incontestable worldwide interconnections in modern society, sociology persists in its refusal to recognize this global system as society. Sociologists habitually refer, as in everyday speech, to "Italian society," "Spanish society," and so on, although names such as "Italy" or "Spain" should not be used in a theory, if only for methodological reasons. Talcott Parsons gave the well-considered title *The System of Modern Societies* to one of his publications.[214] Although Immanuel Wallerstein uses the term "world-system," he means a system of interaction between different regional societies, also with reference to modernity.[215] In particular, authors who attribute a central role to the modern state in societal theory (why ever?) refuse on these grounds to recognize the global system as society.[216] The phenomenon of modern society is then relegated to the figure of "response to globalities."[217] I have already spoken about this fixation as one of the current epistemological obstacles to a theory of society. Political scientists, too, general speak only of "international relations" or the "international system,"[218] thus focusing primarily on the nation-state; if they exceptionally refer to world society they mean a system that is differentiated segmentarily into nation-states and not functionally differentiated into various functional systems.[219] On the other hand, it is difficult to deny that, setting aside all regional specificities and all differences in political ideology, what we mean when we speak of "state" schools, and so on, is predetermined by modern worldwide "culture."[220]

If we ask why a regional concept of society is retained, the response is generally to point to the drastic differences between regions in their state of development. Neither this fact nor its importance are to be denied. A closer look, however, shows that sociology has fallen victim to an artifact of its comparative methodology. Comparison at the *regional* level will understandably reveal regional differences, which will increase in the course of time. If, in contrast, we undertake a *historical* comparison, congruent trends will be discovered such as the worldwide dissolution of family economies in all strata, the worldwide dependence of lifestyles on technology, worldwide, unprecedented imbalances in demographic development. The functional differentiation of society also has so strong a hold on world society that it cannot be regionally boycotted by even the most drastic of political and organizational means. This has been demonstrated most conspicuously by the collapse of the Soviet empire.[221]

Depending on the comparative perspective adopted, we can throw light on divergence or similarities in regional development. This discrepancy cannot be resolved methodologically, and we must know that we reproduce it with our choice of comparative perspective. For this very reason, a theory must be sought that is compatible with such differences and that can interpret them. Such a theory will not claim that regional differences are gradually disappearing (convergence thesis), for there is too little indication that this is so.[222] On the other hand, the assumption of a world society is not refuted. The dissimilarity argument speaks not against but for world society. The interest in development, like the interest in maintaining the cultural diversity of individual countries, is itself shaped by society, and this is particularly evident when we consider the typically modern paradox of simultaneously striving for change and conservation. Turning again to Spencer-Brown's concept of form, we can also say that development is a form whose one side (according to current understanding) consists in industrialization and whose other side consists in underdevelopment.

It is the differing state of development in the various parts of the globe that a theory of society needs to explain, and this explanation cannot follow the "plurality of nations" pattern offered for thousands of years. The point of departure must be the unity of the system of society that produces these differences. For example, if we compare modern society with traditional societies, we note a trend toward transferring educational and training processes to schools and universities and toward using these institutions as centers to promote careers and life opportunities.[223] However, this new mobility allows regional differences to intensify inequalities.[224] And museums or museumified knowledge are now everywhere considered the context within which and against which new art has to assert its newness. At the same time, the idea of the universal museum has failed, and the contexts that permit novelty to be seen in functional equivalence are reinvented over and over again in innumerable, also regional, refractions. Only the opus/context structure has become established in the world society perspective, but precisely this structure now permits contexts to be differentiated that offer varying possibilities for expressing various innovations. The extent to which individual regions share in the advantages and disadvantages of functional differentiation clearly varies greatly, and where disadvantages are involved, differentiated functional systems such as politics and the economy already appear to obstruct one another. But this does not justify positing the existence of different regional societies; for it is the very logic of functional differentiation and comparison not with other societies but with the advantages of fully realizing functional differentiation that brings these problems to light.

A glance at the methodology of functional comparison also justifies taking the system of world society as our point of departure. If we assume the existence of regional societies, we shall get no further than listing and compiling their specificities. We shall be able to show different cultural traditions, geographical peculiarities, natural resources, demographic characteristics, and so on, in comparing countries on the basis of these rather descriptive categories. If, in contrast, we take world society and its functional differentiation as our starting point, we find pointers for the problems confronting individual regions. We are better able to see and especially to explain why certain regional data make a difference and why given differences grow or diminish depending on how they interconnect with world-societal givens. This will certainly not result in linear causal attributions, which systems theory has long since considered obsolete.[225] But it will give us a better understanding of surprising, unpredictable, nonlinear causalities, such as "dissipative structures," "deviation-amplifying effects," the disappearance of initially significant differences, and, vice versa, the substantial effects of minimal differences, not least the random factor of regional "policies." Problems for comparison can naturally also be formulated in abstract terms, and systems theory is known for taking such initiative. In examining a system as complex as modern society, however, it is of considerable advantage to work with empirically saturated problem concepts even at the level of the overall system, for example, in investigating how the central machinery of the modern state can be introduced into regions divided on ethnic, religious, or tribal lines; or whether and how jobs can be saved under global economic conditions in regions with high consumption and correspondingly high wage expectations; or what institutions of the science system promote the internationalization of research topics in the absence of global research facilities.[226]

From the standpoint of this conceptuality and this comparative methodology, to continue arguing in species-theoretical terms, to make the attribution of individual countries to a society conditional on the "similarity" of prevailing living conditions is obsolete thinking. It would be useful only if the "nature of the thing" offered the corresponding criteria and imposed the conceptuality. No one today would accept this precondition. Theory must then take account of the consequences. The modernity of society lies not in its characteristics but in its forms; that is to say, in the distinctions it uses to direct its communicative operations. And typical modern concepts of concern such as development or culture draw attention to quite specific distinctions (and, as we can say on the basis of the theory of observation, without seeing that we then do not see what we cannot see in this way). It is not surprising that certain differences are brought to the fore while others remain invisible. At the level of distinguishing between distinctions (or observing observations) the process remains contingent. But every society conceals its contingencies from itself, and modern society—albeit with less self-assurance because with less tradition—conceals the contingencies of development and culture from itself. Instead, it observes itself and concerns itself in the context of the preferred distinctions.

In premodern society, far-reaching interregional contacts involved a few family households, either from the nobility or from a few major trading houses. Trade dealt above all in "prestige goods," which demonstrated and intensified stratificatory differentiation. In this fashion, the external contact of regional societies was linked to their internal differentiation. This differentiation was based, first, on the segmentary differentiation of family households, and, second, on their classification, be it in terms of stratification, urban/rural differences, or occupations. This made it possible to single out certain households for cross-border contacts. In today's society, interregionality is based on the operation of or cooperation between organizations, especially in business, the mass media, politics, science, and transport. The economy is closely interlinked worldwide not only through its markets (financial markets, commodity and product markets, and increasingly even labor markets): it also increasingly creates organizations that operate worldwide, seeking to profit from the differences that exist.[227] Even mass tourism is organized. At first glance, intellectuals could appear to be an exception; but what would they be and who would know their names without the mass media? Organizations, too, are differentiated social systems—we shall be coming back to this—but with their intrinsic dynamics they permeate the functional systems of society. They evolve in function of the need for decisions and the necessity of communicating decisions to set points of departure for further decisions. They place themselves between society and its functional systems on the one hand and face-to-face interactions on the other. And they make worldwide interlinkage unavoidable in all sectors of society. Since this occurs *within* society and *against* society, however, it is hardly possible to hold to a regional concept of society.

Even if no regional societies can exist under modern conditions, we could perhaps consider a regional differentiation of the world societal system—as if society were divided into subsocieties. This, too, cannot stand up to closer examination. Primarily regional differentiation would contradict the modern primacy of functional differentiation. It would come to naught because functional systems cannot be contained within uniform spatial boundaries applicable to all. Only the political system along with the legal system of modern society can be regionally differentiated in the form of states. All others operate independently of spatial boundaries. The very definiteness of spatial boundaries shows that they are respected by neither verities nor diseases, neither education nor television, neither love nor money (if borrowing requirements are also taken into account). In other words, the total phenomenon of the comprehensive system society cannot be repeated within spatial bounds as a microcosm in a macrocosm. The importance of spatial boundaries lies in the interdependencies between the political system and the legal system, on the one hand, and the other functional systems, on the other. They take effect via the influence of differences in currency rates and central bank systems on the economy, via educational qualifications on education and on occupational regulations. Such differences can very well be understood in the context of a world society and be intensified or weakened by political means. But we would misjudge their specificity if we were to see them as differences between regional societies or as the result of regional differentiation of the societal system.

Only if we proceed on the assumption of a societal system that embraces the entire world can we explain that there are still regional differences today, and especially today (and much more so than in times of archaic tribal societies), but that they do not take the form of system differentiation. They are to be explained by differences in the involvement in and reaction to the dominant structures of the world system of society. They vary greatly from region to region and cannot be dealt with in detail in the present context. Nevertheless, certain general points can at least be mentioned for future investigation.

(1) As modernization in the sense of the diversification of needs proceeds, regions become dependent on the world economic system for production and sales, labor and financing.

(2) Under the regime of functional systems, rational modes of selection in particular enhance variance (rather than equality). Whoever has money or an income can borrow more easily. Small differences in performance in the early stages of schooling grow as education proceeds. In centers of scientific research, whoever does not work with state-of-the-art information facilities is left behind and can at best take belated cognizance of what has been done elsewhere. The Nobel prizes in the sciences show a marked regional distribution. The result is a center-periphery pattern, which, however, need not necessarily remain stable; the focus can shift.[228] This invention or reconstruction of a tradition of one's own is a world societal phenomenon that reacts to modern possibilities of comparison.[229]

(3) The sharp opposition between traditional and modern societies has had to be abandoned. There are various conditions under which tradition-bound structures have a favorable effect in the transition to modern society. World society selects from tradition, so to speak, what benefits it in such fields as stratification, organization, work ethics, or religion.[230] Hardly any autochthonous ways of life are still extant; what we do find are states that can be explained in terms of differential effects arising from the meeting of world-societal structural requirements and operations and special regional geographical and cultural conditions.

(4) Adaptation to the development status of world society through politically driven industrialization and the concomitant urbanization leads to the dissolution of old stratification structures based on landed property. Similarly, small-business family economies in both the agricultural and crafts sectors are dissolving worldwide into mobile money and mobile individuals. They are (temporarily?) replaced by a sharp inclusion/exclusion difference with corresponding impoverishment among large sections of the population; the state becomes a mechanism for perpetuating this difference, especially in pursuit of development policy that seeks to seal a country off from the world economy.[231]

(5) This inclusion/exclusion difference has serious effects, first, because it is provoked by the functional differentiation of world society, and, second, because it hampers, if not prevents, the regional establishment of conditions for functional differentiation. It presents the development of sufficiently big and differentiated regional markets as the precon-

dition for market-oriented mass production, making peripheral countries so dependent on exports that their economies suffer considerable fluctuation. Furthermore, it results in wide sections of the population being denied inclusion in the legal system, so that the legal/illegal code of the legal system cannot be enforced or can be enforced only to a very limited extent. We can accordingly not rely on legal programs (legislation, including constitutional law) to really regulate the attribution of right and wrong, even though they naturally do so to a substantial extent—but then on the basis of the inclusion/exclusion difference.[232] In all, this means that money and the law are formative resources in politics only in a very limited (and often "corrupt") sense. People find it correspondingly difficult to prepare for the realities of life in the educational system of schools and universities. What they learn remains abstract and legitimated largely by foreign models. This in turn transfers career recruitment to other mechanisms specific to certain strata or contact configurations. Traditional sociology still explains all this in terms of stratification; but stratification is a principle of social order, whereas the division of society in terms of inclusion/exclusion, insofar as it is no more than a state of transition in political development, can breed turbulence of a nature quite different from that produced by efforts merely to achieve social advance, leveling, or redistribution.

(6) Differences in involvement in and dependence on the modernization of world society give impetus to seemingly anachronistic tendencies, especially in religion and the ethnic movements developing within nation-states. The *universalism* of functional systems operating in world society does not exclude a wide range of *particularisms*, indeed, it tends to encourage them. The ease with which world society changes structures is thus compensated for by longer-established and at any rate strongly demarcatory ties.

(7) There are, of course, still problems of intercultural communication, linguistic difficulties in understanding, and misunderstanding at the interaction level. But this has nothing to do with the coming into being of a world society;[233] they are to be expected in all cultural contacts. The hypothesis might, however, be defensible that the diversity of cultures together with the diversity of their ethnocentrisms can today be considered known and that problems of understanding are therefore less often attributed ethnocentrically to others.

These arguments in favor of world society can be well substantiated empirically. All that is lacking is a theory that could take them up and process them. The much discussed concept of the capitalist world system elaborated by Immanuel Wallerstein assumes the primacy of the capitalist economy,[234] thus underestimating the contribution made by other functional systems, especially science, as well as communication through the mass media. This is not adequately corrected if, taking up a stratification-oriented distinction from the nineteenth century, we play culture off against industry.[235] Only in reviewing the widely differing globalization tendencies in individual functional systems does the scale of change compared with all traditional societies become apparent. In view of such heterogeneous sources of "globalization," a uniform concept of society is wanting. The systems-theoretical concept of society as an operationally closed, autopoietic social system that includes all other social systems, and hence all communication, seeks to fill this gap.

11. Demands on Rationality

The humanistic tradition of Europe gave a very specific form to the concept of rationality, and hence to the expectations addressed to it, and at the same time concealed the specificity of this form by a self-evidence that admitted no other way of thinking. According to this traditional notion, ratio was part of human nature. As a natural being, the human being was defined in distinction to the animal. Unlike today, the concept of nature included a normative component. A normative concept of rationality was thus grounded in a normative understanding of nature. In the Aristotelian context, nature was understood as a movement directed toward an end (*telos*), which, however, that did not necessarily ensure that this end would be attained. Until well into modern times, "history"—as opposed to "poetry"—was understood as a collection of facts and experiences that teach us what can go wrong. Translated into our conceptual language, *telos* was thus considered a two-sided form, namely, a state of rest, of satisfaction, of perfection, which could be attained or not. The opposite of perfection was corruption. The positive value of the natural state faced a negative value (*sterēsis*, *privatio*) that indicated a lack, a failure.

From a sociological point of view, it is no accident that this concept found exact correspondence in the nobility theories of the time and above all in theories about the education of the nobility. People were noble by birth into a family of ancient wealth, and one had under all circumstances to avoid forfeiting one's nobility through disgrace. But this alone was imperfect nobility. Perfection, the *telos* of nobility, was achieved only through special deserts, through the *bene e virtuose vivere* made possible by hereditary nobility but not guaranteed.[236] Education and moral instruction on personal conduct had the task of supporting the noble on his path to rational perfection and preserving him from the temptations of corruption. The noble was expected to invoke his ancestry only when he had proved his worth through his own achievements.

With all these aspects—later to be variously refined—elaborated for instruction and education, for ethics and rhetoric, the concept of natural rationality offered a stable tension. A continuum of rationality was accordingly posited that could span all differences—even those between action and occurrence and between thinking and being. In retrospect, we can see that the tension between reality and rationality was absorbed and stabilized in the teleological form and in the difference between perfection and corruption. The special problems of the nobility, with their double criterion of birth and merit, were countered by distinguishing the differences between perfection/corruption and perfection/imperfection. The solution found was accompanied by the cantillations of ethics, knowing what to praise and what to blame, and leaving rhetoric to cope with the values thus lost. This made it possible to communicate paradoxically, so to speak, to establish one's own intentions and attitudes on the good side of the world—and accordingly to imply that not everything was as good as it appeared to be. But as always with paradoxical communication, the paradox itself was discounted in communication or treated in rhetoric as mere intellectual training. The ambivalence and inconsistency of communication was consistently treated as incommunicable or relegated to the field of religion, where it could be dealt with as a problem of original sin and of the presumed degeneracy of this world.

In its structural conditions (noble society) and in its semantics, this world has passed away. However much we might admire bygone times, we have to accept this; for we live today. But if this is so, can we continue to adhere to a normative concept of reasonable rationality, as Jürgen Habermas proposes? And if we can, what distinctions could serve to reformulate this concept of rationality?

The unbroken faith in rationality showed first cracks in the seventeenth century. The old continuum of rational nature (well-ordered creation) fractured. The claims of rationality—and in this Descartes is the authority—were reduced to mental states, hence to subjects. This made it possible to understand purposes as notions of control, as corrections to the course of the world and consequently as deviations and no longer as perfect states in nature itself. For the first time, this made the choice of purpose (and no longer the means for fulfilling evident purposes) an acute problem. Soon a distinction was drawn between motives and purposes, motives (in contrast to interests) came to be regarded as inscrutable, and thought was given to the corresponding problems of communicating sincerity and of the criteria for authenticity. Not only the continuum of rational nature but also the continuum of the rational subject was thus split by a difference, namely, that between motive and purpose, so that further inquiry was concerned only with distinctions that breached the continuum of rationality. This dissolution of purposive rationality led initially to the conception of other, better (more rational?) sorts of rationality—for instance, value rationality (disciplined by consequential considerations) or communicative rationality (disciplined by reasonable grounds). It has now reached the point where we have to admit that purposiveness can be judged only in relation to a given point in time.

We remain impressed by eighteenth-century efforts to reclaim rationality and to secure it as a guiding principle for the conduct of life. In the face of resistance—which tells us a great deal! The violations of the rationality continuum persisted. It was the century of the Enlightenment—and of sentiment. The century of Newton—and of Münchhausen. The century of reason—and of history. And it came to an end with Hegel's problem of bifurcation. Everywhere rationality was now the marked side of a form that had another side to it.[237] More clearly than before, the insistence on rationality became paradoxical communication, but this communication continued to seal itself off, for there were no good arguments against rationality. Crossing the boundary to the other side of the form was treated as "cynicism."

Further cracks had already begun to appear in the eighteenth century, for example, in attempts at a theory of humor.[238] Since the nineteenth century, continued reductions have relegated the rationality concept to subsystems of society, to either the economic calculation of utility relations between means and ends (optimization) or the application of scientifically established knowledge. Toward the end of the nineteenth century, finally, the rationality concept itself began to dissolve, permitting the development of general skepticism toward it (Max Weber). This, too, took place by means of a differentiation technique. The rationality concept itself was divided, for example, along the lines of the old distinction between poiesis and practice, into purposive rationality and value rationality or, belatedly echoed by Jürgen Habermas, into the rationality of strategic action and that of communicative action (monologistic versus dialogistic rationality).[239] Thanks to the passing of other concepts of rationality, Habermas could, even toward the end of the twentieth century, persist in the thesis that the theory of society and the theory of rationality are mutually dependent—"that *every* sociology with a claim to societal theory, if it proceeds radically enough, faces the problem of rationality both at the *metatheoretical*, the *methodological*, and the *empirical level*."[240] Rationality is thus not only a problem of historical semantics but even today makes unreasonable demands on the concept of society. The question that then fails to be raised, typically for nineteenth-century differentiation techniques (Hegel excepted), is that of the unity of the difference, the question of what is meant by rationality per se. Instead, a distinction is made only between rationality and irrationality, between consciousness and subconsciousness, between manifest and latent functions, once again without noticing that the question of the unity of each of the differences needs to be put.

Another distinction, now more widespread, is that between substantive and procedural rationality.[241] In the face of growing complexity and criterial uncertainty, we are told, one should switch from substantive to procedural rationality. This will not help much if by procedure we understand a chain of means and ends. However, a set procedure has the advantage that, despite an uncertain future, we can begin and as things develop orient ourselves retrospectively on the results already achieved.

I shall not, therefore, engage in a discussion of these various fractures of the old European rationality continuum but accept the development of rationality semantics as outlined to indicate that the societal system has changed so radically in the transition to modern times as to affect the understanding of how reality relates to rationality. And just as the modern concept of world can be qualified neither as positive nor as negative because every qualification is an observable operation in the world, this can well be said of modern society, too. This is precisely what the concept of autopoietic communication systems propounds for the purposes of science. For when applied to society, this concept means that *all* communication—rational, irrational, arational, by whatever criteria—continues the autopoiesis of society. This need not mean that we have to abandon any expectations of rationality and face reality bereft of criteria. The failure of the old European concept need not mean that the problem disappears; and the insufficiency of reconstructions to date can well be attributed to the transitory situation and the lack of an adequate theory of society. Even the natural sciences, even physics, no longer see any possibility of providing society with a basis for rational judgment in the form of assured knowledge.[242]

If the criteria for rationality are thus uncertain and this affects the concept of rationality, "pluralistic" solutions offer themselves. Setting criteria (and not merely determining preferences in the sense of rational choice theory) then depends on the given observer, who describes behavior as rational or irrational. But this provides no stable solution; it merely dissolves the problem. Reestablishing the unity of the plurality of observers would require all to proceed rationally in accordance with their own criteria in determining their criteria of rationality (in utilitarianism, for example, to show the utility of utilitarianism itself). Today, however, we lack the logical and theoretical means for such reflexive loops—not to mention the problem of how they are to be handled in everyday life. At any rate, classical bivalent logic does not suffice for a more demanding concept of rationality capable of reacting to this situation.[243] It would have to be able to include the observer who judges rationality, thus reformulating the problem at the level of second-order observation.

As always, our reaction in this situation can only be sharp abstraction. If we adopt the proposed difference-theoretical approach, the problem of rationality is likely to lie in the question of the unity of the distinction used. Optimization of the relationship between means and ends or consensus between ego and alter, communicative rationality in Habermas's sense, would then be no more than special cases of a more general principle, and systems theory, too, with its form, with its distinction between system and environment could lay claim to rationality.

As the congruence of the social structure and semantics of traditional society dissolve and the associated plausibilities lose their binding force, a freer conceptuality becomes possible. The problem of rationality can be put in more abstract terms. It can no longer be understood as orientation on the ways of life of a center or apex, and thus no longer as approximation to an idea or, with reference to some normative requirement, as fulfillment or deviation. For the erosion of such ideal conceptuality also affects the counterconceptuality of an imperfect, corrupt, deviant, and resistant reality. The traditional form of rationality, that is to say, the distinction whose one side it marks, dissolves. Instead, the problem of the relationship between reality and rationality becomes acute, because every cognitive and every actional operation as observation requires a distinction in order to indicate the one (and not the other) side of the difference. It must use the distinction that guides its observation as a difference (and not as a unity, not in the undifferentiatedness of what has been differentiated, not in what is common to both sides). What it may not do is to proceed dialectically in Hegel's sense; it must exclude itself as observation from what it observes. The observer, regardless of the distinction he uses, becomes the excluded middle. But it is the observer, he alone, who with his autopoiesis guarantees the reality of his own operations and hence the reality of everything that must be presupposed as world in the mode of simultaneity! The practice of indicative differentiation does not occur in the distinction. It cannot be indicated except by another distinction. It is the blind spot of observation *and for this very reason the locus of its rationality.*

There is no satisfactory solution to a problem thus posed. Nor does it help to draw once again on the distinction between thinking and being or that between subject and object. Theory cannot purge itself merely by treating its object, in this case, society, as paradoxical and thus, so to speak, eliminating the paradox in order to be rid of it. For all concepts with which theory analyzes its object (system, observation, blind spot, meaning, communication, and so on) also apply to theory itself. The level of analysis on which the above inquiries have been operating imposes autological conclusions. But precisely because the problem of rationality is formulated as a paradox and because the communication of rationality is possible only as paradoxical communication, ways out, remedies can be found that can be regarded in this perspective as functionally rational. The problem of rationality is split by reference to a fundamental paradox. Because paradox leads to nothing but itself, it follows that something has to be done about a problem not to be mastered in *observation* and it has to be done *operationally.* And always has been! For every paradox is paradoxical only for an observer who has already systematized his observations. In other words, the paradox cannot "unfold" itself; it finds itself in observation, but only on the basis of a distinction, which (renouncing the question of its own unity) it has already unfolded. For example, the distinction between system and environment. The course of the world can be set in motion only operationally. Or, as Heinz von Foerster has put it: "*We* can decide only *those* questions that can in principle not be decided."[244]

The concept of reentry of the form into the form or of the difference into what has been differentiated offers a way out as resolution of a paradox.[245] Since the form in the form is both the form and not the form, we are dealing with a paradox, but with an unfolded paradox; for we can now choose among distinctions (not all are suitable) whose reentry can be interpreted. An observer of this reentry then has a double possibility of describing a system both from within ("understanding" his self-description) and from without, and thus of adopting both an internal and an external standpoint.[246] Of course, he cannot do both at the same time, for he has to use the internal/external distinction. But this impossibility is compensated for by the possibility of observing his own observation from the given other position.

In retrospect, we realize that this figure of reentry of the form into the form has always underlain the concept of rationality as a covert structure without becoming an argument.[247] A distinction was drawn between being and thinking; and thinking as the condition for rationality was also expected to be congruent with being. In this official version, rationality was congruence itself; and in this regard, I have spoken of the old European continuum of rationality. But—before the invention of an extramundane subject that exploded the old European tradition—thinking itself had to be. Hence, the distinction between being and thinking was based on a reentry of the distinction into what it distinguished, into thinking. And was not this figure perhaps always the covert reason for pretensions to rationality? The same is true for the distinction between nature and action, which could also achieve convergence only on the condition of action being considered rational if it was in keeping with its own rational nature. However, this structure could not be taken into consideration in the description of rationality as convergence. The old European tradition therefore produced only a parallel ontology of being and thinking, of nature and action. It could only assume they were interrelated and thank God for it.

What distances us from tradition is thus only the *discovery* of this reentry.[248] It requires more abstract conceptual means, which in turn give cause to distance ourselves from the anthropological version of rationality articulated in terms of thinking and acting and to move on to a more formal, systems-theoretical description.

If purposive rationality is copied into itself as form, this means that rationality itself is conceived of as a means. But to what end? The purpose itself must clearly be externalized so that rationality can serve it. This had been prepared by the distinction between purpose and motive. Furthermore, we could say that rationality serves self-description as rational. Or legitimation. Or the justification of action. In all these variations rationality is, as it were, Gödelized. It relies on *externally* specified meaning to describe itself *internally* as closed, as complete distinction.[249] Including this external specification in the calculus can only repeat the problem (Russell's and Tarski's attempts to solve the problem by drawing a distinction [*sic*] between levels get us no further). With the implementation of its reentry rationality is therefore always "ideology" from the outset. It remains dependent on operations it does not itself perform and that it cannot explain. For every reentry places the system in a state of "unresolvable indeterminacy."[250]

Systems-theoretical analysis can supplement this interpretation of the fate of modern rationality and state it with greater precision. Applied to the distinction between system and environment, the rule of reentry requires the distinction between system and environment to reoccur in the system. *In* the system! It therefore requires no recourse to an all-embracing system, no ultimate world guarantee of rationality, and therefore no "dominance" as the form of its realization. The system itself produces and observes the difference between system and environment. It produces it by operating. It observes it in that this operation in the context of the system's autopoiesis requires a distinction to be drawn between self-reference and other-reference, which can then be "objectivized" to a distinction between system and environment. The system can as always connect its own operations only to its own operations, but it can obtain directive information either from itself or its environment. There can be no doubt that this is actually possible, even, indeed especially, in operationally closed systems. It is a matter of trying out distinctions operationally—trying out in the sense that their use produces differences that either continue or do not continue in the form of systems.

Very similar views are to be found in the conceptuality of more recent semiotics. In this field, the primary difference is set by signs. Efforts to render the world legible with the aid of relative few signs are considered rational; signs for which, however, a practically infinite number of combinations is available. Tradition had thought of signs as referring, pointing to something given, something "present." Critics of this tradition, such as Jacques Derrida, retain only the operational fact of takeoff, of supersession, of the generation of *différence* through *différance*. The sign is based on its other side, which is not available for indication—Spencer-Brown's "unmarked space," the blank paper, the silence in which sounds make their mark.[251] Keeping silence silent remains the precondition for the combination game of signs that uses its own distinctions. As we see, it is a question of producing difference through indifference. The only functioning distinctions are not the final distinction, not even if they add up to the distinction between system and environment. Or, as Ranulph Glanville put it: "When the final distinction is drawn (i.e. the ultimate) there has already been drawn another, in either intension or extension, namely the distinction that the final distinction is NOT the final distinction since it requires in both cases (identical in form) that there is another distinction drawn; that is, there is a formal identity that adds up to re-entry."[252]

If we accept the concept proposed above, system rationality presupposes such reentry of the form into the form. But it is not achieved by this alone. We must also keep in mind that rationality has to be defined and pursued in the context of a distinction of reality. It is therefore due to a distinction that is not the final distinction. Autopoiesis must continue under the condition of reality. If not, the corresponding reality is lost. In operating autopoietically, the system does what it does and nothing else. It draws a boundary, forms a form, and leaves everything else aside. It can thereupon observe what has been excluded as environment and itself as system. It can observe the world on the basis of the distinction between self-reference and other-reference and in so doing perpetuate its own autopoiesis. Self-observation can never reverse what has happened, for it uses and continues it itself in the context of autopoiesis. It can never overtake what it has produced autopoietically as a difference. In actual operation, it divides the world, the unmarked space, into system and environment; the result eludes observational capture—just as, in traditional terminology, no eye is in a position to see the *plenitudo entis*. After all this reformulation of the problem, rationality no longer appears paradoxical, it appears impossible.

However, this has the advantage of allowing us to consider how to approach the issue. A system can develop internal complexity and thus irritability. It can supplement the system/environment distinction on both sides through further distinctions and thus extend its observational possibilities. It can reuse indications and thus condense references or not reuse them and thus delete them. It can remember and forget and hence react to irritation frequencies. With all this, the reentry of the distinction into what has been distinguished can be enriched and rendered more complexly connective. In contrast to traditional concepts, it is not a matter of approximating to an ideal, no longer a question of equity, of education, of the self-realization of a subjective or objective mind. It is not a matter of attaining unity (for this, as we have seen, would be a return to paradox or its substitute, namely, impossibility). System rationality means exposing a distinction, that between system and environment, to reality and testing it against reality.

We can illustrate this with a look at the ecological problems of modern society.[253] First of all, it must be assumed that, for example, the market economy functions as an operationally closed system and can therefore not at the same time optimize the "ecological system" (if this is a system).[254] It would certainly not be rational to ignore these conditions, to turn a blind eye to them. Nor can the problems be resolved by refraining from intervening in the environment or even eliminating the difference between system and environment, thus discontinuing the operation of society. This would mean aspiring to rationality as the final catastrophe (it is not difficult to imagine the same principle in a smaller format, for example, proposals to cease power generation, chemical production, and so on). A rational approach to the problems can be sought only in society and only under the condition of continued societal autopoiesis; and this always implies maintaining difference. This problem reoccurs within society at the level of its individual functional systems. Here, too, the opportunities for rationality lie in maintaining and exploiting differences, not in eliminating them. The irritability of systems must be intensified, which can take place only in the context of its self-referentially closed operation. But this is precisely what systems theory is after when it treats the distinction between system and environment as the form of the system. More than in any other theory of society, this focuses the theoretical conception on ecological problems and in exactly the same sense on human problems. Centering thus on difference sharpens the eye for the problems mentioned in a way that dashes all hopes that they could be resolved and thus disappear. Only if we accept this can we deal with problems as work programs and seek to improve the position of the societal system relative to its human and nonhuman environment in accordance with criteria that have to be constructed and varied in society itself.

These considerations also show how much the rationality problem of modernity has to do with the differentiation form of the societal system. If in the transition to predominantly functional differentiation, modern society has to renounce a guidance system, an apex, or a center, it will no longer be able to generate a uniform claim to rationality for itself. This does not prevent functional systems, each for itself, from pondering the unity of the difference between system and environment. In the process, the natural environment and the human environment can also come under scrutiny, and both ecological and humanistic sensibilities show these possibilities and their limits. However, in this question, too, system references must be kept apart: no functional system can reflect on society in itself because this would require the operational limitations of all other functional systems to be taken into account in each and every one.[255] Under modern conditions, societal rationality literally means a utopia. It no longer has a locus in society. But this at least we can still know, and, of course, there is nothing to be said against (indeed, this argument strongly favors) giving greater consideration to the macrosocietal environment in the functional systems of society. For no one else can do it.

A system rationality based on the paradox of observation makes no claim to "reason." For a competence concept of this sort, the subject is lacking. "Reason" was a title attributed to nescience where means and ends were in contradiction. In this sense, reason was taken to be innocent. It claims to be "critical." However the emotive term "critique" hides a weakness that we can no longer ignore. Reason has to rely on world states, in practical terms texts, being submitted to it for assessment. However, the problem is that criticism of states does not bring us to a rational concept for changes. This is apparent wherever we look today—in corporate production planning and in ecological policy, in the design of works of art and that of theories differing from the usual. Routines are always required that allow the need for change to be recognized and thus guide intervention. However, this provides no indication for the rationality of change let alone a concept for rational adaptation to change. Criticism of routines tends rather to dismantle the cognitive basis for the perception of a need for change. This is likely to be one reason why evolution theories always prove fascinating where the claims of rationality cannot be upheld.

Nor can reason be understood as a set of criteria (or an institution for determining criteria) for deciding *manifestly* before and after communication whether this communication is to be accepted or not. Acceptance or rejection is always a new, discrete communication. Reason can therefore at best be retrospectively cited to symbolize successful agreement; and it is needed above all where interests are to be disregarded.

If we consider the basic paradox of observation and the reentry of distinctions into themselves, the problem of the blind spot remains, the need to render the paradox invisible. Every observation must unfold its own paradox; in other words, it must replace it with an adequately functioning distinction. Every theory that claims to describe the world, and in this sense aspires to universal application, has to take account of this necessity for invisibilization. It must take it into account at least in others (as their "ideology," their "subconscious," their "latent need"). It must therefore be formulated on the level of second-order observation. But then the "autological" recourse to one's own observation cannot be avoided.

Looking back, we can now better understand why the rationality continuum of the old European tradition had to be abandoned. Every observation (including cognition and action) is tied to the selection of a distinction, and selection necessarily means leaving something out of account. The labels "pragmatism," "historicism," "relativism," and "pluralism" were applied to this in the twentieth century. They were, however, formulated as restrictions on universalistic rationality claims. But if every observation is obliged to resolve its own paradox and can give no reasonable (innocent) grounds for doing so, incompleteness theorems of all types lose the smack of falling too short, which would in itself be desirable. We now have to assume the universality of selection constraints, the universality of differentiation and boundary drawing. Reason that refuses to acknowledge this is not far from totalitarian, if not terrorist, logic. And it, too, has its (well-concealed) invisibility theorem. For it cannot say what is to happen with those who refuse to accept what reason proposes.

Rationality appears to have been the vanishing point at which, in view of society's growing complexity, one could still believe in an ultimate harmony (business still benefits from this in legitimizing its self-description on the basis of assumptions about the rationality of its decision-making practices). On this assumption, however, we also see that the perspective of rationality registers the dissolution of this notion of ultimate harmony—first, through the assumption of an "invisible hand" that guarantees good results, then, through evolution theory up to and including reduction to subjective preferences that can be assumed to be socially interdependent but not stable. Finally, we must even question whether relating the problem of rationality to the individual is tenable—be it in the sense of rational choice or of communicative understanding. For this, too, is perhaps only a traditional element; we would expect rationality from members of an organization or professions, but hardly from people in their private lives. Sociology can offer no hold on this decreasing order, and quite certainly not by means of concepts such as ethics, culture, or institution. Systems theory can at least make use of the reduction to system references to discover for which system the question of rationality weighs most heavily. The answer is likely to be clear: for the comprehensive social system of society and its forms of respecifying overly general criteria, namely, organizations and professions.

However, this is not to assert that, through norms, rules, or directives, society can provide guidelines for what would earn subsystems of society the epithet of rational. As we shall repeatedly see, society steers itself by means of fluctuations that force functional or regional systems to process dissipative structures and thus to organize themselves. Quite different paradoxes and quite different distinctions, at any rate, other distinctions, between self-reference and other-reference are likely to play a role. This must be left to more concrete investigation. However, this does not change the fact that we must apply the concept of rationality primarily to the system of world society if we wish to understand how the context is reproduced for other system rationalities.

But whatever we decide about the concept of rationality and its conditions, the appeal to rationality serves in ongoing communication to mark the nonnegotiability of a position. There is a need for it. At the same time, we speculate in such a procedure with the inertia of the communication process. It will not abandon its topic and turn to the conditions for rationality merely because someone claims that something is rational or not rational. Even if conceptual clarification leads nowhere, this need not discourage an appeal to rationality in ongoing communication. It is, so to speak, the ever-fertile breeding ground for the need to clarify the conditions of rationality.

2

Communication Media

1. Medium and Form

Setting aside for the moment the fact that a system of society actually exists and reproduces communication through communication, such a state of affairs is extremely improbable. Only communication makes itself probable. It cannot occur as an isolated event. Every communication presupposes other operations of the same type to which it can react and which it can stimulate. Without recursive reference of this sort, it would have no occasion whatsoever to take place.

This means above all that communication cannot be connected to communications arbitrarily, for otherwise communication would not recognize communication as such. There must be probabilities to guide expectations if the autopoiesis of communication is to be possible. However, this merely shifts our problem to the question of how communication itself can overcome the improbability of its own occurrence.

The improbability of a communicative operation is shown by the requirements that have to be fulfilled for it to come about. Communication is a synthesis of three selections, as we have seen.[1] It comprises information, utterance, and understanding. Each of these components is in itself a contingent occurrence. Information is a difference that changes the state of a system, thus generating another difference. But why should one particular piece of information and no other impress a system? Because it is uttered? But the selection of a particular item of information for utterance is also improbable. Why, given the many possibilities for meaningful activity, should anyone turn to someone at all, and why with this particular utterance? Finally, why should anyone concentrate his attention on another's utterance, seek to understand it, and adapt his behavior to the information uttered when he is free to refrain from doing so? All these improbabilities are then multiplied in the time dimension. How can it be that communication attains its goal rapidly enough? And, above all, how can it be that one communication is succeeded by another (not the same!) with expectable regularity?

If the individual components of communication are in themselves improbable, their synthesis is all the more so. What gives anyone the idea not merely of perceiving another person, whose behavior may be dangerous or perhaps odd, but also of observing him with regard to the distinction between utterance and information? How does the other come to expect observation and adapt to this expectation? And how is anyone to feel encouraged to venture an utterance (and what one?) if understanding the meaning of the utterance enables the understander to reject it? If we consider what is probable for the participating psychic systems, it is thus hardly possible to explain that communication takes place at all.

Questions of this sort are in principle to be addressed to evolution theory and systems theory. This will be dealt with in detail subsequently. But communication itself also has to cope with its immanent improbability. How communication is possible and what is suitable for communication is determined by the resolution or rather transformation of this problem.

It is hardly ever posed so drastically. It is usually deemed sufficient to explain the occurrence of communication through its function and to see its function in *relieving and expanding the cognitive faculties of living beings*. For compelling biological reasons, living beings exist as individuals. But they not live independently of one another. The more highly developed species are endowed with independent mobility and the faculty of distal perception. Where this is the case, it can bring evolutionary success not only to increase the reach of one's own perception,[2] but also to exchange additional information instead of procuring all information alone. The literature has a number of terms for this state of affairs, including "vicarious learning"[3] and "economy of cognition."[4] The view is taken that we can obtain much more information more rapidly with the aid of others than if we rely only on our own senses. Recent theories on "hominization" correspondingly stress that the evolutionary branching off of "Homo sapiens" is to be attributed not directly to superior abilities in dealing with external nature but to the special *cognitive* requirements of the *social* field in which the primates evolving toward humans existed.[5] The resulting challenge was met by the simultaneous development of *extreme social dependence* and *a high degree of individualization* achieved by building up a complex order of meaningful communication, which then determined the further evolution of humanity.

The argument is helpful but not a sufficient explanation. It offers us particulars about the environment of the communication system that is society (or of corresponding systems of animal communication). If living beings did not have to exist as individuals, if there were no advantages in distal information, and if it were not helpful to expand the range of one's own sensory apparatus—even if adapted to distal perception—through distal perception of the distal perception of other living beings, no communications systems could have developed. The environment that makes this possible explains a great deal. But it does not explain the autopoiesis of communication, the operational closure of communicative systems, any more successfully than chemistry can explain the autopoiesis of life. Even in general terms, stating the function of something cannot explain its existence or the structures by means of which it makes itself possible. In particular, a functional explanation that points to needs or advantages in the *environment* does not suffice to explain how the *system* functions. As soon as we realize the extreme improbability of something coming about and functioning, we must, while accepting the need for a conducive environment, seek the explanation in the system itself.

If we want somewhat greater conceptual precision, we soon see that the advantages of socially expanding the cognitive faculties of living beings cannot be achieved by making them dependent on one another. The long tradition of talking about "relations" between living beings (including humans) obscures this state of affairs. Living beings exist individually; they exist as structurally determined systems. From this point of view, it is a constellationally determined accident if the one, although it does what it does, can benefit the other. Dependency means multiplying improbabilities by each other. Advantages are therefore only to be gained by living beings becoming dependent on a *higher-order system* under whose conditions they can choose contact with one another and thus escape dependence on one other. For humans, this higher-order system, which is not itself a living being, is the communication system society.[6] In other words, at the level of the emergent system, there had to be an intrinsic mode of operation (in this case, communication), an intrinsic autopoiesis, a self-produced continuability of operations; otherwise the evolution of "vicarious learning" possibilities would never have succeeded.

This also means that a "transmission" of information from one living being to another (or from one consciousness system to another) is impossible.[7] Communication can therefore not be understood as a transmission process. Items of information are always time differences constituted within the system, that is, differences with respect to states of the system, which are the result of interaction between self-referential and other-referential, but always internally processed indications. This is true of neurophysiological system formations and even more so of communication systems.

Communication systems constitute themselves with the aid of the distinction between *medium and form*.[8] This distinction replaces the concept of transmission, which proves implausible for systems theory.[9] Moreover, it spares us the search for "ultimate elements," which nuclear metaphysics à la Heisenberg tells us do not exist anyway. Ontological points of reference, the subject of controversy between reductionism and holism, are replaced by a distinction dependent on the observer. When we speak of "communication media," we always mean the operational use of the *difference* between medial substratum and form.[10] Communication is possible only—and this is the answer to the improbability problem—as the processing of this difference.

Like the information concept, the (closely associated) distinction between medium and form is always an *intra*systemic matter. And as with information, there is nothing in the environment corresponding to the medium/form difference (although there are naturally conditions of possibility in the environment and corresponding structural couplings). Thus, communication presupposes no ultimate identities (atoms, particles) that it does not itself constitute through its own distinctions. Above all, neither "information" nor "medium/form" "represent" physical states of affairs of the environment in the system. This is true of perceptual media ("light" is not a physical concept) and all the more so of all communication media, as we shall see. It also means that complexity adequacy always has to take account of how the information processing system structures its own autopoiesis.

The distinction between medial substratum and form decomposes the general problem of structured complexity with the help of the distinction between loosely and strictly coupled elements.[11] This latter distinction assumes that not every element can be connected to every other; but it reformulates the selection problem this poses before tackling it, once again by means of a further, prior distinction, in order to describe forms (in this narrower sense strict coupling) as a selection in the field of a medium.

Such a distinction already underlies the perceptual processes of organisms.[12] They require specific perceptual media such as light or air or electromagnetic fields that can be tied to certain forms by the perceiving organism and can then appear and be exploited as certain things, certain noises, specific signals, and so forth, on the basis of complex neurophysiological processes. Already at this point, the medium can become form: light is let into the cathedrals and becomes form to play on pillars and arches. The physical structure of the world must make this possible, but the difference between medium and form is an achievement of the perceiving organism itself.

On a quite different basis, we find the same distinction underlying the operation of communicative systems. As I have pointed out in explicating the meaning concept and in analyzing language,[13] there is a medium specific to the system here, too, and related forms that make their mark in the medium. Loosely couple words are joined to become sentences, thus gaining a form that is temporary in communication, a form that does not consume but reproduces the word material.[14] The distinction between medium and form translates the improbability of the system's operational continuity into a *difference that can be handled within the system,* transforming it into a framework condition for the autopoiesis of the system. The system operates in tying its own medium to its own forms without consuming this medium (just as our seeing things does not consume light). The actualized forms, the things seen, the sentences spoken, couple the elements of the system for momentary use but do not destroy them. The difference between medium and form is maintained in operational use and thus reproduced. What counts is the difference itself and not only the form condensed in the operation. For the possibility of seeing colors or pronouncing words presupposes that these entities are not consumed in the operation but are reproduced in their availability for use in the context of other forms.

At this point we need to recall that by "form," we understand the marking of a distinction. The distinction between medium and form is hence also a form. The distinction implies itself, it makes every theory that works with it autological. To explain what we understand by medium and form, we have to use language; we accordingly use the distinction between medium and form. From the point of view of traditional epistemology, this would be an error rendering everything that follows from it unusable. We shall encounter the same problem in the discussion in the chapters to come of the distinctions between variation and selection (evolution theory) and between system and environment (theory of system differentiation). For theories taking a universalistic approach, autologies of this sort are unavoidable, and if we come across them, this is no objection: on the contrary, it is evidence for the theoretical standing of the conceptuality.

It is all the more important to describe the distinction between medium and form as precisely as possible so that in each case we can establish what difference an operation uses and where its blind spot, which it cannot itself observe, is to be found. We do this with the aid of the distinction between *loose and strict coupling of elements*. A medium consists of loosely coupled elements, whereas a form joins the same elements in strict coupling. Let us take the example of action as a medium and imagine society as the totality of its actions. Freedom is then based on the strict coupling of actions in their attribution to individual persons who are to be recognized by the form of their actions; and loose coupling would offer the possibility of recruiting actions for purposes as they arise, because they are not bound to persons. Societies that guarantee a high measure of freedom end up with action becoming unavailable for collective purposes.[15] It is only seemingly a paradox that this leads to gigantic government, needing a great deal of money to carry out its programs in the face of freedom.

Coupling is a concept that implies time. We should speak of coupling and uncoupling, of an only momentary integration, which gives form but can be reversed. The medium is bound—and released. Without medium, there is no form, and without form, no medium. Over time, it is possible to reproduce this difference repeatedly. In whatever objective shape, on whatever perceptual basis, the difference between loose and strict coupling enables the temporal processing of operations in dynamically stabilized systems, thus making autopoietic systems of this type possible. With regard to this repeated binding and releasing of the medium, we can also say that the medium "circulates" in the system. It has its unity in movement.

This temporal process of repeated coupling and uncoupling serves both to continue autopoiesis and to form and modify the structures it requires—as with a von Neumann machine. It therefore circumvents the classical distinction of structure and process. This means not least that the unity of the system can no longer be defined in terms of (relative) structural stability, although system maintenance remains the issue, but in terms of the specific conditions for a medium to form forms.

The same temporal reference is also apparent in the general medium of meaning, which serves to produce both psychic and social forms. Since meaning can always be actualized only as event and this takes place in horizons that appresent many further actualization possibilities, every meaning experienced or communicated at the moment is a form, that is to say, the marking of a difference and hence a determination. At the same time, however, following references to an "and-so-on" of further possibilities manifests a relationship of loose coupling, which can be bound only by further actualizations. Strict coupling is what is realized at present (even if as concrete memory or anticipation). Loose coupling is to be found in the possibilities of transition from one to the other not thus determined.

Circulation arises where the form is stronger that the medial substratum. It imposes itself in the field of loosely coupled elements—and regardless of selection criteria, rationality considerations, normative directives, or other value preferences—in fact it does so simply as strict coupling. Unlike Jürgen Habermas in his theory of communicative action, I avoid building pretensions to rationality into the concept of communication,[16] postulating only that there is a *connection between the assertive force and temporal transience of the form*. Communication media entail no bias in the direction of rationality—any more than do the concept of system or that of evolution. At this elementary level, all that can be said is that what happens happens. On the other hand, forms are less permanent that the medial substratum. They endure only through special arrangements such as memory, writing, and printing. But even when a form is preserved because of its importance—and here the concept of semantics comes into play—the free capacity of the medial substratum remains available for ever-new couplings. Unbound (or scarcely bound) elements are innumerable; words, for example, can be used at will without depleting a limited fund of possibilities for use. However, frequent use also "condenses" the meaning of words, so that the combinatorial capacity, the type and reach of possibilities for use are subject to variation in the course of processing the difference between medial substratum and form, and hence in the course of the history of a language.

Finally, it must be noted that it is not the medial substratum but only forms that are operationally connective in the system. The system cannot handle formless, loosely coupled elements. This can also be said of the perceptual media. We do not see light but things, and when we see light, it is by the form of things.[17] We do not hear the air but noises; and the air itself has to make a noise if it is to be audible. The same is true of communication media. In the case of language, it is not words but sentences that make sense that can be processed in communication.[18] In the distinction between loose and strict coupling, there is not only temporal but also substantive asymmetry; and this asymmetry is one of the conditions for the autopoiesis of the communication system society.

Communication systems process communication on the basis of this in itself asymmetrical form of the distinction between medial substratum and form. They focus attention on the meaning of what is happening and seeking connection. Thus society emerges, and thus society reproduces itself in the medium of its communication. This more complexly structured concept replaces the usual notion of a transmission medium whose function it is to "mediate" between organisms existing independently of one another. The old sense of "*com*municatio," the establishment of "commonality" of experience, is therefore abandoned or reduced to the status of a side effect. This is the consequence of the view that it does not suffice to see the function of communication in expanding and relieving living beings' cognitive faculties. Indeed, it is difficult to see how living beings, including humans, can have anything at all in common in the dark inwardness of their consciousness.[19] Instead, the concept of communication media is intended to explain that and how the improbable is nevertheless possible on the basis of communication: the autopoiesis of the communication system society.

2. Dissemination Media and Success Media

The inquiries that follow are based on a distinction that needs an introductory explanation. Societal communication produces various media/forms depending on what problem is to be solved. I speak of "dissemination media" [*Verbreitungsmedien*] with reference to the *scope of social redundancy*. Dissemination media determine and extend the circle of those receiving information. To the extent that the same information is disseminated, information is transformed into redundancy. Redundancy makes information superfluous. It can be used to confirm social belongingness: people relate what is already known to show their solidarity. But this does not involve any gain in information. We can ask anyone who has received the information. If we ask repeatedly, no new information arises.[20]

Dissemination can take place in face-to-face interaction. Writing increased the circle of recipients in an initially still controllable manner. But with the spread of literacy, it was soon impossible to know who had read what and remembered what texts contained. The invention of the printing press and then the advent of modern mass media compounded the anonymization of social redundancy. When in doubt, we must now reckon with disseminated information being known and cannot once again communicate it. New information is continually needed to satisfy the mass media system, which has its own autopoiesis to thank for the self-generated loss of information.[21]

Not only does time pass faster as the dissemination media generate social redundancy, it also becomes uncertain and finally impossible to ascertain whether uttered information is accepted or rejected as the premise for further behavior. Too many, immeasurably many, are involved, and we can no longer determine whether a communication has had a motivating effect and to what end. There is controversial discussion on the subject in the mass media, and their system loves conflict. But this can at most simulate but not elucidate which communications are accepted throughout society and which are rejected or simply forgotten.

In this situation, evolution can stagnate or it can come up with solutions to the new problems. Consequent on the invention of writing, it seemed politic to tauten religion for more intensive deployment as a homogenized motivation tool. However, this demanded too much of the cosmology of this instrument. Society finally found a quite different solution, only superficially integrable with religions, in a new type of media, which we call success media, namely, *symbolically generalized communication media*.

Symbolically generalized communication media establish a novel kind of link between conditioning and motivation. They gear communication in a given media area, for example, in the money economy or the exercise of power in political office, to certain conditions that enhance the chances of acceptance even in the case of "uncomfortable" communication. For example, goods are supplied or services rendered if (and only if) they are paid for. Government authorities are obeyed under the threat of physical force and because it must be assumed that society regards this threat as legitimate (e.g., as lawful). The institutionalization of symbolically generalized communication media thus raises the threshold for the nonacceptance of communication, which is very low when communication extends beyond face-to-face interaction. In the cultural self-description of society, too, these success media play such a prominent role that no information at all is gathered about how much communication is afterward ignored or how much information is simply forgotten. Society then describes itself as if general consensus secured by principles, codes, and programs can be relied upon. As if there were a "public opinion." The rest is left in the dark in the form of "pluralistic ignorance."[22]

Language alone does not decide whether the reaction to communication is acceptance or rejection. As long as language is used only orally, that is to say, only in face-to-face interaction, there is enough social pressure to say pleasant rather than unpleasant things and to inhibit the communication of rejection. If communication is only oral, language also acts as an "intrinsic persuader" (Talcott Parsons). Symbolically generalized communication media develop only when societal evolution has overcome this threshold to allow complexity to develop in greater spatial and temporal dimensions, even though in the same society. Communication must then be increasingly geared to still unknown situations. Society helps itself if evolution helps it, first, with system differentiation,[23] and, second, with the formation of special media for restricting contingency by linking conditioning and motivation, namely, symbolically generalized communication media. The differentiation of these media also drives system differentiation, providing occasion for the outdifferentiation of important societal functional systems.

In this brief overview of the hypotheses that will be guiding our inquiries, I note solely that they draw theoretically on the assumption that society is an *operationally closed social system based on communication*, and that its *evolution therefore follows the problems of the autopoiesis of communication*, the conditions for which evolution is constantly changing.

A complex research program is hence envisaged, which is pursued in the coming sections and chapters with all the necessary detours across a wide range of issues.

3. Language

The fundamental communication medium that guarantees the regular autopoiesis of society in its promise of continuation is language. Although there is communication without language—by means of gestures or the interpretation of basic behavior, for example, of how a person handles things whether or not communication is intended—we can well ask whether such communication could exist, whether we could observe a distinction between utterance behavior and information, if there were no language and hence no experience with language. Furthermore, interpretable behavior is always so specific to the situation that there is hardly any scope for differentiating between medium and form; and this is precisely what language does. In any case, the autopoiesis of a communication system, which requires the regular prospect of further communication, is impossible without language, even though it permits, where enabled, nonlinguistic communication.

A pre-linguistic communication medium that did not yet constitute meaning can have lain only in the totality of the behavioral options of individuals in each other's presence. Movement in space will have played a considerable role. Following George Herbert Mead, we could also speak of a recursive sequence of gestures, in which not the single act but recursivity (connection with what has preceded) prompts emergent effects.[24] In such episodic contexts, we also find species-specific signals, which are, however, of very limited use. Signals are not yet signs, do not yet point to something else; they are only a factor activating "anticipatory reactions" owing to typical, repeated complexes of present and future events, which are, however, not recognized as complexes.[25] Such conditions can enable the morphogenesis of relatively complex social orders if reactive patterns of behavior are reapplied to their own outcomes. Participants do not need to be able to recognize the structures that consequently emerge and to react *to them*. The potential for form building must therefore have been correspondingly limited, but apparently sufficient to establish hierarchies and individual partner preferences.[26] In the pre-linguistic field, indeed, even in relations between humans and animals, we find what is probably the most important preparation for the evolution of language: the perception of perception and, in particular, the perception of being perceived. Even in developed societies, even today, these are still indispensable forms of sociality, especially in relations between the sexes. At this level, sociality uses the complexity and focusability of perception and generates a present—almost without a future. Even if we can assume this as, so to speak, a pre-prehistorical given, and accordingly that life in society adapted to this possibility, this social state of affairs would have allowed of no metacommunication, no communication relating to communication; no, for example, confirmation of the receipt of an utterance, no repetition of the same utterance, no development of sequential, "punctuated" complexity in which communication presupposes that it has already operated successfully with other content.[27] It remains to be seen whether, under these circumstances, we can already speak of autopoietic closure of a social system independent of the course of life—for example, enduring beyond the death of whole generations—and whether and to what extent we can already speak of "language" in Humberto Maturana's sense, of coordinating the coordination of living beings' behavior in their individual existences.[28] In any case, language in the usual meaning of the term with its clear preference for acoustic media and the optical media deriving from them is a singular historical construction of evolution based on a stringent selection of resources.[29]

However, this is not the place to launch into a study of the evolution of language; I merely assume that, as in all evolution of autopoietic systems, a sort of auxiliary construction made takeoff possible.[30] The use of gestures and sounds as *signs* presumably played a role. Signs are also forms, that is to say, marked distinctions. According to Saussure, they distinguish the signifier (*signifiant*) from the signified (*signifié*). In the form of the sign, that is to say, in the relation of signifier to signified, there are references: the signifier signifies the signified. The form itself (and only the form should be called a sign)[31] has no reference; it functions only as a distinction and only when it is in fact used as such.

Signs are therefore structures for (repetitive) operations that require no contact with the outside world. They do not, as so often assumed, serve within the system to "represent" states of affairs in the outside world. The distinction between signifier and signified is rather an internal difference that does not require what is signified to exist in the outside world. Its specific nature lies rather in the *isolation* of this distinction, which has the effect of stabilizing the relationship between signifier and signified regardless of the context in which it is used.[32] The involvement of other meaning references, other contexts (mediated, for example, by the materiality of the sign vehicle) are left out of account. What is decisive for the cultural invention of the sign, as for technology, is a relationship with the world characterized by differentiation, isolation, and consequent repeatability. This also explains why errors are possible. The smallest deviation or confusion can put signs out of action (it suffices to say line or site or seen instead of sign to make what we mean incomprehensible). The generation of redundancies, of limitations to the surprise effect in the use of signs thus depends on the accuracy with which known patterns are copied. But this can be achieved, like isolation itself, only through the arbitrary determination of signs.

The evolution of a stereotyped use of signs is, however, only one precondition for the evolution of language. It fails to explain important properties of language, above all, the most important: the operational closure of the communication system that uses language. The recursivity of gesture sequences, which can be realized only episodically, develops into the recursive use of signs, producing a world that can be referred to over and again even after substantial interruptions. The preconditions and opportunities that lie in the evolution of the form "sign" must therefore be carefully distinguished from the coming into being of the operational closure of a communication system that has language at its disposition.[33] Language generalizes self-reference, and does so with the aid of signs, which themselves *are* this generalization; they do not consist in reference to something *else*.

Giving a sign in particular situations that make this comprehensible may have given occasion and opportunity for frequent repetition, but something quite different has resulted. We see the improbability threshold in the question of how anyone comes to observe another from the standpoint of a difference between information and utterance behavior.[34] Our point of departure is accordingly not the speech act, which occurs only when one can expect the act to be expected and understood, but the situation of the utterance recipient, of the person who observes the utterer and attributes the utterance, *but not the information*, to him. The recipient of the utterance must observe the utterance as indicating a piece of information, thus the two together (as form of the distinction between indicator and what is indicated) as sign (even though other, for example, purely perceptual, possibilities of observation are available to him). This does not necessarily presuppose language. The housewife, for example, bravely swallows the burnt fare to indicate (or so one presumes) that it is edible. However, the facts of communication remain vague and ambiguous, and the utterer can, if questioned, deny having intended to make an utterance; and for this very reason he chooses nonverbal communication. But this also means that it is difficult to add another utterance to the first and thus form a communication system.

Language changes this. Whereas before the development of language, living beings lived in *structural* coupling, and were therefore subject to co-evolution, language also enables *operational* coupling, which can be reflexively monitored by participants. This increases the possibilities of exposing oneself to certain environments or withdrawing from them, and enables participants' self-organization to dissociate from what is communicated. One remains perceivable but comprehensible only in what one wittingly contributes to linguistic communication. With the normalization and recursive stabilization of these coupling operations, a special autopoietic system of linguistic communication takes shape that is self-determined in its operations and fully compatible with the deliberate participation of individuals. Co-evolution between individuals and society now develops, which overdetermines any co-evolutive relationships between individuals (e.g., between mother and child).

Far-reaching changes also take place at the level of the perceptual media. Speech is a behavior specialized in communication, differentiated out for this function and consequently highly perceivable. In the acoustic (and, in the case of the written word, the optical) perceptual medium, language is so distinctive in form that when used, there can be no doubt about it, nor can the relevant perceptions be imputed to others. Every participant knows of himself and of his interlocutor that linguistic specifications of meaning are chosen contingently (which repeatedly confirms that "only" signs are involved). A second mode of selection is imposed on what can be acoustically or optically perceived and thus distinguished. The "material" of language, too, is formed and perceivable only because this is so; but it is also invested with references that function independently of the setting and thus make repeated use possible. Linguistic signs are always possible in various guises. At the same time, however, they take on a form that enables queries and, if writing is used, text interpretation. The conclusion of communicative episodes can hence be delayed and the succession of elementary statement sequences can be directed back on itself.[35] This makes the language process in its self-determination independent of participants' perceptions, which it presupposes. The system shields itself from the noise of perceptions through its own recursions, admitting only irritations that it can handle in its own language. In linguistic guise, communication reproduces what it needs for autocatalysis, namely, double contingency, thus continually renewing its own prerequisites, whatever had made it possible to start. Neither the speaker nor the listener can deny the fact of communication as such. The receiver can at most misunderstand or have difficulty in understanding or interpret, or subsequently communicate in some other way about the communication. The problems of communication feed back into communication. The system closes itself. A normally entropic development of approaches to communication in the direction of noncommunication is reversed by language and directed toward building up complicated, interpretable ways of communicating on the basis of what has already been said. The autopoiesis of a communication system, in itself improbable, thus becomes probable. At the same time, however, it retains its improbability in that, given the host of other possibilities, every statement made is extremely improbable. The clear external boundary of the system leads to the development of structured complexity, which in turn makes every single event in the system improbable. But this is precisely where the system can help itself by processing recursively and ensuring that the choices actually available are limited.

Speech is tied to audition, which, unlike vision, imposes the temporal sequencing of communication, the establishment of order in temporal progression. The distinctions evoked must lend each other meaning in succession; recursion requires time and cannot result from the world we see at the same time—not even if we see someone speaking. Language accordingly requires flexible organization that does not already predetermine possible sequences at the structural level: in other words, grammar. Even sign language is adapted to this temporal flow, not to mention the written word. The acoustic medium therefore demands a higher level of abstraction from the outset and hence requires the meaning of individual components to be fixed more definitely. This alone makes repeatability possible, and this alone, despite nonsimultaneity, despite a nonsimultaneity that differs from that of movements in the world outside, allows a context of meaning to be produced, a second world of communication to be superimposed on the first, visual world.

Language therefore has a quite peculiar *form*. As a form with two sides, it consists in the difference between *sound* and *meaning*. Whoever cannot handle this difference cannot speak. As always with forms in my definition, we find a condensed referential complex of the two sides: the sound is not the meaning, but with this not-being, as it were, it *determines* what meaning is spoken about in each case. Vice versa, the meaning *is* not the sound but *determines* what sound is to be selected if this meaning and no other is to be spoken about. In Hegelian terms, language is determined by a "difference-in-itself" and, we can say, differentiated out by the specifics of this very difference.

In the first place, linguistic communication is hence the processing of meaning in the phonic medium. We speak of medium in this regard not because sounds are forms in the perceptual medium of the consciousness but because they are condensed into words that can be used repeatedly and as such are then available in loose coupling. This in turn presupposes grammar and perhaps Chomsky's deep structures,[36] which ensure that there is sufficient scope for building sentences and that the process is nevertheless not arbitrary, but that sufficient redundancy is available for recursion, for rapid understanding, and, above all, for rapid language acquisition.

If a difference between medium and form specific to language is to be established, the medial substratum of language, the difference between sound and meaning must be *underspecified*.[37] Without underspecification, there would be nothing more to say, because everything would always have already been said. This problem is resolved by differentiating between words and sentences. Although words, too, are constellations of sounds with meaning, they do not yet determine what sentences they will be combined to form. Only through this difference does language lend communication the capacity for temporary adjustment to temporary situations; and the capacity for temporary meaning constructions, which can later be confirmed or withdrawn. Only then can we expect that communication will connect with communication and that there will always be something to say.

Mere perceptual media are bound by the simultaneity of perception and what is perceived. This is also the case when we perceive others' perception; and it is also the case for simple forms of perceiving indexical signs. The operationally determined simultaneity of observation and the world that is observed cannot be overcome, and this is also true where meaning (as in hearing) arises only through sequencing. The future reference of perception depends on the environment sufficiently guaranteeing through its constants that a now-reaction adequately prepares the future. Only language permits this simultaneity premise to be overcome and enables the preparatory synchronization of temporally distant events—independently of whether language has forms at its disposition with which the difference between past, present, and future can be expressed (e.g., through the inflection of verbs). For language makes it possible to look ahead or to restrict what can later be said. In the first place, it is simply a matter of temporally decoupling the recursive course of language from the temporal sequences of the environment, of differentiating an eigentime of the communication system that makes it possible to distinguish the communication process taking place in the system from sequences of environmental events. Only when this is ensured can linguistic forms arise that express temporal relations, for example in the simple form of if-then conditionalization. Language can, in more or less elaborate form, also refer to something that can no longer or not yet be perceived. And it is this that allows synchronization to be problematized, making learning by trial and error possible.

Only this outdifferentiation of an eigentime of linguistic communication achieves what must be regarded as the most important evolutionary accomplishment of linguistic communication. With the aid of language, things can be said *that have never been said before*. "Elvira is an angel." We understand a sentence, unlike gestures and unlike simple behavior or the use of things, even if it is completely new to us.[38] Strictly speaking, it is not even important whether the sentence is original in the history of the world and has never been uttered before. What is decisive is that the meaning and context of earlier use do not need to be remembered. In other words, language facilitates forgetting. It relieves the social memory and therefore constantly frees capacity for new communication.

This capacity for new, never used meaning is naturally not boundless. It generates contexts on which it becomes dependent. But however little possibility there may have been in the early stages of evolution of saying something never before heard, it provides an evolutionary potential that can be increasingly exploited as society becomes more complex and differentiated, hence creating special conditions for recognizing and understanding novelty.

This was already fully developed when language was only spoken (oral). In today's written cultures, it is hard to imagine situations where language was only oral. For sounds are extremely unstable elements. Moreover, their reach is limited, requiring speaker and hearer to be present. Space and time must be present in compact, situational forms to make spoken language possible. The moment sentences are pronounced, they vanish into inaudibility. System formation on the basis of communication therefore needs provision for reuse, in other words, memory.

This suggests, and in a certain sense correctly, that societies that have to rely on oral communication remain dependent on purely mental memory. But this does not explain enough and, incidentally, applies even more so in written cultures, which function only if all members can constantly remember how to read and write. A social memory must therefore be developed beyond (which does not mean independently of) mental memory. It consists solely in the *delayed* reuse of words and the expressed meaning formed with their aid.[39] Psychic systems are used, as it were, only for intermediate storage. What is decisive for social memory is the retrieval of memories in later social situations; and over extended periods of time, the psychic substratum can change.[40] If we want to comprehend what advantages the invention of writing has brought, we must first of all understand the preceding mechanism that all recall has to perform through the temporal form of delay.

However, if distinct phonic perception and its reactivation in the course of later communication are ensured, this does not yet explain how language organizes its recursive use, how it can enable communication. Old European sign theory had argued in terms of external relations. It had reckoned with a world holding the language community of humanity and had attributed a representational function to language. Recognizing names and giving names accordingly presupposed a knowledge of nature.[41] If this is abandoned—and recent linguistics has done so—what, if not the world, guarantees the sustainability of language?

The solution to this problem might lie in the concept of "eigenbehavior" taken from mathematical logic.[42] It refers to a stability arising in the recursive procedure of applying the procedure to the results of the procedure.[43]

Language comes about through the reuse of sounds and groups of sounds. To be more precise, in the course of reuse it first generates the identity of words, condenses language-specific identities; in the same move, it also confirms these condensates in ever-new situations, generalizing them. This process of language formation therefore differentiates an eigenbehavior of the communication system and in second place produces a language-dependent order of perceptual tasks for the individual consciousness.

This reuse succeeds only if words are not confused with things—however much one had initially operated with the auxiliary assumption of a mysterious relationship between words and things and a corresponding influence of language on things. It is, after all, obvious that language functions only if we become aware—and become aware that others have become aware—of the fact that words *are not* the objects of the factual world *but* only *indicate them*. This gives rise to a new, an emergent difference, namely that between real reality and semiotic reality.[44] Only then can there be a real world at all, because only then is there a position from where reality can be indicated as reality, that is to say, distinguished. This does not mean that reality is a mere fiction and that, as some have felt, it "does not exist in reality." But it does mean that we must introduce this distinction between real reality and semiotic reality if anything at all—even semiotic reality—is to be indicated as real.

However, this distinction, which alone lends the world its severity, its fatefulness, its inadequacy, must itself be generated. It is not given simply because it is called on as a transcendental condition of possibility. To this extent, we follow the "linguistic turn," which replaces the transcendental subject by language—now we say by society.[45] The eigenbehavior of the communication system society stabilizes the imaginary space of meanings, which the recursive application of communication to communication does not destroy but establish—thanks precisely to its eigenvalue, hence through the experience that it is one's awareness of others' awareness of the nature of language that produces the results that enable recursive communication to continue, that make the autopoiesis of society possible. This does not necessarily succeed. But systems of this type arise and evolve only if it does succeed. We could also say that language arises in a sort of self-fulfilling prophecy—not in the classical sense of the term propounded by Robert K. Merton and thus not as a mere methodological problem of empirical social research but as constitutive for society as such.[46]

With the aid of what is already form, that is to say, with words, a new medial substratum can be generated—a very large, only loosely coupled set of such words, which are then linked into strictly coupled forms, that is to say, sentences, with the medial substratum in the given coupling not being consumed but renewed by use. Every sentence therefore consists of components that can be reused at will, ongoing sentence building regenerating the lexical inventory of a language, condensing and confirming and thus enriching the meaning of words, but also relegating never reused words to oblivion. Only sentences are connective in the recursive network of linguistic communication; they can be anticipated with a vague idea of word structure and recalled as fixed meaning. They can be quoted, their gist can be passed on, they can be confirmed or withdrawn; and in this sense they transport the autopoiesis of the system through the coupling/decoupling of the lexical inventory. They form the emergent level of the communicative constitution of meaning, and this emergence is nothing other than the autopoiesis of the linguistic communication that it creates in its own medial substratum.

It is for this function that the peculiar structures of language are created whose details occupy the linguists, but which function as latent structures and are not themselves objects of communication. If we ask about these linguistic structures, we are normally referred to restrictions on the use of words, to syntax, to grammar, and the like.[47] The corresponding deep structures, too, result from the urgency involved in the use of language, including the urgency of social language acquisition by succeeding generations.[48] It is easy to see that this condensed complexity serves to generate improbable probabilities. For it makes every specific sentence extremely improbable, but also quite normal that this is so in every communication. However, this paradox unfolds only in communication; it does so through the autopoiesis of the communication system, hence through the restrictions imposed on what can meaningfully be said by recursion to previous communication and the prospect of later communication.

If we assume that language structures the autopoiesis of communication, a radical and much simpler structure comes into focus. I shall call it the (binary) code of language.[49] Language offers a positive and a negative version of everything that is said.

This duplication serves as a structure concerned exclusively with linguistic communication and which can be learned mentally only by participating in communication.[50] Moreover, coding presupposes that language has already constituted identities, hence that it can distinguish and indicate, so that what is affirmed and negated can be established. Coding changes and expands the need for identities; it must be able to presuppose negation-proof identities. It is no longer only a matter of enabling recognizability (including the recognizability of words) for perception and its memory. Identities must now be required to remain the same when communication shifts from affirmation to negation or from negation to affirmation. This allows the repertoire of possible communication to extend beyond the perceivable that can be pointed to; and only thus can communication generate controversy (and hence sociocultural evolution). In contrast to classical logic and the corresponding ontology, there is therefore no primordial distinction between being and nonbeing or between positive or negative referring operations. The world itself cannot be qualified in terms of positive and negative. For this very reason we must distinguish if we wish to indicate something; in other words, a distinction does not negate what it does not indicate. It presupposes it as "unmarked space."[51]

To understand this achievement it is also important to realize that the use of negations does not yet lead to logical inconsistency.[52] It merely opens a contingency space; it is to be assumed in communication that everything that is affirmed can also be negated and vice versa. Only on the basis of this assumption can positive and negative propositions be tested for their truth value, and only for this purpose can a "logic" be developed in addition to other tools. This presupposes, as an added invention, the law of the excluded middle (*tertium non datur*).

We do not know whether this is an evolutionary condition for the genesis of negation or only a successfully used side effect: in any case, negation permits the domestication of the determinate/indeterminate schema, one of the fundamental distinctions enabling us to deal with meaning.[53] Through negation we can indicate something in such a way that it remains uncertain what is actually going on. "No one in the desert" does not tell us what else there is in the desert, or where people really are, or who is meant at all. The communication is nonetheless immediately comprehensible and ready to be dealt with further—for example, as a warning. Even the simplest of societies are apparently quite essentially concerned with normalizing the unusual and stabilizing their own pathologies through repetition. For this purpose, negative reference builds bridges to normality.

However, all this remains an internal problem of the communication system society. Since nothing negative exists in the outside world, and hence nothing indeterminate, the coding of language amounts to the doubling of propositional possibilities. The first question would thus be: What is this all about? Why does language afford itself this luxury?

In this structure, we see a *compensation for problems resulting from the outdifferentiation of the communication system* of society, *hence a condition and consequent arrangement of autopoietic autonomy.*

An autopoietic, self-referential system requires such a code to symbolize its own self-reference and to ensure the interruption of its constitutive circularity. The two values can be translated into each other to negate calls for a positive operation of the system, and the position is logically equivalent to the negation of its negation. At the same time, however, this tautological structure implies a latent propensity for interruption. It makes the system sensitive first to chance, then to self-organization, offering an indication of whether yesses or noes are appropriate. Society thus comes into being through this breach of symmetry intrinsic to language, to which conditionings can then connect. The mere relation of the values would not yet constitute a system, but it is generated only with regard to its capacity to prompt system formation.[54]

This state of affairs, in itself complex, but clearly capable of evolving, also regulates the coming into being of time.[55] The system needs time alone to cross the boundary between the two values (for the negating of something that remains identical). And this holds all the more for the unfolding of the tautology, for the asymmetricizing conditioning, because the given starting situation has to be kept in sight while projecting the bistability of the system into the future. In order to continue its autopoiesis, such a system needs (to use Spencer-Brown's terminology) "memory" and "oscillation," and to distinguish (observe) these two conditions, it forms the difference between the time horizons past and future, which can be observed *simultaneously* from the operationally current present as its past or future. On the one hand, it must know in each case whether a yes version or a no version of communication is to be assumed and what this means in the current context. On the other, it is not yet certain whether the meaning communicated will subsequently be accepted or rejected. And even if, by and large, we can expect the world to continue as it is, the future of communication itself can be presented only through an oscillation function realized in dependence on what is involved at the time. These are historical universals given with the coding of language, which can assume widely varying semantic forms depending on the social structures realized.[56]

It is no exaggeration to say that linguistic coding is the muse of society. Without doubling all signs that fix identities, evolution would never have been able to form society, and we hence find no society without this requirement.

The outdifferentiation of a society that uses language and employs signs gives rise to the problem of *error* and *deception*, of the *unintentional* and *intentional abuse of signs*. It is not only that communication occasionally miscarries, goes astray, or takes the wrong track. The problem, since it can occur *at any time*, is *always* present[57]—a sort of universal problem of the type discovered by Hobbes with his example of violence. With this in mind, it is understandable that society morally appreciates sincerity, truthfulness, and the like, and in the communication process has to rely on trust.[58] But this only confirms that what nevertheless remains possible should not occur. If we ask how the communication process itself reacts to this problem, we realize the advantage of coding, for it makes it possible to doubt what has been uttered, to refrain from accepting it, to explicitly reject it, and to express this reaction understandably, thus reintroducing it into the communication process. Reference to psychological and moral qualities such as uprightness and trust retains its sense, but because no communication process can test psychic premises of this sort (the test itself would destroy what it seeks), the conditions have to be psychologically deconditioned and treated as topics of communication itself. This requires the yes/no coding of language.

Since the problem is a general one affecting all use of language, solving it through coding must also be a general solution. The entire language is coded; this means that every sentence can be negated. Coding transforms the general uncertainty about the misuse of linguistic signs into a bifurcation of connective options. Further communication can be based on either acceptance or rejection. There are only these two possibilities; but for this very reason we can also express indecisiveness or defer the decision, leaving it up to further communication. Without binary coding, not even deferral would be possible, for we would be unable to recognize what is deferred.

The coding of linguistic communication has such far-reaching consequences that it is worth while considering some of its characteristics. Above all, it affects the *entire* system of linguistic communication. Whatever is contributed faces the alternative of acceptance or rejection. "Every word pronounced evokes its opposite."[59] If we wish to avoid this risk, we have to eschew communication.

This generality and inevitability of coding also means that it does not serve to sort good news from bad. Bad news can very well be formulated positively ("the faucet is leaking") and thus, as communication, left to face the alternatives of acceptance or rejection. The precondition is that what is to be accepted or rejected is kept identical (this shows once again that the code is a duplication rule). In accepting or rejecting something, modifications can, of course, be made, especially if we wish to tone down rejection ("the faucet isn't leaking, it just wasn't turned off properly"). But communication always proceeds along thematic identities, and this, too, is an effect of coding. It has a thematically disciplinary effect, because it requires us to ensure that the same thing is being talked about.[60]

Coding as such contains no preference for yes-versions or no-versions, just as language as such is not there to favor the acceptance of communication over rejection. In principle, yesses and noes must therefore be equally easy to understand. It could be that the production and understanding of sentences containing negation take somewhat longer for the information to be processed and require somewhat more mental effort,[61] but in practical terms, this is hardly likely to count if there are reasons for a negative statement. More important are the *social* conditionings for the use of negation; and any difficulties psychic systems may have are only one more indication that they are operations of systems in the environment of society.

That coding relates to communication and not to the views and attitudes of participants can also be formulated as a *self-correction proviso of the communication process*. Correction (negation of preceding communication) is not necessarily incumbent on the recipient of the utterance. The utterer, too, can correct what he has himself said in further communication. Furthermore, correction need not concern explicitly and precisely remembered communications. It can also concern expectations resulting from earlier communication, so that negation is already expressed in the initiative taken to communicate and take the form of negating an external state of affairs ("the faucet wasn't properly turned off"). We presume that all negations directly referring to states of affairs in the world are occasioned by earlier communication and by the assumption that the communication process takes place under the influence of remembered communication and therefore has to be corrected through negation.

Two other peculiarities of linguistic communication follow from its coding. The first is that all use of negation at least implicitly presupposes *distinctions* to allow the options available if something is negated to be established. If something is referred to as "not red," other colors come into question; and, conversely, a positive statement such as "the car traveled slowly" has its prescribed negatives (one cannot, e.g., negate this by saying it traveled on four wheels).[62]

The prospect of yes/no bifurcation can also be directed by *marking*.[63] We mark the components of a communication that we assume offers informational value and the possibility of objecting and leave others unmarked. In particular, value attitudes assumed as a matter of course to be shared are generally communicated without being marked.[64] Erroneous markings are typical of speakers insufficiently familiar with the cultural or situational context of communication and therefore unable to assess probabilities correctly. But the problem of this intensification arises only because communication is coded and therefore seeks to control where it has to reckon with acceptance or rejection, surprise, and resistance.

However, the most important effect of coding is probably that the elementary operation of a communication is concluded with understanding and that the message of acceptance, rejection, or indecision *requires further communication*. For the understanding of a communication is the precondition for its being accepted or rejected; and which path communication chooses at this point can be made clear only by further communication. In understanding, interests converge, for one normally has no particular interest in speaking incomprehensibly or in failing to understand.[65] Thus only the yes/no bifurcation offers the opportunity to bring interests into the communication process, and the common interest in comprehensibility is acceptable only because it immediately precedes this bifurcation.

In sum, linguistic communication has its unity in the yes/no coding. When taken seriously, this excludes derivation of an ideal norm for the endeavor to reach agreement from language itself.[66] Only the autopoiesis of communication is necessary, and this autopoiesis is guaranteed not by a telos of agreement but by the binary code. For a coded communication there is no end but only the option reproduced in all understanding to continue via acceptance or via rejection. In other words, coding excludes every meta-rule, since the communication of such a rule could be received affirmatively or negatively.[67] The coding of language overcomes the evolutionary improbability of an operationally conclusive communication system. As far as this is possible in the system itself, it guarantees the autopoiesis of societal communication by transforming it into the freedom to say yes or no, with far-reaching consequences, to everything that has been determined. In complex societies, what therefore evolves are not obligations for consensus but symbolically generalized communication media.

4. Morality and the Secrets of Religion

Coding closes the system. It leaves everything else open. But the decision whether to accept or reject communicated offers of meaning cannot be left open. The bifurcation the code imposes leads the system to develop conditions pointing to when acceptance or rejection is more appropriate. As systems theory knows,[68] conditionings are among the most general requirements of all system formation. They establish nonarbitrary relationships in the sense that determining certain characteristics limits the scope for determining others. In other terms, considering how we obtain information about a system, we speak of redundancies limiting the variety of the system: where a certain characteristic occurs, others are either more or less probable.

In this theoretical framework, we can also say that the linguistic code is the form through which a system exposes itself to self-conditioning. The coding of language therefore means that the self-conditioning of society develops structures that enable expectations to be formed about the acceptability and rejectability of communications. Only such structures allow the improbability of communication to be transformed into probability. Only such structures permit the closed system to be opened up to influences from the environment. There is still nothing in the environment of the system corresponding to the operation of linguistic communication or to the binary code of the system; but self-conditioning by forming structuring expectations allows the system to take account of success and failure and thus to react to irritation from the environment.

Even the simplest societies appear to make provision for developing the linguistic code in two different directions. The one consists in applying the code to communication itself, hence in the *prohibition of communication* deemed necessary for *secrecy*,[69] which we assign to religion. Here, the other side of communication is placed under a taboo and hence made accessible for communication again. Such a taboo makes it possible to include exclusion. This does not exclude communication with gods, but it typically takes the form of offerings and sacrifices explained through prayer.[70] The other solution to the same problem, initially scarcely distinguishable but increasingly superseding the first, lies in a *further coding*, namely a *moral code* that sets forth what is to be accepted and what is to be rejected. The taboo is displaced by a distinction that offers broader societal connectivity.

Religion has to do directly with peculiarities of observing. All observation must draw distinctions if it is to indicate something, and in so doing it, separates off an "unmarked space" into which the ultimate horizon of the world withdraws. The transcendence accompanying all that can be comprehended thus shifts with every attempt to cross the boundary with new distinctions and indications. Never within reach, it is always present as the opposite side to everything determined. And this very unreachability "binds" the observer, who also escapes observation, to what he can indicate. In whatever cultural guise, the reconnection of what cannot be indicated to what can be indicated is *religio* in the broadest sense of the term.

In its origins, religion can best be understood as semantics and praxis concerned with the distinction between the known and the unknown. This distinction classifies the world without considering that this classification differs for every observer, every settlement, every tribe. By allowing the unknown to appear in the known, giving access to the inaccessible, religion formulates and practices the situation in the world of a societal system aware of being surrounded in space and time by the unknown. Reaching beyond everyday life, it can process self-reference and other-reference in society for society. It is accordingly "decisive" for how the operationally closed societal system in its dependence on communication sets itself up in relation to the world.[71]

Even before the mediatory figure of the "symbol" had been invented, the figure of the "secret" was able to represent the unknown in the known. The semantic form of "being-in-something," easy to render plausible, served this purpose: the divinity was not the phenomenon as such, it was *in it*.[72] This mysterious figure was protected by bans on communication and by corresponding rites and sanctions. The Baktaman offer a good example of a society structured almost exclusively by the communication ban—one of the rare cases in which communication has been studied in a society still unaffected by contact with civilization.[73] The result is simple: communication problems are resolved or at least structured by suppressing communication. The essential knowledge considered worthy of preservation, knowledge of sacred matters, is made accessible only to men, and then only after they have passed through a seven-stage initiation rite, so that, given the high mortality rate, only a small section of the population who can separate themselves off and control one another in the men's house gain possession of this knowledge.[74] Only in this protected domain does socially structured complexity arise. Other fields, including illness and empathy with fellow humans, remain semantically undeveloped. The result is organized mistrust along this main cleavage between knowledge and ignorance that differentiates society. Community life must assert itself against this structure, families are not formed, there is no segmentary structuring and hardly any means for expressing commonalities. "The striking fact of Baktaman life is the absence of such common premises and shared knowledge between persons in intimate interaction."[75]

The sacred is not to be found in nature, it is constituted as a secret (later it will be said that it cannot be adequately described in words).[76] Secrecy keeps arbitrariness and irresponsibility in dealing with nonempirical knowledge—a variant of the deception risk—within limits. In this fashion, the knowledge to be kept secret is produced. In other words, knowledge must be protected against communication because it is generated in the first place only through this protection. Otherwise, it would soon be discovered that holy bones are only bones (high religions explain that a mystery cannot be profaned by revelation because what the curious have before them is a triviality, *not the mystery itself*).

We are well justified in assuming this to have been an evolutionary dead end, offering hardly any further scope for development. The package of improbability, propitiousness, and risk of communication is handled all too directly. The problem is at least attenuated by limiting potency and by exclusion. At the same time, however, we see certain lines of development branching off in refined form. A very common reaction, indeed, a complementary institution to the recognition of unfathomable secrets, is to be found in the widespread techniques of divination. They typically keep to the surface of phenomena, to lines drawn in space or time from which they attempt to infer about the depths, about the past or future, about distant things, about things inaccessible to the senses. Divination techniques presuppose the difference between surface and depth, between visible and invisible; at the same time, however, they sabotage this difference through knowledge about how to cross the boundary. Only against this normal backdrop of older religiousness, incidentally, can we grasp how dramatically religion has been recast by the self-revelation of God. This dogma of revelation can be understood only if we take account of what it is directed against.

Another solution to the same fundamental problem, a functional equivalent of the communication ban upheld by awe and fear, lies in the invention of the *symbolic* presentation of the unity of visible and invisible, present and absent. A symbol is not only a sign (like, e.g., a word). It not only indicates unity, it effects unity.[77] The underlying paradox is precisely concealed. Symbols can therefore not be replaced by concepts, because this would result in a contradiction in the concept. But for this very reason, the form of the symbol (and not the form of the concept) is appropriate when it comes to dealing rationally with what cannot be expressed in words.

The cultic form of *ritual* has the same origin. Rituals enable communication-avoidance communication. The literature stresses that forms are stereotyped and other possibilities are excluded, thus reducing contingency to necessity.[78] The opening for a yes or no to the meaning offered is replaced by the directive to avoid errors with grave consequences. Even more important is that ritual is not performed as communication at all. It takes effect as an object—as a quasi-object in Michel Serres's sense.[79] It does not differentiate between utterance and information but provides information only about itself and correctness of performance. It presents itself in a well-chosen, striking form of perception (like language). But this takes place not just anywhere but only where it is believed that no communication can be risked.

The practice of secrecy and the restriction of communication to the statement that this or that is a secret have found ample emulation. The name of God is kept secret, even if only to uphold the monopoly of access. For the same reason, formulas for enforcing rights are subject to secrecy wherever disclosure would lead to open conflict about the law. Lifting controls on important communication is always a risk. However, the dense, "political" communicative relations in the cities of the ancient Mediterranean basin appear to suggest an increase in the field of public communication and its separation from the practice of the mysteries by recognized cults.[80] This co-existence spared society the notion of a radical break, a substitution of religion with politics and law. The evolution of Roman civil law began with enactment of the Twelve Tables and publication of the promising *legis actiones*. Even in early modern times, the technique of secrecy was used to protect the infant sovereign state. But now there was the printing press. Secrecy now had itself to be kept secret and could no longer serve to mark the big things.[81] Only in religion has the secret preserved its original meaning; for religion presupposes that exposure does not destroy the secret but punishes the curious with incomprehension.

Still under the dominance of the schema known/unknown (occult, secret), wisdom teachings developed with the aid of writing into highly complex structures in the transition from archaic to highly cultivated societies—above all, in Mesopotamia and China.[82] They were based on divination practices used partly for political and partly for (hardly to be distinguished) ritual purposes, and partly for everyday situations in the normal conduct of life. Divination and writing were closely linked, because no distinction was drawn between the nature of the thing and the written character, the latter being considered the form of this nature; nor could such a distinction be drawn before the advent of purely phonetic script.[83] Divinatory signs, like writing and early ornamental forms of art, were considered visible line-work pointing to something invisible. In China, openly displayed "objects" (the bones or entrails of sacrificial animals, bird flight, dreams) of sufficient complexity served as signs of other, hidden states of affairs. The latent function of divination was to neutralize other influences on decision-making, for instance, the accidents of personal memory or the pressure of social influences. We could also speak of a random mechanism intrinsically capable of learning.[84] The result was the development of a fully rationalized system of behavior toward the unknown, of "divination," with multiple safeguards against the probability of deception and error—for example, the vast number of specific conditional programs (if/then) that left selection and combination choices open (Mesopotamia); the gradual trend toward abstracting divination, toward restricting the assessment of signs to either favorable or unfavorable; built-in self-fulfilling prophecies, which are fulfilled precisely through the failure of those involved to believe them or their efforts to evade them (Oedipus); or incorporated ambiguities (Greece) that make misunderstanding almost normal and confirm the oracle only *post factum*. However, the guiding schema of surface/depth (open/secret, known/unknown, clear/unclear) was duplicated, was repeated in the signs for states of affairs, and always involved a doubled relation to the object[85]—*and not observation of observations.*

What is most striking about the text corpus of wisdom teachings and what determined the expectations they raised about the wise is that knowledge was now understood as self-referential, although it remained at the level of first-order observation in the immediate view taken of the world.[86] Despite the use of writing there was still no "holy scripture" that confined further evolution to the interpretation of canonized texts. The world of the gods was disciplined by copying societal structures into it—especially in the form of the family, political rule by a principal god,[87] and the notion of heavenly bookkeeping.[88] These analogies to societal structures, not the specific meaning of a text, made it possible to pass on religious knowledge. The wise man could (it was his art) ask questions and interpret answers; he was not moved, not "de-ranged" (*ver-rückt*) by a spontaneously active god.

Since education was still oral, and texts could be understood only with the aid of the wise, wisdom was, despite the existence of texts, not generally accessible; nor, however, was it strictly secret. It was grounded in particular qualities of the wise, in the way in which they knew what they knew, and how they brought life and teaching into line with it. Wisdom presented knowledge against the backdrop of ignorance and hence self-referentially. Its relation to the world, however general, could be handled only situationally and hence in similar fashion to the popular wisdom expressed in proverbs. The many pronouncements were not related, contradictions were not monitored, not systematized. Wisdom was not the outcome of logical analysis, of a methodology for avoiding inconsistencies. Inconsistencies in the use of wisdom either went unnoticed or were not considered disturbing—because one knew anyway that one did not know and that all knowledge could do was transfer something from the domain of the unknown to that of the known. Precisely this acknowledged insufficiency was compensated for by living by wisdom, guaranteeing it through purity,[89] and presenting it and attesting to it in given situations as the rule of the wise for the conduct of life—with the difference that without wisdom, one would behave differently. Reference to the conduct of life also ensured that the wise man maintained a certain distance from the normal conduct of the upper stratum, indeed, lived in a certain sense outside the class system, for example. as prophet or monk, as admonisher and warner;[90] and it must naturally be assumed that the authenticity of his statements was not called into doubt but inferred from his wisdom itself. Second-order observation was precluded, both for coordinating views with those of others and for controlling for differences between views of one's own. Wisdom was a cultic form of naïveté. Outpourings were direct and for this very reason, as the written culture of the eighteenth century would say,[91] made a "sublime" impression.

Among the most important evolutionary effects of the practice of divination was its circular relationship with writing. Sometimes writing developed in the first place only because divinatory signs could already be "read" and had only to be separated from their objects (heated bones, tortoise shells) in the form of ideograms.[92] Sometimes writing, invented initially for registration purposes, found so complex a field of application in divination and its need for records that phonetization was introduced, but also blocked—as in Mesopotamia. In any case, the symbiosis of divination and writing is among the characteristics that distinguish advanced civilizations markedly from late archaic societies, although oral communication long remained dominant.

We can well ask ourselves how the wisdom culture that developed in this form related to the differentiation techniques of all meaningful communication. On the one hand, it is inconceivable without differentiation of what is hidden, and also tended itself to develop a code of favorable/unfavorable signs. On the other, it clearly lacked the relation to binary schematisms that characterized the *prudentia* of the Greco-Roman tradition, which had determined old European semantics until well into modern times. For *prudentia* are concerned with rationality in a quite different sense, namely, with advice on modes of behavior that found themselves *confronted by a difference*—that between past and future or by moral difference, namely, the possibility that others can act both well and badly. *Prudentia* can then relate to the time dimension and the social dimension in a quite different sense than wisdom, and in an evolutionary sense can therefore be regarded as a "preadaptive advance" for new types of rationality.

Another, less direct sort of reaction to linguistic coding not doomed to esotericism has generally proved more successful: morality. Contrary to the everyday understanding we bring home from church, the symbiosis of religion and morality must be understood as a cultural artifact that is and remains precarious and contingent. When it comes to imagining a high god, for example, in the African religious circles influenced by monotheistic religions, the moral ambivalence of the sacred is preserved and imputing bad will to the high god is avoided even though he allows bad things to happen.[93] In high religions, the tension between religious and moral coding is suppressed. On their fringes, however, the independence of the two semantics is repeatedly manifest—for example, in forms of cult widespread in Central and South America that work with states of trance, which make no distinction between black and white magic, generate possession as a morally ambivalent state, and are fully geared to procedure and effect.[94] The congruence of religion and morality with which we are familiar is presumably useful only to solve a communication problem caused by language offering both a yes- and a no-version of everything that can be said. There can therefore be no justification without negatability, and morality must accordingly shift its basis to the incommunicable secrets of religion (and those who disregard this necessity, like Kant or Bentham or the value ethicists of our times, are punished with the unproductive maxims).

Morality is always symmetrized meaning. It operates under the prohibition of self-exemption. Whoever calls for morality must accept its application to his own behavior. As always, the exception is God. The religious justification of moral rules does not know this constitutive rule. It preserves its secret by not subordinating itself in turn to morality. It proceeds on the assumption of asymmetry. Jesus modifies the law that adulteresses are to be stoned in a scripture invisible to others; and by the new rule: "He that is without sin among you, let him first cast a stone at her."[95] The rule stands—and is beyond communication. It does not read: "He that is without sin among *us* . . ." For then Jesus would himself have had to cast the first stone.

The problem with all secrets is that they cannot be constructed but only deconstructed. They cannot feed into communication without raising the temptation to open what is closed to have a look. Prohibitions may well be imposed, but they can point to the possibility of contravention. The asymmetry of construction and deconstruction exposes the great secrets of society to a ruinous evolution, necessitating ever-new substitutes. Among the most important mitigating devices is the figure of the paradox, which is secret and no longer secret in that it blocks and does not reveal what can be done with it.

From a historical point of view, the most important solution is probably to shift the secret of religion into the (unacknowledgable) paradox of morality.[96] Morality itself can, indeed must, largely forgo secrets (and hence religion). If it is to fulfill its own function, it cannot be secret, it must be known. Only for morality's own paradoxicality, for suppression of the question why it is good itself even though it provides for good and bad behavior, does morality initially require religious foundations in the will of God, who for His part is constrained to do only good.[97] Religion itself is moralized so that it can justify morality; and why wickedness exists at all when God could make the whole world good with a word remains the ultimate secret of religion. At the same time, this alliance between morality and religion has the advantage of compatibility with the written word and with the objectification of the world.[98] Mystifications can thus be largely replaced by structured complexity, at least at the more concrete levels of meaning in communication.

Above all, we are dealing with a novel code in relation to language, namely, the distinction between good and bad behavior. Like the linguistic code itself, this code has only two values, positive and negative. But the moral code is in orthogonal relation to the language code, with the result that both the acceptance and the rejection of a communication can be both good and bad. Therein lies the improbability of morality when compared with the restriction of communication discussed above, and specifically the improbability that the risks arising from language can be controlled in this manner.

I shall speak of morality wherever individuals treat one another as individuals, that is to say, as distinguishable persons, and make their reactions to one another dependent on a judgment about the person and not about the situation. In this sense, morality is a societal universal, since there is no society in which individuals do not distinguish one another as individuals.[99] Variable is, of course, how personality is interpreted and what is attributed and not attributed to the individual, and in *this* regard the evolution of society brings about evolution in morality. As always, morality is not a special sort of norm, indeed, it does not even depend completely on normativization (there are primarily meritorious moralities); it is a coding based on the difference between respect and disrespect and which regulates the corresponding practices.

A fully developed morality is already a quite complicated mechanism of social coordination and not, as present-day ethics would have us believe, merely the application of rules that can be justified by reason. Like the coding of language, the moral code of good and bad, when used in communicative practice, generates a quite complex structure of conditionings, specifically, moral complexity.[100] Several distinctions have to be practiced at the same time and in relation to one another. First, there is the social dimension, that is to say, the difference between ego and alter. On *both* sides of this form *another* two-sided form is used, namely, that of respect and disrespect. This gives expression to the actual moral quality of the communication. Both ego and alter can be both approved of and disapproved of owing to their behavior. This generates an artificial range of combinatory possibilities,[101] which urgently needs to be narrowed. Morality (in the usual sense of the word) accordingly comes about by reducing the complexity of morality.

To achieve such reduction, conditions for respect or disrespect are formulated—in the form of descriptions of behavior, in the form of virtues and vices, in the form of purposes or of rules.[102] The rule also applies, as a principle of morality, that such conditions also apply to whoever sets them. Anyone who informs others of the conditions under which they are respected or disrespected is himself bound by them. Therefore the *symbolically generalized* form good/bad suffices for the code of morality without reference to the inner attitudes of the person whose behavior is being judged.[103] The moral failings of the heroes of antiquity (matricide, patricide, and so on) were presented as fate, not guilt. They proved the power, not the morality of otherworldly powers. Interpersonal self-reference and symbolic generalization of the moral code have dramatic effects—first, on the disciplining of moral demands, but also on the insistence and obtrusiveness with which they are upheld when once installed, and on the inevitability of their conflict.

Further refinements are decidedly culture-dependent and serve to adapt the moral regime to the given stage of societal development. The moral symmetry of ego and alter can thus be re-asymmetrized in adaptation to societal stratification. What applies for the nobility does not apply for the commons. Heroes and ascetics, knights and the monks had possibilities to distinguish themselves that could elicit the admiration of the common man, but which could no longer bind him. Morality then takes on meritorious traits. Or, in adapting to the division of labor in society, it separates off an area with the aid of a distinction between respect and regard in which achievements expected only of specialists are recognized and judged. One does not need to be as good at math as a mathematician.

Finally, in the Middle Ages (and probably under the influence of regular confession), morality comes under the control of consciousness. After all, it now only dealt with the "inner" side of behavior, hence presupposing that people knew the rules and, even as far as their *own* behavior was concerned (note this extravagance!), had to consider *inwardly* if they wished to respect or violate morality. This finally even made it possible under the combined pressure of theology and morality to demand the *inconsistency of contrition* (*contritio*) in relation to a person's *own* behavior and to develop a priestly advisory apparatus solely in order to achieve this.

Since the High Middle Ages and certainly in modernity, the *specification of accountability* has been held up as a condition for qualifying an action as moral. It must supposedly be borne by inner consent.[104] This considerably restricts morality's area of application and detaches it from social status. The heroes of the old world were entirely responsible for how they behaved—not least because their social status guaranteed them independence in their conduct. Since the Middle Ages, this link to social inclusion has been progressively abandoned, to be replaced by a novel combination of universality and specification—a typically modern syndrome.

After the introduction of printing, the link between religion and morality also weakened. The religious civil wars, conducted with moral fervor on both sides, demonstrated this to the whole world. In the seventeenth century, morality came to be problematized psychologically, and in the eighteenth century, in terms of justification theory. In parallel, religion was no longer thought of as organization of the world to be understood communicatively in appropriate fashion, but as a special type of communication conveying special meaning and performing special functions. The perspective shifted from first- to second-order observation. Religion was now seen as a particular sort of reductive structure, and thus as contingent. People were no longer bound by it because the alternative was to live in error and sin. One could believe in it—or not.

As a result, we have now attained a state of society where moralizing continues to be widespread, where, indeed, the "genteel" discretion the upper classes had acquired with such difficulty has been abandoned. But this moralizing no longer generates societal integration, any more than religion itself does. The good/bad code is in use; but it is, so to speak, running idle. Consensus is lacking on the criteria for assigning the values good and bad. The bistability of the code, excluding all other values, guarantees abstractness, accessibility, invariance. But religion no longer prescribes the programs, necessary for this very reason, that regulate what behavior is to be judged positive or negative; and no substitute has been forthcoming. Moral communication still claims to speak for society. But in a polycontextural world, it can no longer do so in unanimity. It is not as if immorality were spreading at the cost of morality. There are always good moral reasons for rejecting the forms for which morality has opted.

This precarious situation of morality in today's society is matched at the semantic level by the individualization of moral reference, its insistence on inner conviction (as opposed to external coercion), hence on self-motivation. This individual ethic is detached from religion and distinguished from law. This leaves us with the question of how moral perspectives are to be coordinated at all in society. If "ethics" are now everywhere in demand, in business, in politics, in ecological issues, for doctors, for journalists—we miss any in-depth specification of what social mechanisms could provide such amoral coordination of morality. And for this very reason, institutions that appear to do so, such as television, must keep their function latent.

But we are jumping ahead to very late conditions. Morality appears to be a universal with which society reacts to the improbability of communicatively propounded meaning being accepted. Very simple forms for moralizing communication can be expected even in simple societies that are not yet rule-oriented, let alone acquainted with "internal" accountability, but that are content to concretely categorize people and behavior with little consistency. Even then, judgment of a behavior will have had the surplus effect of tying both actor and speaker down to certain expectations. The function of such morality in society may well be minor (at any rate, we are not obliged to accept Durkheim's views), but we shall have to reckon with a generative mechanism that, connected to the yes/no coding of language, ensures that conditionings develop to indicate which communications are to be accepted and complied with and which not.

Only in historical retrospect do we call the functional cycle operating with communication bans "religion" and that which codes behavior as good and bad "morality." The theoretical reconstruction I have proposed should, however, keep us from projecting too much modern-day meaning via these terms into societies whose way of communicating was organized quite differently from ours.

5. Writing

Language developed to be spoken, as a medium of oral communication. Communication was therefore tied to systems of face-to-face interaction, but as a society grows, the social relevance of physical presence diminishes. Having to rely on oral communication also had far-reaching consequences for the social structures and differentiation forms that could be attained under these conditions.

In the case of oral communication, sociality is, as it were, automatically ensured. Speakers and listeners hear the same, and in hearing what he says, the speaker includes himself among his listeners. This is also true, and particularly so, for staged and stylized communication: for storytelling (terms such as "oral texts," "oral literature" are inappropriate and comprehensible only in retrospect) and for the reading aloud of texts that have already been written down. Communication extracts the narrative from the performer, as it were; we recognize this from the forms it requires, such as rhythm, music, set phrases, and, above all, an audience, without which even a personal memory of the singer would not function. A very limited and standardized vocabulary appears to suffice for normal communication, too.

Another characteristic of oral communication is that metacommunication necessarily co-occurs. We had already postulated that metacommunication is not possible in a pre-linguistic exchange of signals. However, as language evolves, it becomes the focus of communication, at any rate, the focus of face-to-face communication. We cannot speak without conveying that we are speaking and wish to be heard and understood. Now provision can be also made for disturbances, interruptions, repetitions, for special accentuation. Whenever communication takes place, the stress is thus on the fact that communication is taking place. Noncommunication would be paradoxical communication, namely, the communication of noncommunication; and the paradox would typically be interpreted as a refusal, and thus taken to be intentional communication—with serious consequences for those who really only want to be left in peace. Translated into our conceptuality: the autopoiesis of communication, namely, that it takes place at all, is at the same time the subject of metacommunication and usually also a communal norm that is difficult to evade—unless by the very simple means of being absent. But whoever is present has to take part in communication even if he has nothing to say. Then it is not so much information that matters but rather keeping communication going at all.

Furthermore, the voice, to put it in extreme terms, contradicts the recognizability of meaning. It can be heard only at the moment of speaking, after which it falls silent. Oral communication therefore obtains the necessary redundancies from the personal identity of speaker and hearer, from assumptions of consistency gauged from people and further processed in the schema of conformity and deviation. Only written communication comes under pressure to provide for the necessary redundancies itself, and this requires a quite different sign and word culture. At the same time, however, this releases individuals in great measure from having to answer for recognizability, while enabling special communication contexts to be differentiated out for very personal communication.

Having to rely on oral communication also limits the possibilities for conserving and remembering, and thus what the narrative tradition of such societies can develop in the way of semantics. The spatial boundedness of communication and its dependence on presence has important consequences. What counts in possible (useful or dangerous) interaction is proximity. Greater distance means declining utility and increasing dangerousness, and finally a boundary to the unknown. One knows or suspects that other people live beyond the mountains, but they do not belong to one's own society and their language is often difficult or impossible to understand. There can be no ties with them, no *religio*, no morality in their regard.[105]

Under these conditions, notions of space and time are difficult to keep apart and ultimately merge. The world is "concentrated" in space and time around an inhabited center. Time can be experienced in concrete events, like space in concrete places, and is also ordered in terms of proximity/distance.[106] As in space, there is a countable, conditionable near time and an unreachable, dark remote time in which past and future cannot be distinguished. The near past goes back as far as the individual memory (i.e., the memory we can presuppose and activate in others in communication), and the near future reaches as far as present behavior manifestly conditions future states of affairs.[107]

Orally communicating societies can presentiate their religion through ecstasy, through states of trance, whose non-everydayness impresses those present.[108] They dispatch shamans on journeys to unknown worlds. Nor are they slow with sacralizations.[109] Initially, this means only that there are limits to the comprehensible everyday world at which questioning is discontinued or compensated for by a sort of defensive meaning. Such meaning has to be accepted; no recourse is possible to the assumption that there are texts (or people versed in texts) and hence authorities who could explain what it is about. Further oral communication would merely meet with resistance against a hopeless undertaking (what can one say?) or with more or less circular confirmation of the accepted meaning. This is also particularly the case where no elaborated religion is yet available that covers the sacred with myths, symbols, and explications. A very pragmatic approach to the sacred when it is no longer appropriate is by no means excluded; it forms part of the picture. Orality is characterized by the capacity to forget, to devalue, to adapt. The sacred therefore has no inherent guarantee of endurance, of veneration, of tradition; and if it does become tradition, this is the first step toward dissolution of its sacrality.

Also characteristic of orally communicating society is that a great deal of communication takes place simultaneously (occurs and passes) and can therefore not be coordinated. "One must think of many different informants passing on information simultaneously."[110] The intelligibility of communication depends on the given situation. There can therefore be few consistency constraints and hardly any postulates of consistency monitoring and consistency assurance. The framework of knowledge about the world is restricted anyway, so that agreement in substance can be assumed without further ado; there are few occasions and possibilities for making a personal effort in this direction. Even esoteric knowledge, even mythologies, even divination teachings, even genealogies are passed on from generation to generation without inconsistencies posing a problem. The notion of a uniform collective memory is therefore unlikely to fit in with the reality of such societies; it is rather to be explained by the assumption that societies without writing must have had some functional equivalent to the written word.

This state of affairs changed gradually but fundamentally with the invention and dissemination of writing. Writing also increased the number of differences that a society could use, conserve, and recall. This also multiplied the things or aspects of the world that could be indicated. Nevertheless, the increase was not only quantitative. The change is so profound that it is not possible to give oral communication the form of written text (in analogy to a text in one language being translated into another).[111] Of course, the *meaning* of an oral communication can be written down, and now even electronically recorded. But not the *communication* of the meaning. Indispensable elements of oral presentation, especially the simultaneous involvement of speaker and listener, the simultaneous utilization of several perceptual media, above all audition and vision, and the use of changes in the tone of voice, gestures, pauses, and the constant possibility of the audience intervening, of "turn-taking," cannot be translated into the form of a written text. What is essential is that the simultaneity of speaking and listening consists, not simply in a chronometrically measured process, in regular progression from second to second, minute to minute, but in a structured process with accelerations and decelerations, with acoustically filled stretches and with breaks, with periods of waiting and points in time that build up and release tension. It is this joint experience of a structured sequence that gives speakers and listeners the impression of experiencing the same thing. Reading, too, does not take place evenly, but with meticulously varying speed; but these differences have no social relevance.

Nor is there any one-to-one equivalence between oral and written communication. Even in the case of phonetic script, phonic units cannot be represented as optical units. It is not a question of representing units but of reconstructing differences. It is not the sounds that are fixed in writing but the differences between sounds. Writing is therefore possible only as a system that can represent all possible or at least the usual differences between sounds. Only thus, and not in the form of one-to-one representation, can the difference of perceptual media be used for hearing and seeing. Furthermore, written texts, as we know, require an independent analysis of the phonetics of speech that takes account of the circumstance that differences cannot be exactly copied when translating into another medium.

Only if this is taken into account can one grasp that and how the difference between sound and meaning, which is at stake, can be translated into another medium. Whereas language in general takes form as the difference between sound and meaning, writing makes it possible to *symbolize* precisely this difference in *another* perceptual medium, that of vision. By "symbol" in this context, I mean neither a sign nor the representation of something by something else on the basis of natural similarity. Symbols mark a form. An *i* is not an *r*—which in speech we often cannot hear and therefore cannot know. This means that written characters express the unity of a difference in such a way that that we can continue to operate with this unity and hence make other distinctions. The introduction of written language allows quite novel operations, namely, reading and writing, *precisely because in these operations a distinction has to be made, not between sound and meaning, but only between combinations of letters and meaning.* Before writing was invented the form of language could not be symbolized. The realization that sound and meaning were not identical had to suffice; and this means that the distinction itself was a difficult one to make. There was always a tendency to take the word itself for the meaning, to consider names lucky—or unlucky, and to attempt to influence things themselves through speech. Once writing had been invented, only the gods could still directly change things with words:[112] And God said, Let there be light: and there was light.[113]

The translation of language into an optical medium reinforces an element that, with retrospective reference to Saussure, we can also attribute to the spoken word: namely, that language lives from the difference between its signs and not from conformity with nonlinguistic reality. Oral cultures could, indeed had to, ignore this because they could not reflect on their medium. With the introduction of writing, the nature of written language as sign and word, the spaces between words, their combination (grammar), in short, the remoteness from the world become a problem that was addressed in communication—to begin with as criticism of the innovation, but finally as restriction of form underlying all improvements to the efficiency of the communication system.

With the written word, telecommunication begins, the communicative accessibility of those present in space and time. Now the distinction between words and things was given an additional dimension. Telecommunication made it possible to transport signs instead of things. It works more rapidly, and with less effort, and the energy needed for transmission, initially only force times the time needed to learn to write and to write, does not have to be produced where transmission takes place. Writing had already offered these advantages, but the printing press and modern electronic communication were to enhance them immensely—albeit it with the critical consequence that societal communication now comes to depend in broad areas on industrial energy production.

Writing thus achieves a great deal more than we imagine offhand. In particular, it achieves more than is conveyed by writing. First and foremost, written communication makes metacommunication optional. Metacommunication no longer necessarily accompanies communication (if not in the trite form of inference that a written text is written to be read). Textual and contextual references (e.g., author, sender, addressees) have to be introduced explicitly; and there is no social expectation of direct transition to active participation, to response, or to intimation that the text has been understood. The assumption that the real meaning of communication lies in metacommunication, namely, in participation in communication, is accordingly abandoned. Instead, we expect information and stop reading if our expectation fails to be met for too long.

The reader confronts the utterance process in reduced form: as text. The composition of a text often takes place at a remote place and time. Concrete motives for communicating therefore become less interesting (who wants to know why Thomas Aquinas wrote his *Summa*s, and what use would it be if we knew?). Instead, new scope for interpretation opens up, which can be exploited in very different ways. Where questions about the motivation and context of communication play a role (e.g., when we ask whom or what the text was actually written to attack), they serve to interpret the text.

That we can have *differing* opinions about *identical* texts hence makes it possible to differentiate texts and inhibit immediate reactions. For although the written form leaves the link between the two selections information and utterance intact and is therefore suitable for communication, it makes it possible to postpone understanding and allows it to be realized at any time, anywhere, by anyone without interaction. As a dissemination medium, written language extends the reach of social redundancy; it enlarges the circle of recipients while limiting what can still be spoken about informatively (i.e., surprisingly). In using writing, society thus *waives* the *temporal and interactional guarantee of the unity of the communicative operation*, and this waiver requires *compensation* for what has been abandoned. This leads to an immense, unpredictable expansion of connectivity potential. Greater demands are made on the textualization of utterances that have to be comprehensible even under hardly foreseeable conditions, but that are nevertheless not suitable for monitoring the reactions of the reader. Finally, where writing is used not only for recording purposes but also for communication, problems arise with the self-authorization of the written text that represents an absent source.[114]

In oral communication it was possible to assume that information, utterance, and understanding were generated operationally at the same time, even where information concerned something that was no longer immediate but had to do with the distant past. Myths, too, which were set in times immemorial, were present as narratives and it therefore did not matter that the story could presuppose, indeed, had to presuppose, that it was known. The sense of communicating myths lay not in surprise but in participation. This is different in the case of written communication, because temporal distances between utterance and understanding occur and have to be reflected on. Utterances must be geared to be understood not immediately but later, not in the course of their own flow but in accordance with a later reader's interest. For understanding, too, it can be important to remember that the utterer had a future in mind that was already past for the understander. This double reflection disciplines not only the textual version of communication (it must remain understandable, for example, abstracted from time); it also enhances the surprise quality of the information. Above all, it abstracts the notion of the world as what is to be assumed simultaneous with communication, for example, as being, nature, the omnipresence of an observer god.

It must hence have been difficult and is now even more difficult to understand written communication as communication. Since the world is still only actual in terms of points in time, we are now theoretically obliged to decide when written communication really takes place. We could say: whenever writing and reading take place. But they can no longer occur simultaneously. Communication is realized only when understanding brings it to a conclusion. If this is so, it may seem important or unimportant to reconstruct when an utterance has been written, by whom and why. In any case, written communication works only in retrospection on itself. It must therefore accept an inevitable belatedness. It has to cope with recursions that are no longer self-evident. It has to construct redundancies, take note of what has been "pre-scribed" [*Vor-geschriebenes*] and keep it on hand as a prerequisite for further writing.[115] All this makes communication independent of spatial integration (physical presence), while having to cope all the more with time problems. Not only the medium of writing is stable; the forms given shape in this medium, namely, texts, are also still relatively stable. Texts thus serve as a secondary medium for actual form formation, which is realized only through interpretation.

Using writing thus presupposes a double utilization of the distinction between medium and form: first, in connection with language, a set of written characters for still undetermined but regulated coupling options, which serves as a medium for text production. At this first stage, writing must function physically and is susceptible to destruction; all the more so because the recognition value of signs depends on the precision of their reproduction. In the second stage, meaningfully comprehensible texts have to be produced that can be read differently, interpreted in various ways. Here, too, there can be errors of reproduction, which interpretation can correct or not, as the case may be. And interpretation can generate new texts, which give rise in turn to a tradition in need of interpretation. But final form formation in individual understanding is just as transient a process as communication itself; and it regenerates communication only through the continuous use of the medium of writing.

Of course, writing did not develop as a means of communication, for this would have presupposed readers. As so often, a provisional function intervened to sustain the innovation until it had developed sufficiently to assume its final function.[116]

The oldest extant, albeit controversial "writing" from a Balkan culture of the late sixth millennium (almost two thousand years before the first writings in Mesopotamia) appears to have served purely sacred purposes, namely, commerce between priests and gods.[117] It may have involved some sort of management of religious secrets. There is no indication that such writing was involved in the communication problems of everyday life—hence offering evidence for the evolution of new achievements that attained their final function only at a later date through a shift in function. Probably the best known reason for the development of written language already directed toward societal communication was the need of large, complex economic households to keep records; and subsequently to aid memory in other matters—for example, to back up messages that themselves still had to be delivered orally.[118] In the beginning, this presupposed no direct relation to language, but only the marking of objects.[119] In China, the point of departure appears to have lain in divination practices, which had developed into a highly complex decipherment of signs (on appropriately prepared bones, tortoise shells, and so on). People could therefore read before they could write, and the practice of divination had a very concrete and differentiated relationship with the problems of everyday life, and a corresponding need for a wealth of signs. Increasing artificiality may have developed in elaborating the meaning of the lines, then also in the representation of question and answer on the magic corpus. The signs then had only to be detached from their substratum and adapted for artificial use, an evolutionary mutation that apparently took place in a very brief space of time.[120] In Mesopotamia, too, the use of writing for recording divination programs (wisdom teachings) contributed crucially to its development, in this case to the beginnings of phonetization and then to the blocking of transition to a fully phonetic script.[121] All this was possible without having to consider communicative uses for the written word.

The communicative use of writing presupposes readers, and hence the spread of literacy. Long before this can be attained, we must therefore reckon with a politically and religiously expressive use of writing, where written language, certainly closely associated with notions of magic, impresses an illiterate population. This was the case in the Egypt of the Old Empire, but in many other places, too, especially with the diffusion of writing to hitherto uncivilized or little civilized areas.[122] Writing was then established on a functional level where pomp, images, and buildings were also designed to impress.

Nor was the conversion of the Phoenician syllabic script into an alphabet inspired by the wish to produce literature or the need to jog the memory of singers but, as we now believe, by economic conditions, which were developing rapidly in the eighth and ninth centuries BCE.[123] The wish for a written record of orally performed epics presumably did not come from the singers themselves.[124] After all, it was hardly in their professional interest, and there could be no question of reading aloud. Here, too, there was a shift in context, and literary production, not economic convenience, determined the historically significant impact of the alphabet. It was now possible to do without the rhythmically bound form, without dependence on the links between music, memory, and communication.

However, since at least the second millennium before Christ, writing had also been used communicatively, for example, in the form of letters (which initially presupposed a messenger and served as mnemonics) and in the form of texts that explicitly addressed a reader with the intention of telling him something. Communicative use developed parasitically, benefitting from a universal script that had already been developed, adding a further function to it, and, above all, new occasions for writing and reading.

The development and dissemination of writing thus shows typical characteristics of an evolutionary process in the course of which functions were complemented, substituted, or even exchanged. Unlike speech, however, writing did not rely on the co-evolution of the human organism; it could thus become established relatively rapidly in only a few thousand years. Over this period, it led to a far-reaching transformation of communication options, and thus to a fundamental reorganization of the societal system, which now had to be grounded in oral and in written communication. The implications of this historical turning point have been discussed from many perspectives in recent decades.[125] However, its theoretical ramifications become apparent only if we consider society as a communication system.

The importance of writing lies in a completely new sort of temporality in the communicative operation. What is achieved can only very superficially be described in such terms as permanence, stability, and memory (I naturally do not deny that this was the perspective from which oral cultures had to experience the benefits of writing). Writing does not alter the fact that everything that happens, happens in the present and simultaneously. No system can act outside its present and in a nonsimultaneous world. But precisely these shackles of the present lend writing its importance. For different presents, which are for each other future or past, can now be combined in every present through writing (and only through writing). What was future when the text was written or what is future in the narrative of the text can already be past when it is read; and we can know that the writer or the hero could not know what has meanwhile happened.[126]

Nevertheless, this does not provoke doubts about the unity of time. But writing generates a *novel presence of time*, namely, the *illusion of the simultaneity of the nonsimultaneous.* The merely virtual time of past and future is present in every present, *although something quite different is simultaneous for it than for the present.* And precisely this illusion of the written culture to which we are accustomed makes it difficult to return to the basic insight that everything that happens happens in the present and simultaneously.

Writing imposes a fixing of time—which passes nevertheless—in texts, which survive the passing of time; which hence remain the same at a point in time in which something that was previously future is past. A written culture must therefore break with any direct living-with-time. It must offer descriptions of time that resolve the paradox of constant reference to the transitory. It must be able to refer to time as if we had it before us like a thing or movement. It must adopt a perspective, and integrate it in its time semantics, which lies both within and outside time. Among other things, this requires the original congruence of space and time to be dissolved. When guided by texts, the observer, although still in the world—that is, at a particular point in space and time, "here and now"—relates to space and to time in a quite different sense and is personally affected in various ways.[127]

This concerns the observational not the operational aspect of communication. Communication is and remains an event bound to a point in time; nothing changes this. A communication system can attain dynamic stability, that is, stability due to continuation, only through ever more and different communication. Here, too, nothing can change. Unlike a mere record, communication is completed only through understanding. This, too, remains; and for this reason it must initially have been far from self-evident to use writing not only for recording but also for communicating. The effect of writing lies in the spatial and temporal uncoupling of utterance and understanding and in the dramatic increase in connectivity options that it engenders.

The direct consequences are (1) to waive the beneficent immediate disappearance of the spoken word, and thus the ease of forgetting; and (2) to gain scope for reorganizing sequences. For all communication runs on very narrow-gauge lines and is strictly sequential. One speaks after the other, otherwise no communication process could be organized. In principle, this also applies to written language. But writing conserves what has been uttered for sequences that cannot be foreseen at the moment of utterance, for parallel continuations, and, above all, for indirect connections. The systems that reproduce themselves in this manner thus operate more "connectionistically" (to use the current term) than sequentially. As I have indicated, the preconditions for this are to be found in reorganization of the difference between medial substratum and form.

I have defined the concept of communication medium in terms of the difference between medial substratum and form, the difference between loose and strict coupling. In the case of oral communication, this difference can refer only to single communicative events—to this or that which is said. Writing, in contrast uncouples the communicative event itself. This produces a new sort of medial substratum, which makes quite new demands on strict coupling through sentence forms. The elementary unity of communication is dissolved and can become communication again only through recombination. To put it more simply: where the material substratum suffices, written sentences can be read at any time by any number of unknown readers; but these sentences must themselves establish the context needed to understand them, they must be understandable in themselves. They must put the reader "in the picture" about many things that can, indeed must, be taken for granted in oral communication, where stating what is visible and known to everyone would have no information value (it would, for example, make no sense to describe the scenery for those standing in it anyway, whereas written forms, even where they simulate oral communication, for instance, in dialogues, must at least indicate who is speaking at a given moment).

In oral communication, including long recitations for ritual purposes or on solemn occasions, it will have been assumed that the world in which communication takes place and the world *about which* communication takes place are not in principle different but constitute a continuum of reality. Long after the introduction of writing (and even printing) a concern with purely fictional texts was considered reprehensible. However improbable narratives might be, they were concerned with the world everyone had before them, with the communicatively extended situation that was presupposed and shaped in narration. Only when topics were given written form did purely textual problems of composition arise.[128] In the factual dimension, the adoption of the written form prompted efforts to eliminate the inconsistencies that only now came to light. Situational forms of imparting meaning become cosmologies, gods entered into family relations with one another, genealogies were reconstructed,[129] and in the High Middle Ages, all theology found itself committed to theoretical consistency, with far-reaching consequences for controversies, school formation, ecclesiastical intervention, and finally for schisms. The incentives for more abstract content in communication that this produced can hardly be overestimated.

Probably the most important tool for assuring consistency is (paradoxically) the introduction of distinctions. And thus a reduction in unreasonable consistencies.[130] Writing is highly effective in drawing distinctions. This is the basis for its semantic effectiveness. And this is the basis for the conceptual typification of single words, and also for a tradition that reduces demarcations, divisions, categories, sorts, and types—namely, the tradition of ontological metaphysics; and this provides the basis for also passing down what has been excluded, controversy, and dissent as resources for redefining problems.

From a social point of view, many more people can thus be reached with *one* communication than would be possible if it were restricted to physical presence. In order to stress this, I have called writing (and hence the printing press) a *dissemination medium*. However, this should not take us back to the idea that the medial aspect consists in the transmission of information from one person to others. The effects of writing cannot be explained in terms of the mere multiplication of addressees, however important this aspect might be. It lies in the reordering of time and culture. Above all, writing increases uncertainty about understanding intended meaning.[131] "Whenever one has the potential to read one has the potential to be uncertain,"[132] and this applies not only for the reader but a fortiori for the author's anticipation of understanding. The semantics induced by writing then has to do with the reduction of this uncertainty.

Finally, if we wish to assess the semantic effects of writing and attribute them to written language, we must analyze the particularities of written communication much more precisely. We must limit ourselves to only a few points.

Since writing is always also a technical mnemonic, it modifies the importance of memory.[133] If we are to grasp this, we must understand that the memory of psychic and social systems can not simply be seen as storing past states or events and keeping them available.[134] What is past is and remains operationally unavailable. The memory, too, can be used only in given, actual operations, and thus only in the present. The real function of memory lies not in preserving the past but in regulating the relationship between remembering and forgetting; or, as Heinz von Foerster puts it, in the constant selective re-impregnation of one's own states.[135]

It is memory that makes the eventness of communication possible at all—in both oral and written communication. For as an event, communication refers to itself, but can do so only by understanding present as different from past and future and reaching back or forward into these nonactual time horizons.[136] This in turn is possible only if there is a material basis in neurophysiology or the substrata of writing *that is not remembered as such*. For written communication, too, does not recall writing,[137] but only the texts that are used as communication.

From this perspective we can better understand what the invention of writing means for the differentiation of a specifically social memory and for the re-equilibration of the relationship between remembering and forgetting this made necessary. Whereas pre-writing cultures had to preserve their memories in objects and officiations (quasi-objects) of all sorts and were only in this fashion able to become independent of mortal human memories, the use of writing makes discriminating between remembering and forgetting a matter of decisions to be made. For writing something down always means that something else is not written down. Writing is self-made memory. It can remember more and leave more to be forgotten than before. Writing aids the memory but it burdens it, too. It enables communication to be constantly reimpregnated by rereading texts or referring orally to texts presumed available (even if difficult of access). The prevention of forgetting is also a process that accelerates learning. This in turn imposes the development of semantic schematisms that resolve more inconsistencies, and that can at the same time cope with more redundancy and more variety. This produces a more abstract conceptuality, which oral communication would never have been able to develop alone.

Time, for example, is treated chronometrically in order to accommodate various events at various points in time. What is decisive is that *all* movements, regardless of their speed and regardless of their beginning and end *can be related to the same temporal measure*, even if this is itself a movement, for example, of the sun or a clock. It follows that no movement can move time itself.[138] The being of time is a metaconstruct beyond all movements.

As soon as the keeping of records began to solve problems of memory, it is hardly possible to understand time any longer as a power of forgetfulness (*lēthē*) to be escaped only with the aid of the muses. The old (and necessary) link between oral performance and music is replaced—and destroyed—by writing.[139] The rhythmically supported time of recalling other times is replaced by the notion of a measurable movement, that of a describable dimension in which this simultaneity of the nonsimultaneous is ensured. On the other hand, where oral modes of passing on knowledge (especially in teaching) prevail, a psychic memory is indispensable. The sacred nature of memory enters into a complicated relationship with the techniques of the art of remembering. The solemn, formulaic mode of expression typical of oral cultures wanes or is reserved for poetry (as opposed to prose).[140] Formulation can thus adapt better to expressive requirements. On the other hand, the veneration of memory cannot be abandoned. The sacred quality of memory assumes a new form as remembrance of a founding past,[141] so that highly developed memory training can become established alongside an artificial recording practice.

At the same time, the past gains unprecedented power over the present as recorded history and as existing text. With reference to the China of the tenth to thirteenth centuries, Jacques Gernet writes of a "retour du passé," inevitably calling to mind the recording of the Homeric epics.[142] The same can be said of Mesopotamia.[143] In the old European tradition, symbolizing what is absent by means of writing enables the past to be present, origins (e.g., of noble families) to be actual, and hence the legitimating force of *archē*, *origo*, *Grund* to take effect. The consequences are notoriously ambivalent: one is oriented on the past, which draws attention to what is different in the present. History becomes a drama of the presence of the past, the simultaneity of the nonsimultaneous. Among the losers is the segmentary system of the family clan, whose influence on the imperial bureaucracy declines in the face of writing-oriented and therefore verifiable knowledge.[144]

In the social dimension, writing came to prevail over the possibility and necessity of roles continuously switching between speakers and listeners ("turn-taking"). This has far-reaching consequences. Communication was de-reciprocated; it was linearized and thus became capable of organizing very long but diverging sequences (which has to happen and requires competence). A new sort of authority arose. Self-confidently assuming the role of speaker time after time no longer counted for so much.[145] Authority instead now developed in the form of pretension to and assumption of the ability to know more and to say more than could enter into the necessarily sequential structure of communication. Authority was now the "capacity for reasoned elaboration,"[146] which, like a shadow, long accompanied the still relatively rare written utterance. At the same time, problems developed in linking this form of authority with the status positions that had developed in society through societal differentiation for the representation of society.

Liberation from having to switch roles in speaking and listening also made the corresponding roles of writing and reading into *unsocial* activities. Writing as such became a special type of skill, and thus a problem, as the difficulties various scriptoriums in the Early Middle Ages experienced in coordinating their different ways of writing show.[147] Only communication itself is social. A person necessarily has to write and read on his own, and even when others are there watching, observing him too intensely is pointless, indiscreet, and suspicious.[148] The writer or reader, acting alone and without social pressure, also has more time and opportunity to exercise care in doing justice to the formal exigencies of the text. Expanding the medial scope for combination means greater selectivity in the forms to be included, and this needs monitoring. In general, the problem now is that a full understanding requires grasping the context, understanding what the selection was made from. As we know, shortcomings in this regard are now quite normal.

Writing thus makes it possible to shift the focus from communication to information. In oral communication, the talented distinguish themselves by an ability to talk even when there is nothing to say. And in simple societies, there is not enough information to keep communication going. Communication serves essentially to activate and confirm social convictions and mutually positive attitudes. People chatter, and anyone who persistently remains silent is regarded as dangerous because he refuses to betray his intentions.[149] With writing, this primary dependence on communication declines along with the certainty engendered by the physical presence of interlocutors that everyone already knows everything or is at least acquainted with the nature of things. Only now is information conveyed with increasing intensity, producing the artificial redundancies that make it possible to obtain information from someone or other who happens to have read it.

Compared with the close merging of reciprocity and time in oral communication, the factual dimension accordingly becomes more important. Written texts have a more objective relationship with their subject matter, which makes it possible to take note of the subjective way in which the topic is handled and to attribute it to the author. The "object"—and only now are there "objects"—stays put and lets itself be tackled from all sides. Greater demands are made of persuasion than in the rhapsodic flow of speech. The written text must reckon with more critical attitudes, with knowledge of other texts, and with time for criticism. It must reckon with readers who know better. The word remains authentic, and does so in a new sense directed against falsification; but it can no longer guarantee itself. It must refer in the text to other sources of reliability. Writing generates concepts for cognition and for right thinking.[150]

Compared with oral communication, which is articulated by a voice filling a space, writing occupies only a tiny section of reality. In the medium of its perception it is more clearly differentiated and can therefore also be more easily laid aside or disregarded for the moment, and postponed as communication. The spoken word intrudes, imposes itself, demands and receives precedence. It is far more identical with the situation than the written text, but for this very reason, it can also not outlast the situation. For written utterances, it is not even necessary for the writer to be still alive, and one of the earliest, specifically communicative uses of writing was to allow the dead to speak to the living. The Egyptians, in particular, made intensive use of this possibility of self-perpetuation beyond death in their funerary inscriptions.

Yves Barel refers to another, long-term effect of writing as "potentialization."[151] The textual fixation of meaning solidifies what has once been formulated even if it is rejected or not used. Whereas practically only what rapidly impresses the communication process survives in oral communication, writing can delay the decision to accept or reject, can socially diversify and also record what does not convince. It takes the form of a mere possibility of meaning. And it is quite possible to rediscover this possibility at a later date, to take it up again, to rethink it when its time has come. To the extent that communication produces and records such potentializations, semantics as a whole is "modalized." Reality is seen on the basis of its potentiality: partly as necessity, partly as contingent realization, partly also as mere possibility. To begin with, one is satisfied with rejected or extremely remote ("monstrous") possibilities. Antiquity had, however, already reacted to writing with a theory of modalities.[152] It seems that only with the advent of printing did explicit "nowheres," fictions, fantasies, such as those of Sir Thomas More, Giordano Bruno, the modern novel, the utopias of the late eighteenth century, and the "poetry" of the Romantics, come to be considered publishable and to justify their existence as unrealizable, mere possibility.[153] And then it finally made sense to use the question about the conditions of possibility as a lever to uproot the ontological view of the world and its metaphysical description.

Finally, we should recall that written language no more doubles the world than spoken language does. Despite all system differentiation, there is not one world that we perceive mentally and another that is a correlate of the spoken word and yet another that is a correlate of the written word. New autopoietic modes of operation and observation evolve in one and the same world. The new accomplishments are registered, not as multiplication of objects, but as differentiation and refinement of observation. This is why the evolution of writing gradually prompts the *evolution of higher-order modes of observation*; in particular the observation of other observers who are not as wise as Socrates and write down what they observe. An awareness of the usefulness and necessity of writing down one's own observations developed very early on, especially in the medical writings of antiquity—precisely because what was important in this field more than elsewhere was to make one's own observations available for other observers.[154] Over the long term, systems thus developed on the basis of writing that converted their own autopoiesis entirely to second-order observation: the functional systems of modern society.

These complex characteristics of written communication were naturally not realized in one fell swoop. Even the transition from written record to written communication must have been a problem that took time to resolve. To begin with, being able to write and read was no more that a sort of craft, a matter of special roles, and not everything that could be said could also be written, because the need to keep records and the need to aid communication were also specific needs. Only the development of phonetic script produced an exact and full parallel between oral and written communication. It duplicated not the world of objects spoken about but the communication itself, so that we can speak of a secondary coding of language in terms of oral/written.[155] After an intermediate stage of syllabic scripts, which, depending on the nature of the language, still had to accept ambiguities and reading problems, and (as in the case of the Cretan-Mycenaean linear B script) were often supplemented by ideograms, the final form was achieved in Europe with the letters of alphabetic script.[156] Letters not only make the distinction language requires between sign and meaning. In relation to the phonetics of language, they are still artificial, but for this very reason they enable phonetic script to be completely standardized. The advantages were immediate: the alphabet was easy to learn, so that the ability to read and write could spread without presupposing role-specific skills; and, above all, it allowed new words to be formed (e.g., making adjectives and verbs into nouns, combining words into compounds). Language could thus immediately adapt to all the expressive requirements that arose in cultural development and was much less of an obstacle than ever before to conveying what one wished to say.

In retrospect, the special achievement of the alphabet as perfect phonetic script has perhaps been overestimated. A universally untypical evolutionary development branched off to make history. But why did this happen in the light of so many cultures producing systems of writing they found functional? It is difficult to give a satisfactory answer. What is striking, however, is that alphabetized writing soon went beyond the narrow, functional contexts of long-distance trade and temple and palace administration in political centers of government to become a system of writing used by the public.[157] Not only the alphabet but also the limitation of the horizon to perceivable cities with their specific laws of life (*nomoi*) is likely to have contributed. In any case, a society accustomed to the written word develops, which can use the general medium of writing to differentiate special areas—above all, a city government organized on the basis of offices with changing incumbents, and that finds continuity in its locus and its written laws. But the written word is then no longer a special resource of political rule: the same system of writing can be used for many other purposes—above all, as a medium for a culture of debate in many fields, from medicine and geometry to poetry, theater, rhetoric, and philosophy.

Naturally this does not mean that the whole population learned to read and write. These skills spread only long after the introduction of the printing press and only in the mid-nineteenth century did they become universal in a few countries of the world. However, what counted was not complete coverage, and, even in the Athens of the classical period, literacy was widespread enough for literary texts with a far-reaching impact to be written for unknown readers and unforeseeable situations and for controversies, even in such specialized fields as medicine, to be conducted in writing.[158] The direct consequences included training in criticism on the basis of second-order observation, observation of other observers.

The consequences, in both the short and long terms, were immense. Writing, too, could after all also be understood as communication—and no longer only as a form of recording and an aid to oral communication.[159] Communication as written text—and not only as ongoing oral communication—could then become the subject of communication. Translation and monitoring became possible. Novel sorts of consistency constraints developed, since texts could be read over and over again and could be compared. For example, genealogies—a tried and tested means of symbolizing unity and difference in a structure[160]—had to be freed from contradictions.[161]

But writing is suitable not only for communication: it also enables oral communication to be represented in written texts. This had been recognized and exploited at an early date, for example, in the old Egyptian tomb inscriptions by means of which the dead "speak" to the living; and above all in the philosophical and literary form of the dialogue, which in the written version is represented as if it were being conducted orally, with all the advantages of multiple perspectives without any obligation to reach agreement. Finally, the special literary form of the novel develops, in which the characters themselves act communicatively. We thus find communication in communication, real communication as a copy of fictional communication and fictional communication in real communication, which at the same time allows us to forget that the fictional communication is fabricated by the real communication.[162] This makes it possible to communicate, not only the advantages, but precisely also the failures of oral communication.[163]

All this does not call the predominance of oral communication in society into question. The oral recitation of written texts is common if for no other reason than because the capacity for routinized, effortless reading cannot be expected of the public. But oral communication is enriched in the so-called literate cultures by the possibility of reference to written texts, even if the texts are not on hand. The boundary between the communication system and the environment is drawn all the more distinctly; for if one were still able to assume that extrahuman forces communicate with one another and address humans, they are unlikely to write books or leave notes.[164]

From a formal point of view, written texts change in comparison with the texts of the solemn oral address and naturally even more in comparison with everyday speech. They can do without formulaic modes of expression (needing completion), they are worded more concisely (and consequently more carefully), they waive redundancies, but they have to replace situational self-evidence by explicit statement. In semantics, too, the effects are hard to overestimate. Everything becomes different when conveyed in writing. We have already noted that time becomes a dimension. It enables heterogeneous situations to be joined in sequence, thus enabling greater complexity in myths that can still be presented as a unity. The return to unity becomes a problem; the God concept is only one possible solution. We cannot go into all this in anything like adequate depth at this point. It can be said, however, that the most momentous innovation was the wedding of religion and morality.[165]

Advanced civilizations are societies with moralized (and moralizing) religion. They formulate the unity of the world as a good principle, as a good spirit, and a good god—and "good" is always understood as contrasting with bad. It will be difficult to prove that this merging of previously separate semantics of the secret, the holy (in the double meaning of the enthralling and the awesome) and the supernatural with the moral code can be attributed directly to writing. The need to legitimate differentiated palace economy and/or military systems of dominance offers a more likely explanation. But if this was the inducement, the elaboration into religious-moral cosmologies required the production of appropriate texts, and hence presupposed writing. Heaven itself was assumed to engage in moral bookkeeping, so that nothing, either good or bad, was forgotten.[166] On this basis, moralizing religion was then able to gain stability and endurance even where critical of the powers that were and "prophetic," and quite independently of specific political interests, of the rise and fall of empires. In response to its own problems, including what later came to be called theodicy—how a good and omnipotent God could permit evil in the world and allow the righteous to suffer—it increasingly developed in the evolution of ideas.[167] And it was this problem that brought religion and morality together; for the answer is: we cannot understand it, it is a mystery, we have to accept it.

As we have mentioned, the first religious reaction to writing had been the development in the Near East of an elaborate culture of divination, which, assuming that fate was written down, specialized in the reading of signs. Prophets, in contrast, had a quite different relationship with their god: he inspired them concretely with instructions and warnings, in brief with acts of will, which they learned in dreams and visions and reported orally.[168] In opposition to the elitist culture of divinatory sign reading, a new form of communication developed on the spontaneous basis of an old familiarity with dreams and states of trance, and thus on the basis of an oral culture, in which the initiative no longer lay in questions and answers but in acts of will by the divinity himself. However, this sort of communication was very rapidly reabsorbed by writing, through written reports of such events (including the reactions of those involved), so that for those who had not been present, a tradition of faith developed in which the unbelievable was to be believed—now, however, with a quite different, communicatively active, caring, intervening God, an observer God.

It gradually became more difficult to imagine God as a speaker, even when scripture preserved His words. For what would happen if He suddenly said something that contradicted scripture? And who would be legitimated to hear it and inform others? Sacred writings must then themselves be legitimated as the word of God, as dictated or delivered scripture. In the end, doubts even arise about whether He had ever really spoken.[169]

The revolutionary importance of the new dissemination medium writing should not, however, lead us to imagine that communication important for society was immediately transferred from oral to written language. The opposite is true. Communication continued to be understood as oral communication, and the discovery of the uses to which writing could be put was to take centuries, even after the introduction of the alphabet.[170] Writing was not seen as serving to record new thoughts or new knowledge or even what occurred to the writer only when writing. Despite a well-developed written culture in the monasteries and universities, no one in the Middle Ages thought yet of a creative use of writing; one thought primarily of commentary, analysis, and explication.

In the light of texts recorded in writing, the importance of oral communication was also enhanced. As interpreted by the Talmud, the revelation on Mount Sinai was to be seen as a double one: revelation of a text to be handed down in writing and to be interpreted orally.[171] Both faithfulness to the text and interpretative flexibility could appeal to the same revelation; and it also legitimized the difference. Where this religious mystification of the unity of difference is not used, the written word attracts a great deal of criticism: it is claimed to undermine the cultivation of memory; to replace Mnemosyne as the mother of the Muses;[172] to be sterile, unable to add anything to the truth and certainty of an opinion; to have nothing to say when one has questions: one cannot turn to a text, for it does not respond.[173] Higher knowledge, it was said, remained necessarily unwritten, in law (*nomoi agraphoi*) as in philosophy.[174] For this reason, the development of writing skills initially stimulated the parallel development of oral communication.[175] Precisely when the public could be expected to have textual knowledge, the techniques of persuasion and rhetoric were particularly strongly cultivated—although *logographoi* [speech writers] were then employed to set out in writing the texts to be presented orally. Thus the technique I have mentioned for training the memory developed, along with the concomitant *topos* that imagines "places" where words, phrases, sayings, and arguments that might be useful can be "found." The shift of important communication from rhapsodic speech to dialogue, and thus to a social model of establishing the truth, is to be seen in this context.[176] This shift can be considered the point of departure for the development of a logical terminology, which in turn abstracts from the social situation of dialogue. The sophists competed with the philosophers, the speakers with fact-oriented thinkers, for the upper hand in educating the nobility. The controversy was concerned with oral teaching and with its use in oral communication, but it is recorded in textual form and has left behind a semantics that occupies those who call themselves "philosophers" to this day. Even the printing press did not make rhetoric obsolete, but in the sixteenth and seventeenth centuries provided it with new motifs—for example, that the truth cannot impose itself by its own force, but must rely on appearance and on dissimulation.[177] Until well into the eighteenth century, eloquence was held to be more important than detailed factual knowledge and book learning in the education of the nobility, and the view was taken (especially in religious matters) that there were important communications that should be reserved for oral delivery.[178] Written and oral communication were available as alternatives, and this very functional equivalence made it possible to develop and refine each mode of communication in its specific potential.

These thoughts about the evolutionary gain built into society by the new medium of writing also mark the threshold from which discrepancies between textually fixed semantics and social circumstances have to be expected. After the invention of writing, it can no longer be assumed that social structure and semantics are in constantly synchronized agreement. Especially when stimulated by internal problems and inconsistencies, semantics can change more rapidly and possibly anticipate or even initiate potentials for development in society. But they can also conserve obsolete traditions and thus prevent the production of historically and factually appropriate descriptions.[179] The difference itself then stimulates the observation and description of societal states in both directions. The discrepancy is reproduced in the evolution of society. This has to be imputed to writing having desynchronized the old temporal rhythm in the autopoiesis of societal communication, which is addressed inter alia under the heading "Evolution of Ideas" below.[180]

We can summarize the effects of writing as follows:

(1) Writing intensifies the *differentiation* of the societal system by processing communicative signs in a manner possible only in society and by the resulting expansion and self-determined restriction of scope for selection.

(2) Writing changes the possibilities for establishing a social memory independent of the neurophysiological and psychological mechanisms of the individual human. The recording of memories and repeatability in objects and officiations (rites, celebrations) is not immediately given up; but the constant selection of what is written down now produces remembering and forgetting in the form of decisions that are subject to criteria and monitoring.

(3) Because interactional control is eliminated, writing increases the *risk of self-deception and deception by others* and the *risk of communications being rejected.* More information normally means less acceptance, and only remedies internal to society can counteract this.

(4) Writing leads to *greater differentiation and elaboration of the various dimensions of meaning* with the aid of specific distinctions; it objectifies the time dimension, objectivizes the topics of communication regardless of who is being spoken about and when, and separates off a social dimension where the views and opinions of participants in a communication process can be reflected upon.

(5) Writing uses abstracted signs and thus enables signs to be applied to signs, hence a special sort of double (operational and reflexive) closure of communication.

(6) Writing "modalizes" the understanding of reality, vastly expanding and correspondingly restricting what is treated in communication as necessary or contingent reality.

(7) Writing symbolizes what is absent, and in this context "symbolize" means that both what is absent and what is present is accessible for operations of the system. This provides a basis for second-order observation that is free of restrictive face-to-face social control and permits criticism to an extent that exposes social structure and the semantics of society to far-reaching transformation.

6. Printing

Two thousand years after the alphabet had come into use, the printing press gave an immense boost to the dissemination of the written language. We still have no clear picture of the significance of this turning point in the practice of societal communication.[181] At any rate there was more to it than an increase in the mere number of books and readers, which had already set in in the High Middle Ages.[182] We can rightly speak here of a shift from quantity to quality.

Communication, one should remember, is to be understood in terms not of the action of uttering but of understanding. Written language accordingly presupposes readers if it is to be used not only to record but also to communicate.[183] This makes it clear that the immense increase in what would come to be called the reading public revolutionized societal communication.

And in a relatively brief space of time. To realize the direct effects of printing, it suffices to observe the first century following the invention of the printing press. Printing made it possible to reproduce in volumes that enabled market mechanisms to be used for distribution; in other words, the production of texts was guided by demand and thus detached from the personal interests of the writer or his client. This was, however, not a necessary effect of the technology as such. In contrast to China and Korea, where printing was in the hands of the ruling bureaucracy, and was thus limited to disseminating material produced centrally,[184] in Europe distribution was organized on a decentralized basis via the market and price. Under these conditions, it was possible to translate the Bible, have it printed, and set up schools to teach as many people as possible to read it. The problem was only that readers who could read the Bible could also read other texts, so that it became necessary and possible to make framework decisions on preferred reading, which as distinctions could no longer be made only in religious terms. The dissemination technology could no longer be controlled through preferred content, and consequently no longer by "authority."

That in Europe it was the economy that did the selecting means that everything that sold could be printed and that the religious and political censors had to impose market controls, which very soon proved unsuccessful. Not all territories had such a market. In Russia, printed books became cheaper than manuscripts, and thus competitive, only in the eighteenth century.[185] But this remained an exception. On the whole, the speed of innovation was impressive, even for contemporary observers, who took note of changes in their lifetimes and therefore tended to exaggerate.[186]

Nevertheless, it is not easy to discern what was really new and what had a far-reaching impact on how society communicated. The rationalization of book production had already begun in the big copying workshops of the late Middle Ages. Only in this context (and not as a singular event) is the invention of the printing press to be understood at all. It saved time and expense and avoided the mishearings and slips of the pen that occur in dictation. The relationship with the text probably changed because the tactile element, the movement of the hand, the personal, bodily effort and formative action were relegated to the background by the typographical end product. The hand continued to play a role at best in preparatory work, but this, too, was now concerned with printing. The reader was no longer present with a manuscript. The almost physical presence of the writer was limited to the production of the setting copy.

Above all, however, the technical advantages had economic consequences. Lower prices created a market that in turn created a need; for only when texts were available was it worthwhile learning to read or maintaining one's reading skills through practice. The technology of the printing press generated the supplementary technology of reading, that is, a technology of the minimal motor function of perception, which is not constantly interrupted by decisions. It could be relied upon without further examination. One now hoped (and the books themselves recommended their use to this end) to learn without the aid of others whenever convenient. Reference in books to books and the quoting of specific passages were facilitated and encouraged by the fact that the books could be assumed to be available.[187] The ponderous apparatus of glosses, post-glosses, and comments that were added page for page could be abandoned. Indeed, browsing more extensively through new reading matter for information and entertainment gradually superseded the intensive, repeated reading of the same texts that vested them, as if automatically, with authority.[188] Instead of *repeating* reading, it seemed more useful to *compare* different, now easily accessible texts. Texts now had to be "interesting."

Since books were distributed via the market, claiming that they contained something new became an important selling point—at first, mainly for small, cheap texts such as pamphlets, ballads, and accounts of crimes on the occasion of executions. The buyer clearly did not want something he already knew. And this was true not only for scientific and technical innovations but notably for fictional literature chosen for its entertainment value, which people did not buy if they had already read it. The book market favored alleged novelty, regardless of whether originality and novelty were endorsed by the arts and sciences.[189] The self-advertising of printed products under their own names is likely to have contributed not inconsiderably to the corresponding "change of values." As early as the seventeenth century, it was becoming difficult to understand the pleasure taken in the repeated narration or performance of familiar stories, in the enjoyment of recognition.[190]

Printing and school instruction on the basis of printed texts required the language to be standardized.[191] Since the sixteenth century, national languages had been developing, which were soon to become tools of political nationalization and increasingly replaced Latin as the language of knowledge transfer.[192] Moreover, printing now made it appear worthwhile to record texts transmitting knowledge that had formerly been passed on orally. This was particularly the case with craft technologies. In print, this knowledge was now presented as the state of the art and as encouragement to improvement. But the literature existing in manuscript form was also gradually published in print, and this, too, was to have far-reaching consequences. First, the complexity of existing material became apparent, for example, in jurisprudence. The material could be reviewed, sorted, compared, improved. Typical lower-class jargon could be indicated and class differences confirmed.[193] Regional legal customs were recorded for printing and thus withdrawn more and more from the hands of local (manorial) jurisdiction. Arrangements could now be made centrally. Only now did it become apparent how confused, contradictory, and almost unlearnable existing arrangements were, and an urgent need developed for an overall picture and simplification, for new methods, for systematization, for sorting out what was obsolete and of no use. This led to new demands for intellectual mastery of the material, but also to pedantry. Gradually, the conviction spread beyond the entertainment sector that new knowledge was better than old. When copying texts by hand, each successive copy was worse, because old errors were overlooked and new ones were added. New editions of printed material, in contrast, could be expected to eliminate the errors of preceding ones; what is more, printed knowledge was an inducement to increase and improve existing knowledge. In other regards, too, printing affected temporal orientation. For example, it now made sense to address communication to *many people living at the same time*. The prefaces of printed books clearly indicate that this possibility was felt to be a new one. The process of increasing and improving knowledge made it independent of the physical presence of people at the place where the knowledge was gained and thus independent of the social prestige of these people.[194] Finally, it can be assumed that printing (and especially the inexpensive printing of tracts) contributed considerably to the rapid spread of religious heresies.[195] It led to the public articulation of radical demands, which, once known, could hardly be withdrawn.[196] At any rate, the traditional, practically exclusive channels for the exercise of political influence—whether by corporations, such as guilds or municipalities, or by local magnates and patron/client systems—were undermined. Printed pamphlets were clearly no longer intended for specific addressees but for the public as a whole. And even the practice of petitions, which was retained and developed, made use of printing from the seventeenth century on and thus helped prevent decisions being made on recommendation and in secret.

With all this, printing covertly furthered the trend toward individualization of participation in societal communication, and did so in two regards. If something was known, but there was someone who did not know it, he had himself to blame. He had not read enough. He lacked education. On the other hand, when something was known, this was an incitement to draw attention to oneself as an individual with dissenting opinions or new interpretations. Only in the eighteenth century were these consequences of printing, namely, education and criticism, now also formulated in positive terms, to produce an independent semantics of enlightenment and individualism, because this gave hope of "natural" safeguards for the already irreversible structural transformation of society then taking place.[197]

One effect of printing, already mentioned, was the standardization of national languages employed over wide areas. Strongly varying local dialects making mutual oral understanding difficult, if not impossible, are still to be found even in the twentieth century, but people can read the same books. Only now do rules (and a sense of rules) for the "correct" use of language develop, up to and including the absurdities of complete academic governance of the written word [*Dudenisierung*], whose modification can then be decided only by experts and authorities.

More than a culture based on manuscripts and oral tradition, printing reveals inconsistencies in tradition and thus leads indirectly to arrangements for the semantic resolution of contradictions. This can be achieved, for example, by linearizing chronologized time, making it possible to separate things by situating them in time and thus making them "historically" compatible. In the longer term, this destroyed myths of origin, which had assumed the presence of origin and a past existing simultaneously with presence, without sequential (or with only briefly remembered sequential) order. This affected the justification and motivation of the nobility by dynastic origins and ultimately transformed tradition into an ideological option that had, so to speak, to be explained against the advance of time.

The numerous evident effects of printing are difficult to assess in their totality. In many regards they were still outcomes of the adoption of writing that had failed to come to bear only because of insufficient dissemination, and that now, with the lifting of this limitation, were suddenly triggered, as it were, by delayed reaction. This is likely to have been the case with everything that we might describe as descriptive and explanatory texts, which have to supply everything that is necessary for understanding them within the text itself. Until the advent of printing, the primacy of oral communication had been assumed, and writing had been seen above all as a means of registering and recording matters that were then to be communicated; or at least no clear distinction had been made between recording medium and communication medium.[198] *Communicatio* meant establishing agreement, making known—and after the invention of the printing press, it could also be claimed that the machine itself "communicated." Finally, printing made it impossible to understand writing as mere recording. The self-recommendation of books (which, as in the past, initially "spoke" on their own behalf, addressing the reader as books) showed the difference. Although more precise research on this question is lacking, we may assume that the understanding of communication changed, and if this was the case, it could well have been the most momentous effect of the printing press. For how communication is understood is how society is understood.

It took well over two hundred years after the invention of printing for its function to become apparent as a technical infrastructure for the maintenance and updating of a societal memory[199]—separate from what individuals more or less accidentally recall and that dies with them. In order to make this memory generally available, "public" libraries were set up. The associated guarantee of stability, independent of the succession of generations of individuals, is renewable and open for a future it does not itself determine. It replaced the guarantees of stability that older, orally communicating societies had found in the family and spatial structures of the community; and it replaced it by forms that could be used by the various functional systems, by science and by literature, by the legal system with its increasingly legislative activities, and, finally, by the economy, through the printing of bank notes. It was the technical grounding of this form of distributing and conserving knowledge that made it possible to uncouple it from already structured forms of societal differentiation; and it could therefore be left up to the given functional system whether to use it and how.

Further developments followed step by step. Negative effects of reading books were noted—for instance from women's delight in love stories or knights' pleasure in tales of chivalry (*Don Quixote*). Production began to be oriented to the reader.[200] But for the time being, the belief persisted that communication was interaction. Interaction remained the model for social rationality, however insular this might appear in a society that was already acquainted with a carefully calculated money economy, reasons of state, and theory-guided scientific research. The Enlightenment still espoused the interaction model, and thus ultimately that of oral communication; but for the mutual disciplining of those physically present it substituted the assumption of a rational interest ascribed to the individual members of the reading classes. The concept of the human being was accordingly generalized. This was then outbidden by the theory of transcendental consciousness, the paradoxical assumption that self-reference is generalizable. It was only the Romantics, who—seeking to include infinity, incommunicability, and deviant views of reality in communication—adapted to written and printed language; only then was the failure to communicate to become a favorite theme in literature.

When the entire population might be expected to have attained literacy, this development would be taken a stage further. Only in the mid-nineteenth century did an inexpensive, daily mass press begin to publish, requiring a deliberate lowering of the understanding threshold, which in Japan also required a (not always observed) limitation to the written characters that could be assumed to be generally known.[201] I have discussed some of the consequences elsewhere apropos of public opinion.[202]

Finally, we can assume that the concept of action had to be modified if it was to include the writing of books for the printing press. Activities could no longer be easily regarded as following the pattern of interaction between physically present interlocutors, who could draw on numerous implicit pointers to understanding. In the course of the eighteenth century, it also became clear that the author could not appear in his own text, because he already knew the end of the story and by referring back to himself would repeatedly interrupt the course of events. He therefore had to limit himself to the role of "author" external to the text (just as an artist had to sign a work). If the concept of action was to include this case (and how could it avoid doing so?) it had to be decontexted and freed of all narrative restrictions. But what then is the unit of action? Where does it start, where does it end? In effect, action could no longer be anything else but the embodiment of a subjective intention—with the result that the legitimacy of action could now be called into question.

7. Electronic Media

In our century, the use of electricity that technology offers has broadened options for communication and, above all, reduced the obstacles to natural communication based on the human organism. The energy needed for communication can now be produced and supplied quite independently (e.g., in quite different places) of the operational implementation of communication. The technical network of energy flow is completely neutral to communication; in other words, information is produced outside the network and can only be disturbed by "noise." Causal relations between technological physics and communicated information are freed of overlap and take the form of structural coupling. In the first place, this means that the communication system society is becoming more and more dependent on technologically determined structural coupling with its environment. Susceptibility to failure is increasing, and with it the technical and economic cost of safeguards against breakdown. On the other hand, this has led to the technically induced but use-determined, endogenously dynamic proliferation of communication options, and has done so almost simultaneously in several regards. It is still too early to judge the consequences, but we can at least describe the structures of these innovations.

Telecommunication—from telephone to fax and e-mail—reduces the remaining spatial (and therefore temporal) restrictions on communication to more or less zero. The technical possibilities are supplemented by recording facilities, which also permit utterance and reception to be separated, permitting different temporal arrangements on the two sides and hence facilitating communication. Electronics calls neither oral nor written communication into question, merely providing more potential applications, albeit at the cost of the restrictions imposed by the technology.

The really momentous change, however, appears to lie in the invention and development of electronic machines for information processing. Under the spell of a long humanistic tradition, the issue had first been defined in terms of whether the computer and its "artificial intelligence" achieved anything comparable or superior to human consciousness and how superiorities and inferiorities were distributed across the various areas of performance. The human subject has always been the vanishing point for the humanities. The question is whether this is the right definition of the problem and whether the computer will not sooner or later emerge victorious from this competition if society grants it "equal opportunities." Quite another question is whether and how computers can replace or outbid *communication*, an achievement constitutive of society. They would have to treat knowledge as form, and thus know what other computers do not. At the cybernetics conferences of the 1950s, claims had already been made that human consciousness could be constructed as a machine if only it were possible to say precisely enough what the machine was to do. But this means that the area of research that came to be called "artificial intelligence" is concerned only with programming. This shifts the problem to linguistic communication, which has the advantage of also operating with fuzzy expressions, as long as self-correcting operations can be undertaken should the need arise. Communication is the ongoing processing of the difference between knowledge and nonknowledge, with no need to establish what stocks of knowledge/nonknowledge the individuals or machines involved have. They are both outcome and precondition of communication. There are good arguments, at least at present, for the indispensability and superiority of oral and written communication, which can, however, use the computer to enhance their own capabilities and concentrate on essentials that cannot be delegated to technology.

But comparing computer performance with consciousness or communication is probably a secondary issue. I leave aside the question of whether working or playing with computers can be understood as communication; whether, for example, there is double contingency on *both* sides. Nor do I consider whether and how we have to change the concept of communication if we wish to include this case. More interesting is how societal communication is affected if influenced by computer-mediated knowledge. What we actually observe are worldwide, connectionist networks for collecting, assessing, and accessing data, for example, in medicine, which address specific topics but are not spatially limited in operation. This offers a further argument for the fact of a world society, which intensifies and accelerates communication in a fashion impossible without these new dissemination media.

Compared with what tradition had defined through religion and through art, the computer changes above all the relationship between (accessible) surface and depth. It is no longer a matter of *craquelure* that allows divination or of ornaments that emphasize meanings. The surface is now the monitor, which makes extremely limited demands on the human senses, whereas depth is the invisible machine, capable of reorganizing itself from one moment to the next, for example, in response to use. The link between surface and depth can be established by commands instructing the machine to make something visible on the monitor or as printout. The machine itself remains invisible.

We can only assume that this structure considerably influences both the possibilities of and restrictions on communication. On the one hand, it requires specific skills in coupling surface and depth. Only for this reason can we describe the invisible machine as "virtual reality" (only presupposed ability [*virtus*] distinguishes virtuality from mere possibility). On the other hand, the structure can be used only if it sets off changes (information) in psychic or social systems. Mediation appears to require forms to be temporalized. Fixed forms are no longer taken as given, to be judged true or false, useful and useless, and so on, by the codes of functional systems. Every determination produces an unmarked space and hence another side that can be determined only through further operations (with the same consequences). Although they can be understood and used as such in applied contexts, these "transclassical" [*transklassischen*] machines are more than just powerful tools.[203] What is involved is the marking of forms that enrich distinction and indication with unforeseeable consequences for the communication system society. At any rate, as ability increases, so does inability (as measured against it). The possibilities of arguing by accessing the invisible machine are clearly diminishing and the susceptibility to failure is increasing.

Further technical inventions, namely, cinema and, in the telecommunication field, television, enable *moving pictures to be communicated.* Sound can also be synchronized with pictures so that the whole reality can be multiplied and reproduced for secondary experience with guaranteed faithfulness to the original. Optical and acoustic reproduction, so strictly separated by writing, now merge. The guarantee of reality, which language had had to forgo because everything that is said can be contradicted, shifts to moving, optically/acoustically synchronized pictures.[204] Although we still have to watch the replay and understand that there is no sense in contradicting the pictures or destroying them—the screen quite obviously presents an alibi reality—photography also guarantees correspondence between the photographed reality and the reality that appears in the picture. The whole of communication thus mediated once again becomes dependent on real time. A film can only be shot when what is to be filmed actually happens—neither beforehand nor afterward. And we can view it only when it is screened or broadcast. This "relapse" into quasi-oral temporal relations can rapidly be compensated for by cutting and recording techniques. The problems caused by technology can be resolved by technology. But this dependence on real time produces a certain credibility bonus: there is no time for complex manipulation or to check for such manipulation either during shooting or viewing. This does not exclude a general suspicion of manipulation, but such a suspicion must remain distant and abstract, and therefore lacks evidence in communication.

The result of these inventions is that the entire world has become communicable.[205] The phenomenology of being is replaced by the phenomenology of communication. We see the world as visual communication suggests it to us—even if not so dramatic, not in such high contrast, not so flawless, not so colorful, and, above all, not so select. The world we perceive, both the normally perceived world and the television world, pales under the constant drive to outbid.[206] What is more, the very aspect that had been fascinating in language now declines, namely, the possibility and necessity of distinguishing between information and utterance. Although we still see people talking on television, indeed, even viewers again play a part in the medium, be it only as ridiculous background laughter indicating that there is something to laugh about,[207] the entire arrangement evades the controls that had been developed over thousands of years on the basis of distinguishability between utterance and information. For this reason, the yes/no coding of linguistic communication also fails. We can be positively or negatively affected by a film, we can find it good or bad, but, in the overall complex of what is perceived, the intensification is lacking that would allow a clear distinction to be drawn between acceptance and rejection. Although we *know* that it is communication, we do *not see it*. This can raise suspicions of manipulation, which cannot, however, be substantiated. We know it, we live with it. Television produces a produced form that binds all everyday means of persuasion. And the other side of the form is precisely the suspicion of manipulation.

Since audiovisual transmission can convey perception completely, the possibilities and necessities of individual imagination do not come to bear.[208] At the same time, individual-mass reception obviates communicative efforts to persuade. Similarity of purpose is established before the screen but naturally does not exclude differences of opinion any more than does the natural perceptual world. There is therefore little sign of culture and worldviews homogenizing, but shifts in attunement are perhaps taking place in more rapid rhythm.

What then is communication if everything can be communicated, and if in important, impressive fields, the difference between information and utterance that is constitutive of communication becomes unrecognizable? Does the totalization of communication lead, as Baudrillard claims, to the disappearance of communication? Or does the blind closure of the system of societal communication only now become full reality? Is communication then only invisible assistance in the self-observation of the world, and is society the boundary per se across which the world observes itself?

Let us leave these speculative questions aside and consider how under these conditions the selectivity of communication reorganizes itself. In many cases (with the exception of telephony), technology imposes unilateral communication. This is partly inevitable due to the interposition of technical apparatus, but also partly a necessity of mass communication that printing had also had to accept.[209] This changes the process of selection, and does so on *both* sides of the apparatus. One no longer selects in communication but *for* communication. The sender chooses topics and forms, productions, and above all the time and duration of transmission as he sees fit. The receiver chooses what he wants to see and hear. Communication then takes place as in a hypercycle of mutual selection; but, where it occurs, it can no longer correct itself.

While this shows how far we have moved away from oral communication (without, it should be repeatedly stressed, replacing or eliminating it), the latest invention goes a step further. We are talking about communication mediated by computers. It makes it possible to separate the input of data into the computer and the retrieval of information so strongly that no identity of any sort remains. As far as communication is concerned,[210] this means that the unity of utterance and understanding is abandoned. Whoever feeds something in does not know (and if he did, he would not need the computer) what will be taken out on the other side. The data have meanwhile been "processed." The receiver, too, needs just as little to know whether something is intended for his attention and what. This means that the *authority* of the source with all the required sociostructural safeguards (stratification, reputation) becomes superfluous, is indeed annulled by the technology and replaced by the *unknownness* of the source. The possibility is also lost of recognizing the intention of an utterance and of nurturing suspicions or drawing other conclusions that could lead to the communication being accepted or rejected.[211] What we have is the absorption of uncertainty subject to limited self-monitoring. What is more, human bodies (at least in the current state of the art) are tied to connection points even where they are portable devices. As with television, this could lead to a reduction in chance contacts between freely roaming bodies.[212] All this has driven the *social decoupling* of the medial substratum of communication to an extreme. In our conceptual terms, this means that a new medium is emerging whose forms depend on computer programs. Although these programs do not decide how the medium concentrates the communication itself into forms, for this involves the events of information input and retrieval, like the grammatical rules of language, the programs are forms that restrict the possibilities of strict coupling and can thus extend them into the unforeseeable.

Whereas writing achieved the spatial (and hence also temporal) decoupling of the communication components utterance and understanding, albeit under the strict condition that the factually same information is concerned (however this might then be "hermeneutically" modified), the computer can include the factual dimension of the meaning of communication in the decoupling. What this can lead to currently eludes the boldest speculation. Nevertheless, new trends in the cognitive treatment of such matters are already apparent, which are beginning to influence the form of ordering knowledge. The point of departure is a basically operational and then procedural understanding of reality[213]—with or without "autopoiesis." This leads to the notion of a no longer comprehensible complexity and subsequently to work on cognitive structures that abstract from time and, for example, in the form of calculi, postulate reusability at other points in time. Such temporally abstract models of fundamentally time-dependent (historical) operational sequences explode the classical concept of movement, which is to be recognized only in the difference to what is fixed, thus the distinction between moving/unmoving, dynamic/static, and so on. What takes its place, if we can indeed understand the conversion of knowledge in terms of such a substitution process, cannot be established with any certainty, despite the progress made in such fields as the cognitive sciences, artificial intelligence, computer linguistics, and the new mathematics of the unexpectable—at any rate, not for a sociologist, who can only respond to societal facts that are already in evidence. From the point of view of a theory of society, we can at best formulate the problem of this new ordering of knowledge as radically as necessary.

The new media of this century have considerably expanded the worldwide possibilities for communication. They have therefore intensified the discrepancy between possible and actual communication. Hence they intensify the selection problem to which society reacts by both organizing and individualizing selection.[214] They dissolve the cogent unity of communication in a way that would not have been considered possible only a few decades ago. This increases the importance of the difference between medium and form (i.e. the form of the difference between medium and form). Modern society accordingly appears to have reached a limit beyond which nothing can be communicated any more—with one old exception: sincerity.

For if we cannot say that we do not mean what we say because we then cannot know that others cannot know what is meant when we say that we do not mean what we say, we can also not say that we mean what we say because this is either a superfluous and suspicious tautology or the negation of a negation that is incommunicable anyway. This paradox of communication cannot be avoided. But it can be circumvented, dissolved, replaced by an apposite distinction. This is achieved by institutions that we choose to call symbolically generalized communication media.

8. Dissemination Media: Summary

If there are sustained trends in the evolution of dissemination media that begin with the invention of writing and culminate in modern electronic media, they can in brief be identified as the trend from hierarchical to heterarchical organization and the waiving of the spatial integration of societal operations.

While reliance was placed on hierarchical order in developing societal differentiation, in empire building, urban ascendancy, and stratification, the dissemination media were already working on delegitimizing it, or more precisely, on an alternative project. With hierarchies, it suffices to watch and influence the apex, because, more or less rightly, it can be assumed capable of asserting its will. Heterarchies, in contrast, are based on the interconnection of direct contacts discriminating (observing) on the spot. The invention of the printing press still left uncertainty about this opposition between hierarchy and heterarchy. In China and Korea, the printing press was a dissemination tool in ruling bureaucracies. In Europe, which had from the outset set its sights on the economic exploitation and market distribution of printed material, the authorities sought to resolve the conflict by means of censorship. Their failure, inevitable with the multiplicity of printing centers in various territories and with the rapidly increasing complexity of printed communication, finally obliged all hierarchies, including those of politics and the law, to come to terms with a fundamentally heterarchically communicating society. Since the eighteenth century, this state of affairs has been celebrated as the primacy of "public opinion." As far as differentiation forms are concerned, this corresponds with the transition to functional differentiation.

Modern computer technology takes us an important step further. It also attacks the authority of the experts. In principle, everyone will in future be able to check the statements of experts such as physicians and lawyers on his own computer. They may very well claim there is no scientific evidence for the efficacy of certain medications—and we find it nonetheless. Or that there are no court rulings on certain legal issues—and we find them nonetheless. Although it is difficult to check how knowledge finds its way into the computer, it can at any rate not be turned into authority. Naturally, this does not change the fact that everyone who relies on communication in one way or another has to depend on trust. But in the age of electronic data processing, this trust can no longer be personalized, no longer implemented in social status; it is now only trust in the system.

In the decentralized order of a heterarchy, too, there is no lack of far-reaching and above all highly consequential events. A single selection can permit or obstruct many others. An item of news—such as the dropping of the atom bomb—can change the world. There are also places under observation, like the stock exchange, that are more worth observing than others. Important things can also gain prominence here, but only in the context of simultaneous nonknowledge, only in contexts that cannot be monitored. There are indeed constants, repetitions, intensifications; and, above all, if we may describe the single event as observation, a shift in the functioning of the system to the level of observing observations.[215] If we now have only observers to observe, this is in the first place a drastic reduction; but at the same time a reduction that in any case gives us the option of whether we wish to attribute what is observed to the observer and his distinction, or to what he observes. Is what is transmitted "right," or is it selected, stylized, falsified, invented by a special sense of mission. Here, too, the only help is in observing observations, including one's own observations.

As a result, this situation has profoundly unsettled the semantics with which society reproduces meaning worth conserving. The confidence in established forms has dissolved, resuscitation efforts have proved vain. Society appears to be trying out new eigenvalues that promise stability under the conditions of heterarchy and second-order observation. And a decisive role in this is likely to fall to the selections of the dissemination media, for they at any rate are compatible with a heterarchical order.

A second, just as far-reaching consequence of the evolution of dissemination technologies and the corresponding media lies in the waning need for societal operations to be spatially integrated. By integration, I mean restriction of the degree of freedom of systems.[216] Writing had already made the understanding of and response to communication independent of the physical presence of the utterer. However, in the Middle Ages, semantic evolution still depended on which libraries housed what manuscripts and what chance led readers to the rare texts to gain inspiration from the ideas they conveyed. The bodies of individuals and thus their presence in particular places did indeed play an important role. This changed gradually with the spread of printed writings. When in the eighteenth century, the integration of society was left to "public opinion," this amounted ultimately to waiving spatial integration, if not integration itself. For "public" means nothing other than giving access to anyone, relinquishing control of access, with consequent structural uncertainty of spatial integration.

Spatial integration means that the degree of freedom of systems, that is, the set of possibilities they can realize, depends on the locus in space where each operates and hence on specific local conditions. Every change in these conditions, every movement costs time and draws on scarce resources. One sends messengers, in the sense of the ancient Greek *theōroi*, to learn what is communicated elsewhere (e.g., at Delphi). Until well into modern times, with its world of states, spatial complexes and demarcations also served to define experimental fields for structural innovation, and hence to reduce risks should their diffusion become possible.[217] However, with the advent of writing and printing, and then with increasing travel and external studies by members of the upper classes, spatial distance and spatial boundaries lost their restrictive character. Landscape become an object of "subjective" pleasure, home becomes a topic of "nostalgic" plaint. As spatial integration dwindled, so did the certainties that built on it. Sojourn in certain places became the contingently experienced result of journeys, changes of residence, migratory movements, and the special spatial conditions that one can find anywhere and everywhere require an adaptation of behavior that the individual can evade through mobility and by substituting other conditions.

Where this has become a normal condition in society, sociological theory must also adapt to it. System boundaries can no longer be understood as edges of the system, as skins or membranes by which the system fortifies itself, so to speak. Boundaries are not parts—subdivisions, one might almost say—of the system, as if there were also "inner" parts that benefit from having no contact with the environment. Rather, a social system is nothing other than the one side, the inner side, the operating side of the form of the system, and with every operation of the system, the distinctness of the system as opposed to the environment is reproduced. The autopoiesis of a meaning system is nothing other than the reproduction of this difference.

9. Symbolically Generalized Communication Media, 1: Function

Classical social theories have answered the question of what makes social order possible by reference to *normative* conditions: to natural law, the social contract, or consensual morality. This has also been true for sociology, for Durkheim, and for Talcott Parsons. However, Parsons pointed the way to an alternative, which is not, however, unchecked but assigned to the still normative meaning of codes and shared symbolic values. It lies in the theory of symbolically generalized media. As soon as we reformulate the problem underlying this segment of theory, we can recognize that it is in fact an alternative, a functional equivalent to the usual normative safeguard of social cohesion (which naturally cannot mean that norms can be replaced by media).

Symbolically generalized communication media do not (like law, above all) serve primarily to safeguard expectations against disappointment. They are independent media relating directly to the problem of the improbability of communication. However, they presuppose the yes/no coding of language and assume the function of rendering expectable the acceptance of a communication in cases where rejection is probable. They come into being only when there is writing and when the rejection of communicated meaning proposals therefore becomes even more probable. They react to the problem that more information normally means less acceptance.[218]

Even if the linguistic code gives a proposed meaning an equal chance of being accepted or rejected, an accepted meaning can be expected to have a better chance of being repeated than a rejected one. Communication registers a success and, if repetition is sufficiently tenable, will remember it.[219] Moreover, an accepted meaning proposal has a better chance of generalization because the accepting communication and all subsequent communications take it over in another context and have to adapt it accordingly. Acceptance and rejection therefore set off different recursions. This explains that either rejection prompts the development of, at best, conflict management institutions, which have to be geared to unpredictable individual differences of opinion and disputes, or a positive semantics of accepted meaning develops that matures, as it were, in a process of reuse, concentration, abstraction. This does not mean that the development path produces "reasonable" results, for, as always, evolution depends on starting points and bifurcations; but it does seem likely that society itself gives good marks to positive results such as "nature," "reason," and "reality," and can then at best take a "critical" view of them.

Symbolically generalized media are one of the results of this process. In a very abstract sense, they are a functional equivalent of morality, conditioning the likelihood of acceptance or rejection. Whereas, owing to its conflictuality and dangerousness, morality presupposes prepared terrain with a high degree of plausibility, symbolically generalized media are differentiated in order to motivate against plausibility. This explains why morality tends toward standardization, whereas symbolically generalized media develop from the outset in the plural and for problem-specific constellations. To achieve the probability of highly improbable meaning selection, a multiplicity of specialized codes has to be developed. Borrowing a term from biology, we might also speak of "adaptive polymorphism."

The formula "symbolically generalized," coined by Parsons, is not apposite in every respect. Parsons applies "symbolic" to the difference between ego and alter, and thus to the social dimension, and "generalized" to the difference between situations, and thus to the factual dimension of the meaning being processed. The idea (similar to Wittgenstein's concept of rule) is that social agreement can be attained only if the underlying commonalities last for more than a single situation. To this extent, I concur. Incidentally, however, the theory of symbolically generalized *communication* media presented here does not follow on from Parsons's theory of interaction media (or media of interchange), which is committed to the theoretical architecture of his AGIL paradigm.[220] Instead, I proceed on the assumption that linguistic coding only structures, and does not solve, the general problem of the improbability of successful communication, which is rather exacerbated by the clear opposition between acceptance and rejection. The general concept of communication medium is also applicable to this case. Symbolically generalized media are also media insofar as they require the difference between loose and strict coupling and enable forms to be formed on the basis of a loosely coupled medial substratum. However, we are dealing neither with special languages nor dissemination media, but with a different type of medium: a different *form*, a different sort of *distinction*, other sorts of *code*. Before I go into detail, these differences must therefore be clarified.

Especially since the nineteenth century, "symbol" and "symbolic" have been used in a very general and diffuse sense, often almost synonymously with "sign." This makes the concept superfluous. In order to restore its precise meaning, I shall limit it to cases where a sign connotes its own function, and hence becomes reflexive. Its own function is to represent the unity of what indicates and what is indicated. Symbolization therefore expresses—and hence makes amenable to communication—that unity lies in difference, and what is separated belongs together, so that what indicates can stand for (and not only point to) what is indicated, standing in the grand tradition for the sacred.

In the context of the "symbolically generalized communication media" concept, I therefore (like Parsons) mean by "symbolic" that these media bridge a difference and supply communication with opportunities for acceptance. Unlike language, they are not satisfied with securing sufficient understanding under highly complex conditions and communication selected only ad hoc. They presuppose this. In many cases understanding makes it extremely improbable that communication will be accepted—for example, in the case of improbable assertions, of requests for handouts, of arbitrary instructions for conduct. If we had to rely only on language in such situations, failure could be expected and the corresponding communication would not take place. In other words, language itself can realize only a small part of what is linguistically possible with its own resources. Everything else would fall victim to discouragement if there were not additional arrangements of a different sort. Symbolically generalized media transform no-probabilities into yes-probabilities in miraculous ways—for example, by enabling us to offer payment for goods or services we would like to obtain. They are *sym*bolic insofar as they use communication to effect a match that is per se improbable. At the same time, however, they are *dia*bolic, because, in achieving this, they generate new differences. A specific communication problem is solved by rearranging unity and difference: whoever can pay gets what he wants; whoever cannot pay does not.

In other words, symbolically generalized communication media coordinate selections that cannot be linked without difficulty and therefore initially exist as a loosely coupled set of elements—selections of information items, utterances, and understanding content. They achieve strict coupling only through the form specific to the given medium—for example, theories, proofs of love, laws, prices. They must not only function symbolically but (as the above examples show) also be generalized, since in anticipation of further autopoiesis, the corresponding expectations can be formed only if the form covers a range of situations. Even a proof of love does not count only for the immediate present, and certainly not if it is always offered in the same form. What is ultimately at stake is always to encourage, indeed, enable, communication through added opportunities for acceptance; and thus to gain terrain for society that would otherwise remain unworked owing to natural infertility.

The achievement of these media and the forms typical of them can therefore be described as the ongoing *enablement of a highly improbably combination of selection and motivation.* But these terms do not describe psychic states (what the payer feels when handing over money is irrelevant to the success of communication) but social constructions, which manage on the assumption of corresponding states of consciousness.[221] They are realized in communication itself through recursion. That communications are accepted therefore means only that their acceptance is taken as the premise for further communication, whatever might go on in the individual consciousness.

The combinatorial problem is solved by resolving the circular relationship between selection and motivation (each determines the other) by making the *conditioning of selection into a motivational factor.* We can accept a demand for communication if we know that its selection obeys certain conditions; at the same time, the person who utters this demand can enhance the probability of acceptance by conforming to these conditions and thus encouraging himself to communicate. The double problem of deceit and acceptance is thus resolved at the same time, or at least normalized. We enhance the certainty that these conditions will be respected, although they are themselves highly selective and are far from covering every desired constellation; we signal this self-determination by using symbols that attest to use of the medium, and thus earn the prospect of communication being accepted. For example, we appeal to truth. Or we manipulate symbols of power (now chiefly the subjection of power itself to the law) in a way that demonstrates superior, effectual power. Measured against the vast number of possible linguistic communications, conditions that couple selection and motivation are the exception. Nevertheless, they are unlikely to be too rare, for otherwise there would be no expectations, no socialization, no related system formation. Symbolically generalized communication media can therefore differentiate only in sufficiently large, complex societies. They accordingly require, not only the linguistic code as the structure of their referential problem, but also writing to set off differentiation and, as we shall see, printing to develop to the full.

In the classical age of Greece, the alphabetization of writing and the consequent spread of literacy had provoked two responses without addressing the difference between them. The question had become acute of how to motivate the acceptance of communication where its selectivity is manifest and can no longer be disputed. As I have indicated, the sole solution lay in strengthening oral communication's resources for persuading and convincing. In the course of time, mediated for the Middle Ages primarily by Cicero and Quintilian, this led to an *alliance between rhetoric, topic, and morality*. The viewpoints to be used in speech (*topoi*, "commonplaces") had to be found and amplified, and this had to be taught and learned.[222] Since these terms referred initially to advances of the speaker, an artistic approach had imposed itself. If we take a closer look at their meaning and function, we see that a unity of cognition and motivation was still in mind—hence a solution to the problem of motivation through selection.[223] For implementation (contrary to sophistic teaching), the structure of truth and morality was decisive. It could succeed only in the context of good, since truths (as well as virtues) support each other, whereas errors (like vices) contend with one another. The expertise and personal virtue of the speaker were thus considered more important than any tricks. More important, that is, for amplification.

Printing put an end to this syndrome of rhetoric, topic, and morality, and hence to amplification, since it made too much complexity apparent at the same time.[224] But this took another good two hundred years. Initially, the printed book revived the old form.[225] As in the past, amplification depended on the general being considered more valuable than the particular. As in the past, *topoi* steered motivation in the direction of factually, temporally, and socially congruent generalization. As in the past, important communication was morally dichotomized, placed in a scheme easy to deal with orally. As in the past, this admonition and teaching confirmed itself in the endeavor to praise virtues, blame vices, and treat passions as disturbance. The amplification of communication served to amplify morality and vice versa. In the far-reaching debates of the sixteenth century on the understanding of history and poetry, an epideictic, amplifying function still presupposed both modes of description. The "heroes" of literature had to function as commonplaces, for their individualization would have disturbed their amplifying function. There was no anticipation at all of the individual confronted by the platitudes of the *topoi* becoming stubborn and recoiling into their own ego. Gradually, however, opposing trends also made themselves felt (e.g., Montaigne's *Essays*). Amplifications "which are in effect nothing else but either exaggerations, or cumulations of reasons"[226] now appear in an ambiguous light, and printing begins its sabotage by reproducing the once so popular set (*copia*) of *topoi* as surplus and surfeit, finally lending the semantics of *copia*/*copie*/copy the negative slant it has today.[227]

But what if it no longer works?

We see the alternative in the development and differentiation of symbolically generalized communication media. This, too, can be traced back to impulses given by alphabetic script. We therefore return to the Greek sources.

Obviously, the spread of written culture had both offered the possibility of artificial word formation and accordingly made it advisable to differentiate terminologies in terms of different problems to allow novel means of persuasion to be described.[228] To show how this fits together, let's take a brief look at the most important innovations.

As far as *knowledge* [*Wissen*] is concerned, the Greek language had had an invented word even in Homeric times—*alētheia*—which negated the condition of being covert, concealed, forgotten [*lēthē* = forgetfulness].[229] It was thus not a state but the result of an effort. In the oral tradition, truth was tied to rhythm and to the memory rhythm facilitated, and this alone allowed it to be saved from oblivion, to be truth. In written culture, this association with feasibility (*technē, poiesis, sophia*) was retained in the classical period's "consciousness of ability" [*Könnens-Bewußtsein*].[230] But if truth itself was already a negation, how was it to be negated again to arrive at a coding in terms of true/false?

Opposing concepts—especially *pseudos* [falsehood]—were initially meant interactionally and dialogistically. It was a matter of truthfulness or mendacity, of the correct or false presentation of knowledge. In other words, there was originally only this behavioral orientation with no notion of a relation between statement and reality independent of behavior. The correct presentation of reality is a duty of conduct, and the opposite behavior violates this duty, is an ill-considered utterance, if not a lie.[231]

Only with the aid of writing can topics be so objectivized that controversial discussion about them is possible. It is presumably because of such dialogues that one becomes accustomed to second-order observation, which reserves to itself the right to check whether knowledge held to be true is correctly or wrongly accepted as knowledge.[232] This then differentiates a communication problem that uses distinctions of its own, between strict knowledge (*epistēmē*) and opinion (*doxa*), for example, which occur in no other field of meaning.[233]

The semantics that develops around the also newly coined word *philia* takes us into a quite different problem field.[234] It is generally translated as "friendship," but in broader contexts, we might also think of solidarity. Unlike the Romans, the Athenians had early broken with the archaic segmentary structures of nobility.[235] The archaic ethos had required a person to summon up sympathy and engagement for what was close to him, including weapons, animals, women, gods (and *philos* had originally meant just this), whereas remoter entities could be treated indifferently and arbitrarily. To this must be added the urban polity rule that one had to treat the friends of one's friends as friends and the enemies of one's enemies as enemies—a rule that was still in effect in Rome when Cicero wrote *De amicitia*.[236] Friendship was differentiated out of these archaic structures based on birth and descent and at the same time generalized as a general notion of belonging together relating to society.[237] The counterconcept of enmity receded (i.e., a code forms: friend or not) and the problem of the criteria for choosing friends came to the fore. Being close to someone was then no longer a *condition* for friendship but the *consequence of choosing* a friend. General societal sociality remained a precondition, but friendship was built into it as an intensive form. The concept could then no longer be extended to animals or gods. From Aristotle onward, a specialized, tradition-setting distinction restricted and structured application, that between friendships of utility, friendships of pleasure, and friendships of virtue. And demands for the ruthless primary orientation of this code arose—for example, in the question of whether friendship was juster than justice; or whether one could expect help from a friend in breaking the law, in desecrating a temple, or in similar misdeeds.

Communication specializing in the economy had always been concerned with property and had practiced the transfer of property in the form of barter. A new situation developed with the invention and spread of coinage, initially in Lydia, then in Greece from the seventh century BCE.[238] Minting gave money an easily recognizable, special form and made it independent of the meaning of a relatively generally usable commodity.[239] For the first time, coinage connected long-distance with local trade and was temporarily able to combine politics and economics in a commercial loop in the form of *tyrannis* [despotic rule].[240] Backing by precious metal remained indispensable for another twenty-five centuries, but it became unnecessary for the issuer of the money to guarantee its redemption. Money's acceptance as tender in the marketplace, facilitating transfer of goods and rendering of services that would not otherwise have occurred, developed from its initial use in palace and trading-house transactions.

It is somewhat more difficult to judge the differentiation of a special medium for political power with a specialized semantics, precisely because of the superabundant terminology. In this field institutional, role-related, legally constituted differentiation was most advanced, but the attention value gained led to these structures being identified with the city itself. There were offices and assemblies capable of making decisions. The concepts needed only to follow. Elaborate consideration was paid to the guiding aspects of the urban order, namely, *isonomia* and *homonoia*, and to their importance for law and democracy. This discussion was marked by the replacement of *themis* by *nomos*, which for its part enabled a distinction (not yet understood as being hierarchical) to be drawn between *physis* and *nomos*.[241] The differentiation of political legal principles, which then, however, required the *establishment* of a corresponding order, is apparent above all in the turn against influences stemming from stratification and (as we may well be permitted to add) from networks of friendship. Despite stratification, equality before the law was to apply.[242] All this held only for the exercise of political power and not as a maxim explaining knowledge or the choice of friends. But since it was formulated with reference to urban life, the terminology was much more differentiated than in other cases and also more strongly tied to the self-description of society, to the "political identity" of the Greeks.[243]

If a sufficiently sharp distinction was not made from self-description of the (urban) societal system in political semantics, too great a distinction was drawn in the fields of property and making money. The difference between *oikos* and *polis* prompted this skewing. It excluded any talk about "political economy," which would at best have sounded paradoxical to Greek ears.[244] On the other hand, as typical in aristocratic societies, trade was underrated and, not least, political sources of funding were available, for example, tribute. This was certainly not in keeping with the structural differentiation of the societal system, which in Athens was very advanced,[245] and a terminology relating to the money economy was accordingly in use that still reflected the prevailing understanding of society not in assessment of the autonomy of the money economy but only in evaluation of the corresponding activities.

In retrospect, these differentiations can be understood. It is easy to understand, for example, that truth and love had to be distinguished, for love would disturb truth, just as truth would disturb love. However, before such a semantics evolved, the very opposite had been plausible. Did a person not have to trust what someone close to him said more than what anyone else might say? It therefore remains for evolution theory to say how such a radical change in plausibilities could take place. We can do no more than speculate.

The spread of the alphabetic script may have been what led to such far-reaching, issue-focused diversification of semantic forms, but this does not suffice to explain it. What must also be considered is that the powerful alliance between religion and morality that ruled in other advanced civilizations had not developed in Greek cities.[246] Nor was there any organization of the clergy (such as churches) extending beyond the individual city. Whether religion in Greece can be described as a private matter is a moot point.[247] At any rate, no religion focused on scripture had developed. Written culture had simply developed alongside what there was in the way of religion, and only in the Hellenistic empires of late antiquity did new mystic forms of cult arise that sought to be resistant to the written word, and finally Christianity, a new religion of faith that spread with the aid of canonical texts.

Nevertheless, it cannot be claimed that symbolically generalized communication media were already fully developed in antiquity. To judge this, however, we must first outline what was required, not least that these media introduce the autocatalysis of functional systems. At any rate, to anticipate a concept from evolution theory,[248] significant predevelopments had been achieved. And I would note that referential problems had been singled out that were later to prove key issues in media development: truth, love, power/law, and property/money.

To begin with, however, the forms chosen for this purpose had to accept major restrictions, because they were developed for a specific society in history and had to harmonize with its descriptions of the world and itself. This explains, first, why the political was overrated (remarkable when considering the structural givens), with society being defined as political and the economic being reduced to household and commerce. But in the field of *philia*, too, forms were similarly adapted: the "highest" variant of friendship was the friendship of virtue, directed toward satisfying the demands of living together in the urban polity. And what could be accepted as truth was determined by bivalent logic and the corresponding ontology, an arrangement of relatively low structural diversity, allowing account to be taken of the communicative restrictions of observing observations in this society, without the logic permitting this to be known and articulated.

10. Symbolically Generalized Communication Media, 2: Differentiation

I interrupt this historical account to return to my systematic exposition, for we still lack any explanation for the diversity and differentiation of symbolically generalized communication media.

If we wish to analyze the forms of differentiation for symbolically generalized communication media, we must remember that we are dealing with the special problem of a connection between selection and motivation that has become improbable. *From this point of view, all symbolically generalized communication media are functionally equivalent.* However, precisely this viewpoint requires that the problem not merely be described by enumerating the components of each communication, namely, information, utterance, and understanding. Other, connecting forms are needed, and it is these forms that generate the specification and differentiation of symbolically generalized communication media.

Forms of self-observation of the communication process are used for this purpose. To begin with, the improbability problem has to be put in the social form of "double contingency," which has been described in terms of the positional concepts ego and alter. Why? The normal answer is that ego and alter already exist anyway, that they are different persons who communicate with each other from time to time. Whoever means no more than this should avoid the ego/alter terminology, which conveys precisely that *every* person is always *both* when (and only when) he engages in communication. But why, to be more exact, do we have this doubling up? The answer is that the self-reference of social systems requires an immanent duality to allow a circle to form whose interruption can permit structures to develop. Inspired by the thermostat, which can only control because it allows itself to be controlled, Ranulph Glanville postulates this principle for objects per se.[249] We can leave this open. Social systems clearly need *self-constituted* twoness if they are to be structurally determined;[250] and this cannot be an essentially predetermined twoness (qua human being) imported from outside. For the problem at issue, the improbable acceptance of selections, this means that every selection has to take into account that it has to reckon with other (conforming or adverse) selections. Otherwise, a specifically *social* solution to the problem cannot be reached.

It must also be established where responsibility lies for the selection whose conditioning is to motivate. This means that selection has to be *attributed*. Attributions never involve the inner activity (the autopoiesis) of systems, but only their behavior as seen by an observer and relating to the environment.[251] They are always artificial activity, which, although it finds suggestive conditions in real qualities, is never fully determined by them. The process of attribution itself is hence socially conditioned, and the attribution of attribution is one of those endless questions that are not admitted but hidden and made invisible by "reasons."[252]

The complicated structure of preconditions for symbolically generalized communication media alone shows that they must be a late development, and that theoretical reconstruction cannot feed into the media semantics themselves. They require immediately convincing symbolization, whereas we are seeking to observe what *cannot* be observed with the semantics of the media.

Differentiation of the media follows from binarization based on the two possibilities of attribution: internal and external.[253] Since communication can observe itself only if a distinction is drawn between information and utterance, the accent of attribution can be placed either on information (experience) or on utterance (action); and this is true for both sides: for those who initiate a communication and for those who have to decide on (the communication of) its acceptance or rejection. If a selection (by whomsoever) is attributed to the system itself, I speak of *action*,[254] if it is attributed to the environment, of *experience*. Symbolically generalized communication media are then categorized according to whether they assume the two social positions ego and alter to be experiencing or acting. The two distinctions present no everyday knowledge. It is not a matter of completely classifying phenomena. Attribution is tied to experience or action and participation marked as ego or alter (with reference to persons who are always both) only when needed. It takes place only in contexts of use, that is, only when necessary for the autopoiesis of the communication system. Bringing communication problems to a point in constellations that come into question for media formation thus activates distinctions of attribution as experience or action and of marking as ego or alter that would otherwise not occur and could also not be explained by the "nature of things."

The resulting constellation can be compiled in the form of a table.

Ego / Alter	Experience	Action
Experience	Ae → Ee Truth Values	Ae → Ea Love
Action	Aa → Ee Property/Money Art	Aa → Ea Power/Law

With the aid of attributions, the communication process can be captured and the problem of double contingency asymmetricized and thus *de-tautologized*. Communication runs from alter to ego.[255] Alter must first utter something, only then can ego understand and accept or reject. This basal unity is abstracted out, although double contingency is always constructed as a circle,[256] and communication as the unity of information, utterance, and understanding is generated in recursive interconnection with other communications.

Only where attributions place causality is conditioning possible. In this respect, the attribution scheme directs (not determines!) the conditioning of selection and, through selection, the motivation that can be expected. It therefore makes a difference whether alter and ego are conditioned as acting or experiencing (both are naturally always both). As the table shows, we must therefore in principle take four constellations into account: (1) alter sets off corresponding experience in ego through communication of his experience; (2) alter's experience leads to corresponding action by ego; (3) alter's action is only experienced by ego; and (4) alter's action occasions corresponding action by ego. By "correspondence," I do not mean similarity, let alone repetition, but only complementarity. For a communication is successful if its meaning is taken over as the premise of further behavior, and in this sense communication is continued by other communications.

The attribution-theoretical basis of this typology already implies that it is not a matter of classifying all situations that occur in reality. In fact, attribution questions rarely arise and only in recursive contexts in which other decisions depend on them.[257] In the special situation in which an improbable operational coupling of selection and motivation has to be made, this is a precondition for relevance. But it is always a question of specific problems for which conditioning of selection is important for motivational purposes, and *it then depends on these problems what attribution constellations are activated in each case.*

In the long term, the most important consequences of this specification of attribution constellations are likely to lie in the *dissolution of old multifunctionalities*. Older societies ground the authority to attain unusual aims in role accumulation, in access to other roles. A person is respected, has many friends or such as aspire to be friends, can help with resources or contacts or refuse to do so. Social statuses of this sort are broken up and other roles decoupled when achieving unusual aims depends on the conditioning of selections and in particular on whether alter and ego are conditioned with respect to experience or to action. For the appropriation of other roles is then felt to be out of place, and eventually explicitly discredited as corruption.

The differentiation of symbolically generalized communication media thus requires a *reference problem* and an *attribution constellation.*[258] Among other things, this explains the historicality of the context in which symbolically generalized communication media develop, and its dependence on society. At the same time, it shows that no media can develop if reference problems and attribution constellations do not converge—for whatever reason. We presume that this has hindered the development of a religious communication medium—despite all the extravagant demands made of specifically religious communication and in spite of all differentiation (e.g., through asceticism and "rejection of the world").[259]

In anticipation, I have already named and classified the symbolically generalized communication media identifiable in the above table (p. 201). I now present them in order. Comprehensive treatment with the necessary substantive and historical details is beyond the scope of a theory of society and must be left to specialized monographs.[260]

A medium for *truth* does not only form because every communication presupposes knowledge, utters knowledge, generates knowledge. We can communicate about news when it matches types already known. In such event, problems arise at best of truthfulness, of error, and of interest in deception. The special semantic apparatus of a truth medium has to be developed and deployed only if new, unheard-of knowledge is to be asserted; or if we wish to deviate from or criticize extant knowledge. We then shift to a level of second-order observation and sort observers' knowledge into true and untrue. Statements must then be modalized by reference to the medium—for example, we say it is true, can be proved, and so on, that asbestos is harmful to health. The question of what the case is must then be supplemented (not replaced!) by a statement on how we can reliably establish what the case is. Reference to the medium points to possibilities of respecification through methods and theories. If we no longer expect doubts, we can again use the short form of statement (asbestos is harmful to health), but we can nevertheless return at any time to the level of second-order observation. Where a truth medium has been differentiated, it is available for all statements and it is only a question of specific occasion whether it is used or not. Truth (like every symbolically generalized medium) is a medium that constructs a world and not a means limited to certain purposes alone.

We speak of truth only when the selection of information is attributed to none of the participants. Truth presupposes external selection (and it should be noted that all autopoietic systems that are operationally involved nevertheless function as operationally closed systems). Reduction to external selection shows that the medium of truth tolerates no differing opinions.[261] The truth content of a statement can therefore not be derived from the will or interest of one of the participants, for this would mean that it is not binding for others. The return to the level of second-order observation is also determined by waiving the actional deforming of matters (which naturally does not exclude thematizing actions as the object of experience any more than it does action specialized in research). The immense apparatus of theoretical generalizations and methodological rules is intended to neutralize the influence of action on the result of investigations; for only then can results be presented as truth. In other words, if we allowed surprising, unaccustomed, puzzling knowledge to be introduced by action and made subject to compulsory acceptance, arbitrariness would have free rein. In this case, we would have to do without medium-specific conditioning. Surprising as it may seem at first, reduction to experience therefore considerably *limits* permitted possibilities and *in this manner* provides the point of departure for wide-ranging conditioning.

In the case of values, it is doubtful in the first place whether a symbolically generalized communication medium exists,[262] or even if such a medium can be seen to be developing; suitable terminology dates back only two hundred years or so.[263] The problem referred to is clear: the operational closure of psychic systems. In this respect, the experience of double contingency in social encounters makes it extremely unlikely that a common basis can be found and contacts continued. Nor can this be achieved through negotiation, as some now believe, but only through recursive consolidation of corresponding assumptions in the communication process itself. The same problem occurs where the medium separates off a value semantics of its own from assumed common values. There must, one feels, be "inviolate levels,"[264] beyond all contingencies, which shift when contingencies are discovered here, too. This implies that values cannot be conceived of as independent of action, but, vice verse, actions must be conceived of as dependent on values. Among attribution constellations, only reference to experience is therefore to be considered. The pragmatic context of value theory, one might say, leads us astray. Also harmless is the assertion that values have normative meaning; that they are not mere preferences but prescribed preferences. There can be no question of values being in a position to select actions. They are far too abstract and, from the standpoint of action situations, always take the form of a conflict of values.[265] Their function is only to provide orientation that no one calls into question for action in communicative situations. Values are therefore nothing other than a highly mobile set of viewpoints. They do not, as ideas once did, resemble fixed stars, but rather balloons kept on hand to be inflated when called for, especially on festive occasions. We therefore cannot speak of "unconditional preferences."[266] Although they do not explain the conditions of application, they are subject to deliberation, so that how they can be realized has to be determined from case to case.

Not everything that is needed in the way of congruence to keep communication going can be provided through the medium of truth. But the difference between truths and values was clarified only in the course of the nineteenth century. Only then was a semantics of validity universalized,[267] parallel to that of being, and one of the reasons is likely to have been the differentiation of science. The forms for the respecification of science are to be found in theories and methods. There is no use for them in the field of values. This respecification takes place through ideologies and argumentation;[268] in contrast to theories and methods, ideology commits the big crimes and argumentation engages in the petty stratagems. This imposes differentiation of the media and at the same time excludes taking truth itself as a yardstick in the field of values (ideologies, arguments). For this would have to mean placing the value of all values in their truth.

Unlike truths, values are introduced into the communication process not by assertions, which can then be questioned and tested, but by supposition. Communication avoids "marking" values,[269] because this would convey the possibility of contradiction. No one asserts that health, peace, or justice are values in order to generate the yes/no bifurcation of acceptance or rejection. One does not provoke, one suggests.[270] If health is a value, we may still consider washing regularly to be harmful and discuss the question. In other words, values are actualized by allusion and their indisputability consists in this. If this no longer works, they have to be abandoned. Values therefore convince because objections are lacking in communication, not because we can justify them. They make it possible to waive justification. Where necessary, they rely on "gag rules," that is, on tacit agreement that certain conflicts of values are not spoken about and the corresponding values are used only in separate contexts.[271] Values are the medium for assuming common ground, which limits what can be said and demanded without determining what should be done.

As always with symbolically generalized communication media, what matters is social not psychic ordering. Values are socially stable because they are psychically unstable.[272] However, they lack important qualities that characterize other media, for example, a central coding (such as true/untrue) and, associated with this, the ability to form media-specific functional systems (such as science). Their directive value is low because no value can determine an act or even, as we might say with Pascal, excuse an act.[273] All this shows that indications of value demonstrate that even an important reference problem in combination with an appropriate attribution constellation does not suffice to generate a fully functioning communication medium.

While values bind too weakly, *love* binds too strongly. In our modern understanding, which differs markedly from the *philia/amicitia* tradition,[274] love requires a loving ego to adapt action to what alter experiences; and, above all, of course, to how alter experiences ego.

To adapt our own action to what others experience is a matter of course, especially when we know we are being observed. The schooled eye anticipates the expectations of others. We do not wait until they manifest themselves in action, we anticipate them. This makes fast coordination possible, skipping communication, as it were, for example, when working with others or in road traffic. Lovers, too, can be recognized where such communicationless coordination also works in nonstandardized situations. A brief glance suffices.

This may be based on familiarity. The specific reference problem of love goes far beyond this. It postulates that one can find agreement and support for a *personal* worldview over and beyond the anonymous world of truths and values. The problem becomes acute with the growing individualization of personal views and motives for action, and this becomes not only a psychic matter (which it always is) but also a social one. One is then expected to take account of all possible idiosyncrasies in communication and thus to accept them in experience, too. Furthermore, love demands visible commitment through his/her own action from at least one other (ego). In this case, it is not the specific but the special, the particular that is vested with universal relevance. This can happen only in the form of a couple relationship. In its form and the substance of its expectations, this is a highly improbable structure,[275] and for this very reason it requires a strong, extravagant medium. It was introduced into culture under the heading "passion" and is nowadays called "romantic."[276]

Appropriate semantics was developed, first for the nobility, then for the upper middle classes.[277] However, as love became a requirement of marriage, this semantics had to be made accessible to all, in other words, trivialized. This has ended with mass-produced illusions more or less at variance with people's experience of life.[278] The improbability of love—that every gesture, bodily and verbal, has to serve to observe, even to observe the observation of love—becomes pathological in marriage. This brings to light the improbability of this solution to the problem of making personal idiosyncrasies acceptable. In present-day parlance, one might say that it is a matter of concerning oneself with the otherness of the other and, if not "enjoying" it, at least confirming it with no intention of adaptation, reeducation, improvement. But even if this succeeds, it would merely shift the problem to another question: how we are to deal with someone who is dissatisfied with himself, is unhappy and seeks confirmation of this. From this point of view, it is certainly no accident that paradox has become a key problem of therapy, because in trying to solve this problem, love fails.

This clarifies the differentiation of the medium. It has nothing to do with truth,[279] and certainly nothing to do with money. Whatever the real motives might be, if they deviate, they cannot be named; otherwise, it is simply not love. This very differentiation makes love a universal medium, a medium for constructing a world seen through the unique eyes of the other.

Love, because asymmetrically constructed, is one-sided love and therefore often (should we say normally?) unhappy love. But everyone knows the semantics in its more concrete demands, and everyone knows the word. To this extent, declarations of love are binding on communication. And since the sincerity/insincerity of such declarations is incommunicable anyway, a modus vivendi can establish itself—albeit depending on the consensus not being tested too insistently.[280]

The opposite case, that the action of alter is experienced by ego, is to begin with trivial and unproblematic. We see that the neighbor is mowing his lawn. So what? Although, in contrast to the media discussed so far, it is not the world of the other that is involved but the arbitrariness of the other. But why should we not be able to observe and accept that others act as they do? It would be unfortunate if every act we witnessed were to cause us consternation. We would have to close our eyes.

However, this changes immediately where action consists in appropriating scarce goods that the bystander might be interested in himself. And this problem intensifies to the extent that both take a long-term interest in their future and, in the face of scarcity, wish to secure now what could be possibly be needed later. If one or more take their share, the bystanders are always in the majority. If they have the upper hand, why should they hold back? Whether they can later reach agreement among themselves is a problem for later.[281]

For this reference problem, societal evolution has created the medium of property, which it later transformed into the medium of money to make it more available and easier to coordinate. Even property is therefore a communication medium and cannot be adequately understood if seen only as a means to satisfy the needs of the owner.[282] The medium of money then ensures acceptance of others' acquiring what they wish with their money, or simply making money with money without knowing why. Anti-monetary emotions from Luther to Marx, and their social success, teach us how improbable any expectation of such acceptance is. But it works nevertheless.

Money probably developed not for its function in mediated exchange, but as a sign for performance imbalances, to begin with, probably in household economies. Public debt was already the primary tool for money creation in the eighteenth century, and "bank" notes were initially designed as (transferable) promissory notes. But then one increasingly had to know who the debtor was, and whether his solvency was to be trusted. Only in very recent times has this restriction been abandoned. The debtor, if we can still use this term at all, is the economy itself, which owes itself the money it has circulating. Solvency can no longer be ensured other than in the form of a guarantee of the usability of money, hence in the form of the autopoiesis of the economic system. The function of the symbolically generalized communication medium money is so improbable that it could never have served as an enabling factor in evolution, but became manifest only in an already functioning money economy.

Whereas property could still be uninteresting—why do I need an orchard with twenty apple trees?—the medium of money universalizes both scarcity and interest. That one can always use more money was known as early as Aristotle. It was only the monetarization of property, which puts a monetary value on all property, even one's own labor, that enables the scarcity medium property/money to expand into the form to which we are accustomed today. Money serves as a medium for observing scarcity, and payments are forms that operationalize the medium.[283] In this sense, much more is scarce in today's "affluent society" than in the past,[284] and money has assumed the form of a world construction, is a "God-term," as Kenneth Burke puts it.[285]

In contrast to the usual economics perspective, we accordingly do not see the social function of property in the immediacy of access to material goods or services, or the social function of money in the mediation of transactions. There is naturally no disputing this as factual situation and historical genetic motive. But the function of the corresponding generalized symbolic medium lies elsewhere, as always in overcoming an improbability threshold. *Everyone* must be motivated to *accept the experience of extremely specific selections* by someone or other—from furnishing the living room and buying a certain screw to an international company being taken over by another. Otherwise, the economy would not have been able to function in the past and would certainly be unable to satisfy today's demands.[286]

Whereas property as a medium is still tied to the natural divisibility of things and can therefore not be very widely dispersed, the medial substratum of money is the given smallest monetary unit, which can, moreover, be determined arbitrarily as required. This permits standardization that abstracts from individual preferences. Thus the functioning of the medium is based on a difference between social and psychic valuation: precisely because the social valuation of money is quantitatively standardized and fluctuates in accordance with its own conditions, money can individually be variously valued, which means it can relate to variously felt requirements. The medium can thereupon be coupled to specific forms according to the prices that are to be paid in transactions. It should be noted that transactions are monetarily calculated *by both sides* when it comes to the exchange of goods for money. This is shown by the universality of the medium and its clear specification. Finally, it should be noted that the form in which a transaction is set is dissolved immediately afterward; for once in the hands of the recipient, the money is free for other combinations at will.[287] No other medium attains this extension and this speed of dissolution and recombination, of loose and strict coupling.[288] And it is hence understandable that money is often seen (notably by Parsons) as a model for an effective symbolically generalized medium.

For the constellation in which alter acts and ego correspondingly experiences, there is another medium that, perhaps because of this closeness to the attribution form of money, places great value on not appearing to be "useful," namely, art. The constellation is clear: the artist acts, bringing the viewer a certain experience. But what is the problem?

The old European answer was that the purpose of the work of art was to arouse astonishment and admiration, and to do so in the sense of passions that allow of no reference to their opposite. However, this presupposes that society is established in a world in which there are astonishing and admirable things, especially in the fields of religion and politics. In the Middle Ages, there was accordingly a special sort of truth provided for *res artificiales* (in relation to forms in the imagination of the producer/artist), but not a special medium.[289] Since the seventeenth century, this solution has been criticized, without the aesthetic reflection that then transpired being able to offer a convincing alternative.[290] A figure immanent in aesthetics, for instance, the representation of the general in the particular, cannot yet tell us why art is differentiated for communication, and in this case for the generation of improbable willingness to accept. And it is a fortiori insufficient to follow the thesis current in the art world itself, and above all in literature, that "modern" art has to do in a specific manner with the individual in modern society.[291]

It perhaps helps to take a far more radical approach, going back to the circumstance that every experienced meaning offers an abundance of possibilities for further experience, only a few of which are or can be realized. What we perceive is already the way it is and not otherwise. What we do is directed by purposes, and why not by others, or even by none? What art aspires to could therefore be described as the *reactivation of eliminated possibilities*.[292] Its function is to allow the world to appear in the world, to portray unity in unity, be it improved or (as now preferred) worsened. Although this happens through every thing, every captured meaning, it happens only in such a way that the one points to the other and the world remains invisible to itself. The work of art lays claim to this illuminating and concealing function of meaning, but heightens it so that the invisible also becomes visible and, if it succeeds, that the world is portrayed in the world. For this very reason, the normal references of daily life, the purposes and utilities have to be breached to distract attention from these distractions. The portrayal of the world in the world modifies the world itself in the sense of what is "not necessary as such." The work of art supplies its own proof of necessity—and thus withholds it from the world.

This requires such strict forms that we see more and differently than usual. Art points out that the scope of the possible is not exhausted and it therefore generates a liberating distance from reality. We might call this "fictionality," but the term does not convey enough. Art does not remain fiction: it generates a reality with a right to its own objectivity. Once again, it is a matter of constructing a world, of a specific universalism that confronts total reality.

In contrast to other symbolically generalized communication media, art uses perceptual media or, in the case of narrative literature, visualization. But in these perceptual media, it generates its own forms through its own dissolution techniques, or more precisely, its own forms of distinguishing between medial substratum and form.[293] As a result, widely differing types of art develop: music, painting, lyric poetry, dance, sculpture, architecture, and so on. But they are all based on a common principle, namely, the incorporation of media in media, and the consequent new possibilities for strict coupling, new possibilities of form. Whether art can motivate people to accept the selections it offers then depends on the individual work of art, making it plausible that it itself (as opposed to the world) has to be the way it is, even though it is made and no model for it exists anywhere. In this sense "originality" has been demanded of a work of art since the seventeenth century; originality now being decided not in comparison with nature, not in the quality of imitation, but in comparison with other works of art.[294] In the form of a demand made of the individual work, art is differentiated as autonomous and self-referential. And in the form of a demand made of the individual work, because this is the only way to unfold the paradox of the necessity of the only possible.

To ask about the truth of the work of art is therefore just as inappropriate as asking about its use. Both questions would direct attention to conditioning completely alien to art. The work of art imitates nothing, accomplishes nothing, proves nothing. It demonstrates that and how the arbitrariness of beginning captures and cancels itself, makes itself necessary. However one begins, with production or examination—once one begins, what follows is no longer unrestricted. It becomes *necessità cercata* [willing necessity].[295] For this very reason, a work of art has to be conceived as the self-conditioning of the arbitrary, as action whose communication binds experience.

Art must, of course, pay for rendering transparent with intransparencies of its own. Its function, too, unfolds a paradox. It makes something visible by making something else invisible—something else, which is to say, the unity of the distinctions that it uses itself as form. As art articulates what it articulates, distinguishing something from something else in the process, brightness from darkness, fates from trivialities, dissonance from consonance, the world withdraws behind what has been distinguished into the unity of the difference—and remains invisible. Art, too, can only observe, can only injure the world through its own cuts.

The last attribution constellation, that of the medium *power* is also at first trivial, but it, too, holds the seed for unfolding improbable possibilities, which can, however, be realized only if a symbolically generalized communication medium is available. First of all, it is quite normal that actions follow on from actions, for example, when we hand over an object, work or play together, eat what is served, or act in traffic in accordance with how others are driving. It often helps to recognize the immediately subsequent acts of others, and rhythmic coordination typically develops. We extrapolate ongoing movement and place our own act at the suitable moment. This is how the famous "turn-taking" in oral communication is organized. We might occasionally exceed the demand threshold, but then ad hoc positive or negative adjustments are always possible. The reference problem of power arises only in the special case where *the action of alter consists in a decision about the action of ego that is required to be obeyed*: in an order, an instruction, perhaps in a suggestion backed by the threat of sanctions.[296] This does not alter the fact that action on both sides is attributable; the instruction should not be only experienced or replace the action of the recipient. It should, although obviously a contingent selection, be adopted as premise for one's own conduct; and on the additional condition that arbitrariness lies not in alter's decision but specifically in the determination of ego's action.

Power generates itself as a medium by doubling the possibilities of action. The course of action desired by alter is confronted by another, namely, the imposition of sanctions, which neither alter nor ego can want, but that is less disadvantageous for alter than for ego. But the form of power is nothing other than this difference, the difference between carrying out instructions and the alternative to be avoided. If the sanctions are sufficiently generalized (e.g., the use of physical force or dismissal from employment), the medium consists in a relationship of loose coupling between a multiplicity of power goals and sanctions, and the use of power then determines the form in which the medium is temporarily strictly coupled. The limits of power therefore lie where ego begins to prefer the avoidance alternative and itself asserts power to force alter to renounce or to impose sanctions. Once again, we see, on the one hand, a loose coupling of elements that as threats are not consumed in use but renewed, and, on the other, tight temporary coupling; that is, forms of combining (explicit or guessed) instructions and compliance with them. What is improbable in such an arrangement is that it normally works, even though the parties have completely different interests and although the action of instructing occurs as a decision, hence as contingent; although it pursues no other goal than to specify ego's action, and finally even without the exercise of power requiring investigation in the individual case as to whether, in the light of the type of instruction, compliance can be expected or not.

Both truth and money neutralize dangerous, conflictual power communication by demanding only experience of ego,[297] and social utopias therefore favor the notion that society can be steered only by truths or only by the market. However, this would mean waiving important possibilities of ordering, namely, everything that can be organized through conditioned arbitrariness in the way of long chains of action. For neither truth nor money can determine what the recipient does with what is received—and precisely this is the function of power.

As in the case of property/money, a secondary coding has proved its worth, namely, the *legal coding of power*. The central institutions of politically organized coercive power have to be made available to private parties where they are in the right, even if (note the improbability of this construction!) the legal content has not been politically monitored at all but has come about in contract form. What is more, political power itself can be subject to the law, so that it can assert its own means of coercion only if it is in the right, and can amend the law itself only if this takes place under conditions that are provided for in the legal system. The prevailing term for these achievements is the "rule of law," the *Rechtsstaat*. Only through this self-referential juridification of power does the political medium of power become a self-inclusive medium of world construction—quite independently of the liberal ideology that had initially launched the concept as a condition of freedom, earning snide comments in the process.

Although there are highly generalized means of power (threats) that can be used for many purposes, clear limits to their application are apparent. Perhaps the most important is the dependence of the power holder on information. Even if he can do what he wants, it is far from certain what he can want to want. All political systems that set out to control the economy politically through production plans and price fixing face the problem, for example, that they can obtain no information on economic efficiency independent of their own decisions, and therefore develop into a vast network of internal manipulations whose economic failures become political problems. In other words, power—at the political level but also at the organizational level—has to rely on differentiations and on information sources independent of power, because all information would otherwise change into power.[298] It is not sufficient for power to be informed only self-referentially, only on the basis of the schema success/failure of its own plans or that of compliance/noncompliance with its instructions. The medium of power therefore has *immanent* reasons for not setting itself up as a universal medium for controlling society, but for insisting on specification of its own *universal competence*.

All symbolically generalized communication media accordingly arise from trivial, everyday situations, initially performing only relatively undemanding special services ad hoc, and are thus not yet really media. This starting position is particularly important for evolution-theoretical considerations. It integrates media theory with evolution theory. For it explains that the possibilities for a more improbable combination of selection and motivation lie fallow, as it were, in the general redundancy of meaningful communication, but can be used as soon as the need arises, as soon as the reference problems mentioned become acute, as soon as, for whatever reason, one discovers the combinatorial possibilities that can be realized with medium-specific dissolution and form-building. In my view—at this juncture no more than a subject for future research—such a development and differentiation of symbolically generalized communication media require both the dissemination media to have achieved the development status of writing and printing and the prevailing form of system differentiation to set them off. Symbolically generalized communication media develop to the full only where the system of society is functionally differentiated; for only then can the media serve as catalysts for the differentiation of the functional systems of society. Only then does what is condensed as semantics in the use of media occupy the place that had previously been taken by morality for the description of society. And only then do we find moral critique of this very state of affairs.

11. Symbolically Generalized Communication Media, 3: Structures

For modern society, for a society with fully developed symbolically generalized media, there is no super-medium that could relate all communication to an underlying unity. Morality (some say ethics) might come to mind. But any attempt to cure all the moral weaknesses of society with ethics (thus with reflection on morality) borders on the ridiculous. At any rate, proof of suitability has yet to be established and, what is more, we do not typically think about morally coded behavior, that is, good and bad, but only about good conduct, which is naturally welcome but unfortunately does not come alone.

As far as communication media are concerned, the unity of society manifests itself, not in morality, not in concrete morals, but in the non-arbitrariness of the structural arrangements that translate the function of symbolically generalized communication media into possibilities for autopoietic systems. From a methodological point of view, this means that we find viewpoints for comparing the various media and with the aid of these viewpoints have to test the forms in which modern society realizes itself as a communication enterprise. We do not assume that, owing to logical or theoretical constraints, all characteristics have to be realized equally in all media. The theory remains open for evolutionary distinctions. But for this very reason, it offers a framework for inquiry if one notes that (and asks why) certain media have not realized certain structural characteristics or have done so less successfully. We have already seen that only extravagant cases of extremely improbable communication can be involved. But at the given level of evolution, society as a whole depends on the problems of transforming improbabilities into probabilities being solved in one way or another. The following points may be made here:

(1) Symbolically generalized communication media require a *uniform code* (central code) for the entire media field.[299] A code consists of two opposing values, and at this level (naturally not "in life") excludes third and further values. This converts the possibility—indefinite but tending to increase—of the communicated meaning proposal being rejected into a hard either/or, that is, transforms an "analog" situation into a "digital" one; what is gained is a clear choice to be made, the same for both alter and ego. It is not their opinions that are coded but the communication itself; and this is done in a fashion that has to rely on learning ability, namely, on the specification of criteria for the correct attribution of positive and negative values (whereas the uncoded starting situation could bring only increasing disappointment, resentment, and conflict).

Unlike many other codings, this is a *preference code*. In contrast to the general yes/no code of language, the positive value is expressed as a preference for this value (and not for the opposing value). This expresses the fact that communication is *directed against probability*. The initial improbability of communication being accepted is not also communicated and therefore remains latent.

Like other distinctions, codes function as two-sided forms, which an observer can use or not use. They also have the character of a distinction, in that they can be indicated on only one side and not at the same time on the other, and only thus can they serve as connecting and starting point for a further operation. By equating what is distinguished, the observer would generate a paradox (namely, the paradox of the sameness of the different) and point out to himself that this cannot be. The particularity of codes as compared with other distinctions is that the transition from one side to the other, the crossing of boundaries, *is facilitated*. If a positive value such as true is accepted, there is no difficulty in determining by another operation what is consequently untrue, namely, the opposing statement. In other words, we need no additional conditioning to move from the value to the opposing value and back. Logic can consequently treat this to-and-fro as not having taken place.[300]

What mainly facilitates crossing the inner boundary of the codes is that no moral consequences ensue. The result is not that one passes from good to bad, let alone that one becomes wicked.[301] However, learning this is a protracted evolutionary process. As long as society is still stratificationally differentiated, thus presupposing integration at the apex to which moral qualities are attributed, the moral neutralization of media codes cannot be achieved.[302] And the facility of crossing to the opposing value will be lacking, which imposes insistence on systemic control criteria.

In this facilitation of crossing from one side to the other, we see a variable of decisive importance for the semantic evolution of media codes. The facilitation of crossing from a value to an opposing value and back (without the base value changing in the meantime) makes the code itself an invariant structure. At the same time, gluing together positive values or negative values of different codes becomes more difficult (i.e., more contingent). Whether someone who is beautiful also tells the truth, whether someone who is rich is also powerful, also good, also healthy is a question that depends on further conditions that are not systemically guaranteed and that observers have to treat as an accident, which they cannot assume to be stable. To this extent, the evolution of media codes toward schematized crossing (I shall also be referring to this as "technicization" with regard to the context-independence of the operation) also explodes a premise important for all hierarchically stratified societies, namely, the assumption that all positive values come together at the apex (in the nobility, the ruler, God).

Facilitation of crossing to the other value makes the operation context-free, giving it too much leeway, which then has to be restricted. In the course of evolution, codings therefore develop a supplementary semantics of criteria determining the conditions under which positive and negative values are correctly attributed. I shall be calling this conditioning "programs."[303] They attach themselves as a vast semantic apparatus to the respective codes; and while codes achieve simplicity and invariance, their program area, in supplementation, so to speak, becomes charged with complexity and changeability. In this sense, the semantic "stocks" of law or science, for example, consist of programs.

Codes indicate the medium responsible for their functional areas and thus a limited but loose coupling of possibilities. They take part in every operation, which could otherwise not be attributed to the medium and possibly not to the relevant functional system. They can hence not be forgotten, whereas on the program level both remembering and forgetting are possible, depending on how often the programs are called up or, if not, deleted from memory. Only codes are necessarily regenerated. Only they define the unity of the medium and perhaps that of the functional system through a specific difference, whereas programs can change.

Fixing the preference or "dispreference" [*Dispräferenz*] that distinguishes the code can disregard psychic realities. However, it must proceed on the assumption, for example, in the case of the money code, that there is interest in utility, or in the case of love, that there is interest in self-realization. But as long as such motivational assumptions do not become improbable in communication, medium-oriented communication functions. Precisely because of this preference orientation, symbolically generalized media are suitable *guidance* media. They perform their guidance function by *fixing* preferences and by exposing them to *variable* conditioning. By varying conditioning, we can ascertain whether a communication makes a difference in relation to a specific preference or not, and can readjust if need be—show more commitment to demonstrate love, offer more arguments to prove a truth or more money to obtain a desired object, or vary the content of an instruction or threat to assert power in achieving our ends. Structurally decisive for all this is the *difference between fixed preference code and variable conditioning* (programs).

The more abstractly the code is formulated, the more weakly the preference is likely to be developed (consider, for example, the falsification principle in science, which admits as truth only what remains when enough has been falsified). But the positive value always symbolizes the *connectivity* of medium-specific operations, whereas the negative value symbolizes only the *contingency of conditions* for connectivity. With Gotthard Günther,[304] we can therefore also say that media preference codes consist in a designation value and a reflection value *to the exclusion of third possibilities*. Something can be done with truths, love, property, power. The corresponding negative values are available only for control purposes and provide the context through which the connection practice of the positive side can become rational selection (what would be the use of money if we had to pay at any price and could not not pay?).[305]

As with all codes, this is a duplication rule that doubles what is or happens in a positive and a negative version. However, that it is mere duplication cannot be taken into consideration, for the user of the code has to use it as a twoness and not as a unity.[306] This duplication (also a reflection that has to be deleted) provides the basis for developing a medial substratum with loosely coupled elements (e.g., sums of money that can be paid or not paid), which tolerates only certain forms of strict coupling (and not others); in the case of money, for example, transactions at certain prices. The unity of the code consists here, too, in its form: the other side is always connoted when the first is indicated; and this requires binarity, for even three-way constellations are confusing.

Binarity enables the opposing value to be included in the value, and the value to be included in the opposing value. The value is then both identity and difference, namely, itself and not the opposing value (as is also the case on the other side). This leads to a self-iterative, self-referential relation, and thus to a form that dissolves the difference between identity and difference in difference, in a certain distinction between positive and negative value that can be distinguished from other distinctions of the same sort, from other codes. This in turn differs radically from all attempts to reduce difference to unity, be it to a religious formula, be it "mind" [*Geist*] as a formula for what is differentiated in itself. As a result, the media (distinguished from one another) lead to a semantics that can no longer be controlled by religion.

Despite this formal symmetry of positive and negative values, there is an important (but difficult to discover) distinction from the general yes/no coding of language. It manifests itself in the first place as preference for the positive value. Important, but hidden by this, is a confusion of two levels that a logical thinker should keep separate. The positive value functions as a preference, and hence as a symbol for connectivity, *and at the same time, it functions as legitimation for the use of the code itself.* It symbolizes what is distinguished from the opposing value *and also legitimizes the distinction itself.* Preference codes—and this makes their strictly logical treatment difficult—frustrate a logically necessary differentiation of types.[307] But this is still too superficial a description. In radical terms, codes unfold a fundamental paradox, that of the unity of a distinction, by prescribing the form of a binary schematism, from which third values are excluded, in which the value and the opposing value can be identified and their simultaneous application to the same object is forbidden as contradictory.[308] But this presupposes that the unity of the distinction itself is not questioned, but its use legitimized, along with the preference value. In effect, the observer who uses the distinction remains unobservable to himself; he must only commit himself to the positive value. The underlying paradox is both unfolded (binarized, digitized) and concealed. But then it constitutes one of the main incentives for reflection theories such as become necessary when correspondingly differentiated functional systems have to show how they understand and solve their communication problems. And this becomes necessary in modern societies, which can no longer rely on macrosocietal givens (stratification, morality) but find themselves confronted in their functional systems by problems of self-legitimation, of autonomy, of applying the code to itself.[309]

The more strictly codes are formed, the more strongly they differ from normal evaluation in society. Consider the code of the medium property/money. What counts economically is only who is owner and who not. And since for every item of property everyone else is a nonowner, the code offers immense redundancy in possibilities for change. In the societal and political view of the economy, in contrast, the distinction between rich and poor—a quite different form—appears to be important; and the economy has been observed since the eighteenth century primarily with regard to a growing gap between rich and poor, which now (unlike in a stratified society) has lost its function. The Marxian critique of the political economy can therefore also be read as a critique of the outdifferentiated economy from a macrosocietal point of view.

The final stage of this differentiation, in which only few media are involved, is reached when a negation suffices to cross the boundary, to convert the value into the opposing value.[310] Within the code, crossing to the opposing value is facilitated—but subject to renouncing any implication for the values of other codes. The values of codes are not interconvertible. Monetary wealth cannot be converted into love, nor power into truth or vice versa.[311] I call facilitation of crossing from value to opposing value and back as *technicization* of the medium—in the sense of easing information processing in accepting and taking account of all the concrete meaning relations that are implicated.[312]

We might think of logic primarily as a form for scientific calculus. But this is a special case of technicity. Other methods attain a substantial level of technicization through a structure that I call secondary coding; the foremost cases are the secondary coding of property through money and the secondary coding of power through law. In both cases, the positive value is again duplicated, in that we can use property in money to pay or not to pay, and can exercise power lawfully or unlawfully—but not, of course, if we have no property at all or no power at all. Secondary coding goes along with abstraction. Since the monetarization of property, the economy has been interested only in the abstract difference between property and nonproperty in relation to specific things or rights. This difference keeps the economy running, because even the wealthiest person is a nonowner in relation to most things. The difference between rich and poor, where it does not serve to motivate work, is a problem left to politics to resolve. Instead, the "critique of political economy" addresses the monetary technology of "capitalism," which allows it to offset material and labor costs in operational accounts, disregarding the fact that the contributions made by material and labor to the production process differ in significant ways. It is important to keep an eye on these secondary codings as extensions of technicization, for while they cannot be understood as applications of logic they are nevertheless indispensable for the modern rationality and distinctness of the corresponding media codes.

Other media take pride in being *not technicizable*, and they see this not as a deficit but as a particular quality. This is the case with love and with art. It is not by chance that in these two cases, the general is stressed in the particular—in love in the special subject, in art in the special object.

From a historical point of view, this contrast intensified from the eighteenth century on in response to the development of technicized media. One of the consequences is that the counterstructurally formed media of love and art have to do without some of the characteristics of the other media, above all, the assured capacity to form systems.

With all these particularities, codes also realize the general properties of every form: drawing a boundary, the crossing of which is possible but requires time. Coded media are therefore always temporalized media. We must start from a value or from the opposing value, we must, for example know whether we own a thing or not; but then we can cross over with a further operation to the opposing value, can sell or buy to find ourselves in a later situation, which in turn offers time for further operations. The diversification of media therefore always generates a diversification of time, and hence eigentimes in the various media fields that do not have to be coordinated among themselves, even though everything that happens in fact happens at the same time.

(2) I treat another characteristic of preference codes separately, for they not only serve to compare symbolically generalized communication media among themselves but also provide insight into the effects of their differentiation. I mention the *self-placing* of the code in one of its values, which for the sake of this function is described as the positive value.

The unity of the code (as of every distinction) consists in a form that separates two sides. It can therefore, to be exact, not be represented on only one side. Preferences do this nonetheless and by doing so block the question of the unity of the code and the problem of applying coded operations to the code itself.[313] *Instead*, they postulate that the communication of a truth is a true communication. Whoever loves cannot and may not avoid declaring his love. To assert what is lawfully right is legitimate. Exchangeability (availability) is a quality of property, so that even giving property away is still covered by property. The same trick is played for opposing values: proof of an untruth is itself a true operation, and so on. The code, so to speak, gives itself permission to operate *without having to take recourse to higher values.*

Self-placement is not thematized; it remains latent. It eludes the risk of provoking a yes or a no as utterance. In this very sense, the positive and negative sides of the code are "values." Self-placement uses and intensifies the asymmetry of the code, the difference between positive and negative values.[314] A little cheating—and the code can assert its autonomy, can avoid looking back on its paradox and with all this can count on a high degree of plausibility. Where would it get us if we were to deny that we do not have the right to distinguish between right and wrong?

But we are not interested in this form because of its ingenuity. Its main achievement, from a symbolic point of view, is that it uncouples the code from strict dependence on social structural asymmetries. The differences between town and country, nobility and commons, patron and client, man and woman, parents and children cannot be preference-coded in this fashion. Although, in dependence on given societal structures, they assert asymmetry and the superiority of the one side, they have to rely directly on societal structures or, as seventeenth-century nobility theories would have put it, on imagination. We could hardly say that a communication by a gentlewoman to her coachman (and vice versa) is a noble communication. Instead of this simple self-placement, elaborate verbal forms, ceremonial, and so on, repeatedly reintroduce the difference of status into communication. It works; many examples demonstrate it. But this solution depends on concrete face-to-face interaction. It cannot be translated into writing, and printing relegates it fully to the periphery of societally important communication. The preference-coded communication media now prove to be clearly superior evolutionary advances, and it is understandable that after the introduction of printing, they contributed more and more to converting the differentiation form of society to preference-coded functional systems.

Not only symbolically generalized communication media but also morality developed a preference code. Communication that indicates that something is good or bad is a good communication. This is an important element in the engagement technique of morality, for the person who describes something as good or bad has difficulty, if the communication is good, in correcting himself. Since Aristotle, this problem has been resolved via a cognitive detour: one always wants what is good, but one may err. This, too, is an elegant solution, and we soon recognize that it lends independence from asymmetries in societal structures. Nobility and commons, townsfolk and peasants, rich and poor, men and women, however the expectations they have to meet might differ, are all subject to moral judgment.

This similarity between morality and symbolically generalized communication media explains a competitive situation that persisted until well into the eighteenth century or, if we take laggards seriously, has continued to this day. The differentiation of media that had begun in classical Greek urban culture was, at least in the Aristotelian texts, but also in the presuppositions of rhetoric, held together by an ethic of the urban way of life. Since it was a matter of societal criticism, critiques of the estates in the eighteenth century still primarily cite morality. Nevertheless, the functional differentiation of the societal system clearly uses the codes of the media, not the code of morality; and obviously does so because not unity but difference is concerned. In other words, the media have to rely on the *neutralization of moral propositions* because fusioning would otherwise occur and the onus of motivation would pass (in this regard rather unreliable) to morality.[315] If communication nonetheless takes place that opts morally for or against the values of the communication media, we learn nothing about these values but something about the moral convictions of the person communicating in this fashion. A not unpernicious syndrome appears to establish itself, in which society uses the codes of symbolically generalized communication media at a demanding level for its reproduction and activates morality for criticizing precisely this state of affairs (e.g., criticism of the orientation on money).[316]

(3) Through coding alone, symbolically generalized communication media are self-referentially structured and differentiated as closed operational contexts. This is to be distinguished from *processual reflexivity*, which is in evidence in all fully developed media. Normal communication is already reflexive, in that it can apply to itself and its own outcomes at any time.[317] In other words, it orients itself in the self-produced network of its own reproduction. In the domain of symbolically generalized communication media, special conditions apply that lend this possibility greater scope by limitation to single media. Processes in the communication field of a medium can also be applied to themselves; they can be their own object. In the medium of truth, there are research on research and true (or untrue) statements about the truth (or untruth) of statements. Value relations can themselves be evaluated, for example, from the point of view of their ideological function. From the ideal, we deduce who needs it.[318] That one loves love for the sake of love, loves oneself and one's lover as lovers (and even only as such!) is a well-known postulate of the love semantic. That we can procure money for money is just as current as the application of power to power, for example, in the form of political choice or the internal organizational phenomenon of the power of pressure exercised by subordinates.

The examples also show that such forms of reflexivity amount to indirectness. They therefore found little acceptance in the course of history, becoming fully established only in modern society. This is understandable when we consider that this reflexivity is not one case of application among others but the form in which the medium acquires distinctness and autonomy and asserts itself against the demands of family and class systems. We cannot engage in serious research without methods and theories at our disposition that are themselves the outcome of research. Real love requires loving to be loved, and so forth. The medium must first be applied to itself before it is ready for operational deployment. To put it in another way, media generate a self-substitutive order. Results in a media field can be changed only through operations of the same medium. We cannot invalidate truths against payment but only through research. To this extent, too, the medium is responsible for itself, for its own results.

Media can only be handled reflexively, that is, applied only to their own processes and results, if the necessary apparatus of distinctions and indications is available. Confusion with the objects of other media must be obviated. We must be able to love loving and not only to think loving. But if media are differentiated by their own coding, they generate the special semantics they require in the process.[319]

In such cases, the observer sees an unfolded paradox, and thus an ultimate undecidability. All power comes about by submitting to power, and supreme power comes about through submission to the lowest power. We call this democracy. The truth code itself, by reason of the fact that we are considering it, is the object of true or perhaps untrue statements. In order to generate goods in abundance, money must be kept scarce, whereas in reality the opposite is the case. Value relations demonstrate their untenability if we attempt to act in accordance with them only to realize that this cannot be done unless we violate other values. But the paradox on which media are based does not lead to their operations being blocked. On the contrary, it is the condition for creative unfolding, for media-specific distinctions, or for temporal sequencing that transfers what cannot be at the same time into a succession. First a law applies, then no longer; and no one objects that what is right is wrong and what is wrong is right. It is only a matter of lost opportunities.

(4) One of the most important resolutions of paradox lies in the differentiation of first- and second-order observation.[320] One of the most notable characteristics of symbolically generalized media is that they make such a differentiation possible. One researcher observes what other researchers

observe. Whoever loves has a prime interest in finding out whether his/her lover (still) loves. Prices offer the possibility of observing how others observe the market and whether they buy or do not buy at a certain price.[321] Modern art can be understood only if we recognize how artists use their means, that is, how they observe what they do.[322] And power relations are fully dependent on the mutual observation of observations; otherwise, one would have to threaten or provoke threats in order to find out which communications are covered by power. What is at issue in all these cases is not that participants in media-mediated communications are observed like objects with regard to their own characteristics in order to foresee how they will act. Interest focuses only on observing what they observe; and in many instances, this includes observing what they do not observe.

As soon as there is second-order observation, all observation in the given media field relates to this level. The first-order observer, too, knows that he is observed by a second-order observer (who may be himself).[323] For the truth medium, this requirement is subsumed under the heading "empirical knowledge." All conditioning of the medium must therefore come to bear at the second-order level. This unblocks first-order observation and gears it to surprise, with immense consequences.

Under all these conditions of self-referential circularity, the medium remains a distinctive unity determined by coding. Elementary operation, structure formation, structural change, crossing in the code and change of level are carried out in the same medium.[324] In this sense, media lay claim to universal competence for all communications that fall within their field of application. They do so in the sense of "provided that" abstractions: where problems and attribution constellations of the truth medium are concerned, this medium alone is competent. Put in terms of Talcott Parsons's pattern variables,[325] the media therefore combine "universalism" and "specificity," and Parsons rightly considers this a typically modern constellation, which older societies could not attain.[326] Universalism is concerned with worldwide application, not limited by external circumstances; specificity is concerned with the distinction (in this instance, the code) underlying observation.

(5) Media codes are open to all information and utterances that fall within their particular domain. They rely on and are geared to random stimulus. Moreover, they must be able to guarantee that both values in the system are usable, both right and wrong, and that in the process of specifying acceptance demands, there is repeated crossing between code values. The un-

truth of certain statements is thus among the most important arguments in the search for truth; their rejection alone cannot fulfill the function of the medium. This also means that a positive value cannot in itself have the function of a criterion (in the classical sense of *kritērion, kanōn, regula*) that guides the selection of this same value. It will generally be acknowledged today that truth is therefore not a criterion of truth.[327] But having property is also no sufficient reason for economic activity. More typical today is for whoever seeks to keep his property to lose assets and whoever wishes to keep or increase his assets to have continually to change his plans in property matters. The medium is considered a transaction medium, property is not a blanket term for various types of goods. Nor is power superiority itself, or the mere lawfulness of exercising power, a criterion for the use of power. In analogy to money, Parsons speaks of the need to "spend" power, and the reason for doing so cannot lie only in the positive value of the code.

There must accordingly be further conditions that determine the circumstances under which assignment of the positive value is right or wrong and the circumstances under which assignment of the negative value is right or wrong. I shall call such conditions *programs* and correspondingly distinguish between coding and programming for all symbolically generalized communication media. This distinction solves many problems that would be insoluble from a more simple teleological, goal-directed, value-pragmatic perspective. It is also the condition for media to generate complexity.

It is easy to see that it is a distinction of distinctions, thus a form for forms. Coding ensures the differentiation and specification of a medium in distinction to others, and programming can therefore only be code-specific. For the truth medium, for example, programs take the form of theories and methods; for legally coded power, the form of laws, court rulings establishing precedents, and contracts; the medium of money is respecified in the form of investment programs and consumption programs, monitored by means of balance sheets and budgets. For the medium love, memories of a common history appear to assume the function of limiting possibilities. All this requires further research. What is important to note at this point is only that such programs have to be assigned to one and only one code and cannot shift from medium to medium. A theory is not yet a law, and whoever invests in a love affair does not act entrepreneurially.

Coding and programming, as we have seen, also differ from the point of view of invariance and variability. We cannot change a code. Any attempt to do so would only mean that we are basing communication on another symbolically generalized medium, or on none at all. At the program level, in contrast, variability can be organized. The examples mentioned above will have sufficiently demonstrated this.

Finally, it should be noted that all the values that are excluded by the binarity of the code at this level can be reintroduced as aspects of program selection. A work of art must satisfy its own code as coherent/incoherent or, in traditional terms, as beautiful/ugly. But in choosing the subject, one can "politicize" or keep an eye on marketing potential.

(6) Symbolically generalized media, like all communication, operate in structural coupling with the consciousness of the psychic systems that participate in communication. This structural coupling also involves the living bodies of participants. In interaction systems, for example, they must be physically present in order to contribute to communication.[328] Communication therefore continually refers to persons and presupposes that this reference is covered by the reality of highly complex but opaque autopoietic systems. Since this also applies vice versa for psychic systems, we can, to borrow a term from Parsons's theory of the general action system, speak of interpenetration.

We can call the need to take account of corporeality in communication *symbiosis*, and the corresponding means of expression, *symbiotic symbols*. Symbiotic symbols organize how communication allows itself to be irritated by corporeality; hence, how the effects of structural coupling are processed in the communication system without this breaching the closure of the system and requiring a noncommunicative mode of operation. Differentiation of symbolically generalized media suggests corresponding differentiation of the symbiotic symbols used in the media field; for reference to corporeality is required in the given highly specified sense, whereas the physical involvement of people can be disregarded.[329]

As far as truth is concerned, the symbiotic symbol refers to *perception* that is physically possible, or, more precisely, to the possibility of perceiving perceptions. This is, of course, no ultimate decision-making authority, as was assumed by older empiricist theories; for even if it is established that perception has taken place, there can always be controversy over what was perceived.[330] Nor does what research achieves correlate with the set and unambiguity of scientifically established perceptions.[331] But the perception of the perception of others is a source of irritation and cannot simply be ignored.

In the field of the love medium, we find an exact analogy in the symbiotic use of sexual references. In the case of love, as in the case of truth, we find symbiotic symbols not securing communication on a deeper motivational basis but acting as a source of irritation that has to be built into the semantics. In perception as in sexuality, the modern differentiation of these media therefore enhances the value of their symbiotic symbols.[332] They are no longer assigned in the context of a hierarchical world architecture to the "lower" (because shared with animals) domain of sensuality, but included in the conditioning of the media. For sexuality, the lead distinction is then: with or without love. In the first case, this can end up in marriage; in the second, in a counterculture of obscenity.[333]

As far as symbiosis is concerned, property and money relate to *needs*. Even in earlier times, it was recognized that no property system can simply ignore the acute physical needs of others. Life at the subsistence level gave certain rights, and where necessity demanded, there was the doctrine that theft in need [*Notdiebstahl*] should not be punished.[334] The transition to the money economy changed this line of reasoning; it was now assumed, first, that everyone could satisfy his needs by working for wages if he chose, and, second, that a generalized concept of need had been established covering everything that could be produced for whatever purpose. Symbiosis with people dying of hunger is not taken into account in the conditioning of the economy medium and thus becomes a political problem.

In the case of power, the symbiotic symbol is *physical force*. In every society, there are many other sources of power, for example, the regular advantages that one can threaten to withdraw, but there is nothing that can be done against superior physical force. The political system, which power uses as a medium, must therefore concentrate decision-making on the deployment of physical force; today, this is done with the aid of law. With Parsons, one may regard control over physical force to be the basis of security (real assets) for the power medium.[335] At the same time, however, it is a source of irritation, for whoever wishes to use physical force as a symbiotic symbol and not as a personal form of conduct cannot ignore the occurrence of violence whose conditioning he does not control. The demonstrations of recent times, with their propensity for violence (or merely the mass presentation of physical presence), illustrate this problem.

The various symbiotic symbols of the different media have much in common. In all cases there is a close link between usability and disturbability that follows from the systemic activation of structural couplings. In all cases, the symbol, because it is a symbol, is an object of cultural interpretation. Thus a cheeky look can be interpreted as the onset of physical force, or a day without beer and tobacco as a state of emergency. Much depends on trained sensitivity. Whoever wishes to "see" inscriptions or murals in the gloom of Egyptian tombs needs some experience, and this means that the medium depends more strongly on the specific nature of structural couplings. Above all, however, symbiotic symbols require a *ban on self-gratification*. They have to rely on the body being used in accordance with social conditionings and not directly for what the consciousness suggests. This explains why the positive sexology of the eighteenth century also provoked an almost neurotic attitude toward masturbation; that only few decades previously, science, which depends on controlled perception, had to reject all reference to intuition in the sense of a self-gratifying approach as a variant of "fanaticism";[336] and, of course, that the political power of the "sovereign" state could tolerate no unauthorized use of force in its own territory and allow only international wars. It is striking that bans on self-gratification relate to the coding of media. For Pascal, this meant that, because science lacks intuitive-direct access to truth such as claimed by religion, it has to take the arduous path of refuting opposing assumptions.[337] And it is also clear in the case of power that a generally stabilized difference between superiority and inferiority can be maintained only if not everyone has the means of physical force at their disposal, and the power question always first has to be settled in combat.

Finally, we note something surprising: through symbiotic symbols, media become dependent on *organization*. This is obvious where control over physical force requires decisions to be made, as well as military or police organization. But the preparation of perceptions relevant to truth also now requires organization if we do not want to be at the mercy of chance. The same applies for the market-mediated satisfaction of needs. And very recently even sexuality has made itself dependent on organization, namely, on the services of the pharmaceutical industry. Behind the external reference and irritation given by structural coupling to consciousness and body, society itself once again emerges. Ultimate security lies not in controlling the body, as the old theory of the passions and reason teaches, but in the functioning of organizations.

(7) The function of symbolically generalized communication is to condition selections in such a way that communications are accepted, even though this is improbable as an exigency. With respect to actual motivational success, however, a symbolic medium can be used too much or too little. In the first case, we speak of *inflation*; in the second, of *deflation*.

Parsons proposed generalizing this distinction, originally usual only with reference to money but conceptually not very well developed.[338] In the context of the general theory of the action system, embodiment in the "realia," the "things" that make action possible,[339] suffices, and, incidentally, the analogy with monetary inflation and deflation. However, we find ourselves in a theoretically more difficult situation. What does "too much" or "too little" successful motivation mean?

We see the problem not in the extent of "backing" for the medium by "things" (this would not suffice even for money theory), but in *trust* in relation to the *further use* of the meaning reduced by communication (circulation).[340] This may, but need not, depend on such "backing"; above all, the various media differ considerably on what can provide such backing.

Inflation occurs when communication overdraws its line of trust, when it assumes it has more trust at its disposal than it can generate. Deflation occurs in the reverse case, when the possibilities of gaining trust are not exploited. In the case of inflation, the medium reacts by devaluing symbols (in the economy, measured against price increases). In the case of deflation, the medium reacts with too strongly restrictive conditioning, which means reducing circulation. Calculating with the reusability (= liquidity) of media symbols requires that others' calculations be calculated. Inflation and deflation can therefore be expected if the medium is geared to second-order observation. Borderline cases of inflation are reached where inflationary correction (devaluation) can no longer be expected to suffice and the acceptance of the symbols is refused. Borderline cases of deflation are reached where conditioning intervenes so strictly that no more communication is permitted. Then, too, we refuse acceptance, because under such conditions, we know that the results will be no use to us. In cases of hyperinflation or hyperdeflation, the original improbability of communications with particularly substantial demands reemerges—but now in developed societies, which can no longer bear with it. Only these borderline cases of correction failure can be described as mistrust, whereas in other cases it is a matter of maintaining trust with increasing effort.

Truth is inflated where it proposes more possibilities for use than can be realized.[341] For value relations, we find an impressive example even before their differentiation, namely, in the devotional movements of the seventeenth century,[342] and another in the contemporary invention of the "fashion" concept. For present-day conditions, values can be considered inflation-proof, since they suffer no harm and we cannot devalue them if we see they are no use to us. We follow the advice of fashion and move on to other values. *Love* is inflated where it proposes more regard for the world of the other than can be put into practice in real life. This is where the novel, and today pulp fiction and films of that ilk ensure permanent inflation—without provoking any deflationary countertrends in literature. We have inflation of the *money medium* where money cannot be reused at the value at which it had been accepted.[343] Inflation in *art* occurs especially where the artist renounces "difficulty" in producing works and the scarcity this entails, where art is accordingly abstracted from skill. Inflation might then be accompanied by deflation where fashion, reputation, and the gallery business overestimate some artists and underestimate others. In the case of *power*, finally, inflation consists in promising political action that cannot be taken.[344] The modern technique in political communication of only radiating good intentions in itself reflects permanent inflation, and symbols are devalued by what politicians say being discounted from the outset. From time to time, it is then good to remind politicians that only gods can change things through words.

This overview shows that the media's function of offering a prospect of improbable motivation tends to inflate. Established media impose trust and trust in the trust of others, and for this very reason, they have high inflation tolerance. This is why it is not much use to look for states of equilibrium in which there is neither inflation nor deflation and to consider such states optimal. Inflation and deflation can also occur at the same time, and only highly centralized media such as money render this improbable ("stagflation" has, however, been discussed in this connection). Deflation tends rather to take the form of corrective movements—for instance, insistence on empiricism over "grand theory" in American sociology, regionalization movements in politics, fundamentalism in religion. At any rate, inflation/deflation is also a form with two sides and a dividing line that is to be understood only as a boundary to be crossed and not as a perfect state of affairs.

(8) If symbolically generalized media claim to be universally applicable and in this sense to be operationally closed, they must offer the possibility of symbolizing the inclusion of exclusion, just as arithmetic has the zero symbol at its disposal, so that the nonnumber can be symbolized as a number. This zero method is applied particularly strikingly in the case of money. If money serves to observe scarcity, that is, to transform scarcity into operations, there must also be nonscarce money in a money system. Today, this is no longer realized through external references, with scarce commodities such as gold restricting the amount of money available. Instead of such commodity money, the credit of the central bank serves to regulate the money supply within the system based on nothing, as it were, by either expanding the money supply or reducing it (making it more expensive). What is decisive is that this zero method is not understood as a license for arbitrariness or as admitting external (in this instance, political) influence, but is tied to the self-reflection of the system in its concrete, historical situation.[345] This does not work automatically, but only when it is communicated.

If we recognize the principle, we find the same state of affairs in the case of power. Power depends decisively on the possibility of imposing negative sanctions, especially physical coercion. In the actual use of these sanctions, however, power fails because one cannot achieve what one really wants to achieve with them. The practice of power therefore requires constant reflection on the nonuse of the means of power, a continuous balancing act between showing strength and avoiding the imposition of sanctions. And this, too, is a communication problem. One has to threaten without threatening; one has to attempt to manage with a reference to structures and conditions without being definite about what one would do if instructions are not followed.

In the case of truth, we have a similar problem: that we have to be able to forget in order to be able to remember. The truth medium stylizes this necessity as a selection problem and advances reasons for the preferred selection. But there can be no grounds for forgetting that would not prevent forgetting itself. For the medium love, historical semantics have found paradoxical formulas that indicate the improbability of the medium, while making it clear that the improbability of love assumes pathological forms in marriage. Love demands that every (verbal and bodily) gesture serve the observation of love, indeed the observation of the observation of love. But no long-term relationship can sustain such an endurance test. Modes of dealing with one another must therefore be found that make the nonproof of love possible, with the communicated understanding for this conduct counting as proof of love.

(9) Universalization and closure through a zero method is at the same time a semantic and communicative precondition for the differentiation of medium-specific, operationally closed functional systems. A final aspect in comparing media is therefore whether and to what extent they can serve as catalysts in system formation. There are obvious links between the differentiation of media and that of the functional systems of modern society. It is obvious that the modern economy requires the secondary coding of property by money and modern politics the secondary coding of power by law. On the other hand, these two examples alone show differences that suggest system formation obeys its own laws. The political system and the legal system are thus differentiated as different autopoietic systems with differing codes;[346] not so property and money. There is therefore no automatic congruence between medium formation and system formation, but instances in which a system is characterized by the use of a medium are much to the fore.

Probably the most important condition for such a link is that the code of a medium be suitable for defining the unity of a system in distinction to other systems of its environment. Media without central coding, especially value relations, have no prospect of forming distinguishable systems. For whether an operation assigns itself to politics or the economy, to law or to an intimate relationship is decided in accordance with the code on which it orients itself.

However, this alone does not suffice. The operations that the medium makes possible (despite the improbability of combining selection and motivation) must be suitable for initiating and closing an autopoietic reproduction context. They must be able to organize recursive anticipation and recursion, and thus occur not only now and again and in isolation. In other words, media must be able to concatenate communications. They must do so independently of the sameness of the communication partners and their memory. Moreover, it is useful if the concatenation is not strictly linear in a one-to-one sequence but open to ramification and unpredictable constellations. The engagement that is generated in communication must be relevant for others, and in such a way that the decision on what it is for has to be taken only later. Art has difficulty satisfying this requirement, and its potential for system formation is therefore meager. Money, in contrast, satisfies the condition optimally. It retains its value even though each payment deletes memory of the structures (prices, transaction conditions) that had motivated it,[347] and it nevertheless remains ready for use and in quite different denominations without the slightest doubt that a payment is always an operation of the economic system.

Also important in this context is the technicity of the code we have dealt with above, that is, the independence of the crossing between positive and negative values in innumerable concrete meaning constellations, its psychological and moral deconditioning—all without loss of definiteness of the option between positive and negative value, without evasion in vague generalizations that need interpreting. In this regard, too, money is an optimal case, for when we pay there can be no doubt about the fact and amount of payment.

True knowledge and law are given in qualitative units but they, too, guarantee bifurcation capacity and reusability. But they require authorities (publications, organizations) to which they can refer when the distribution of code values is unclear. Whoever regularly takes aspirin to guard against heart attacks can justify his action to his astonished fellows by citing medical research. And if we are denied parking space on the lot of an office building even though we are stockholders (in other words, so we thought, owners) of the company in question, this is a matter to be settled before the courts and not on the stock exchange. When it comes to highly technicized codes and corresponding programs of this sort, laymen typically find that what matters is not what they had first thought. This means not least that moral evaluation, too, has to step back because the assignment of positive and negative code values cannot be coordinated with the distinction between respect and disrespect.[348] But it depends on this technical efficiency whether and to what extent media can form highly complex, operationally closed, self-defining and self-reproducing systems.

The reuse of a selection once made has also been called *circulation* of the medium. The expression is understandable only in a historical context, for there is no question of a "circle."[349] Ultimately it is a matter of the dynamic aspect of the medium/form difference. Although each coupling of the medial substratum to forms releases the medium itself for new forms, more than mere pulsation must be achieved in autopoietic systems; and precisely the symbolically generalized media are geared to do something with what has been previously achieved. They serve as already reduced complexity, as absorption of uncertainty, as premises for further operations. Every sum of money received is available for further payments. If truths are established, we can rely on them without have to test them again, and in the case of effectual power everyone can expect not to be the only fool to do what he is told.

On the other hand, and to this extent the concept of circulation is deceptive, this does not mean that connective operations are foreseeable. Circulation is not a concept that offers prospects of calculation and planning. Whoever pays cannot foresee what the recipient will do with the money, and if under certain circumstances, this is nonetheless factually or legally under control, what at the latest the following recipient does cannot be predicted. Even the conditional programs of law hardly extend our field of vision.[350] Consider only the difficulty of estimating how a change in divorce law will affect power relations in marriages. Although the circulation of media symbols serves system formation, for symbols can circulate only in systems, it would be wrong to conclude that the system can be controlled. The technical efficiency of the medium in the structure of its codes and in the dispersal of binding effects speaks against rather than for controllability.

These differences in the capability of various symbolically generalized communication media to form systems shape modern society. Together with other factors, they lead to uneven growth among functional systems and hence to the uneven operation of functions as regards communication effort and visibility without any covert rationality or hierarchy of functions being responsible. Society does not rise like dough; it does not grow evenly, become evenly more differentiated, more complex, as nineteenth-century theoreticians of progress believed (and were able to believe because they saw society only as the economic system). Rather, it complexifies certain functional areas and allows others to wither. This imbalance has repeatedly given rise to critiques of civilization—whether in terms of religion, like [post-Napoleonic Hegelian] "Restoration philosophy" [*Restaurationsphilosophie*], or in terms of reason, like Jürgen Habermas. Recent cybernetic and systems-theoretical research has, however, shown that this is a quite normal phenomenon, which can be corrected only by evolution.[351]

From an evolution-theoretical standpoint, too, it is important to distinguish between symbolically generalized communication media and the system formed through them. Media can come into being and be differentiated before there are any corresponding functional systems. The programming and specialized terminology of the coding needed to build systems can be provisionally prepared. We can trace the beginnings of this back to antiquity. Such predevelopments are particularly evident in the extent of the money economy in antiquity and again since the High Middle Ages, but also in the beginnings of conceptual systematization in juristically elaborated Roman and English case law. Without such preliminary work, the transition from a stratified society to a functionally differentiated society would scarcely have been possible, and—as always with such "preadaptive advances"[352]—it is essential that a provisional context be available to stabilize achievements without systems already having been formed, which will then finally lead to the operational closure and autopoietic autonomy of the corresponding functional cycles. For if system formation takes place, we can assume that there have always been operations of the type necessary for this to occur, and we can set out gradually to dismantle the restrictions that an older order has imposed—for example, the fragmentation of the manorial and clerical systems of jurisdiction, or the dual currency systems of the Middle Ages, or serfdom and the aristocratic prerogative of landownership.

12. Symbolically Generalized Communication Media, 4: Self-Validation

Since the beginning of their development, symbolically generalized communication media have reacted *differently* to *different* problems. In this they are not only unlike religion but also differ from one another. As society has evolved, the corresponding demarcations have emerged more clearly; especially as media have tended to form focal points for the differentiation of functional systems. This put an end to the religious (or cosmological or nature-related) grounding of the media and their semantics. Their codes could also no longer be aggregated into a single societal code of morality. This ultimately raises the question of the basis for willingness to accept media symbols and to assume the corresponding restrictions as premises for further communication. The issue of generalized acceptance has been discussed particularly with regard to the medium of money.[353] But it concerns all other media as well.

All communication is an operation that takes place concretely under the direction of specific meaning intentions. It is concerned with the truth of certain statements, compliance with certain instructions, the purchase of certain objects, certain signs of love—or indifference. Individual communications of this type are, however, never self-motivating, they draw on a recursive network of reusability of the same medium. In each and every case, the medium therefore has to be both condensed and confirmed in a paradoxical because contrary operation of generalization through specification. Media symbols thus generate, we could say, the eigenvalues of their own recursivity. When they are reused, such medium-specific eigenvalues develop—for example, as the value of per se valueless money symbols. Eigenvalue formation is the result of reuse, the application of operations to the result of previous operations of the same medium. But are eigenvalues also the condition for the possibility of such reuse?

It is difficult to accept such a circular argument. If we consult the theories developed for individual media, we learn that external references are typically used. A power holder must actually be in a position to send troops. A lover must actually be in a position to mobilize the appropriate feelings. For truth theories, despite all skirmishing with "constructivism," some sort of backing by external reality appears to be indispensable. Only in the case of money have theories of this type become increasingly questionable once backing by precious metal had been recognized as superfluous and the backing of certain currencies by foreign exchange had proved to amount almost to self-validation owing to the volatility of international money.

An additional argument appeals to necessary trust. What goes by this name is expected to build bridges between external reference and internal usability and between generalization and specification. Trust in external safeguards makes it possible to rely on the medium for not yet specified situations. This is a complicated argument concealed by psychological plausibility. It is still a question of dissolving the difference between specification and generalization by means of externalization, be it by trusting in the trust of others and consequently operating under the protection of "pluralistic ignorance."[354]

These considerations can be considerably simplified if we concede that a medium can use the *future* of its own operations as a *focus for externalizations.* Future is and remains external in that it can never become reality but is always only held in abeyance.[355] As far as realized reality is concerned, every system always finds itself at the end of its history.[356] At the same time we can test at every moment, in every present, whether the future still holds what it promised. Whether others are still willing to accept money can, however, be tried out only in the present, but in every present. Lovers swear to be eternally faithful—at the moment for the moment. But here, too, one situation follows another, and we can (however self-destructive this might be) check over and again whether the oath is still valid. Truths can already be revised tomorrow; but if new truths are to be convincing, they must be able to offer an explanation for what, as one now knows, the old truths had wrongly explained, for otherwise there would be not competition for substitutes.

We can accordingly very well assume that media validate themselves and even derive certain form requirements from this self-validation. We need only a sufficiently subtle theory of time that determines the present as the boundary between past and future. Whenever discontinuities between past and future become relevant (and only thus can future acceptability become a problem), the present is the breaking point and the locus for examining and renewing expectations; and also the only locus in time where real action can occur simultaneously with the world. Symbolically generalized communication media, like all communication, use only the present to bridge the difference between specification and generalization (condensation and confirmation). And this can happen only under the guidance of expectations that the medium produces and reproduces itself. We can accordingly speak of self-validation.

The problem therefore lies, not in the tautological-paradoxical formulation, which can be resolved temporally, but rather in whether social experience blocks generalized media-specific expectations of the future from being reproduced in all circumstances. There is no lack of indications to this effect: see the stability of mafia-like positions in opposition to state power or the frantic speculation resulting from the negotiability of all investments. The self-validation of media eigenvalues must therefore be seen as a risky evolutionary achievement, whose capacity to satisfy expectations in all media fields in all circumstances must be considered uncertain.

13. Moral Communication

Insomuch as society manages its most important functional areas through symbolically generalized communication media, which are responsible only for special problems, the importance of moral communication in society changes. This is easy to understand. But a convincing concept has yet to be developed. This, too, can happen only from the perspective of an external observer, and hence not in morally convincing let alone binding fashion. In what follows, the author is therefore not to be understood as wanting to risk his self-esteem.

Moral communication does not differ from other modes of communication by referring to a certain sort of rule, maxim, or principle to be distinguished as moral from other sorts such as legal rules. Such a mutually exclusive demarcation cannot be made, especially for law. In other words, morality is not, for example, applied ethics. It establishes its medium by reference to conditions under which people respect or disrespect themselves and others.[357]

The possibility of calling on or expressing respect and disrespect is highly diffuse. The form of the medium is defined by its concern not with recognizing the particular skills or achievements of specialists but with including people per se in societal communication. This at least belongs to the expressive style of morality, regardless of whether moral offenses are actually sanctioned by exclusion or by breaking off or reducing contact or not.[358] It is also indispensable to take double contingency into account and, for bridging purposes, to proclaim the same respect/disrespect conditions for both ego and alter—from whatever side. These requirements are united in the form of binary coding, distinguishing (equally for both sides) good and bad behavior or, where inner attitudes toward one's own behavior are also taken into consideration, good and evil behavior. Even if society provides plentifully for morally neutral behavior, morality itself contains no third value and therefore allows substantial fluctuation in the field of moralization. Wearing jeans to the theater is no longer regarded as a breach of morality, whereas what detergent and what sort of paper we use can be moralized about from an ecological standpoint.

Both printing and the differentiation of specially coded symbolically coded communication media have confronted this field of moral communication with new constellations. Morality is now no more than morality.

Its cosmological and therefore magical underpinning has been lost, as has the intimacy of negative moral judgment with the impure, disgusting, despicable. Offenses become explicable and their evaluation can therefore be derived from the circumstances.[359] The magical forms of effectiveness and of combating evil have disappeared.[360] We can obviously no longer assume that someone's behavior is inspired by evil spirits or is in some other way simply damnable or that it belongs on the dark side of the world like the devil or witches. We can and must inquire into the *motives* of behavior, and this attenuates censure by further considerations.

In the seventeenth century, there were increasing signs that the moral code was being de-ontologized and coming to be seen as a unity. Without vice, there can be no virtues. Moral judgments were themselves judged.[361] The cosmic struggle in *Paradise Lost* in which God attempts to make something good of all evil, and the devil, threatened as a principle, seeks in response to discover something evil in good, in fact takes place in the human soul—and ends in a draw. At approximately the same time, morality was released from the custody of religion, thus losing both heteronomous restrictions and security. This began to emerge in the *science de moeurs* and the courtesy theories of the seventeenth century, becoming fully apparent in the shift in leadership from religion to morality in the semantic priorities of the eighteenth century. Morality was now appealed to when religious tolerance needed to be achieved, and religions themselves were left to cultural comparison if not summoned before the judgment seat of morality. Detached from the old ties to (good) manners, such as one still finds in Montesquieu or his admirer Lord Kames, the concept of morality changed in meaning in the eighteenth century. It was no longer used almost synonymously with "social" (in expressions such as *certitude morale* [moral certitude], *personne morale*, for legal personality, or "ius est facultas moralis agendi" [law is the moral capacity to act]) but developed a profile of specific requirements. It even assumed politically subversive and generally "emancipatory" functions.[362] Morality consequently found itself in a justificatory crisis, which was initially addressed by a theory of the nature of man and his social = moral sensibilities (Shaftesbury, Hutcheson, Adam Smith) and finally by novel ethical theories aiming to provide reasonable standpoints for justifying moral judgments. Old doubts passed down in the apocryphal or speculative literature of theology about whether good and evil can be distinguished at all as principles now surfaced: Mandeville,

Sade. But precisely now, when the absence of a religious safety net made it so important, such doubts were unable to impose themselves against a morality that held itself to be good.

This can be dealt with only in outline here.[363] If we wish to trace the consequences that changes in the communication system society have had for morality, we cannot rely solely on analysis in the context of the history of ideas. However important such indicators might be, we require a more formal conceptuality, since we are concerned to assess the relationship between dissemination technologies and the symbolically generalized but problem-specific communication media and morality. We therefore take recourse to the distinction between medium and form (see § 1 above). The both specific and universal medium of morality is provided by the coded distinction between respect and disrespect. Its elements are communications that express whether certain persons are to be respected or disrespected. The form of the medium's elements (i.e., the form *of* the medial substratum as opposed to the forms developed *in* the medium) differs only through the specific coding respect/disrespect, good/bad, and through distinction from mere recognition of skills or achievements. Both reference to individual persons (one cannot respect or disrespect humankind) and the formality of the code difference guarantee the loose coupling of medium elements. The highly individualized reference to persons in modern society strengthens this loose coupling. We cannot disrespect a whole family because one member is in prison or the daughter has had a child out of wedlock. Owing to this loose coupling, the medium itself is highly stable. It would therefore be a mistake to claim that the importance of morality is diminishing in modern society. The medium of morality is and remains available, both in face-to-face interaction and in communication by the mass media. Television, in particular, has led to the conspicuous everyday topicality of moral communication.

Decisive changes are to be found in the relationship between the medial substratum and the forms developed with the aid of the medium and that regenerate it. Whereas the medium is stable and available for all possible communications, the conditions for respect and disrespect—the rules for the forms developed in the medium—tend to be unstable and are in any case no longer fully amenable to consensus. The police have different ideas than drug takers, students than the top management of big corporations, members of a profession than their clients. There are also stark differences, for example, in ethnic and religious viewpoints, and not least differences in the moral acceptance of the relativity of all moral judgments and the consequent normativization of restraint and tolerance. The difference between medial substratum (loose coupling) and medial forms (strict coupling) is thus fully exploited, and this leads in moral communication to the simultaneity of consensus and dissent, stability and instability, necessity and contingency.

In older societies it would have made little sense and met with little understanding to distinguish in this fashion between medial substratum and temporary medial forms. Instead, the problem was articulated in the shape of a hierarchy in which upper norms were seen as invariant and lower norms as varying with time and situation. The problem was built into the norm system itself, and law, as we shall see,[364] was conceived of as natural law, compliance with which converged with morality. The collapse of such a hierarchy of *leges* cannot, however, be taken to mean that everything had now become variable and contingent. For the very reason that contingency observations spread, compatible "values" are reformulated. The short-circuited collapse of difference between top and bottom in a hierarchy raises the question of what external reference points survive. "Supertangling creates a new inviolate level," according to Douglas R. Hofstadter.[365] And logical undecidabilities have to be "Gödelized," in other words, cured by externalization.

As far as morality is concerned, we now typically find unarticulated (assumed) consensus in value relations. no one says he is against peace, against justice, against honesty, against health, and so on. But this makes no provision at all for conflicts between values. Decisions on value conflicts—and only in the event of conflict are values relevant at all—must depend on the given situation; they are made ad hoc, only in subsystems of society or by individuals. In this regard, moral dissent typically arises about the forms of morality, about the conditions for approval and disapproval. Inequalities (for example, in granting loans) are justified on the grounds that they are required by the functional logic of the economic system and for the optimal exploitation of economic resources to cover demand (wealth); others are opposed to inequalities because they mean that the people who most need loans are not granted them.

Be that as it may, it cannot be said that the moralization of communications in modern society is arbitrary. On the one hand, there are structurally determined occasions for moralization—for example, where the coding of communication media is threatened, as in "fair play" in relations between government and opposition (Watergate, Barschel [the alleged murder in 1987 of a former minister-president of the German state of Schleswig-Holstein]) or in sport (doping). Most striking, however, is the relation of consensus to dissent, of necessity to contingency, of stability to instability. It seems that both sides of these distinctions have to be capable of morality. Morality actualizes itself in the unity of the difference between the two sides of these distinctions, while the unity itself (and thus the paradox of the distinctions) eludes communication. The fact that values amenable to consensus become relevant only in a conflict between values for which a consensual solution is then no longer available cannot itself be evaluated. We cannot make a principle out of the fact that principles are practicable only within limits whose admission cannot be specified on the same level of abstraction. The representation of this problem with the aid of the distinction between stable medial substrata and temporary, hence unstable forms, which actualize themselves in this medium, is a theoretical representation of the problem that is not itself capable of morality. But this very presentation shows how the hypercomplexity of modern society affects morality.

Moreover, it also shows what morality and symbolically generalized communication media have in common. For money, too, the medial substratum of the means of payment, the acceptability of money in the autopoiesis of the economic system, must and can be much more enduringly guaranteed than the forms that develop with the aid of this medium, namely, the prices paid. Only inflation and deflation can possibly cause the collapse of this difference if they short-circuit the value of money and prices in circular interdependence. Similarly, one can imagine morality inflating or deflating with the immediate risk of a transition to violence because the simultaneous actualization of stable media and unstable forms can no longer be maintained.

This being the case, the most important change in the function of moral communication is likely to have been that morality can no longer serve to integrate society with regard to its optimum state. This is excluded alone by the fact that special symbolically generalized communication media obey their own binary codes, whose positive/negative values cannot be equated with morality. In relation to their respective codes, power holders, property owners, lovers, and successful researchers are not also established as morally better; and society would not accept treating people without power, without property, incapable of love, and so on, with moral contempt for this reason. Where the incongruence of all codes among themselves and in relation to the moral code becomes apparent, society has to renounce considering itself a moral institution.

But this does not exclude moralizing communication. There is much to suggest that morality now assumes a sort of alarm function. It emerges where urgent societal problems come to notice that cannot obviously be solved by means of symbolically generalized communication media and in the corresponding functional systems. Society clearly recruits moral communication for serious problems caused by its own structures and above all by its differentiation form. As long as this served to justify center/periphery differentiations or stratification, the impression could be upheld and cultivated that society was morally integrated at its center or its apex. This notion can no longer be maintained in modern society. Moral communication now has free rein and is directed to where disquieting realities are apparent: the social question in the nineteenth century, the stark worldwide differences in prosperity, and the ecological problems of this century, which seemingly cannot be overcome either economically or politically. This leads to an inflation of moral communication, albeit highly selective. Its code is easily actualizable without clear directives; its criteria (rules, programs), however, are no longer amenable to consensus. Morality takes on "polemogenous," war-generating traits: it arises from conflicts and encourages conflicts.

Among the most important problems to attract morally charged attention today are practices that sabotage the separation of code values and thus the codings of symbolically generalized communication media. This holds for undermining the right/wrong distinction through corruption and for corresponding phenomena in the field of party politics (Watergate). It holds true for the use of insider knowledge in stock-exchange transactions and for the widespread practice of doping in competitive sport.[366] In all these cases, the problem is transformed into a scandal by reporting in the mass media and is thus morally upgraded. On the other hand, the spread of these phenomena (scandal feeds on other cases not being discovered) leads to helplessness in practical terms. Easy to arouse indignation does not yet provide practical advice on what to do. The improbability of the coding has its correlate in the probability of sabotage.

Against insider scandals of this type it helps little to draw the net of ethical regulation ever tighter in response to experience of such cases. Only the law can help, which threatens offenders with serious sanctions (if it can be applied without corruption).

One now speaks of "ethics" to cultivate the illusion that there are reasoned and practicable rules for making decisions in cases of this sort. In reality, however, ethics performs the function of a utopia in the exact, paradoxical sense of Thomas More's *Utopia*. It indicates a *topos* that is not to be found, a place that does not exist. Under the name of ethics, society creates the possibility for itself of introducing the negation of the system into the system and of talking about it respectably. That such an oppositional if not outright negative ethics exists is proved by the autonomy and operational closure of the system, which is also in a position to deal with the negation of the system in the system. For society cannot be negated from without, only destroyed.

14. Effects on the Evolution of the Societal System

If we want to know to what extent and with what consequences symbolically generalized media determine modern society and condition its further evolution, we must consider not only imbalances in their own growth. In other respects, too, their workings are limited, for in their very limitation lie the opportunities they offer. Society is not a zero-sum game. It develops complexity with the help of appropriate complexity reduction.

We have already dealt with the most important aspects; they need only to be sifted out and presented. Above all, however normalized the use of media may be (e.g., in handling money), they never order all of everyday behavior. Love has to prove itself in everyday life, not as everyday life. If we wish to enjoy art, we first have to know where to find it. The power holder also needs a room, a desk, a telephone.[367] Where media organize the autopoiesis of systems, there is always far more communication in these systems than the autopoietic minimum (just as a cell contains far more chemical molecules than those that carry out autopoiesis in the strict sense). The value added by system formation consists in this assignment of everyday behavior to an autopoietic process. The autopoiesis of the economy consists in the reproduction of payments through payments;[368] but there is naturally no economic system that provides for this and nothing else.

I have repeatedly stressed that none of the media codes can achieve congruence with the moral code, that property owners do not deserve greater approval than nonowners (not least because everyone is nonowner of almost all goods, however wealthy he might be). Inasmuch as the systemic differentiation of society relies on symbolically generalized media, this distance from morality is functionally necessary, while morality itself becomes a free-floating, disturbing and supportive orientation; at any rate, it does not become a final principle of reasonable justification.

In view of this situation, the congruence of morality and religion with its heaven/hell theology passed down from the high cultures cannot endure. One cannot and need not prevent preachers from moralizing. It is always good to stand up for the good. The predicaments of religion in a "secularized" society are often bridged by morality. But religion itself would be well advised to keep aloof from morality. It is to be doubted whether the old mechanism of demanding inconsistent behavior, namely, sin and remorse, suffices, and whether it suffices to hold out the prospect of the Last Judgment as a surprise for the righteous and the sinners. In any case, religion has long had a code of its own in the immanence/transcendence duplication rule (which it naturally cannot think of as a duplication rule) standing orthogonally to morality, as do the preference codes of the media.[369] Even with this code, religion cannot achieve control over symbolically generalized media. In other words, it is also unable to offer a supercode, but only a way of its own to describe the world.

Finally, it should be noted that symbolically generalized communication media are suitable only for functional areas in which the problem and the success aspired to lie in communication itself. The function is fulfilled if the selection of a communication is taken as the premise for further communications. Such media are therefore unsuitable for areas of communication whose function it is to change the environment—whether altering the physical, chemical, and biological circumstances, changing human bodies, or modifying consciousness structures. There are therefore no symbolically generalized communication media for technology, for medical care, or for education. In these cases, the problem that sets off the autocatalysis of symbolically generalized media, namely, a very high probability of rejection, does not occur at all. At least for medical care and for education, special societal functional systems have differentiated, which have to manage without their own communication media and are above all heavily dependent on organized interaction. None of these three problem areas is governed by a single communication medium, by either truth or money, although the current state of development would be inconceivable without differentiated science and without a money economy.[370] We must therefore assume that, however important symbolically generalized communication media are, the functional differentiation of the societal system cannot simply comply with the media paradigm but has to be guided by the problems that society has to resolve at its given level of development.

These thoughts on the societal context of symbolically generalized communication media can finally help us to solve the puzzle of the value medium. As we have seen, it is not a fully developed symbolically generalized communication medium. It lacks a central code and thus the clear distinction between coding and programming; it lacks symbiotic symbols (which does not exclude calling life a value), and it lacks potential for system formation. What nevertheless justifies us in speaking of a medium is the loose coupling of innumerable possibilities for action in accordance with value positions that then take shape in the individual case by weighing up values. There is also no doubting the independence, differentiation, and specific universalism of the medium. In the value medium, all the values of other media such as truth or wealth, love, beauty, or power are only values among other values, and the specific contingency management of the other media is inapplicable when it comes to values as values. On the other hand, the motivation of acceptance in the case of values is not generated but presupposed.

In these value relations, we see a connecting medium between the fully operational communication media and the rest of society. Hence the possibilities for their direct implementation in everyday behavior through inconspicuously obvious reference to values; hence the possibility of reference to morality and religion, as recently shown in a discussion of "civil religion";[371] hence their far-reaching relevance, which also condemns education, medical care, and lately even technologies to put values into the balance. It is therefore necessary to do without central coding. The specific modernity of values lies ultimately in the fact that as form and in all applications, they lead not to unity but to difference. Finally, we note that "strange loop" (Hofstadter) that consists in the *highest* values having to be secured at the *lowest* levels of societal communication, and not through justification, not through nonmarking, but through mere suggestion.

The combined effect of all communication media—language, dissemination media, and the symbolically generalized media—is to condense what we might overall call "culture." Condensation in this context means that the meaning used remains the same through reuse in various situations (otherwise there would be no reuse), but is also confirmed and enriched with implications that can no longer be reduced to a simple formula. This suggests that the overflow of meaning is itself the result of the condensation and confirmation of meaning, and that communication is the operation that thus creates its own medium.

These considerations leave us with a certain skepticism about the possibilities of a theory of culture. The surplus reference actualized in all meaning and precisely the concreteness of the condensations involved allow only selective processing. Something has to be said—and this means something else has to remain unsaid. We can imagine interpretative or "hermeneutic" procedures that condense their own meaning in dealing with meaning and in going through their own results. But this merely restates the initial problem, albeit in a more ingenious manner.

Structural analysis of the possible forms of culture could start with the problems of comparison and controlling. The expansion of possibilities for comparison and control began with writing and continued with the printing press and modern machine information processing. Always involved is the comparison of input with memory (both being *internal* units). Comparative "control" does not imply governing causality. On the contrary, it tends to raise awareness that such dominance is wanting.

If we consider the semantic forms with which society reacts to the increase in possibilities for monitoring, we first of all come across purpose-oriented semantics. After the alphabet had been introduced, teleology was invented as a means for ordering more complex materials over time from a uniform perspective. The thought was that natural movements have a natural end when they come to rest in a state of perfection, and one can then compare information to see what it has to say about the attainment of this end or the failure to do so (perfection must be conceived of as corruptible and nature as normative). We know this theory pattern from Aristotle.

The intensification of possibilities for comparing and control brought by printing sabotaged this teleology of nature. To some extent, orientation on a temporal end (and then also on a temporal beginning) was completely abandoned and knowledge of nature restructured with the aid of laws of nature and/or notions of equilibrium.[372] And to some extent teleology was subjectivized, so that purposes no longer concerned the natural, good end of a natural (including human) movement, but mental (and hence memory-based) anticipation, which in turn brings about human action with corresponding consequences.[373] The modern rationality of feasibility is then applied to the question of whether and to what extent this succeeds. One of the consequences of this bifurcation of extended and mental existences associated with Descartes is renunciation of the notion of a world rationality, with the result that an extremely restless culture of opposing developed. One had held onto everything one had expected in the form of a giant memory and now had to recognize in the light of new information that it had not come about. The system then had to activate new means or correct its memoirs to update what it could expect. Comparing the actual status of things with the desired status became an enduring problem, and the continuous need for correction gradually ruined what had been presupposed in the way of ties. Ultimately, only values remained as forms of the self-confirmation of culture.

Whether the invention of the computer, which first of all only expands the possibilities of monitoring, in the sense of comparing information and memory, can change this remains to be seen. It is also uncertain what will condense from these possibilities in the way of culture. That the computer can raise the average level of expectation fulfillment if it also stores expectations is unlikely. What can be achieved is to improve and accelerate the organization of complexity. This allows expectations, too, to be better pretested before being stored—but still only with the aid of the technique of comparative monitoring, that is, always only in relation to the past. There is little danger of this leading to a calculated culture, for meaning forms condense only in communication itself. We must more likely assume that the acceleration of monitoring operations will be the element to which culture has to react—which it must do by renouncing a positive evaluation of temporal stability.

However, structural analyses of this sort can only provide examples. At best, they record single perspectives that fail to do justice to the overall complex of modern culture, being unable to reduce it to a basic problem. We can still work with genetic analysis, even if we have to manage without a description of phenomenal complexity in the case of highly complex states of affairs of this type. We can inquire how things come about—even if we cannot explain why things are the way they are. It is useful for the purposes of such genetic analysis to use a systems theory that demands precision in determining the operations that produce and reproduce the system with its boundaries. This chapter has accordingly been devoted to the concept of communication. In the next chapter, we turn to a related theory called "evolution," which likewise provides only genetic analysis without explaining phenomena.

3

Evolution

1. Creation, Planning, Evolution

Society is the outcome of evolution. We can also speak of "emergence."[1] But this is only a metaphor, which does not explain anything but presents us logically with a paradox. Accepting this, we can describe evolution theories as transforming a logically insoluble problem into a genetic one.[2] However unsatisfying the explanations offered by evolution might be by the logical, theory-of-science and methodological standards of causal explanation and prediction, no other theory today is in a position to explain how the structures of the social system develop and reproduce.

So far, I have only mentioned a word and referred to a rather confusing discussion.[3] Our inquiry will be guided by the *paradox of the probability of the improbable.*[4] For statisticians, this is a triviality (or a false application of statistical concepts). After all, every totality of characteristics, for instance, the particularity of a given person, is, if we consider the conditions for these characteristics to come together, extremely improbable: the result of a chance meeting. However, this holds in every case and is therefore quite normal. Statistics can and must ignore this problem. For evolution theory, however, the resolution of this paradox is the point of departure. The improbability of isolated individuals or isolated families surviving is transformed into the (lesser) improbability of their structural coordination, *which is when sociocultural evolution begins.* Evolution theory shifts the problem to time and attempts to explain how it is possible that ever more demanding and ever more improbable structures develop and function as normal.[5] The basic proposition is that evolution transforms low probability of origination into high probability of maintenance.[6] This is merely another way of putting the more familiar question of how (despite the entropy principle) entropy can give rise to negentropy. To put it in still another way, it is about the morphogenesis of complexity.[7]

This definition of the problem, involving time and geared to dynamics, precludes simply gauging evolution from its structural results, for example, from its effects on the distribution of energy and power or on the coordination of integration levels in society.[8] Although it is important to take such results into account, for instance, in the form of the distribution of action potential among "levels" or "subsystems," they are precisely what evolution theory has to explain. Describing the differences that come about is not itself a theory of evolution, not even if the material is ordered in historical sequence, presented as a succession. We therefore see the problem in the *morphogenesis* of complexity.

More recent evolution theories explain the morphogenesis of complexity neither in terms of a corresponding *law* (which can be empirically verified) nor in terms of the *rationality advantages* of complexity, which would suggest a purposive if not intentional interpretation of evolution. It is assumed rather that evolution behaves *recursively*, that is, applies the same procedure iteratively to its own results. But we must then define more precisely what sort of "procedure" we are talking about. In what follows, this is attempted with reference to the neo-Darwinian schema of variation, selection, and restabilization.

Another assumption for which we claim empirical evidence is that in the course of evolution, the biomass to be found on earth and, since the advent of language, the quantity of communicative events have increased. This is to begin with a purely quantitative statement and accordingly easy to verify. In explaining the finding, we must assume that quantitative increases of this sort are possible only through differentiation. And in the field of linguistic communication, it must be added that the possible amount will increase enormously if communication can also run negatively, that is to say, in the form of denying or rejecting communications.[9] Behind the assumption of quantitative growth therefore lies the precondition of nonarbitrary structural differentiation. We can couch this in the usual terms of complexity enhancement, for example, with Darwin, in terms of the differentiation and specialization of parts, provided we drop the additional assumption that higher complexity serves to improve the adaptation of systems to their environment. This points us in certain directions but does not yet explain why improbabilities come to be transformed into probabilities and why such differentiation-driven quantitative increases take place. Evolution theory thus faces a problem, but this merely sets the framework within which solutions to this very problem are to be sought.

Evolution theory does indeed operate with causal assumptions, but it renounces explaining evolution in terms of causal laws. On the contrary, nonrepeatability assumptions are built in, and in this sense, it is a theory of the historically unique development of systems. For evolution comes about through the use of transitory, impermanent conditions. This very possibility provides the opportunity for developing an improbable order over time. Evolution is, as it were, a theory of waiting for useful chances, and this requires systems capable of persisting and/or reproducing, and that can maintain themselves—and wait. Time is accordingly one of the essential preconditions of evolution, and this means among other things that close temporal ties between environmental states and system states have to be interrupted. We now call this "loose coupling."

Evolution hence means that the number of preconditions on which an order can depend increases. Through a process of self-reinforcing deviation from basic assumptions of even distribution, an order emerges in which positions, dependencies, and expectations can be expected with greater or lesser certainty in dependence on this same order. If meaningful communication becomes possible at all, every specific utterance being equally probable at every specific point in time becomes improbable. Specific probabilities condense into expectabilities, but given that all expectations are fundamentally uncertain, they are in themselves still evidently improbable.

There are various theories on offer relevant to this problem against which evolution theory has to hold its own. People have long admired the world's complexity and produced creation theories in response.[10] With hindsight, this had a major theoretical advantage. One could distinguish the world, describe it as a work, as the unity of the totality of all visible and invisible things, while always explicitly or implicitly recalling another side to the distinction: God. The genesis of complex order was ascribed to an intelligent cause and uncomprehending admiration of the world diverted into uncomprehending admiration of God. Order is the execution of a plan. The unity of order is mentally duplicated in cause and effect. The cause is God the Creator, and the effect, in which the cause reveals itself, is the world. But this explanation satisfies only those who believe in it.

Creation theories have to be elaborated in sufficient detail to allow both redundancy and variety to be derived from them. They have to help process the *diversitas temporum* and be open to both positive and negative aspects. Only thus can they generate information under the impact of daily events. The traditional distinctions between good and bad events and between the perfection and corruption of nature did justice to these demands. They could be supplemented by theological theories about the special providence of God, which, for example, give sense to prayer. In the early modern age, these plausibility conditions dissolved under the theoretical and methodological pressure exerted by the demands of both research in the natural sciences and the human scope for action. The Aristotelian theory of natural final purposes was abandoned. The thesis of the divine creation of the world therefore lost all resonance as a complement to everyday experience and action. It no longer generates information and serves only—as it were, to spare traditional religion—as concluding formula for indicating the otherwise unobservable unity of the world.[11] After a protracted phase of religious quarantine and search for new symbioses, evolution theory asserted itself from the second half of the nineteenth century despite its theological offensiveness. Creation theory renounced explaining the world and withdrew into theology. Specific problems now arose in this domain. The "nothing" of *creatio ex nihilo* could not be left in the past. It was constantly needed to allow being to be being. *Creatio continua* requires constant re-creation, also from nothing. But evolution theory has no need to concern itself with this.

Another obstacle lay in the ontological cognitive presuppositions of tradition, combined with the low resolution capacity of science. One spoke of the species and genera of living beings that had to be treated in accordance with the schema being/nonbeing. Nature and creation had fixed forms of being and substances. Variation was possible only in the domain of the accidental. Event-like breaches were understood as "miracles"—as naturally improbable happenings by means of which God drew attention to Himself. More or less legendary mixed forms went by the name of "monster," but they were denied any classificatory value. At best, they had the function of providing roundabout proof of the perfect order and harmony of nature: this is what you get when something goes wrong! It was this order of species that had blessed rabbits with enough offspring to feed foxes, something that theologically could not otherwise be explained.

Ontology and its bivalent logic also dictated that a distinction was to be drawn between moveable and immovable (between mutable and immutable) things. All theories of change had taken this distinction as their point of departure, which was summed up in the paradox of the unmoved mover and was at this point implemented in concepts of potency (will, power) and interpreted religiously (omnipotence). It was simply out of the question (as long as the movement concept was retained) to think of everything as moved and to forgo any counterconcept. Or one was obliged to introduce a two-sided form into the concept of movement, distinguishing between faster and slower movement.

As long as living beings, like all things, were defined in terms of fixed generic characteristics, they preserved the memory of their origin. With the transition to evolution theories, indeed, even with Lamarck, things, so to speak, lost their memory. They owe what they are to some variations or other, which repeat themselves in other forms and can lead to other forms. This means history! Evolution theory offered scientific proof for this—thus rousing the theological ire of the nineteenth century and its progeny. The eighteenth century had already extenuated much. To avoid entanglement in theological dogmatics, the Creator was now called "Providence." And he was allowed time. He had not created the whole world all at once. He was still at it.[12] But no longer with works and wonders, no longer with "signs," but with an "invisible hand." At the same time "history" was discovered. Finally, the increasing resolution capacity of geological/biological research also called the typological rigidity of species and genera into question. On the one hand, it was and remained clear that there were narrow limits to cross-breeding. This corresponded to a new concept of the population as a polymorphous unity. On the other hand, history provided more and more evidence of the variation and diversification of species. And this imposed the idea of seeing evolution theory as a theory of history. In Darwin, it dissociates itself from the assumption of a compact creation of species and genera as a gradualistic concept of evolution, which understands the coming into being of species and genera as a gradual, continual process.[13] Finally, coordination, the possible coexistence of the differentiated, is explained historically—and not as the result of a corresponding intention.[14] It is this that makes it interesting for the contemporary theory of society. The "invisible hand" is now replaced by the invisible forces of history, the subliminal changes of evolution, the latent motives and interests, which can be rendered visible only with the aid of scientific theories.

But what alternative is there to creation theories? What distinction can replace the unity of origin and the difference between moved and unmoved as the lead distinction in the theory of historical change? From the seventeenth to the nineteenth centuries, a semantic alternative had initially been sought in theories of progress. Today, this is considered behind the times, not least in evolution theories.[15] The emergence of evolutionary advances cannot be assigned to any consistently evaluated line of progress. But if progress is not to be assumed, what then is the architecture of an evolution theory? Even biology had found it difficult for almost a century to comprehend the complex design of natural selection.[16] As the systemic contours of the course of life became apparent, the distinction between natural and artificial that had initially guided Darwin was succeeded by a distinction between outside and inside, so that the concept of natural selection came to mean external selection. When taken up by the theory of society, this concept blends with existing notions about historical processes (in the plural or singular), the nineteenth century tending to adopt a fatalistic view of history and no longer simply to accept that "man makes history."

Since the eighteenth century, this problem had been contemplated in the form of stage models of historical development. Although not quite consistent with the meaning of the term, I shall be calling them development theories. What is involved is a sort of "operationalization" of progress theories—for how is one to prove progress empirically other than by comparing different stages of the historical process?[17] The *unity* of the history of society is reconstructed as a *distinction* between epochs, and what does not fit is incorporated with the anomaly-absorbing concept of the simultaneity of the nonsimultaneous.

This corresponds to the notion of history as a process, which gained binding form in Hegel's philosophy of history. It was still based on the idea of a hierarchy of lower and higher activities extended into the temporal dimension. On the basis of the distinctions this brings, the theory can show the same to be acting in different domains. It incorporates—in the guise of logical metaphysics—the element of negation, by which the higher domain in awareness of itself interprets *for itself* the lower domain as insufficient, as deficient, as pain, as something to be overcome. In this negation, it discovers and realizes its "freedom" as its *own*. It thus discovers a contradiction *in itself* and can choose to perish by this contradiction or, as philosophy advises, to "sublate" it. Such inner reflection requires "mind" as the principle of becoming. The mind moves by its ability to distinguish, including the "absolute" final ability to distinguish itself in itself. The mind thus only enriches itself, it deletes nothing. It forgets nothing. Nor does it forgo the realization of possibilities. It is perfect because in the end only exclusion is excluded and everything possible becomes real.

No theory has ever again attained this closed form, and all later theories have therefore to be distinguished from it. All post-Hegelian theories must accordingly provide not for the exclusion of exclusion but for the inclusion of exclusion. In the empirical sciences, which, without being preoccupied by the mind, operate with inductive concepts of epoch, the notion of process unity has given rise to innumerable controversies that are no longer relevant today—for example, on the characterization (and then naturally on rejection of the characterization) of this process as continuous, as unilinear, as regular, as necessarily progressive.[18] Where such definitions are advanced in evolution theory, they can only be rejected.[19] But they are based on a confusion that can probably be rectified with a minimum of conceptual care.

Such divisions into epochs and development theories in general are seen with increasing skepticism.[20] The same holds for the global process theories that have been inspired and borne by them. But whatever we might think of them, they are not evolution theories.

Another approach, which also does business under the name of evolution theory, pursues a quite different explanatory goal. At issue is the problem of differential evolution, that is, the question why some societies develop and others do not; for example, why "states" emerge in some societies and not in others. Certain variables, especially population growth, to which others are added (e.g., ecological conditions or social organization) typically serve as point of departure in explaining why differential development has taken place.[21] Another schema also sold as evolution theory is the distinction between innovation and diffusion.[22] The research interests pursued, particularly by archaeologists and prehistorians, are perfectly legitimate. It is only confusing that this also goes by the name of evolution theory, which blurs the line dividing it from theories addressing the morphogenesis of complexity.

Although these differences are now hardly recognized in social anthropology and sociology,[23] from the Darwinian perspective they are quite clear.[24] Evolution theory (however far it may now have left Darwin behind) uses a quite different sort of distinction to replace that between moved and unmoved. It distinguishes not between epochs but between *variation*, *selection*, and *restablization*.[25] It explains, to use the old terminology, the origin of forms of being and substances in accident. It frees the order of things from all ties to an origin, to a formative beginning. It simply reverses the conceptual framework of world description.

That a distinction is made between variation, selection, and restabilization makes sense in a way that conceals the distinction itself. The distinction explains that and how it is possible to use temporary and passing constellations. It serves to unfold the paradox of the probability of the improbable with the aid of *another* distinction. The concepts variation and selection shift the problem to another level and thus displace the question of the unity of the distinction between probable and improbable. They put the initial paradox in a more manageable form: naturally erratic, logically abstruse, creative. The paradox becomes less recognizable, it is rendered invisible, and its place is taken by another distinction that offers prospects of empirical inquiry. For we can now ask about the conditions under which the mechanisms of variation and those of selection separate and can then be distinguished by an observer.

As always, a distinction that serves for observation requires a blind spot. It finds it where the boundary has to be drawn that separates the two sides of the distinction. The dividing line has to be drawn unobservably because the observer has to connect to one side of the distinction or the other. In the case of the distinction between variation and selection and that between selection and restabilization, the boundary is called *chance*, which means negation of any systemic connection of evolutionary functions. We can accordingly not know (not observe) whether variations lead to the positive or negative selection of innovation; and just as little whether restabilization of the system after positive or negative selection will succeed or not. And the very proposition that one cannot know, cannot calculate, cannot plan characterizes a theory as an evolution theory.

As long as we proceed like Darwin on the assumption of "natural selection" by the environment, we have a certain guarantee of stability.[26] Not all, but well-adapted systems were therefore considered stable as long as the environment did not change. There was no question of a special function. This changes if we abandon the principle of natural selection and switch evolution theory to the co-evolution of structurally coupled, autopoietic systems.[27] Such systems have to provide their stability themselves if they are to continue taking part in evolution. Three evolutionary functions or mechanisms are now needed, of which variation and selection refer to events, while restabilization refers to the self-organization of evolving systems as an essential precondition for variation and selection.

Considering two distinctions, between variation and selection and between selection and restabilization, is a first step toward resolving the problem of unobservability that we label "chance," namely, in the form of the downstream concept of restabilization, which comes to bear only when variation and selection interact "by chance" and in turn reacts randomly (systemically uncoordinatedly) to this chance interaction as unity of the distinction. If the theory had had only one of these distinctions at its disposal, it would, so to speak, not have got past chance, and would have had to refer via this concept to the environment of the system. Only the coupling of two distinctions centered on the concept of selection allows the theory to conceive of evolution as an endless process in irreversible time, in which every stability achieved—the more complex it is, the more this holds true—offers a starting point for variation.

It is above all obvious that both positive and negative selection produces a stability problem. In the case of positive selection, a new structure has to be built into the system with consequences that have yet to prove their worth. In the case of negative selection, the system "potentializes" the rejected possibility. It has to live with its rejected option, even though it could have taken it and other systems have perhaps done so or would do so. This might have been a mistake, and this remains so. Selection does not necessarily guarantee good results.[28] In the long run, it has to pass the stabilizability test.

This account suggests that restabilization is the end of a sequence. But stability is also required for the start, as precondition for varying something. The third factor of evolution is therefore both beginning and end, a concept of its unity, which, because it amounts to structural change, can be described as dynamic stability. In a temporally abstract model, evolution theory describes a circular relationship. It thus also indicates that and how time intervenes as an asymmetricizing factor. From a superficial point of view—which, however, completely suppresses the initial paradox—it appears for this very reason to be a process.

Having clarified these points, it hardly needs to be stressed that evolution theory is not a theory of progress. It accepts the emergence and destruction of systems with equanimity. Darwin had also (albeit not completely consistently) refused to use expressions like "higher" and "lower" to characterize species. Even the idea that evolution improves the adaptation of systems to their environment cannot be understood as progress because we would have to assume that the environment changes continuously and triggers ever-new adaptations. It is just as doubtful whether specialization can continue to be seen as a sort of evolutionary attractor, which (but how in fact?) leads to more and more specific competencies, roles, organizations, systems being differentiated. It seems that the economic theory of the division of labor and the restriction of competition through market diversification has imposed itself on evolution theory and, above all, through Spencer, been generalized into a historical law—only to provoke evolution theory to discover the evolutionary advantage of the unspecified.[29] Such ideas need not be rejected across the board; but with the aid of evolution theory, we must examine whether and to what extent they are tenable.

These definitional considerations have consequences for the explanatory goal of evolution theory. Evolution theory provides no interpretation of the future. It enables no predictions.[30] It presupposes no teleology of history—with regard to either a good or a bad end to it. It is not a control theory, which could help in deciding whether we should let evolution be or correct it.[31] It is concerned solely with how we explain that more complex systems develop in a world that always offers and retains other possibilities; and perhaps why such systems fail. In very simple terms, it is concerned with explaining structural changes.

Here one normally thinks of unplanned structural changes. However, planning theory offers no alternative to evolution theory. Evolution theory also deals with systems that plan themselves. There is no disputing that planning or, more generally, intentional anticipation of the future, play a role in sociocultural evolution. We then speak of forward induction.[32] But, in the first place, the basis for forming intentions is typically, if not always, deviation from established routines (thus not at all a spontaneous self-realization of the mind); it is hence itself a result of evolution. Moreover, the future does not comply with intentions but only takes the intentionally created facts as the starting point for further evolution. Evolution theory therefore assumes—and is not far from reality in doing so—that planning cannot determine the state in which the system will end up as a result of planning. Planning, when it takes place, is accordingly an element of evolution, for even the observation of models and the good intentions of planners put the system on an unforeseen course. Evolution theory would say: what structures result will emerge through evolution.

If we wish to understand structural changes evolutionistically, we have to forgo the notion that structures are something "fixed" as opposed to something "in flux." (An observer, however, can see it thus, but if we want to know *what* he sees as structure we have to observe the observer). Structures are conditions for restricting the area of connective operations, and are hence conditions for the autopoiesis of the system. They do not exist in abstraction, not independently of time. They are used or not used in progressing from operation to operation. They condense and confirm through repetition in various situations a wealth of meaning that eludes exact definition; or they are forgotten. Structures appear "stable" (to the observer) inasmuch as there are other structures that invite reuse.[33] But structures always realize themselves only in directing (restricting the possibilities for) progression from operation to operation. And it is this operational context (in our case communication) that exposes the structures of society to evolution.

No extraordinary effort is therefore required, as the classical theory would have to see it, to change structures despite their immanent stability. They can become obsolete if other channels of operational connections come to be preferred. Their use can be limited to certain situations or extended to new situations. Evolution is always and everywhere.

2. Systems-Theoretical Basis

Recent developments in evolution theory since its Darwinian beginnings have been influenced above all by gradual realization of the extent to which evolution theory has to take recourse to systems-theoretical premises and has accordingly been drawn into the controversy between systems theories.[34] Systems theory treats variation and selection as "sub-dynamics of the complex system."[35] The nineteenth century had preferred a semantics of demography, of populations, of heredity. The more uncertain the semantics of subjectivity and freedom, the more certain life and corporeality were. Without this background, Darwin's interest and, above all, the interest of ideologies in Darwin are inconceivable. With the innumerable variants to be found, the individual serves as the final reference, and this also holds for attempts to combine action theory with evolution theory.[36] This does not take us beyond the theories of the nineteenth century, which claimed the individual for the self-regulation of the evolutionary process, thus for development theories that present themselves as theories of history and often explicitly rejected the expression evolution. Even more than in the refusal of religious explanation, this appears to be the unifying element of most nineteenth-century theories of evolution or history (with the exception of Hegelian derivatives), and hence the undisputed starting point for all controversies.[37] In comparison, systems theory imposes sharper abstractions but also greater conceptual precision.

We return to our general point of departure: systems theory does not have to do with a particular type of object but uses a certain distinction, namely, that between system and environment. In essence, evolution means nothing other than that structural changes, precisely because they can take place only intrasystemically (autopoietically), are not at the disposal of the system but have to impose themselves in an environment that the system itself cannot probe, at any rate cannot include in its planning. The evolutionary diversification and reproduction of systems is at the same time a diversification and reproduction of environments.[38] Only the *difference* between system and environment makes evolution possible. In other words, no system can evolve from within itself. If the environment did not constantly vary *differently* than the system, evolution would come to a rapid end in "optimal fit."[39] It also follows that, although evolution does not have to *effect* the adaptation of the system to the environment, such adaptation is *required* as a sort of minimum condition. But this says no more than that systems that no longer exist can also not evolve. It should above all be noted that the difference between system and environment lends every change a *multiplication effect*. It changes a system and at the same time the (relevant or irrelevant) environment of other systems. Every change is accordingly very likely to set off a whole series of effects, which in turn generate effects independently of one another, and for which the same holds true.[40] The world becomes dynamic from within, precisely because of the simultaneity of what happens and because of the associated impossibility of coordination. If, in other words, both the system that we observe and the systems in its environment evolve (co-evolve), the result is the "co-evolution of unsustainability";[41] and observers can react only by observing "chance occurrences." Only against this backdrop can we understand what role "chance" plays in evolution theory.

If we take this difference-theoretical starting point seriously, an old dispute about the relative weight of external and internal causes (exogenous and endogenous evolution) becomes obsolete. With the aid of the "population" concept, older evolution theory had localized the causes for variation within the system. On the one hand, this led to the view that demographic variables, mainly the irresistible human drive to multiply, are the factors that trigger all higher evolutionary development, for example, the transition to agriculture, the division of labor, the formation of hierarchies. Such single-factor explanations are now considered obsolete.[42] Even from the perspective of our concept of society, however, we would have to operate with variables such as communication density or frequency and diversity of information produced, and, above all, to take account of circular relationships amplifying deviation.

But this demographic interpretation of the population concept has overlooked the most important innovation it introduces. A population—and in this the concept supersedes the older typological essentialism of species and genera—consists of *individuals*, and this means of *differing* individuals. It is thus a polymorphous unity. The source of variation is not seen, as in later social Darwinism, as the occasional occurrence of particularly creative, innovative, assertive individuals, but as the diversity of individuals in the collectivity of the population. For the biologist this means that the genetic heterogeneity of populations explains evolution better than perhaps "natural selection." Possibilities are therefore available for the population to reinforce this or that characteristic in order to adapt to changing requirements. We are thus dealing, if such a term is allowed, with a collective individualism and not with an individualism that places emphasis on the single being. The possibility of variation lies in variety and not in the sufficiently probable chance of there being exemplars among a large number of individuals that distinguish themselves as being particularly innovative.

Then again, the selection mechanism is transferred to the environment, and in this sense, one speaks of "natural selection." However, if we formulate systems theory radically as a theory of the production and reproduction of a difference between system and environment, this distribution of internal (variation) and external (selection) factors cannot be upheld. Merely criticizing the concept of "natural selection" and setting out beyond Darwin from that position does not suffice either.[43] Moreover, the converse approach is just as unconvincing, namely, advocating the "natural selection" concept, and hence orientation on external causes, in sociological theory,[44] which had hitherto clearly favored endogenous causes.[45] Causal propositions always presuppose selection, thus the attribution of causes and effects, and hence an observer. But evolution neither makes such attributions nor observes itself.

The system reference of "social systems" also allows the dispute between more demographic-ecological evolution theories and those oriented rather on culture to be decided. Whoever is interested in human beings as a living population (in the fight against bugs, lions, bacteria, and so on) has to adopt a demographic orientation. In contrast, we can speak of the social system society evolving only if we conceive of it, not as living, but as a communication system, which reproduces meaning in each of its operations, presupposes knowledge, draws on its own memory, uses cultural forms. It is therefore a matter, not of meaningful scientific controversy, but of a choice of system reference, that is, of a decision on the object of evolution-theoretical analysis.[46]

Apart from these rapidly settled questions, systems theory also intervenes substantively in evolution theory in deciding to base the research program of the theory on operationally closed, autopoietic systems.[47] This theory first of all allows us to explain that there is scope for evolutionary structural development in systems. Autopoiesis itself makes only minimal demands; in the case of the system of society, it requires only that communication take place with regard to further communication. But this can happen in widely differing structures.[48] Structures are necessary because they narrow the scope for suitable connective operations to such an extent that progression from operation to operation can be achieved. We could also say that they are necessary complexity reductions. However, this selectivity of structure formation also provides the opportunity for different developments. The *need for structural selection compatible with auto-*

poiesis—and this is only the other side of the coin—explains the *chance of differential evolution*. Types of autopoietic operation and corresponding system formation—such as life, consciousness, and communication—are, as it were, one-off inventions of evolution, which have proved their worth through their potential for structural development. Their worth lies, however, in the specification of widely differing forms, which develop in the medium of autopoietic necessity and can further specify. This interplay between self-continuation and structure formation enables and imposes evolution without any need to posit "natural selection" or other sorts of external structural determination. It is therefore not a question of almost optimal, or at any rate competitive, adaptation to the environment. Under similar ecological conditions very differently endowed living beings can survive.[49] Moreover, this resolves an old controversy in theory, namely, the dispute about the higher evolutionary potential of the underspecified.[50] In reality, there is no nonspecific reproduction. But there is a difference between autopoiesis and structural determination.

This fundamentally contradicts the research program of sociobiology. The genetic determination of life is an undisputed point of departure. But it does not follow that social orders are also determined from this position (although it must naturally be conceded that no social order can survive that requires people to walk on their hands rather than on their feet). The genetic determination of life is rather compensated by a societal order of social systems endowed with high (can we say higher?) degrees of freedom. And this order develops structural determinations of a particular type.

In another regard, too, the distinction between systems theory and evolution theory provides useful insights—especially if we take the concept of operationally closed autopoietic systems as the basis. For these systems practice a self-referential, circular relationship between structure and operation. They generate structures through their own operations, but on the assumption that structures guide the determination of connecting operations. From a temporally abstract point of view, such a theory is empirically empty. Evolution theory, in contrast, asymmetricizes the relationship between structure and operation, because it is concerned only with changing structures, and autopoiesis plays a role only as a boundary concept. In this context, exertion of influence on an operation can provide the point where the system can mutate by chance. Evolutionary selection, in contrast, is the procedure that decides whether a structural change is accepted or rejected. If we see autopoietic systems as resulting from evolution (and what is to be said against it?), we have to consider the restrictions on possible structural change that permit empirically substantial theories to be formulated.[51] We shall be pursuing this issue above all with regard to evolutionary change in the forms of societal differentiation.

While these reflections can elucidate the links between systems theory and evolution theory, the theory of operationally closed, autopoietic systems finds itself in other regards in flagrant contradiction to the usual way of thinking in evolution theory. How is an operationally closed system of society to evolve if it cannot use its own operations to start or stop, but either operates autopoietically or not at all? How is it to come about gradually? For transitional situations, there is no "half" life, no "little bit" of communication. A living being is either alive or not. Communication either takes place or not. The concept demands such uncompromising stringency.[52]

We should recall that autopoietic systems always perform their operations only in the actual present. The recursive interconnection of operations also takes place in the present on the basis of currently available conditions and connectivity options. For the operation (and this also holds for communication if it is to be an autopoietic operation), there is accordingly neither a beginning, because the system must always have already begun if it is to be able to reproduce its operations from its own products, nor an end, because every further operation is produced with an eye to further operations.[53] Only an observer (and this can be the operating system itself) can make out a beginning and an end if he takes a corresponding before/after construction as his basis. Only when the system is operating and has built up sufficient complexity to describe itself in the temporal dimension can it "postcipate" its beginning. The determination of a beginning, an origin, a "source," and a (or no) "before" is a myth fabricated in the system itself—or an account by another observer.[54]

Where autopoietic systems are involved, evolution can therefore not be understood as a mere meeting of particulars where what already exists enables something to be added that could not have been done without this precondition. We do not have to completely exclude such a development; but it alone cannot explain the speed of evolution. Autopoietic systems make evolution possible, rapid evolution, precisely because they close themselves off on the basis of their own distinctions and can thus recruit their own requirements whenever the *simultaneous* environment suffices.

Anyway, the time dimension is not a system/environment schema in the sense that systems exist in time, and past and future constitute their environment.[55] The system/environment difference can be observed solely in the factual dimension. The observer can think of them as difference extended into the past or future and imagine a beginning and an end, but only as present operation simultaneous with the given environment.

This shifts the issue (in relation to "objective" thinking about time). Autopoietic systems can come into being when presents occur in which recursive reproduction can be installed. This is of course not possible on the basis of just any past history. In order to recognize what is required, the autopoietic operation has to be indicated with sufficient precision. For example, communication (and hence society) is always set in motion whenever utterance and information can be distinguished in observation (which hence becomes "understanding"). This is also possible pre-linguistically, but language imposes this distinction so compellingly that the understander, when he speaks himself, can rely on the very mechanism that allows him to understand. The result is recursive closure, which uses no elements of any sort from the environment but operates with an emergent distinction. It is also easy to demonstrate that the consciousness, too, reproduces itself through such recourse.[56]

This "exclusivity" of language offers major advantages in relation to the environment. It allows the system constantly to address a continually changing environment, and thus not to adapt its structures once and for all to lasting or recurring environmental states, but (like an organism's faculty of sight) to attune itself *temporarily* to *temporary* states on account of structural conditions prevailing only in the system and not in the environment.[57] All subsystems established in society can then specialize in particular opportunities. When the evolution of this condition "began" can no longer be objectively and definitely determined; such a critical moment is construed in the system itself as an event to which the closed system owes its existence and criteria. Only a specially endowed observer will then be able to ask about prior developments, preconditions enabling and favoring closure, and provide an answer in accordance with *his* cognitive possibilities.

This basic procedure can be varied in many ways wherever autopoietic systems can form. A class of nobility closes itself off by means of endogamy or some other mechanism—but naturally only if the families in question can be identified. Only then are genealogies constructed going back to heroes or gods or family primogenitors.[58] The differentiation of a legal system requires dispute events and dispute resolution events to have occurred that point to rules for future practice, even if what is recalled as having happened had nothing to do with applying rules.[59] Science can develop as an independent autopoietic system only if there is already sufficient knowledge for critical review to ascertain whether this knowledge is true or untrue.[60] The first coins were minted, not for purposes of exchange, but as clearing units in household economy contexts. Money came into use originally as a sign for performance imbalances, as a substitute for gratitude, as it were.[61] But once there was a sufficiently large quantity of such coins, and a barter economy was well enough developed to stagnate, owing to the difficulty of finding suitable items to exchange, a money economy was able to differentiate itself—however small the extent and complexity of transactions may initially have been. With the differentiation of an economy based on coinage, an economic development set in that can be attributed neither to the prior state nor to the "invention" of coinage, but only to its own recursive network, which could count on a willingness to accept money however its value was guaranteed. Or, to conclude with an example from early modern times: the state differentiated under the heading of sovereignty presupposed governmental structures of an older sort, but understood itself in retrospect as completely new—as if there had always been sovereign legal concentration and only the abuses of the nobility had ruined the old system.[62] With the proclamation of the sovereign state, especially in the France of the second half of the sixteenth century, the historians took up their work. The present needs a past that fits.

Analysis thus shows that the problem of the gradual beginning can be solved only if we revise the underlying concept of time. Just as drastic changes are needed to adapt the concept of adaptation.

Evolution theory beyond Spencer and Darwin has already had serious reservations about the assumption that the best adapted (or perhaps the least badly adapted) systems are chosen by "natural selection" for survival.[63] It has also been found irritating that some species of living beings can apparently exist unchanged for millions of years, while others evolve under the pressure to adapt.[64] Furthermore, in many cases, adaptation precedes need—an explanatorily essential insight for evolution theory. For instance, even before the invention of DDT, there were insects adapted to it that could survive exposure.[65] In general, biological critique of older adaptionism was limited to asserting that not all phenotypical changes in living beings could be explained as better adaptation.[66] Revision of the concept was first called for by the theory of autopoietic systems, for which adaptation is a precondition rather than a result of evolution; and if a result, then at best in the sense that evolution destroys its material if it can no longer guarantee adaptation.[67] The onus of explanation is now on the concept of "structural coupling," which has always guaranteed adaptation sufficient to continue autopoiesis. Although the mobility of living creatures harmonizes with earth's gravity, knowing that does not tell us in what form this opening is exploited, whether as dinosaur or as insect. In many respects (e.g., speed), societal communication thus depends on structural coupling with consciousness systems, without this determining what is communicated and how the autopoietic system of society draws its boundaries with the environment. No steadily improving adaptation of survivors is hence to be expected from evolution; and a glance at the ecological problems of modern society is likely to provide enough evidence to deny such an assumption any plausibility. Precisely because autopoietic systems are operationally closed systems, they have broad scope for developing structures that prove compatible with autopoiesis. On the basis of adaptation, more and more daring disadaptations can thus arise—as long as autopoiesis itself is not interrupted.

These considerations make it essential and possible to redefine the importance of the concept of complexity for an understanding of evolution. The old idea that evolution is a process that leads from simple to complex conditions is untenable, if only because there are no simple conditions; and because less complex and more complex systems obviously still co-exist today, so that the former have not been replaced by the latter (e.g., owing to "better" adaptability). Where we find directional indications of this sort, we are dealing with simplifying self-descriptions of modern society, and such descriptions are especially plausible for today's society, because it is now a single, global system that tolerates no "simple" societies within or beside itself. Evolution itself needs no directional specifications. It is not a purposive process anyway.

In any case, evolution theory is perfectly compatible with the observation that highly complex systems are destroyed or abandoned,[68] that they often have too little evolutionary capacity, and that evolution not infrequently replaces highly complex arrangements by superior simplification.[69] With regard to language, in particular, the thesis of increasing complexity in the course of evolution cannot be maintained.[70] Despite all these objections, there is no denying that complexity tests occur in the course of evolution, and that more complex systems come into being alongside others. Complexity is an epigenetic product of how autopoietic systems operate.[71] Under conditions still to be clarified, it permits more (or "softer") structural couplings between system and environment and consequently more differentiated system irritabilities. But complexity can never be a selection criterion itself (it is too complex).[72] In particular, we must therefore always ask, "what kinds of situations would give positive selective value to increased or decreased complexity,"[73] and only because *both* are possible can highly complex systems *also* develop in the course of evolution.

This redefinition of the relationship between evolution theory and systems theory can take account of the fact that new developments often occur abruptly, very rapidly, and under special conditions, and hence do not result from the structures already realized of large systems or populations.[74] We need think only of the particularities of the peripheral Hebrew or Greek cultures of the ancient world, what Parsons has called "seed-bed societies."[75] Finally, the perhaps most important, or at any rate, potentially upsetting, concept in evolution theory requires systems-theoretical reintegration: the concept of *chance*.

The importance of chance in evolution theory could be understood as meaning that the theory is grounded in a postulate of ignorance—ignorance of the microphysical, chemical, biochemical, neurophysiological, psychological processes that ultimately determine what happens.[76] This reduces the problem to an epistemological formula and makes it a paradox (knowledge grounded in nonknowledge). But this is only a special case of a far more general law, namely, that systems always manifest limited (reduced and enhanced) response capacity and, one might say, are accessible to one another only through "windows." Phrasing it differently, in order to generate the information needed to guide them, all systems have to perform measurements. For this reason, a system substitutes full knowledge of the environment by preparedness for something that is chance *for it*. Only this makes evolution possible.

In contrast to older assumptions, the concept does not therefore serve to negate causality; it does not imply causeless occurrence. "Chance" is therefore no makeshift causal construction, for example, a cause advanced (as it were to complete a causal schema in explaining the world) if we can give no cause. We ascribe no causal-theoretical importance to the concept of chance. In extremely abstract terms, we can speak of chance as a difference-theoretical boundary concept. Chance then means that determination of the one side of a distinction has no meaning for determination of the other side. This is how Hegel understands the concept of chance and correspondingly the counterconcept of necessity. A narrower definition suffices us, relating to the distinction between system and environment. By "chance," we understand a form of correlation between system and environment that eludes synchronization (i.e., also control, "systematization") by the system.[77] No system can take account of all causalities. Their complexity must be reduced. Certain causal relations are observed, expected, preventively induced or averted, normalized—and others are left to chance. In other words, the "irregularity" of chance is not a global phenomenon, and it is consequently not useful to bring it up in the discussion of determinism/indeterminism. It presupposes system reference, for only thus can an observer say for whom something is chance.

This rather negative characterization is complemented by a positive one. Chance is the capacity of a system to use events that cannot be produced and coordinated by the system itself (hence not in the network of the system's autopoiesis). From this point of view, chances are risks, occasions, opportunities. To "take a chance" means to win structuring effects from it with the means of systemic operations. Measured against existing structures, these effects can be both constructive and destructive (insofar as this can be distinguished at all in the long term). In any case, the observation of chance events expands the information-processing capacity of the system, thus correcting as far as possible the tightness of its own structural formations without sacrificing the orientational advantages of these strictures.

However, this does not yet tell us how it happens. There are very general ideas about it in systems theory. The "order from noise" principle is one of them;[78] the notion that structural couplings channel irritations is another. Systems theory is thus ready to receive evolution theory. But this naturally does not explain how evolution is possible.

3. The Neo-Darwinian Theory of Evolution

The independence of evolution theory lies in the independence of its distinctions. Since Darwin, one has spoken of *variation* and *selection*. Since selection is double-edged, however, either protecting what exists or changing it, we need a further concept, which I shall call *restabilization*. As our framework theory teaches (see § 1 above), this involves a paradox resolution program, the unfolding of the paradox of the probability of the improbable. These terms therefore refer to forms, to identifiable distinctions, and particularly in this context, this is likely to be immediately understandable. Variation does not simply mean change (for this would then already be evolution), but the production of a variant for possible selection. Similarly, selection in the context of evolution theory does not mean simply the pure fact that something happens the way it does and not otherwise; the term refers to selection on the occasion of a variation that occurs in the system. They are corresponding concepts that are not used outside evolution theory, and this immanent reference of its lead distinction gives the concept of evolution its form.

Whereas stage models shift difference into mere succession and can describe the historical process only as the unity of these differences, evolution theory itself presupposes the generation of difference over time and can thus allow the difference principle to become reflexive. However variation operates empirically, it generates a difference, namely, a deviation from what has hitherto been usual. This difference imposes a selection—against or in favor of innovation. In turn, the selection, if it opts for innovation, imposes cascades of adaptation or demarcation movements in the system, and, if it opts for the status quo, confirmations of this option, since what had previously been a matter or course has become contingent. The distinctions of evolution theory therefore refer to differences that process differences. And it is this structure that makes it unnecessary to speak of a final goal or a law of historical movement.

We arrive at similar notions if we set out from the problem of genetic or cultural *transmission*.[79] Authors of this inclination tend to proceed on the assumption of a generation change and see the problem of evolution primarily in bridging this break dictated by life. This brings us to the question whether there are transmissible equivalents in culture for the role of genes in biological evolution. And we then speak of populations rather than systems. But here, too, at the next theoretical stage, the problem of coping with deviant transmission arises, the question of whether malformations are simply eradicated or in rare cases lead to structural innovations. And only this is really evolution that goes beyond the mere autopoiesis of life or society.

The distinction between variation, selection, and (autopoietic) stabilization gives us the point of departure for a general theory of evolution that still completely ignores what sorts of system can effect a separation of these evolutionary functions. They can be both living systems and societies.[80] For every application of evolution theory, the system reference must therefore first be determined. If it is a matter of society, all living systems belong in the environment of the system.[81] The way in which variation, selection, and restabilization are separated and divided could differ. For the evolution of living beings, we could consider various types of system—of genetically programmed cells as the object of variation, of the survival of organisms as the object of selection, and of ecologically stable populations as the object of restabilization. In societal evolution, there is no indication of any sort for this type of separation guarantee. The medium of meaning alone, with its immense referential and connective capacity, makes such isolated evolutionary functions at various levels of the system improbable.[82] Critics of neo-Darwinism accordingly reject the proposition that variation and selection can be separated for social systems—mainly with the argument that individuals anticipate the future.[83] However, this does not exclude systems that operate meaningfully from separating variation, selection, and restabilization. The question is only how they do so.

This question has hardly arisen let alone been satisfactorily answered in the social sciences, where they have taken up the Darwin schema at all.[84] I propose relating the various components of evolution to various components of the autopoiesis of the societal system as follows:

(1) *Variation* varies the *elements* of the system, in this case communications. Variation consists in the deviant reproduction of elements by the elements of the system, in other words, in unexpected, surprising communication.

(2) *Selection* concerns the *structures* of the system, in this instance, expectations that steer communication. From deviant communication it chooses meanings promising for developing structures, which are suitable for repeated use, which can form and condense expectations; and, by attributing deviation to the situation, consigning it to oblivion or even explicitly

rejecting it, it discards innovations that appear unsuitable as structure and hence for guiding continuing communication.

(3) *Restabilization* concerns the state of the evolving *system* after selection, whether positive or negative. This has primarily to do with the societal system itself in relation to its environment. Consider, for example, the primal development of agriculture with consequences that had to be "systemically viable" in the social system of society. Or the avoidance of agrarization (for ecological or other reasons), which led to the emergence of "nomadic peoples" on the periphery of already politically developed peasant societies. In the course of societal evolution, the restabilization function shifted more and more to subsystems of society, which have had to prove their worth in the intrasocietal environment. The problem was ultimately the permanence of system differentiation.

Elements, structures, and the unity of the reproduction context are necessary components of an autopoietic system. There are no elements without a system, no system without elements, and so on. This raises the question how evolution is possible at all if it requires access *differentiated* by variation, selection, and restabilization to these individual components. With this question, we also reconstruct the thesis of the improbability of all evolution and the improbable probability of the system forms it generates.

The concept of the autopoietic system alone shows that these components of the system structure and evolution have a circular relationship to one another. Although the distinction between variation, selection, and restabilization suggests temporal succession, and is also so intended, it is just as correct to say that variation presupposes stability or, if you will, normal reproduction. Evolution is therefore always only the modification of existing states; and if we try to capture it with concepts such as innovation or emergence we are left with abstracted descriptions in which we must ask ourselves why the focus is on discontinuity and not continuity.

Just as artificial is episode formation that starts with variation and describes restabilization as its result. Only selection—in keeping with its key position in the concept of evolution—cannot describe the beginning or the end of an evolutionary episode. An autopoietic system can neither begin nor end a structural change with selection. In very simplistic terms, we can therefore also describe evolution as structural selection, and, when we consider that structures steer the selection of operations, as the selection of selections.[85]

4. The Variation of Elements

To this day, the sociological literature has failed to produce a satisfying explanation of evolutionary variation—just as biology initially understood mutation only as an abrupt and inexplicable change in genotype. Older sociology was satisfied to point to the practically infinite possibilities of variation in individual behavior.[86] Even today, action theoreticians argue—either against systems theory or with the intention of complementing it—that any explanation of societal change requires recourse to highly motivated individual action, hence localizing it (together with the individual agents?) in social systems.[87] On closer analysis and, above all, with a better understanding of the individuality of organic-psychic systems, this is untenable. The concept of successful evolutionary variation also speaks against it. On the one hand, recent biological research suggests that the conditions of genetic variation are also subject to highly complex fine-tuning.[88] But such regulation can take place only within the evolving system itself. On the other hand, a theory of operationally closed systems cannot accept that the variation mechanism lies in the organic-psychic environment of society. The high systemic complexity and extrasocietal autopoiesis of human organisms and psychic systems allow, indeed, oblige, us to consider that they collaborate in societal evolution by chance—despite the socialization of these individuals and their dependence on society. If we want to clarify evolutionary variation, we must turn to the system of society itself and look for the conditions of possible variation in the basal operation of this system, in communication.

Also unacceptable is a further proposition, more at home in the sociology of the twentieth century, to understand intellectuals as disruptive factors, in accordance with a pattern developed in the eighteenth century, and to put them at the service of variation.[89] This brings us from the individual to the role. The production of deviating ideas gains a certain regularity, an almost businesslike nature. Intellectuals accordingly regard "critique" as a positive attitude. What they find more difficult is the insight that specialization in variation demands renouncing responsibility for selection.[90] More important, however, is another objection: evolutionary variation is far too broad, too much of a mass phenomenon to be left to special roles. Intellectuals may well act as amplifiers, but they are too strongly determined by fashions, polemics, and the semantic consistency of their ideas to be able to generate sufficiently open variation if put to the test. Prague structuralists of the prewar period rightly renounced ascribing a decisive role in the evolution of literature and art to writers and artists as outstanding personalities.[91] However indispensable this factor of chance, they claimed, it failed to explain the frequent occurrence of "pleiads" at certain periods, differences in position, or the nature of controversies; and these are, after all, decisive variations in evolution. Historical "greatness" is a description fabricated to explain variation, a societal construction.

The primary variation mechanism is already to be found in the linguistic nature of communication (and in this we see parallels to the requirement of chemical stability in genetic mutation). Already as variation, language makes variation dependent on complex fine-tuning. Linguistically, communication has to be approximately correct, it has at any rate to be understandable. Variation hence lies neither in the occasional slip of the tongue nor in slips of the pen or typographical errors. Such occurrences are far too rare and trifling to give a society sufficient opportunity for selection. Linguistic communication has to condense meaning in advance with the aid of acceptable words and sentence constructions in which minor technical errors disappear; and evolutionary variation comes about only where linguistically successful meaning proposals are called into question in the communication process or flatly rejected. Variation can lie in an unusual utterance, but also, and presumably more frequently, in the unexpected nonacceptance of an utterance in view of a situation that makes this possible or likely. In any case, it must be linguistically understandable—with regard not only to the meaning that is directly negated but also with regard to the whys, wherefores, and whatnows.

To put it more precisely and consider it with respect to its communicative use, the variation mechanism consists in the invention of negation and the yes/no coding of linguistic communication this makes possible.[92] We note the improbability of the evolutionary achievement. In first place, linguistic communication is, after all, a positive, actually experienceable event in the real world; and a differentiating event that indicates something determinate. What we can initially observe is only the operation of distinguishing itself—quite independently of the question of whether it refers to something, what this something is, and whether it does so positively or negatively. What is not indicated remains in the "unmarked state" of the world and is not negated (for this would require indication).[93] The possibility of understanding a communication as negation, let alone the possibility of taking such a possibility into account in anticipation, is a very contingent result (our argument is circular!) of its own evolution.

As we know, there is no environmental correlate for negations. They come about only for internal use. This holds true a fortiori for the linguistic code, which ensures that every communication is concentrated *as communication* (and not, e.g., owing to its external reference) on a bifurcation of acceptance or rejection of the meaning proposed. Purely linguistically, this is not be prevented, however much rhetorical effort is invested. In contrast to an environment-related use of negation ("I haven't seen him") the coding directs communication toward itself. It is a matter of acceptance or rejection of the meaning it conveys and not of whether communication has taken place or not. Through coding, communication itself becomes reflexive and in this form can also put pressure on environment-related negations by discussing whether an assertion to this effect holds true or not. Once introduced, the coding can never be eliminated as an element in the autopoiesis of linguistic communication. It grows with the possibilities of linguistic communication, hence with society. The more possibilities for expression and understanding the development of a complex semantics provides, the more stimulus for rejection this produces.

This need not mean that the yeses and noes are originally equally probable. The coding creates a surplus; society helps itself out by inhibiting the noes. Whatever is linguistically possible and understandable is nevertheless not always appropriate. Where inhibition does not take effect or institutional disinhibition restores the possibilities of rejection, the variation mechanism finds room for maneuver, and only by this complicated detour of surplus production, inhibition, and disinhibition can it adapt to the given status of societal evolution.

Variation therefore comes about through communication that rejects the content of communication. It produces a deviant element—nothing more nor less. The process focuses on the expectation of acceptance already articulated or implied or expected in communication. It thus looks into the past—with its back to the future, like the prophets of Israel. This separates variation from selection; for a proposed selection would itself be a positive meaning proposal, which is in turn subject to the bifurcation of acceptance and rejection. Variation is therefore not the spontaneous genesis of innovation ("new" will still long be a suspect category, almost to be equated with aberrance)[94] but the deviant reproduction of elements of the system. And deviation is a recursive concept, for it presupposes something to deviate from.

Rejection *contradicts* the expectation of acceptance or simply the assumption of continuity in "business as usual." All variation therefore occurs as contradiction—not in the logical sense, but in the more original, dialogical sense. It can occur only as self-contradiction of the system.[95] It resigns itself to the requirements of the system's autopoiesis—it communicates!—it ensures the continuation of communication, even if with freer connectivity options and with an immanent tendency toward conflict.

Day in, day out, corrective variation of this sort takes place on a massive scale, the correction of opinions expressed, or conflicts also vaguely hinted at and then mostly avoided. It is thus important to keep the trifling nature of evolutionary variation in mind. Like all operational elements of dynamic systems, communication, including deviant communication, is a situation-bound occurrence whose importance normally passes very rapidly. The concept of variation hence provides no answer to the much too compact question of how great, epoch-making ideas or inventions come into being. Evolution makes no large, abrupt leaps (even though its results can be so interpreted in retrospective observation). But it requires material amenable to evolution to be produced on a massive scale and normally to disappear again unused. This alone ensures that selection has sufficient chances, that minor chance events reinforce each other frequently enough, and that one variation can support another taking place at the same time.

It should also be noted that variation, unlike selection, is not communicated as such. It is not conveyed with regard to selection.[96] It is explained somehow—but not by its evolutionary function. There are also practical grounds for this. If variation were to take place only or largely with an eye to selection chances, it would run a high risk of disappointment; for social reality is extremely conservative and does not lightly negate what exists and has proved its worth in the light of something unknown whose prospects of consensus have yet to be tested, and that cannot be tested in the given situation. Rejection must seek justification elsewhere. The ban on usury is not respected—not because this serves the evolution of the economic system but because legally and ecclesiastically tenable ways of circumventing it can be found. Or one simply dissociates oneself and opts out: NIMBY. This naturally does not exclude deviations from usual practice being proposed for selection (and in fact, it is misleading to describe sociocultural evolution as "blind"). But the proposal itself is not the selection; and, anyway, only a small part of variation occurrences relevant to evolution take such intentional form.[97] Only through the noncoordination of variation and selection, in other words, by avoiding communication on this relationship, can evolution become sufficiently probable and lead sufficiently rapidly to the development of an order that is in itself improbable. It is in this sense that we can also describe the relationship between variation and selection as *chance*: the determinacy of variation tells us nothing about the chances of selection.

If evolution produces more complex societies, this therefore cannot mean that more "useful" variations now have to be generated. The greater the complexity, the more improbable it is that any kind of innovation can fit in structurally. The chance coordination of variation and selection therefore has to be maintained; the alternative would be to switch to planning. In the functional area of variation, however, the dialectic of surplus production, inhibition, and disinhibition is adapted to the conditions of higher complexity by the means of higher complexity. In other words, additional facilities for massing and accelerating variation are needed (as where biochemical mutation is complemented in the evolution of life by bisexual reproduction). In societal evolution, this has happened in two ways: through the dissemination medium writing and by enhancing conflict competence and conflict tolerance in society (to put it another way, by renouncing the externalization of all conflicts as typical in segmentary societies).

Where writing is accepted as a dissemination medium (and not only for recording purposes), this has a double effect. Communication can be given greater spatial and temporal reach and is freed from the constraints of interaction, which means that it gains greater liberty in producing (writing) and receiving (reading). Greater dissemination makes it possible to change *many* things, indeed innumerable things, with *one* change. The notion that we can change something directly with a word is consequently lost or reduced to certain magical-religious practices. Moreover, the resulting increase in the unobservability of effects has to be institutionally safeguarded. As with all techniques, this raises religious problems, such as that narrated in the Prometheus myth. The rigidity of traditional holy law dissolves in the flames of writing, for example, and the now "valid" law makes legislation possible; but how?[98] Or when the ethos of the nobility was written down and, as in early modern times, even printed, the nobility soon found itself confronted by indeterminable people who had read the books and were therefore (!) better acquainted with what had previously been only pretension, could handle it with greater "virtuosity," and judge it critically.

Written and hence interaction-free communication need not and cannot take account of physically present interlocutors, but must replace the aids to understanding provided by the unity of the face-to-face situation. It must explicate more clearly and only by means of the text itself. This leads to new types of linguistic form and above all to the formation of concepts with their own unforeseeable consequences. As long as God was only designated by a name that one had to know in order to invoke Him, it was possible to solve the problem by keeping the name secret. If we have a concept for God that is fixed in writing, the concept can condense experience, demand specification, lead to consistency problems—in short, provoke everything that occupied medieval theologians.

The other possibility for enhancing variation competence mentioned above, namely, the generation and toleration of intrasocietal conflicts, also had to be asserted against structurally obdurate reservations; and even today conflict is frowned upon by all but a few sociologists. Conflicts test the potential for rejection. They lead to the all-round integration of participants' behavior, to continual observation of observation, and hence to an intensive exchange of information. If a no wins a conflict, we can assume that it has passed a first test and proved sustainable.[99] Nevertheless, conflicts easily get out of control and disturb the intrasocietal environment. In older societies, face-to-face violence was much more frequent than today, and a propensity for violence was correspondingly subject to severe repression.[100] This must have affected the willingness to say no; for if a person dares to refuse after others have already committed themselves in communication, conflict is at the door. The others will insist, look for and find arguments and allies, and all of a sudden a system forms within the system: a conflict. In small societies formed in the intimacy of interaction, conflict repression is therefore vital for survival. With increasing size and complexity, as Late Archaic societies already showed, this condition was eased. However, this can happen only under similarly complex conditions, which make it possible to attain more conflict and more peace at the same time.

One widespread attempt in this direction was to shift the problem of deviation to the level of social roles and to solve it there through the differentiation of success roles on the one hand and failure and misfortune-related roles on the other. The former became celebrity roles and were then engaged for conflict regulation,[101] and the latter were neutralized by assumptions regarding the evil eye, witchcraft, and the like.[102] This situation was superseded only by the development of political decision-making powers with complicated consequences for the now necessary balance between religion and politics.[103]

With the development of effectual political rule, it becomes possible to strengthen the rejection of communicative offers of meaning while mitigating the consequences of conflict. Legitimate force arises to combat illegitimate force.[104] The form found to achieve this is a structurally secured asymmetry—be it on the basis of property or on the basis of power secured by followers. Whoever has the resources can say no, can elude demands for help or handouts without having to reckon with conflict.[105] He can concentrate his resources. This achievement is restabilized by stratification of the societal system.[106]

Another possibility is *to permit conflicts but to defuse them through social regulation and the influence of third parties on the outcome of disputes.* To this end, arbitration procedures, ultimately, the rule-bound settlement of disputes, became established, which, epigenetically, as it were, produced semantic material that eventually became known as "law" and used for the autopoiesis of a legal system.[107] The wealthy man can reject a communication anyway; but the poor man can now also do so, if he is *in the right.*[108] Contrary to the "moral functionalism" assumptions of a Durkheim or certain philosophers of law, the prime function of the law is not the moral integration of society but the intensification of conflict possibilities in forms that do not endanger social structures.[109] The enhancement of conflict competence can be used differentially, and in older societies it serves mainly to develop stratificatory differentiation.

Hardly comparable is a third possibility of highly complex society, namely, the *differentiation of conflict grounds and conflict topics.*[110] There can be deep-seated structural reasons for the repeated outbreak of conflicts, but the conflicts themselves seek other occasions and topics, because the structural trigger is anyway no "solvable problem." The insistent search by some sociologists for the "real" reasons of conflict, their Marxist heritage, in other words, has concealed the fact that this very difference between grounds and topics is an achievement provided the system is big enough to endure conflicts.[111]

Among the imponderables provoked by these extended possibilities of variation is the corresponding transformation of the semantics and its consequences. The more possibilities of rejection are admitted, the greater is the need for nonnegatability. But the very search for what is necessary, if it can be observed as a search (and writing guarantees this), produces ever-new contingencies. Religion, inasmuch as it is under the aegis of theology, joins in this dangerous course.[112] Reality, which had been considered nonnegatable per se, falls under suspicion of being mere creation, mere "appearance," a mere correlate of consciousness, or now a mere "construction." The differentiation of special functional systems gives rise to related contingency formulae that can assert system-specific indisputability, for instance, scarcity for the economic system, legitimacy for the political system, justice for the legal system, limitationality for the science system.[113] But tying such formulae to particular special functional systems leaves open their meaning for society as a whole. The saving formula since the mid-nineteenth century has been values. But they are exposed to the same process of corrosion. Once in the world, they allow discussion of the "reevaluation of values" or "value change."

All these reflections on forms of variation presuppose that deviations can be perceived at all. All variation thus depends on a predetermined semantic, on the memory of the system, which informs all communication about what is known and normal, what can be expected, and what not. What stands out is hence guided by already established structures. This precondition is all the more important because it operates unseen. The unity of the distinction between expected and unexpected, normal/deviant is not itself addressed. Finely ramified semantics, in particular, as in religious or legal dogmatics, feed problems back into themselves to rougher or more fundamental distinctions, but do not result in the differentiation schema being called into question. The choice is then apparently between tradition and variation, old and new. In favorable cases a variation can assert itself. But it will hardly be possible to ask why the question is put the way it is and not otherwise.

Dependence on a predetermined semantics is an essential precondition for recognizing deviations, and thus for evolution. Nevertheless one can imagine that difficulties arise on the threshold to radical change. Whenever the invisible hand of tradition (and for many fields this means religion) determines how to draw distinctions between conformity and deviation, variations are likely that categorize problems wrongly, for example producing exceptions from rules that as rules have lost their importance (e.g., exceptions to and ways round the [ecclesiastical] ban on charging interest on loans). This also means that in times of radical change, the radical nature of structural change cannot be observed and, in retrospect, communication employs distinctions that are no longer appropriate. Where the early modern age saw its problem in bringing innovation in almost all functional areas into harmony with a fundamentally religious positing of the world, or to taking its distance from them, we now ask ourselves whether it was indeed this problem that decided the transition to our modern, functionally differentiated society.

On the basis of this situation, can we expect society to describe the world and itself ever better, and hence to learn to control the formation of categories prescribing what is experienced as old and what as new? In a certain sense, the question answers itself. The fact that we can put it merely shifts the problem to another level of abstraction without definitively solving it. What we can observe, however, is a different sort of reaction, namely, intensification of differentiation between variation, selection, and restabilization, which not by chance takes place by degrees where far-reaching structural breaks occur, for example, the spread of an easily manageable system of writing or a change in the differentiation form of society. Although we do not notice that a schema revision is due, evolution itself evolves; it autonomizes selection and restabilization vis-à-vis variation and thus creates a higher degree of freedom in dealing with not understood or insufficiently positioned problems.

When in premodern societies one came under the pressure of enhanced possibilities of variation, it could always be assumed that selection had to be guided by the One, True, and Good. People could believe themselves accommodated in a cosmos of essences. The means might be uncertain or they might fail, but there was no doubting the goals, "quia ex se patet quod optatur" (because what is desirable is obvious in itself). But this trust in the only right selection, which ultimately brought perfection, peace, stability had been secretly reensured by stratification and the center/periphery differentiation of the societal system, safeguards that no longer hold. Instead, one begins to value what is new as such,[114] to understand "critique" to mean rejection of what is criticized, and to understand "alternatives" no longer as mere options but as variants to be deemed better than what exists without closer inspection. In sum, variation suffers semantic hypertrophy—and society consequently develops a built-in disappointment with itself. For variation alone cannot effect evolution.

As a result, however, something quite different from mere reevaluation took place in relations between old and new. In fact, society has now adapted to modes of selection that not longer offer a prospect of stability. It differentiates between selection and restabilization—simply because the pressure of innovation is growing and has to be dealt with more rapidly. If we are to assess this process, however, we must first examine the functional vehicles of selection and restabilization as such.

5. Selection Through Media

The concept of evolution takes form in the distinction between variation and selection. "Form" necessarily implies "another side," which means in this case that where variation occurs, selection is necessary. The interest of the nineteenth century in evolution was an interest in selection, whether natural or unnatural;[115] and the interest in selection was an interest in the *production* of a unity or unities, now that they could no longer be taken as given.

Since variation and selection are coupled only "by chance," a theory of evolutionary selection can be elaborated separately.[116] Here and there, a structural innovation occurs, "whatever its causes."[117] Different initial situations may also be said to be "equifinal"—rather misleadingly, because this naturally does not mean that established forms converge in the course of evolution. It should only be noted that the selection function depends solely on the fact of variation, not on which concrete activating factor brings it into the world.

Like variation, selection is possible only if and as long as the system exists, that is, if and as long as the adaptedness of the system can be maintained. In evolutionary selection, this boundary condition (which does not serve as a selection criterion!) is expressed in the form of the reusability of selection viewpoints. They recall and condense the test experience of the system and make it available internally.[118] For this purpose, they must be abstracted from concrete situations, but also so conceived that they "fit" many, concretely different situations—regardless of whether their earlier use and worth is remembered or not. Furthermore, not least for understanding the problem on hand, a high degree of conformity with existing structures is required. The compatibility of the innovation is examined. However, evolution is accommodated by the difficulty of testing consistency and can generally be recognized only when the innovation has been introduced and has led to problems in practice. At any rate, the case that modern social critique has in mind, namely, that an innovation is preferred because it deviates, must be considered a rare exception.[119]

Every variation necessarily leads to selection. Even if no positive selection takes place, selection takes place because operation-bound variation passes away without changing structures, and everything remains the way it was and is. What is selected is the existing state—and not the innovation. Selection itself is hence a two-sided form: if not positive, then negative. That it is a form also distinguishes it from variation, which for its part is form because it can occur—or not occur. The form of evolution (variation/selection) is therefore a second-order form, a form formed of forms.

The fundamental condition of all evolution is hence that the facilities for variation and those for selection do not coincide, but remain separate. In cybernetic terms, the operation connects with the system in the form of feedback. This feedback can be negative or positive, it can concern keeping within a given range of fluctuation in system states or amplifying deviation, developing complexity, which then comes to bear with its own problems.

History can be reversed neither by negative selection (= selection of nonselection) nor by negative feedback. The system never returns to its earlier state. It can only remember and compare. It can attribute variation to the situation and explain why the opportunity for change was not taken. But this cannot prevent a conservative course from being regretted later or the problem addressed anew, indeed, it rather points in this direction. In any case, repetition creates a different situation.

Whether evolutionary selection tends in one direction or another is decided through its own mechanisms. It is accordingly by chance that a variation is relevant for selection through its own determinacy alone.[120] Above all, no purposive relationship may be installed, with the result that a variation is carried out only for the sake of selection. This may well motivate variations, and communications anticipating useful outcomes are naturally not excluded.[121] But if evolutionary structural changes then occur, this is due not to the achievement of a purpose but to the system reacting by structural changes to the efforts to achieve it. Evolution makes use of calculated optimism to stimulate variation. But what is selected as structure is not yet decided for this reason alone.[122]

The separation of these evolutionary functions is already ensured by their relating to different components of the societal system: variation to elements, that is, communications, and selection to structures, that is, the formation and use of expectations. This means above all that no one-to-one relationship is to be assumed between variation events and selections (just as little as between mutations and the selection of phenotypical characteristics in organic evolution). Communication, especially when it is observed, is much too diffuse in its effect. A single no cannot yet change structures, and if this does occur, it would be an extremely rare exception that cannot explain the tempo of evolution. Contradiction to assumed expectations can attract attention, can confer social prestige, can encourage repetition or parallel action, and together with other conditions can overall change (or consolidate) structures quite different from those originally rejected. An existing social order always plays a part in the structural effects of rejecting communication. And only this can explain why in the evolution of life, as in the evolution of society, the results are always entirely coherent, not to say harmonious.

Returning to the problem of the probability of the improbable discussed at the outset of this chapter, we now see much more clearly how this overall effect comes about. The rejection of a demand for acceptance, like a negation of anticipated rejection in an attempt to achieve it nonetheless, is among the highly probable events of daily life. Variation in this sense occurs constantly. Only through selection of a structure using, confirming, condensing this event does something improbable come about, namely, a marked deviation from the initial state. It is clear that classical theories of linear causal laws cannot explain such phenomena. It is not that suitable causes necessarily produce effects where necessary constraints are present; events that repeatedly occur are used occasionally (on the whole often enough) by processes of circular deviation amplification to build structures that had not previously existed.[123] And the "no" has the attention value needed to trigger this. However complex mediation might be, there are indeed links between communication and structural formation; or, at any rate, what is never communicated can never influence structure formation. But, given prior structures, if communication actualizes a deviant variant, this can set into structure—*or not*, as the case may be. Variation as such generates *both* possibilities, *through its very determinacy*. It clears the way for selection; otherwise it would be no variation. But what mechanisms ensure that this is not the end, but that society provisionally opts for one or other of the possibilities? This question allows historical specification of the selection process, the possibility of recognizing the dependence of evolution on the societal formations it has itself created.

Darwinian theory had a simple answer: variation takes place in the system, but selection as "natural selection" through the environment. This simple opposition now finds hardly any proponents. Biologists, for example, have resolved it with game theory assumptions. It is above all incompatible with an elaborated systems-theoretical conceptuality. If we accept the theory of operationally closed, structurally determined systems, we must assume that systems can change their structures only through their own operations, however they react to occurrences in the environment in the form of disruption, disturbance, disappointment, deficiency, and so on. We must therefore examine society itself for selection mechanisms.

For all societies, including the most primitive, the primary selection mechanism is the differentiation of interaction systems and societal system.[124] No criteria are needed and there are no authorities for carrying out corresponding tests. The question is only whether what turns up in particular interaction systems, convincing owing to their situation, prevails in society as a whole, and if so in what form.

In face-to-face interaction, diverging opinions, if expressed, can hardly be ignored (tact, humor, and so on are relevant inventions, but come late in civilization). Since communication is attributed to a person as an action, we must reckon with its recurrence or with corresponding connective behavior inside or outside the system. Conflicts then arise that deplete resources. The system is too small to tolerate conflicts within it; it becomes a conflict. Or the system grasps the opportunity and sets out on the suggested course. Within interaction systems, the probability of structural transformation through communicative events is therefore very high—practically so high that there can be no evolution, because selection cannot be independently installed, but is taken in by practically every variation. Interaction can experiment with all sorts of peculiarities, because it can be certain that society will continue to exist anyway.

But society not only carries out interactions, it is also the societal environment of interactions.[125] This intrasocietal difference prevents everything that presents itself, that pleases, that displeases in interaction from affecting the structures of the societal system. All meaning—and especially what can be person or role—is constituted *transinteractionally* with an eye to use outside current interaction. This is already taken into account in interaction, and, compared with what can happen in interaction, very little innovation can pass this filter for diffusion throughout society.

In early segmentary societies, it was still relatively clear what could happen elsewhere in society or be acceptable. When society becomes more complex, it loses this easy possibility of self-assessment. Unlike in simple societies, however, there can now be "subcultures" in which deviations can sustain themselves, and also subsystems drawing their own boundaries, which have to be crossed if an innovation is to have societywide resonance.[126] In contrast to the usual diffusionist theories, we are dealing here with a *different sort* of use, made possible by boundaries, of a stimulus that is initially volatile or with only limited scope for expansion (e.g., the use of an established stone-working technique for large-format religious purposes). However, the evolutionary situation undergoes a profound change only with the invention and spread of writing. Since not all communication still takes place in interaction systems, and writing gives negation new opportunities, only corresponding amplifiers in the field of selection can ensure that evolution remains possible.

To begin with, religion could absorb the pressure. It was able to offer criteria for judging whether letting oneself in for variations could cause difficulties with otherworldly powers; and it could be assumed that the mundane world was open to experiment (e.g., with new production techniques) on condition that the domain of the sacred was spared. However, one had to know what pleased the gods and spirits and what did not. Major religious innovations took place. The archaic arbitrary behavior of sacred powers was limited and disciplined—as arable farming and city building disciplined society. The gods of Mesopotamia acted in accordance with adopted plans; they accepted governmental structures and family orders for themselves too. Through religion, society put itself under pressure to adapt and develop sanctified selection criteria for intercepting and sorting out wild variations. This function could perhaps be performed by a single god attributed the ability to observe and judge everything, so that it could not be wrong to accept his criteria.

We have this need to reorganize selection to thank for the world religions still practiced today. Each for itself, they are religions for everyone, for all human beings. They intensify the moral demands on God and on humans, as if it were crucial to hold onto the unity of the selection context of a culture and fix it with the aid of "canonic" texts.[127] Morality allows scope for interpretation and legal casuistry. Religion itself finds forms of vying radicalness and can thus take its distance from both the ruling bureaucracy and social stratification. Consider the relation of Buddhism to the caste system or the Augustinian theory of the two *civitates*. The combination of evidence and duration, problematic for all meaning, is shifted to transcendence. With the help of its texts, religion was converted into (largely orally practiced) tradition, and through ritualization (especially in India) or popular versions, it was made accessible to broad sections of the population. And because what had been written down was passed on orally, the text showed a stability not (or only imperceptibly) varied in oral transmission, whose obviousness conceals that there could be other possibilities.

While this solution predominates and has proved highly persuasive, there are other approaches, too, to a different, functionally equivalent amplification of the means of selection. This lies in the development of function-specific, symbolically generalized communication media. Selection tests whether one can invoke feasibility and, in considering the consequences, truth; whether the innovation can be financed and whether the power available suffices to assert it against any resistance.

What needed to be said about symbolically generalized communication media was said earlier (Chapter 2 §§ 9–12), so we can limit ourselves here to a few considerations. Symbolically generalized communication media can secure the acceptance of communications with highly exigent content, even under improbable conditions, by conditionalizing motives for acceptance and rendering them expectable through conditionalization. This is based on a process of dissolution and recombination, thus an enormous enhancement of combinatorial possibilities in search of forms that are nevertheless binding. Money is a good example, but power, backed by the threat of superior physical force, also has this structure. Similar thematic openness, bordering almost on the arbitrary, is generated with the methodization of scientific truth, and art is also reputed to be able to give shape to something in the "soft, simple element" of imagination that is not to be found in this guise in nature, which serves as model.[128]

In their basal structure, the media are loosely coupled, gigantic sets of elements with which tradition can be circumvented. This offers the chance to formulate new selection criteria that manage without perfection, peace, and stability. "Profit" hence becomes a selection viewpoint for the use of money, even though profit itself is unstable and depends on the exploitation of unstable, continuously changing market situations. All reliance on perfection is abandoned, whether in the quality of work or goods, in the entrepreneurial lifestyle and the income that goes with it, or, finally, in a human instinct that reason must tame and put to use. What remains are profitability calculations bound to single forms. For example, they require differentiable assets, which as such cannot even consider the stability of the economic system. In parallel, passionate love proclaims sovereignty over its own realm, represses object- and quality-related concepts of love, the love of God and the love of virtue, and sets store rather by the lesson of experience that it cannot last long.[129] Seventeenth-century political theory focused on opportunities (referred to at the time as "coups d'état")[130] and justified the need to concentrate power in the state mainly from this point of view. Finally, science, too, relaxed its assertion of certainty lying in the nature of objects and in cognition itself (initially indispensable in holding its own against religion) to find truth only in the free market of inductive inference, falsification experiments, and constructions.

The striking parallel development in these semantic innovations points to a link with functional differentiation. What interests us in the present context is only that in this manner selection is uncoupled from any prospects of stabilization, that a boundary is thus once again drawn, a dividing line between selection and stabilization functions.

It is obvious that this socially (and, as it later proves, religiously) ruthless broadening and narrowing of scope for selection can provide an answer to the problem that the enormous increase in possibilities for variation has caused. If deviations occur in the ambit of such media, they have no particular difficulty in noting and imposing them—provided that they satisfy the special conditions that apply for the medium in question. A new invention is introduced—for instance, the printing press—and money is already available for calculating the costs and benefits of a business program to be put into effect with this invention where economically feasible. Money can offer resistance only in quantity, but not, for instance, by intervening in the printing process. Or a new research question is launched, and tried and tested techniques are available that alone decide the extent to which results can be provided in the form of true or untrue propositions. Or one has read novels and knows what love is about. All that is then lacking is a person around whom the emotion can crystallize.

Whereas religion places its hopes in the unity of selection criteria and, where necessary, is willing to pay for it with stagnation, the development of societal complexity under the regime of symbolically generalized communication media depends on which media are more suitable than others. Considerable disbalances must accordingly be expected. It cannot at any rate be assumed that the system of society develops evenly in all areas, that every possible meaning is unfolded sooner or later, and that all needs and interests are finally satisfied at a higher level. Such illusions of a total ascendency of "humanity" prevailed in the eighteenth century and, if we count "communism," even in the nineteenth. We have in the meantime bid farewell to these notions, which have no successors. Certain functional areas must be expected to solve their selection problem more successfully than others, to adapt more rapidly to the tempo of modern societies or to accumulate achievements better than others.[131] The outcome is the dominance of technology or of money or of special rationalities that are not fully satisfying.

Despite all the semantic differences between religion and symbolically generalized media, they do appear to have something in common. In both domains, selection establishes itself at the level of *second-order observation*. Religion observes God as observer of humankind, symbolically generalized communication media direct the observing of other observers, for instance, in the markets of the economic system or in the field of knowledge assertions. The selection arrangements now needed distance themselves from the immediacy of variation events as an observer who observes what other observers observe. But if this is the technique employed in reaction to increasing complexity, it can, if successfully practiced, be expected to dissolve direct trust in reality. How, then, can the outcome of selection obtain stable form?

6. The Restabilization of Systems

As long as selection events are oriented on determined, only temporarily disturbed states, it does not make much sense to speak of a third evolutionary function. Selection itself ensures stability, and if it fails to do so (as is to be expected in a world determined by corruption or sin), selection has to be repeated over and again and as well as possible. The early modern state had still been described in the light of this task, and "peace" was the concept recommending it.[132] For where peace is secured, it can be left to each individual to safeguard his spiritual welfare and earthly livelihood. In the evolution-theoretical literature, too, selection and stabilization are often combined in a single concept. The talk is then of "selective retention" or "stabilizing selection."[133] This was plausible as long as biology, not to mention economic theory, understood selection to be natural selection by the environment and the outcome to be "optimal fit." Stability was described as "equilibrium," which used homeostatic mechanisms to balance out disturbances and reestablish a state of equilibrium. However, this required a fixed equilibrium point not displaced by any deviations that might occur. On condition that the environment itself did not change, this then needed no further provision for stabilization *after* structural change. This view is now hardly upheld.[134] It is dynamic systems that are amenable to evolution, systems far from being in equilibrium and that can reproduce. This is all the more true if we are obliged to abandon this premise, if we understand selection (as we do) to be a purely internal process. For what guarantees the assumption that only the prospect of stability can successfully select? And, above all, what guarantees this in a society that describes itself in relation to a difference between past and future states and has to cope daily with the experience of very rapid structural change? Does not today's society orient its selections only on what appears to be useful at the moment or temporarily?[135]

For living beings, the function of restabilization is performed by the formation of populations—population being understood in this context as the reproductive isolation of a gene pool that can accept variations to a limited extent and include them in reproduction. Each population can produce offspring only within itself, snakes and cats cannot produce snats. The Lamarckist thesis of the heritability of acquired characteristics is considered to have been refuted. This is what the closure of the population (in the strict systems-theoretical sense) is based on, as well as on the closure of its strong *ecological autonomy* (= stability). Very few ecological factors still intervene, namely, only those that can inhibit reproduction.

Current theorizing on societal evolution has produced few ideas for describing the restabilization function more precisely. Without any profound awareness of the problem, some authors rely on the normal continuity of facts and inventories,[136] others rely on the nineteenth-century distinction between mind and matter and explain stability in terms of cultural transmission and heredity.[137] Here, too, the lack of a sufficiently elaborated systems-theoretical conceptuality is apparent; for stability can best be determined with regard to systems.

We assume that the selection process already leads to the formation of structures. A further problem can therefore lie only in the relation of structures to systems whose autopoietic operations take place independently of structures. It should also be considered that both positive and negative selections can cause a restabilization problem, which accordingly reacts to selection per se. This is obvious in the case of positive selections that change structures. Innovated structures have to be adapted to the system and must be compatible with its environmental conditions without advance knowledge (upon selection) of whether and how this can be managed. In 1789, unrest in Paris was observed as "revolution" and described with a concept especially modified for the purpose. The consequences could be neither stopped nor controlled, and can probably best be described as a hundred years of failed follow-up revolutions, which, however, succeeded in transforming the French political system into a representative democracy. Codification of law, the abandonment of the economy to effectual intrasystemic forces, secularization in the religious field, privatization of the great families were also compensatory developments that can be understood as restabilizing revolutionary innovations.

But also where revolution selects negatively, where rejection prevails as it did in Prussia, restabilization is necessary, for example, in the sense of the *Kulturstaat* program for schools and universities. To put it in more general terms, variations can disappear into the unseen, but selections are normally retained by the system's memory, and one has to cope with the knowledge that something possible has not been realized. Conservational tendencies can thus be described and criticized as conservative ideology.[138] In these cases, too, (negative) selection does not yet decide that and how the system can adapt to itself and to its environment (e.g., to the expectations of individuals). It may well be that the innovative impact of a rejected innovation is much greater in the long run than the effect of an innovation that is realized—to the advantage or disadvantage of the system.

At any rate, the term "restabilization" refers to sequences of building structural changes into a system whose operations are structurally determined; and it takes into account that this also takes place through variations and selections, but always through operations of the system itself. In each case, selection, whether positive or negative, leads to an increase in the complexity of the system, to which the system has to react by restabilizing.

Such problems of structural compatibility (or "structural contradictions") are now the daily fare of sociologists, and it is therefore surprising that they have not received due attention.[139] System formation itself helps reduce problems of structural compatibility. It produces form, that is, boundaries on the inner side of which reduced complexity and a high degree of indifference toward the outer side can be gained. Incompatibilities can then be externalized—by blaming them on someone or by attributing them to God and entrusting them to the mystery of God. In this functional position, we often find specific institutional, indeed, organizational, inventions. For instance, banks serve the evolutionary restabilization of the money economy, which had dissolved the old maxim of reciprocity. And the modern "state" serves to restabilize long prepared political centralization. This trick of differentiation in already differentiated systems can be repeated, so that evolution leads to ever more contingent (and thus improbable) system formations in order to keep the burden of structural incompatibilities as light as possible and to distribute them among various systems. The cost, however, is structural incompatibilities among systems. This initially occurs in the relatively clear form of town/country differentiation and stratification, which help to legitimize this very process. Under today's functional differentiation regime, the problem assumes more drastic forms, and the overall system of society can then only register that this is so.

The function of evolutionary restabilization, like the formation of populations of living beings, is therefore subject to historical specification. It makes use of system differentiation, albeit with considerable residual problems, and develops solutions that vary depending on the dominant differentiation form. Whereas the cumulative deposition of more and more structures and the repetition of system formation in systems led to increasing form binding,[140] a change in forms of system differentiation, thus through evolutionary transition from segmentary differentiation to center/periphery-differentiation, to stratification, and eventually to functional differentiation, can provide new latitude for dissolving and recombining such forms, giving chances for new structures of more favorable complexity. This is also apparent in the parallel form changes in religion (*religio* = bind).

Externalization can naturally never be the final solution to a problem. Problems return in altered form in relations between system and environment. We can study this in the ecological problems in which modern society has become involved, but also in intrasocietal problems, for example, discussion of the now dubious "externalization of costs" through the money economy. It is therefore worth taking a closer look at how the process of restabilization proceeds in building new structures into the fabric of existing structures.

Here, too, the system benefits from already reduced complexity. Structural contradictions become apparent at certain points, for instance, in the late Middle Ages in the growing dependence of the nobility on money or in the age of the welfare state where politics becomes dependent on the successful operation of the economy, being able to attain success in its own right only by withdrawing more and more resources from economic calculation. "Inflation" is then the consequence of externalizing political conflicts,[141] but at the same time a problem for whose permanent supervision and continual handling specific skills and tools can be developed. Innovations are then, as it were, kept under surveillance on the inflation monitor, and we see relatively soon whether things are still in order or not. Specific techniques can be found for dealing even with highly generalized problem-distribution mechanisms—for which the money economy is notorious—and with a wide range of civilizational diseases. Conditions remain confused. In introducing new structures (e.g., automatic data-processing in more and more fields of society), we cannot always foresee what will happen; and when something does, it is usually too late to withdraw the innovation. Still, we can always invest in dealing with the resulting problems. Motorized traffic requires liability laws and insurance, rescue and ambulance services, specialized accident hospitals, upgraded and downgraded ("traffic calming") streets. Overall, society switches its stabilization efforts to reactive procedures. Society has become too complex and too opaque to set stability as an attainable goal.

It is no accident that the differentiation of selection criteria that no longer offer stability goes hand in hand with transition to the functional differentiation of the societal system. Selection and restabilization are separated more strongly than ever before. The multifunctional problem-solving by family households and morality is broken up and replaced by functional specifications. The stability of functional systems and of the organizations, professions, and roles differentiated within them on the principle of the division of labor is compatible with a wide range of variations and selections. It is based on the circumstance that a function, once differentiated out, can be fulfilled at an advanced level only in the facility provided for this purpose. The function itself is the point of reference for the limitation of functional equivalents, and for the function itself there is therefore no functional equivalent (unless with reference to a more general problem, for which the same then applies). Research can, for example, now only be carried on "scientifically." The amateur is no more. When political or economic organizations set up research institutes, the operations performed there proceed nevertheless in the science system—or they are not research institutes but possibly covert advertising organizations or addresses where deserving politicians can be put out to pasture. The order of such systems is then organized *self-substitutively* in the sense that their structures can be replaced only by other structures with the same function and of the same type: theories only by other theories, legislation only by other legislation, political platforms only by other political platforms. The stability principle this embodies takes the form of demand for a substitute solution. Anyone who wants to abolish nuclear power stations consequently faces the question of how power is to be generated by other means.

With the shift of the restabilization function to functional systems, stability itself becomes a dynamic principle and indirectly a major initiator of variation.[142] Under the condition of functional equivalence and the net superiority of new forms, functional systems are amenable to change. Even if they do not themselves bring innovations into the world, they have strong potential for reacting to innovation by innovation. This is increasingly so where organizations form within functional systems which can change themselves and their decision-making by means of decisions.[143] Already in the markedly stratificatory order of the Middle Ages, corporations such as the Church, monasteries, orders, cities, guilds, and universities assumed innovative functions—initially, because, thanks to their corporate stability, they were able as co-residential communities to keep themselves outside the estates system. Society was already experimenting with forms of dynamic stability, which were not provided for in their differentiation form.[144] But this very offside position of corporations also meant that their innovation potential was limited to themselves and that in the transition to modernity, they tended to be registered as rigid and obdurate. The order of estates and corporations was replaced more and more by the order of organizations *within* functional systems; and it was this turn of events that gave the primary societal subsystems themselves the possibility of developing conditioned dynamic stability.

In the course of this stage of evolution, functional systems switch their mode of selection to *essentially unstable criteria*. Selection can no longer be grounded in the quality of what is selected, but only in the criteria of selection. *Reasons of state* are invoked to allow politics to bow to situational constraints and let stable norms of morality or natural law fall by the wayside. The orientation of the economy on profit allows the continuous adaptation of production to market conditions. Any balance lies in a now only mathematical theory of equilibrium. The notion that love is a *passion* abandons intimate relationships to their own, at all events finite, temporal development. Balance lies in the assumption that love leads to marriage, but that this path can unfortunately not be taken by anyone who is already married. Since the second half of the eighteenth century, one has spoken of *style* to describe a both factual-formal and temporal unity, a unity that itself contains points of departure for possible deviations, which are allowed provided they succeed as works of art. Law now finds its validity principle in *positivity*, with the result that other decisions can bring other law into force. In early modern times, the same destabilization of criteria also shows itself in religion, thus depriving it of the possibility of offering other systems aids to stabilization. The medium of religion lies in the relationship between its boundary identities God and the soul. In Christianity, it could be elaborated as belief in revealed truths on the basis of biblical texts and glossed through the institutional order of the Church, through confession, moral casuistry, and so on. However, since the late Middle Ages, with its theological controversies, and since the ever stronger individualization of the soul (individuality = self-reference), the possibilities of forming forms in this medium have been problematic. Specifically, this means that the conditions for salvation of the soul become a problem to which the texts of tradition no longer provide a satisfactory answer. Neither the confidence conveyed by the Church, with its administration of grace , nor the life counseling offered by the Jesuits suffices, neither the invocation of faith (*sola fides*) nor the certainty that one hoped to find in seeking salvation by one's own efforts. Selection criteria, that is, the programs for programming coded functional systems, are geared throughout to instability, and this means that new "inviolate levels" have to be inserted—semantically in the form of the nineteenth-century conceptuality of value, structurally in the form of the autopoietic autonomy of functional systems.

Such immanent but open-ended safeguarding of stability manages without certainty about the world. Nor does it require reference to a description of society. Only function-related packages of alternatives are differentiated; all-too-abstract problem formulations prove ineffective because not informative enough for assessing the extent of change in the process of ongoing restabilization. What is striking from an evolution-theoretical point of view is that functional systems are geared to variation in order to stabilize, so that the stabilization mechanism also operates as an engine of evolutionary variation.[145] This accelerates societal evolution to an unprecedented extent. As in a short circuit, stabilization and variation appear to coincide. Only thus could selection criteria be chosen that do without any commitment to a morality binding on society as a whole or to considerations of stability; and only thus could a seriously posited semantics conceive of and welcome innovation, critique, change, and hence variation as such free of deviation. The opponents of society benefit not least of all from society encouraging itself in this historically unprecedented manner. The result is an unusually high frequency of change in the structures of the societal system perceptible within the lifetime of individuals. "We need an annual supplement to the Decalogue," groaned Edward A. Ross.[146] This fits the assumption in evolution theory that the extent to which variation, selection, and restabilization are differentiated correlates with the tempo of evolutionary change.

After all this, the concept of system stability needs to be redefined. Recognition of structural contradictions and the concept of dynamic stability were steps in this direction. Over and above this, however, it is questionable whether stability can be described at all in terms of a bivalent logic such that stable relates to unstable the way A relates to non-A. Self-referential systems are always so constructed that they provide options whose alternatives are also available and whose unity must therefore be described as paradoxical. And only because this is so can changes be set off from without. Liquid water contains within itself the possibility of freezing into ice or evaporating; and only because of this can external changes in temperature cause these effects. The form of communication offers the possibility of reacting to meaning proposals by accepting or rejecting them; and only because this is so can external changes affect society through the states of consciousness of psychic systems. This does not amount to a dialectical theory positing that, on account of the logical instability of its self-generated internal contradictions, a system works on synthesizing them itself. Evolution rather leads to systems in which every internal operation realizes something determinate at the cost of something else, thus making it possible to "cross" the internal boundaries of the distinctions used if the occasion or opportunity to do so arises.

In describing modern, functionally differentiated society, this can no longer be left out of account, because it concerns not only the external relations of the societal system but also its internal relations. Magoroh Maruyama is therefore perhaps right in assuming a quite new, nonstationary situation. In the past, too, he claims, there had been both imperceptible change as well as occasional sudden and radical change, but always from one stationary state to another. Societies were therefore always able to describe themselves as stationary and to accept a corresponding epistemology of constant order. Only the transition to modern society effected a "metatransition," a transition from a stationary state to a nonstationary state; and an appropriate epistemology was only now developing.[147] The distinction between various forms of system differentiation in combination with the theory of the evolutionary differentiation of evolutionary functions could offer an explanation.

This description is, however, still very one-sided. The other side to it is the conservatism of this very society. The methodology of planning reactive changes—let alone freely chosen, purposive planning—fails to keep pace. In decision theory, only "bounded rationality" is still in demand. Methodology becomes a brake, develops uncertainty, and complexity is defined—and practiced—as a lack of information. Inasmuch as the channeling of restabilization lies in the hands of organizations, that is, operates by decision and has to be secured against "postdecisional regret,"[148] innovation faces resistance. Meaning is established retrospectively after action has been taken and decisions made.[149] But, for better or for worse, society does not evolve at the level of its organizations.

The outcome is an unusual, unique case for evolution theory. Although evolution has never exhausted the possibilities of its basal substratum—this holds for proteins, for photosynthesis, for meaning, and for language—the result has always been the diversification of structurally determined systems. The fullness of being lies in the multitude of realized possibilities. Societal evolution has produced innumerable tribal societies. Depending on how one counts, there are some twenty to thirty examples of advanced civilizations. In contrast, there is only a single case of a functionally differentiated society. Thus evolution in only one case? This appears to amount to forgoing all redundancies and the avoidance of all safeguards. If this society no longer exists, there will be no others—unless new forms emerge from within it. We shall have to examine the possibilities of intrasocietal evolution,[150] but this alone is clearly not an adequate answer to the question posed. The answer can be found only in this society itself, for example, in its ability to take the pace, to find replacements for failures, to capitalize contingency reserves, and, above all, to exert a socializing influence with these requirements and to make the consciousness systems of human beings acquainted with these matters. For it is all too understandable if under such circumstances people accustomed to other things in a long-living culture become nervous.

7. Differentiation of Variation, Selection, and Restabilization

As I have sought to show, societal evolution requires and realizes a differentiation of evolutionary functions, which means to say their realization through various circumstances. In the course of evolution, and with growing differentiation of evolutionary functions, the separation problem shifts. In segmentary societies without writing, it must have been difficult to separate variation from selection, for face-to-face interaction was the only form of system available for communication and the segmentary form of system differentiation ensured that similar conditions could be assumed everywhere in the intrasocietal environment. In highly cultivated societies, both writing and differentiation on the basis of inequality facilitate this primary process of separation. However, this very circumstance makes it difficult to distinguish selection from restabilization. Selections are understood as answers to disturbances and as restoration of a state of rest, a stable state of society. If a dividing line is drawn between selection and restabilization, and this enables the transition to a primarily functional differentiation, the problem shifts anew. Now, as we have seen, it becomes difficult to distinguish between restabilization and variation. The forms of societal differentiation clearly correspond to priority problems in separating evolutionary functions.

The coming into being of distinct forms of intrasocietal system differentiation is thus a result of evolution. Differentiation forms are themselves evolutionary advances. On the other hand, they have an effect on evolution itself inasmuch as they have specific difficulties in establishing a separation between evolutionary mechanisms. Differentiation forms differ in the extent of structural complexity that makes them possible, and in the semantics with which they react to the associated problems. This affects the possibilities of separating evolutionary mechanisms institutionally. Highly cultivated societies that rely on center/periphery differentiation, for example, can already formulate and apply criteria; but they have to defend the inequalities built into them and fend off unrest, and therefore need a stability-focused semantics to guide selection. Only under the regime of functional differentiation do selection criteria arise that have a destabilizing effect. But then the difference between stabilization and variation collapses, for stability now has to be grounded primarily in flexibility, changeability, decidability. With these shifts in the transition from one differentiation form to another, the frequency of structural changes also changes, along with the tempo of evolution. Time itself seems to pass more quickly.

These considerations alone show that the separation and (chance) reconnection of evolutionary functions depend neither on laws of nature nor on the necessities of a dialectical process.[151] There is no eternal world order that provides for this to happen. Evolution is due to evolution.[152] It makes itself possible by developing the conditions for the differentiation of its mechanisms. How everything began, we must leave to the "big bang" theory or like myths to explain. For all later onset points of evolution, system/environment differences can always be presupposed and hence the multiplication mechanism that allows only such systems to emerge that can adjust to the mix of phenomena they can construe as disorder or order, as chance or necessity, as expectable or irritating, and thus also as variation, which triggers pressure for selection. The theory of self-referential evolution thus no longer places the "reason" for what happens at the beginning (*archē, principium*). It replaces this traditional way of explaining things by a difference-theoretical one, namely, specification of the difference of evolutionary functions and the optimal localization of special conditions for their separation in the empirical reality of evolving systems. In this way, evolution theory generates a practically endless research program for historical studies.

If evolution is not a process and if it requires circularity of function, theory abstracts from time. However, there can be no doubt that evolution takes place in time. This means not only that structural change can be dated—by reference to longer or shorter periods of time. It takes place not only in time but also uses historical situations that arise from evolution itself, and that are possibly unique or manifest a certain typicality that makes a multiple emergence of evolutionary advances probable—the eye, the last will and testament, and so forth. Such situations offer both opportunities and restrictions; they offer possibilities for selection whose reproduction, however, is possible only under certain conditions. Preadaptive advances, evolutionary advances, and history are relevant here. At the moment, we note only that evolution theory is not based on a linear concept of time, even if it relies on time measurements for dating, but that the time in which structural innovations occur assumes the form of a historically unique present in which a combination of opportunities and restrictions is available; available in combination, for there are no opportunities without restrictions, just as there is no variation and selection without stability. In other words, evolution is possible only in empirical concretion, even though evolution theory cannot supply a causal explanation for what then changes and appears to be new.

Systems theory provides the same insight. In view of the systemic basis of all evolution, in view of the indissoluble link between elementary operations, structure formation, and operational closure of the system delimited against the outside world, the differentiation of evolutionary functions cannot mean that causal separation takes place. It does mean, however, that the functions variation, selection, and restabilization are not coordinated, cannot be adjusted to one another by the evolving system; this would mean that only so much varies from the outset as can be selected to contribute to "system maintenance." Forgoing this sort of expedient coordination means that from the point of view of the system, it is by chance that variations lead to positive or negative selection, and that it is also a matter of chance whether and how these selections, which apply their own criteria, can be stabilized in the system. "Chance" in this connection means that the evolving system is uncontrolledly responsive to the environment at these inner boundaries. Chance, possibly transient environmental conditions, can have an impact, and in this way the system can, without planning to do so, use opportunities to carry out structural changes in a communicatively plausible manner that would be impossible in other historical situations. Thus the introduction of writing produced new possibilities and gave rise to new problems for the existing difference between competent and incompetent roles in dealing with sacred matters—for instance, that of consolidating a tradition held to be holy. Thus, it probably made a difference for the development of talmudic Judaism and how it handled interpretation of Holy Scripture that the political unity of the Jewish people had been destroyed, that no discriminating political support and stabilization of theological controversies, as in the case of Islam and Christianity, were to be expected. Thus, the regional and political segmentation of Europe (the failure of the imperial idea in the face of resistance from the Church in the eleventh and twelfth centuries) produced an abundance of differential progress in individual regions, which served to experiment with progress, providing models for other regions in deciding their path to functional differentiation. Thus, there was a nation-state in France at a very early stage, but a literature on the theory of art developed only after the establishment of the Académie royale de peinture et de sculpture (1648), both, it should be noted, on the Italian model. These considerations explode the classical theoretic distinction between endogenously and exogenously induced evolution, which is untenable anyway from a systems-theoretical point of view. It has to be replaced by a more complex theory, namely, by the hypothesis that, in differentiating evolutionary functions, an evolving system will accept more external influences, will react more to historical situations, and will therefore evolve faster (but always purely internally).

If it is true that evolution comes about through the separation of its functions (through realization of its form), we can conclude that operationally necessary chance, so to speak, gains a higher degree of organization in the course of evolution. It becomes more and more likely that the improbable, the chance event, will occur, because the highly complex structures of evolved systems offer more possibilities for deviation and more possibilities for coping with deviations.[153] It follows that evolution begins to speed up as it takes its course. This naturally cannot mean that all systems or all types of system begin to change more and more rapidly in the course of evolution. The lizards alone would protest. It can only mean that morphogenetic transformations also occur more rapidly as evolution proceeds and generate forms that can handle a faster rate of change in the environment and in the system itself.

At this point at least, evolution theory has to rely on close cooperation in research with systems theory. Systems theory would say that the greater system complexity (achieved through evolution) is, the more probable innovation will be. The necessity of the form variation/selection/restabilization corresponds to the necessity of the form system/environment. The two necessities place chance such that the determinacy of variation means nothing for the determinacy of selection and the determinacy of the environment means nothing for the determinacy of the system. In other words, evolving systems are structurally determined systems, and in higher organizational forms, systems that can establish an internal representation for externally induced chance. I have spoken of "irritation." Hence, the greater tempo of evolution corresponds not, for example, to more and more overlap, interlinkage, dedifferentiation at the system boundaries but to operational closure and self-organization accompanied by increasing irritability.

The thesis that system stabilization is the precondition for variation or, in brief, the thesis of the evolution of evolution mediates in the notorious controversy between Lamarckism and Darwinism. Be that as it may, evolution is based on self-made starting positions, one could say on a past added up to make a present, which limits what is possible in each case. This also holds for the surviving populations of organic evolution. Lamarck's achievement had been in asserting the concept of change in structural characteristics set off by environmental changes against the older notion of fixed essential characteristics of species and genera.[154] Lamarck called the most important structural characteristic of all living beings that replaced fixed type characteristics *irritabilité*.[155] This characteristic also described the relation of the system to the environment. Nothing has since been changed. The dispute that later genetics decided, it would appear,[156] against Lamarck was only about the secondary aspect of the heritability of acquired characteristics, to which Lamarck devoted hardly any attention. In the theory of sociocultural evolution, however, it had never been possible to renounce "Lamarckism" anyway, because in this field the possibility of structural change through the interaction of memory and learning cannot be disputed.[157] As I have noted, organic and sociocultural evolution certainly differ in how they invest the functions of variation, selection, and restabilization. But for the general theory of evolution, the ongoing circular interlinkage of these functions and thus the autopoiesis of evolution itself are the decisive aspect, which comes to bear when we assume that the genetic endowment of the individual organism can no longer be changed through its mode of living.

This interim appraisal summing up the inquiry thus far brings us back to general evolution theory. At the same time, the overview raises new questions, to which we must now turn our attention. One concerns the relation between continuity and discontinuity, in other words, the relation between the gradualness and erraticism of evolutionary changes. Both are clearly to be found. It obviously makes little sense to start a scientific controversy at this point and to leave it to the professors to take sides. It is a further distinction with which the initial paradox of the probability of the improbable is resolved and transferred to a research program. The next section is devoted to this topic, under the heading of *evolutionary advances.*

Another question we shall then be examining is the unity or plurality of societal evolutions. Since society is only one system, there can be only one societal evolution. But this does not exclude that there are other evolutions in the system of society that use society as already ordered intrasocietal environment, which thus arise from the evolution of society itself. With considerable doubts about the details, I shall be affirming this.

8. Evolutionary Advances

If we wish to describe evolution in general, to define it as the enablement of higher complexity suffices. But this amounts only to an almost useless blanket phrase. We must therefore explore more precisely what enables higher complexity and how. This transfers the question to a level on which the system is described as a unity (it "is" complex), the level of system structures. On this level, too, we need a concept that can indicate the result of evolution, a concept for a structural arrangement markedly superior to functional equivalents. Consider the eye or money, the opposable thumb or telecommunication. Consolidated gains of this sort, which are more compatible than others with complex conditions, I call *evolutionary advances*.[158]

That there are better and less good solutions has to do with the problem of complexity. From a purely functional point of view, the solutions are after all "equivalent." There are two different levels of assessment to the concept of evolutionary achievement, and neither presupposes absolute validity.[159] A solution must be suitable. Writing, for example, must be suitable not only for recording purposes but also for communication. The suitability of a solution depends on the specifications of the problem (with respect to writing, for example: suitable for all communication, easy to learn, phonetically autonomous, readable without great demands on interpretation). Beside this level of assessment, there is that of evolutionary advantageousness. Here it is a matter of the relation to the complexity of the system that accepts and practices the evolutionary advance. From this point of view, advances reduce complexity in order to organize greater complexity on the basis of restriction. Thus a road network reduces possibilities for movement to enable easier and faster movement and hence increase the options for movement concretely available. Enhancement by reducing complexity: evolutionary advances choose reductions that are compatible with greater complexity, indeed, often making it possible in the first place (and often only very gradually). The formula is so general that it offers many potential applications, for instance, greater complexity of the environment accessible to the system or greater complexity of the system itself and greater independence (less integration) or more varied options for intervention.[160] Above all, however, an increase in complexity means an increase in combinatorial options, typically bringing together various societal functions. This can contribute to the rapid stabilization of such advances where they have become visible and usable. In any case, by complexity, I mean a complexity situation that is historically relative. Keeping to our example, a road network makes more complexity available by improving possibilities for movement and integrating long-distance traffic into the general complexity network of society. In this regard, there are strategically crucial evolutionary advances that enable greater complexity in very many areas of society. Examples are agriculture, writing, the printing press, telecommunications.

There are no clear causes for any evolutionary advance, not even for the genesis of agriculture. A wide range of initial situations can have an "equifinal" effect favoring form finding. This presupposes that there are limited possibilities in evolution for realizing gains in complexity.[161] This is clearly due to the peculiar combination of renunciation and gain, of reduction of complexity to build up complexity. This gives direction to evolution in the sense of increasing complexity, although at the same time societies without certain evolutionary advances may very well survive (i.e., not succumb to unsolved problems).

This complicated concept of evolutionary achievement takes account of criticism leveled at a purely functionalistic concept of evolution. Suitability is not the sole "cause," as it were, of better solutions to problems being gradually found and asserting themselves. In relation to function, there is, after all, always an abundance of possible solutions. It is the surrounding complexity that narrows the choice to those that are more advantageous than others. And the complexity already attained determines the form in which problems present themselves for which alternative solutions come under consideration. Suitable structures are fixed in the form of evolutionary advances, and to the extent that independent gains in complexity are realized, the advance is built in irreversibly. It can no longer be given up without catastrophic effect.

Evolutionary advances accordingly do not come about because they are suitable for solving certain problems. The problems arise with the advances. Only when there is magic does one see what it can be used for. Only when municipal offices are established to get rid of kings does filling them have to be politicized and do conditions have to be created that will later be celebrated as "democracy." The concept therefore does not contain the notion of a search for ever better solutions to problems. It rather also explains that societal evolution can be left with not very suitable or quite unsuitable achievements if they satisfy the level of aspiration set with them or, as in the case of magic, perform functions that are not in view at all.[162]

A number of known facts can be better explained in this way than by teleological theories (or functionalistic theories constructed on teleological lines). We need not dispute that solutions to problems can be purposively sought. But far-reaching evolutionary advances mostly do not come about in this manner.[163] Discoveries are often made, evolutionary advances often develop under false or peculiar perspectives (situational perspectives offering little prospect of complexity).[164] One example, mentioned above,[165] is the origin of Chinese script in the complex interpretation patterns of divination practices. In another example, money had existed in other forms (e.g., bookkeeping tallies) long before coinage developed in the context of the domestic economies of emporia and palaces. Marking the metal was initially intended only to indicate ownership—and not, for instance, to affirm an official political or religious guarantee of value. But once these protocoins began to circulate outside the household to which they belonged and where they could be used—and, moreover, small change came to be needed—within a few decades, other forms of coinage followed, which had to take on new functions, and above all, to guarantee value. The suddenness of the breakthrough, which revolutionized all business and even political forms (e.g., the transition to the *tyrannis*), is impressive.[166] Another example: the invention of the synallagmatic contract presupposes acquaintance with reciprocity relations, but replaces the institutionalization of duties of gratitude by the legal institution of the *synallagma* as the basis for the incurrence of obligations actionable in the case of default in performance, and which can also be enforced against third persons. The contract is suitable for a law of transactions with a regionally broader reach, and it made it possible (in Roman civil law and again in the development of European law in the eleventh and twelfth centuries) to separate legal protection by criminal law and by civil law. To begin with, action under the terms of a contract was allowed in only a few, strictly defined cases; then the innovation was, as it were, released on parole and rapidly expanded from the late Middle Ages on.

It is often the case that formulations, and thus legitimation, are found only after the corresponding practices have been successfully introduced and have become usual. Innovation is facilitated by nameless introduction. We can thus speak of a political concept of "public opinion" only from the second half of the eighteenth century on, and its spread throughout Europe only after the French Revolution. But the real innovation lay in the use of the printing press for political pamphlets or, in seventeenth-century England, for the dissemination of petitions addressed to Parliament. For this alone made it clear that not only the addressee was being spoken to, and that handling matters confidentially was out of the question.

Evolutionary advances tend to reinforce the results of evolution. They cannot be got rid of. New possibilities for dealing with complexity are gained and other societal institutions adapt to them. Eliminating them would have far-reaching, destructive effects and is hence as good as excluded. At this level, innovations have to be able to step in as functional equivalents, and this typically takes place, not in the form of complete substitution, but rather as supplementation and specialization—as when banknotes came to be used alongside coins, and then instead of banknotes, money guaranteed by the state and bank accounts.

Important improvements to complexity arrangements in systems often originate in the need to cope in a changing environment. In the case of the alphabet, transcription of the entire cultural heritage appears to have been initiated by efforts to improve mnemonic techniques for business purposes, and then also for oral texts, perhaps in competition among a multitude of singers and poets. Such processes are particularly likely where restrictions offer chances of complexity, because at the moment of innovation, there is no foreseeing what can be done with it, so that there must be *other* grounds, which can later cease to apply. In such cases, we therefore typically find the emergent structure suitable for several functions, which need not be realized at the same time.[167] Evolution accordingly benefits from the possibility of realizing multifunctionality sequentially, and thus of exploiting it for functional specification. An already known structure is then only "co-opted" in a later context.[168]

Even in the evolution of living systems, such a switch of identical characteristics from one adaptation context to another is typical rather than rare. The same is true of societal evolution. Here, too, it appears to be almost the norm that the emergence of evolutionary advances is favored, indeed enabled in the first place by predevelopments, by "preadaptive advances."[169] Major achievements in all communication media offer examples. But the same is also to be found in many details. The guilds, so important for adapting the household economy to municipal or to territorial politics, came into being as religious fraternities and only later assumed this mediating function.[170] As long as family formation took place in a system of stratification, the semantics of passionate love could initially be developed only for extramarital relations. It was only when partners could be freely chosen—a development favored in Europe by the older idea of founding a new family in each generation, by the claim to economic autonomy (substitutable by approval of the liege lord), and by an above-average marrying age—that the notion of sexually based love could be given the final function of providing a basis for marriage. An arrangement favorable to complexity was thus permitted to arise, and it was only later, when it came to be exploited to a more complex end, that was it discovered what it was suitable for. This concretizes J. B. S. Haldane's somewhat vague assertion that "every now and then an evolutionary advance is rewarded by a large increase in numbers."[171]

The interpretation and also the invention of traditions often serve in the unrecognized introduction of innovations.[172] Perhaps the most famous example is the Protestant Reformation. Another would be the abolition of manorial jurisdiction in France on the grounds of the "abuse" of a right falling under the "sovereignty" of the king. Innovation is thus spared having to be legitimated and enforced as such. It appears in the guise of a past it belongs to.

Evolutionary advances can thus be introduced as if on a trial basis and mostly without any possibility of assessing their implications; and this is in keeping with the premise of evolution theory that the coordination of variation, selection, and stabilization has to be left to a random factor. If we examine the context for the emergence of evolutionary advances more closely, we discover further conditions. They include the "law of limited possibilities."[173] Only when the field of suitabilities that come into question is too limited can we distinguish better solutions from less useful ones. Theoretically, this means that evolutionary advances are to be expected only in the context of resultant structural problems—and not simply from the point of view of better possibilities for agreement or better complexity reductions as such. The restrictions this implies are compensated to a certain degree by the possibility of "equifinal" developments.[174] One and the same achievement can develop on the basis of differing initial situations. For if the solution is both short on alternatives and compatible with many different situations, and can hence be used as a generalized institution, it is not improbable that it will be found frequently and therefore able survive any failure of supporting systems.

Thanks to this concurrence of limited possible solutions with equifinality, advances in the field of societal evolution are amenable to diffusion. They can exceed their context of origin and be copied elsewhere. This phenomenon of diffusion has wrongly been played off against evolution theory. Diffusion presupposes evolution and relates only to evolutionary advances, which for their part can then become important for the differentiation of evolutionary functions (e.g., writing). It cannot be overlooked that evolutionary advances often acquire their final form and prominence only through diffusion. In the process of diffusion, they are empirically tested, refined, and generalized. Thus important political notions of the Greeks like *homonoia* and democracy appear to have originated in the course of founding colonies, hence in the copying of urban patterns.[175] This state of affairs is even more obvious in the development of phonetic scripts through constant copying and adaptation to other languages. It may well be that the discovery of original forms, purely historical derivations, for example, the search for original, autochthonous state-building, yields little because the advance acquired the form in which it provided the basis for further evolution only during diffusion.

It is an indispensable prerequisite for all this that the social system be already sufficiently complex to provide for the *interruption of interdependence* between various solutions and thus to enable *temporal shifts*. This allows conditions that have just occurred historically to be used and later decoupled as superfluous. In such an event, evolutionary advances are relative consolidations, which prove their worth with regard to structure-dependent problems provided they are constant.

The concept of evolutionary advances has nothing to say about the relative weight of the corresponding arrangements. They include agriculture, but also the fountain pen, which obviates the need for an inkwell; the potter's wheel; the extension of family consciousness by the invention of grandfathers; the computer; purgatory, to tide us over the period until the Final Judgment; and the printing press, not to mention pagination (already introduced), which made possible the subject index and easier references in books. The concept alone provides no overall view. We can nonetheless ask whether there are such things as "epoch-making" advances and, if so, what characterizes them.

Changes in certain structures have far-reaching, "catastrophic" effects on the complexity of the societal system. These structures are the dissemination media of communication (extended by writing, then the printing press, and now telecommunication and electronic data processing) and the forms of system differentiation (segmentation, center/periphery differentiation, stratification, functional differentiation). Taken alone, each of these distinctions provides no epochal structure of world history. Although certain irreversible sequences can be discerned (no printing press before the invention of writing, no direct transition from segmentation to functional differentiation), the distinctions alone do not impose a specific course of events. There can indeed be evolutionary advances that set off dramatic changes in form—for instance, when, in a society that already knows differences in rank, the notion of the equality of families is introduced, thus initiating the end of the nobility, with all the advantages of centralized interdependence. Thus, to put it paradoxically, hitherto impossible possibilities arise whose use lifts society gradually onto a level of greater complexity.

If evolutionary advances intervene in these fundamental structures, whether of the dissemination media of communication or of system differentiation, and enable transition from one to the other, the observer gains the impression of certain formations of society that are clearly distinct from one another. In very simplistic terms, he can then distinguish illiterate from literate cultures, or strongly stratified societies from segmentary societies, or from modern society, which is based on the operational closure of functional systems. But since there are two areas of such distinctions, communication media and differentiation forms, epochs can still not be clearly demarcated. We can say that modern society begins in the fifteenth century with the transition from the large, well-organized workshops for manuscript production on the late Middle Ages to the production of texts with the aid of the printing press. Or we can say that modern society begins in the eighteenth century with observation of the collapse of stratification and the new formation of operationally closed functional systems. The facts and circumstances do not permit any more definite turning points. If we want to know how modern society demarcates itself historically, we have to observe it from a second-order level. We have to describe how it describes itself.

9. Technology

If we define evolutionary advances in terms of proving their worth under conditions of increasing complexity, they come close to what we usually call technology. Evolutionary advances require a certain decoupling from given conditioning relations—*amour passion*, for example, needs to be decoupled from family interests. The same applies for technology. We can go so far as to take technology (technics, techniques technizability, and so on) as the superlative form of evolutionary advances, as giving form to what is most important. That romantic love can be compared with technology, indeed, be placed on the same level of specific special characteristics as technology, is at first surprising, and differences can naturally not be denied; but we can take account of these differences through additional distinctions, especially distinguishing various communication media.

In describing technology as an evolutionary achievement we reject notions that the "world," "society," and "civilization" have themselves become technical.[176] This is difficult to imagine if it means that only technically mediated relations now occur. That the development of technology affects what is experienced as world, society, civilization is naturally not to be disputed; but totalizing concepts can be neither conceptually nor empirically redeemed. The concept of evolutionary achievement serves us as a bridge.

It is now probably agreed that the evolution of technological achievements cannot be explained simply as applied science.[177] There are many other, especially economic, factors in play, and science is often, indeed, mostly, not in a position to say how specific technical problems can be solved. We often find the reverse to be the case: that specialized fields of scientific research owe their initiation to technological developments (steel production—metallurgy; computers—computer science). This is not to underestimate the contribution of the knowledge that science produces. It lies in a "unique combination of opportunities and constraints."[178] It also lies in the provision of expert competence that increases awareness of problems and alternatives. But this does not yet supply a recipe for technological developments but only provides an evolutionary chance, a heightening of probabilities.

If technical arrangements are preferred in societal evolution, this appears mainly to be because, although they involve artificial objects, they *save consensus*. What works, works. What proves its worth has proved its worth. Agreement does not have to be reached. In coordinating processes, technology also saves the always difficult and conflictual coordination of human action. Whatever the chance causes of technical inventions, evolution steps in and drives the structural development of society in the direction set. That this can also entail risks, and that these risks can be variously assessed, is a late insight, and some would say all too late an insight, which can then help only with additional technology.[179] Technical coupling divides consensus problems into problems of purpose and problems of means and costs. We can then develop relational rationalization strategies to examine whether the purpose justifies the effort. The evolution of technology follows a structuring of rationality geared to this end, and rationalization is nothing other than a form of solving still unresolved, so to speak, marginal questions of consensus.

But what is technology? A look at the history of the concept shows firstly that the problem (and hence the concept) of technology has always been determined by counterconcepts, whose task it was to cover what technical performances are differentiated from; and whenever denotations are determined by counterconcepts, this betrays the presence of an observer, whose interests can be investigated.[180] This is particularly the case, for example, where technology is defined as a substitute for organs (Gehlen following Kapp).[181] In a world still understood in religious and cosmological terms, technology was distinguished from nature. In the Greek understanding of the concept, there are also aspects of violation of a natural order, insistence on human ability against a nature coming to be in itself and of itself. This was religiously deproblematized through concepts of progress. Since that time, technology has been regarded as something "artificial."[182] In Christian thinking, the concept of nature was set against a different counterconceptuality. Nature was distinguished from grace with the possibility of understanding the unity of the distinction as God. This set the technology concept free to be developed as imitation of increasingly recognizable natural law.

This corresponds with an increasing shift since the late Middle Ages from what-questions to how-questions, universally disseminated by printing, itself an achievement celebrated as technology. The beautiful world was no longer only the object of religious admiration, with practical problems of coping. Its manifestations raised the question of how they came into being, and how one could produce corresponding effects oneself. In the early Renaissance, this shift was first conceived of as an interest in recuperating the knowledge and skills of antiquity. But if we once know how something can be produced, we can vary our goals and undertake to produce new, unprecedented phenomena. Modern science formulates its understanding of nature in terms of method and experiment; but the theory of the art of government also sets out from the question of how power is to be gained and how power positions are to be maintained. The technology-related semantics of imagining and producing, of *Vorstellen* and *Herstellen* (Heidegger) fully favors the assumption of an externally positioned subject who uses technical possibilities from outside without himself functioning in the manner of a technostructure.

In early modern times, technology was hence understood as the application of knowledge about nature to human ends, almost, indeed, in parallel to Divine Creation, or as the copying of the archetypes Creation had provided. This made it possible to call for a science of "technology" to deal with the subject matter.[183] It was this close link between nature and technology that suggested the now usual opposition drawn between technology and humanity. For subjectivist philosophy, for Romanticism, for Husserl's phenomenology, indeed, for Habermas, this opposition is decisive, generating a technology aversion, a characterization of technology as a necessary evil. The warning is that man should not allow his view of himself to be determined by technology; he should rebel against the resulting dependence as against domination per se; he should, if he wishes to save his humanity and his self-determination, free, "emancipate" himself from an alienation caused by technology and domination. Even today, many a complaint is to be heard that technology is not sufficiently under control (remarkably, the market is left out of account or declared inadequate as a controlling force),[184] but criticism from the right or the left has no basis in a clear definition of the problem. The moves toward technology assessment that have been developing for some time now shift the problem, without having solved it, to the future.

Meanwhile, the classical efforts by the humanities and social sciences to address the subject of "technology"[185] have failed to free themselves from this situation.[186] They have proceeded either on the assumption of a concept of culture or one of action, and have thus limited and externalized the phenomenon of technology to a material substratum. Focusing the concept of technology on the use of energy (and energy in a new sense = work)[187] has enhanced the resolution capacity of the conceptuality but has changed nothing with respect to the counterconceptuality in relation to human concerns. Modern electronic communication technologies, as well, and in particular, are based on the clear separation of technical networks from information and thus on the cultural semantics that is communicated with their aid. Research into "artificial intelligence" is concerned with the manipulation of "symbols," not with the forming of meaning.

However, there are now increasing signs that this opposition between technology and nature or technology and humanity (technology and reason, technology and "life-world," etc.) is obsolete. If the natural sciences have themselves dissolved the (observer-independent) concept of nature, and technology and nature mingle inseparably and unpredictably in the ecological context, it no longer makes any sense to order phenomena in terms of the distinction between technology and nature.[188] Technology becomes nature again, a second nature, because hardly anyone understands how it works, and because this understanding can no longer be assumed in everyday communication. How (and why) should we distinguish genetically engineered organisms from others? Only so that we can communicate that we are against them? Henry Adams counted "Niagara Falls, the Yellowstone Geysers, and the whole railway system" among the wonders that nineteenth-century America had to offer.[189]

In other regards, too, technical artifacts are, on the one hand, something special that is particularly characteristic of modern society, while on the other they are achievements that cannot be explained in themselves. Numerous detailed studies on technological developments in the nineteenth and twentieth centuries have shown that the discovery of the forms that finally imposed themselves was far from obeying a logic of technology-immanent improvement, but can be explained only in terms of responsiveness of the social environment, of demand for and use of the technology.[190] At the same time, this means that technology does not rule over society as an anonymous power, but that society makes itself dependent on technology, in a manner not rationally planned, by becoming involved with it. If, however, life and the survival of humankind depend all too clearly on technology (in both a positive and negative, destructive sense), it is implausible to place the really human aspect on the other side of the distinction that defines the concept of technology. Awareness of the problem is changed above all by high-risk high technologies but also by the limits to predicting technically supposedly safe performance. This requires safety technologies that can be realized mechanically only to a limited extent. We therefore need a broader concept of technology not geared exclusively to predictability and rationality in this narrow sense. This holds a fortiori if we include action formalization of the more general sort, regulatory technologies, condition programming, calculation technologies, and so on. Especially calculation technologies oriented on money make the development of the economy unpredictable, even for the immediate future. Research aimed at new knowledge, particularly where it addresses technical realizations, produces unforeseeable effects. The problem appears to be more and more whether and how the typical characteristics of technology can still and repeatedly be secured in the face of the growing need for technology. Or is technology as a form of evolutionary achievement coming up against insurmountable limits?[191]

Looking for a concept that fits this situation and this interest, we might consider understanding technology as *functioning simplification*. It may be a matter of causal technology or information-processing technology. Causal technologies are not only concerned with recognizing the effects of causes that somehow occur and that can possibly be foreseen; the causes themselves have to be "de-randomized," removed from chance and producible in almost any state of the world.[192] For information-processing technology, calculations, at any rate, conditional programs, are to be considered in borderline cases that are redundant to the extent that, given the information provided for, we can know what then has to happen. In any case, it is a process of effective isolation; the elimination of the rest-of-the-world; leaving undisputed realities out of account—whether they be other causes and effects or other information; hence restrictions that cannot be deduced from the reality of the world.[193] Functioning can be ascertained if the excluded world can be prevented from having an effect on the intended result. The decisive distinction that determines the form "technology" is now that between controllable and uncontrollable states of affairs. To put it in extremely abstract terms, it is a question of the successful reduction of complexity. Whatever else might happen, technology supplies the intended results. However, we also know, as noted above,[194] that complexity itself can be captured in no reduction, can be represented in no model. Even if it works, we must also expect something to be left over. "Successful" reduction thus amounts to harmless ignoring. With this *concept* of technology, we by no means deny that the *deployment* of technology is subject to numerous social and cultural conditions. The sociology of technology has in recent times demonstrated this in many ways.

A somewhat different but compatible description of technology uses the distinction between strict and loose coupling, which I have already taken as the basis for the concept of medium. Nowadays (in contrast to older notions of "natural law"), we see that the stability of organisms and of ecological "equilibrium" requires the avoidance of strict couplings, in other words, robustness in absorbing disturbances.[195] For technology, in contrast, strict coupling is a condition. Hence we see a reformulation of the old problem of relations between nature and technology, and the advantage of (as well as the motive for) this new version is to throw light on the problems of technical intervention in natural systems and in relations between systems. In brief, this suggests that the increase in knowledge about nature can lead only to an increase in ignorance about the effects of technical interventions; this applies explicitly to the effects of modern medicine.

If technology is geared to strict (as opposed to loose) coupling, the material basis on which it works is irrelevant as long as it works. It may involve physical, chemical, biological, neurophysiological, or also conscious processes, provided that they are set up in such a way that decisions are not constantly required *ad interim*. Consider, for instance, the link between the printing press and reading technology, with its unnoticed, enormously fast dovetailing of perception and the mini-actuation of eye movements. Reading is a good example of how very much the distinction between matter and mind or between technology and human being can lead astray. The problem is rather how to reintroduce alternatives and hence decision-making requirements into an automated process—for example, how to bring a reader to notice that he is not understanding what he is reading. A technology that is planned and set up to be as trouble-free as possible has the problem of coming by disturbances that draw attention to problems that are important for the context of functioning. And whenever decision-making requirements are inserted in technicized processes, strict coupling is interrupted by loose coupling.

Technology (always provided that it works) thus makes it possible to couple completely heterogeneous elements. A physically actuated signal may set off communication. A communication may bring a brain to cause levers to be moved. And all this happens in (almost) reliably repeatable manner. Technology therefore operates orthogonally to the operational closure of autopoietic systems. This is likely to explain why societal evolution takes recourse to technology in order to secure couplings between the societal system and its environment to which internal processes of information processing and social technization can connect. This does not contradict the theorems of the theory of autopoietic systems, for technology, too, can be observed and installed only if a system determines which of innumerable elements are to be coupled.[196] Technology accordingly provides good evidence in support of my initial thesis that operational closure does not mean causal isolation, but makes it possible to realize couplings with the environment within the system through disposition over intrasystemic elements. And this also makes it possible to control the system's sensitivity to sources of disturbance from the environment at the risk of disregarding important matters.

In contrast to the traditional concept of technology oriented on ability, action, and decision-making, the emphasis is not so much on gaining new possibilities and, in the concept of technical rationality, on choosing between alternatives, but on the isolation of such a selective area. The world does not only consist of alternatives to be accepted and rejected; it is first of all the wilderness of what happens simultaneously—and for this reason alone, uncontrollably: other simultaneously real causes and effects, other sources of information. Simultaneity is chaos. Superseding this chaos therefore always requires distantiation in time and space.[197] And before any technical forms are developed that can be inserted in this time-space (dechaoticized) world, systems have to be formed that take their distance from the other realities that they can treat as environment.

At first glance, this concept of technology appears to be too broad. For example, impassioned love can hardly be understood as a functioning simplification (that is nonetheless exposed to chaos). But, in a sort of concurrent thematization, this has always also been perceived; we need think only of the Don Juan theme. The concept of technology must only be freed of any humanistic counterconceptuality, for this change in the concept is to enable new relationships to be seen.[198] Various advantages are associated with the form of technology. They include expansion of the scope of possible options; comparability and repeatability of the same in various situations; associated with this: the possibility of gathering experience, learning, refining, hence of bringing an initial discovery into a form that can no longer be improved; the determinability of errors—be they in design or in operation; the limitability of input to what is needed, thus the planability and rationalizability of resource allocation; and, finally and above all, a certain degree of intrasystemic control over external relations that the system sees, with the conversion of risks of differentiation into risks of technology. Technization therefore combines generalizations and specifications in a specific way, namely, for use in widely differing situations and in often very different purposive contexts with a high measure of precision in specifying functional conditions, repair potentiality, replacement requirements. The reach of a technological development—such as the computer or laser technology—can then be determined by the extent of generalization and diversification under existing specifications and conditions of operational integrity.

I shall not speak of the evolution of technology. Technological developments are oriented on presumable improvements and come about far more quickly than is typical for evolution. Think only of the present use of genetically modified organisms. Evolution in the strict sense occurs only when technological achievements are inserted in a natural or societal environment without it being possible to foresee what will happen.

The importance of technology for societal evolution can be explained by a very specific relationship between redundancy and variety, which in turn influences societal communication.[199] Artificial redundancies are created (it works or it doesn't), with subsequent variety. New goals, new values, new calculations, new errors become possible. More and more communication can concern itself with sounding out this specific way of increasing redundancy and variation and take inspiration from corresponding success. But the assessment of rationality remains tied to precisely this form of increase and cannot be projected to macrosocietal rationality. This may give repeated cause for criticism of technology, which for its part, however, gives an impression of helplessness if society has reasons (e.g., military and economic) to prefer the exploration of technological possibilities.

Over the past two centuries, technological development has sped up enormously, but above all, the advent of the computer has marked a turning point. Nineteenth-century machinery was oriented on energy efficiency and time-saving. It was based on an extended action schema. This drew on the notion of the human body as work energy and on the possibility of accelerating the transport of things and bodies. As has often been described, this led in the second half of the nineteenth century to the development of machine-based big industry. It has become apparent in recent times that the computer has fundamentally changed this concept. It has shifted technology from bodies and things to signs whose meaning consists in making other signs accessible.[200] The time problem lies no longer in the need for transport but in the necessity of a sequence of orders that are required to make the invisible machine in the computer work and make its results visible. On the level of a universal network of machines, we then have simultaneity, which, however, has to be dissolved into places and points in time by user request. The unambiguity of machine switching processes is transformed back into the ambiguity (meaningfulness) of use contexts. Thus, the old problems of energy and time-saving do not become completely unimportant, but they are now decisive neither for further technological development nor for its societal effects.

Mostly but not always in dependence on computers, there are also tendencies to use the simplification of technology to build highly complex technical systems, which, although constructed, raise difficult problems in analyzing and interpreting any disturbances that occur. Since technology functions continuously, the consequences of a disturbance often occur at quite different points in the system and can cascade. The control of technicized processes cannot then limit itself to correcting defective behavior or sorting out defective products; it therefore becomes more difficult to organize it in the form of hierarchical supervision.[201] It needs more intelligence, and especially in the event of unexpected incidents, rapidly available intelligence to ward off damage. These problems can be solved neither by means of complex control systems, which extremely rarely come to bear, nor by calling on higher authorities. From the outset, error tolerance or, where risks are involved, redundant safeguards have to be built into systems.

The universal spread and concrete presence of technologies best explain why there is so much talk today of "innovation."[202] The observation of functioning technology is an important source of ideas about what can be done differently and how. This explains the often noted influence of practitioners and clients on technological development, for example. When it comes to innovation, even organizations are regarded as functioning technologies. The consolidated past is present as a comprehensible present, inspiring consideration of how changes can bring better results. The concept of innovation transforms this possibility into a general societal recommendation. Existing processes are treated retrospectively as a realized technology which still has certain defects or possibilities of improvement. If we abstract from technological realizations, the concept of innovation loses its hold and assumes ideological form to the effect that new is better than old.

Society has meanwhile grown accustomed to technology. This is not to say that society itself has become a sort of technology, as we sometimes read.[203] Any such thesis would be easy to refute. It also flies in the face of all everyday experience. Only dependence on functioning technology has increased, with the result that any breakdown of technology (especially energy supplies) would also lead to the breakdown of our familiar society.

In other words, technological development has led to innumerable *non-natural self-evidences*. We take it for granted that the cistern will refill when we flush the toilet. This in turn produces strange dependencies. "The more options we develop for ourselves, the less the institutional structure (and here we would have to add especially the technical structure) with whose aid we develop them is available itself as an option."[204] This state of affairs can be described with the help of the *structural coupling* concept. This means that societal communication has to presuppose technology and be able to rely on technology in all *present* operations, because other possibilities are no longer available in the problem horizons of the operations. And the time needed to replace technology by initiating retrogressive development would be so long, and the factual consequences would be so serious and unpredictable in detail, that a switch to other external references of society is practically excluded.

The result of this dependence on technology is that the structural coupling of the physical world and society can no longer be captured by the concept of nature, just as if there were an *analogia entis* grounded in nature. The nature concept is replaced in this context by the paired concepts energy/work and energy/economy. Technology consumes energy and performs work and in this manner links physical givens with society. As always, this structural coupling also couples the channeling of irritations. Technology itself defines and changes the boundaries of the conversion of energy into work. The risks that have to be accepted increase, and the future depends on technologies that are not yet available.

The social consequences of this switch to risks provoked by technology and reinforced by organized decision-making are difficult to overestimate. The technology of evolutionary advance was introduced into a society that was neither structurally nor semantically ready for it. Although the future is still uncertain in the given present in all societies, this uncertainty could nevertheless be appresented in older societies as coming from outside. This led to the rewarding of social solidarity,[205] which, as it were, offered a safety net for coping with any dangers. When, however, risks are involved, which society takes with decisions considered rational because they are necessary to take advantage of opportunities or to prevent worse happening, the consequences are precisely the opposite.[206] Conflicts develop between decision-makers and interested parties, between risk calculations mostly worked out by organizations and those who bear the consequences without being taken into account. What constitutes a risk for decision-makers is, for the parties possibly affected, a danger that comes from outside but originates within society itself, namely, in the decision taken, and is hence attributed to it.

As long as solidarity is needed and in demand, absolute criteria whose social conditionality is not addressed provide orientation. They are criteria of religious, moral, or tribal (ethnic) content. They, too, are socially discriminating, but such that a distinction can be drawn between conformity and deviation and those deviating can be excluded and expelled as unbelievers, as barbarians, as heathens, as *saraceni*, or, at a later date, as unreasonable. They are owed neither solidarity nor moral duties. The shift to risk perspectives changes this form of discrimination radically. Now divergences in perspective are within society. With regard to the future, they divide society into varying decision-makers and affected parties; and what is rational for the one is for the other a convincing reason for protest and resistance. Now, too, there are newly developing solidarities, but they assume a fundamentalist guise. Such solidarity unfolds in awareness of religious or ethnic otherness; but this takes place in a world society, which people know they are dependent on as far as communication, supply, services, and, of course, technology are concerned.

What is more, technical links in mass production, transport, and energy and information supply cross traditional, regional-society boundaries. Apart from and in interplay with the functional differentiation that dissolves spatial bounds, technological developments are among the most important conditions that have made a "global system" in the form of a world society inevitable.[207] In our context, this means that less and less reliance can be placed on ethnic or national solidarity or concentrations of interests in coping with problems of technology impact. From a political point of view, there is completely new potential for threats and sanctions, consisting in cutting regions off from the advantages of technical supply, or, vice versa, refusing to collaborate on ecologically controlled or less risky technological development.

Well-meaning treatments speak of pluralism or of the diversity of postmodern discourses. But this addresses only the social dimension. However, it cannot be denied that the root of the problem lies in the time dimension and particularly in the various forms of realizing future uncertainty. Technology enables and imposes decisions that have an uncertain future at their disposal, and solidarity or even common value orientations cannot be expected for such decisions.

In the context of evolution theory, this understanding of technology amounts to a renunciation of adaptationist concepts. Technology does not enable society to adapt progressively to its environment as it is. By multiplying possible options, it serves to develop the endogenous dynamics of the societal system. The concept remains completely open on the question of what happens next. Warning signs can no longer be ignored in the field of risky high technology. In view of the continuous dependence of all technology on energy, it is extremely questionable whether technologies will always be found to guarantee an adequate energy supply.[208] And it cannot be excluded that chaos will catch up with technology in its further evolution.

For this reason, technology concepts geared to nature or mind or the human being as counterconcept now get us no further. The really interesting question is rather whether in the logic of evolution, the achievements of technology are irreversible, and every failure can therefore by compensated for only by new technologies; or whether technology is to be understood as a store of possibilities we can draw on again at any time as the need arises. Under present economic conditions, there is much to be said for irreversibility, given the scarcity of resources and the unpredictably high costs of retrogression (compared with the opportunities and costs of new development, which are easier to calculate). But these are economic arguments, of which no one can at present say whether they will withstand the future development of the societal system or be dismissed by necessity when the energy needed to supply technology no longer suffices.[209]

In the age of the steam engine it was not steam that was the problem, but the engine. This appears to change where the operating conditions of technology and, with them, the generation of energy become a problem. The cosmology now required had already been indicated by the law of entropy. For the theory of society and its concept of evolution, the corresponding problem lies in the reproduction of improbable structures.

10. The Evolution of Ideas

Societal evolution has thus far been spoken of in the singular, despite the many societies in the past that evolved together in the fashion of a species or population and, as it were, constituted the varietal pool for societal evolution. The issue of whether further evolution can take place within a societal system is a separate one, requiring the description of further instances of unplanned structural changes, aided by differing variation, selection, and restabilization. Because such evolution, assuming it is possible, cannot take place in society independently of society, a co-evolutionary relationship would have to be assumed, and the theory of macrosocietal evolution geared to this additional complication.[210]

The distinction between the dissemination media of communication and forms of system differentiation raises two further questions. The subject of this section is whether the separating out of written communication allowed fixed, recorded semantics that was handed down, and hence variable, to evolve independently.[211] I shall be referring to this as the "evolution of ideas."[212] The next section then goes on to investigate whether independent evolution at the level of societal subsystems is possible, too. Current knowledge on both questions is more than scant.

Regardless of the concrete historical conditions for a special evolution of ideas, isolating it ultimately goes back to the distinction between operation and observation. Since all observations can be realized only in the form of factual operation (in this instance, communicating), the societal system is operationally closed at this level, with the possibility of evolutionarily divergent structure formation, triggered by further operational closures within the operationally closed societal system. Communication is possible only as an observing operation. It has to rely on the meaning of the difference between utterance and information being understood and hence processed for further communication. Observations, too, are *real* events, and thus operations. They can be realized connectively only in operationally closed systems. Otherwise, they would not take place at all. Their reality value therefore lies not, as all tradition interested in cognition had assumed, in the reality of their objects, which are observed and described as either true or false, either accurate or inaccurate. It lies *solely in the reality of the observational operations themselves*, in other words, in the testing of resistance, which is to be found not in the objective outside world but *exclusively in the recursive interconnection of system operations themselves.* We could also say that it lies in the successful processing of irritations, which as such do not yet contain any information about the environment.

Just as observations are a special sort of operation and draw their reality from this, semantics are a special sort of structure. Further to the distinction between operation and observation, we must therefore draw a distinction between the corresponding structures: the structures of system differentiation and the semantic structures that identify, fix, and remember meaning worth preserving or consign it to oblivion. As observations, the operations that condense and confirm semantics are blind to their own operating. For they cannot observe themselves without coming up against the paradox of the unity of the different.[213] However, the fact that operations produce differences can be observed and described by an observer; and this also holds for differences that are generated by other observational operations.[214] The relationship between operation and observation is therefore doubly circular, and the two circles are separated by latencies. While observations are operations that reproduce the operating systems autopoietically but cannot observe themselves, *all* operations can be observed by observations aimed at doing so, for otherwise we would know nothing about them.

This double circle takes effect in the morphogenesis, in the evolutionary development, diversification, and dissolution of structures. At the operational level, system differentiations are produced that continue differentiation of the societal system internally, enriching it with complexity. At the semantic level, structures arise that steer the observation and description of these results of evolution, that is to say, provide them with distinctions. The semantics requires latencies. Its own self-description must distinguish what it describes without being able to include the unity of what is differentiated in the description. The result is divergence between the evolution of system differentiation and the description of its outcomes. The structural breaks that the evolution of new forms of system differentiation generates are not observed and described in the change itself, because how the innovation differs cannot also be captured. The semantics grants structural innovation a certain honeymoon period until it has so consolidated that it can hold its own as order in its own right. There are numerous other temporal incongruities between system structural and semantic evolution—including how newly invented ideas are learned and tested in the semantics before being deployed in the structural context of differentiations.[215]

These considerations lead us to ask whether we can speak of evolution in the domain of semantic structures, too, and what conditions in the history of society could have actuated an endogenous dynamic in the evolution of ideas.

If, in the context of the autopoietic social system society, we assume that communication serves to reproduce communication, we must expect situations to arise in which the old way of letting this happen no longer suffices. Structures are reproduced as tradition, but current conditions betray that the descriptions of structure determined by tradition no longer fit. A discrepancy is apparent: the possibilities of present reproduction are no longer adequate for what is to be reproduced.[216] Time breaks lead to factual differentiation. Such circumstances reveal differences between social structure and semantics. This puts the semantics under pressure to adapt but also enables ideas to be fixed ahead of time, before being assigned social functions.[217]

This can happen only if there is enough memory capacity, if society disposes of writing in adequate measure. In the evolution of ideas, the invention and spread of writing was the starting point for independent evolution, and the advent of the printing press was the turning point that triggered far-reaching semantic adjustments. Before writing had been introduced, meaning was so concretely instituted that the specific form of stability (fixing in writing) that could set off a special form of variation did not exist. Semantic structures change by adapting their use to situations and by forgetting. Where ideas have already been fixed in writing, they can only have a disturbing effect on institutions, rituals, interpreted situations geared to nonwritten communication.[218] The primacy of the oral tradition (above all in teaching) was maintained for thousands of years after the invention of writing, but writing itself made such novel demands on the explication of thought (to be understood only from the text) that it produced new words, new concepts, ideas about ideas (hence "philosophy"). Despite the primacy of the oral tradition and although it was not really realized (above all conceptually!) that writing and reading are communication, this invention broke the prepotence of the spoken word. The effects are particularly apparent in the world of religious ideas.[219] To begin with, however, there were still major limitations to the use of writing, also among the upper classes and in the cities. They lay partly in its restriction to special roles,[220] partly in its limitation to learned languages otherwise no longer in common use (Sanskrit; Latin in medieval Europe), which were held to be indispensable for appropriate expression and thus merged with the form of the ideas themselves to form a unity. In some societies, cultural elites then emerged with a problematic (mostly religiously safeguarded) relation to the predominant ascriptive status order.[221] Only where these sociostructural restrictions on the use of writing were lifted could increasing demands be made on the plausibility of ideas and thus on the more intensive co-evolution of written material and system differentiations.

The possibilities thus initiated but inhibited by such restrictions were abruptly made available by the printing press. Above all, additional capacity for control and storage was gained. It was now broadly apparent how much knowledge there already was. For no more than a few decades, efforts continued to put all the old aids to memory into print, the commonplaces, quotations, sayings, and so on, everything that had been passed on as topic.[222] Finally, it was realized that printing had made this pointless and superfluous. But morality, established in this domain, where it had enjoyed drawing on the possibilities of rhetoric, now had to be reformulated on the basis of principles. In theology, the more that was published, the greater were the doubts about the old "disputed question" technique, that is, providing authoritative solutions to contradictions between opposing opinions.[223] The possibilities for comparison also grew. Different books could be put side by side and read almost at the same time. This brought new intransparency and a need for methodical access.[224] Around 1600, the word "system" began its career—initially, in the form of a book title and declaration of the intention to write a book with properly ordered contents.[225] As always when control capacity is increased, the power of the past over the present grows; *contrarotulare* means to compare texts fixed in the past against present information. But precisely this makes it possible to recognize what is new and to appreciate it. The distinction between new and old (*moderni/antiqui*) is taken out of the context of the encomiums in which it was at home.[226] Applied to history, it is temporalized.[227]

Thought in written form, accessible to the anonymous reader in print, has in its favor the weight of a tradition and the power of being (presumably) known; moreover, it offers an incentive to express other views on the same subject or problem. In the printed word, we can discover and actualize latent potentialities for other opinions. And this is particularly true where acute (especially politically acute) situations suggest the advisability of instrumentalizing such innovations.[228] Political criticism of the assertion of parliamentary sovereignty by Westminster, for example, led to the introduction into the discussion of the term "unconstitutional," with unforeseeable consequences for the then necessary distinction between illegal and unconstitutional, for the separation of powers, civil rights, judicial review, and much more.[229] But this move presupposed an understanding of "constitution"—a term already introduced for other reasons—that differed from that in Roman law.

These indications serve above all to recall the importance of the turning points brought about by the introduction of writing and the printing press.[230] For a theory on the evolution of ideas (in contrast to more detailed studies of issues in the history of ideas), they are important because they concern the separability of evolutionary functions and hence the conditions for ideas to evolve independently. But what still needs to be clarified is whether variation, selection, and restabilization can be separated specially for the evolution of ideas, and what forms evolutionary mechanisms assume in this case.

The point of departure for variation is the fixing of the material in writing and the freedom this gives to both writing and reading from surveillance by an interaction system. Writing makes objective, almost mannerly, criticism possible. When writing and reading, we also have more time than when we are under pressure to act in interaction. Surplus activity typically develops in relation to the text, which tends to find expression in critical rather than merely receptive communication. However, this very high probability of deviation rapidly dissipates, since few readers react to what they have read in writing let alone in print.[231] Those whose calling it is to criticize are under all the more pressure to do so. The Enlightenment was carried by *gens de lettres*.

It should also be noted that the conditions for the structural coupling of consciousness processes and communication processes change in written communication. Since the environment can irritate communication only by means of communication, such a change is extremely important. It acts selectively, for most consciousness systems switch themselves off in writing and reading. They do not know how to go on, they tire, they give up. Those who stay the course are specialists, who skillfully convert texts into texts, as it were, as annex to the communication process, but who have their difficulties and have to make a substantive and stylistic effort to remain recognizable as individuals.[232]

These problems are usually addressed under the "text and interpretation" schema. Especially since the advent of new—no longer in the old sense "grammatical"—philologies in the eighteenth century, the relation of text to interpretation has become the subject of thoroughgoing secondary reflection. The associated scientific endeavors go by the name of "hermeneutics." This cannot be addressed in due detail at this point. On the problem of variation in the evolution of ideas, there is nonetheless agreement that it is important for text and interpretation to stabilize one another. Immanent circularity and not an external subject has been the decisive factor since Hans-Georg Gadamer at the latest. As in all other cases of evolutionary variation, considerable provision is thus made here, too, for the stability of deviating variants. If they are to come into question at all, they must satisfy the postulate of the unity of text and interpretation; they must be able to prove themselves to be interpretations of the text. At the same time, however, the figure of the hermeneutic circle shows that this does not decide finally whether and which ideas will prevail. This can be seen as evidence that here, too, the evolutionary functions of variation, selection, and restabilization have been successfully differentiated.

Whereas the variation of ideas is largely endogenous through the production of texts from texts, evolutionary selection has to rely on criteria of *plausibility* or, even more stringently, on *evidence*.[233] It may seem plausible, indeed evident, that plausibility and evidence are crucial for the evolution of ideas. Stimulated by this remarkable autology, we must nevertheless ask why this is so.

Plausibility is secured by using common schemata or scripts in the sense of modern cognitive psychology.[234] It is a matter of descriptions of something as something, but also of causal attributions relating certain effects to certain causes and hence provoking moral judgments, demands for action, evaluations. Schemata are the form in which communication develops judgments and condenses memory. But since schemata do not yet determine their use in communication, because in any case they cannot be applied schematically, this concept does not yet explain how plausibility is gained and can be revised where necessary in certain historical situations.

Before the age of the mass media, which now address this problem, conceptually feasible forms of thought had already been developed in skepticism and rhetoric, which also served as arguments for the evidence of the ontological description of the world. Skepticism was regarded as futile, as foundering on its own autology. Rhetoric was the only description of communication whose self-reflection was allowed.[235] It could present itself as rhetoric and face practical testing in the given society. It was no coincidence that paradox, skepticism, and rhetoric experienced a renaissance after the introduction of printing. This lasted from the sixteenth century until well into the seventeenth and began to lose ground only with the incipient self-awareness of modern society in the eighteenth. But what has taken its place?

No direct semantic successor is in sight, an indication of the radical nature of the structural break. Instead, we find abundant offers of uncertainty: contingency philosophy, relativism, historicism, the use of ideological distinctions, and, recently, such disparate offers as "postmodernism" or "deconstructivism," which appear to prove that things cannot continue like this or any other way. But we can substitute the distinction between paradox and the unfolding of paradox, and analysis of historical (social historical) conditions of plausibility and evidence, for such information.

Cognitive schemata require coordination with the unwritten givens of the internal and external environment of the societal system. Thus in aristocratic societies, one cannot very well deny that the noble "lives better" and therefore "is better" than the peasant. Any child can see that. The limitations to technical and professional skill, the differences in the nature of things, the heavens above, the earth below—all this provides a framework for testing plausibilities and curtailing extravagance. Ideas are plausible if they make immediate sense and do not have to be further justified in the communication process. This is now the case, for example, for the "values" of the moment. We can speak of evidence when something makes sense to the exclusion of alternatives. What is important is that sporadic confirmations of this sort do not impose the acceptance of more complex communication. At the beginning of the nineteenth century, the new pauperism caused by industry could be accepted as a natural law determined by progress, or it could be combated as the consequence of arbitrary rule—but the fact of it could not be disputed. The position is similar for present-day discussion on ecological problems.

As time passes more rapidly and ever more structural changes accumulate, only *situational* evidence will suffice. The trial of Galileo Galilei or the causes of the American War of Independence, the Lisbon Earthquake, which gave Voltaire a welcome occasion to address the question of theodicy: the insight supplied by present evidence suffices for selection. However, on this basis, it cannot also assume the function of restabilization.

As a consequence of these plausibility tests, selections in the evolution of ideas are markedly dependent on the environment, and hence subject to conditions that they can control neither in written form nor argumentatively. For the same reason, the evolution of ideas always leads only to historical semantics. It remains dependent on social structures, which are determined by the predominant form of system differentiation. Plausibilities convey a sort of reality index, and anyone who does not submit to it has little chance. Innovations have to be introduced with them, not against them. All the same, printing increases the complexity of the possible so fast and to such an extent that innovations can for their part select their plausibilities. Furthermore, a high degree of self-gratification sets in. One cites, giving the impression that others have already taken care of plausibility.

Especially in the seventeenth and eighteenth centuries, the literature, which should have been offering something new, vibrated with this problem. The new aphoristically and fragmentarily formulated morality was clearly geared to what found favor in the salons. The same can be said of the mania for *portraits* and *caractères*.[236] For a while, "common sense" becomes a criterion of knowledge,[237] and "evidence" becomes a buzzword, especially among the physiocrats. Ridiculousness was accordingly proposed as a criterion for sorting plausible from implausible communication.[238] It is not difficult to guess that all this was in quest of covert reinsurance in oral communication. Only the parallel development of new scientificity and Romanticism put an end to the discussion. For the Romantics, "fragment" had a quite new and fundamental sense, namely, that of protest against totalizing worldviews. And Romanticism is also to the forefront in cultivating the plausibility of the implausible. This leaves disposition over plausibilities to writing, printing, and finally to the mass media. Oral communication loses its function as supervisory authority with the upper classes.

Plausibility, let alone evidence, can be secured for semantic structural change only if the changes to which changes in conceptuality react are sufficiently clear. Innovation requires not only temporal but also factual awareness of difference.[239] Only when this condition is met can discontinuities be marked. In the course of rapid and far-reaching structural changes such as in the transition from stratificatory to functional differentiation, adequate self-observation and self-description are difficult if not impossible. Discontinuity is then not marked. Instead, old names continue to be used, for example, the term "state," possibly with attributes such as "constitutional" or "modern," which do not affect the substance. In this manner, meaning is so enriched that the concept ultimately becomes indefinable. The evolution of ideas cannot follow structural evolution fast enough, coping instead with inconsistencies and, in this regard, imprecise concept reference.

The stability of ideas is initially expressed through the normativization of the expectations leveled at communication and behavior. With the help of normativization, one can claim that something is right even if in individual cases it is not. God and the Devil obviously agreed that humanity would otherwise not manage.[240] Even what nature demands is normatively supported, that is, regardless of deviating cases. Statistics—which does the same in a different way and therefore makes it possible to abandon the normative concept of nature—began only in the seventeenth century, in a society in which it was increasingly necessary to work with artificially generated plausibilities.

As in societal evolution in general, selection aspects and notions of stability are at first difficult to separate in the evolution of ideas. Interest in the consistency of statements already develops with the spread of writing—but this works in both directions: stabilizing and, in the case of inconsistencies, destabilizing.[241] The movement of skepticism that reacts to this, which itself owes its existence to writing,[242] can only shake its head, but not change anything. Only after the arrival of the printing press, and only in the seventeenth century, do things begin to move. I have already mentioned the invention of statistics. It demonstrates clearly that there can be forms of certainty in uncertainty that undermine the old opposition between dogma and skepticism.[243] Leaving aside religion, the concepts of dogma, dogmatics, dogmatism, dogmaticism (note the successive degree of rejection) are hence negatively connoted.[244] In parallel, the new order concept of system is relativized and used in the sense of purely subjective projection.[245] With Shaftesbury, we can then say: "The most ingenious way of becoming foolish is by a system."[246] Ideas, in particular, which owe their selection only to situational plausibilities, depend on novel forms of stabilization in mobile systems. They endure beyond the favor of the moment—or not. In any case, they can no longer base their selection on a stable world order. But then it seems advisable to watch the current state of affairs for opportunities to innovate. As with societal evolution in general, the evolution of ideas also tends to collapse if, even though variation, selection, and stabilization can be separated, the difference between stabilization and variation begins to diminish.

At the end of the eighteenth century, the old form of the evolution of ideas with text-related variance, plausible or evident selection, and normative or dogmatically unquestioned stability also appears to have come to an end. The French Revolution sent a message that could be heard everywhere; and although it changed little in societal structures, its effects on the world of ideas in the period that followed can hardly be overestimated.[247] In Königsberg and Berlin, new attempts were made to safeguard the world of ideas with a philosophical concept of science. In fact, however, the reflective endeavors of functional systems assumed the lead.[248] Economics and politics, science and the law, now each have their own histories of ideas, written, also, in historical retrospective. The extent to which they pursue an independent evolution of ideas within functional systems requires special investigation. At the macrosocietal level, at any rate, we can hardly speak of a corresponding general evolution of ideas any longer.

General trends can be identified. With Bernhard Barbar, we can perhaps speak of a tendency toward greater abstraction, stronger systematization, and greater comprehensiveness of idea complexes.[249] It is also apparent that plausible ideas and concepts now have to cope with more disorder in the environment of the societal system and intrasocietal environments of the functional systems within the societal system. In search of something permanent and necessary, ever-new contingencies are revealed, up to and including the contingency of natural laws themselves. In many areas, especially in art and literature, an individualism plagued by self-doubt is considered a symptom, if not the very nature, of modernity, and ideas are accordingly expected to be individual-friendly in their formulation (undogmatic, consensual, open to learning). Reference problems and code problems, thus the distinctions self-reference/other-reference and distinctions such as true/false, good/bad, right/wrong can no longer be brought into line—as the failure of logical positivism and then of analytical philosophy to integrate the concept groups of reference, meaning, and truth demonstrates. This is likely to tally with the assumption that the points of convergence holding ideas together recede increasingly into the distance[250]—or, alternatively, have to be introduced into societal differentiation, hence being differentiated in step. If the two courses are embarked upon at the same time, more universality (especially including history) and greater precision can be realized than in the older literature.

The trends by which the evolution of ideas reacts to itself have recently acquired the empty title of postmodernism (Toynbee, then Lyotard). This can mean renouncing comprehensive claims to unity and a transition to radically differentialist approaches. It is thus likely to confirm that the end of dialectic cannot be stopped even by a negative dialectic that, as a principle of progress, announces the end of progress.[251] The outbidding logic of progress and its avant-garde, who reflect on and disavow it, can be followed only by an underbidding logic. What is past is stripped of its historical situating, and hence of its status of having been overcome, its temporal nature. It can thus be used capriciously—in music by Stravinsky or Schnittke, in social philosophy by old-style anti-liberals (Carl Schmitt, Leo Strauss, Alasdair MacIntyre);[252] or, most recently, in such fields as civil society with particular emphasis on women. Philosophers react to the disaster of all the ethics of modern times (Kant, Bentham, Max Scheler)—with Aristotle. One might suspect this of being a vogue that has passed its peak. But perhaps a sense develops in the constant deconstruction and reconstruction of forms for the limits to combinatorial options, for a thoroughgoing construction of interrelations. And this circumstance would once again point to evolution. For who could say how this will happen, and what then?

Contrary to the earlier distinction between population evolution (applicable to both human beings and animals) and cultural evolution (only human artifacts), I shall resist the temptation to distinguish stages or epochs within the evolution of ideas; at least not in the sense of a self-generated historical sequence of cultural epochs or historical types. If we can afterward reconstruct historical divisions of this sort, this is due solely to sociostructural evolution, or, to be more precise, to the dominance of certain differentiation types. These types of differentiation can be assigned to certain semantic forms.[253] But this does not justify concluding that an independent cultural evolution generates a type sequence of its own in parallel to sociostructural evolution. After all, the evolution of ideas has to rely in its selection mechanism on "plausibility." It can deduce this plausibility only from observing society. From the logic of its own determinations, it can win critical or innovative potential and thus lead to "preadaptive advances." Or it can continue to pursue its own traditions even where they are long since obsolete—for example, the notion, associated with hopes of upward social mobility, so enduringly beloved of "middle-class society," that we live in a stratified society with linear transitions between "down" and "up." These temporal shifts are important for a sufficiently realistic theory of "sociocultural" evolution. But this does not mean that the semantics is strong enough in itself, as it were, from an "intellectual history" or ideation-causal point of view, to produce epochal divisions. It only observes what is produced in societal autopoiesis—but using its own distinctions, constructive and deconstructive, and including time-related concepts such as "modern" or divisions such as antiquity/Middle Ages/modern age.

11. The Evolution of Subsystems

We come up against quite different problems when we ask whether independent intrasocietal evolution with differentiation of variation, selection, and restabilization is possible at the level of societal subsystems. In this case, too, our results will be historically differentiated and run counter to our assessment of the evolution of ideas. Subsystem evolutions begin only with the functional differentiation of the societal system, for only with this form of differentiation is the combination of operational closure and high internal complexity attained at the level of subsystems that gives the differentiation of evolutionary functions sufficient hold.[254]

In some, albeit few, cases, attempts have been made to apply the conceptuality of evolution theory to the functional systems of modern society. From the perspective of the history of science, such attempts have been motivated by the collapse of older theoretical notions, especially by doubts about the immanent rationality of the subject matter. Evolutionary epistemology for the functional system called science provides the most striking example. An alternative to Neo-Kantianism and to logical-methodological theories geared to deduction had already developed along with pragmatism in the late nineteenth century.[255] A particular attraction appears to have been that the legitimation of "chance" provided an opportunity to include innovations and escape the corset of a methodology adapted to control and not to discovery. As a result, attention focused almost exclusively on the variation function. Evolution theory, with its schema of variation and selection, also offered a possibility of breaching the justificatory circle that threatens all theories of knowledge without having to take recourse to an unquestioningly self-assured authority: that is, without having to invoke reason.

Having for decades gone along with the ups and downs of "Darwinism," and having itself to fight for survival, evolutionary epistemology is today one of the few remaining theories on offer in this field. However, it ranges from biologically inspired epistemology (which I shall disregard) and theories of the Popper or Kuhn type, which do not operate with the variation/selection schema, to not very elaborated cases of applied general evolution theory.[256] At present, the bottleneck lies both in the inadequate elaboration of a general evolution theory, as well as in unsolved problems of "constructivism," and, as a sociologist might be permitted to note, in the unsettled relationship between science and society.[257]

Attempts have been under way to apply evolution theory to the economic system for some forty years now.[258] Here, too, the collapse of an older theory, namely, the theory of price determination by the market with (quasi-) perfect competition, has clearly been the incentive.[259] This shows that the starting point is not the economic system itself, but the individual enterprise and its decisions, and that population theoretical notions are therefore in play. If economic decisions are no longer made by the market, but in enterprises under conditions of lacking information and uncertainty, it seems obvious to treat decisions as chance variations[260] and to attribute the selection of corporate success, that is, of the surviving population, to "natural selection" by the market.[261] Meanwhile, however, it has been realized that adaptive strategies within firms and selection by the market offer no meaningful theoretical alternative, but that the two always take effect together. This view has established itself in both "population ecology" and in a narrower (late-Darwinian) understanding of economic evolution.[262] However, it raises problems of "structural drift," and these cannot be adequately handled by traditional research approaches, which concern themselves with the entry and exit of firms in the population.

The more recent theoretical discussion in economics, which has given considerable impetus to evolution-theoretical considerations, amounts to criticism of neoclassical "orthodoxy."[263] The blame is placed on the fixation of prevailing opinion on a link between equilibrium models and optimization strategies, which can comprehend the economic decision only as reaction and not as innovation. Close ties result between evolution theory and research into technological change, which cannot be satisfactorily treated by traditional neoclassicism. This gives rise to a new version of criticism directed at the conventional premises of rational behavior. The loss of the historical dimension is also lamented. On the other hand, no common opposing standpoint has yet been found, and any recourse to neo-Darwinian theoretical notions of biology in particular is rejected.[264] A discussion between only reactive or primarily proactive (creative) theoretical interests is unlikely to prove productive, for both ultimately confirm the unpredictability of evolution. What is especially convincing, however, is that interests have to be diversified for transactions, that is, for the way in which the economy operates, to be possible and this is precisely what evolution can be expected to achieve.

For research into other functional systems, practically no evolution-theoretical approaches are to be found. We might at best mention the legal system,[265] and here, too, the incentive lies in the failure of preceding deductive theories, whether they draw on natural law, analytical approaches, or analytical jurisprudence. An evolution-theoretical treatment of the political system of modern society is lacking,[266] although development toward and in the welfare state could offer good possibilities for such a project.

The status of research renders any assessment difficult. We must therefore make do with a number of questions that arise when seriously addressing studies on co-evolution between the societal system and the functional systems differentiated within it. This entails analyses of system differentiation.

The theoretical point of departure would have to lie in the societal nesting of operationally closed autopoietic systems, hence in the question of how it is possible for a social system within another to establish its own autopoietic reproduction on the basis of operational closure. Only where this is possible, and only where adequate internal complexity develops on this basis within subsystems, can the differentiation of variation, selection, and restabilization find a hold. I presume that here, too, the variation mechanism lies firstly in the observation of communication as (provoking) negation and is systematized only with the setting in motion of functional differentiation by binary codings—now in the coding of function-specific operations with the aid of such distinctions as true/false, propertied/unpropertied, lawful/unlawful, rulers/subjects, aesthetically consonant/disconsonant (beautiful/ugly).

These special codes provide for differentiation while facilitating the code-specific switch from one side to the other. This allows keeping an eye on the opposing case to become daily routine. But this circumstance also means that which of the code values (for example true or false) is chosen to indicate its own operations is impossible to predict and depends on the system's programs.

Formally speaking, binary coding does not mean that external considerations are excluded. The binary structure of code values is in orthogonal relation to the distinction self-reference/other-reference, and therefore does not prejudice the criteria by which code values are assigned. Otherwise, no society could take the risk of reacting to certain problems with binary codings. But inasmuch as the codes inaugurate the need for criteria, it can and must become apparent that such criteria first have to be found. Even if it is only a matter of decorating everyday objects: what is beautiful and ugly first has to be tried out. Even where situations involving superior power arise in tribal or religious settings and have to fulfill the conditions of the societal context, how this power is exercised is not yet determined. Or, in the case of norm projections invoking conventionalities, latitude for judgment arises as soon as controversy develops. The stringent coding to the exclusion of third values generates open contingencies that create a need for meaning and at this very point become susceptible to evolution. If a variation intervenes here, it is likely to be considered for selection. The adoption of external selection criteria is then felt to be methodologically less and less appropriate—a partly continuous, partly abrupt switch, which depends on the societal reach of the criteria and on the tried and tested eigenvalues of the domain of special evolution, and is accordingly delayed or furthered by them.

Binary codes therefore appear to be hinges for opening the gates to subsystem evolutions in society where favorable circumstances occur; and writing, as we have seen,[267] will have had an important role to play in this. Binary structures have speed advantages: they offer the fastest way to develop complexity and, at the same time, the simplest form of ordering memory. Since language is already binarily coded, memory is easy to update. On the one hand, binary decisional situations occur often enough and have enough practical relevance in life not to have to rely on corresponding functional systems already existing in autopoietically closed form. On the other, they entail a sufficiently specific need for criteria, so that special evolutions can take off as soon as recursive reference to criteria of the same type comes into play. That artistic criteria, even in the case of poetry, are not suitable for deciding questions of truth was recognized at the latest in early modern times (that legal matters cannot be settled in the form of vase paintings and the artistic portrayal of judicial scenes provides no legal argument will already have been realized).[268] Property was still long treated as an instrument of power, while the power of political office, consolidated in the territorial state, had since the late Middle Ages no longer been able effectively to control events in the economic marketplace. As early as 1200, England experienced inflation that influenced the development of law and, above all, broke the complex feudal structures of landed property in the interest of clear property relations suitable for borrowing and liability.[269] However, inflation itself is not a problem for the courts to decide; evolution of the economy and of the law, because codes and underlying programs differ, go their separate ways.

Whereas at the code level, that is, in the mechanism of self-variation, systems are determined by eigenvalues—for this defines their distinctness from other systems—at the program level they are adaptable. Theories and legal rules or contracts, investment or consumption programs, political agendas are more or less sensitive to the societal environment. Here, too, systems are structurally determined and closed, for only they themselves can decide and apply their programs. But in selecting programs that serve to select operations, they can be irritated and influenced by the environment. To express this, one often speaks of "interests." As always, stability lies in the autopoiesis itself. It is thus not a static but a dynamic stability. The ability to change structures (especially programs), often against resistance from their own organizations, opens the way to restabilizing innovations. The short-circuit I have noted for the functionally differentiated societal system is thus repeated at this level: stabilization facilities are so dynamized that they also serve the function of evolutionary variation. Precisely this appears to be the outcome of co-evolution between societal evolution and subsystem evolutions: society cannot defend itself (it has no organ for this purpose) against the pace dictated by functional systems.

The coding and programming of functional systems is both result and condition of their evolution. Such a circular relationship is typical and inevitable for evolution-theoretical accounts, but does not satisfy as historical explanation. We must return to the insight that evolution has to rely on transient situations that can be used for takeoff even if they later lapse or lose their fundamental importance.

Particulars can be clarified only by detailed historical studies. We must make do with examples. In the second half of the sixteenth century, printing, having more broadly informed the reading public and more widely disseminated religious, political, and humanistic propaganda—irreversible changes in relations between individuals, who no longer participate only in court circles and territorial-state politics—is likely to have contributed much to the transition to modern theater. At any rate, the theater simulated this situation with the new fixed architectural division between stage and auditorium and, on stage, political themes and characters abandoned to their fate. For the endogenous dynamics of the visual arts that began to develop in the Renaissance, the social upgrading of artists through courtly contacts is considered to have been an important stimulus.[270] The American mass media system began its historical career with advertising free sheets containing added and therefore ideologically neutral news;[271] there must therefore first have been a market without further sociopolitical interests. In early modern times, European universities profited from the switch from a religiously determined clientele system to a political, territorial-state one, which could provide greater freedom in professional training;[272] and then again in the nineteenth century from the switch to the "unity of research and teaching," thus to science. As long ago as the eleventh and twelfth centuries, the legal system achieved remarkable independence from the feudal system, which still controlled politics, and from the dogmatic premises of religion, because it was employed as an instrument for differentiating religion (canon law) and politics (common law, city charters, feudal rights) and for developing broad organization of government for both the Church and the emerging territorial states (England, Sicily). It therefore had to satisfy the relevant requirements for precision and adaptability.[273]

That evolution can recruit opportunities that may later lapse when a new format of autopoiesis and self-organization is secured therefore breaks the circularity of the evolution-theoretical explanation and moves on to historical analysis. This naturally does not mean that there is an automatism that exploits every opportunity; nor does it mean that one can return to a purely narrative sequence. A theory of self-referential systems and self-evolving evolutions is needed to formulate the problem.

Inasmuch as subsystem evolutions are set into motion on the basis of special functions and codings, and then ensure evolutionary structural changes within these systems that are no longer coordinated between systems, the conditions to which the evolution of the societal system reacts change. That societal evolution is increasingly the result of subsystem evolutions must have considerable impact. It certainly does not mean that we can no longer speak of societal evolution, because, after all, the subsystems themselves carry out the (deviating) reproduction of society. It is also, from the point of view of the system reference society, still a matter of language, of symbolically generalized media and of the relationship between system and environment. What can be observed, however, are changes in the semantic self-description of society.[274] Since the end of the nineteenth century, no one has dared presume progress. Despite all the controversy about "social Darwinism," evolution itself was still described in terms of positively connoted structural characteristics (for instance, survival of the best adapted), but this sort of postulate can now be advanced only ideologically, only controversially. And behind the increasing uncertainty about the future, the presentiment is emerging that an evolution of evolutions per se will produce unforeseeable states of affairs.

In the second half of the twentieth century, society as a whole can be characterized only by the specific problems that arise at the level of this system with the extrasocietal environment: with the ecological conditions for ongoing restabilization and with increasingly intractable, alienated individuals. Evolution is no longer expected to produce ever better adaptation. The facts speak for the contrary. The question can therefore only be how society is to maintain the state of adaptedness required to continue its own autopoiesis under conditions of high complexity and improbability. Subsystem evolutions can give no answer. They make it much more likely that science will generate more and more knowledge, leading to more and more uncertainty; that the economy will generate more and more capital looking to be invested, but which is not invested; that, in the course of democratization and thematic universalization, the proportion of decisions taken in politics to refrain from a decision will increase; that the law will be embedded in a framework where it is subjected to renewed deliberation and "weighing up" of how it is to be determined, and whether it ought to be applied at all. In all these cases, acceleration and delay multiply simultaneously, producing friction that makes synchronization more and more difficult. For a young generation with a long life expectancy, the perspectives become blurred.

We have at any rate to abandon an idea that long dominated in modernization research after World War II, the notion that modernization trends in the individual functional systems, namely, political democracy, the market-oriented money economy, the rule of law, dogmatically unhampered scientific research, uncensored mass media, school education for the entire population according to individual aptitude, and so on would trigger a wave of development in which the achievements of the various functional systems would mutually support and confirm one another. The contrary is more probable. Following Richard Norgaard, I have already spoken of the "co-evolution of unsustainability."[275] We could also say that evolution can confirm only itself.

All this enhances the impression that only evolution will get us further, but the question is how and where to. If this cannot be answered, not even in such a simple schema as better/worse, the resulting uncertainty will become a factor that reacts to evolution in similarly unforeseeable manner, possibly quite differently, depending on the subsystem evolution concerned.

12. Evolution and History

Evolution theory describes systems that reproduce themselves from moment to moment in many individual operations, using or failing to use and changing or failing to change structures. All this happens in a present and in a world that exist simultaneously (and can hence not be influenced). For its operational reproduction, such a system requires no history to begin with. Having got as far as I have in writing this book, I only need to find the next sentence. Here it is.

Evolution theory, like systems theory, therefore assumes that uncounted operations (counting would be another operation) take place simultaneously and, by producing further operations, reproduce the system. The special interest of evolution theory is in deviant reproduction as a condition for structural change. To begin with, this has nothing to do with historiography, which makes it understandable that from the standpoint of the history of science, evolutionism and historicism are at loggerheads.[276] Conceding the difference in perspective, the controversy is unnecessary. Characteristically, historians look for *new* knowledge in the past (instead of keeping it in memory only through ritually maintained contact). They combine narration with causal explanation with the proviso of doing justice to accessible sources. No theory of societal evolution can or wants to compete with this. For the sociological perspective and especially for systems-theoretical analysis, causal explanations are so difficult that they are inadvisable at the level of general theoretical propositions, and for narration, the sociologist lacks improvisational talent. This is particularly true because the societal system has to be understood as a self-referential system (a nontrivial machine in Heinz von Foerster's sense)[277] in which transformations do not simply take place: their taking place is also observed and communicated. As a result, intentions (however inappropriate) develop that seek to prevent the change or to promote it.[278] The theory of societal evolution can accordingly not undertake to explain the cause of the course of history or merely of certain events. The objective is only to provide a theoretical schema for historical studies, which, under favorable circumstances, may point to causally relevant origins. But hypotheses for such transitions would first have to be developed with regard to certain historical states of affairs. They can neither be derived from evolution theory nor, correspondingly generalized, can they "verify" evolution theory. The "variation—selection—restabilization" differentiation schema of evolution theory is circular. All historical analyses must, however, set out from specific situations and, for the purposes of evolution-theoretical explanation, show how opportunities and restrictions in these situations interlock.

To give an example, in the historical and social-science literature dealing with Europe's special path [*Sonderweg*] since the Middle Ages, hence with the origins of modern society, factor theories confront one another that single out religion, economics, political state building, or law. When considering the Middle Ages, the differentiation of functional systems has clearly been the schema to assert itself. Where a primary factor is postulated, the relevance of others is recognized and attributed to it. Immanuel Wallerstein, for example, takes the segmentation of the European world of states to be a consequence of the international division of labor in the economy.[279] Max Weber derives the primacy of religious orientation from a need to legitimate unleashed economic motives.[280] More recent authors give primacy back to politics and see the decisive factor in the prevention of empire building and in the segmentary, territorial-state order of the political control of force.[281] For just as good reasons, the early differentiation of a systematized legal culture is posited as a European peculiarity that generates deviation.[282] These controversies will persist as long as such primacy theories are advanced. Methodologically, it should be noted that many good arguments but no hypothesis of a particularly important factor can be derived from the sources. And theoretically, we must ask whether it makes any sense at all to attribute the transition to functional differentiation (if that is what is at issue) to primacy of one of the functional systems, however historically relative.

A theory of societal evolution renounces causal explanations (or limits them to minimal sectors of macrosocietal evolution). It replaces the causal schema by the assumption of circular evolutionary conditions.[283] In every historical situation, society is a nontrivial, historical machine, which uses variation, selection, and restabilization in accordance with the momentarily given state of affairs. What matters is only that these evolutionary mechanisms can be separated, and this requires a minimum of complexity in the system. The result is a trend toward deviation amplification in which, returning to our examples, the early territorial-state organizations (such as the Norman states of England and Sicily or the republics of Italy) were able to use legal instruments also deployed by the Church in combating the theocratic ambitions of the Holy Roman Emperor, and that owed their essential impetus to the chance rediscovery of ancient Roman texts and their glossing for teaching purposes. The development of the money economy (for instance, banking) used the same instruments, which at the same time, however, freed the concept of property from its basis in feudal law in the course of the first monetary inflation in England (around 1200).[284] Much depended on a system of territorial-state jurisdiction that also functioned outside the cities (e.g., with respect at least to loans secured by land), and thus also on the consolidation of political control over a territory that was itself not vast enough in its impact to be able to regulate trade. Typical of these early forms of functional differentiation therefore appears to be that evolutionary advances of a very specific sort develop within the ambit of particular functions and act on other evolutionary possibilities as chance events that can be used in the historical situation.

In other words, evolution theory stresses the rather improbable, opportunistic tendency for structural changes, which, all in all, transform improbable opportunities through integration in systems into probabilities of maintaining and developing their possibilities. At any rate, no historiography can manage without the notion of structural change. It will also have to consult evolution theory; and the question can only be whether the resolution capacity of evolution theory takes the need for sources in historical research and its propensity for putting unanswerable questions so far that any account of a meaningful, coherent history in which what comes later is explained by what comes earlier cannot be achieved in this roundabout way. Historians have anyway dissociated themselves from any notion of "universal history."

History is made when events of importance in society are observed with regard to the difference between before and after (hence as events and, more precisely, as breaks). It presupposes that the difference in time thus revealed cannot simply be dissolved by disidentification in the sense that the society existing after the event is a different one than that before. Thus the Persian wars made the Greeks aware of their identity beforehand and afterward—an identity that united the many cities of Greece. The earliest Western historiography documents this. More and more, events that make history could also be structural changes in the system—for instance, the great politico-economic reforms in early Greece and in Rome, or the announcement of a religious reform, which in the face of resistance was, in historical retrospective, to become the revelation of a new religion. The difference between before and after makes it possible to celebrate the unity of the different. Even the "revolutions" of modern times can make history in this fashion, as success for people or success of ideas.

The old world was able to safeguard this unity of the difference between before and after in the horizon of time itself with the aid of the difference between transient time and eternity.[285] Eternity could describe the position simultaneous with all times from which God observed humankind and their history, whereas the advent of difference (the emergence of time as the one side of this difference) was explained as the break with God, the Fall of Man.[286] In timeless time, eternity, lay the real meaning of history and also the certainty that everything is going the way God wishes it to go.

In the transition to modern society, this safeguarding of the meaning of events in a timeless eternity breaks down. In the seventeenth century, we find this position occupied by the notion of a *conservatio* as a natural result of natural processes. In other eyes, in Milton's *Paradise Lost*, it is assumed that the meaning of history has to be explained to man (Adam, the reader) in the midst of history; for Adam was not able to observe the beginning and cannot yet observe the end; but he needs orientation now. The eighteenth century reacted to this by rethinking historical time and history, with history itself becoming part of history and having to be rewritten in every age.[287] The space of history was now too small for what one would now like to, indeed, have to, do to persist in the future. The nineteenth century found itself confronted by the same problem, and solved it partly through the notion of unique historical processes and "individual laws" of history,[288] partly through evolution theory. No further progress had been made even by the end of the twentieth century.

Expecting evolution theory to meaningfully interpret the unity of difference is asking too much of it scientifically. Its real achievements lie in the theoretical specification of the problems of structural change. It does not even offer a theory of the historical process, let alone any substantive directional indications—for example, in the sense of concepts of progress or decline. It provides no information about the future—in either a comforting or discomforting sense. If it can nevertheless contribute to the self-description of modern society, and this can happen only in close association with systems theory and communication theory. Such a combination of theory can produce historically fruitful questions. Only thus can the demand for sufficiently complex analytical tools and conceptual precision be met. And only thus can a *specifically scientific* contribution be made to the self-description of modern society, which can be also be put to the test in science itself, through research.

Whether evolution theory or not, every theory of history leads to the reorganization of data requirements. The need for data is independent of the source situation, for it arises from the theory. This might drive historians to distraction or to renounce theory. The problem presents itself differently for the sociology of societal history. It has no intention of writing history, nor does it seek to establish sufficient coherence in relations between events. Its problem is that the time dimension of the societal system can be excluded or ignored by no theory of society. It knows that all systems that reenter the distinction between system and environment into the system require a memory function that informs them of the present as the result of an unchanging history. It is thus concerned, not with the coherence of events, but with consistency in the theoretical apparatus of societal theory. I have mentioned one example of this problem in discussing the links between evolution theory and systems theory. The consequence is a considerable data deficit with corresponding verification difficulties. However, substantial possibilities for reinterpreting sources are also created.

13. Memory

The evolution theory used above treats society as if it could be observed from without. This may well be due to its origins in biological research. But sociologists, too, often uphold the claim of their discipline to scientific status as if they could observe society from the outside and had at best to take account of "intersubjective" agreement and the effects of the communication of their observations on society. In principle, historians recognize that all history is written in current and continuing history; but their concept for self-reference is and remains history, not society. They are satisfied to work with provisional historical accounts, which, although not taking their perspective from the end of history, do set out from the state of knowledge at the time of writing. A sociology concerned with the theory of society will have to revise these assumptions, which means it will have to observe them again. Here we are concerned, however, only with how society reenters its evolution into evolution; that is to say, what role the fact that transformation is observed and commented on plays in evolutionary transformations.

I have repeatedly emphasized that evolution theory does not demonstrate causal sequences (though it does not exclude observers maintaining that they can discover links between causes and effects). What is more, evolution theory is unable to confirm a further form of the usual historical account of continuity, namely, that innovations explicitly assert themselves *against* existing structures, thus mobilizing a historical process. For this would presuppose an observer who singles out certain distinctions from others, for example, who speaks of a rising social class that differentiates itself both upwardly and downwardly. This is not to deny that time-related distinctions occur, for example, between old and new or between before and after. But what needs to be clarified is why certain distinctions are preferred over others. For this we need a theory that goes beyond merely observing and explaining continuities and discontinuities, lasting influences, or marked breaks, and that can ask how such distinctions can be made in an already evolving system and what decides that this distinction is made and not that.

This presupposes that the system can distinguish itself. If the complexity of the societal system then permits the distinctions the system uses to reenter what it has distinguished,[289] the system becomes opaque to itself.

It can no longer adequately observe itself with the operations that generate and change its own state. This holds true particularly dramatically for the time dimension, for the very reason that complexity is now increasingly "temporalized," in other words, has to be developed and reduced successively. This is only another way of putting the common thesis that no system can control its own evolution. *Instead* the system uses an additional facility in current (present) operations, which can be called "memory," following Spencer-Brown.[290] In any case, a system that establishes historical causes for its present state or wishes to describe this as differing from early states, for example, as "modern," requires a memory to process the distinctions.[291] But what is memory?

I use the term "memory" here neither in the sense of a possible return to the past nor in the sense of a store of data or information we can draw on as need be.[292] I am talking about a function in constant but only present use that tests all incipient operations for consistency with what the system constructs as reality. In the field we are dealing with, these operations are communications, and thus not neurobiological changes in the state of the brain nor what enters the awareness of a single consciousness. The function of the memory is therefore to limit possible consistency checks and at the same time to free information-processing capacities in order to open the system to new irritations. The main function of memory therefore lies in *forgetting*, in preventing the system from blocking itself by congealing the results of earlier observations.[293]

Forgetting should not be understood as a sort of loss of access to what is past; for this would mean that time is fundamentally reversible. Forgetting has a positive function, because time acts both irreversibly and cumulatively.[294] The link between these two properties must be both preserved and interrupted, and precisely this is the function of memory, or, to put it more exactly, the double function of remembering and forgetting. Without forgetting there would be neither learning nor evolution. This double function is already built into ongoing reimpregnation (psychologists often say "reinforcement"). On the one hand, a compact impression of familiarity, of acquaintance with things is developed through repetition of the communication, the language it uses, its references. On the other, how things were when certain impressions or demands and irritations were new, surprising, unfamiliar, is forgotten. The repetition itself generates both remembering *and* forgetting. But it is always a question of preconditions for the operation under way, not of jumping about in time. In chess, for instance, we can set out from the present positions of the pieces on the board and do not need to remember how they reached them. Chess problems are accordingly presented in newspapers without going into the history of the game. It would be far too complex if this history had to be remembered to enable the game to continue, even though it might be useful to recall the last moves of one's opponent in sequence the better to guess his strategy. This example shows that the present suffices largely as representation of the past. But this is a highly stylized borderline case, which demonstrates how very much forgetting enables complexity to be overcome. The situation is different for even the simplest language games. We cannot enter an ongoing conversation and join in without being introduced to the history of the interaction or being able to guess it. A conversation cannot constantly forget itself; but this has repercussions for complexity and, we can perhaps say, for the relative rulelessness of the system.

If the present has to be accepted as congealed past, this generally suffices—on condition that enough identities (in our examples, the potential moves of the various chessmen; the possible uses of words) guarantee that a forgotten past that is with us only as present can be linked to a future. Identities are special achievements that disburden memory. Only exceptionally are identities so condensed that they are available for repeated use. Only exceptionally do "objects" develop in the recursive operating of the system as system-specific "eigenvalues" by which the system can observe stability and changes.[295] Only exceptionally is forgetting therefore inhibited. And only exceptionally are memories provided with a time index, which prevents too much heterogeneous material as a permanent property of objects from generating too many inconsistencies. Thus, only exceptionally are the system's eigenvalues dissolved through time markings such as past/future or even through datings to allow temporary objects, limited-term entities, episodes, and so on, to arise, whose present relevance can again be filtered.

The present is nothing other than the distinction between past and future. It is not an independent period but takes up only the operational time necessary to observe distinctions in the time horizons of past and future (in whatever factual regard). If the memory can exercise its function only in current operation, that is, only in the present, this means that it has to do with the difference between past and future, that it manages this distinction—and does not, for example, operate in relation only to the past.[296]

We can therefore also say that the memory controls the resistance of the system's operations to the system's operations. With its consistency checks, it notes what, after processing of this internal, self-organized resistance, the system takes to be "reality" (in the sense of *res*). And this in turn means that it examines which reality provides the system's perspective on the future.

Can we visualize this more precisely?

We go a step further with the thesis that the transfer function of memory relates to *distinctions*; or, more exactly, to indications of something as opposed to something else. The memory operates with what has been successfully indicated and tends to forget the other side of the distinction. Although it can also mark distinctions as forms, for instance, the distinction between good and evil, it tends to forget what this distinction was distinguished from. The particularity of discrimination in the forgetting/remembering schema is determined not least by language and is insofar a characteristic of social systems. Although the subject/predicate structure of our language does not exclude always mentioning what all components of a sentence are distinguished from, this would be extremely long-winded. Even the perceiving consciousness when remembering concentrates on things or events rather than on the settings in which they were embedded when perceived; or it remembers these settings as complex arrangements for which further links are lacking. This has proved worthwhile, not least because the things that we consciously remember or the topics to which communication can return can be taken out of their context by identification and confirmed as worth repeating, whereas concrete situations never repeat themselves—although there can be no indication without distinction, no singling out, no observation.

Throwing light on the background to the distinctions a system uses to observe shows how the memory contributing to this process distinguishes between and links past and present. Whereas the distinction itself remains unmarked in the past (which, as we have seen, also holds for the distinguishing of distinctions), in the area that functions as future, the distinction is used to enable oscillation, the crossing of the internal boundary.[297] If, for example, in extradomestic ("political") matters talk has explicitly or implicitly been only of men, a future can be conceptualized that remembers that men are to be distinguished from women, and that the boundary can be crossed and recrossed within this distinction, that oscillation is possible. In the present, the function of memory is then to remember the distinction or to substitute the distinction man/unmarked by the distinction man/woman, or to remove this distinction from the context of the *polis/oikos* distinction (see Plato's "community of women") in order to gain a past that provides the future with scope for oscillation.

Memory is not the system, for the system must already be running if it is to be able to remember anything; and the remembered past is consequently not the past of the system. An external observer can always add another past or treat the past remembered in the system as fictional. Logicians and linguists (as external observers) will be tempted to distinguish "levels" and to advance a principle of nonconfusion; which is more plausible in this context than elsewhere, for by forgetting, memory distinguishes itself from the level of system operations.

We need such a general theory of memory, suitable also for mathematical, neurobiological, and psychological purposes, if we are to ask how the memory of society and its subsystems work. I am not talking about so-called "collective memory," which consists only in consciousness systems subjected to the same social conditions remembering by and large the same states of affairs.[298] Social memory does not consist in the traces communications leave behind in individual consciousness systems.[299] It is an achievement of communicative operations themselves, of their own, indispensable recursivity. A social memory is reproduced only by every communication actualizing determinate meaning; it is assumed that communication is in a position to make something of this meaning, that, so to speak, it already knows it. At the same time repeated use of the same references ensures that this will also be so in future cases.[300] The ongoing reimpregnation of communicatively usable meaning and the corresponding forgetting presupposes that consciousness systems collaborate, but does not depend on what single individuals remember and how they refresh their own memories by participating in communication. Individuals are, in other words, free to associate identical topics with widely differing memories and thus to influence social communication as if by chance. Although social memory would not function if there were no consciousness systems endowed with memory (just as consciousness systems for their part have to rely on neurophysiologically reproduced memory), it is not based on the memories held by consciousness systems, for they are much too diverse and cannot be brought down to a common denominator in communication. Although we can assume that the scope of social evolution for variation is limited where individuals have a strongly developed collective memory at their disposal and communication can presuppose that all participants have sufficiently similar memories, this does not explain how evolutionary variation is possible at all and how social communication separates remembering (past) and oscillation (future).

Every society has to rely on its own, self-produced memory taking part in all operations; for no society could make the continuation of its own operations dependent on first clarifying (and how, if not by means of communication?) what is given participants neurophysiologically and psychologically as known, as familiar, as past facts. Illiterate societies rely on "objects" or "quasi-objects."[301] What is meant is neither topics of communication expressly spoken about from case to case, nor the mere materiality of matters in the outside world, but determination of the meaning and correct form of objects (houses, tools, places, and ways, or names of natural objects, but also of human beings) to which communication can refer without doubts arising about what is intended and how to deal with it. The memory function is marked by the assumption that there are "correct" forms and "correct" names and that knowledge of names gives power over objects. Ornaments can intensify this labeling and build bridges for directing mental attention. There are also "quasi-objects," rites or celebrations or narratable myths, in other words, stagings whose special function it is to provide the operations of the system with memory in a manner not foreseeable in detail. The narrative traditions of illiterate societies now so thoroughly investigated also serve not to transfer knowledge but to prepare narrators and audience for something they already know and reactualize as memory. The required memory performance of singers is tied to the form of communication, to rhythm, music, formalisms, ready-made phrases already adapted to rhythms, stagings, and so on, and could not even be brought to awareness independently of communication.

There was hence memory of this sort long before writing was invented.[302] The memory of early societies is above all topographical memory.[303] A topographical memory suffices as long as the problem lies in providing scenes for repeatable action (for example, sacred places or temples for worship). It provides places, including buildings, that enable and separate interactions.[304] In this lies the structure to be taken as known, which regulates meetings (and the avoidance of meetings). An area of society is also demarcated, an inhabited "civilization" in opposition to an unknown and therefore "wild" environment, and nonobjectivated events can be forgotten. Since this state of familiarity (like all memory) operates unnoticed, the only special problem that remains is the personal wish not to be forgotten. In Mesopotamia, it was addressed initially to the gods, and later to posterity.[305] Writing merely complements the object-bound memory with a more mobile memory, which can constantly be regenerated, but which, when it comes to writing matters down, also requires decisions to be made between remembering and forgetting, for which criteria and controls have subsequently to be developed.

Neither illiterate nor literate societies had been able fully to grasp their dependence on self-produced memory, even though there was a highly developed cult of memory and corresponding techniques for learning to remember. Only in modern societies has a sufficiently general concept of culture developed that is suitable for distinguishing social memory from other social functions.[306] Without an adequate theory of memory at his disposal, Talcott Parsons had a ground-breaking intuition. His general theory of the action system provides for a function of "latent-pattern maintenance," latency meaning that patterns of order have to be maintained and handed down even if they are not actualized at the moment. According to Parsons, this is the task of the cultural subsystem of the action system. Culture must accordingly have existed since the formation of human society began, and the problem is only that and how a cultural system and a social system differentiated in the course of evolution that contributed differently to enabling action.[307] However, the concept of culture does not yet explain precisely enough how this bridging function is performed. To discover this, we must take recourse to a theory of memory, and this raises the question of what we gain by calling social memory culture.

Let us therefore reformulate the problem and ask why society invents a concept of culture to describe its memory. For culture is a historical concept,[308] and modern society would have to recollect when and why it introduced it. It presumably did so to reorganize its memory and adapt it to the requirements of modern, highly complex, endogenously dynamic society.

For "culture" as an independent domain in opposition to "nature" was spoken of only from the second half of the eighteenth century,[309] in reaction to increasingly universalistic, historical, and regional comparisons, which included extreme cases ("wild," prebiblical times), and process the material from the point of view of a "culture" necessary for humankind.

The phenomenon addressed has yet to be successfully demarcated, for example, semiotically in relation to "signs" in general or sociologically in relation to "action."[310] This could suggest that culture is indeed nothing other than the memory of society, hence the filter of forgetting/remembering and the appropriation of the past to determine the variation framework of the future. This could also explain why culture does not understand itself as being the best of all possibilities, but rather as responsible for steering the possibilities of comparison, and thus obstructing the view of other possibilities. In other words, culture prevents us from considering what we could do instead of what we are accustomed to. The invention of a special concept of culture would accordingly be due to a situation in which society has become so complex that it has to forget more and remember more and has to reflect on this, and therefore needs a sorting mechanism that can satisfy these requirements.

This brings us to the concept of "cultural capital" introduced by Pierre Bourdieu.[311] For capital is nothing other than accumulated past, which can be treated as a disposable resource without the learning and appropriation processes themselves having to be remembered. The concept of capital conceals the possibilities of comparison, which were originally the concern of the culture concept, and replaces them with the social comparison of the prestige value of symbolic goods, so that the concept of cultural capital covers only a narrow segment of what the culturally formed memory means for society.

The influence of the memory on structural developments goes largely unnoticed. Memory is not named as their cause. Thus incipient political centralism in early Mesopotamia might be attributable to the deeds of kings being the main subjects of reports and to these reports being handed down,[312] but their selectivity is naturally not to be seen as the cause of royal rule. The problem of memory is instead seen mainly in memory losses. To begin with, it was mainly people who wanted to prevent being forgotten. Only later did one want to preserve existing factual knowledge and skills from oblivion. In the old *memoria* theory, a key problem was already how to prevent forgetting, at any rate, forgetting truths. The so-called Renaissance with its refined theory of memory had discovered that things in the arts and sciences had once been better *in this world* (!) and that the level then reached had once again to be attained. The proof of this possibility lay in the past.[313] However, this tradition-dependent concept was overtaxed.

Rethinking of the problem began with Giambattista Vico [1668–1744],[314] and toward the end of the eighteenth century resulted in the newly formulated concept of culture.

This can be conceived of as a special "sphere of subject matter" that is comprehensible to science (even be it only to the "humanities"). The discussion continues. If, however, we assume that interest in "interesting" comparison was the activating factor, it is evident that a new sort of differentiation technique is in play. Triadic relations are needed, if not trivalent logics, namely, a comparative perspective from which what is the same can be recognized despite major, often extreme diversity—no longer in the schema of natural similarities between species and genera but in that of functional equivalences. For example, there is now a function of religion that can be fulfilled in very different ways. And there is a cultural symptomatology that reads cultural phenomena as symptoms for something else.[315] The broad radius of comparison stimulates a culture of suspicion to which sociology can then connect.[316] And tradition is now no longer the self-evidence of what memory presents, but a form of observing culture.[317]

With this new semantics of "culture," a newly formed thinking about difference appears—newly formed in the form of comparisons. Older societies, too, had grounded their institutions on judgments of like and unlike, thus cognitively safeguarding these institutions.[318] Depending on the state of familiarization in the societies in question, this could happen in various ways and without the concept of culture. The culture concept switches, and hence mobilizes orientation, from sameness to comparability. At least when it began, this still allowed one to presuppose a multiplicity of societies that could be compared in their regional and/or historical diversity. This comparison has far-reaching effects. In the course of time—for example, in the empirical research of ethnology, not to mention the research of the Durkheim school into classifications—it demolishes the supposition that there can be any natural basis in the nature of things for judging likeness and unlikeness. Formally, this interest in comparison burdens itself with the advance determination of comparative standpoints and the question of the social conditionality of this decision. Initially, one appears to have had enough self-confidence to locate comparisons regionally (centered on Europe, if not on a single nation) or historically, which required a special concept of zeitgeist or modernity. Or the mass of material was processed strictly "scientifically" (in ethnology, the historical sciences, the humanities); and it had to be accepted that the scientific status of these efforts had to be distinguished from the established natural sciences. Yet all this produced conceptual problems that would not have arisen (or arisen differently) in a systems-theoretical approach that regards society itself as difference.

The differentiation technique of culture, relating to comparisons and developed on the basis of comparisons, has considerable consequences for how society reacts to its own evolution. To an unprecedented degree, cultural comparisons inhibit forgetting. Not only truths are saved from the embrace of forgetting but, one could say, all sorts of things. More is recognized as like than before, but this no longer provides certain orientation. Memory thus loses the function of providing leads. It loses the function of checking for consistency in the ongoing operations (communications) of society. This task has to be left to the special memories of the functional systems, which can no longer be mutually integrated.[319] The reality construction of society as a whole thus remains indeterminate.[320] It is transferred to a functional system, the system of the mass media. What can now be offered as overall formula for reality construction is that there is no longer any such formula.[321] As we know, Hegel had no heirs.

But this does not mean that every link between past and future is broken; for this would also mean that the two time horizons can no longer be distinguished, since they would be "unmarked states" for each other.[322] Something along these lines seems to be envisioned when the legend of the "end of history" is invoked; but it is in stark contradiction to what society assumes and reproduces every day in its communications. At this point, the theory of societal memory outlined above might be of help.

It seems that our culture operates by reading distinctions into the past, which supply frames in which the future can oscillate. The distinctions indicate forms that determine what the "other possibility" to a determinate something would be. Concretion of the distinctions used in each instance remains variable; but in order to vary distinctions, they have to be distinguished, marked as forms, and thus submitted to the same conditions of oscillation *within* implicitly or explicitly presupposed distinctions. There appears to be no binding "primary distinction" any more[323]—neither that of being and nonbeing nor that of truth values, neither that of science nor that of morality.[324] *But this does not mean that distinctions are not necessary.* The consequence is only that we are obliged to observe who uses what distinctions for setting their past for their future.

Whereas we assume that evolution happens the way it happens, and that it does so in a fashion that leaves the coupling of past to future to chance in the forms of variation/selection/restabilization, the operational memory of the system is concerned precisely with the coupling of past and future; but to couple these time horizons, it first has to distinguish between them. Evolution knows no beginnings. Memory (and possibly evolution theory, where it serves as system memory) may well find order and satisfaction in the construction of beginnings (e.g., Homer). Breaks then serve as distinctions that make it possible to consider what has come before to be insignificant. For its part, memory is a product of evolution; but it cannot remember this. It builds a manageable, self-constructed time difference into what has happened. The forms in which this occurs, that is, the distinctions with which memory operates, evolve with evolution and take effect within it. But they generate no representation of evolution, they do not represent it; they can therefore not control it. The future remains evolutionarily indeterminate and unpredictable. But memory can nevertheless determine the future as the sphere of possible oscillations, thus making the operations of the system dependent on the distinctions that are used in each case for indicating one side (but not the other), and that hence point to which boundary can be crossed.

Evolution is and remains unpredictable. Memory cannot change this. It can only adapt with various forms, depending on the irritation and acceleration coefficients that arise from evolution. An ontologically no longer comprehensible, identifiable culture locating itself in itself appears to be the form that the memory of society has invented and accepted in order to adapt the historical constructions and future perspectives of society to the conditions that have developed from the transition to primarily functional differentiation and from the threatening collapse of the distinction between stability and variation. It is thus justified and justifiable to retain a usage already introduced and to describe societal evolution also as "sociocultural evolution."

Notes

ABBREVIATIONS

Luhmann, *Aufklärung* Niklas Luhmann, *Soziologische Aufklärung*, 6 vols. (Opladen, 1970–1995)
Luhmann, *Gesellschaft* Niklas Luhmann, *Die Gesellschaft der Gesellschaft* (Frankfurt, 1997)
Luhmann, *Gesellschaftsstruktur* Niklas Luhmann, *Gesellschaftsstruktur und Semantik*, 4 vols. (Frankfurt, 1980–1995)
Luhmann, *Systeme* Niklas Luhmann, *Soziale Systeme: Grundriß einer allgemeinen Theorie* (Frankfurt, 1984)
Spencer-Brown, *Laws* George Spencer-Brown, *Laws of Form* (1969; new ed., New York, 1979)

PREFACE

1. Trans. under the title *Social Systems* (Stanford, CA, 1995).
2. Trans. under the title *Law as a Social System* (Oxford, 2004).
3. Trans. under the title *Art as a Social System* (Stanford, CA, 2000).
4. Niklas Luhmann and Raffaele De Giorgi, *Teoria della società* (Milan, 1992).
5. See Mary B. Hesse, *Models and Analogies in Science* (Notre Dame, IN, 1966).

TRANSLATOR'S NOTE

1. Niklas Luhmann, *Soziologie des Risikos* (Berlin, 1991), trans. Rhodes Barrett under the title *Risk: A Sociological Theory* (New York, 1993).

CHAPTER 1: SOCIETY AS A SOCIAL SYSTEM

1. In similar vein, Lars Löfgren uses the term "autolinguistic" to mean a form that has to be logically "unfolded" in distinguishing between levels. See Löfgren, "Life as an Autolinguistic Phenomenon," in *Autopoiesis: A Theory of Living Organization*, ed. Milan Zeleny (New York, 1981), 236–249.

2. Following Gotthard Günther, see, e.g., Fred Pusch, *Entfaltung der sozialwissenschaftlichen Rationalität durch eine transklassische Logik* (Dortmund, 1992).

3. To this day! See Friedrich H. Tenbruck, "Emile Durkheim oder die Geburt der Gesellschaft aus dem Geist der Soziologie," *Zeitschrift für Soziologie* 10 (1981): 333–350. To emphasize relations and dynamics, Georg Simmel writes only of "sociation" [*Vergesellschaftung*]. Max Weber places so much (and such "tragic") weight on differences between the value spheres, life orders, etc., of society that he manages without a superordinate concept of unity. See Hartmann Tyrell, "Max Webers Soziologie—eine Soziologie ohne 'Gesellschaft,'" in *Max Webers Wissenschaftslehre*, ed. Gerhard Wagner and H. Zipprian (Frankfurt, 1994), 390–414

4. See Helmut Schelsky, *Ortsbestimmung der deutschen Soziologie* (1959; 3rd ed., Düsseldorf, 1967), 93ff. See also Horst Baier, *Soziologie als Aufklärung—oder die Vertreibung der Transzendenz aus der Gesellschaft* (Constance, 1989).

5. See Friedrich H. Tenbruck, *Geschichte und Gesellschaft* (Berlin, 1986).

6. See Peter Bürger, *Prosa der Moderne* (Frankfurt, 1988).

7. At least in organizational theory, this is now recognized as the unfolding of a paradox. See *Paradox and Transformation: Toward a Theory of Change in Organization and Management*, ed. Robert E. Quinn and Kim S. Cameron (Cambridge, MA, 1988), esp. the article by Andrew H. Van de Ven and Marshall Scott Poole.

8. See also Michael Mulkay, *The Word and the World: Explorations in the Form of Sociological Analysis* (London, 1985); John Law, ed., *Power, Action and Belief: A New Sociology of Knowledge?* (London, 1986).

9. For more detail, see Niklas Luhmann, "Warum AGIL?" *Kölner Zeitschrift für Soziologie und Sozialpsychologie* 40 (1988): 127–139.

10. See Richard Münch, "Moralische Diskurse: Das unvollendete Projekt der Moderne," in id., *Dynamik der Kommunikationsgesellschaft* (Frankfurt, 1995), 13–36.

11. See Warren Weaver, "Science and Complexity," *American Scientist* 36 (1948): 536–544.

12. See Gaston Bachelard, *La formation de l'esprit scientifique: Contribution à une psychanalyse de la connaissance objective* (Paris, 1947), 13ff. See also the reflections on counteradaptive results of adaptive change in Anthony Wilden, *System and Structure: Essays in Communication and Exchange* (1972; 2nd ed., London, 1980), 205ff.

13. Severe criticism of these premises dating back to the nineteenth century is to be found in Charles Tilly, *Big Structures, Large Processes, Huge Comparisons* (New York, 1984). However, it remains theoretically unproductive, because along with the premises it also abandons the concept of society itself.

14. The problem this posed for sociology was really clear from the outset. Durkheim writes, e.g., in *Les règles de la méthode sociologique* (1894; 8th ed., Paris, 1927), 127: "la société n'est pas une simple somme d'individus, mais le système

formé par leur association représente une réalité spécifique qui a ses caractères propres." What was at issue was only to define the specificity of this association. For can one conceive of an association without associates? As long as this theoretical gap is not filled, relapses will occur. Even more recent systems theories that introduced the concept of self-reference sometimes proceed on the assumption that social systems consist of people. To cite a philosopher, a physicist, a biologist, and a sociologist, see Pablo Navarro, *El holograma social: Una ontología de la socialidad humana* (Madrid, 1994); Mario Bunge, "A Systems Concept of Society: Beyond Individualism and Holism," *Theory and Decision* 10 (1979): 13–30; Humberto R. Maturana, "Man and Society," in *Autopoiesis, Communication, and Society: The Theory of Autopoietic System in the Social Sciences*, ed. Frank Benseler, Peter M. Hejl, and Wolfram K. Köck (Frankfurt, 1980), 11–13; Peter M. Hejl, *Sozialwissenschaft als Theorie selbstreferentieller Systeme* (Frankfurt, 1982). Such confusion renders it impossible, however, to define with any precision the operation performing autopoiesis in the case of organic, neurophysiological, psychic and social systems. To be sure, it is typically conceded that the entire human being is not part of the social system, but only so to the extent that he interacts with others or actualizes consensual (parallelized) experiences. See, e.g., Peter M. Hejl, "Zum Begriff des Individuums—Bemerkungen zum ungeklärten Verhältnis von Psychologie und Soziologie," in *Systeme erkennen Systeme: Individuelle, soziale und methodische Bedingungen systemischer Diagnostik*, ed. Günter Schiepek (Munich, 1987), 115–154 (128). But far from improving things, this makes them worse: for it now becomes quite impossible to say what operation this "to the extent that" distinction performs; it is clearly neither cell chemistry nor brain, nor consciousness, nor societal communication—at best a differentiating observer. One typical solution is to ignore system-constitutive operations altogether and to tackle theory construction only at the level of "variables," whose selection, however, then escapes theoretical control. See, e.g., B. Abbott Segraves, "Ecological Generalization and Structural Transformation of Sociocultural Systems," *American Anthropologist* 76 (1974): 530–552.

15. Based on the current state of knowledge, we must presumably say that what is experienced and referred to as reason, will, sentiment, etc., is an interpretation after the fact of the outcome of neurophysiological operations, most likely serving to prepare them for conscious further processing, but by no means the decisive cause of human behavior. See, e.g., Brian Massumi, "The Autonomy of Affect," *Cultural Critique* 31 (1995): 83–109.

16. See J. H. Plumb et al., *Man Versus Society in 18th-Century Britain: Six Points of View*, ed. James L. Clifford (Cambridge, 1968).

17. Georg Simmel, "Über sociale Differenzierung" (1890), in id., *Gesamtausgabe*, vol. 2 (Frankfurt, 1989), 109–295 (126).

18. On the current discussion, see Lea Campos Boralevi et al., *Contrattualismo*

e scienze sociali: Storia ed attualità di un paradigma politico, ed. Antonio Carbonaro and Carlo Catarsi (Milan, 1992).

19. See John Rawls, *A Theory of Justice* (1971), German trans. under the title *Eine Theorie der Gerechtigkeit* (Frankfurt, 1975), 27ff.

20. See Emile Durkheim, *Le suicide: Etude de sociologie* (1897; Paris, 1987).

21. This view owes much to the "social behaviorism" of George Herbert Mead, which is, however, repeatedly built into the usual consensus theory and consequently misunderstood in its essential point. However, Mead is primarily concerned with the generation of permanent objects as stabilizers of behavior in flux from event to event and only secondarily with whether such objects can also function as symbols for concordant views—but as symbols precisely because consensus can never be controlled under the conditions of the simultaneous eventness of experience and action. It is in the first place a theory of time and only in the second place a social theory based on necessary fictions. The question is how sociality is possible at all under the condition of simultaneity (= uncontrollability). And the answer is: through the constitution of objects as eigenvalues of behavior flowing in time. See esp. George Herbert Mead, "A Behavioristic Account of the Significant Symbol" (1922) and, with reference to Whitehead, "The *Genesis* of Self and Social Control" (1925), trans. under the titles "Eine behavioristische Erklärung des signifikanten Symbols" and "Die Genesis der Identität und die soziale Kontrolle," in Mead, *Gesammelte Aufsätze*, vol. 1 (Frankfurt, 1980), 290–298, 299–328. On criticism of social contract theory on the basis of a concept of "quasi-objets," see Michel Serres, *Genèse* (Paris, 1982), 146ff. However, Serres is concerned only with the special case that certain symbolic objects are specially constituted for the purpose of social coordination. My reflections go far beyond this.

22. For the best-known example, see Martin Heidegger, *Sein und Zeit* (1927; 6th ed., Tübingen, 1949), § 10 (45ff.).

23. Günter Dux, *Geschlecht und Gesellschaft: Warum wir lieben: Die romantische Liebe nach dem Verlust der Welt* (Frankfurt, 1994) is particularly trenchant (and thus rather atypical).

24. The objections are quite widespread and are made particularly by authors who take individuals/persons as their point of departure. See, e.g., Tim Ingold, *Evolution and Social Life* (Cambridge, 1986), 119ff. But they typically take the form of objections to the systems-theoretical concept of society—as if systems theory were obliged to set the boundaries of systems in space and time. We therefore have a double problem: (a) to explain why sociologists disregard evident reservations about the territorialistic concept, and (b) to formulate systems theory as the basis of society in such a way that in determining the boundaries of society, it does not have to rely on space and time.

25. Immanuel Wallerstein, a strong critic of the concept of a state society, points out that in the twentieth century, the language area encompassing the Federal Republic of Germany, the German Democratic Republic, and Austria had

sometimes been a single society and sometimes several societies. See Wallerstein, "Societal Development, or Development of the World-System," *International Sociology* 1(1986): 3–17, repr. in *Globalization, Knowledge and Society*, ed. Martin Albrow and Elisabeth King (London, 1990), 157–171. On the other hand, precisely Wallerstein stands by a regional understanding of society, apart from which he speaks only of a world-system.

26. See only Wilbert E. Moore, "Global Sociology: The World as a Singular System," *American Journal of Sociology* 71 (1966): 475–482; Roland Robertson, *Globalization: Social Theory and Global Culture* (London, 1992).

27. Anthony Giddens, *The Consequences of Modernity* (Stanford, CA, 1990), 12ff. (16); see also 63ff. in extenso on "globalization."

28. See (with application to the development of cybernetic systems theory) the concept of skeuomorphs borrowed from archaeological anthropology in N. Katherine Hayles, "Boundary Disputes: Homeostasis, Reflexivity, and the Foundations of Cybernetics," *Configurations* 2, no. 3 (Fall 1994): 441–467. "A Skeuomorph is a design feature, no longer functional in itself, that refers back to an avatar that was functional at an earlier time" (446).

29. This is advised by Italo Calvino in his *Lezioni americane: Sei proposte per il prossimo millennio* (Milan, 1988), 6–7. See also Niklas Luhmann, "Sthenographie," *Delfin* 10 (1988): 4–12; also in Niklas Luhmann et al., *Beobachter: Konvergenz der Erkenntnistheorien?* (Munich, 1990), 119–137.

30. Kenneth Burke, *Permanence and Change* (New York, 1935).

31. Formulated in terms of language and text, see only Paul de Man, *Resistance to Theory* (Minneapolis, 1986).

32. It can, of course, be denied that expectations of a theory of society can be satisfied in the manner. See Thomas Schwinn, "Funktion und Gesellschaft: Konstante Probleme trotz Paradigmawechsel in der Systemtheorie Niklas Luhmanns," *Zeitschrift für Soziologie* 24 (1995): 196–214. But then we would have to state more exactly *and justify* what is expected of a theory of society.

33. For more detail, see Niklas Luhmann, "Was ist der Fall, was steckt dahinter? Die zwei Soziologien und die Gesellschaftstheorie," *Zeitschrift für Soziologie* 22 (1993): 245–260.

34. An instructive outline of the limits to these methodological conceptions is provided by Karl E. Weick, "Organizational Communication: Toward a Research Agenda," in *Communication and Organizations: An Interpretive Approach*, ed. Linda L. Putnam and Michael E. Pacanowski (Beverly Hills, CA, 1983), 13–29.

35. For its part, a skeptical description of this concept is a tradition. See, e.g., Herbert Blumer, "Sociological Analysis and the 'Variable,'" *American Sociological Review* 21 (1956): 683–690. On the other hand, renouncing this restriction leads to a sort of overdetermination of research findings that makes it difficult if not impossible to achieve generalizable results. The dispute between schools has been going on for decades.

36. For an overview of recent interest in these questions, see Michael Smithson, *Ignorance and Uncertainty: Emerging Paradigms* (New York, 1989). Linguists tend to have more understanding than sociologists of the fact that when language is used, the selection area, and thus what is not said, is always actualized as well. See, e.g., M. A. K. Halliday, *Language as Social Semiotic: The Social Interpretation of Language and Meaning* (London, 1978), e.g., 52 and elsewhere.

37. This might be one of the reasons why sociology finds it difficult to switch from action to communication.

38. See p. 14 above. For a similar correction of typical procedure in research on "artificial intelligence," see *Revue internationale de systémique* 8, no. 1 (1994).

39. Such an assumption is rapidly refuted as final theoretical figure, although in specific regards everyone can naturally ascertain that he does not know something. But this is a question of memory—be it that we search for something we have forgotten, be it that we believe we can remember that we never knew anything specific.

40. See esp. Henri Poincaré, *La science et l'hypothèse* (Paris, 1929).

41. "The theorist could succeed in furnishing the necessary linkages with observation language by drawing selectively from the storehouse of 'what everybody knows,'" Kenneth J. Gergen writes, after scathing criticism of the procedures and results of the usual empirical social psychology (Gergen, *Toward a Transformation in Social Knowledge* [New York, 1982], 103–104). The methodological problem lies, of course, in the word "selectively."

42. In so-called pragmatism, the argument often runs differently, in an effort to balance out theory relativism (renunciation of paradigms, pluralism, and so on) by maintaining a knowledge-securing understanding of method. See, e.g., Nicholas Rescher, *Methodological Pragmatism: A Systems-Theoretic Approach to the Theory of Knowledge* (Oxford, 1977).

43. See Niklas Luhmann, "Sinn als Grundbegriff der Soziologie," in Jürgen Habermas and Niklas Luhmann, *Theorie der Gesellschaft oder Sozialtechnologie—Was leistet die Systemforschung?* (Frankfurt, 1971), 25–100; id., *Systeme*, 92–147; "Complexity and Meaning," in id., *Essays on Self-Reference* (New York, 1990), 80–85.

44. See also Gilles Deleuze, *Logique du sens* (Paris, 1969), e.g., 87ff.: "Le sens est toujours un *effet*"; "Le sens n'est jamais principe ou origine, il est produit." For Deleuze, this is closely related to the thesis that meaning can be gained only by resolving a paradox.

45. See Spencer-Brown, *Laws*, esp. 56ff.

46. Cyberneticians would speak of the reintroduction of output as input in the same system.

47. For reasons that lie in systems theory, I go beyond Spencer-Brown with this distinction.

48. It is a moot point whether this also applies to living systems that, while

operating free of meaning, are capable of discrimination. See, e.g., Madeleine Bastide, Agnès Lagache, and Catherine Lemaire-Misonne, "Le paradigme des signifiants: Schème d'information applicable en immunologie et en homeopathie," *Revue internationale de systémique* 9 (1995): 237–249, esp. the formulation: "La structure vivante est capable de recevoir l'objet sémantique non pas comme objet matériel affectant le soi, mais comme information sur cet objet, appelant dès lors le traitement et la régulation active par l'ensemble du système" (241). Only thus can the concept of information justifiably be used with reference to living systems.

49. In Husserl's transcendental phenomenology, the methodological correlate consists only in the distinction between the phenomenological reduction, which only dissolves the claim to being in consciousness, and the eidetic reduction, which captures what appears in variations to be identical. See Edmund Husserl, *Ideen zu einer reinen Phänomenologie und phänomenologischen Philosophie*, vol. 1, in *Husserliana*, vol. 3 (The Hague, 1950), esp. 136ff.

50. The "linguistic turn" in philosophy is hence to be understood as a correlate of a societal development that denies plausibility to substance ontology and its transcendental refuge. This also implies a transition from "What . . . ?" questions to "How . . . ?" questions, the problematization of the translatability of languages, and, in general, the need recognized since de Saussure to replace identities by differences.

51. This need not be automatically understood in the sense of "omnis determinatio est negatio." Negation is always a specific operation that presupposes the identity of what is to be negated, which we could also affirm. We have not yet come to the already specific distinction between positive and negative meaning processing, and drawing a distinction itself points to the co-constitutive relevance of what is not indicated.

52. The exception that tradition offers is the concept of God. On its acceptance outside theology, see, e.g., Sir Thomas Browne, *Religio Medici* (1643; London, 1965), 40, 79. For this very reason, "God" must be an extraordinary concept.

53. This formulation with reference to politics is to be found in Bernard Willms, "Politik als Erste Philosophie oder: Was heißt radikales politisches Philosophieren?" in *Der Begriff der Politik: Bedingungen und Gründe politischen Handelns*, ed. Volker Gerhard (Stuttgart, 1990), 252–267 (260, 265–266).

54. See also Deleuze, *Logique du sens*, 83ff.; *non-sens* reflects on what Deleuze calls "donation du sens" (87).

55. On this concept, see Yves Barel, *Le paradoxe et le système: Essai sur le fantastique social* (1979; 2nd ed., Grenoble 1989), 71–72, 185–186, 302–303.

56. This includes this statement itself. We can also speak only in a certain manner about "infinite" or "indeterminable," namely, in the context of certain (and not other) distinctions such as infinite/finite or indeterminate/determinate.

57. See Louis H. Kauffman, "Self-Reference and Recursive Forms," *Journal of Social and Biological Structures* 10 (1987): 53–72 (58–59).

58. See Winfried Menninghaus, *Lob des Unsinns: Über Kant, Tieck und Blaubart* (Frankfurt, 1995).

59. See Alois Hahn, "Sinn und Sinnlosigkeit," in *Sinn, Kommunikation und soziale Differenzierung: Beiträge zu Luhmanns Theorie sozialer Systeme*, ed. Hans Haferkamp and Michael Schmid (Frankfurt, 1987), 155–164.

60. This provides an answer to the old question of whether there is a criterion for meaning that enables the meaningful to be distinguished from the meaningless, and, if so, whether this criterion is itself meaningful or meaningless.

61. The term "eigenbehavior" is used here in the sense of Heinz von Foerster, *Observing Systems* (Seaside, CA, 1981), 273ff.

62. See in more detail Niklas Luhmann, "Gleichzeitigkeit und Synchronisation," in id., *Aufklärung*, 5: 95–130.

63. This possibility exists regardless of time measurements; but time measurements can be introduced in addition to determine distances from the present, making it easier to judge the no longer actual or not yet actual relevance of temporally distant events.

64. I note in anticipation that this temporal form of conveying redundancy and variety has become extremely important in modern times because the natural hedging of redundancies by means of necessities and impossibilities has had to be increasingly abandoned, while the uncoordinated irritability of societal communication, i.e., variety, has grown.

65. See Spencer-Brown, *Laws*, 5.

66. In both the old European and the later subjectivized meanings of *securus*. See Emil Winkler, *Sécurité* (Berlin, 1939).

67. See also Niklas Luhmann, "The Paradoxy of Observing Systems," *Cultural Critique* 31 (1985): 37–55.

68. This could give occasion to consider the specialization of science in (unusual) comparisons, be they quantitative or functional. It is a matter of marking differences in the domain of what is still comparable.

69. All other beings are "something but by distinction, " according to Browne, *Religio Medici*, 40.

70. Spencer-Brown, *Laws*, 1.

71. As Ranulph Glanville and Francisco Varela show in "Your Inside Is Out and Your Outside Is In" (Beatles [Lennon–McCartney, "Everybody's Got Something to Hide Except Me and My Monkey"] 1968), in *Applied Systems and Cybernetics*, ed. George E. Lasker, vol. 2 (New York, 1981), 638–641, the same is true for all similar paradoxes of the absoluteness of the universal (which excludes nothing) and the elementary (which includes nothing) and of the beginning and end of the world. This brings us close to arguments that prompted [the fifteenth-century Neoplatonist] Nicholas of Cusa [Nicolaus Cusanus] to engage in theological reflection.

72. It should be noted that such presupposition of presuppositions in the same

form is, of course, paradoxical only if it remains in the form and if this form is understood as a closed description of the world, because it otherwise amounts to infinite regression.

73. See chap. 2, § 1.

74. Spencer-Brown, *Laws,* helps clarify this.

75. Spencer-Brown accordingly formulates (only!) two axioms: (1) "The value of a call made again is the value of the call"; and (2) "The value of a crossing made again is not the value of the crossing" (ibid., 1–2).

76. Trading opposing concepts like this is proposed by Christopher Alexander, *Notes on the Synthesis of Form* (Cambridge, MA, 1964).

77. We return to this in the discussion of the distinction between medium and form in chap. 2, § 1.

78. Fritz B. Simon, *Unterschiede, die Unterschiede machen: Klinische Epistemologie: Grundlage einer systemischen Psychiatrie und Psychosomatik* (Berlin, 1988), esp. 47ff., is both explicit and comprehensive.

79. It follows that the distinction between system and environment cannot be ranked in importance, cannot be "hierarchized"—or if it can, then in what Hofstadter calls a "tangled hierarchy" [Douglas R. Hofstadter, *Gödel, Escher, Bach: An Eternal Golden Braid* (Hassocks, Sussex, UK, 1979)], See Olivier Godard, "L'environnement, du champs de recherche au concept: Une hiérarchie enchevêtrée dans la formation du sens," *Revue internationale de systémique* 9 (1995): 405–428.

80. See Heinz von Foerster, "On Self-Organizing Systems and Their Environments," in *Self-Organizing Systems: Proceedings of an Interdisciplinary Conference*, ed. Marshall C. Yovits and Scott Cameron; (Oxford, 1960), 31–50, German translation in Heinz von Foerster, *Sicht und Einsicht: Versuche zu einer operativen Erkenntnistheorie* (Braunschweig, 1985), 115–130; Henri Altan, *Entre le cristal et la fumée* (Paris, 1979).

81. Henri Altan goes so far as to say that organizational changes in the system can therefore only be explained externally. See id., "L'émergence du nouveau et du sens," in *L'auto-organisation: De la physique au politique*, ed. Paul Dumouchel and Jean-Pierre Dupuy (Paris, 1983), 115–130. See also Henri Altan, "Disorder, Complexity and Meaning," in *Disorder and Order: Proceedings of the Stanford International Symposium*, ed. Paisley Livingston (Saratoga, CA, 1984), 109–128.

82. For a summary, see Humberto Maturana, *Erkennen: Die Organisation und Verkörperung von Wirklichkeit* (Braunschweig, 1982). For an overview of the recent discussion, see John Mingers, *Self-Producing Systems: Implications and Applications of Autopoiesis* (New York, 1995).

83. In German, we can speak of *Ausdifferenzierung*. There is no equivalent in English. This perhaps explains why insufficient attention has hitherto been paid to this aspect of autopoiesis. After all, Maturana draws a clear distinction between autopoiesis and autopoietic organization (structure formation).

84. Today, the perfect example is the brain. For a brief introduction, see

Jürgen R. Schwarz, "Die neuronalen Grundlagen der Wahrnehmung," in *Systeme erkennen Systeme*, ed. Schiepek, 75–93.

85. This is now generally accepted, but the specificity of Gödel's argumentation is often overlooked. See also the systems theoretical arguments of W. Ross Ashby, "Principles of the Self-Organizing System," in *Principles of Self-Organization*, ed. Heinz von Foerster and George W. Zopf (New York, 1962), 255–278; repr. in *Modern Systems Research for the Behavioral Scientist: A Sourcebook*, ed. Walter Buckley (Chicago, 1968), 108–118.

86. Michel Serres, *Le parasite* (Paris, 1980), trans. under the title *Der Parasit* (Frankfurt, 1981), 365.

87. This *operational* understanding of social systems differs radically from the approach that defines social systems in terms of a multiplicity of interacting elements and the maintenance of their network even where elements are eliminated. See Milan Zeleny, "Ecosocieties: Societal Aspects of Biological Self-Production," *Soziale Systeme* 1 (1995): 179–202. The consequence is that organisms, even cells, can be taken to be social systems. I'd rather avoid this conceptual overreach.

88. For detailed conceptual clarification, see Luhmann, *Systeme*, 191ff. We shall be coming back to this issue whenever greater depth of focus is needed in our analysis.

89. For application in literary studies, see Henk de Berg, *Kontext und Kontingenz: Kommunikationstheoretische Überlegungen zur Literaturhistoriographie* (Opladen, 1995); id., "A Systems Theoretical Perspective on Communication," *Poetics Today* 16 (1995): 709–736.

90. See Gotthard Günther, "Cognition and Volition: A Contribution to a Cybernetic Theory of Subjectivity," in id., *Beiträge zur Grundlegung einer operationsfähigen Dialektik*, vol. 2 (Hamburg, 1979), 203–240, with the important insight that no operationally closed system can renounce taking an active role in relation to its environment (212).

91. On the influence of these and other metaphors on the concept of communication, see Klaus Krippendorff, "Der verschwundene Bote: Metaphern und Modelle der Kommunikation," in *Die Wirklichkeit der Medien: Eine Einführung in die Kommunikationswissenschaft*, ed. Klaus Merten, Siegfried J. Schmidt, and Siegfried Weischenberg (Opladen, 1994), 79–113.

92. See Michael Hutter, "Communication in Economic Evolution: The Case of Money," in *Evolutionary Concepts in Contemporary Economics*, ed. Richard W. England (Ann Arbor, MI, 1994), 111–136 (115): "The self-referential nature of the process implies its logical closure. Understanding appears always complete, because it contains its own foundation. Understanding operates blindly, and it has to. The sense of completeness is an eminently helpful property; without it, we would probably die of fear and insecurity."

93. With regard to theory comparison note that we can manage without the classical distinction between process and structure, which had to distinguish be-

tween two levels and therefore had no possibility of indicating the (production of the) unity of the system—unless it be purely linguistically through the conjunction "and" between process and structure.

94. What consequences this has can also be illustrated with the mathematical concept of recursive functions, which underlies the modern mathematics of the unexpectable and the compensation of incalculability by the systemic production of eigenvalues. See Heinz von Foerster, "Für Niklas Luhmann: Wie rekursiv ist Kommunikation?" *Teoria Sociologica* 1, no. 2 (1993): 61–85, with the result: communication is recursivity.

95. There continue to be good reasons for retaining these concepts when system *models* are to be described. But they take us no further than model building. In their operational reality and fluidity—especially in the wealth of their *ignored* possibilities—systems are much more complex than can be shown by a model. I must therefore reject Pierpaolo Donati's proposal in *Teoria relazionale della società* (Milan, 1991) that systems theory be replaced by a theory of relations, as well as Karl-Heinz Ladeur's suggestion in *Postmoderne Rechtstheorie: Selbstreferenz—Selbstorganisation Prozeduralisierung* (Berlin, 1992) for supplementing it (see, e.g., 165).

96. Spencer-Brown, *Laws*, 10, 12.

97. See chap. 2, 190ff, in this volume.

98. See Jacques Derrida, *Marges de la philosophie* (Paris, 1972), esp. 1ff., 365ff. For a comparative analysis, see also Niklas Luhmann, "Deconstruction as Second-Order Observing," *New Literary History* 24 (1993): 763–782.

99. "C'est que cette unité de la forme signifiante ne se constitue que par son itérabilité, par son possibilité d'être répétée en l'absence non seulement de son 'référent', ce qui va de soi, mais en l'absence d'un signifié déterminé ou de l'intention de signification actuelle, comme de toute intention de communication présente" (Derrida, *Marges de la philosophie*, 378).

100. The question of how exactly this is to be understood must remain open. At any rate, the nervous system can observe only the organism from which and in which it lives. It discriminates states of the organism without any access to its environment. Consciousness appears to have developed to resolve the resulting conflicts in information processing. It sees an external space, a time that goes beyond the present moment, it imagines what is absent in order to settle contradictions that would otherwise arise (e.g., those resulting from binocular vision or the consistency checks of memory). But this solution can work, even for animals, only if the consciousness does not live somewhere bounded in space.

101. Similarly, for the "self," Gregory Bateson, *Mind and Nature: A Necessary Unity* (New York, 1979), trans. under the title *Geist und Natur: Eine notwendige Einheit* (Frankfurt, 1982), 163ff.

102. I am speaking here about the memory of the communication system itself and not about neurophysiological or psychic processes. By using its own resource of communication, the communication system can then substitute the memory

performance of single psychic systems, finally creating its own memory with the written word.

103. In the sense of Foerster, *Observing Systems*, 304ff.

104. Aristotle *Politics* 1252a5–6.

105. E.g., as in Mary B. Hesse, *Models and Analogies in Science* (Notre Dame, IN, 1966), 157ff.

106. See preliminary work on this in Luhmann, Systeme.

107. One can, of course, argue that this is impossible anyway owing to the complexity and operational speed of consciousness systems, and that evolution has for this very reason come up with communication as a solution, which also gives consciousness systems the possibility of developing their own complexity. This, too, holds true. However, the argument presented in the text still means that communication does not allow one to recognize the state of the participants' consciousness but only to guess or fabricate it to an extent that permits communication to continue. Apart from that, the argument excludes redundancies in relations between people just as little as in relation to things: one knows her footfall and his hat, and the one knows how to annoy the other.

108. See also Alois Hahn, "Verstehen bei Dilthey und Luhmann," *Annali di Sociologia* 8 (1992): 421–430.

109. Alois Hahn points this out with the concept of agreement [*Verständnis*] that can include consensus fictions, but that can use other means, too, to enable the continuance of communication where psychic states diverge. See Hahn, "Verständigung als Strategie," in *Kultur und Gesellschaft: Soziologentag*, ed. Max Haller, Hans-Joachim Hoffmann-Nowotny, and Wolfgang Zapf (Frankfurt, 1989), 346–359.

110. Further decomposition into single words or phonetic components of words (phonemes) is naturally possible and can be important for linguistics. But we are then speaking not about communication but about language—language as the subject matter of communication. From the point of view of communication, sound units or words are only (loosely coupled) media of communication, which work in communication only if coupled with utterances of determinate meaning (forms). For detailed treatment, see chap. 2 § 1.

111. See Foerster, "Für Niklas Luhmann," 61–88.

112. For more detail, see Luhmann, "Gleichzeitigkeit und Synchronisation."

113. Esp. George Herbert Mead, *Mind, Self, and Society From the Standpoint of a Social Behaviorist* (Chicago, 1934).

114. See Maturana, *Erkennen*, esp. 258ff. See also 155, where language is described as "recursive structural coupling of the nervous system with its *own* structure" (emphasis added).

115. This is also seen and accepted by Peter M. Hejl, *Sozialwissenschaft als Theorie selbstreferentieller Systeme* (Frankfurt, 1982).

116. See Philip Lieberman, *Uniquely Human: The Evolution of Speech, Thought, and Selfless Behavior* (Cambridge, MA, 1991), esp. 36ff.

117. For more detail, see Luhmann, *Systeme*, 191ff.; and see also chap. 2, § 1, in this volume on language.

118. The reason is that the concept of action, which is generally understood as presupposing actors, blurs the boundaries between systems and environments. But this does not rule out reintroducing the concept of action as a construct of an observing system, where the system can localize actions as points of imputation in the system and in the environment.

119. Pierre Livet, "La fascination de l'auto-organisation," in *L'auto-organisation: De la physique au politique*, ed. Paul Dumouchel and Jean-Pierre Dupuy (Paris, 1983), 165–171, endorses such *clôture épistémologique*, but notes that it does not ensure the consistency of a uniquely correct self-description.

120. A similar exclusion of all states of consciousness, subjective intentions, or emotions is to be found in Jean-François Lyotard's discourse theory, where the basic unit is the sentence (*phrase*), which concatenates with other sentences (*enchaînement*). See Lyotard, *Le différend* (Paris 1983). However, Lyotard explicitly ignores the systems-theoretical notion that the concatenation itself necessarily involves generation of a system/environment difference that would have to be *taken into consideration* in the system (in the discourse?).

121. See the examples discussed in Niklas Luhmann and Peter Fuchs, *Reden und Schweigen* (Frankfurt, 1989).

122. In distinguishing between logical and existential paradoxes in *Le paradoxe et le système*, esp. 19ff., Barel seems to be saying the same thing. Existential paradoxes are inevitable in systems capable of self-referential operations.

123. Wil Martens, "Die Autopoiesis sozialer Systeme," *Kölner Zeitschrift für Soziologie und Sozialpsychologie* 43 (1991): 625–646, takes the view that they could at least contribute the components of the elements of social systems (thus to communication, information, utterance, and understanding). But even this is not possible. From a causal point of view, there is naturally such an extraneous origin. But this origin cannot be communicated as well. It does not enter into the meaning of the communication but remains in the environment as the social system emerges. This is only another way of formulating the principle that the autopoietic process *necessarily* draws system boundaries.

124. We shall shortly see that this statement has to be modified by the concept of structural coupling within the scope of this situation.

125. This broadens what linguistics and literary theory call the "resistance of language to language" (Wlad Godzich, foreword to de Man, *Resistance to Theory*, xvii).

126. I say "typically" because it should not be excluded that, where sufficiently complex, the system obtains information about itself, which is to say, surprises itself with itself. The distinction between self-reference and other-reference thus refers in the first place only to the individual operation and not simply to the system. Whereas the utterance cannot be otherwise understood as internal to the

system, the information component can be either external to the operation or external to the system.

127. On the function of this reentry and the coming into being of an "imaginary" space that alone can then represent unity, see Spencer-Brown, *Laws*, 56–57, 69ff. See also Louis H. Kauffman, "Self-Reference and Recursive Forms," *Journal of Social and Biological Structures* 10 (1987): 53–72 (56–57); Jacques Miermont, "Les conditions formelles de l'état autonome," *Revue internationale de systémique* 3 (1989): 295–314.

128. From this point of view, it is not by chance that the theory of operationally closed systems arose at the same time as the matching, very general "constructivist" concept of cognition for which the old objections to supposedly realityless idealism no longer apply.

129. The emphasis is on *structural* entities as opposed to merely *operational* entities (events). This means that objects can remain identical in progression from communication to communication; however, not because the natural conditions of the external world guarantee their persistence, but because they are generated through the other-reference of the system (as "topics" of communication) as *structural* entities *of the system*.

130. Maturana, *Erkennen*, 143ff., 150ff., 243–244, 251ff.; id. and Francisco J. Varela, *Der Baum der Erkenntnis: Die biologischen Wurzeln des menschlichen Erkennens* (Munich, 1987), esp. 85ff., 252ff.; Mingers, *Self-Producing Systems*, 34ff. The difficulty of distinguishing between own operations and causalities taking effect through structural couplings has been repeatedly pointed out. See, e.g., Stein Bråten, "Simulation and Self-Organization of Mind," *Contemporary Philosophy* 2 (1982), 189–218 (204). We try to solve this problem by defining the concept of communication as precisely as possible.

131. See, e.g., Humberto R. Maturana, "Reflexionen: Lernen oder ontogenetische Drift," *Delfin* 2 (1983): 60–72 (64).

132. See Gregory Bateson, *Steps to an Ecology of Mind: Collected Essays in Anthropology, Psychiatry, Evolution, and Epistemology* (Chicago, 1972), trans. under the title *Ökologie des Geistes: Anthropologische, psychologische, biologische und epistemologische Perspektiven* (Frankfurt, 1981), 376–377; Anthony Wilden, *System and Structure: Essays in Communication and Exchange* (1972; 2nd ed., London 1980), 155ff. and passim.

133. At this point, critics might have an Aha! experience, which I want to preclude. The statement does not limit the basic constructivist thesis and is not a reversion to an ontological concept of the world. I am only explaining the implication of a theoretical mode of observation that makes use of the autopoiesis concept. The point of departure remains a differentiation-theoretical one: that the system/environment distinction must be introduced into a world that would remain unobservable without any distinction being drawn. And by "reality," in this connection, I always mean a result of consistency checks.

134. That this does not exclude the steering of perception through communication should be noted in passing. For this requires effort on the part of consciousness, whose own autopoiesis is continually irritated by (perceptual) participation in communication.

135. See Jurgen Ruesch and Gregory Bateson, *Communication: The Social Matrix of Psychiatry* (1951; 2nd ed., New York,1968), 23–24, 208ff.

136. For an early critical treatment, see Klaus Merten, *Kommunikation: Eine Begriffs- und Prozeßanalyse* (Opladen, 1977), 43ff. Many of the presuppositions of the transmission concept are now questioned by cognitive psychology, e.g., the assumptions that communication expresses existing thoughts in words, that words function in the transmission process as vehicles of a certain semantic content, that understanding is the inverse process of converting words into thoughts, and, moreover that "semantics" denotes a process of representation both in the psychic system and in communication. On these points, see Benny Shanon, "Metaphors for Language and Communication," *Revue internationale de systémique* 3 (1989): 43–59. The consequence is that we have to understand semantics in terms of pragmatics (in terms of the autopoiesis of communication), and not, as is generally the case, the other way round.

137. For more detail, see Niklas Luhmann, "Die Form 'Person,'" *Soziale Welt* 42 (1991): 166–175.

138. Spencer-Brown, *Laws*, 10.

139. For more detail, see Niklas Luhmann, "Individuum, Individualität, Individualismus," in id., *Gesellschaftsstruktur*, 3: 149–258.

140. See W. Ross Ashby, *An Introduction to Cybernetics* (London, 1956), 206ff.; id., "Requisite Variety and Its Implications for the Control of Complex Systems," *Cybernetica* 1 (1958): 83–99.

141. For detailed treatment, see Luhmann, *Systeme*, 286ff.

142. Since in the concepts of autopoiesis and structural coupling, I draw on Maturana's ideas, a remark on demarcation is needed at this point. Maturana and I share the rejection of a purely denotative, as well as a purely structuralistic, concept of language, and, like Maturana, I give primacy to the concept of operation. In contrast to Maturana, however, my argument here treats structural coupling through language, not as a relationship between living beings, but as a relationship between consciousness and communication. The nervous systems of various living beings can be structurally coupled even without language. I thus dispense with the construction of a "super-observer" of language, which is needed in Maturana if the relationship of language to reality is to be described (Maturana, *Erkennen*, 264ff.), avoiding the question of the structural couplings of this observer. Instead, I take the autopoietic system of communication as my starting point, which depends on structural couplings with consciousness systems, which can in turn be coupled with one another through language and through perceptions of other types. This is naturally not to deny that every consciousness depends on structural

couplings with its own nervous system. I dispense with the super-observer based on the much simpler assumption that in communication systems, language is one of the things about which communication is possible.

143. C. Wright Mills proposed that there be a separate discipline, which he called "sociotics." See Mills, "The Language and Ideas of Ancient China," in id., *Power, Politics and People* (New York, 1963), 469–520 ("sociotics," 492–493); id., "Language, Logic, and Culture," *American Sociological Review* 4 (1939): 670–680. However, this never went beyond suggestions and numerous detailed studies. The systems-theoretical approach has the advantage of rendering the vague concept "culture" superfluous, and of making the distance between psychic and social systems extreme. However, this raises the question of what concepts tolerate this.

144. Wilhelm von Humboldt, "Ueber die Verschiedenheit des menschlichen Sprachbaues und ihren Einfluß auf die geistige Entwicklung des Menschengeschlechts," in id., *Werke*, vol. 3 (Darmstadt, 1963), 368–756 (425ff., quotation, 438).

145. See Frederic C. Bartlett, *Remembering: A Study in Experimental and Social Psychology* (Cambridge, 1932), inspiration for far-reaching research.

146. See, e.g., Roger C. Schank and Robert P. Abelson, *Scripts, Plans, Goals and Understanding: An Inquiry into Human Knowledge Structures* (Hillsdale, NJ, 1977); Robert P. Abelson, "Psychological Status of the Script Concept," *American Psychologist* 36 (1981): 715–729.

147. See Arthur C. Graesser et al., "Memory for Typical and Atypical Actions in Scripted Activities," *Journal of Experimental Psychology, Learning, Memory and Cognition* 6 (1980): 503–515.

148. See Joseph W. Alba and Lynn Hasher, "Is Memory Schematic?" *Psychological Bulletin* 93 (1983): 203–231.

149. See esp. Talcott Parsons, Robert F. Bales, and Edward A. Shils, *Working Papers in the Theory of Action* (Glencoe, IL, 1953).

150. Chapter 2 will deal with this in detail.

151. On the relationship between presentation and concept, see likewise "Of the Schematism of the Pure Conceptions of the Understanding," bk. 2, chap. 1, in Kant's *Critique of Pure Reason* (*Kritik der reinen Vernunft*, "Von dem Schematismus der reinen Verstandesbegriffe," B176ff.). Kant speaks of homogeneity [*Gleichartigkeit*] because his problem lies in subjective consciousness.

152. See esp. Brian Massumi, "The Autonomy of Affect," *Cultural Critique* 31 (1995): 83–109.

153. This refers to the section on "Sense-Certainty" in Hegel's *Phenomenology of Spirit* ("Die sinnliche Gewißheit," in Hegel, *Phänomenologie des Geistes*, ed. Johannes Hoffmeister, 4th ed. [Leipzig, 1937], 79ff.). According to Hegel, consciousness thus contradicts itself when it says to itself, "This is a tree," because in the next moment, it will say (and knows that it will say), "This is a house." On this tension between what is meant and the way it is meant, see also de Man, *Resistance to Theory*, 61–62, 86–87, on the basis of Walter Benjamin's essay on translation.

154. However there are economists, too, who think differently. See, e.g. Ronald H. Coase, *The Firm, the Market, and the Law* (Chicago, 1988), 4.

155. This followed the new appreciation of sensory perception through modern aesthetics that began with Alexander Gottlieb Baumgarten (*Aesthetica*, vol. 1 [Frankfurt a/O, 1750; repr. Hildesheim, 1970]) and accompanied the differentiation of an autonomous art system. For more detail, see Niklas Luhmann, *Die Kunst der Gesellschaft* (Frankfurt, 1995), 13ff.

156. See Steve Woolgar, "Reconstructing Man and Machine: A Note on Sociological Critiques of Cognitivism," in *The Social Construction of Technological Systems: New Directions in the Sociology and History of Technology*, ed. Wiebe E. Bijker, Thomas P. Hughes, and Trevor J. Pinch (Cambridge, MA, 1987), 311–328.

157. Ibid., 327n5.

158. See in chap. 1, § 3 above.

159. See A. Moreno, J. Fernandez, and A. Etxeberria, "Computational Darwinism as a Basis for Cognition," *Revue internationale de systémique* 6 (1992): 205–221.

160. See W. Ross Ashby, *Design for a Brain: The Origin of Adaptive Behaviour* (2nd ed., London, 1954); id., *Introduction to Cybernetics*; id., "Requisite Variety and Its Implications"; id., "Systems and Their Informational Measures," in *Trends in General Systems Theory*, ed. George J. Klir (New York, 1972), 78–97.

161. This naturally presupposes a still undefined concept of cognition. Maturana avoids the problem by adopting too general a concept of cognition. However, it is useful to keep the question of specifically cognitive mechanisms evolving within systems open.

162. For the moment, I leave aside societal-historical constraints on the understanding of knowledge in favor of a more general framework concept. There are societies that treat the "knowledge of names" as knowledge. I include both opinions (*doxa, certitude morale*) and certain, indisputable knowledge insofar as this enables and facilitates the handling of information.

163. This argument can be repeated for consciousness systems. They, too, cannot monitor or even register their neurophysiological condition. Neuronal processes are strictly tied to their locus; but the consciousness has to omit all information about this locus, has to delocalize cognition if it is to give the impression of being able to perceive something "outside."

164. Including the conditioning of conditionings. See Ashby, "Principles of the Self-Organizing System."

165. With this shift, we can also answer the question that could not even be put in the traditional context, namely, that of the reality of cognitive and volitional operations *that face resistance*. See Jacques Miermont, "Réalité et construction des connaissances," *Revue internationale de systémique* 9 (1995): 251–268 (262–263).

166. In the early twentieth century, the scientific community was shocked by this idea in Poincaré's *La science et l'hypothèse* (e.g., 133).

167. For evidence from the United States, see Timothy W. Luke, "On Envi-

ronmentality: Geo-Power and Eco-Knowledge in the Discourses of Contemporary Environmentalism," *Cultural Critique* 31 (1995): 57–81.

168. We shall be coming back to this in chap. 2.

169. For more detail, see Niklas Luhmann, *Ökologische Kommunikation: Kann die moderne Gesellschaft sich auf ökologische Gefährdungen einstellen?* (Opladen, 1986).

170. See Wolfgang Krohn and Johannes Weyer, "Die Gesellschaft als Labor: Risikotransformation und Risikokonstitution durch moderne Forschung," in *Riskante Entscheidungen und Katastrophenpotentiale: Elemente einer soziologischen Risikoforschung*, ed. Jost Halfmann and Klaus Peter Japp (Opladen, 1990), 89–122.

171. On older societal formations, see also Roy A. Rappaport, *Ecology, Meaning, and Religion* (Richmond, CA, 1979), esp. 145–173.

172. Again I would point out that this concept of organizing differs from that of Maturana; here it means the production of ordered (connective) selections. See also Karl E. Weick, *The Social Psychology of Organizing* (Reading, MA, 1969), trans. under the title *Der Prozeß des Organisierens* (Frankfurt, 1985), albeit with an insufficiently explicated criterion (11).

173. See for an overview of efforts at more precise treatment in two essays by Eric Bonabeau, Jean-Louis Dessalles, and Alain Grumbach, "Characterizing Emergent Phenomena," 1 and 2, *Revue internationale de systémique* 9 (1995): 327–346, 347–371.

174. See, e.g., Thomas J. Fararo, *The Meaning of General Theoretical Sociology: Tradition and Formalization* (Cambridge, 1989), esp. 139ff.

175. See Helmut Willke, *Systemtheorie entwickelter Gesellschaften: Dynamik und Riskanz moderner gesellschaftlicher Selbstorganisation* (Weinheim, 1989), 10.

176. There is a great deal of literature on the *broader* question of how complexity can be formally modeled and measured, for example, as the need for information an observer requires to fully describe a system. At this juncture, I shall set such reflections aside, since their usefulness for the theory of social systems is not yet sufficiently established.

177. For more detail, see Niklas Luhmann, "Haltlose Komplexität," in id., *Aufklärung*, 5: 59–76.

178. If we regard "human beings" as elements, the problem is less drastic, because one human can contact many others. But the problem becomes more acute if we take time into consideration and ask how many people someone can be in contact with at any one time.

179. On this problem, see W. Ross Ashby, *Design for a Brain* (2nd ed., London, 1960, repr., 1978), esp. 80ff. on ultrastable systems.

180. See, e.g., Lars Löfgren, "Complexity of Descriptions of Systems: A Foundational Study," *International Journal of General Systems* 3 (1977): 197–214.

181. Basically, the concept of operation sabotages the classical concept of complexity because it sublates the distinction between element and relation into one concept (operation = selective relationization as elementary unity). This is perhaps

why complexity is less talked about than in the past. Nevertheless, systems theory cannot do without the concept, because it is needed to represent the relationship between system and environment.

182. For a comprehensive treatment, see esp. Edgar Morin, *La méthode*, 4 vols. (Paris, 1977–1991). See also id., "Complexity," *International Social Science Journal* 26 (1974): 555–582.

183. E.g., by Jean-Louis Le Moigne and Magali Orillard, "L'intelligence stratégique de la complexité, 'En attente de bricolage et de bricoleur,'" *Revue internationale de systémique* 9 (1995): 101–104. However, the contributions that follow this introductory article hardly do justice to these aspirations.

184. This incidentally explains, albeit indirectly, the renewed interest in the conditions for the possibility of repeatability. See only Gilles Deleuze, *Différence et répétition* (Paris, 1968).

185. See also Henri Atlan, *Entre de cristal et la fumée: Essai sur l'organisation du vivant* (Paris, 1979).

186. See Karl E. Weick, *Social Psychology of Organizing*; id., *Sensemaking in Organizations* (Thousand Oaks, CA, 1995).

187. This is incidentally one of the many reasons why neither mechanistic (machine-theoretical) nor mathematical calculatory (now often referred to as "machine") descriptions of society suffice.

188. With some justification, Henri Atlan has therefore propose describing complexity in terms of the H function in Shannon's information theory, in other words, as the measure for the information that is still lacking for a complete description of the system. See Atlan, *Entre le cristal et la fumée*; id., "Hierarchical Self-Organization in Living Systems: Noise and Meaning," in *Autopoiesis: A Theory of Living Organization*, ed. Milan Zeleny (New York, 1981), 185–208.

189. For this way of putting things, see Barel, *Le paradoxe et le système*, 71: "un système s'actualise, les autres, de ce fait, se potentialisent." In Husserl's phenomenology, this state of affairs is formulated from the standpoint of transcendental consciousness. The intentional activity of the consciousness can identify an object only with reference to further possibilities of experience, only in "horizons" of other possibilities.

190. Spencer-Brown expresses the same double meaning in elegant fashion in distinguishing between "condensation" and "confirmation." The repetition of an expression brings nothing new but merely condenses it (—>). Read backward (—>), the same equation can be understood as the unfolding of a tautology. Spencer-Brown speaks of "confirmation" (Spencer-Brown, *Laws*, 10). What I would like to stress more strongly is the *diversity* of the repetition situations that arise from the recursively connected operations that are differentiation systems.

191. See the chapter "Scope and Reduction" in Kenneth Burke, A *Grammar of Motives* (1945; Cleveland, 1962), 59ff., and Jerome S. Bruner et al., *A Study of Thinking* (New York, 1956), esp. 12.

192. I have deliberately chosen this counterconcept to creation, for I do not wish to exclude that complexity *negates*, and in this form of negativity then potentializes, and can thus be saved for later actualization. Of course, we can say that something complex (e.g., physical movement in swimming) is quite simple; but we then give others the opportunity to deny this.

193. See, e.g., Aegidius Romanus [Giles of Rome], archbishop of Bourges, *De regimine principum* (Rome, 1607), 403, 411–412.

194. Plato *Timaeus* 92c.

195. Using concepts such as imitation or diffusion to describe this process achieves too little and encourages the idea that it is a unidirectional process. In fact, the action of conveying also changes the conveying system. Which not least shows that, within its reach, communication—being always circular—produces world society.

196. See Jan Assmann, "Der Einbruch der Geschichte: Die Wandlungen des Gottes- und Weltbegriffs im alten Ägypten," *Frankfurter Allgemeine Zeitung*, 14 November 1987, on Egypt after the Hyksos wars.

197. See Shmuel N. Eisenstadt, *The Political Systems of Empires* (New York, 1963).

198. Nicholas of Cusa [Nicolaus Cusanus], *De visione Dei*, IX, says: "extra te igitur, Dominus, nihil esse potest" (Nikolaus von Kues, *Philosophisch-Theologische Schriften*, vol. 3 [Vienna, 1967], 130).

199. Cf. Ludwig Wittgenstein, *Tractatus logico-philosophicus* 6.45: "The sense of the world as a limited whole is the mystical" (id., *Schriften*, vol. 1 [Frankfurt, 1969], 82 [trans. RB].

200. Friedrich Schlegel argues, e.g., that only what can be determined through distinctions can enter the consciousness, and that we are not obliged to renounce the concept of world in rejecting the notion of "things apart from ourselves" (id., Jena lecture on *Transzendentalphilosophie* [1800–1801], in *Kritische Friedrich-Schlegel-Ausgabe*, vol. 12 [Munich, 1964], 37).

201. This world concept cannot be captured with traditional bivalent logic. It cannot be described as simultaneously positive and negative; this would run counter to the exclusion of contradictions, nor is a third value available to denote world. In retrospect, tradition hence had no choice but to see the world as an aggregate of objects (*aggregatio corporum, universitas rerum*).

202. On this tradition and its phasing out in the eighteenth century, see Reinhart Koselleck, "Zur historisch-politischen Semantik asymmetrischer Gegenbegriffe," repr. in id., *Vergangene Zukunft: Zur Semantik geschichtlicher Zeiten* (Frankfurt, 1979), 211–259; Rudolf Stichweh, "Fremde, Barbaren und Menschen: Vorüberlegungen zu einer Soziologie der 'Menschheit,'" in *Der Mensch—das Medium der Gesellschaft?* ed. Peter Fuchs and Andreas Göbel (Frankfurt, 1994), 72–91.

203. See further Luhmann, *Gesellschaft*, vol. 2, chap. 5, § 12.

204. Robertson, *Globalization*, 60, objects that this concept treats the global

system as "an outcome of processes of basically intra-societal origin." This is correct, but it merely shows that what is at issue is the concept of society. The opposing side in the controversy must show that a concept of society is possible that provides for communication external to society. This brings us back to the problems that arise if, despite all concessions to globalization, we insist on a multiplicity of societies.

205. For a similar argument, see Rudolf Stichweh, "Zur Theorie der Weltgesellschaft," *Soziale Systeme* 1 (1995): 29–45.

206. See Franco Cassano, "Pensare la frontiera," *Rassegna Italiana di Sociologia* 36 (1995): 27–39.

207. Kant's theses regarding the infinity of space, the incompleteness of creation, and "the inevitable tendency of each completed world system to move little by little toward its downfall" (id., *Allgemeine Naturgeschichte und Theorie des Himmels* [Leipzig, 1755], 118), were an important step in this direction.

208. From the rich literature on the history of ideas, see, e.g., Pierre Duhem, *Le système du monde: Histoire des doctrines cosmologiques de Platon à Copernic* (1913–1959; new ed., 6 vols., Paris, 1979–1988). Also Rodolfo Mondolfo, *L'infinito nel pensiero dei Greci* (Florence, 1934); Charles Mugler, *Deux thèmes de la cosmologie Grecque: Devenir cyclique et pluralité des mondes* (Paris, 1953); A. P. Orbán, *Les dénominations du monde chez les premiers auteurs chrétiens* (Nijmegen, 1970); James F. Anderson, "Time and Possibility of an Eternal World," *Thomist* 15 (1952): 136–161; Anneliese Maier, "Diskussionen über das aktuell Unendliche in der ersten Hälfte des 14. Jahrhunderts," *Divus Thomas* 25 (1947): 147–166, 317–337.

209. The objections to this are well known. Such a position is denounced as "relativist," and justifiably so if one has one of the numerous consciousness systems in mind. But I am talking about a correlate of communication, not of consciousness—about the problem of unity that always arises when information is obtained from distinctions, not about doubting the reality of things.

210. See Spencer-Brown, *Laws*, 5.

211. In other words, it is logically naïve to combat the worldwide proliferation of fundamentalism with an ethic of pluralism. Fundamentalism is a contagious disease that tends particularly to infect its opponents too. See Peter M. Blau, "Il paradosso del multiculturalismo," *Rassegna Italiana di Sociologia* 36 (1995): 53–63.

212. Henri Bergson, *L'évolution créatrice* (1907; 52nd ed., Paris, 1940), esp. chap. 1, takes a similar view with regard to mechanistic and finalistic descriptions of the world.

213. In a very specific sense, Hegel therefore speaks of "world history." See esp. Joachim Ritter, *Hegel und die französische Revolution* (1957), in id., *Metaphysik und Politik: Studien zu Aristoteles und Hegel* (Frankfurt, 1969), 183–255. Reflecting on the problem of colonization, Ritter writes: "For Hegel, industrial bourgeois society is therefore destined by its own law to become world society; *the relation of freedom to humanity and the human species that is decisive for the relation of politi-*

cal revolution to world history is grounded in this potential universality of bourgeois society" (222; [trans. RB]). The thought that the individuality of the human being implies world society is already to be found in John Locke, who writes: "he and all the rest of mankind are one community, make up one society distinct from all other creatures, and were it not for the corruption and viciousness of degenerate men, there would be no need of any other, no necessity that men should separate from this great and natural community and associate into lesser combinations" (id., *Two Treatises of Civil Government* [1680–1690; London, 1953], II, § 128, 181).

214. Talcott Parsons, *The System of Modern Societies* (Englewood Cliffs, NJ, 1971).

215. What is then specific to the modern world-system is only the unrestricted possibility of accumulating capital. See Immanuel Wallerstein, *The Modern World-System,* vol. 3: *The Second Era of Great Expansion of the Capitalist World-Economy, 1730–1840* (San Diego, CA, 1989); id., "The Evolution of the Modern World-System," *Protosoziologie* 7 (1995): 4–10. In the framework of this tradition, Christopher Chase-Dunn, *Global Formation: Structures of the World-Economy* (Oxford, 1989), also defines a world system as "intersocietal and transsocietal relations" (1), but the glossary lacks an entry on society. See also Christopher Chase-Dunn and Thomas D. Hall, "The Historical Evolution of World-Systems: Iterations and Transformations," *Protosoziologie* 7 (1995): 23–34 (23).

216. See, e.g., Anthony Giddens, *The Nation-State and Violence* (Cambridge, 1985); id., *The Consequences of Modernity* (Stanford, CA, 1990), 12ff.

217. A formulation and research topic of Robertson, *Globalization.* See also Roland Robertson and Frank Lechner, "Modernization, Globalization and the Problem of Culture in World-Systems Theory," *Theory, Culture and Society* 11 (1985): 105–118. On "globalization" without underlying societal theory, see *Global Culture: Nationalism, Globalization and Modernity,* ed. Mike Featherstone (London, 1990). See also Giddens, *Consequences of Modernity,* esp. 63ff., on "globalization" understood as the abstraction and disjoining of space/time contexts. Wherever "globalization" is talked about, what appears to be meant is a process that assumes that no world society yet exists. See explicitly Margaret S. Archer's foreword to *Globalization, Knowledge and Society,* ed. Martin Albrow and Elisabeth King (London, 1990), 1.

218. Kurt Tudyka, "Weltgesellschaft—Unbegriff und Phantom," *Politische Viertelsjahresschrift* 30 (1989): 503–508, for example, specifically defends the concept of the "international system" against the newly fashionable concept of world society. However, his arguments are unconvincing. The concept of world society admittedly needs clarification, since an adequate theory of society is lacking. But the concept of an international system is even more unclear, since we neither know what a nation is nor are given any explanation of how an "inter" can be a system. It is far more useful to speak of a "system of states" [*Staatensystem*] (cf. Klaus Faupel, "Ein analytischer Begriff der Entspannung: Große Poli-

tik, Machtpolitik und das Ende des Ost-West-Konflikts," *Zeitschrift für Politik* 38 [1991]: 140–165). It is then clear that only the political system of world society can be meant. And, indeed, "détente" exists, not as a state of world society, but, if at all, as a state of its political system. Also to be noted is the concept of "transnational society" as used by Gerhart Niemeyer, *Law Without Force: The Function of Politics in International Law* (Princeton, NJ, 1941), by which, however, he means only a network of private interests.

219. See, e.g., John W. Burton, *World Society* (Cambridge, 1972), albeit noting: "But the study of world society is not confined to relations among states or state authorities. There are important religious, language, scientific, commercial and other relations in addition to a variety of formal, non-governmental institutions that are world-wide" (19). But the author's orientation on a nation-focused differentiation schema and representation of the cohesion of this world society in terms of the weak concept of "relations" prevents him from pursuing this insight in sufficient depth.

220. See George M. Thomas et al., *Institutional Structure: Constituting State, Society, and the Individual* (Newbury Park, CA, 1987), esp. John W. Meyer, "The World Polity and the Authority of the Nation-State" (albeit with an unclear concept of society).

221. See Nicolas Hayoz, "Fictions socialistes et société moderne: Aspects sociologique du naufrage programmé de l'URSS" (thesis, Geneva, 1996).

222. In earlier times, too, hopes were placed from a European point of view in a world society promising equivalent standards of living and civilization. "The disturbed *balance* of his own forces makes the individual miserable, the *inequality* between citizens, *inequality* between nations makes the Earth miserable," we read in Jean Paul's *Hesperus*. "An eternal balance in Europe requires the four remaining parts of the world to be in balance, which, disregarding minor librations, one can promise our globe. In future neither a savage nor an island will be discovered. One nation must deliver the other from its juvenility. The more equal culture will conclude commercial agreements with more equal advantages" (Jean Paul, *Werke*, ed. Norbert Miller, vol. 1 [Munich, 1960], 871, 872).

223. See Francisco O. Ramirez and John Boli, "Global Patterns of Educational Institutionalization," in Thomas et al., *Institutional Structure*, 150–172; John W. Meyer et al., *School Knowledge for the Masses: World Models and National Primary Curricular Categories in the Twentieth Century* (Washington, DC, 1992). Even if we consult textbooks from developing countries on the organization and planning of school/university systems (e.g., Vicente Sarubbi Zaldivar, *Una sistema de educación superior para el Paraguay democrático* [Asunción, 1994 (?)]), we find ourselves on familiar ground.

224. From the perspective of comparative education studies, see Jürgen K. Schriewer, *Welt-System und Interrelations-Gefüge: Die Internationalisierung der Pädagogik als Problem vergleichender Erziehungswissenschaft* (Berlin, 1994).

225. See Morin, *La méthode*, vol. 1 (1977), 269–270 and passim.

226. See Rudolf Stichweh, "Science in the System of World Society," *Social Science Information* 35 (1996): 327–340. Stichweh finds that it is research disciplines and the external contacts of single investigators not exactly favored by home organizations that become operative.

227. Now a much discussed topic. See, e.g., Hans-Christoph Froehling and Andreas Martin Rauch, "Die Rolle Multinationaler Konzerne in der Weltwirtschaft," *Zeitschrift für Politik* 42 (1995): 297–315.

228. See esp. Edward Tiryakian, "The Changing Centers of Modernity," in *Comparative Social Dynamics: Essays in Honor of S. N. Eisenstadt*, ed. Erik Cohen et al. (Boulder, CO, 1985), 121–147.

229. See *The Invention of Tradition*, ed. Eric Hobsbawm and Terence Ranger (Cambridge, 1983).

230. Far-reaching discussion on the subject began in the 1960s, and Japan has been one of the favorite examples. See, e.g., Reinhard Bendix, "Tradition and Modernity Reconsidered," *Comparative Studies in Society and History* 9 (1967): 292–346; Joseph R. Gusfield, "Tradition and Modernity: Misplaced Polarities in the Study of Social Change," *American Journal of Sociology* 72 (1967): 351–362; S. N. Eisenstadt, *Tradition, Change and Modernity* (New York, 1973).

231. See further Luhmann, *Gesellschaft*, vol. 2, chap. 4, § 12.

232. See, e.g., Volkmar Gessner, *Recht und Konflikt: Eine soziologische Untersuchung privatrechtlicher Konflikte in Mexico* (Tübingen, 1976); Marcelo Da Costa Pinto Neves, *Verfassung und positives Recht in der peripheren Moderne: Eine theoretische Betrachtung und eine Darstellung des Falles Brasiliens* (Berlin, 1992); id., *A constitucionalização symbólica* (São Paulo, 1994).

233. A different view is taken by Horst Reimann, ed., *Transkulturelle Kommunikation und Weltgesellschaft: Theorie und Pragmatik globaler Interaktion* (Opladen, 1992). However, the contributions to this volume lack a concept of society and therefore any possibility of testing what could have changed through the globalization of communication.

234. See Immanuel Wallerstein, *The Modern World-System,* vol. 1: *Capitalist Agriculture and the Origins of the European World-Economy in the Sixteenth Century* (New York, 1974); id., *The Capitalist World-Economy* (Cambridge, 1979); id., *The Politics of the World-Economy* (Cambridge, 1984).

235. See Mike Featherstone, ed., *Global Culture, Nationalism, Globalization and Modernity* (London, 1991); Robertson, *Globalization*. For an overview of this discussion, see also Gianfranco Bottazzi, "Prospettive della globalizzazione: Sistema-mondo e cultura globale," *Rassegna Italiana di Sociologica* 35 (1994): 425–440.

236. See just Annibale Romei, *Discorsi* (Ferrara, 1586), 58ff.

237. Even in Kant, it has been supposed. See Hartmut Böhme and Gernot Böhme, *Das Andere der Vernunft: Zur Entwicklung von Rationalitätsstrukturen am Beispiel Kants* (Frankfurt, 1983).

238. Associated, however, with the individualization of the mode of communication and consequently with the nonbinding character and imprescribability of this solution to the paradox problem. The extravagance and willfulness of humorous utterances were long insisted on, and the English word "humor" was translated into German as *Laune* [mood, whim, caprice]. See Johann Gottfried Herder, "Viertes Kritisches Wäldchen," in id., *Sämmtliche Werke*, ed. Bernhard Suphan, vol. 4 (Berlin, 1878), 182ff.

239. Summarized in Jürgen Habermas, *Theorie des kommunikativen Handelns*, 2 vols. (Frankfurt, 1981).

240. Ibid., 1: 23; emphasis in original.

241. See, e.g., Herbert A. Simon, "From Substantive to Procedural Rationality," in *Method and Appraisal in Economics*, ed. Spiro J. Latsis (Cambridge, 1976), 129–148.

242. On the decline of classical concepts of rationality in the light of the universalization of risks, see Klaus Peter Japp, *Soziologische Risikotheorie: Funktionale Differenzierung, Politisierung und Reflexion* (Weinheim, 1996), esp. 67ff. On the consequences of the loss of certainty for the demands of rationality, see also Ilya Prigogine, "A New Rationality?" in *Laws of Nature and Human Conduct*, ed. id. and Michèle Sanglier (Brussels, 1987), 19–39. The solution of taking probabilities as one's point of departure is not very helpful, for there are no possibilities in the everyday life of society for calculating them. Although known things and processes are probably kept stable microphysically, this does not necessarily produce a critical concept of rationality.

243. See Elena Esposito, "Die Orientierung an Differenzen: Systemrationalität und kybernetische Rationalität," *Selbstorganisation* 6 (1995): 161–176.

244. See Heinz von Foerster, "Wahrnehmung," in *Philosophien der neuen Technologie*, ed. Ars Electronica (Berlin, 1989), 27–40 (30).

245. "Reentry" in Spencer-Brown's sense (*Laws*, 56ff., 69ff).

246. On such oscillation, see Stein Bråten, "The Third Position: Beyond Artificial and Autopoietic Reduction," in Felix Geyer and Johannes van der Zouwen, *Sociocybernetic Paradoxes: Observation, Control and Evolution of Self-Steering Systems* (London, 1986), 193–205; François Ost and Michel van de Kerchove, *Jalons pour une théorie critique du droit* (Brussels, 1987), esp. 30ff.; Michael Hutter, *Die Produktion von Recht: Eine selbstreferentielle Theorie der Wirtschaft, angewandt auf den Fall des Arzneimittelpatentrechts* (Tübingen, 1989), esp. 37ff.

247. More comprehensive treatment in Niklas Luhmann, "Observing Reentries," *Graduate Faculty Philosophy Journal* 16 (1993): 485–498; also in *Protosoziologie* 6 (1994): 4–13.

248. In the version proposed by Spencer-Brown, the form calculus moves between hidden reentry at the beginning and open reentry at the end, both of which, as boundary conditions, so to speak, elude calculation. To begin with, the operator is introduced as the unity of indication and distinction (hence as the dis-

tinction in which, in the sense of "perfect continence," the distinction also occurs as what is to be distinguished). And at the end, this is justified by disclosing the figure of reentry, so that we can understand the calculus as a model of a self-closing system that represents nothing but only processes itself.

249. Or with Spencer-Brown's definition of distinction as "perfect continence" (*Laws*, 1).

250. Ibid., 57.

251. See, following Saussure, Ranulph Glanville, "Distinguished and Exact Lies" (i.e., lies in the double sense of untruth and situation, N.L.), in *Cybernetics and Systems Research 2*, ed. Robert Trappl (Amsterdam, 1984), 655–662; German trans. in Glanville, *Objekte* (Berlin, 1988), 175–194 and 195.

252. Glanville, "Distinguished and Exact Lies," in *Cybernetics and Systems Research 2*, 657.

253. See § 8 above in this chapter.

254. See, e.g., *Revue internationale de systémique* 4, no. 5 (1994), and Richard B. Norgaard, "Environmental Economics: An Evolutionary Critique and a Plea for Pluralism," *Journal of Environmental Economics Management* 12, no. 4 (1985): 382–394. But the "plea for pluralism" ultimately means the necessity of political decisions, hence a shift in system reference.

255. See Georg Kneer, "Bestandserhaltung und Reflexion: Zur kritischen Reformulierung gesellschaftlicher Rationalität," in *Kritik der Theorie sozialer Systeme*, ed. Michael Welker and Werner Krawietz (Frankfurt, 1992), 86–112.

CHAPTER 2: COMMUNICATION MEDIA

1. See chap. 1, § 5, in this volume.

2. Extensive research by Donald T. Campbell draws on such a theory of evolution. See, e.g., with reference to the psychology of Egon Brunswik, Donald T. Campbell, "Pattern Matching as an Essential in Distal Knowing," in *The Psychology of Egon Brunswik*, ed. Kenneth R. Hammond (New York, 1966), 81–106; id., "Natural Selection as an Epistemological Model," in *A Handbook of Method in Cultural Anthropology*, ed. Raoul Naroll and Ronald Cohen (Garden City, NY, 1970), 51–85; id., "On the Conflicts Between Biological and Social Evolution and Between Psychological and Moral Tradition," *American Psychologist* 30 (1975): 1103–1126.

3. See Alfred A. Lindesmith and Anselm L. Strauss, *Social Psychology* (3rd ed., New York, 1968), 284ff.; Albert Bandura, "Vicarious Processes: No Trial Learning," in *Advances in Experimental Social Psychology*, ed. Leonard Berkowitz (New York, 1968), 76ff.; Justin Aronfreed, *Conduct and Conscience: The Socialization of Internalized Control over Behavior* (New York, 1968), 76ff. Older research is also to be found under the rubric "imitation."

4. See, e.g., Donald T. Campbell, "Ethnocentric and Other Altruistic Motives,"

in *Nebraska Symposium on Motivation, 1965*, ed. David Levine (Lincoln, 1965), 283–311 (298–299).

5. See also Eve-Marie Engels, *Erkenntnis als Anpassung? Eine Studie zur evolutionären Erkenntnistheorie* (Frankfurt, 1989), 83ff., with further references.

6. It is hence not only a system of concentrated dependence on political dominance in Hobbes's sense. Nor is it only a system of diffuse and optional dependencies such as that which developed with the transition from the barter economy to the money economy. These are examples of successful evolutionary advances in our context. But they do not bring us to a theory of society, or if so, then to a theory defined in terms of a primacy of politics or a primacy of economics.

7. On this still quite novel view, see Benny Shanon, "Metaphors for Language and Communication," *Revue internationale de systémique* 3 (1989): 43–59. See also Humberto R. Maturana, *Erkennen: Die Organisation und Verkörperung von Wirklichkeit: Ausgewählte Arbeiten zur biologischen Epistemologie* (Braunschweig, 1982), 57–58; or Klaus Kornwachs and Walter von Lucadou, "Komplexe Systeme," in *Offenheit—Zeitlichkeit—Komplexität: Zur Theorie offener Systeme*, ed. Klaus Kornwachs (Frankfurt, 1984), 110–165 (120): "Information appears as a process whose effectiveness is conditionally determined by thermodynamic boundary conditions and already existing information. The distinction between sender and receiver, as strictly formulated in Shannon's information theory, is thus nullified."

8. For further discussion of this distinction with respect to functional systems, see also Niklas Luhmann, *Die Wissenschaft der Gesellschaft* (Frankfurt, 1990), 53ff., 181ff.; id., *Die Kunst der Gesellschaft* (Frankfurt, 1995), 165ff.

9. It also replaces or at least complements Saussure's distinction between *langue* and *parole*. This distinction can be generalized to a difference between structure and event. But it is then apparent that it lacks everything that systems theory achieves, namely, an explanation of how events produce structures and how structures direct events. The distinction between medium and form is situated in this intermediate sphere. It presupposes both elementary events capable of coupling (*paroles*) and the necessity of a structured language for carrying out this coupling and varying it from moment to moment.

10. The term "communication media" is used here in keeping with established usage. Where greater precision is important and only the one side of the distinction is to be indicated in opposition to (and not in unity with) the other, I shall, as above in this chapter, speak of "medial substratum."

11. This brings us close to the distinction drawn in the natural sciences between equilibrium and states of nonequilibrium, particularly as used by Ilya Prigogine and equated with the distinction between entropy and negentropy or between disorder and order. These formulations give the impression that we are dealing with different, incompatible states. However, if we consider chaos research, developments in the natural sciences have already taken us beyond this. The problem shifts to the theory of time, and, in particular to the question of how we are

to understand "simultaneity" in relation to "time." At any rate, the medium/form distinction presupposes that states of loose and tight coupling exist simultaneously and have to be distinguished substantially. It is not a theory of the genesis of order as a development from medium to form.

12. The distinction used in the text was first developed with reference to perceptual media. See Fritz Heider, "Ding und Medium," *Symposion* 1 (1926): 109–157.

13. See chap. 1, § 3 and § 6, in this volume.

14. Gracián's version of this reads: "Dos cosas hacen perfecto un estilo, lo material de las palabras y lo forma de las pensamientos, que de ambas eminencias se adequa su perfección" (Baltasar Gracián, *Agudeza y arte de ingenio*, discourse LX [1649; Madrid, 1969], 2: 228).

15. See on this Mancur Olson, *The Logic of Collective Action* (Cambridge, MA, 1965).

16. In Habermas, this leads to forms of communication that do not comply being *nevertheless admitted*, but—the theory sees no other way out—*having to be devalued*, for example, as mere "strategic" action. For the full exposition, see Jürgen Habermas, *Theorie des kommunikativen Handelns* (Frankfurt, 1981), and much secondary literature.

17. Older optics had voted for exactly the opposite, understanding light particles as input, as sensations penetrating from without. Today, in contrast, we deny that stimuli can be perceived. On this turnabout in theory, see James J. Gibson, *The Ecological Approach to Visual Perception* (Boston, 1979), 54–55.

18. I naturally do not deny that there can be one-word sentences, exclamations, etc. It suffices to shout "Careful!" and answer "Why?"

19. This is almost a citation of Hegel, who speaks of the "dark inwardness of thought" in *Vorlesungen über die Ästhetik*, vol. 1 (Frankfurt, 1970), 18,—without, however, coming the same conclusions.

20. See Gregory Bateson, *Steps to an Ecology of Mind: Collected Essays in Anthropology, Psychiatry, Evolution, and Epistemology* (Chicago, 1972), trans. under the title *Ökologie des Geistes: Anthropologische, psychologische, biologische und epistemologische Untersuchungen* (Frankfurt, 1981), 524–25.

21. For more detail, see Niklas Luhmann, *Die Realität der Massenmedien* (2nd ed., Opladen, 1996).

22. See Floyd H. Allport, *Institutional Behavior: Essays Toward a Re-interpretation of Contemporary Social Organization* (Chapel Hill, NC, 1933).

23. See Odd Ramsöy, *Social Groups as System and Subsystem* (New York, 1963).

24. What I am calling "recursivity" here, Mead calls "conversation in gestures" or (clearer) "of gestures"; see George H. Mead, *Mind, Self & Society from the Standpoint of a Social Behaviorist* (1934; Chicago, 1952), 14, 63.

25. On the concept of "anticipatory reactions," which presupposes no expectancy, see Robert Rosen, *Anticipatory Systems: Philosophical, Mathematical and Methodological Formulations* (Oxford, 1985). Gerd Sommerhoff had earlier spo-

ken of "directive correlation"; see id., *Analytical Biology* (London, 1950), 54ff., and *Logic of the Living Brain* (London, 1974), 73ff. Such anticipatory adaptation to a not yet visible future (trees lose their leaves before it snows) naturally functions only on the basis of regularities in environmental processes. It is not suitable for merely temporary adaptation to temporary situations.

26. With reference to the status of research, see Bernard Thierry, "Emergence of Social Organizations in Non-Human Primates," *Revue internationale de systémique* 8 (1994): 65–77.

27. See Jurgen Ruesch and Gregory Bateson, *Communication: The Social Matrix of Psychiatry* (1951; 2nd ed., New York,1968), 208ff.

28. What is more, in describing recursive interactions between organisms as "language," Maturana presupposes an observer who can establish that behavior amenable to coordination is selected. See , e.g., Humberto R. Maturana, "The Biological Foundations of Self-Consciousness and the Physical Domain of Existence," in Niklas Luhmann et al., *Beobachter: Konvergenz der Erkenntnistheorien?* (Munich, 1990), 47–117 (92ff.). In this version, the concept of language is close to the social-psychology/sociological concept of double contingency.

29. From a historical point of view, this would mean that linguistic research can address not only language structures but would also have to expand its theoretical basis, e.g., to take account of functional analysis or a general semiology subsuming language as a special case.

30. See further Luhmann, *Gesellschaft*, vol. 2, chap. 3, 230–31, 565ff.

31. German linguistic aesthetics makes this difficult to abide by, so that the corresponding literature repeatedly confuses *Bezeichendem* (signifier) with *Zeichen* (sign). This fosters the error of French semiologists (e.g., Roland Barthes, Julia Kristeva) in restricting themselves to a mere rhetoric of referenceless signs. The above considerations should make it clear that semiotics requires a more complex deep structure, which we can obtain with the aid of the two-sided form concept. See also Niklas Luhmann, "Zeichen als Form," in *Probleme der Form*, ed. Dirk Baecker (Frankfurt, 1993), 45–69.

32. Following Saussure, it is usual to speak of the arbitrary determination of signs (*l'arbitraire du signe*). This can, however, be misunderstood. See the critical comments by Roman Jakobson, "Zeichen und System der Sprache" (1962), repr. in id., *Semiotik: Ausgewählte Texte, 1919–1982* (Frankfurt, 1988), 427–436. Arbitrariness exists only in the relationship between signifier and signified. This is a condition for the insulation of the sign use. The sign itself (as form of this distinction) is, however, dependent on tradition and on a high degree of redundancy in connectivity. If it had to be recreated from moment to moment, it would be neither learnable nor usable. Arbitrariness and tradition do not exclude one another; on the contrary, they are interdependent—like medium and form.

33. Thus also Kenneth E. Boulding, *Ecodynamics: A New Theory of Societal Evolution* (Beverly Hills, CA, 1978), 128–129.

34. In his semiotics, Charles S. Peirce uses the more formal, difficult to interpret concept of "interpretant."

35. This also means that the clarification of meaning and interpretation have no claim to another "quality" or "level of meaning" of the system; they have to be processed like everything that is communicated, namely, as a sequence of communicative operations. This is naturally not to deny that psychic systems can at times behave uncommunicatively and reflectively.

36. This is not to say that I agree with Chomsky's thesis that such structures must be *innate*, because the speed of language acquisition cannot otherwise be explained. See Noam Chomsky, *Aspects of the Theory of Syntax* (Cambridge, MA, 1965), trans. as *Aspekte der Syntax-Theorie* (Frankfurt, 1969), esp. 68ff. What Chomsky seeks to explain in terms of innateness, I explain in terms of structural coupling and the consequent intensification of (origin-specific) irritations and irritation processing.

37. On the underspecification of language as a condition for the possibility of conversation, see Gordon Pask, "The Meaning of Cybernetics in the Behavioural Sciences (The Cybernetics of Behaviour and Cognition; Extending the Meaning of 'Goal')," in *Progress in Cybernetics*, ed. John Rose (London, 1970), 1: 15–44 (31).

38. This is shown by the difficulty the arts face in obtaining scope for creating "new" works of art and for making them comprehensible in their originality. That only original works of art count as art and that, if we are to appreciate them, we have to recognize how they differ from preceding art and from perceivable nature make extremely high demands on trained observation. This includes inhibiting forgetting because only knowledge of preceding art makes it possible to recognize the novel value of a work. This possibility is built into linguistic communication from the outset.

39. See Klaus Krippendorff, "Some Principles of Information Storage and Retrieval in Society," *General Systems* 20 (1975): 15–35.

40. In what sense there can be a "collective memory" going beyond this is a question that has attracted attention—and skepticism—for some time. See Rosalind Thomas, *Oral Tradition and Written Record in Classical Athens* (Cambridge, 1989), 4ff. One question that plays a role is whether memory is available for optional access (as in the case of the written word) or only in the form of fixed sequences of individual reproductions (as in the case of narrators and singers).

41. See the discussion in Plato *Cratylus* 292–297.

42. Following David Hilbert, see Heinz von Foerster, "Objects: Token for (Eigen-) Behaviors," in id., *Observing Systems* (Seaside, CA, 1981), 274–285. However, language is not the issue in this case but the calculation of the identity of objects by reusing the results of previous calculations. To the best of my knowledge, the obvious implications for language have yet to be explored.

43. However, in transferring the concept to the theory of empirical systems, it must be noted that recursivity can then no longer be understood as strictly exclusive. We must then argue in terms of the operational closure of the system.

44. Instead of semiotic reality, we could speak of imaginary, imagining, construing, constituting, etc., reality.

45. The outline of such a program is to be found in Max Adler, but without a sufficiently elaborated theory of society. See Max Adler, *Das Soziologische in Kants Erkenntnistheorie: Ein Beitrag zur Auseinandersetzung zwischen Naturalismus und Kritizismus* (Vienna, 1924); id., *Kant und der Marxismus: Gesammelte Aufsätze zur Erkenntniskritik und Theorie des Sozialen* (Berlin, 1925); id., *Das Rätsel der Gesellschaft: Zur erkenntnis-kritischen Grundlegung der Sozialwissenschaften* (Vienna, 1925). And Wittgenstein's *Tractatus* must be mentioned if we are concerned with genealogy.

46. See Daya Krishna's little-noted essay "'The Self-Fulfilling Prophecy' and the Nature of Society," *American Sociological Review* 36 (1971): 1104–1107.

47. That these structures themselves evolve (an example is the merging of the Greek aorist into one of the forms of the Latin perfect with retention of the acoustically conspicuous *s*) cannot be dealt with in this context.

48. Chomsky, as we know, developed the theory of such deep structures with respect to the innate competence for language acquisition in an attempt to explain the speed with which such acquisition proceeds. The brief description in the text proceeds on the reverse assumption: that the need to learn rapidly from generation to generation must have been a constraint on the evolution of language, and that only those structures survive that make this possible—whatever neurophysiological conditions prevail. In other words, only languages whose self-organization manifests enough redundancy to permit rapid communication and rapid language acquisition can exist.

49. Sociologists tend to adopt the linguistic concept of code, which probably goes back to Vico's work on historical symbol structures and in present-day usage owes much to Roman Jakobson and Morris Halle, *Fundamentals of Language* (The Hague, 1956). See, e.g., Bernhard Giesen, *Die Entdinglichung des Sozialen: Eine evolutionstheoretische Perspektive auf die Postmoderne* (Frankfurt, 1991), and id., "Code und Situation: Das selektionstheoretische Programm einer Analyse sozialen Wandels—illustriert an der Genese des deutschen Nationalbewußtseins," in *Sozialer Wandel: Modellbildung und theoretische Ansätze*, ed. Hans-Peter Müller and Michael Schmid (Frankfurt, 1995), 228–226. In referring to the general context for the use of signs and symbols, I speak in what follows of semantics, reserving the concept of code for strictly binary structures. It should accordingly be clear that I am not using the linguistic but the cybernetic concept of code. See, e.g., *Wörterbuch der Kybernetik*, ed. Georg Klaus and Heinz Liebscher, 4th ed. (Berlin, 1976), s.v. *Kode*.

50. This is not to deny that in psychic systems, even in animals, there are pre-linguistic irritations when expectations are disappointed, when consistency checks fail.

51. In the sense of Spencer-Brown's calculus of forms in *Laws*.

52. As an exception—and the status of an exception is decisive in this respect!—

the concept of God has been discussed. As in the theory of the proofs of the existence of God, His existence is seen as a necessary predicate of the idea.

53. See Philip G. Herbst, *Alternatives to Hierarchies* (Leiden, 1976), 88, who assumes a fundamental implication relationship between the irreducible distinctions being/nonbeing, internal/external, and determinate/indeterminate.

54. On "if conditionality" as a condition of self-organization, see W. Ross Ashby, "Principles of the Self-Organizing System," in *Principles of Self-Organization*, ed. Heinz von Foerster and George W. Zopf (New York, 1962), 255–278.

55. See George Spencer-Brown, "Self-Reference, Distinctions and Time," *Teoria Sociologica* 1, no. 2 (1993): 47–53.

56. See further Luhmann, *Gesellschaft*, vol. 2, chap. 5, § 12.

57. Roy A. Rappaport, *Ecology, Meaning, and Religion* (Richmond, CA, 1979), 229, puts it as follows: "The problem of falsehood is not merely that of falsehood itself, nor even of its direct effects, as devastating as they may be, but of the corrosive distrust bred by falsehood's mere possibility."

58. See, e.g., Campbell, "Ethnocentric and Other Altruistic Motives," 298–299.

59. From Ottilia's diary in Johann Wolfgang von Goethe, *Die Wahlverwandtschaften* (*Elective Affinities*), in *Goethes Werke*, ed. Ludwig Geiger (6th ed., Berlin, 1893), 5: 500.

60. Everyday experience teaches us that this discipline is not always complied with. At the same time, however, the irritation that then arises shows that the requirements of orderly communication have been violated, and that there is little sense in continuing to talk in this fashion.

61. See G. A. Miller, "Language and Psychology," in *New Directions in the Study of Language*, ed. Eric H. Lenneberg (Cambridge, MA, 1964), 89–107 (102ff.).

62. On this condition of processing indeterminacy (without outward penetration), see Bernard Harrison, *An Introduction to the Philosophy of Language* (New York, 1979), 113ff.

63. On "markedness" in this sense, see John Lyons, *Semantics,* vol. 1 (Cambridge, 1977), 305ff.

64. See further p. 205 in this volume.

65. It must be admitted that there can be an expressive interest in incomprehensible modes of expression, e.g., in religiously inspired communication; or, for instance, that skeptical rationalists have a mania for claiming that they cannot understand what one is saying, which for them amounts to the charge of metaphysics. But then one wants it at least to be understood that one does not want to be understood or cannot understand and deems this to be for good reason.

66. I once again cite Jürgen Habermas—with all the emphasis on the yes/no position of the addressee. See, e.g., id., *Nachmetaphysisches Denken: Philosophische Aufsätze* (Frankfurt, 1988), 146: "Without the *possibility* of taking a yes/no position, the communication process remains incomplete" [trans. RB].

67. I therefore find myself on Lyotard's side versus Habermas and [Karl-Otto] Apel in the current controversy, albeit for a different reason.

68. See esp. Ashby, "Principles of the Self-Organizing System."

69. On secrecy as security behavior in a very broad sense, see Klaus E. Müller, *Das magische Universum der Identität: Elementarformen sozialen Verhaltens. Ein ethnologischer Grundriß* (Frankfurt, 1987), 310ff.; id., "Die Apokryphen der Öffentlichkeit geschlossener Gesellschaften," *Sociologia Internationalis* 29 (1991): 189–205.

70. Similarly, statues were brought into temples in Mesopotamia to remind the gods not to forget the names of the dead. See Gerdien Jonker, *The Topography of Remembrance: The Dead, Tradition and Collective Memory in Mesopotamia* (Leiden, 1995), esp. 71ff.

71. On the transfer of this condition into the coding immanent/transcendent of a functionally differentiated system of religion, see Niklas Luhmann, "Die Ausdifferenzierung der Religion," in id., *Gesellschaftsstruktur*, 3: 259–357.

72. See, e.g., John S. Mbiti, *Concepts of God in Africa* (London, 1970), 8: "He may be in the thunder, but he is not the thunder."

73. See Fredrik Barth, *Ritual and Knowledge Among the Baktaman of New Guinea* (Oslo, 1975). Size of the tribe: 183 persons, all of whom know one another. Period under study 1967–1968. First fleeting contact with passing Europeans, 1927. First local patrol, 1964. Since then repeated three times. Rumors about "pacification" and for some years now more and somewhat more secure contact with neighboring tribes—that is all. From a methodological point of view, it was attempted to avoid all manipulation through questions and to observe the ways of communicating as such. This makes the findings exceptionally valuable for us.

74. Many much more developed societies have also stressed that difficult, important knowledge has to be kept from women. "He [the good husband] keeps her [his wife] in wholesome ignorance of unnecessary secrets" for "the knowledge of weighty Counsels" is "too heavy for the weaker sex to bear," we read in Thomas Fuller, *The Holy State and the Profane State* (Cambridge, 1642), 9.

75. Barth, *Ritual and Knowledge*, 264–265.

76. "Le sacré est par excellence ce qui ne saurait être circonscrit par des mots. D'où le rapport constamment évoqué entre le sacré et le secret," Marie-Madeleine Davy says of the Middle Ages in *Essai sur la symbolique romane* (Paris, 1955), 39. This is to read the constitutive relations in reverse, starting with the result.

77. Although symbol was usually defined as sign (*signum*) in the Middle Ages, what was always meant was that this sign *itself effected* access to what was otherwise out of reach. Today, signs are, conversely, often referred to as "symbols," but this only goes to show that people have forgotten (or irrationalized) what "symbol" originally meant.

78. See, e.g., Anthony F. C. Wallace, *Religion: An Anthropological View* (New York, 1966), 233ff.; Mary Douglas, *Natural Symbols: Explorations in Cosmology*

(London, 1970), esp. 50ff.; Roy A. Rappaport, *Ecology, Meaning, Religion* (Richmond, CA, 1979), esp. 173ff.

79. See Michel Serres, *Genèse* (Paris, 1982), 146ff.

80. See Jean-Pierre Vernant, *Les origines de la pensée grecque* (Paris, 1962).

81. The "hermetic" movement of the early modern age can be understood as an attempt to do this *nevertheless* and thus to eliminate the emerging structural uncertainties. However, precisely because of this anachronism, it had to present itself as "ancient wisdom" and dissolved as soon as source research delved into its origins.

82. See Jean-Pierre Vernant et al., *Divination et rationalité* (Paris, 1974); Jean Bottéro, *Mésopotamie: L'écriture, la raison et les dieux* (Paris, 1987), esp. 133ff., 157ff.

83. This, too, is good evidence of how much evolution depends on *temporary constellations*.

84. See also Omar K. Moore, "Divination—A New Perspective," *American Anthropologist* 59 (1957): 69–74; Vilhelm Aubert, "Change in Social Affairs" (1959), in id., *The Hidden Society* (Totowa, NJ, 1965).

85. "Elle voit des choses à travers d'autres choses," Jean Bottéro writes in "Symptômes, signes, écritures en Mésopotamie ancienne," in Vernant et al., *Divination et rationalité*, 70–197 (157).

86. The first half of this statement and a profound treatment of its implications are also to be found in Alois Hahn, "Zur Soziologie der Weisheit," in *Weisheit*, Archäologie der literarischen Kommunikation, 3, ed. Aleida Assmann (Munich, 1991), 47–57.

87. See, e.g., Madeleine David, *Les dieux et le destin en Babylonie* (Paris, 1949); Bottéro, *Mésopotamie*, 241ff.

88. On this point and on the differences between oriental and Christian versions, see esp. Leo Koep, *Das himmlische Buch in Antike und Christentum: Eine religionsgeschichtliche Untersuchung zur altchristlichen Bildersprache* (Bonn, 1952).

89. A knowledge of signs (names) calls for purifying (*kathairein*). See Plato *Cratylus* 396e–397a.

90. On the development of cultural "elites" not based on the units of the prevailing social structure, and that may therefore exacerbate the difference between secular and transcendental, see (following Max Weber) Talcott Parsons, *Societies: Evolutionary and Comparative Perspectives* (Englewood Cliffs, NJ, 1966), 98–99; also Shmuel N. Eisenstadt, "Social Division of Labor, Construction of Centers and Institutional Dynamics: A Reassessment of the Structural-Evolutionary Perspective," *Protosoziologie* 7 (1995): 11–22 (16–17). Weber himself summarized this differentiation problem above all in the (theoretically unproductive) concept of "charisma," which refers to the spontaneous genesis of authority determined not by origins, class, or social status. On the ensuing (largely exegetically critical) discussion, see *Max Webers Studie über das antike Judentum: Interpretation und Kritik*, ed. Wolfgang Schluchter (Frankfurt, 1981).

91. See, inevitably, Edmund Burke, *A Philosophical Enquiry into our Ideas of*

the Sublime and the Beautiful (1756; London, 1958). See also Samuel H. Monk, *The Sublime: A Study of Critical Theories in XVIIIth-Century England* (1935; 2nd ed., Ann Arbor, MI, 1960). The thrust was then against the rule-aesthetic and against the pompous style of merely glorifying societal forces of order (that were no longer such) with only an overtone of nostalgia for lost authenticity. Today, however, this is the primary motive when postmodernism attempts to correct itself by a gesture reaching for the sublime.

92. This is how Léon Vandermeersch, "De la tortue à l'achillée: Chine," in Vernant et al., *Divination et rationalité*, 29–51, explains the development of a sufficiently complex system of writing in China through the mutation of divinatory signs.

93. See Mbiti, *Concepts of God*, 16–17.

94. It should be noted that these are twentieth-century developments.

95. John 8:7.

96. This process is apparent in the myth of paradise and original sin. It remains God's secret why he wished to forbid the capacity for moral discretion. But the prohibition was clear; this remains the unacknowledgable paradox of morality, which is there only to be contravened.

97. From a statistical point of view, gods who concern themselves with the moral affairs of humans and in so doing commit themselves to good and against evil are clearly in the minority. Only 25 percent of the societal systems recorded by George P. Murdock in the *Ethnographic Atlas* (Pittsburgh, 1967) know a high god who sits in moral judgment over humans. The interest in a morally qualifying high god may have to do with economic development and with the need for trust in property and trade relations. See Ralph Underhill, "Economic and Political Antecedents of Monotheism: A Cross-Cultural Study," *American Journal of Sociology* 80 (1975): 841–861.

98. If we keep the original meaning of *res* in mind, we could also speak of "reification" in this connection. What is involved is the constitution of external references independent of how they are spoken about. Martin Heidegger reminds us that the "thing" is mysterious in itself; see specifically id., "Das Ding," in *Vorträge und Aufsätze* (Pfullingen, 1954), 163–181. The advantage of *Dinghaftigkeit* [thingness, materiality] is, however, that one does not need to respect this secret either communicatively or otherwise.

99. A different view, albeit without sufficient empirical backing, is taken by Sighard Neckel and Jürgen Wolf, "The Fascination of Amorality: Luhmann's Theory of Morality and Its Resonances Among German Intellectuals," *Theory, Culture & Society* 11, no. 2 (1994): 69–99. The error appears to have to do with the relationship between morality and societal differentiation. But even if there is no scope for expressing personal respect and disrespect *between* Indian castes or tribes in segmentary societies, this does not mean that such scope does not exist *within* the subsystems in question. The opposite is so probable that it can be taken for granted.

100. Whether the results are then formulated in abstraction from principles or in moral casuistry is another question and at any rate presupposes a corresponding morphogenesis of moral complexity.

101. This scope becomes enormous if moral expectations are also expected, for then both ego and alter can attract approval or disapproval merely by applying morality rightly or wrongly to others or to themselves.

102. The advanced forms of this list can naturally be attained only if writing is available.

103. This is manifested semantically in changes in the concept of person (persona as opposed to anima), which accepts self-referential components (consensus with oneself as opposed to remorse) and then tends to merge with the concept of individual. See esp. Hans Rheinfelder, *Das Wort "Persona": Geschichte seiner Bedeutungen mit besonderer Berücksichtigung des französischen und italienischen Mittelalters* (Halle, 1928).

104. Explicitly, for example, in the ethics of Abelard; see Peter Abelard, *Ethics* (Oxford, 1971), esp. 4. The theological justification is that one cannot harm God but can scorn him by consenting inwardly to sin.

105. On differences in the spatial form proximity/distance that differentiate the forms of reciprocity, see Marshall D. Sahlins, "On the Sociology of Primitive Exchange," in *The Relevance of Models for Social Anthropology* (London, 1965), 139–236. On the consequences for morality, see also F. G. Bailey, "The Peasant View of Bad Life," *Advancement of Science* 23 (1966): 399–409.

106. See, e.g., Werner Müller, "Raum und Zeit in Sprachen und Kalendern Nordamerikas und Alteuropas," *Anthropos* 57 (1963): 568–590; John Mbiti, "Les Africains et la notion du temps," *Africa* 8, no. 2 (1967): 33–41; Robert J. Thornton, *Space, Time and Culture Among the Iraqw of Tanzania* (New York, 1980). The same can be said of advanced civilizations, especially China and India.

107. See Rüdiger Schott, "Das Geschichtsbewußtsein schriftloser Völker," *Archiv für Begriffsgeschichte* 12 (1968): 166–205. However, it can be assumed that even before the invention of writing, an interest in better elaboration and depth of field in time relations developed with the differentiation of large politico-economic households, and this might have been a reason for introducing a technique of written records. See also, e.g., Burr C. Brundage, "The Birth of Clio: A Résumé and Interpretation of Ancient Near Eastern Historiography," in *Teachers of History: Essays in Honor of Laurence Bradford Packard*, ed. H. Stuart Hughes (Ithaca, NY, 1954), 199–230; François Châtelet, *La naissance de l'histoire: La formation de la pensée historienne en Grèce* (Paris, 1962). The same can be posited about the emergence of archaeological interests in the later Mesopotamia; see Jonker, *Topography of Remembrance*, esp. 153ff.

108. The evolutionary originality of this (ultimately neurophysiological) phenomenon and its occurrence throughout the world and in all periods are remarkable. This includes the many new occurrences of trance-based cults in the

twentieth century. Only religions of the Book appear to see this as a problem and to be able and obliged to replace cultic repetition by reports of such events, such as the stories of the prophets in the Old Testament or the Pentecostal miracle in the New Testament. Repetition becomes a matter of reading scripture.

109. This is also true of cultures that already have writing, but whose communication still takes place orally even in important matters. See Werner Glinga, "Mündlichkeit in Afrika und Schriftlichkeit in Europa: Zur Theorie eines gesellschaftlichen Organisationsmodus," *Zeitschrift für Soziologie* 18 (1989): 89–99.

110. See Thomas, *Oral Tradition and Written Record*, 197.

111. For more comprehensive treatment, see Dennis Tedlock, *The Spoken Word and the Work of Interpretation* (Philadelphia, 1983).

112. For Greece, see Marcel Detienne, *Les maîtres de vérité dans la grèce archaïque* (3rd ed., Paris, 1979), 53ff.

113. Gen. 1:3. The assumption that in so doing, God consulted a text, namely, the Torah, is a specialty of the Jewish tradition, a sort of (naturally subsequent) hypostatization of scripture. There were differences laid down in writing (a sort of original text) before the Creation.

114. With reference to the transition to monumental inscriptions of political and legal texts in Greek cities, Marcel Detienne speaks of "autoréférence. L'écrit renvoie à sa propre lettre; il évoque des lois contemporaines ou plus anciennes; il recommande d'obéir à ce qui est écrit, de se conformer à ce que dit la stèle" (*Les savoirs de l'écriture en Grèce ancienne*, ed. id. [Lille, 1988], 18); see also ibid., "L'espace de la publicité: Ses opérateurs intellectuels dans la cité," 29–81 (49ff.), on *autocitation* and *autodéfense*.

115. The paradigmatic text here is *Don Quijote*, the second part of which treats itself as a printed book known to all. Literary scholars speak in such cases of an "intertextuality" unavoidable in the use of writing, but whose refinement can be intensified.

116. On such preadaptive advances and evolutionary functional changes, see chap. 3, § 8, in this volume.

117. See Harald Haarmann, *Universalgeschichte der Schrift* (Frankfurt, 1990), 70ff. It appears that inscriptions on statues in temples in Mesopotamia were also initially seen as communication with the gods—a "notch" (*Einkerbung*), so to speak, in their memory—and only later as messages to future generations (see Jonker, *Topography of Remembrance*, 178–179). For the prehistory of engravings, see Alexander Marshack, *The Roots of Civilization: The Cognitive Beginnings of Man's First Art, Symbol and Notation* (London, 1972). For early forms of registering transactions thousands of years before the invention of writing in the real sense of the term, see also Denise Schmandt-Besserat, "An Archaic Recording System and the Origin of Writing," *Syro-Mesopotamian Studies* 1, no. 2 (1977): 1–32.

118. For an overview and further references, see Jack Goody, *The Logic of*

Writing and the Organization of Society (Cambridge, 1986), trans. under the title *Die Logik der Schrift und die Organisation von Gesellschaft* (Frankfurt, 1990), esp. 89ff.

119. On the Sumerian beginnings, see Jean Bottéro, "De l'aide-mémoire à l'écriture," in id., *Mésopotamie*, 89–112.

120. See Léon Vandermeersch, "De la tortue à l'achillée: Chine," in Jean-Pierre Vernant et al., *Divination et rationalité* (Paris, 1974), 29–51. See also Haarmann, *Universalgeschichte*, 126ff.

121. See Bottéro, "Symptômes, signes, écritures," in Vernant et al., *Divination et rationalité*, 70–197.

122. See, e.g., Margaret R. Nieke, "Literacy and Power: The Introduction and Use of Writing in Early Historic Scotland," in *State and Society: The Emergence and Development of Social Hierarchy and Political Centralization*, ed. John Gledhill, Barbara Bender, and Mogens Trolle Larsen (London, 1988), 237–252.

123. See Alfred Heubeck, *Schrift* (Göttingen, 1979); id., "Zum Erwachen der Schriftlichkeit im archaischen Griechentum," in id., *Kleine Schriften zur griechischen Sprache und Literatur* (Erlangen, 1984), 537–554; Walter Burkert, *Die orientalisierende Epoche in der griechischen Religion und Literatur* (Heidelberg, 1984); Joachim Latacz, *Homer: Der erste Dichter des Abendlandes* (2nd ed., Munich, 1989), 24ff., 70–71. On the uncertainty of sources, see also William V. Harris, *Ancient Literacy* (Cambridge, MA, 1989), 45ff. The superiority of alphabetic script over other systems of writing, which had also managed to considerably reduce the number of signs they used, was not immediately apparent in the competitive situation prevailing at the time when it was introduced (e.g., it failed to catch on in Cyprus). See Anna Morpurgo Davies, "Forms of Writing in the Ancient Mediterranean World," in *The Written World: Literacy in Transition*, ed. Gerd Baumann (Oxford, 1986), 51–77.

124. See Martin L. West, "Archaische Heldendichtung: Singen und Schreiben," in *Der Übergang von der Mündlichkeit zur Literatur bei den Griechen*, ed. Wolfgang Kullmann and Michael Reichel (Tübingen, 1990), 33–50 (38–39, 47–48). Walther Heissig, *Oralität und Schriftlichkeit mongolischer Spielmanns-Dichtung*, Vorträge der Rheinisch-Westfälischen Akademie der Wissenschaften G 317 (Opladen, 1992), also reports that written records were not called for by the singers themselves but by Mongolian nobles pursuing a rather archival (twentieth-century!) interest in collecting, safeguarding, and preserving. On the other hand, a knowledge of writing is now mentioned as a guarantee of faithfulness to the original and truth value. This applies particularly with regard to Chinese sources, thus for loans from another culture.

125. For important ideas, see Alfred B. Lord, *The Singer of Tales* (Cambridge, MA, 1960), Eric A. Havelock, *Preface to Plato* (Cambridge, MA, 1963), and Walter J. Ong, *The Presence of the World: Some Prolegomena for Cultural and Religious History* (New Haven, CT, 1967). As an example of the present-day discussion

among experts, see *Formen und Funktionen mündlicher Tradition*, ed. Walther Heissig (Opladen, 1995).

126. Such time shifts are evident, above all, and much discussed, in the *Odyssey*. However, we cannot really know to what extent they go back to the written version of the epic, or whether they were not already present in retarding interpolations in oral versions, albeit then less with a view to establishing the unity of a historical time.

127. This deformation through writing is illustrated by the discussion of time in Aristotle *Physics* 4.10, which poses the question of the being or nonbeing of time, without asking why precisely this (ontological) distinction—for its part, certainly dependent on writing—should inform the account (see also Hegel in the *Encyclopädie der philosophischen Wissenschaften* § 258). Furthermore, writing allows the adverb *nyn* (now) to be substantivized (*to de nyn* in [Arist. *Phys.* 4.10] 218a6 and elsewhere). Translations give us not the adverbial "now" but formations such as "now-point" [*Jetzpunkt*]. This in turn makes it possible to ask whether a now-point is part (*meros*) of time or not. Which again provokes controversy as in the paradox that a now-point (whether or not part of time) consists in not-yet-being and no-longer-being, so that time itself, as a unity of being and nonbeing, must appear a paradox in the ontological schema. In the tradition from Aristotle to Hegel, this paradox can then be unfolded through the concept of movement. *But* why the static observation schema of being/nonbeing and then part/whole? And above all, why if one wished to objectivize the meaning, is an adverb nominalized that is used orally as an indexical expression, and that therefore presupposes an observer of the observer involved in the situation? Both deformations are consequences of writing and both prevent, at least initially, reflection on second-order observation in favor of an ontological metaphysics.

128. This is easy to understand if we consider efforts to "textualize" what is now referred to as "oral literature." See Lauri Honko, "Problems of Oral and Semiliterary Epics," in *Formen und Funktionen*, ed. Heissig, 26–40.

129. On the "telescoping" of oral genealogical myths and reconstruction efforts with the aid of writing, see Thomas, *Oral Tradition and Written Record*, 95ff., 155ff. On Mesopotamia, see also Jonker, *Topography of Remembrance*, 213ff. It should be added that genealogies partly serve cultic purposes within families, but above all they provide evidence for the differentiation of prominent families—vis-à-vis both society and one another.

130. See Walter J. Ong, "Writing Is a Technology That Restructures Thought," in *The Written Word: Literacy in Transition*, ed. Gerd Baumann (Oxford, 1986), 23–50 (36ff.), with examples such as the distinction between the person who knows and what he knows; between text and communication; between the word and its phonic realization, between the word and the fullness of being (of the world); between past and present; logic and rhetoric, strict knowledge and ability (wisdom, *sophia*); between being and time, etc.

131. One can, of course, point out with Stanley Fish that oral communication, too, is uncertain with respect to meaning and authenticity. No second-order observer can in principle deny that a first-order observer may be uncertain and dependent on interpretation. See Stanley Fish, "With the Compliments of the Author: Reflections on Austin and Derrida," in id., *Doing What Comes Naturally: Change, Rhetoric, and the Practice of Theory in Literary and Legal Studies* (Oxford, 1989), 37–67.

132. Dean MacCannell and Juliet F. MacCannell, *The Time of the Sign: A Semiotic Interpretation of Modern Culture* (Bloomington, IN, 1982), 119.

133. That it is matter of change and not of creating a previously impossible social memory is also stressed by Jan Assmann, "Lesende und nichtlesende Gesellschaften," *Almanach (des Deutschen Hochschulverbandes)* 7 (1994): 7–12. See also Jonker, *Topography of Remembrance.*

134. This is dealt with in detail in chap. 3, § 18, in this volume.

135. See Heinz Förster, *Das Gedächtnis* (Vienna, 1948); Heinz von Foerster, "Quantum Mechanical Theory of Memory," in *Cybernetics: Circular Causal, and Feedback Mechanisms in Biological and Social Systems. Transactions of the Sixth Conference 1949*, ed. id. (New York, 1950), 112–134. This shift to the *difference* between remembering and forgetting drew Foerster's attention to the need for a macromolecular, quantum mechanical analysis of the neurophysiology of memory.

136. See Heinz von Foerster, "Was ist Gedächtnis, das es Rückschau *und* Vorschau ermöglicht," in id., *Wissen und Gewissen: Versuch einer Brücke* (Frankfurt, 1993), 299–336.

137. This is naturally different for registers, archives, etc.

138. That this abstraction had first of all to be learned is obvious, just as one had to learn to give up commodity money and thus not to confuse the value of money with the value of a given commodity (such as gold).

139. See West, "Archaische Heldendichtung," esp. 43–44.

140. In addition to the literature cited in n. 125 above, see *Oral Literature and the Formula*, ed. Benjamin A. Stolz and Richard S. Shannon (Ann Arbor, MI, 1976); Heissig, *Oralität und Schriftlichkeit.*

141. A protracted process. For various aspects, see, e.g., J. L. Myres, "Folk-Memory," *Folk-Lore* 37 (1926): 12–34; James A. Notopoulos, "Mnemosyne in Oral Literature," *Transactions of the American Philological Association* 69 (1968): 465–493; Jean-Pierre Vernant, *Mythe et pensée chez les grecs: Etude de psychologie historique* (Paris, 1965), 51ff.; P. A. H. de Boor, *Gedenken und Gedächtnis in der Welt des Alten Testaments* (Stuttgart, 1962); Brevard S. Childs, *Memory and Tradition in Israel* (London, 1962); Willy Schottroff, *"Gedenken" im alten Orient und im Alten Testament* (Neukirchen-Vluyn, 1964); Frances Yates, *The Art of Memory* (Chicago, 1966); Herwig Blum, *Die antike Mnemotechnik* (Hildesheim, 1969); Stefan Goldmann, "Statt Totenklage Gedächtnis: Zur Erfindung der Mnemotechnik durch Simonides von Keos," *Poetica* 21 (1989): 43–66; Renate Lachmann, *Gedächtnis und Literatur: Intertextualität in der russischen Moderne* (Frankfurt, 1990).

142. Jacques Gernet, *La vie quotidienne en Chine à la veille de l'invasion mongole, 1250–1276* (1959; repr., Paris, 1978), 247; in this connection, as a consequence of the use of the printing press.

143. See Jonker, *Topography of Remembrance*, esp. 109ff.

144. On the associated dissolution of the old indistinguishability of word and thing, see also David Palumbo-Liu, "Schrift und kulturelles Potential in China," in *Schrift*, ed. Hans Ulrich Gumbrecht and K. Ludwig Pfeiffer (Munich, 1993), 159–167.

145. In cultures that already have writing and no longer need such insistence to develop social structures (especially leadership roles), a counter-*topos* develops. In this regard, reserve is considered good manners, turn-taking is cultivated, *grands parleurs* [big mouths] are warned against—a familiar theme in narrative literature since Plutarch, and, incidentally, one of many indications that the understanding of societal communication still concentrates on the oral medium.

146. The concept and formulation are from Carl J. Friedrich, "Authority, Reason, and Discretion," in *Authority*, ed. id., Nomos 1 (Cambridge, MA, 1958), 28–48.

147. See David Ganz, "Temptabat et scribere: Vom Schreiben in der Karolingerzeit," in *Schriftkultur und Reichsverwaltung unter den Karolingern*, ed. Rudolf Schieffer (Opladen, 1996), 13–33.

148. That this capping of sociality in specializing on communication is a result of evolution is evidenced by the institutions surviving from the transition from ritual to written cultures—e.g., the joint reading and discussion of scripture in the synagogue.

149. See Lorna Marshall, "Sharing, Talking and Giving: Relief of Social Tensions Among !Kung Bushmen," *Africa* 31 (1961): 231–249. See also Bronislaw Malinowski, "The Problem of Meaning in Primitive Language," in *The Meaning of Meaning*, ed. C. K. Ogden and I. A. Richards (10th ed., London, 1960), 296–336 (314): "for a natural man, another's man silence is not a reassuring factor, but, on the contrary, something alarming and dangerous. The stranger who cannot speak the language is to all savage tribesmen the natural enemy." The necessity and habit of talking is the direct correlate of the permanent presence of others whom one knows and meets again.

150. On consciousness and other concepts of cognition as correlates of writing see E. A. Havelock, *The Literate Revolution in Greece and Its Cultural Consequences* (Princeton, NJ, 1982), 290–291.

151. See Yves Barel, *Le paradoxe et le système: Essai sur le fantastique social* (2nd ed., Grenoble, 1989), 71–72, 185–186, 302–303. Among the traditions that pay particular attention to this is the Talmud teaching of the revelation on Mount Sinai intended for scripture *and* for oral tradition. This teaching invited the conclusion that precisely the differences of opinion and minority opinion were to be passed down because they could prove important in the unforeseeable future. See, e.g., Jeffrey I. Roth, "The Justification for Controversy Under Jewish Law," *Califor-*

nia Law Review 76 (1988): 338–387. See also id., "Responding to Dissent in Jewish Law: Suppression Versus Self-Restraint," *Rutgers Law Review* 40 (1987): 31–99.

152. Even if only to deny that possible/impossible can *be* (Diodoros Kronos).

153. On the difficulty of getting this accepted and of gaining recognition for the reality value of the fictional, see, looking at the novel as an example, Lennard J. Davis, *Factual Fictions: The Origin of the English Novel* (New York, 1983). Cf. also Niklas Luhmann, "Literatur als fiktionale Realität" (MS, 1995).

154. See Jackie Pigeaud, "Le style d'Hippocrate ou l'écriture fondatrice de la médecine," in *Les savoirs de l'écriture en Grèce ancienne*, ed. Marcel Detienne (Lille, 1988), 305–329. A compilation of passages from the Corpus Hippocraticum is to be found in Knut Uscner, "'Schreiben' im Corpus Hippocraticum," in *Übergang von der Mündlichkeit*, ed. Kullmann and Reichel, 291–299. On the ensuing understanding of science and method in Hellenistic antiquity, see also G. E. R. Lloyd, *Magic, Reason and Experience: Studies in the Origin and Development of Greek Science* (Cambridge, 1979).

155. See Niklas Luhmann, "The Form of Writing," *Stanford Literature Review* 9 (1992): 25–42; German trans. in *Schrift*, ed. Gumbrecht and Pfeiffer, 349–366.

156. From a historical point of view, we have no complete understanding of how earlier scripts evolved into the alphabet. It can only be assumed that the interruption of written practice after the collapse of the Mycenaean culture and the obligation to choose and adapt a script to a different sort of language played a role. It is now denied that the need to write down oral poetry was the decisive factor. On the importance of literacy for both the functional and the social universal utilization of writing, see Eric A. Havelock, *Origins of Western Literacy* (Toronto, 1976); id., *Literate Revolution*; Egert Pöhlmann, "Zur Überlieferung griechischer Literatur vom 8. bis zum 4. Jahrhundert," in *Übergang von der Mündlichkeit*, ed. Kullmann and Reichel, 11–30 (backdating the general accessibility of writing to the eighth century). It should naturally not be overlooked that nonalphabetic scripts, e.g., Chinese, developed functional equivalents with a different mix of advantages and disadvantages under different linguistic (and also phonetic) preconditions.

157. See Marcel Detienne's contributions to *Savoirs de l'écriture*, ed. id., 7ff., 29ff.

158. See, on its extent, F. D. Harvey, "Literacy in Athenian Democracy," *Revue des études grecques* 76 (1966): 585–635; Havelock, *Literate Revolution*, 27ff. And see now especially the overview in Harris, *Ancient Literacy*, with a very skeptical assessment of the dissemination of reading and writing skills, also in Greek and Roman antiquity. Such speculation about the extent of competence in reading and writing in the population as a whole is, however, of limited interest, since the society in question was a stratified one and literacy was certainly very widespread among the upper classes.

159. The dating of such expansion of the communication concept requires thorough research. At any rate, it is apparent in Galileo—with printing, in the context of the scientific acquisition of knowledge, and with an eye to the unat-

tainable ability of God to know everything at once and not to have to rely on sequential cognition. In the dialogue *Sopra i due massimi sistemi del mondo*, we find at the end of the first day: "Ma sopra tutte le invenzioni stupende, qual eminenza di mente fu quella di colui che s'immaginò di trovar modo di communicare i suoi più reconditi pensieri a qualsivolgia altra persona, benchè distante per lunghissimo intervallo di luogo e di tempo? parlare con quelli che son nell'Indie, parlare a quelli che non sono ancora nati nè saranno se non di qua a mille e dieci mila anni? e con qual facilità?" (*Le opere di Galileo Galilei* [Florence, 1968], 7: 130).

160. See Wauthier de Mahieu, "A l'intersection de temps et de l'espace du mythe et de l'histoire, les généalogies: L'example Komo," *Cultures et Développement* 11 (1979): 415–457.

161. See Thomas, *Oral Tradition and Written Record*, 175ff.

162. See, with abundant material, Hans-Georg Pott, *Literarische Bildung: Zur Geschichte der Individualität* (Munich, 1995).

163. Think only here of Jean Paul's novels *Blumen- Frucht- und Dornenstücke, oder Ehestand, Tod und Hochzeit des Armenadvokaten Siebenkäs* [Flower, Fruit, and Thorn; or, The Married Life, Death and Wedding of the Advocate of the Poor, Firmian Stanislaus Siebenkäs] and *Flegeljahre* [The Teens], or of Benjamin Constant's *Adolphe*.

164. At best they dictate—e.g., the Koran. Then the improbability of the event is acclaimed as its uniqueness. And this compromise is naturally directed toward the still more improbable solution of incarnation: that after the invention of writing, God Himself had to become flesh in order to communicate; in this case, improbability is concealed by the myth of sin and redemption.

165. It was initiated by the differentiation of symbolically generalized communication media, a development that was just as important and later became even more important; see further §§ 9 to 12 of this chapter.

166. Particularly in Mesopotamian and again in old Christian thinking. See, with copious material, Leo Koep, *Das himmlische Buch in Antike und Christentum: Eine religionsgeschichtliche Untersuchung zur altchristlichen Bildersprache* (Bonn, 1952).

167. See, in general, chap. 3, §10, in this volume.

168. On this difference between divination and prophetic communication, see Cristiano Grotanelli, "Profezia e scrittura nel Vicino Oriente," *La Ricerca Folkloria: La scrittura: Funzioni e ideologie* 5 (1982): 57–62.

169. In the late eighteenth century, William Blake writes: "The Prophets Isaiah and Ezekiel dined with me, and I asked them how they dared so roundly to assert that God spoke to them; and whether they did not think at the time that they would be misunderstood, and so be the cause of imposition. Isaiah answer'd: 'I saw no God, nor heard any, in a finite organical perception; but my senses discover'd the infinite in every thing, and as I was then perswaded, & remain confirm'd, that the voice of honest indignation is the voice of God, I cared not for consequences

but wrote'" (Blake, *The Marriage of Heaven and Hell* [1790–1793], in id., *Complete Writings* [London, 1969], 148–158 [153]).

170. Now likely to be the generally accepted view. See esp. Thomas, *Oral Tradition and Written Record.*

171. See George Horowitz, *The Spirit of Jewish Law* (1953; repr., New York, 1973), who attributes to this the civilizability of the crude beginnings of a legal tradition. Also Geza Vermes, *Scripture and Tradition in Judaism—Haggadic Studies* (Leiden, 1973); id., "Scripture and Tradition in Judaism: Written and Oral Torah," *The Written Word: Literacy in Transition*, ed. Gerd Baumann (Oxford, 1986), 79–95; Susan A. Handelman, *The Slayers of Moses: The Emergence of Rabbinic Interpretation in Modern Literary Theory* (Albany, NY, 1982), esp. 37ff.; José Faur, *Golden Doves and Silver Dots: Semiotics and Textuality in Rabbinic Tradition* (Bloomington, IN, 1986), esp. 84ff. However, the distinction between written and oral in this context refers to text types rather than modes of communication. There is nothing to be said against quoting the written text verbatim and recording the oral interpretation in writing.

172. See pointers in Notopoulos, "Mnemosyne in Oral Literature."

173. See Plato *Phaedrus* 274bff. and also the more political reservations about written records in Plato's Seventh Letter [http://classics.mit.edu/Plato/seventh_letter.html (accessed 2 January 2012)]. On the ensuing, far-reaching discussion, see, e.g., Wolfgang Kullmann, "Hintergründe und Motive der platonischen Schriftkritik," in *Übergang von der Mündlichkeit*, ed. id. and Reichel, 317–334 with further information.

174. Criticism of the written word is, of course, written criticism, and only a written culture can come up with the notion of "unwritten" law. See Michael Gagarin, *Early Greek Law* (Berkeley, CA, 1986), esp. 121ff.

175. Also Walter J. Ong, *Interface of the Word: Studies in the Evolution of Consciousness and Culture* (Ithaca, NY, 1977), 82ff.

176. Marcel Detienne, *Les maîtres de vérité dans la Grèce archaïque* (3rd ed., Paris, 1979), 81ff., describes this as a "procès de laicisation."

177. Above all, Baltasar Gracián, in all his writings. Like hardly anyone before him, Gracián—and this is what makes him modern—argues that the world can be observed only by means of the difference between visible and invisible. It is the job of rhetoric to *manipulate t*his difference aesthetically, politically, and cognitively.

178. See Walter J. Ong, "Communications Media and the State of Theology," *Cross Currents* 19 (1969): 462–480.

179. With reference to the present-day situation in social theory, I have spoken in chapter 1 of "epistemological obstacles" (Bachelard's "obstacles épistémologiques"). Another example is the persisting relevance of bourgeois/*bürgerlich* ideas and theories, which, put forward between 1760 and 1820, continue today as value ideologies, with the inevitable disappointment that society is still not reasonably set up, that liberty and equality are still lacking, not to mention fraternity.

180. See chap. 3, § 10, in this volume.

181. On this epoch-making turn, see Elisabeth L. Eisenstein, *The Printing Press as an Agent of Social Change: Communications and Cultural Transformations in Early-Modern Europe*, 2 vols. (Cambridge, 1979); Michael Giesecke, *Der Buchdruck in der frühen Neuzeit: Eine historische Fallstudie über die Durchsetzung neuer Informations- und Kommunikationstechnologien* (Frankfurt, 1991); and id., *Sinnenwandel, Sprachwandel, Kulturwandel: Studien zur Vorgeschichte der Informationsgesellschaft* (Frankfurt, 1992). More skeptical authors point to the slowness with which literacy spread and to the uncertainty about the extent to which existing skills were used. See, e.g., Keith Thomas, "The Meaning of Literacy in Early Modern England," in *The Written Word: Literacy in Transition*, ed. Gerd Baumann (Oxford, 1986), 97–131.

182. *Libri e lettori nel medioevo: Guida storica e critica*, ed. Gugliemo Cavallo (Bari, 1983), provides an overview going back to the fifth century.

183. Communication research and especially historical research tends for understandable methodological and source-related reasons to take the opposing view; for texts are easier to find and analyze than what goes on in the reader. On this problem and the "priority of reading over writing," see Havelock, *Literate Revolution*, 56ff.

184. As shown by the corresponding practices of both the Church and secular rulers, commencing only a few decades after the printing press became known, this was not excluded in Europe either.

185. See Hans Rothe, *Religion und Kultur in den Regionen des russischen Reiches im 18. Jahrhundert* (Opladen, 1984), 34–35. See also Gary Marker, *Publishing, Printing and the Origins of Intellectual Life in Russia, 1700–1800* (Princeton, NJ, 1985), esp. 5–6, 39–40.

186. References in Giesecke, *Buchdruck in der frühen Neuzeit*. However, contemporaries saw the innovation as a technical one. The invention of the printing press was often admired in context with the invention of artillery. See, e.g., Estienne Pasquier, *Les recherches de la France* (new ed., Paris, 1665), 369.

187. However, page numbering, references to pages, and indices had already been introduced in the course of rationalizing manuscript book production in the late Middle Ages. See Bernhard Bischoff, *Paläographie des römischen Altertums und des abendländischen Mittelalters* (Berlin, 1979), 281–282, with further references. As in other regards, it was the printing press that brought existing inventions to full fruition; and it is nevertheless astonishing how long it took until the practice of quotation became established as a normal form of literary discussion.

188. Given the range of reading matter available, this was recommended even in antiquity as a *method*, however, rather than as a stopgap in the absence of texts; see Marcus Fabius Quintilianus [Quintilian] *Institutionis oratoriae libri XII*, 10.1.20 (ca. 95 CE; Darmstadt, 1975), 2: 438. And this was still so in the face of floods of new texts in the eighteenth century.

189. For references, especially concerning "ballads," see Davis, *Factual Fictions*, 42ff.

190. Articulating his sense of the superiority of new texts, John Dryden describes audience reaction to a performance of the unchanging story of Oedipus, for example, "so that they sate with a yawning kind of expectation, till he was to come with his eyes pull'd out, and speak a hundred or more Verses in a Tragick tone, in complaint of his misfortune" (Dryden, *Of Dramatik Poesie: An Essay* [1668; London, 1964], 53–54).

191. See Michael Giesecke, "Schriftspracherwerb und Erstlesedidaktik in der Zeit des 'gemein teutsch'—eine sprachhistorische Interpretation der Lehrbücher Valentin Ickelsamers," *Osnabrücker Beiträge zur Sprachtheorie* 11 (1979): 48–72; id., "'Natürliche' und 'künstliche' Sprachen? Grundzüge einer informations- und medientheoretischen Betrachtung des Sprachwandels," *Deutsche Sprache* 17 (1989): 317–340, repr. in Giesecke, *Sinnenwandel, Sprachwandel, Kulturwandel*, 36–72.

192. Although there had been criticism of the rough medieval Latin and efforts to achieve an elegant style even before the advent of printing, the printing press profiled national languages and engendered awareness of the diversity and variability of the vernacular. See, e.g., Francois Loryot, *Les Fleurs des Secretz Moraux, sur les passions du coeur humain* (Paris, 1614), 70ff.

193. The new playhouses certainly also exploited this possibility. See Jean-Christophe Agnew, *Worlds Apart: The Market and the Theater in Anglo-American Thought, 1550–1750* (Cambridge, 1986), 66–67.

194. See Mervyn James, *Family, Lineage, and Civil Society: A Study of Society, Politics, and Mentality in the Durham Region, 1500–1640* (Oxford, 1974). Also Peter S. Bearman, *Relations into Rhetorics: Local Elite Social Structure in Norfolk, England, 1540–1640* (New Brunswick, NJ, 1993), on the transition from politics based on family relationships to a more abstract (especially religiously oriented) rhetoric that follows this line and was certainly also made possible by the printing press (although this aspect is not dealt with). At the outset, however, even the Royal Society of London was not as certain about this issue as it was to be in the eighteenth century. At any rate, the presence of prestigious personalities (e.g., members of the royal family) were mentioned, as if this might contribute to the quality of the experiments and the knowledge derived from them. See Charles Bazerman, *Shaping Written Knowledge: The Genre and Activity of the Experimental Article in Science* (Madison, WI, 1988), 73ff., 140ff.

195. See Robert Mandrou, "La transmission de l'hérésie à l'époche moderne," in *Hérésies et sociétés dans l'Europe pré-industrielle: 11e–18e siècles: Communications et débats du Colloque de Royaumont*, ed. Jacques LeGoff (Paris, 1968), 281–287.

196. This should be compared with the soft landing of many a council member in the lap of the strengthening papal Church shortly before the invention of printing.

197. See again here Luhmann, *Gesellschaft*, vol. 2, chap. 5, § 13.

198. A pertinent example: *The School of Salernum: Regimen sanitatis Salerni: The English Version of Sir John Harington* (Salerno, 1953, 1966). The study materials

of this famous medieval school of medicine were completely geared to oral transmission and memorizing.

199. For literature on this, see Davis, *Factual Fictions*, 138ff.

200. Whereas in Greece, poets had been able to change the world, Shaftesbury imagined: "In our Days *the Audience* makes *the Poet*; and *the Bookseller the Author*" (Anthony Ashley Cooper, 3rd earl of Shaftesbury, *Characteristicks of Men, Manners, Opinions, Times* [2nd ed., 1714; Farnborough, UK, 1968], 1: 264). Since he had his own books printed, however, the affected rejection of the book market (and not so much of the printing press) is something of a conspiratorial wink at the reader at the level of private, well-considered convictions. Incidentally, Shaftesbury is also reacting to a specifically English tradition that celebrated the poet as a sort of lawmaker and speculates on the publicity effect of printing. See David Norbrook, *Poetry and Politics in the English Renaissance* (London, 1984).

201. I mention this with regard to the advantages and disadvantages of a nonphonetic script.

202. See Luhmann, *Gesellschaft*, vol. 2, chap. 5, § 13.

203. They are "transclassical" in the sense of Gotthard Günther, *Das Bewußtsein der Maschinen: Eine Metaphysik der Kybernetik* (Krefeld, 1963).

204. See Wlad Godzich, "Vom Paradox der Sprache zur Dissonanz des Bildes," in *Paradoxien, Dissonanzen, Zusammenbrüche: Situationen offener Epistemologie*, ed. Hans Ulrich Gumbrecht and K. Ludwig Pfeiffer (Frankfurt, 1991), 747–758.

205. This naturally presupposes that the human perceptual apparatus reacts more strongly to movements than to the constants of its perceptual field.

206. All that remains to human beings, we might assume, is thought, and that can easily go wrong. At any rate, the chief achievement of consciousness, the externalization and ordering of the perceptual world, becomes less important—in other-referential and self-referential contexts: for the inner plausibility of world experience and for the secure placing of the individual in this world.

207. Peter Klier, *Im Dreieck von Demokratie, Öffentlichkeit und Massenmedien* (Berlin, 1990), 106ff., speaks in this connection of re-aestheticization; Wolfgang Welsch, "Anästhetik—Focus einer erweiterten Ästhetik," in *Schöne Aussichten? Ästhetische Bildung in einer technisch-medialen Welt*, ed. Wolfgang Zacharias (Essen, 1991), 79–106, sees anestheticization as a comparative form of aestheticization.

208. An important exception—albeit seldom significant, owing to the quality of broadcasting—would be perception as a work of art and corresponding criticism of artistic means.

209. With significant delay, incidentally; in the sixteenth century, books still exhorted readers to report their experiences in print likewise.

210. I must stress this, because the computer can also be used personally for data processing for the user alone.

211. There are parallels with communication about works of art, which, at least under modern conditions, can also be scattered so far afield that the artist can no

longer foresee the observations of the viewer or indeed wish to leave things open, and the viewer can no longer believe he has understood the work if he believes he has grasped what the artist "meant." See Umberto Eco, *Opera aperta* (1962; 6th ed., Milan, 1988).

212. Mind you, *chance* contacts. This is not to deny that planned meetings and thus face-to-face interaction remain possible and need not be restricted. But what does society owe to chance?

213. See, influentially, Herbert A. Simon, "From Substantive to Procedural Rationality," in *Method and Appraisal in Economics*, ed. Spiro J. Latsis (Cambridge, 1976), 129–148.

214. In this connection, it is striking that a morality has developed uncoupled from religion and law and geared to inner acceptance, and thus fully individualized, which declares its principles or values to be "ethics," but has nothing to say on the question of the social coordination of ethical perspectives. Presumably, as evidenced by the American film industry with its strong moral standardization, one is already covertly relying on a symbiosis of television and morality.

215. On a subsystem of modern society, see Dirk Baecker, *Information und Risiko in der Marktwirtschaft* (Frankfurt, 1988).

216. See further Luhmann, *Gesellschaft*, 2: 601.

217. See Alois Hahn, "Identität und Nation in Europa," *Berliner Journal für Sozialforschung* 3 (1993): 193–203.

218. As a special study on this problem of the undemocratic nature of communication, see Austin Sarat, "Support for the Legal System: An Analysis of Knowledge, Attitudes, and Behavior," *American Politics Quarterly* 3, no. 1 (1975): 3–24.

219. There are similar ideas for successful moves in evolutionary game theory. See D. Friedman, "Evolutionary Games in Economics," *Econometrica* 59 (1991): 637–666; P. H. Young, "The Evolution of Conventions," ibid. 61 (1993): 57–84; Gisèle Umbhauer, "Evolution and Forward Induction in Game Theory," *Revue internationale de systémique* 7 (1993): 613–626.

220. [AGIL is Parsons's acronym for Adaptation + Goal Attainment + Integration + Latency, the key functions required of every society according to him.] For the field of the social system, see Talcott Parsons, *Social Systems and the Evolution of Action Theory* (New York, 1977); ed. Stefan Jensen under the title *Zur Theorie der sozialen Interaktionsmedien* (Opladen, 1980). But this does not cover the media of the general action system. A thorough discussion, with attempts at application, is to be found in *Explorations in General Theory in Social Science: Essays in Honor of Talcott Parsons*, vol. 1 (New York, 1976), pt. 4. For developments on this line of thought, see, e.g., Richard Münch, *Theorie des Handelns: Zur Rekonstruktion der Beiträge von Talcott Parsons, Emile Durkheim und Max Weber* (Frankfurt, 1982), 123ff. and passim; Bernhard Giesen, *Die Entdinglichung des Sozialen: Eine evolutionstheoretische Perspektive auf die Postmoderne* (Frankfurt, 1991), 223ff. Cf. also Jan Künzler, *Medien und Gesellschaft: Die Medienkonzepte von Talcott Parsons, Jürgen*

Habermas und Niklas Luhmann (Stuttgart, 1989). A comparable (but far less elaborated) theoretical approach is pursued under the heading "capital symbolique" by Pierre Bourdieu; see also, e.g., id., *Ce que parler veut dire: L'*économie des échanges linguistiques (Paris, 1982), 68ff. Here, too, however, unlike with Parsons, the economic concept of capital is used only metaphorically, and this is particularly true of the notion that "capital symbolique" is differentiated according to "markets."

221. I refer to what is said about structural coupling in chap. 1, § 6, above.

222. It might have to do with the modern lack of understanding for the problem underlying amplification or with one-sided treatment by philosophy—at any rate, in the renewed modern interest in topic and rhetoric, *inventio* is stressed much more strongly than *amplificatio*. See, e.g., Lothar Bornscheuer, *Topik: Zur Struktur der gesellschaftlichen Einbildungskraft* (Frankfurt, 1976). Even classical literature (e.g., Quintilian *Institutionis oratoriae* 8.4) fails to give due status to *amplificatio*. The *Historisches Wörterbuch der Philosophie* contains a comprehensive article on *inventio* but none on *amplificatio*, only on (logical) *ampliatio*. Amplifying's difficulties with truth are perhaps off-putting. However, examination of the communicative function leads to a contrary assessment.

223. After all, the elaborated tradition supplies two terms for it, namely, *opinio* and *admiratio*, just as if their separation were preprogrammed. "To amplify and to illustrate are two chiefest ornaments of eloquence, and gain of men's minds to the chiefest advantages, admiration and belief," John Hoskins writes in *Directions for Speech and Style* (1599; Princeton, NJ, 1935), 17. In keeping with the hierarchical structure of society, *admiratio* is thus a sort of passion (and hence a motivating factor), albeit a passion that, in contrast to all others, contains *no contrary emotion*, and that can therefore be activated *prior to any binary coding*, as Descartes emphasizes in *Les passions de l'ame*, art. 53 (in id., *Oeuvres et lettres* [Paris, 1952], 723–724). A communication that arouses *admiratio* thus effects undivided understanding and acceptance.

224. I do not claim that this was the only cause. Other experience certainly also contributed—for instance, the now only politically manageable religious conflict, the corresponding consolidation of the schism between churches, criticism of the Latin schools and the growing differentiation of functional systems with their own motivation.

225. See Joan Marie Lechner, *Renaissance Concepts of the Commonplaces: An Historical Investigation of the General and Universal Ideas Used in All Argumentation and Persuasion* (1962; repr. Westport, CT, 1974).

226. Thomas Wright, *The Passions of the Minde in Generall* (1630; Urbana, IL, 1971), 191.

227. See Ong, *Presence of the Word*, 79ff.

228. A similar argument is offered by Jack Goody and Ian Watt, "The Consequences of Literacy," *Comparative Studies in Society and History* 5 (1963): 304–345. See also Jack Goody, "Literacy in Traditional Society," *British Journal of Sociology*

24 (1973): 1–12; id., "Literacy, Criticism, and the Growth of Knowledge," in *Culture and Its Creators: Essays in Honor of Edward Shils*, ed. Joseph Ben-David and Terry N. Clark (Chicago, 1977), 226–243.

229. In comparison with other languages, *alētheia* is a very unusual coinage; see Jean-Pierre Levet, *Le vrai et le faux dans la pensée grecque archaïque: Etude de vocabulaire*, vol. 1 (Paris, 1976), esp. 80ff.

230. *Könnens-Bewußtsein*: Christian Meier, *Die Entstehung des Politischen bei den Griechen* (Frankfurt, 1980), 435ff. See Berkley Peabody, *The Winged Word: A Study in the Technique of Ancient Greek Oral Composition as Seen Principally Through Hesiod's Works and Days* (Albany, NY, 1975).

231. This difference in quality could also explain why Indo-Germanic languages use different roots for truth and for lie. A lie is more than an untrue statement. And only for this reason could the privative alpha be used to indicate truth [*alētheia*].

232. We can concede to Heidegger that an indirectness of "being-relation" decisive for the period following is thus attained. His verdict of guilty—Plato!—can hardly be upheld. See esp. Paul Friedländer, *Platon*, vol. 1: *Seinswahrheit und Lebenswirklichkeit* (3rd ed., Berlin, 1964), 233ff.

233. On attribution to the poet Simonides of Ceos [now Kéa], familiar with money and writing, see Marcel Detienne, *Les maîtres de vérité dans la grèce archaïque* (3rd ed., Paris, 1979), 105–106. Important passages on the further history of the distinction are to be found in Plato *Republic* 6.20–21.

234. On the etymology, see Franz Dirlmeier, *ΦΙΛΟΣ und ΦΙΛΙΑ im vorhellenistischen Griechentum* (Munich, 1931); Manfred Landfester, *Das griechische Nomen "philos" und seine Ableitungen* (Hildesheim, 1966). On the Latin *amicitia*, see also J. Hellegouarc'h, *Le vocabulaire latin des relations et des partis politiques sous la republique* (Paris, 1963), esp. 42ff., 142ff.

235. Moreover, it is now assumed to have been of comparatively little importance in the Greek city, so that the difference to Rome had been long prepared. See Denis Roussel, *Tribu et cité: Etudes sur les groupes sociaux dans les cités grecques aux époques archaïques et classiques* (Paris, 1976); Felix Bourriot, *Recherches sur la nature du genos* (Lille, 1976).

236. Laelius was then considered in Rome as symbolically representing the opposing position, which held friendship also to be possible with (political) enemies of one's (political) friends, thus differentiating friendship from politics and privatizing it. See Fritz-Arthur Steinmetz, *Die Freundschaftslehre des Panaitios* (Wiesbaden, 1967). See also Horst Hutter, *Politics as Friendship: The Origins of Classical Notions of Politics in the Theory and Practice of Friendship* (Waterloo, ON, Canada, 1978).

237. On *philia* as the consequence of the discovery of freedom and thus of given possibilities for differentiation within the city independent of the clans, see also Jean-Claude Fraisse, *Philia: La notion d'amitié dans la philosophie antique. Essai sur un problème perdu et retrouvé* (Paris, 1974).

238. See Fritz Heichelheim, "Die Ausbreitung der Münzwirtschaft und der Wirtschaftsstil im archaischen Griechenland," *Schmollers Jahrbuch* 55 (1931): 229–254; Michael Hutter, "Communication in Economic Evolution: The Case of Money," in *Evolutionary Concepts in Contemporary Economics*, ed. Richard W. England (Ann Arbor, MI, 1994), 111–136.

239. See Michael Hutter, "Die frühe Form der Münze," in *Probleme der Form*, ed. Dirk Baecker (Frankfurt, 1993), 159–180.

240. On this, see esp. Peter N. Ure, *The Origin of Tyranny* (Cambridge, 1922).

241. This change of name shows the politically determined contingency of law as opposed to the behavior-related understanding of truth. On the formal terms for laws (*thesmos, nomos*), see Martin Ostwald, *Nomos and the Beginning of Athenian Democracy* (Oxford, 1969); Jaqueline de Romilly, *La loi dans la pensée Grecque des origines à Aristote* (Paris, 1971), 9ff. See also Meier, *Entstehung des Politischen*, 305ff.

242. See Romilly, *Loi dans la pensée Grecque*, 11–12, 20–21, *citing* Euripides *Hiketides* 432: "But when the laws are written, the poor man and the rich have equal rights. Then when a wealthy citizen does wrong, a weaker one can criticize, and prevail, with justice on his side" (Euripides, *Suppliant Women*, trans. Rosanna Warren and Stephen Scully [Oxford, 1995], 37).

243. See the contribution by Christian Meier to the article on "Macht, Gewalt" in *Geschichtliche Grundbegriffe: Historisches Lexikon zur politisch-sozialen Sprache in Deutschland*, vol. 3 (Stuttgart, 1982), 817–935 (820ff.).

244. See Peter Spahn, "Die Anfänge der antiken Ökonomie," *Chiron* 14 (1984): 301–323.

245. See S. C. Humphreys, "Evolution and History: Approaches to the Study of Structural Differentiation," in *The Evolution of Social Systems*, ed. J. Friedman and M. J. Rowlands (Pittsburgh, 1978), 341–371, esp. in regard to the relationship of politics, economy, and religion.

246. On the lack of a systematic orthodoxy and on the freedom of criticism of the usual magical and religious ideas, see G. E. R. Lloyd, *Magic, Reason and Experience in the Origin and Development of Greek Science* (Cambridge, 1979), 10ff.

247. Humphreys, "Evolution and History," 353.

248. See 309f. in this volume.

249. See Ranulph Glanville, *Objekte* (Berlin, 1988). See Dirk Baecker, "Ranulph Glanville und der Thermostat: Zum Verständnis von Kybernetik und Konfusion," *Merkur* 43 (1989): 513–524.

250. See also, with suspiciously demanding concepts such as mutuality or dialogue, Stein Bråten, "Systems Research and Social Sciences," in *Applied General Systems Research: Recent Developments and Trends*, ed. George Klir (New York, 1978), 655–685; id., "Time and Dualities in Self-Reflective Dialogical Systems," in *Applied Systems and Cybernetics: Proceedings of the International Congress on Applied Systems Research and Cybernetics*, ed. George E. Lasker (New York, 1981), 3: 1339–1348.

251. In this context "behavior" means not only change of an internal state but change in the relationship between system and environment. See Humberto R. Maturana, "Reflexionen, Lernen oder ontogenetische Drift," *Delfin* 2 (1983): 60–71: "Behavior as a characteristic of all or some of its changes of state does not belong to the organism or living being. Behavior is rather a relationship between an organism or living being and an environment in which an observer excludes and observes it. In this sense, the nervous system as an integral part of an organism or living being does not generate behavior but merely takes part in the dynamics of changes in the state of the system that it integrates. For an observer, however, the nervous system participates in generating behavior to the extent that it takes part in changes in the state of the organism or the living being whose change in form or situation he observes and describes relative to an environment" (62).

252. For causal attributions, this is obvious: the attribution of effects to causes is not itself a cause [*Ursache*], a prime cause [*Urursache*] of effects.

253. It should be noted that in this connection we cannot speak of self-attribution/other-attribution because reference to the attributer himself must be avoided. The difference between internal/external can be used to refer to both the attributer himself and (by him) to other systems. The results must, in other words, be objectivizable, *although consensus on attribution imposed on substantive grounds cannot be assumed.*

254. In contrast to "action theories," I thus postulate no "objective" concept of action but naturally assume that at the level of first-order observation actions can be experienced and treated as objects, which does not contradict the so-called subjective concept of action, which says only that actions have to be freely chosen (I say internally attributed), which in my parlance would mean that we have to observe the actor (as observer of his situation) if we wish to understand how he acts. I note this only to show that, contrary to the widespread reservations of action theoreticians, nothing is lost in transition from the level of first-order observation to that of second-order observation and that everything can be reconstructed, albeit in a more complex, structurally more diverse language.

255. I reverse the usual order ego-alter as a reminder that I construct the communication process from the position of the observer, starting with understanding, *and not in action-theoretical terms.*

256. "If you do what I want I'll do what you want."

257. This has always been clear, particularly in the discussion of attribution problems in jurisprudence and political economy (in fact, in all the older research). The attribution research in social psychology that started in the 1960s initially overrated the importance of the question, but we are indebted to it for having intensively investigated the links between cognition and motivation. I shall not offer any references; research in this field is vast, has numerous specialized strands of discussion, and can hardly be covered as a whole.

258. Here lies a major difference from Talcott Parsons's media theory, which fol-

lows from the theory of structural differentiation of the general action system and therefore conclusively defines the causes and number of possible media in cross-tabulation form. But this, too, should not be understood to mean that each society actually realizes the totality of all possible media. See Stefan Jensen, "Aspekte der Medien-Theorie: Welche Funktion haben die Medien in Handlungssystemen?" *Zeitschrift für Soziologie* 13 (1984): 145–164

259. Semantic and organizational equivalents will have to be sought above all in "ecclesiology."

260. See, e.g., Niklas Luhmann, *Liebe als Passion: Zur Codierung von Intimität* (Frankfurt, 1982).

261. Once again, this does not affect the circumstance that opinions *necessarily* differ *in psychic systems.*

262. Resolutely, for the media of interchange, Talcott Parsons, "On the Concept of Value-Commitments," *Sociological Inquiry* 38 (1968): 135–160. On what follows, see also Niklas Luhmann, "Complexity, Structural Contingencies and Value Conflicts," in *Detraditionalization: Critical Reflections on Authority and Identity*, ed. Paul Heelas, Scott Lash, and Paul Morris (Oxford, 1996), 59–71.

263. There is nothing approaching adequate research on word and concept. What we find presents itself as prehistory of the economics concept of value. See esp. Rudolf Kaulla, *Die geschichtliche Entwicklung der modernen Werttheorien* (Tübingen, 1906); Lujo Brentano, *Die Entwicklung der Wertlehre* (Munich, 1908); Fritz Bamberger, *Untersuchungen zur Entstehung des Wertproblems in der Philosophie des 19. Jahrhunderts. I: Lotze* (Halle, 1924). An early history of the concept, which traces the shift from *valeur* (= force, *vigeur*, *Lebenskraft*, etc.) to *utilité,* and thus to comparative rationality is to be found in Abbé Morellet, *Prospectus d'un nouveau Dictionnaire de commerce* (1769; repr. Munich, 1980), 98ff. At any rate, a very general use of the value concept was already current in the second half of the eighteenth century. One speaks, e.g., of the value of purposes.

264. This is the term used by Douglas R. Hofstadter, *Gödel, Escher, Bach: An Eternal Golden Braid* (Hassocks, Sussex, UK, 1979), 686ff.

265. The widespread presentation of the value problem with aid of the subjective/objective distinction hides this very problem: that it is always a matter of both unquestioned assumptions and unresolved conflicts.

266. Thus, but with awareness of the problem, Georg Henrik von Wright, *The Logic of Preference* (Edinburgh, 1963), 31ff.

267. It is not correct to assert that the concepts of "values," *valeur*, etc., were only then generalized beyond their economic context to be applied to cultural, moral, aesthetic aspects (as does, e.g., *La langue française* [Paris, 1976], s.v. *valeur*). We find many examples for its application to duties and pleasures, honor, life, health, etc., even in the eighteenth century and probably earlier. Only the universalization of value reference is really new.

268. The ideology concept as used in the nineteenth century, the argumenta-

tion concept in keeping with more recent usage. See esp. Chaïm Perelman and L. Olbrechts-Tyteca, *Traité de l'argumentation: La nouvelle rhetorique* (Paris, 1958).

269. On "marking" in the linguistic semantic sense, see 137f. [with nn. 63 and 64] above.

270. The methodological counterpart to this practice of value communication lies in the difficulty of gaining a firm footing on questions concerning value attitudes (however refined the planning). One only receives answers to questions; and different answers to different questions.

271. See also, and on the failure of such an understanding in the American slavery conflict, Stephen Holmes, "Gag Rules or the Politics of Omission," in *Constitutionalism and Democracy*, ed. Jon Elster and Rune Slagstadt (Cambridge, 1988), 19–58.

272. See Baruch Fischhoff, Paul Slovic, and Sarah Lichtenstein, "Labile Values: A Challenge for Risk Assessment," in *Society, Technology, and Risk Assessment*, ed. Jobst Conrad (London, 1980), 57–66. On older studies about stability on the basis of susceptibility to disappointment, see also Ralph M. Stogdill, *Individual Behavior and Group Achievement* (New York, 1959), 72ff. Old European thinking on this subject referred to it as *akrasia* (lacking command over oneself).

273. See Blaise Pascal, *Lettres provinciales*, in id., *Oeuvres*, éd. de la Pléiade (Paris, 1950), 427–678.

274. The origins nevertheless go back to tribal societies, in the form of couple relationships transcending family structures, which were tolerated as *exceptions* and therefore *ritualized*—e.g., the famous uncle/nephew relationships or certain forms of male friendship. See Shmuel N. Eisenstadt, "Ritualized Personal Relations," *Man* 96 (1956): 90–95; Kenelm O. L. Burridge, "Friendship in Tangu," *Oceania* 27 (1957): 177–189; Julian Pitt-Rivers, "Pseudo-Kinship," in the *International Encyclopedia of the Social Sciences*, vol. 8 (New York, 1968), 408–413. The ancient Greek form of accepted and at the same time not accepted homosexuality probably expressed less a specific sentiment about sexual practices than the problem of the social acceptance of a regression of sociality to couple relationships.

275. That the intensification of sociality in the form of couple relationships is a case of regression and requires special sanctioning by society is an unusual thought for modern culture, but a well-known state of affairs for sociologists. See esp. Philip E. Slater, "On Social Regression," *American Sociological Review* 28 (1963): 339–364; Vilhelm Aubert and Oddvar Arner, "On the Social Structure of the Ship," *Acta Sociologica* 3 (1959): 200–219; Michael Rustin, "Structural and Unconscious Implications of the Dyad and Triad: An Essay in Theoretical Integration: Durkheim, Simmel, Freud," *Sociological Review* 19 (1971): 179–201. See also the preceding note.

276. Now in ignorance of Romanticism, whose concept of irony had reflected precisely this improbability with a reservation for incommunicable subjectivity. Most people (especially Americans) presumably think of the behavior models presented by the novel when they hear the word "romantic."

277. On the historical background, see Luhmann, *Liebe als Passion.*

278. On this discrepancy, which has apparently not impaired the mass consumption of such illusions, see Bruno Péquignot, *La relation amoureuse: Analyse sociologique du roman sentimental moderne* (Paris, 1991).

279. See Ulrich in Robert Musil, *Der Man ohne Eigenschaften* (Hamburg, 1952), 558–559: "Lovers have nothing new to say to one another; and they know no recognition. For the lover recognizes nothing of the person he loves except that he is transported by her in indescribable fashion into inner activity. . . . This is why there is also no truth for lovers; it would be a cul-de-sac, an end, the death of thought" [trans. RB].

280. See Alois Hahn, "Konsensfiktionen in Kleingruppen: Dargestellt am Beispiel von jungen Ehen," in *Gruppensoziologie: Perspektiven und Materialien*, ed. Friedhelm Neidhardt, *Kölner Zeitschrift für Soziologie und Sozialpsychologie*, special ed. 25 (1983): 210–232; Roland Eckert, Alois Hahn, and Marianne Wolf, *Die ersten Jahre junger Ehen* (Frankfurt, 1989).

281. We see already that regulating this problem by means of property requires another, different type of regulation: the political regulation of power. The separation of the media makes them dependent on one another.

282. This should really be self-evident; after all, we cannot eat property. Anthropological explanations fall short in this case and otherwise, and belong to the terminology that condenses *as a consequence* of the development of property. This is not necessarily a new insight; T. E. Cliffe Leslie writes, e.g., in his introduction to Emile de Lavelaye's *Primitive Property* (London, 1878): "Property has not its roots in the love of possession. All human beings like and desire certain things, and if nature has armed them with any weapons are prone to use them in order to get and to keep what they want. What requires explanation is not the want or desire of certain things on the part of individuals, but the fact that other individuals, with similar wants and desires, should leave them in undisturbed possession, allot them a share, of such things. It is the conduct of a community, not the inclination of individuals, that needs explanation" (xi; quoted from Elman R. Service, *The Hunters* [Englewood Cliffs, NJ, 1966], 21).

283. See Michael Hutter, "Signum non olet: Grundzüge einer Zeichentheorie des Geldes," in *Rätsel Geld: Annäherungen aus ökonomischer, soziologischer und historischer Sicht*, ed. Waltraut Schelkle and Manfred Nitsch (Marburg, 1995), 325–352.

284. For more detail, see Niklas Luhmann, *Die Wirtschaft der Gesellschaft* (Frankfurt, 1988).

285. Kenneth Burke, *A Grammar of Motives* (Cleveland, 1962), 355–356.

286. See the comprehensive natural law discussion stemming from antiquity on the *advantages of the nevertheless unjust* shift from the original community of goods to differential property. On the end of this discussion in the seventeenth and eighteenth centuries, see Niklas Luhmann, "Am Anfang war kein Unrecht," in id., *Gesellschaftsstruktur und Semantik*, vol. 3 (Frankfurt, 1989), 11–64.

287. This does not, of course, exclude decisions on buying and selling being regretted. The rationality of economic calculation has to do with this problem. Ultimately, however, no orientation can prevent subsequent regrets, because conditions and opportunities are always in flux.

288. Closer examination is needed of how psychic systems come to terms with this, especially how they make the necessary calculations. Initial findings indicate better than at school. See Terzinha Nunes Carraher, David William Carraher, and Analúcia Dias Schliemann, "Mathematics in the Streets and in Schools," *British Journal of Developmental Psychology* 3 (1985): 21–29; Terezinha Nunes Carraher and Analúcia Dias Schliemann, "Computation Routines Prescribed by Schools: Help or Hindrance?" *Journal for Research in Mathematical Education* 16 (1985): 17–44; Jean Lave, "The Values of Quantification," in *Power, Action and Belief: A New Sociology of Knowledge?* ed. John Law (London, 1986), 88–111.

289. For made things in general, see, e.g., Thomas Aquinas, *Summa Theologiae* I, q. 16 a.1 (Turin, 1952), 93.

290. "*Astonishment* is of all other Passions the easiest rais'd in raw and unexperienced Mankind," Shaftesbury writes (*Characteristicks*, 1: 264), thus also betraying that this concept of art presupposes a hierarchical architecture of the world and a corresponding society in which uncritical reverence was due from bottom to top.

291. See, e.g., Peter Bürger, *Prosa der Moderne* (Frankfurt, 1988).

292. Following Barel, *Le paradoxe et le système*, 71–72, 185–186, 302–303, we might also say that art discovers, uncovers the *potentializations* of a society, that is to say, what realization of the definite has relegated to the status of the merely possible.

293. See Niklas Luhmann, "Das Medium der Kunst," *Delfin* 4 (1986): 6–15, repr. in *"Ohne Titel": Neue Orientierungen in der Kunst*, ed. Frederick D. Bunsen (Würzburg, 1988, 61–71; id., *Die Kunst der Gesellschaft* (Frankfurt, 1995).

294. In curious contradiction to the etymology of the word, which now no longer refers to a past origin (*origo*) but demands "novelty" for attribution to the artist. See, e.g., Lodovico Antonio Muratori, *Della perfetta poesia italiana* (1706; Milan, 1971), 1: 104ff.

295. Matteo Peregrini came up with this formula to describe service at the princely court; see Peregrini, *Difesa del savio in corte* (Macerata, 1634), esp. 250ff.

296. See Niklas Luhmann, *Macht* (Stuttgart, 1975).

297. See the distinction between market choice and political choice in Geoffrey Vickers, *The Art of Judgement: A Study of Policy Making* (London, 1965), 122ff.

298. See also Niklas Luhmann, "Selbstorganisation und Information im politischen System," *Selbstorganisation* 2 (1991): 11–26.

299. It has already been noted in the preceding section that this precondition is not met by a medium of value relations, and that such a medium can therefore not be successfully differentiated. We have to do with values everywhere.

300. See Spencer-Brown's "law of crossing": "The value of a crossing made again is not the value of the crossing" (id., *Laws*, 2).

301. See Luhmann, *Gesellschaft*, 2: 751.

302. On problems with the corresponding expectations of literature opting for a morally positive position in the eighteenth century, see Niels Werber, *Literatur als System: Zur Ausdifferenzierung literarischer Kommunikation* (Opladen, 1992).

303. See further 226f. in this volume.

304. See Gotthard Günther, "Strukturelle Minimalbedingungen einer Theorie des objektiven Geistes als Einheit der Geschichte," in id., *Beiträge zur Grundlegung einer operationsfähigen Dialektik*, vol. 3 (Hamburg, 1980), 136–182 (140ff.).

305. This thought points to the problem of inflation, which endangers precisely this condition (and therefore the coding itself).

306. In the terminology introduced above (p. 110), this means that the unity of the code serves as the blind spot that is the essential condition for observational operation. And it is only another version of the same state of affairs when we note that all referral of coded operations back to the unity of their own code makes this appear a *paradox*.

307. Some—e.g., the "double bind" theoreticians and Barel, *Le paradoxe et le système*, esp. 53ff.—see sufficient justification in this alone for the paradoxical grounding of social systems. Nevertheless, the *logical* necessity of distinguishing between types, levels, languages, and metalanguages is only a necessity of *logic*, and if logic itself cannot stay the course, this contributes little to proving the paradoxical foundations of real systems.

308. Although the logic used knows the principle of identity, the prohibition of contradiction, and the principle of the excluded middle, it does not know the principle of sufficient reason. And if it lacks this principle (or something in its place), it cannot help itself out with logical axioms but only with metaphysics.

309. See further Luhmann, *Gesellschaft*, vol. 2, chap. 5, § 9.

310. The artificiality of this condition is apparent when one considers that the psychic schematism of willingness and unwillingness, not to mention its neurophysiological basis, does not satisfy it, and these are taken as qualitative distinctions. The absence of unwillingness does not suffice to produce willingness.

311. It should be obvious that interdependencies at the level of operations and programs are thus not excluded. Research can naturally be conducted better with money than without. That interdependencies and dependencies can be realized together is to be explained by the distinction between coding and programming.

312. Similarly, but from a transcendental theoretical point of view, see Edmund Husserl, *The Crisis of European Sciences and Transcendental Phenomenology: An Introduction to Phenomenological Philosophy* (German original, 1954; trans., Evanston, IL., 2000).

313. The associated logical problems are noted under (1) in the text above.

314. An in-depth analysis might discover in this a phenomenon of superposition in the sense of Barel, *Le paradoxe et le système*, 103ff. The preference for connectivity that is given anyway is used a second time to make invisible the paradox that would arise if one had to indicate the difference of the positive and the negative value as a unity, as *the same*.

315. In more detail, see Niklas Luhmann, "Wirtschaftsethik—als Ethik?" in *Wirtschaftsethik und Theorie der Gesellschaft*, ed. Josef Wieland (Frankfurt, 1993), 134–147; id., "Die Ehrlichkeit der Politiker und die höhere Amoralität der Politik," in *Opfer der Macht: Müssen Politiker ehrlich sein?* ed. Peter Kemper (Frankfurt, 1993), 27–41.

316. See further Luhmann, *Gesellschaft*, vol. 2 (*Taschenbuchausgabe*, 1998), chap. 5, § 14.

317. So-called ethnomethodology has taken a particular interest in this, undertaking research that has shown that this reflexivity cannot be used too often and above all not to establish ultimate causes. "Taking for granted" is indispensable. See also Chua Berg-Huat, "On the Commitments of Ethnomethodology," *Sociological Inquiry* 44 (1974): 241–256. In contrast, I aim to show what is to be gained with the differentiation of symbolically generalized communication media.

318. These different forms of reflexivity impose the separation of truths and value relations (or, in the terminology of the nineteenth century, questions of being and questions of validity). See also Niklas Luhmann, "Wahrheit und Ideologie," in id., *Aufklärung*, 1: 54–65.

319. This is also the reason why these media depend on written records and for their full development on printing.

320. See further Luhmann, *Gesellschaft*, vol. 2, chap. 5, § 21.

321. See Baecker, *Information und Risiko*.

322. It is only for this reason that *art criticism* has become a specific profession in which praise of the work of art reflects to some extent on the person who has found out why it is praiseworthy; it is, moreover, a secure profession, because finding fault with the work of art can also earn praise for the critic.

323. On the beginnings of modern science and with regard to printing, see Steve Shapin, "Pump and Circumstances: Robert Boyle's Literary Technology," *Social Studies of Science* 14, no. 4 (1984): 481–520.

324. It is remarkable that this is the very idea on which the von Neumann computer is based.

325. See esp. Talcott Parsons, "Pattern Variables Revisited," *American Sociological Review* 25 (1960): 467–483.

326. As widespread reservations about the universality claim of systems theory show, even people alive today are often not up to this combinatorial problem, though Kant long ago worked exemplarily with "provided that" abstractions.

327. See only Karl R. Popper, *Objective Knowledge: An Evolutionary Approach*

(Oxford, 1972), 317ff. The fact that it is often disregarded at the level of truth theories, and justificatory elements (coherence, consensus, etc.) are built into the truth concept, shows, however, how new and how improbable this insight is.

328. See further Luhmann, *Gesellschaft*, vol. 2, chap. 4, § 13.

329. See Niklas Luhmann, "Symbiotische Mechanismen," in id., *Aufklärung*, 3: 228–244; id., *Macht*, 60ff.; id., *Liebe als Passion*, esp. 137ff.; id., *Systeme*, 337ff.

330. For a remarkable case study, see Harold Garfinkel, Michael Lynch, and Eric Livingston, "The Work of Discovering Science, Constructed with Materials from the Optically Discovered Pulsar," *Philosophy of the Social Sciences* 11 (1981): 131–158.

331. See Alfred North Whitehead, *Modes of Thought* (1939; repr., New York, 1968), 111ff.

332. On the revaluation of sexuality since the mid-eighteenth century, see Edward Shorter, "Illegitimacy, Sexual Revolution and Social Change in Modern Europe," *Journal of Interdisciplinary History* 2 (1971): 237–272; Aram Vartanian, "La Mettrie, Diderot and Sexology in the Enlightenment," in *Essays on the Age of Enlightenment in Honor of Ira O. Wade* (Geneva, 1977), 347–367.

333. On the beginnings and on its foundations in printing, see David Foxon, "Libertine Literature in England 1660–1745," *The Book Collector* 12 (1963): 21–36, 159–177, 294–307.

334. See, e.g., P. J. Montes, "Precedentes doctrinales del 'estado de necessidad' en las obras de nuestras antiguos teologos y jurisconsultos," *La Ciudad de Dios* 142 (1925): 260–274, 352–361.

335. See Talcott Parsons, "Some Reflections on the Place of Force in Social Process," in *Internal War: Problems and Approaches*, ed. Harry Eckstein (New York, 1964), repr. in id., *Sociological Theory and Modern Society* (New York, 1967), 264–296.

336. As the then usual term "fanaticism" suggests, this was an old problem of religion, especially acute in the later Middle Ages because of the rapid increase in visions (uncertified, but useful for Church and monastic politics, and open to inspection as corporeal reality).

337. See Pascal, *De l'esprit géométrique et de l'art de persuader*, in id., *Oeuvres*, 358–386 (369).

338. See Parsons, *Social Systems and the Evolution of Action Theory*, ed. Jensen as *Zur Theorie der sozialen Interaktionsmedien*, esp. 211ff.; Talcott Parsons and Gerald M. Platt, *The American University* (Cambridge, MA, 1973), 304ff. Also Rainer Baum, "On Societal Media Dynamics," in *Explorations in General Theory in Social Science*, ed. Jan J. Loubser et al. (New York, 1976), 2: 579–608. David A. Baldwin, "Money and Power," *Journal of Politics* 33 (1971): 578–614 (608ff.), while taking an otherwise quite critical view of the media concept, also sees this as an issue worth pursuing.

339. For an example of inflation, see also Stefan Jensen, *Systemtheorie* (Stutt-

gart, 1983), 57: "Too many words (symbols) compared with too few 'realia' are circulating—too much is spoken about love and too little love is practiced."

340. For more detail, see Niklas Luhmann, *Vertrauen: Ein Mechanismus der Reduktion sozialer Komplexität* (3rd ed., Stuttgart, 1989). See also *Trust: Making and Breaking Cooperative Relations*, ed. Diego Gambetta (Oxford, 1988).

341. For a case study on the subject concerning the inflation of Kantian philosophy in the last decade of the eighteenth century, see Niklas Luhmann, "Theoriesubstitution in der Erziehungswissenschaft: Von der Philanthropie zum Neuhumanismus," in id., *Gesellschaftsstruktur*, 2: 105–194. Wolfgang Walter, "Vererbung und Gesellschaft: Zur Wissenssoziologie des hereditären Diskurses" (diss., Bielefeld, 1989), discusses another example, attributable to a societally suggested interest in individuals.

342. Alban J. Krailsheimer, *Studies in Self-Interest: From Descartes to La Bruyère* (Oxford, 1962), 113, speaks of the effects of a "debasement of spiritual currency." A fundamentalist countermovement then developed in Jansenism, Pietism, etc. For modern America, Parsons distinguishes inflationary trends (social activism) and deflationary trends ("fundamentalism") in religion. See Parsons, *Social Systems and the Evolution of Action Theory*, ed. Jensen as *Zur Theorie der sozialen Interaktionsmedien*, 212. For similar ideas with regard to modern morality, see Richard Münch, "Moralische Achtung als Medium der Kommunikation," in id., *Dynamik der Kommunikationsgesellschaft* (Frankfurt, 1995), 214ff.

343. For this reason, only general price increases can be taken as an inflation index, because when money is accepted, it is not yet certain what it will be spent on.

344. In the context of a historical case study on the basis of Parsons's theoretical apparatus, see Mark Gould, *Revolution in the Development of Capitalism: The Coming of the English Revolution* (Berkeley, CA, 1987), esp. 54ff. and 230ff.: the English king overextended his power apparatus in the absence of a sufficient administrative substructure, thus provoking the revolution.

345. For a communication-theoretical treatment of this problem, see Hutter, "Signum non olet."

346. It may well be asked, however, whether this is not because of the historical accident that the territorial state emerged in Europe after the eleventh-century differentiation of the legal system, notably in the form of the canon law of the Roman Catholic Church and based on discovery of the sources of Roman civil law. See Harold J. Berman, *Law and Revolution: The Formation of the Western Legal Tradition* (Cambridge, MA, 1983). Global confirmation of this special case has not yet been forthcoming.

347. On the abstractions reacting to this, see Dirk Baecker, "Das Gedächtnis der Wirtschaft," in *Theorie als Passion*, ed. id. (Frankfurt, 1987), 519–546.

348. This is only another way of saying that after differentiating symbolically generalized communication media, society can no longer impose a supercode. But

this does not exclude morality now being free to evaluate what it wants to, and how it wants to, indeed, it makes this possible.

349. Originally, the metaphor of the circle had a cosmological meaning, symbolizing the unity of movement and immutability. The seventeenth century sought to bring this symbol down to earth from the heavens, although the circulation neither of the blood nor of money is strictly speaking circular.

350. Lawyers who practice consequentialist decision-making, and nowadays that includes practically all of them, suffer here from sheer incomprehensible illusions. What counts for the decision are not the actual consequences, but only those that the jurist would like to bring about or prevent with an informed decision. There are nevertheless moderate voices who wish to limit consequentialism to opening or closing decision-making possibilities in the legal system (and thus to regulating circulation of the symbol "legal validity"). See Bernard Rudden, "Consequences," *Juridical Review* 24 (1979): 193–201, and, giving way in this direction, Neil MacCormick, "Legal Decisions and Their Consequences: From Dewey to Dworkin," *New York University Law Review* 58 (1983): 253–258.

351. Magoroh Maruyama, "The Second Cybernetics: Deviation-Amplifying Mutual Causal Processes," *General Systems* 8 (1963): 233–241, and the ensuing research into positive feedback, was an important point of departure. See also Alfred Gierer, "Generation of Biological Patterns and Form: Some Physical, Mathematical, and Logical Aspects," *Progress of Biophysics and Molecular Biology* 37 (1981): 1–47; id., "Socioeconomic Inequalities: Effects of Self-enhancement, Depletion and Redistribution," *Jahrbücher für Nationalökonomie und Statistik* 196 (1981): 309–331; id., *Die Physik, das Leben und die Seele: Anspruch und Grenzen der Naturwissenschaft* (4th ed., Munich, 1988), esp. 121ff.

352. See further chap. 3, § 8, in this volume.

353. See André Orléan, "La monnaie et les paradoxes de l'individualisme," *Stanford French Review* 15 (1992): 271–295.

354. See Floyd H. Allport, *Institutional Behavior: Essays Toward a Re-interpreting of Contemporary Social Organization* (Chapel Hill, NC, 1933). It was not by chance that Allport moved on later to an idiosyncratic social-psychology theory that assumes a distinction between "structure" and "event."

355. See Niklas Luhmann, "The Future Cannot Begin: Temporal Structures in Modern Society," *Social Research* 43 (1976): 130–152.

356. Bernard Anconi, "Apprentissage, temps historique et évolution économique," *Revue internationale de systémique* 7 (1993): 593–612 (597–598), puts it more drastically: "Le système est toujours à la fin des temps," but immediately concedes that this is not in contradiction to the openness of the future.

357. See 145ff. above and, with more detail, Niklas Luhmann, "Soziologie der Moral," in *Theorietechnik und Moral*, ed. id. and Stephan H. Pfürtner (Frankfurt, 1978), 8–116.

358. In the moral critique of modern times, this is where the reproach of hypo-

crisy is raised, which is naturally justified, but does not question that communication takes place in relation to the medium of morality. What is basically at issue is the utopian notion that people actually have to mean what they say.

359. For an overview of the very wide-ranging forms, which diverge not only regionally but also between high and popular culture, see *The Anthropology of Evil*, ed. David Parkin (Oxford, 1985).

360. Whether words like *böse* or "evil" are now used less frequently for this reason is a moot point and probably difficult to prove. See Alan MacFarlane, *The Culture of Capitalism* (Oxford, 1987), 98ff.

361. "No man can justly censure or condemn another, indeed no man truly knows another," Sir Thomas Browne writes in *Religio Medici* (1643; London, 1965), 72. "Further no man can judge another because no man knows himself."

362. On this shift in the meaning of "morality" and for a very far-reaching research complex, see, e.g., Marcel Thomann, "Histoire de l'idéologie juridique au XVIIIe siècle, ou: 'Le droit prisonnier des mots,'" *Archives de philosophie du droit* 19 (1974): 127–149.

363. See also Niklas Luhmann, "Ethik als Reflexionstheorie der Moral," in id., *Gesellschaftsstruktur*, 3: 259–357; also the section of the universalization of morality in Luhmann, *Gesellschaft*, vol. 2, chap. 5..

364. See Luhmann, *Gesellschaft*, 2: 975–976.

365. In Hofstadter, *Gödel, Escher, Bach*, 688.

366. See the comprehensive study by Karl-Heinrich Bette and Uwe Schimank, *Doping im Hochleistungssport: Anpassung durch Abweichung* (Frankfurt, 1995).

367. E.g., Lenin at the Smolny Institute in St. Petersburg in 1917.

368. See Luhmann, *Wirtschaft der Gesellschaft*.

369. More detail in Niklas Luhmann, "Die Ausdifferenzierung der Religion," in id., *Gesellschaftsstruktur*, 3: 259–357.

370. We explicitly maintain this independence of externally directed (naturally always communicative) efforts also for technology, and therefore also see more than applied science in modern technology. See chap. 3, § 9, in this volume. Numerous technological problems—from railroad construction to modern safety engineering—cannot be solved by "reading," but have to rely on constructing and testing the very installations one wants to construct. It goes without saying that this requires scientifically trained personnel. But their training, too, is not research but education.

371. See Niklas Luhmann, "Grundwerte als Zivilreligion: Zur wissenschaftlichen Karriere eines Themas," *Archivio di Filosofia* 46, nos. 2–3 (1978): 51–71.

372. On dating in the early seventeenth century, see Edgar Zilsel, "The Genesis of the Concept of Physical Law," *Philosophical Review* 51 (1942): 245–279.

373. On this branch of the development of ideas, see Niklas Luhmann, "Selbstreferenz und Teleologie in gesellschaftstheoretischer Perspektive," in id., *Gesellschaftsstruktur*, 2: 9–44.

CHAPTER 3: EVOLUTION

1. See Colwyn L. Morgan, *Emergent Evolution* (New York, 1923), or, for a multitude of dimensions or variables of emergence, Anthony Wilden, *System and Structure: Essays in Communication and Exchange* (2nd ed., London, 1980), 351ff. (375). For a more recent overview, see also Eric Bonabeau, Jean-Louis Dessalles, and Alain Grumbach, "Characterizing Emergent Phenomena," *Revue internationale de systémique* 9 (1995): 327–346, 347–371.

2. With respect to the "emergence" of self-organization, see E. Bernard-Weil, "Réévaluation des concepts d'auto-organisation et d'émergence à la lumière de la systémique ago-antagoniste," *Revue internationale de systémique* 8 (1994): 315–335 (316). Dialectical solutions, with their even more opaque logic, are also no help. We would do better to consider attempts to temporalize mathematical calculations.

3. For overviews of the Anglo-Saxon branch of the discussion, see Tim Ingold, *Evolution and Social Life* (Cambridge, 1986), or Stephen K. Sanderson, *Social Evolutionism: A Critical History* (Oxford, 1990).

4. On "l'improbable probable," see Edgar Morin, *La méthode*, vol. 1 (Paris, 1977), 294ff. The already classical paradigm is the chemical improbability of DNA molecules.

5. In the structuralist manner, a corresponding theory of the probability of the improbable could be constructed with the aid of the *force* concept. Universally distributed virtual force is doubled and differentiated into legitimate and nonlegitimate force. This is done not by social contract (Hobbes) but by evolution. In its legitimate form, force (today as state authority) serves to drive out illegitimate force. With this differentiation, force is thus characterized by the inclusion of exclusion, and legitimacy is, from this point of view, not a value concept but this very inclusion of exclusion—a paradox whose resolution constitutes itself as state authority (or its functional equivalent). See also Dirk Baecker, "Gewalt im System," *Soziale Welt* 47 (1996): 92–109.

6. Magoroh Maruyama, "Postscript to the Second Cybernetics," *American Scientist* 51 (1963), 250–256.

7. This is a quite common view. It ultimately goes back to Herbert Spencer's famous formula of "change from a state of indefinite, incoherent homogeneity to a state of definite, coherent heterogeneity" (id., "What Is Social Evolution?" *The Nineteenth Century* 44 [1898]: 348–358 [353]). Comprehensive treatment is to be found in chaps. 14–17 on "The Law of Evolution," of id., *First Principles* (5th ed., London, 1887), 307ff. For more recent views see, e.g., J. W. S. Pringle, "On the Parallel Between Learning and Evolution," *Behaviour* 3 (1951): 174–215; Walter Buckley, *Sociology and Modern Systems Theory* (Englewood Cliffs, NJ, 1967), 50–51, 62ff.; Gerd Pawelzig, *Dialektik der Entwicklung objektiver Systeme* (Berlin, 1970), 135ff.; Gerhard Lenski, "Social Structure in Evolutionary Perspective," in *Approaches to the Study of Social Structure*, ed. Peter Blau (London, 1976), 135–153.

8. E.g., Richard Newbold Adams, *Energy and Structure: A Theory of Social Power* (Austin, TX, 1975).

9. This takes us back to the treatment of yes/no coding in language in chap. 2, 132ff., in this volume.

10. We are talking about cosmologies with the following characteristics: total creation by an author, contingency, dependence. The biblical texts give a much more complex picture. See Michael Welker, *Schöpfung und Wirklichkeit* (Neukirchen-Vluyn, 1995). Taking this further, we could say that creation is the event (or registration) of the difference that can *afterward* begin to act creatively.

11. Hegel argues quite the other way around, seeing a gain for piety in renunciation of detailed final natures: "What is to the benefit of the one is to the disadvantage of the other, and is therefore inappropriate: the maintenance of life and the interests concerned with existence, which in the one case are furthered are in the other case just as much endangered and destroyed. There is a *bifurcation in itself* that, contrary to the eternal workings of God, finite things are raised to essential purposes" (*Vorlesungen über die Philosophie der Religion* I, in Hegel, *Werke*, vol. 16 [Frankfurt, 1969], 21–22). In the world history of the mind, this can only be a temporary shortcoming.

12. See Johann George Sulzer, "Versuch über die Glückseligkeit veständiger Wesen" (1754), in id., *Vermischte Philosophische Schriften*, vol. 1 (1773; repr., Hildesheim, 1974), 323–347. See also Kant's *Allgemeine Naturgeschichte und Theorie des Himmels* (1755), esp. chap. 7. As early as the sixteenth century, we find, with a growing awareness of progress, the view that God, even though he had not created the world gradually, had at least revealed it step by step—not least the printing press, the two Americas, and artillery. See François de La Noue, *Discours politiques et militaires* (1587; repr., Geneva, 1967), 520ff. The change is now, however, believed only to have taken place in the mid-eighteenth century—see Arthur O. Lovejoy, *The Great Chain of Being: A Study of the History of an Idea* (Cambridge, MA, 1936), 242ff., and Wolf Lepenies, *Das Ende der Naturgeschichte: Wandel kultureller Selbstverständlichkeiten in den Wissenschaften des 18. und 19. Jahrhunderts* (Munich, 1976).

13. Today, this has been abandoned both in biology and in the theory of society in favor of a concept of occasional but abrupt structural changes now that we need no longer fear that this brings us too close to miracles of creation. See p. 270 in this volume.

14. On Darwin as a "historical methodologist," see Stephen Jay Gould, "Evolution and the Triumph of Homology, or Why History Matters," *American Scientist* 74 (1986): 60–69.

15. See, e.g., Ingold, *Evolution and Social Life*, 12ff.

16. For a history of evolution theories from a biological perspective, see Peter J. Bowler, *Evolution: The History of an Idea* (2nd ed., Berkeley, CA, 1989). For a systematic state-of-the-art presentation, see Stuart A. Kauffman, *The Origins of Order: Self-Organization and Selection in Evolution* (New York, 1993).

17. Methodologically, this is now based on Guttmann-scalogram analysis, which is, however, never applied to society as a whole but only to special areas such as the division of labor, religion, political order, and law. For an overview, see Robert L. Carneiro, "Scale Analysis, Evolutionary Sequences, and the Rating of Cultures," in *Handbook of Method in Cultural Anthropology*, ed. Raoul Naroll and Ronald Cohen (Garden City, NY, 1970), 834–871.

18. Herbert Spencer, who was at the heart of these controversies, was both cautious and careless in this regard. See, e.g., the criticism of such assumptions in Spencer, *Principles of Sociology*, vol. 1 (3rd ed., London, 1885), 93ff., and id., *First Principles*, 517, with the assertion "that Evolution can end only in the establishment of the greatest perfection and the most complete happiness." A hundred years later, we can still accept this—albeit with the added remark: then it simply doesn't end!

19. Many controversies about evolution theory, which have in retrospect proved useless, have been inspired by this. See, e.g., L.T. Hobhouse, G. C. Wheeler, and Morris Ginsberg, *The Material Culture and Social Institutions of the Simpler Peoples: An Essay in Correlation* (1915; repr., London, 1965), 1ff. The criticism of the style of these controversies is also already half a century old. See, e.g., Leonhard Adam, "Functionalism and Neo-Functionalism," *Oceania* 17 (1946): 1–25.

20. See the discussions in *Epochenschwellen und Epochenstrukturen im Diskurs der Literatur- und Sprachhistorie*, ed. Hans Ulrich Gumbrecht and Ursula Link-Heer (Frankfurt, 1985), or in *Epochenschwelle und Epochenbewußtsein*, ed. Reinhart Herzog and Reinhart Koselleck, Poetik und Hermeneutik, vol. 12 (Munich, 1987).

21. For an example, see William T. Sanders and David Webster, "Unilinealism and Multilinealism, and the Evolution of Complex Societies," in *Social Archeology: Beyond Subsistence and Dating*, ed. Charles L. Redman et al. (New York, 1978), 249–302.

22. Ernst Heuss, "Evolution und Stagnation of Economic Systems," in *The Evolution of Economic Systems: Essays in Honour of Ota Šik*, ed. Kurt Dopfer and Karl-F. Raible (London, 1990), 91–99 (93).

23. See, e.g., Ingold, *Evolution and Social Life*, 102, who, in keeping with the tradition of the evolution concept seeks "to denote the continuous, directed and purposive movement to which the term originally and quite properly referred." See the apposite criticism by Marion Blute, "Sociocultural Evolutionism: An Untried Theory," *Behavioral Science* 24 (1979): 46–59. See also Thomas Dietz, Tom R. Burns, and Frederick H. Buttel, "Evolutionary Theory in Sociology: An Examination of Current Thinking," *Sociological Forum* 5 (1990): 155–171.

24. However, it should at least be mentioned that the concept of evolution came into fashion owing to Spencer rather than Darwin. Darwin himself uses it only quite casually and at any rate not to name his own theory. Even so-called social Darwinism can hardly cite Darwin himself, especially not *The Descent of Man* (1871). In retrospect, see *Darwinisme et société*, ed. Patrick Tort (Paris, 1992).

25. For transfer to the social sciences, see esp. Donald T. Campbell, "Blind Variation and Selective Retention in Creative Thought as in Other Knowledge Processes," *Psychological Review* 67 (1960): 380–400; id., "Variation and Selective Retention in Socio-Cultural Evolution," *General Systems* 14 (1969): 69–85; id., "On the Conflict Between Biological and Social Evolution and Between Psychological and Moral Tradition," *American Psychologist* 30 (1975): 1103–1126 (a selection of mostly epistemologically oriented writings); and with regard to evolution changing cultural "rules," Tom R. Burns and Thomas Dietz, "Cultural Evolution: Social Rule Systems and Human Agency," *International Sociology* 7 (1992): 259–281.

26. Darwin himself held that the evolution of civilization cancelled natural selection. See Patrick Tort, "L'effet réversif de l'évolution: Fondements de l'anthropologie darwinienne," in id., *Darwinisme et société*, 13–46. This would have to mean that civilization as a product of evolution now had to guarantee itself.

27. See also Loet Leydesdorff, "The Evolution of Communication Systems," *International Journal of Systems Research and Information Science* 6 (1994): 219–230.

28. See Julian S. Huxley, *Evolution: The Modern Synthesis* (1942; 3rd ed., London 1974), 485, quoted from C. R. Hallpike, *The Principles of Social Evolution* (Oxford, 1986), 77: "we now realize that the results of selection are by no means necessarily 'good', from the point of view either of the species or of the progressive evolution of life. They may be neutral, they may be a dangerous balance of useful and harmful, or they may be definitely deleterious."

29. See, e.g., E. D. Cope, *The Primary Factors of Organic Evolution* (Chicago, 1896), Elman R. Service, *Cultural Evolutionism: Theory in Practice* (New York, 1971), and G. Ledyard Stebbins, *The Basis of Progressive Evolution* (Chapel Hill, NC, 1969).

30. See Lars Löfgren, "Knowledge of Evolution and Evolution of Knowledge," in *The Evolutionary Vision: Towards a Unifying Paradigm of Physical, Biological, and Sociocultural Evolution*, ed. Erich Jantsch (Boulder, CO, 1981), 129–151. The scientific elaboration of a theory of unpredictable changes requires the admission of self-reference in evolution theory as in systems theory.

31. Such notions, too, are occasionally formulated with the concept of evolution. See, e.g., the idea of a "welfare-oriented evolutionary theory" in Edmund Dahlström, "Developmental Direction and Welfare Goals: Some Comments on Functionalistic Evolutionary Theory about Highly Developed Societies," *Acta Sociologica* 17 (1974): 3–21. The advance made by this version of the theory, to do it justice, is that static final states are no longer in question, but rather variables intended to indicate potential for development, such as learning ability, mobilization of resources, and adaptive upgrading.

32. See, e.g., Gisèle Umbhauer, "Evolution and Forward Induction in Game Theory," *Revue internationale de systémique* 7 (1993): 613–626, on evolution of the economy.

33. I argue that the form of system differentiation is of particular importance in this regard; see further also Luhmann, *Gesellschaft*, vol. 2, chap. 4, esp. 883.

34. Among biologists, Rupert Riedl has been foremost in stressing the need to clarify systems-theoretical premises of evolution theory. See Riedl, *Die Ordnung des Lebendigen: Systembedingungen der Evolution* (Hamburg, 1975), and "A Systems-Analytical Approach to Macro-Evolutionary Phenomena," *Quarterly Review of Biology* 52 (1977): 351–370.

35. Loet Leydesdorff, "New Models of Technological Change: New Theories for Technology Studies," in *Evolutionary Economics and Chaos Theory: New Directions in Technology Studies*, ed. id. and Peter van den Besselaar (London, 1994), 180–192 (180).

36. See Hans-Peter Müller and Michael Schmid, "Paradigm Lost? Von der Theorie sozialen Wandels zur Theorie dynamischer Systeme," in *Sozialer Wandel: Modellbildung und theoretische Ansätze*, ed. id. (Frankfurt, 1995), 9–55 (31ff.); Michael Schmid, "Soziologische Evolutionstheorie," *Protosoziologie* 7 (1995): 200–210 (201ff.); Sanderson, *Social Evolutionism*, 224. However, the empirical reference of this attribution to action remains unclear, since one can scarcely claim that certain actions have evolutionary effects. Anthony Giddens (who is often cited in this connection) is more consistent insofar as he rejects an evolutionistic interpretation of his "structuration" theory.

37. This is not fundamentally different if, with Ingold, *Evolution and Social Life*, esp. 104–105, 114ff., we distinguish between person as meaning-imparting, acting entity and individual as an entity in which a multitude of objective events take place as "the things that happen" (105), as "temporary vehicle for the projection of past into future" (106). Views on the importance of human beings for sociocultural evolution may differ; but the problem is whether evolution theory should make itself dependent at all, for the notion from which it takes its departure, on such a humanistic design.

38. This is further discussed below in this chapter with reference to system differentiation.

39. See pertinent remarks in C. H. Waddington, "The Principles of Archetypes in Evolution," in *Mathematical Challenges to the Neo-Darwinian Interpretation of Evolution*, ed. Paul S. Moorhead and Martin M. Kaplan (Philadelphia, 1967), 113–115.

40. Herbert Spencer had already clearly seen this. See the chapter "The Multiplication of Effects," in id., *First Principles*, 93ff.

41. As formulated by Richad B. Norgaard, "The Coevolution of Economic and Environmental Systems and the Emergence of Unsustainability," in *Evolutionary Concepts in Contemporary Economics*, ed. Richard W. England (Ann Arbor, MI, 1994), 213–225 (220).

42. See, e.g., Gregory A. Johnson, "Organizational Structure and Scalar Stress," in *Theory and Explanation in Archaeology*, ed. Colin Renfrew, Michael J. Rowlands, and Barbara Abbott Segraves (New York, 1982), 389–421: "population

is not necessarily the best measure of scale" (391–392); and see also 407. Nevertheless, the author, with no other theory of society at his disposal, continues to count individuals, families, and small groups as the point of departure for determining the size and the "scalar stress" of a society.

43. See, e.g., Stephen Jay Gould, "Darwinism and the Expansion of Evolutionary Theory," *Science* 216 (1982): 380–387.

44. E.g., Anatol Rapoport, "Mathematical, Evolutionary, and Psychological Approaches to the Study of Total Societies," in *The Study of Total Societies*, ed. Samuel Z. Klausner (Garden City, NY, 1967), 114–143 (133ff.) sees possibilities for retreating from Darwin's notion of "natural selection" with the aid of the meaning concept. Similarly, Stephen Toulmin, *Human Understanding*, vol. 1 (Princeton, NJ, 1972). If one argues more in the context of main-stream sociology, the almost complete neglect of external causes in the theories on historical developments is more striking. This has been increasingly criticized. Anthony D. Smith, *The Concept of Social Change* (London, 1973), 150ff., sees in this the reason for the controversy between historicism and evolutionism. Bernhard Giesen and Christoph Lau, "Zur Anwendung Darwinistischer Erklärungsstrategien in der Soziologie," *Kölner Zeitschrift für Soziologie und Sozialpsychologie* 33 (1981): 229–256, and Michael Schmid, *Theorie sozialen Wandels* (Opladen, 1982), therefore propose reorientation with the help of a concept of external natural selection. But can this *distinction* be at issue at all?

45. Untenably inferring endogenous causality from the unity of sociology's subject matter, Emile Durkheim observes: "que les causes des phénomènes sociaux sont internes à la société." He adds: "C'est bien plutôt à la théorie qui fait dériver la société de l'individu qu'on pourrait justement reprocher de chercher à tirer le dedans du dehors." Durkheim, *Les règles de la méthode sociologique* (8th ed., Paris 1927), 147–148.

46. Mixed forms that transfer demographically tried and tested theory patterns to social systems are then all the more problematic. This sort of theory formation is particularly widespread in dealing with the evolution of organizations. See, e.g., Bill McKelvey and Howard Aldrich, "Populations, Natural Selection, and Applied Organizational Science," *Administrative Science Quarterly* 28 (1983): 101–128; W. Graham Astley, "The Two Ecologies: Population and Community Perspectives on Organizational Evolution," ibid., 30 (1985): 224–241; Michael T. Hannan and John Freeman, *Organizationale Ecology* (Cambridge, MA, 1989); and *Evolutionary Dynamics of Organizations*, ed. Joel Baum and Jitendra Singh (New York, 1994).

47. See Gerhard Roth, "Conditions of Evolution and Adaptation in Organism as Autopoietic Systems," in *Environmental Adaptation and Evolution*, ed. D. Mossakowski and G. Roth (Stuttgart, 1982), 37–48; Hans Rademacher, "Zur Grammatik autopoietischer Systeme," in *Autopoiesis: Eine Theorie im Brennpunkt der Kritik*, ed. Hans Rudi Fischer (Heidelberg, 1991), 53–66.

48. Maturana accordingly distinguishes between the autopoietic organization and the structures of a system. However, I wish to avoid the term "organization" in this connection, because I want to use it differently.

49. Thus salamanders with or without complicated sling-tongue. See David B. Wake, Gerhard Roth, and Marvalee H. Wake, "On the Problems of Stasis in Organismal Evolution," *Journal of Theoretical Biology* 101 (1983): 211–224.

50. See, e.g., Cope, *Primary Factors of Organic Evolution*, 172ff., and Service, *Cultural Evolutionism*, 31ff., for the one view, and Stebbins, *Basis of Progressive Evolution*, 121, for the other.

51. This argument is directed against an objection that is often raised, but is even from a purely methodological point of view quite nonsensical. For no concept—neither autopoiesis nor action, neither control nor socialization, neither purpose nor organization—*as concept* provides the structural limitations within which what is indicated can be realized in any particular case. Apparently, the heat of the controversy about autopoiesis makes one forget that this is also not demanded of one's own concepts. See inter alia Walter L. Bühl, "Politische Grenzen der Autopoiese sozialer Systeme," in *Autopoiesis: Eine Theorie im Brennpunkt der Kritik*, ed. Hans Rudi Fischer (Heidelberg, 1991), 201–225.

52. Gunther Teubner reacts to precisely this problem by attenuating the stringency of the autopoiesis concept in "Hyperzyklus in Recht und Organisation: Zum Verhältnis von Selbstbeobachtung, Selbstkonstitution und Autopoiesis," in *Sinn, Kommunikation und soziale Differenzierung: Beiträge zu Luhmanns Theorie sozialer Systeme*, ed. Hans Haferkamp and Michael Schmid (Frankfurt, 1987), 98–128. Similarly, for biology, Gerhard Roth, "Autopoiese und Kognition: Die Theorie H. R. Maturanas und die Notwendigkeit ihrer Weiterentwicklung," in *Systeme erkennen Systeme: Individuelle, soziale und methodische Bedingungen systemischer Diagnostik*, ed. Günther Schiepek (Munich, 1987), 50–74 (57–58). Our inquiries take another path. See also, deploying the concepts of "self-organization" and "structural coupling," Rudolf Stichweh, "Selbstorganisation und die Entstehung nationaler Rechtssysteme (17.–19. Jahrhundert)," *Rechtshistorisches Journal* 9 (1990): 254–272.

53. See Luhmann, *Gesellschaft*, 2: 816, on interactions envisaged as episodes, showing that episodization is possible only with the help of the distinction between interaction and society, and hence only in a society that is itself infinite.

54. N. Katherine Hayles, "Making the Cut: The Interplay of Narrative and System, or What Systems Theory Can't See," *Cultural Critique* 30 (1995): 7–100, is thus right when she suggests that a transition could be useful to narrative patterns that can give an account of how autopoietic systems, and, among them, observing systems, set themselves as difference. But this solution does not get us very far, although it makes other means of establishing plausibility available and also permits us to inquire into the historical situations in which the narration of autopoietic evolution has been able to take root at all. But ultimately this merely brings us back to the question of who tells the tale.

55. This is seldom said with sufficient clarity. But see, following Heidegger, Anthony Giddens, "Time and Social Organization," in id., *Social Theory and Modern Society* (Cambridge, 1987), 140–165.

56. *After* an accident we know what we have experienced and why we behaved the way we did, just as if everything had happened under conscious control; or we know (but we know!) that we cannot remember clearly enough.

57. See also Donald T. Campbell, "Neurological Embodiments of Belief and the Gaps in the Fit of Phenomena to Noumena," in *Naturalistic Epistemology*, ed. Abner Shimony and Debra Nails (Dordrecht, 1987), 165–192 (175).

58. Greek examples show that it is difficult to determine stable ancestors in the absence of writing. See Rosalind Thomas, *Oral Tradition and Written Record in Classical Athens* (Cambridge, 1989), esp. 155ff. See also Gerdien Jonker, *The Topography of Remembrance: The Dead, Tradition and Collective Memory in Mesopotamia* (Leiden, 1995), esp. 213ff.

59. Harold J. Berman, *Law and Revolution: The Formation of the Western Legal Tradition* (Cambridge, MA, 1983), dates the change (after the break in the Roman civil law tradition) precisely to the second half of the eleventh century. Takeoff became possible when a socially embedded system of jurisprudence coincided over the course of a few decades with chance events such as the rediscovery of the Roman *Corpus Iuris Civilis* [Code of Justinian], the Norman Conquest of England and imposition of royal law, and, above all, Church reform.

60. The account of the development of Greek science in G. E. R. Lloyd, *Magic, Reason and Experience: Studies in the Origin and Development of Greek Science* (Cambridge, 1979), although not at all conceived in this way, can very well be interpreted thus.

61. See p. 208 in this volume.

62. For an instructive example concerning local jurisdiction, see Charles Loyseau, *Discours de l'abus des justices de village, tiré du Traité des offices de C.L.P.* (Paris, 1603).

63. See Gould, "Darwinism and the Expansion of Evolutionary Theory"; Richard M. Burian, "Adaptation," in *Dimensions of Darwinism*, ed. Marjorie Green (Cambridge, 1984), 287–314; Michael T. Hannan and John Freeman, *Organizational Ecology* (Cambridge, MA, 1989), 21ff. A widespread point of criticism amounts to an accusation of tautology (adaptation = survival = adaptation); but this could be dispelled.

64. In this context, the concept of the evolutionary "niche" initially helped, but this merely shifts the issue, for now the distinction between niche and nonniche becomes crucial for theory.

65. For this example, see Theodosius Dobzhansky, "Chance and Creativity in Evolution," in *Studies in the Philosophy of Biology: Reduction and Related Problems*, ed. id. and Francisco José Ayala (London, 1974).

66. See, e.g., Bowler, *Evolution*, 340.

67. See Humberto Maturana and Francisco Varela, *El arbol del conocimiento* (Santiago de Chile, 1984), esp. 71ff.; trans. as *The Tree of Knowledge: The Biological Roots of Human Understanding* (Boston, 1992).

68. See just Joseph A. Tainter, *The Collapse of Complex Societies* (Cambridge, 1988).

69. Anyone who argues that evolution is a process that enhances complexity must consequently refer to these phenomena as "devolution." See Charles Tilly, "Clio and Minerva," in *Theoretical Sociology: Perspectives and Developments*, ed. John C. McKinney and Edward A. Tiryakian (New York, 1970), 433–466. I prefer to restrict the thesis itself.

70. See, e.g., Joseph H. Greenberg, *Essays in Linguistics* (New York, 1957), 56ff.

71. On the basis of other theories, biologists also stress that complexity is epigenetically co-produced, but that the actual effect of evolution consists in the development of system structures. See G. Ledyard Stebbins, "Adaptive Shifts and Evolutionary Novelty: A Compositionist Approach," in *Studies in the Philosophy of Biology: Reduction and Related Problems*, ed. Francisco Ayala and Theodosius Dobzhansky (London, 1974), 285–306 (302ff.). See also id., *The Basis of Progressive Evolution* (Chapel Hill, NC, 1969).

72. This holds for physical-chemical evolution and a fortiori for organic evolution. See Melvin Calvin, "Origin of Life on Earth and Elsewhere," in *The Logic of Personal Knowledge: Essays Presented to Michael Polanyi on His Seventieth Birthday* (London, 1961), 207–231 (214).

73. See Richard Levins, *Evolution in Changing Environments: Some Theoretical Explorations* (Princeton, NJ, 1968), 6.

74. For biology, see Niles Eldredge and Stephen Jay Gould, "Punctuated Equilibria: An Alternative to Phyletic Gradualism," in *Models in Paleobiology*, ed. Thomas J. M. Schopf (San Francisco, 1972), 82–115. See also Kenneth E. Boulding, "Punctuationalism in Societal Evolution," *Journal of Social and Biological Structures* 12 (1989): 213–223.

75. See Talcott Parsons, *Societies: Evolutionary and Comparative Perspectives* (Englewood Cliffs, NJ, 1966), 95ff.

76. Michael Conrad discusses such a "postulate of ignorance" in "Rationality in the Light of Evolution," in *Laws of Nature and Human Conduct*, ed. Ilya Prigogine and Michèle Sanglier (Brussels, 1987), 111–211,

77. The concept of decoupling has a similar function in Bernhard Giesen's quite differently oriented theory of social change in id., "Code und Situation: Das selektionstheoretische Programm einer Analyse sozialen Wandels—illustriert an der Genese des deutschen Nationalbewußtseins," in *Sozialer Wandel: Modellbildung und theoretische Ansätze*, ed. Hans-Peter Müller and Michael Schmid (Frankfurt, 1995), 228–266.

78. See Heinz von Foerster, "On Self-Organizing Systems and Their Environments," in *Self-Organizing Systems: Proceedings of an Interdisciplinary Conference*,

ed. Marshall C. Yovits and Scott Cameron (Oxford, 1960), 31–48; Henri Atlan, *Entre le cristal et la fumée* (Paris, 1979).

79. See, e.g., Robert Boyd and Peter J. Richerson, *Culture and the Evolutionary Process* (Chicago, 1985).

80. This should make it clear, but in view of innumerable misunderstandings and misinterpretations, I would take the precaution of noting that there is *no analogical inference* involved in either the one direction or the other. This means that the fact that living systems evolve does not allow us to conclude that the societal system must also evolve. Such reasoning could be upheld at best in theories that maintain that society consists of living beings.

81. Failure to take this sufficiently into account provoked the dispute over "sociobiology." We can spare ourselves this controversy without have to deny that like other environmental factors, genetic predisposition also affects society, inasmuch as it can disturb communication. In the system reference of living systems, "culture" can be regarded as the continuation of life by other (and probably dubious) means or as learned (as opposed to genetically determined) behavior. See, e.g., John Tyler Bonner, *The Evolution of Culture in Animals* (Princeton, NJ, 1980). All this may also provide "anthropologically" interesting insights. But it permits no conclusions about societal evolution.

82. This reservation has led to objections that variation, selection, and restabilization cannot be distinguished at all in societal evolution, because the one takes place only in meaningful reference back to the other. But this holds for meaning relations generally and does not exclude quite obviously meaningful distinctions.

83. See, e.g., Hallpike, *Principles of Social Evolution*, chap. 2. The effect of confusion about the relations between individual and society, blocking the way to a theory of societal evolution, is evident.

84. Older examples include Albert G. Keller, *Societal Evolution: A Study of the Evolutionary Basis of the Science of Society* (2nd ed., New Haven, CT, 1931), and V. Gordon Childe, *Social Evolution* (London, 1951). And see esp. Donald T. Campbell, "Variation and Selection Retention in Socio-Cultural Evolution," *General Systems* 14 (1969), 69–85; Robert A. LeVine, *Culture, Behavior, and Personality* (Chicago, 1973), 101ff.; Howard E. Aldrich, *Organizations and Environments* (Englewood Cliffs, NJ, 1979), 26ff.; John Langton, "Darwinism and the Behavioral Theory of Sociocultural Evolution: An Analysis," *American Journal of Sociology* 85 (1979): 288–309; Christoph Lau, *Gesellschaftliche Evolution als kollektiver Lernprozeß* (Berlin, 1981). A review of this literature shows that the specification possibilities offered by systems theory are not used.

85. Here we also encounter a much more general concept of evolution in terms of the explanation of synergetic effects, dissipative structures, etc.—in short, of very general processes of difference formation (deviation amplification) that can also be demonstrated in physical (i.e., non-autopoietic) systems—which should

be noted at least in passing. This is not to deny that such a theory could also be applied to social systems; but it is not specific enough for the purpose.

86. As far as I can see, this applies without exception to the nineteenth century, and still to Keller, *Societal Evolution*, 67ff., where we read: "The agent of variation is the individual" (68). Even evolutionary epistemology, which had developed at an early stage, asserts the chance inspiration of certain researchers. See, e.g., William James, "Great Man, Great Thought and the Environment," *Atlantic Monthly* 46 (1888), 441–459, or Georg Simmel, "Über einige Beziehungen der Selektionslehre zur Erkenntnistheorie," *Archiv für systematische Philosophie* 1 (1895): 34–45 ("among the innumerable, psychologically arising ideas are some that . . ." [39]). Even then, as noted above (p. 263), this explanation of variation contradicted the collective individualism of the population concept.

87. See just Uwe Schimank, "Der mangelnde Akteursbezug systemtheoretischer Erklärungen gesellschaftlicher Differenzierung—Ein Diskussionsvorschlag," *Zeitschrift für Soziologie* 14 (1985): 421–434; Michael Schmid, "Autopoiesis und soziales System: Eine Standortbestimmung," in *Sinn, Kommunikation und soziale Differenzierung: Beiträge zu Luhmanns Theorie sozialer Systeme*, ed. id. and Hans Haferkamp (Frankfurt, 1987), 25–50 (41–42); id., "Soziologische Evolutionstheorie," *Protosoziologie* 7 (1995): 200–210. Recourse to individuals now no longer indicates a determinable empirical reality but serves only to present action as a variable. "Action must be conceived of as changeable so that actors can become the vehicles of variation," we read in the reverse perspective in Schmid, "Soziologische Evolutionstheorie," 201.

88. For a brief overview, see Ernst Mayr, *Evolution und die Vielfalt des Lebens* (Berlin, 1979), 47ff. The testing and harmonization required are also often called "selection," but then not in a strictly evolution-theoretical sense of the term. See, e.g., Lancelot L. White, *Internal Factors in Evolution* (London, 1965), or Manfred Eigen, "Selforganization of Matter and the Evolution of Biological Macromolecules," *Die Naturwissenschaften* 58 (1971): 465–523. The effect of this preselection in trying out variations is above all that evolutionary selection is itself curtailed and accelerated.

89. See inter alia Josef Schumpeter, *Kapitalismus, Sozialismus und Demokratie* (Bern, 1946), 47ff.; Theodor Geiger, *Aufgaben und Stellung der Intelligenz in der Gesellschaft* (Stuttgart, 1949).

90. This is recalled, albeit not in an evolution-theoretical but a "political" context, by Helmut Schelsky, *Die Arbeit tun die anderen: Klassenkampf und Priesterherrschaft der Intellektuellen* (Opladen, 1975).

91. See particularly the important contribution by Jan Mukařovský, "Das Individuum und die literarische Evolution," in id., *Kunst, Poetik, Semiotik*, German trans., (Frankfurt, 1989), 213–237.

92. More detailed treatment in chap. 2, § 3, in this volume.

93. Spencer-Brown's calculus of forms in *Laws* requires only this operation of

differentiating distinction; for this reason, it is not a logic but a mathematical theory. To generate the form of a positive/negative distinction, much more complex observational relations are necessary, which cannot yet be predicted at the outset.

94. Etymological references in Johannes Spörl, "Das Alte und das Neue im Mittelalter: Studien zum Problem des mittelalterlichen Fortschrittsbewußtseins," *Historisches Jahrbuch* 50 (1930): 297–341, 498–524. See also Walter Freund, *Modernus und andere Zeitbegriffe des Mittelalters* (Cologne, 1957).

95. For general treatment, see Niklas Luhmann, *Soziale Systeme: Grundriß einer allgemeinen Theorie* (Frankfurt, 1984), 488ff. The position adopted in the text is to be distinguished from the widespread view that structural contradictions give rise to variation of the system—be it in the manner prescribed by dialectics or as a "variety pool" with still indeterminate development possibilities. See inter alia Oskar Lange, *Wholes and Parts: A General Theory of System Behaviour* (Oxford, 1965), 1–2, 72ff.; Claude Lévi-Strauss, "La notion de structure en Ethnologie," in id., *Anthropologie structurale* (Paris, 1958), 303–351 (342ff.); Talcott Parsons, "Some Considerations on the Theory of Social Change," *Rural Sociology* 26 (1961)L 219–239; Walter Buckley, *Sociology and Modern Systems Theory* (Englewood Cliffs, NJ, 1967), esp. 50ff.; Jon Elster, *Logic and Society: Contradictions and Possible Worlds* (Chichester, UK, 1978). There are quite conceivably structural conditions that provide greater stimulus than others to reject communications. But the structure itself cannot be called "contradictory" in either a logical or dialogical sense. It is used or not used operationally to convey connections; and only an observer can construct contradictions in this context.

96. It is often claimed or assumed, however, that the opposite is true, that the coupling of variation and selection is characteristic of sociocultural evolution, and that this is where the "analogy" with biological evolution fails. See (although for the limited field of the evolution of science) L. Jonathan Cohen, "Is the Progress of Science Evolutionary?" *British Journal for the Philosophy of Science* 24 (1973): 41–61 (47–48); Stephen Toulmin, *Human Understanding*, vol. 1 (Princeton, NJ, 1972); Nicholas Rescher, *Methodological Pragmatism: A Systems-Theoretic Approach to the Theory of Knowledge* (Oxford, 1977). Only more precise analysis of communicative operations could settle this difference of opinion.

97. For a test of this thesis in the case of the invention of "constitutions" (initially impressive in their intention and method), see Niklas Luhmann, "Verfassung als evolutionäre Errungenschaft," *Rechtshistorisches Journal* (1990): 176–220.

98. To give an example, the problem was initially solved in ancient Greek law in the form of a trial against the law in force, i.e., in the form of second-order observation to settle the question whether the law was rightly or wrongly applied. See Polybius 12.16, and on late forms of an already routine treatment, Ulrich Kahrstedt, "Untersuchungen zu athenischen Behörden," *Klio* 31 (1938): 1–32 (19ff.); K. M. T. Atkinson, "Athenian Legislative Procedure and the Revision of Laws," *Bulletin of the John Rylands Library* 23, no. 1 (1939): 107–150; A. R. W. Har-

rison, "Law-Making at Athens at the End of Fifth Century B.C.," *Journal of Hellenic Studies* 75 (1955): 27–35; W. G. Forrest, "Legislation in Sparta," *Phoenix* 21 (1967): 11–19. Only very gradually, but at the latest in Aristotle *Rhetoric* 1354a32ff., the difference between legislation and the administration of justice was given a new function, namely, to ensure that the course of justice did not depend on class or cronyism. This was not the sense of the original variation, however, but arose from consideration of its effects.

99. I do not assume that this alone suffices to explain selection, in contrast to game-theoretic evolution theories, e.g., John Maynard Smith, *Evolution and the Theory of Games* (Cambridge, 1982).

100. Of an abundant literature on segmentary societies, see, e.g., H. Ian Hogbin, "Social Reaction to Crime: Law and Morals in the Schouten Islands, New Guinea," *Journal of the Royal Anthropological Institute* 68 (1938): 223–262; Alfred R. Radcliffe-Brown, "On Joking Relationships," *Africa* 13 (1940): 195–210; Max Gluckman, *Custom and Conflict in Africa* (Oxford, 1955); George M. Foster, "Interpersonal Relations in Peasant Society," *Human Organization* 19 (1960): 3–15; Asen Abalikai, "Quarrels in a Balkan Village," *American Anthropologist* 67 (1965): 1456–1469; Sally F. Moore, "Legal Liability and Evolutionary Interpretation: Some Aspects of Strict Liability, Self-Help and Collective Responsibility," in *The Allocation of Responsibility*, ed. Max Gluckman (Manchester, 1972), 51–107.

101. For an example from a copious literature, see Kenelm O. L. Burridge, "Disputing in Tangu," *American Anthropologist* 59 (1957): 763–780.

102. See esp. Mary Douglas, *Purity and Danger: An Analysis of the Concept of Pollution and Taboo* (London, 1966), 111ff.

103. For the solutions found in Mesopotamia, see M. David, *Les dieux et le destin en Babylonie* (Paris, 1949); John G. Gunnell, *Political Philosophy and Time* (Middletown, CT, 1968), esp. 39ff.

104. See n. 5 above.

105. It must be admitted this is still difficult in face-to-face interaction. Apart from avoiding interaction, technical precautions can under certain circumstances provide a solution. A person who rolls his own cigarettes is safer from sponging than someone who pulls them out of a pack.

106. See further Luhmann, *Gesellschaft*, vol. 2, chap. 4, § 7.

107. A case where the evolutionary emergence of autopoietic systems discussed on p. 77 above applies.

108. See Euripides *Suppliant Women*, trans. Rosanna Warren and Stephen Scully (Oxford, 1995), 37.

109. Under present-day conditions, this need not mean serving the interests of the upper class, as the "critical legal studies" movement in the United States assumes. See also Austin Turk, "Law as a Weapon in Social Conflict," *Social Problems* 23 (1976): 276–291. On the other hand, it is not untypical, especially in the countries of peripheral modernity, for members of the lower classes to be found

in the role of defendant and members of the upper class in that of plaintiff. On arrangements for civil-law proceedings in Mexico, see Volkmar Gessner, *Recht und Konflikt: Eine soziologische Untersuchung privatrechtlicher Konflikte in Mexiko* (Tübingen, 1976), esp. 100.

110. For a case study on the organizational level, see Alvin Gouldner, *Patterns of Industrial Bureaucracy* (Glencoe, IL, 1954), and id., *Wildcat Strike* (Yellow Springs, OH, 1954). See also Eligio Resta, *Conflitti sociali e giustizia* (Bari, 1977).

111. Systems that are "too small" from this point of view—whether families or organizations—are now subjected to "systems therapy," which attempts to rearrange their conflicts.

112. This can be discussed from widely differing points of view—e.g., with regard to the increase in undecidable controversies and the associated increase in consistency constraints in argumentation; or with regard to voluntarism with its contingency problems (Duns Scotus, William of Ockham); or with the aid of the so-called *via negationis* of proofs of the existence of God; or in relation to the dissolution of notions of perfection through the concept of actual infinity. We must be content with these pointers.

113. The somewhat unusual term "limitationality" is intended to indicate that limited possibilities must be assumed if we wish to claim that the determination of truths or untruths reduces and not (for which there is some indication) enlarges the range of questions still to be examined. Only under this premise does it make sense, e.g., to demand the "falsifiability" of hypotheses.

114. The radical change took place in the seventeenth century, when although the old prohibition of innovations was maintained for religion and politics, a positive evaluation of novelty asserted itself for everything that was intended to "please." As François de Grenaille, *La mode, ou Charactère de la religion, de la vie, de la conversation, de la solitude, des compliments, des habits et du style du temps* (Paris, 1642), 5, describes the dilemma: "Si la durée fait subsister toutes les parties du monde, la nouveauté les faict estimer." On the corresponding upgrading of "surprise" in the seventeenth and eighteenth centuries from [Antoine Gombaud] Méré [1607–1684] (with doubts) to Dominique Bouhours [1628–1702] and Montesquieu, see Erich Köhler, *Esprit und arkadische Freiheit: Aufsätze aus der Welt der Romania* (Frankfurt, 1966), 267–268. For more detail, see Luhmann, *Gesellschaft*, vol. 2, chap. 5, § 12.

115. This, at any rate, was what interested Henry Adams: "He felt, like nine men in ten, an instinctive belief in Evolution, but he felt no more concern in Natural than in unnatural Selection" (*The Education of Henry Adams* [1907; Boston, 1918], 225).

116. It goes without saying that this is a theoretical abstraction.

117. Talcott Parsons, *Societies: Evolutionary and Comparative Perspectives* (Englewood Cliffs, NJ, 1966), 42.

118. It has already been noted in connection with introduction of the concept of symbolically generalized media (chap. 2, § 9) that this typically happens in the

case of historically contingent acceptance of meaning proposals but not in the case of their rejection.

119. Still, this possibility is likely to have gained greater probability from the fact that the mass media tend to report on deviations, establishing a precondition for deviations to be perceived as normal. This may well facilitate their institutionalization.

120. It is now undisputed in biology, too, that there are many selection-neutral mutations (which biologists often regard as deviating from Darwinian theory patterns). See, e.g., Jack Lester King and Thomas H. Jukes, "Non-Darwinian Evolution," *Science* 164 (1969): 788–798.

121. I have spoken on p. 260 above of "forward induction."

122. See n. 96 above.

123. Foremost among the authors to have associated this procedure with a second cybernetics of positive feedback is Magoroh Maruyama, who states clearly: "A small initial deviation, which is within the range of high probability, may develop into a large deviation of low probability (or more precisely into a large deviation which is very improbable within the framework of probabilistic unidirectional causality" (id., "Toward Cultural Symbiosis," in *Evolution and Consciousness: Human Systems in Transition*, ed. Erich Jantsch and Conrad C. Waddington [Reading, MA, 1976], 198–213 [203]).

124. Consider in comparison the cell as environment of (possible mutated) genes; here, too, it is acknowledged that evolution assumes a direction only thanks to regulation of this relationship. See Ernst Mayr, "Selektion und gerichtete Evolution," *Die Naturwissenschaften* 52 (1965): 173–180.

125. For a more detailed presentation of this form of differentiation, see Luhmann, *Gesellschaft*, vol. 2, chap. 4, § 13.

126. See (taking the example of metallurgy) Colin Renfrew, *The Emergence of Civilization: The Cyclades and the Aegean in the Third Millenium B.C.* (London, 1972), 28, 36ff.: "Innovations occur all the time in any society: new ideas which crop up rather haphazardly, rather like mutations in the organic world. They are not individually predictable. But what is crucial is the response to these innovations. If the innovation is rejected, there is no effective change. But if accepted it can be further modified. . . . Changes or innovations occurring in one field of human activity (in one subsystem of a culture) sometimes act so as to favour changes in other fields (in other subsystems). The multiplier effect is said to operate when these induced changes in one or more subsystems act so as to enhance the original changes in the first subsystem" (28, 37). What factors discriminate in precisely this regard can be discovered only by concrete analysis of specific states of affairs.

127. See Jan Assmann, *Das kulturelle Gedächtnis: Schrift, Erinnerung und politische Identität in frühen Hochkulturen* (Munich, 1992).

128. Georg Wilhelm Friedrich Hegel, *Vorlesungen über die Ästhetik* (Frankfurt, 1970), 1: 215.

129. For details, see Niklas Luhmann, *Liebe als Passion: Zur Codierung von Intimität* (Frankfurt, 1982).

130. See Gabriel Naudé, *Considérations politiques sur les coups d'Etat* (1639), cited from *Science des princes, ou Considérations sur les coups d'état*, 3 vols. (Paris, 1712).

131. See the distinction between cumulative and noncumulative areas of societal change in Eric R. Wolf, "The Study of Evolution," in *Readings in Social Evolution and Development*, ed. Shmuel N. Eisenstadt (Oxford, 1970), 179–191 (187ff.). The cumulative area is equated with that determined by technology.

132. The state *is* peace, nothing other than "una identità e pace temporale delle cose; cioè un esser sempre la stessa essenza," and its perfection consists precisely in this, according to Giovanni Antonio Palazzo, *Discorso del governo e della ragion vera di Stato* (Venice, 1606), 12–13.

133. See Donald T. Campbell, "Blind Variation and Selective Retention in Creative Thought as in Other Knowledge Processes," *Psychological Review* 67 (1960): 380–400; id., "Variation and Selective Retention in Socio-Cultural Evolution," *General Systems* 14 (1969): 69–85; Michael Schmid, *Theorie sozialen Wandels* (Opladen, 1982), 137.

134. It is at least still considered necessary to reject it. See, e.g., Michael T. Hannan and John Freeman, *Organizational Ecology* (Cambridge, MA, 1989), 21–22.

135. See Warren G. Bennis and Phillip E. Slater, *The Temporary Society* (New York, 1968).

136. See, e.g., Thomas G. Harding, "Adaptation and Stability," in *Evolution and Culture*, ed. Marshall D. Sahlins and Elman R. Service (Ann Arbor, MI, 1960), 45–68.

137. In more detail, see Keller, *Societal Evolution*, 287ff., and in more modern terms Robert Boyd and Peter J. Richerson, *Culture and the Evolutionary Process* (Chicago, 1987).

138. On this distinction (but not on the evolution-theoretical basis), see Karl Mannheim, *Konservativismus: Ein Beitrag zur Soziologie des Wissens*, ed. David Kettler, Volker Meja, and Nico Stehr (Frankfurt, 1984).

139. If we look for an explanation in the history of science, it might be that the dispute about evolution theory has long been fought out on the wrong fronts, for example, structure versus process, static versus dynamic, structural fundamentalist theories versus theories of social change; or that the theory of structural contradictions was regarded by class theoreticians as a "conservative" attempt to avoid or at least tone down the only relevant topic, class war. This is hardly now of any interest.

140. Richard Levins, *Evolution in Changing Environments: Some Theoretical Explorations* (Princeton, NJ, 1968), 108–109, writes of evolution as "progressive binding."

141. On a recent discussion of this subject, see Tom Baumgartner and Tom R. Burns, "Inflation as the Institutionalized Struggle over Income Distribution," *Acta Sociologica* 23 (1980): 177–186.

142. With the stress on functional differentiation, I advance a theory also common in biology: that diversity enhances the chance and frequency of variation.

143. See further Luhmann, *Gesellschaft*, vol. 2, chap. 4.

144. For universities, see Rudolf Stichweh, *Der frühmoderne Staat und die europäische Universität: Zur Interaktion von Politik und Erziehungssystem im Prozeß ihrer Ausdifferenzierung (16.–18. Jahrhundert)* (Frankfurt, 1991); for monasteries, Alfred Kieser, "From Ascetism to Administration of Wealth: Medieval Monasteries and the Pitfalls of Rationalization," *Organization Studies* 8 (1987): 103–123; for craft guilds, Alfred Kieser, "Organizational, Institutional, and Societal Evolution: Medieval Craft Guilds and the Genesis of Formal Organizations," *Administrative Science Quarterly* 34 (1989): 540–564.

145. A similar thought is to be found in Michael Fullan and Jan J. Loubser, "Education and Adaptive Capacity," *Sociology of Education* 45 (1972): 271–287 (281–282).

146. Edward A. Ross, *Sin and Society: An Analysis of Latter-Day Iniquity* (Boston, 1907), 40.

147. I am paraphrasing Maruyama, "Toward Cultural Symbiosis."

148. See further Luhmann, *Gesellschaft*, vol. 2, chap. 4, § 14.

149. See Karl E. Weick, *Sensemaking in Organizations* (Thousand Oaks, CA, 1995).

150. See § 11 in this chapter.

151. The relation of evolution theory to dialectic, and thus to Hegel's theory of history, requires more thoroughgoing examination. It should be mentioned that the concept of form marks a distinction and thus shows the connection between the two sides of the distinction to be necessary. Selection therefore necessarily succeeds variation, restabilization necessarily succeeds selection. But this does not mean that a corresponding *process* is necessary. Nor does it mean that within this process only distinctions that are constituted as an "opposition" induce motion. These premises are tenable only if we postulate something like "mind" that from a higher (later) position can put something merely existing into the form of a "lack" in order to cure this lack in itself.

152. That evolution causes evolution is now widely recognized. See, e.g., Erich Jantsch, *The Self-Organizing Universe: Scientific and Human Implications of the Emerging Paradigm of Evolution* (Oxford, 1980), esp. 217ff. This is to be distinguished from self-reference at the theory level, which means that insights into evolution can bring evolution *theory* to understand itself as the result of evolution. On this "autological" element in an evolution theory with a claim to universality, see Löfgren, "Knowledge of Evolution and Evolution of Knowledge." Reason, however, judges such circularity with severity, because it has to defend its own historical privilege of self-justification. See Hans-Michael Baumgartner, "Über die Widerspenstigkeit der Vernunft, sich aus der Geschichte erklären zu lassen: Zur Kritik des Selbstverständnisses der evolutionären Erkenntnistheorie," in *Wandel des Vernunftbegriffs*, ed. Hans Poser (Munich, 1981), 39–64; id., "Die in-

nere Unmöglichkeit einer evolutionären Erklärung der menschlichen Vernunft," in *Evolutionstheorie und menschliches Selbstverständnis*, ed. Robert Spaemann, Peter Koslowski, and Reinhard Löw (Weinheim, 1984), 55–71.

153. See Stebbins, *Basis of Progressive Evolution*, , 117: "The hypothesis that living systems have evolved in the manner just outlined carries with it the corollary that the ability to evolve by means of mutation and genetic recombination, guided by natural selection, must have itself evolved gradually from the ability to change only by frequent and irregular chemical reactions."

154. See Jean-Baptiste Pierre Antoine de Monet de Lamarck, *Philosophie zoologique* (1809; repr., Weinheim, 1960).

155. Ibid., 1: 82ff.

156. I add "it would appear," because we cannot be quite sure whether genetics has said the last word on this subject.

157. See *Revue internationale de systémique* 7, no. 5 (1993).

158. The literature offers a multitude of expressions with similar meaning. Drawing on linguistic usage in paleontology and biology, *Evolution and Culture*, ed. Sahlins and Service, 25, 69ff. speaks of "adaptive advances" or "dominant types." Talcott Parsons speaks of "evolutionary universals"; see esp. Parsons, "Evolutionary Universals in Society," *American Sociological Review* 29 (1964): 339–357, repr. in id., *Sociological Theory and Modern Society* (New York, 1967), 490–520. In James S. Coleman, "Social Inventions," *Social Forces* 49 (1970): 163–173, we find "social inventions." In all cases, it is a question of advantages that are based on restrictions.

159. As we have seen, this distinguishes theories of evolution from theories of progress.

160. The latter double possibility, in relation to the environment, defines the concept of "dominant type" in Julian S. Huxley, *Evolution: The Modern Synthesis* (1942; 2nd ed., London, 1963).

161. This insight goes back to Alexander A. Goldenweiser, "The Principle of Limited Possibilities in the Development of Culture," *Journal of American Folk-Lore* 26 (1913): 259–290.

162. See the chapter on "The Survival of the Mediocre" in Hallpike, *Principles of Social Evolution*, 81ff.

163. And often even simple technical inventions have to be improved. That the commercial success of the railroad was to be achieved only by opening it up to passenger traffic, and that of the telephone only by developing it into a means of two-way communication, making it possible to speak and listen with the same apparatus, was seen only some time after the inventions had been made.

164. Alfred S. Romer, *The Vertebrate Story* (Chicago, 1959), 93–94, illustrates this procedure (called Romer's principle) with reference to lungfish, which, where flooding conditions are changeable, have to return to the water across dry stretches of land, thus gradually qualifying themselves for life on land.

165. See 157f. in this volume.

166. Fritz Heichelheim, "Die Ausbreitung der Münzgeldwirtschaft und der Wirtschaftsstil im archaischen Griechenland," *Schmollers Jahrbuch* 55 (1931): 229–254 (238), speaks of an "abrupt" spread once the minting of small-denomination coins of guaranteed value had begun. See also Michael Hutter, "Communication in Economic Evolution: The Case of Money," in *Evolutionary Concepts in Contemporary Economics*, ed. Richard W. England (Ann Arbor, MI, 1994), 111–136.

167. See Ernst Mayr, "The Emergence of Evolutionary Novelties," in *Evolution After Darwin*, ed. Sol Tax, vol. 1 (Chicago, 1960), 349–380. Gerhard Vollmer, "Die Unvollständigkeit der Evolutionstheorie," in id., *Was können wir wissen?* vol. 2 (Stuttgart, 1986), 1–38, 24ff., speaks of "double functions" (indispensable for evolution).

168. This formulation in Stephen Jay Gould, "Darwinism and the Expansion of Evolutionary Theory," *Science* 216 (1982): 380–387 (383).

169. According to Robert MacAdams, *The Evolution of Urban Society: Early Mesopotamia and Prehispanic Mexico* (London, 1966), 41. On the origin of the concept, see L. Cuénot, *L'adaptation* (Paris, 1925).

170. In the case of China and comparison with England (the same generally applies for Europe in the early Middle Ages), see Hosea Ballou Morse, *The Gilds of China: With an Account of the Gild Merchant or Co-hong of Canton* (London, 1909).

171. J. B. S. Haldane, *The Causes of Evolution* (New York, 1932), 153, quoted from George G. Simpson, "The Concept of Progress in Organic Evolution," *Social Research* 41 (1974): 28–51 (46).

172. See *The Invention of Tradition*, ed. Eric Hobsbawn and Terence Ranger (Cambridge, 1983).

173. See Goldenweiser, "Principle of Limited Possibilities"; Pitirim A. Sorokin, *Social and Cultural Dynamics*, vol. 4 (New York, 1941), 76ff. In biological evolution theory, we find a similar discussion of the extent to which a phenotype already achieved limits the possibilities of further variation (law of homologous variation).

174. On the concept of equifinality, see, e.g., on older biological bases, Ludwig von Bertalanffy, "Zu einer allgemeinen Systemlehre," *Biologia Generalis* 19 (1949): 114–129 (123ff.); id., *Problems of Life* (New York, 1960), 142. The same thought is already to be found in Emile Boutroux, *De la contingence des lois de nature* (8th ed., Paris, 1915), 13. See also W. Ross Ashby, "The Effect of Experience on a Determinate Dynamic System," *Behavioral Science* 1 (1956): 35–42. Talcott Parsons, too, builds it into his concept of evolutionary universals in a double evolutionary and structural sense: "I shall designate as an evolutionary universal any organizational development sufficiently important to further evolution that, rather than emerging only once, it is likely to be 'hit upon' by various systems operating under different conditions" (Parsons, *Sociological Theory and Modern Society*, 491).

175. See Christian Meier, *Die Entstehung des Politischen bei den Griechen* (Frankfurt, 1980), 57ff.

176. See, e.g., Wilhelm Berger, "Am Punkt der Vollendung: Technikphilosophie nach Martin Heidegger und Gotthard Günther," in *Gotthard Günther—Technik, Logik, Technologie*, ed. Ernst Kotzmann (Munich, 1994), 33–54 (33–34). Hans Jonas, *Das Prinzip Verantwortung: Versuch einer Ethik für die technologische Zivilisation* (Frankfurt, 1979), also speaks of "technological civilization," but nevertheless sees latitude in the society thus described for an ethically motivated countermovement.

177. See *The Social Construction of Technological Systems: New Directions in the Sociology and History of Technology*, ed. Wiebe E. Bijker, Thomas P. Hughes, and Trevor J. Pinch (Cambridge, MA, 1987). On the picture at the organizational (and personnel) level, see Henry Etzkowitz, "Academic-Industrial Relations: A Sociological Paradigm for Economic Development," in *Evolutionary Economics and Chaos Theory: New Directions in Technology Studies*, ed. Loet Leydesdorff and Peter van den Besselaar (London, 1994), 139–151.

178. Nathan Rosenberg, *Perspectives on Technology* (Cambridge, 1975), 5; in more detail, 260ff.

179. See Gerald Wagner, "Vertrauen in Technik," *Zeitschrift für Soziologie* 23 (1994): 145–157.

180. For an overview, see Friedrich Rapp, *Analytische Technikphilosophie* (Freiburg, 1978), 30ff.

181. Arnold Gehlen, *Die Seele im technischen Zeitalter* (Hamburg, 1957); Ernst Kapp, *Grundlinien einer Philosophie der Technik* (1877; Düsseldorf, 1978).

182. This also holds, and particularly so (but not only) for the modern tradition—largely saving us the search for a theoretically elaborated conceptuality. In Wolfgang Krohn, "Die Verschiedenheit der Technik und die Einheit der Techniksoziologie," in *Technik als sozialer Prozeß*, ed. Peter Weingart (Frankfurt, 1989), 15–43 (15), we read: "At the heart (of contemporary literature on technology, N.L.) is the concept of the artifact, which as tool, machine, or robot is the means for attaining non-technical goals."

183. See Wilfried Seibicke, *Technik: Versuch einer Geschichte der Wortfamilie um τέχνη in Deutschland vom 16. Jahrhundert bis etwa 1830* (Düsseldorf, 1968), 99ff. The current term *Technologie* in German is a loan from English "technology" and has nothing to do with this tradition. The clear conceptual contours of *Technologie* have thus also been lost. But we can perhaps say that *Technologie* has to do with the application of techniques to the production and utilization of energy.

184. See inter alia Manfred Mai, "Technikblindheit des Rechts—Technikignoranz der Juristen?" *Zeitschrift für Rechtssoziologie* 13 (1992): 257–270.

185. See, e.g., Hans Freyer, *Theorie des gegenwärtigen Zeitalters* (Stuttgart, 1955); id., *Gedanken zur Industriegesellschaft* (Mainz, 1970); Friedrich Georg Jünger, *Die Perfektion der Technik* (Frankfurt, 1953); Gehlen, *Die Seele im technischen Zeital-*

ter; Helmut Schelsky, *Der Mensch in der wissenschaftlichen Zivilisation* (Opladen, 1961); Martin Heidegger, *Die Technik und die Kehre* (Pfullingen, 1962).

186. For a succinct overview, see Bernward Joerges, "Soziologie und Maschinerie—Vorschläge zu einer 'realistischen' Techniksoziologie," in *Technik als sozialer Prozeß*, ed. Peter Weingart (Frankfurt, 1989), 44–89 (esp. 48ff. on Weber, Marx, Sombart, and Freyer).

187. See Herbert Breger, *Die Natur als arbeitende Maschine: Zur Entstehung des Energiebegriffs in der Physik, 1840–1850* (Frankfurt, 1982). In addition, the relation between energy and economics would have to be considered, which is of fundamental importance, e.g., for Freud's theory of a psychic energy budget.

188. There is naturally no denying that the distinction continues to makes sense in the everyday world. A farmer who decided to plant one of his fields with jacket potatoes would be making a category error.

189. *The Education of Henry Adams: An Autobiography* (Boston, 1918), 339–340.

190. In addition to *Social Construction of Technological Systems*, ed. Bijker et al., see also Alain Gras, *Grandeur et dépendance: Sociologie des macro-systèmes techniques* (Paris, 1993).

191. One way of addressing this issue today is under the cautionary heading of "chaos." Technical performance and mathematical calculations inevitably involve imprecision, which in the long term generates deviations from the envisaged course.

192. It is also obvious how very much technological development depends on market development, i.e., on an environment in which we can buy everything we need and therefore have it at our disposition (if not in stock).

193. See also Niklas Luhmann, "Technology, Environment and Social Risk: A Systems Perspective," *Industrial Crisis Quarterly* 4 (1990); 223–231.

194. See chap. 1, § 9.

195. See, e.g., Robert B. Glassman, "Persistence and Loose Coupling in Living Systems," *Behavioral Science* 18 (1973): 83–98. The same applies for social systems and even for organizations. See also Karl E. Weick, *The Social Psychology of Organizing* (Reading, MA, 1969), trans. under the title *Der Prozeß des Organisierens* (Frankfurt, 1985), esp. 163ff.; id., "Management of Organizational Change Among Loosely Coupled Elements," in *Change in Organizations: New Perspectives on Theory, Research, and Practice*, ed. Paul S. Goodman et al. (San Francisco, 1982), 375–408. Older cybernetics (e.g., W. Ross Ashby) spoke of "ultrastability."

196. From quite different, network theoretical and social-constructivist perspectives, see also John Law, "Technology and Heterogeneous Engineering: The Case of Portuguese Expansion," in *Social Construction of Technological Systems*, ed. Bijker et al., 111–134 (131): "'nature' reveals its obduracy in a way that is relevant only to the network when it is registered by the system builders."

197. Perhaps in the sense of time-space distantiation—a concept that Anthony Giddens likes to use, albeit only to characterize modernity; see id., *The Consequences of Modernity* (Stanford, CA, 1990), esp. 14–15, 17ff.

198. It will be recalled that one can, of course, eliminate the resulting similarities by means of added distinctions (in this case, communications media).

199. Not necessarily, it must be conceded, when we compare the wealth of ideas produced by Greek intellectuals, mathematicians, and philosophers with their very limited technical realization (architecture, theater building, the tunnel of Eupalinos [on Samos], military machines, sometimes with forms of calculation that are now unknown).

200. Usually, we speak not of signs but of symbols. Basically, neither term is suitable if we stick to their traditional meanings. This, too, shows the extent of the change. Perhaps we should speak of forms.

201. Karl E. Weick writes that "obtrusive controls require more observables than are ordinarily present with new technologies" (id., "Technology as Equivoque: Sensemaking in New Technologies," in *Technology and Organizations*, ed. Paul S. Goodman and Lee S. Sproull et al. [San Francisco, 1990], 1–44 [34]).

202. Norman Clark and Calestous Juma, *Long-Run Economics: An Evolutionary Approach to Economic Growth* (New York, 1987), e.g., use the concepts of innovation and technological change synonymously.

203. See, e.g., Kurt Klagenfurt, *Technologische Zivilisation und transklassische Logik: Eine Einführung in die Technikphilosophie Gotthard Günthers* (Frankfurt, 1995), 19 ("technologische Zivilisation"). See also *Gotthard Günther—Technik, Logik, Technologie*, esp. 33–34.

204. Claus Offe, "Die Utopie der Null-Option: Modernität und Modernisierung als politische Gütekriterien," in *Die Moderne—Kontinuität und Zäsuren*, ed. Johannes Berger, *Sozialen Welt*, special issue no. 4 (1986): 97–117 (104).

205. Although not under this name, which came into fashion only in the nineteenth century. See *Solidarität*, ed. Giuseppe Orsi et al., Rechtsphilosophische Hefte, 4 (Frankfurt, 1995). In the old European semantics, *philia*/*amicitia*.

206. On the danger/risk distinction, see detailed treatment in Niklas Luhmann, "Risiko und Gefahr," in id., *Aufklärung* 5: 131–169; id., *Soziologie des Risikos* (Berlin, 1991), esp. 9ff. See also Klaus Peter Japp, *Soziologische Risikotheorie: Funktionale Differenzierung, Politisierung und Reflexion* (Weinheim, 1996), 61ff.

207. See (still in the sense of larger regional complexes) James D. Thompson, "Technology, Polity, and Societal Development," *Administrative Science Quarterly* 19 (1974): 6–21.

208. This question had already been discussed in the nineteenth century. See W. Stanley Jevons, *The Coal Question: An Inquiry Concerning the Progress of the Nation, and the Probable Exhaustion of Our Coal-Mines* (1865; 3rd ed., 1906, repr., New York, 1965), esp. 158ff.

209. The preconditions and limits to economic analysis are shown in Richard L. Gordon, *An Economic Analysis of World Energy Problems* (Cambridge, MA, 1981).

210. Such problems of co-evolution are examined on the basis of concrete case studies in Luhmann, *Gesellschaftsstruktur*.

211. It should be made clear that it is *not* a matter of the general importance of "culture" for societal evolution. I have already stated my position on p. 248 above. Nor is it a matter of the development of cultural artifacts per se, for example, markings that we would today call styles. On this subject (using the term "evolution," but without evolution-theoretical apparatus), see esp. Margaret W. Conkey, "Style and Information in Cultural Evolution: Toward a Predictive Model of the Paleolithic," in *Social Archeology: Beyond Subsistence and Dating*, ed. Charles L. Redman et al. (New York, 1978), 61–85.

212. Nineteenth-century writers spoke rather of "cultural evolution" and distinguished this from the evolution of populations; see, e.g., Edward B. Tyler, *Primitive Culture*, 2 vols. (London, 1871).

213. See Heinz von Foerster, "Das Gleichnis vom blinden Fleck: Über das Sehen im allgemeinen," in *Der entfesselte Blick: Symposion, Workshops, Ausstellung*, ed. Gerhard Johann Lischka (Bern, 1993), 14–47.

214. See Niklas Luhmann, "Wie lassen sich latente Strukturen beobachten?" in *Das Auge des Betrachters—Beiträge zum Konstruktivismus: Festschrift Heinz von Foerster*, ed. Paul Watzlawick and Peter Krieg (Munich, 1991), 61–74.

215. For an example, see Luhmann, *Liebe als Passion.*

216. A good case study on this is Aldo Schiavone, *Nacita della Giurisprudenza: Cultura aristocratica e pensiero giuridico nella Roma tardo-repubblicana* (Bari, 1976).

217. See the chapter on "seed-bed" societies in Talcott Parsons, *Societies: Evolutionary and Comparative Perspectives* (Englewood Cliffs, NJ, 1966), 95ff.

218. A brilliant presentation of this problem is to be found in the "condensed description" of a burial ritual and its disturbance by ideas in Clifford Geertz, *The Interpretation of Cultures: Selected Essays* (New York, 1973), trans. under the title *Dichte Beschreibung: Beiträge zum Verstehen kultureller Systeme* (Frankfurt, 1983), 96ff. Another example: the embarrassment the philosopher causes the singer in Plato's *Ion*, who still seeks to represent a shaman culture based on emotion, possession, rapture. Remarkably, it is the philosopher who takes a skeptical view of written culture. See also Heinz Schlaffer, *Poesie und Wissen: Die Entstehung des ästhetischen Bewußtseins und der philosophischen Erkenntnis* (Frankfurt, 1990).

219. For important research on this, see Walter J. Ong, *The Presence of the Word: Some Prolegomena for Cultural and Religious History* (New Haven, CT, 1967); id., "Communications Media and the State of Theology," *Cross Currents* 19 (1969): 462–480; id., *Interfaces of the Word: Studies in the Evolution of Consciousness and Culture* (Ithaca, NY, 1977); id., *Orality and Literacy: The Technologizing of the Word* (London, 1982). See also chap. 2, § 5, in this volume.

220. Parsons, *Societies* , 51–52, speaks of "craft literacy." On the societal role of the "scribe" in Mesopotamia, see also Jonker, *Topography of Remembrance*: they gradually take on the cultivation of the social memory and thus regulate the relation between remembering and forgetting.

221. Shmuel Noah Eisenstadt has pointed this out on more than one occa-

sion; see, e.g., id., "Social Division of Labor, Construction of Centers and Institutional Dynamics: A Reassessment of the Structural-Evolutionary Perspective," *Protosoziologie* 7 (1995): 11–22 (16–17).

222. See Joan Marie Lechner, *The Renaissance Concepts of the Commonplaces: An Historical Investigation of the General and Universal Ideas Used in All Argumentation and Persuasion* (1962; repr. Westport, CT, 1974); Ong, *Presence of the Word*, 79ff.

223. Such doubts are already apparent—e.g., in William of Ockham—before the advent of the printing press. In the sixteenth century, they then develop into the literary form of the paradox, i.e., the undissolved unity of opposing views. On this prehistory of the Renaissance love of paradox, see A. E. Malloch, "The Technique and Function of the Renaissance Paradox," *Studies in Philology* 53 (1956): 191–203.

224. On this background to what was in its time the very impressive "dialectic" of Petrus Ramus, see Walter J. Ong, *Ramus: Method, and the Decay of Dialogue: From the Art of Discourse to the Art of Reason* (Cambridge, MA, 1958). In substance, it is about a method for sequencing binary distinctions, which needs to be looked at more closely, especially today.

225. See esp. the tracts on various subjects by Bartholomäus Keckermann in id., *Opera omnia* (Geneva, 1614).

226. See Robert Black, "Ancients and Moderns: Rhetoric and History in Accolti's *Dialogue* on the Preeminence of Men of His Own Time," *Journal of the History of Ideas* 43 (1982): 3–32, and, more comprehensively, also Elisabeth Gössmann, *Antiqui und Moderni im Mittelalter: Eine geschichtliche Standortbestimmung* (Munich, 1974).

227. On this much discussed turn, see, e.g., Richard F. Jones, *Ancients and Moderns: A Study of the Rise of the Scientific Movement in Seventeenth-Century England* (1936; 2nd ed., St. Louis, 1961); Herschel Baker, *The Wars of Truth: Studies in the Decay of Christian Humanism in the Earlier Seventeenth-Century* (1952; repr., Gloucester, MA, 1969), esp. 79ff.

228. This argument is typical of Quentin Skinner and his school. On methodology, see Quentin Skinner, "Meaning and Understanding in the History of Ideas," *History and Theory* 8 (1969): 3–53; id., "Motives, Intentions and the Interpretation of Texts," *New Literary History* 3 (1972): 393–408; also, e.g., James Farr, "Conceptual Change and Constitutional Innovation," in *Conceptual Change and the Constitution*, ed. Terence Ball and J. G. A. Pocock (Lawrence, KS, 1988), 13–34; id., "Understanding Conceptual Change Politically," in *Political Innovation and Conceptual Change*, ed. Terence Ball, James Farr, and Russell L. Hanson (Cambridge, 1989), 24–49.

229. See Niklas Luhmann, "Verfassung als evolutionäre Errungenschaft," *Rechtshistorisches Journal* 9 (1990): 176–220.

230. For more detail, see in this volume chap. 2, § 5, and Luhmann, *Gesellschaft*, vol. 2, chap. 6.

231. It is noteworthy, moreover, how long this was overlooked, and how regularly the reader was addressed and called upon to express himself, even, indeed particularly, in the first hundred years following the invention of printing. That this expectation was retained even as late as the eighteenth century in the concept of "public opinion" is striking proof of the radical nature of the change, which eluded attention because of the persistence of expectations applicable strictly to oral communication in interactive situations.

232. Participation in modern (i.e., American) journals' anonymous peer review system provides a good test; reviewers occasionally (but rarely) guess an author correctly, almost always based on chance knowledge.

233. Studies in the history of concepts have examined only "evidence," but it is probably not necessary to point out that light and vision imagery and hence traditional epistemology have played a role. See W. Halbfaß, "Evidenz," in *Historisches Wörterbuch der Philosophie*, vol. 2 (Stuttgart, 1972), cols. 829–834.

234. See p. 61 in this volume.

235. This is, incidentally, one of the reasons why a Paul de Man's text-linguistic deconstructivism presents itself as "rhetoric." For this means open to autology.

236. On this stylistic theme, already discussed at the time, see Louis van Delft, *Le moraliste classique: Essai de définition et de typologie* (Geneva, 1982), 235ff.; Niklas Luhmann, "Ethik als Reflexionstheorie der Moral," in id., *Gesellschaftsstruktur*, 3: 358–447 (390ff.).

237. See, e.g., Claude Buffier, *Traité des premières véritéz et de la source de nos jugemens* (Paris, 1724); Thomas Reid, *An Inquiry into the Human Mind* and *Essays on the Intellectual Powers of Man*, in id., *Philosophical Works* (8th ed., 1895, repr., Hildesheim, 1967), 2: 742–803. Also the fashionably long-winded Jean-Baptiste de Boyer, marquis d'Argens, *La philosophie du bon-sens, ou Réflexions philosophiques sur l'incertitude des connoissances humaines*, 3 vols. (1737; The Hague, 1768).

238. See Jean-Baptiste Morvan de Bellegarde, *Réflexions sur le ridicule, et les moyens de l'éviter, où sont représentez les moeurs et les différens caractères des personnes de ce siècle* (1696; 4th ed., Paris 1699); Anthony Ashley Cooper, 3rd earl of Shaftesbury, *An Essay on the Freedom of Wit and Humour* (1709), in id., *Characteristicks of Men, Manners, Opinions, Times* (2nd ed., 1714; Farnborough, UK, 1968), 1: 57–150.

239. That this is not recalled in later linear historiography but has to be reconstituted for it is shown in numerous individual studies in *Kommunikation und Differenz: Systemtheoretische Ansätze in der Literatur- und Kunstwissenschaft*, ed. Henk de Berg and Matthias Prangel (Opladen, 1993).

240. See Kenneth Burke, *The Rhetoric of Religion: Studies in Logology* (1961; Berkeley, CA, 1970), epilogue.

241. Roman civil law handed down in the "digests" is remarkable in *both* regards. It builds on standard decisions, which can very well hold their own, but judgments often conclude with grandiloquent dictums or general explanatory phrases, which were then learned and handed down in the (oral) training system of the Mid-

dle Ages. This gave rise to new consistency concerns, which kept legists and decretists busy but had little to do with the simultaneous changes in legal practice. For material, see, e.g., Rudolf Weigand, *Die Naturrechtslehre der Legisten und Dekretisten von Irnerius bis Accursius und von Gratian bis Johannes Teutonicus* (Munich, 1967).

242. See Jack Goody, "Literacy, Criticism, and the Growth of Knowledge," in *Culture and Its Creators: Essays in Honor of Edward Shils*, ed. Joseph Ben-David and Terry N. Clark (Chicago, 1977), 226–243 (esp. 234).

243. This takes place against the background of a revival of antique skepticism from the second half of the sixteenth century on. See Richard H. Popkin, *The History of Scepticism from Erasmus to Descartes* (2nd ed., New York, 1964), esp. on the dissolution of the distinction between dogma and skepticism by Hartley, Henry Home (Lord Kames), Condillac, and Condorcet, 153; Henry G. van Leeuwen, *The Problem of Certainty in English Thought* (2nd ed., The Hague, 1970). And see also important essays in Benjamin Nelson, *Der Ursprung der Moderne: Vergleichende Studien zum Zivilisationsprozeß* (Frankfurt, 1977).

244. An important contribution to this is a change in the opposing concept. Francis Bacon no longer distinguishes between dogma and skepticism (which leads to confirmation of dogma) but between dogma and experience (which leads to rejection of dogma): "Those who have handled sciences have been either men of experiment or men of dogmas" (Bacon, *Novum Organum* [1620] 1.95, in id., *Works,* vol. 4 [London, 1860], 92).

245. See Mario G. Losano, *Sistema e struttura nel diritto,* vol. 1 (Turin, 1968), 97ff.; Friedrich Kambartel, "'System' und 'Begründung' als wissenschaftliche und philosophische Ordnungsbegriffe bei und vor Kant," in *Philosophie und Rechtswissenschaft: Zum Problem ihrer Beziehungen im 19. Jahrhundert*, ed. Jürgen Blühdorn and Joachim Ritter (Frankfurt, 1969), 99–113. Only against this background can we comprehend that and how the system concept was reestablished, in the context of a new understanding of science, as construction of a manifold from a single perspective, esp. by Johann Heinrich Lambert (see id., *Texte zur Systematologie und zur Theorie der wissenschaftlichen Erkenntnis*, ed. Geo Siegwart [Hamburg, 1988]) and then with broader impact by Kant.

246. Shaftesbury, *Characteristicks*, 1: 290.

247. Distinguishing between social structure and terminology and their consequences would be helpful in resolving the much discussed question of whether the French Revolution changed anything or not (see, e.g., R. Reichardt and E. Schmitt, "Die Französische Revolution—Umbruch oder Kontinuität," *Zeitschrift für historische Forschung* 7 [1980]: 257–320).

248. On the development of such reflection theories, see further Luhmann, *Gesellschaft*, vol. 2, chap. 5, § 9.

249. See Bernhard Barbar, "Toward a New View of the Sociology of Knowledge," in *The Idea of Social Structure: Papers in Honor of Robert K. Merton*, ed. Lewis A. Coser (New York, 1975), 103–116.

250. On the concept of "distal knowledge" developed by Egon Brunswick, see Donald T. Campbell, "Natural Selection as an Epistemological Model," in *A Handbook of Method in Cultural Anthropology*, ed. Raoul Naroll and Ronald Cohen (Garden City, NY, 1970), 51–85.

251. See David Roberts, *Art and Enlightenment: Aesthetic Theory after Adorno* (Lincoln, NE, 1991).

252. On this, see esp. Stephen Holmes, *The Anatomy of Antiliberalism* (Cambridge, MA, 1993). However, the easy time one has of it with these figures is no proof that liberalism itself cannot be deconstructed, too—provided that we refrain from wanting to "overcome" it.

253. See Luhmann, *Gesellschaft*, vol. 2, chap. 5

254. As a precaution, I should note that this question would also have to be examined for stratified societies with regard to the possibility of the subsystem nobility evolving independently. Given the lack of adequate studies, I venture no judgment and, unlike in the case of some functional systems, cannot draw on research in progress.

255. See, e.g., Georg Simmel, "Über eine Beziehung der Selektionslehre zur Erkenntnistheorie," *Archiv für systematische Philosophie* 1 (1895): 34–45. Many scattered remarks by Charles S. Peirce also belong in this context, e.g., in "The Architecture of Theories" (1891), in *Writings of Charles S. Peirce: A Chronological Edition*, vol. 8: *1890–1892* (Bloomington, IN, 2010).

256. See Stephen Toulmin, "The Evolutionary Development of Natural Science," *American Scientist* 57 (1967): 456–471; id., *Human Understanding*, vol. 1 (Princeton, NJ, 1972); James A. Blachowitz, "Systems Theory and Evolutionary Models of the Development of Science," *Philosophy of Science* 38 (1971): 178–199; Donald T. Campbell, "Evolutionary Epistemology," in *The Philosophy of Karl Popper*, ed. Paul Arthur Schilpp (La Salle, IL, 1974), 1: 412–463; id., "Unjustified Variation and Selective Retention in Scientific Discovery," in *Studies in the Philosophy of Biology*, ed. Francisco Jose Ayala and Theodosius Dobzhansky (London, 1974), 133–161. For an overview, see also *Evolutionary Epistemology, Rationality, and the Sociology of Knowledge*, ed. Gerard Radnitzky and W. W. Bartlett (La Salle, IL, 1987).

257. For more detail, see Niklas Luhmann, *Die Wissenschaft der Gesellschaft* (Frankfurt, 1960), on evolution, 549–615.

258. An early discussion on reasons (taxonomic structure, hedonistic action concept) that could induce economics to reject evolution theory is to be found in Thorstein Veblen, "Why Is Economics Not an Evolutionary Science?" *Quarterly Journal of Economics* 13 (1898): 373–397. The real reason would have been that people still had enough confidence in the market's capacity for taking rational decisions.

259. See inter alia Armen A. Alchian, "Uncertainty, Evolution, and Economic Theory," *Journal of Political Economy* 58 (1950): 211–221, repr. in id., *Economic Forces at Work* (Indianapolis, IN, 1977), 15–35; also Edith T. Penrose, "Biological Analogies in the Theory of the Firm," *American Economic Review* 42 (1952):

804–819; Joseph Spengler, "Social Evolution and the Theory of Economic Development," in *Social Change in Developing Areas: A Reinterpretation of Evolutionary Theory*, ed. Herbert Barringer, George I. Blanksten, and Raymond W. Mack (Cambridge, MA, 1965), 243–272.

260. The largely dominant theoretical development seeks *instead* to manage by reducing rationality demands. See esp. Herbert A. Simon, *Models of Man, Social and Rational: Mathematical Essays on Rational Human Behavior in a Social Setting* (New York, 1957).

261. Richard Nelson and Sidney Winter have concerned themselves most intensively with this version of the theory. For a summary, see Nelson and Winter, *An Evolutionary Theory of Economic Change* (Cambridge, MA, 1982).

262. See the contributions to *Organizational Evolution: New Directions*, ed. Jitendra V. Singh (Newbury Park, CA, 1990). For developments in population ecology, see also Michael T. Hannan and John Freeman, *Organizational Ecology* (Cambridge, MA, 1989), and *Evolutionary Dynamics of Organizations*, ed. Joel Baum and Jitendra Singh (New York, 1994).

263. See, e.g., Clark and Juma, *Long-Run Economics*; *Explaining Process and Change: Approaches to Evolutionary Economics*, ed. Ulrich Witt (Ann Arbor, MI, 1992); Geoffrey M. Hodgson, *Economics and Evolution: Bringing Life Back into Economics* (Ann Arbor, MI, 1993); *Evolutionary Economics and Chaos Theory: New Directions in Technology Studies*, ed. Loet Leydesdorff and Peter van den Besselaar (London, 1994); *Evolutionary Concepts in Contemporary Economics*, ed. Richard W. England (Ann Arbor, MI, 1994); Giovanni Dosi and Richard R. Nelson, "An Introduction to Evolutionary Theories in Economics," *Journal of Evolutionary Economics* 4 (1994): 153–172.

264. On recourse to Lamarck, see *Revue internationale de systémique* 7, no. 5 (1993).

265. See Huntington Cairns's little-known *The Theory of Legal Science* (Chapel Hill, NC, 1941), esp. 29ff.; also Niklas Luhmann, "Evolution des Rechts," in id., *Ausdifferenzierung des Rechts* (Frankfurt, 1981), 11–34; Ernst-Joachim Lampe, *Genetische Rechtstheorie: Recht, Evolution und Geschichte* (Freiburg, 1987) (on the anthropological basis); Gunther Teubner, *Recht als autopoietisches System* (Frankfurt, 1989), 61ff. (with reference to recent literature, which, however, uses the evolution concept in very different ways).

266. The brief, stalled reconstruction of late-Marxist "Staatsableitungen" ("derivations of the state") in Philippe von Parijs, *Evolutionary Explanation in Social Science: An Emerging Paradigm* (London, 1981), 174ff., can at best serve as evidence for the typical grounds for theory development: the failure of more demanding preceding theories. See also, with close reference to the theory of society, Hannes Wimmer, *Evolution der Politik: Von der Stammesgesellschaft zur modernen Demokratie* (Vienna, 1996).

267. In chap. 2, § 5.

268. However, this example shows that we may not necessarily presuppose the separation of media codings as an evolution-proof achievement. Consider, above all, the effects of mass media, especially television, on the administration of justice by the courts. Like certain earlier cases (e.g., the Rodney King beating trial), the spectacular proceedings against O. J. Simpson lead one to think that their impact on American jury trial practice can hardly be overestimated.

269. See Robert C. Palmer, "The Origins of Property in England," *Law and History Review* 3 (1985): 1–50; id., "The Economic and Cultural Impact of the Origin of Property, 1180–1220," ibid., 375–396.

270. At least according to Klaus Disselbeck, "Die Ausdifferenzierung der Kunst als Problem der Ästhetik," in *Kommunikation und Differenz: Systemtheoretische Ansätze in der Literatur- und Kunstwissenschaft*, ed. Henk de Berg and Matthias Prangel (Opladen, 1993), 137–158. In other contexts, see also Niklas Luhmann, *Die Kunst der Gesellschaft* (Frankfurt, 1995), esp. 256ff.

271. See Michael Schudson, *Discovering the News: A Social History of American Newspapers* (New York, 1978).

272. See Rudolf Stichweh, *Der frühmoderne Staat und die europäische Universität: Zur Interaktion von Politik und Erziehungssystem im Prozeß ihrer Ausdifferenzierung (16.–18. Jahrhundert)* (Frankfurt, 1991).

273. See Berman, *Law and Revolution.*

274. See Luhmann, *Gesellschaft*, vol. 2, chap. 5, for comprehensive treatment of this topic.

275. See Norgaard, "Coevolution of Economic and Environmental Systems."

276. The theory of history has taken a particular interest in this demarcation. For a subjective, Neo-Kantian understanding of history, see Robin G. Collingwood, *The Idea of History* (Oxford, 1946); for an overview, see also Ingold, *Evolution and Social Life*, 74ff.

277. See esp. Heinz von Foerster, "Prinzipien der Selbstorganisation im sozialen und betriebswirtschaftlichen Bereich," in id., *Wissen und Gewissen: Versuch einer Brücke* (Frankfurt, 1993), 233–268 (247ff.).

278. See also Dirk Baecker, "Nichttriviale Transformation," *Soziale Systeme* 1 (1995): 100–117.

279. See Immanuel Wallerstein, *The Modern World-System: Capitalist Agriculture and the Origins of the European World-Economy in the Sixteenth Century* (New York, 1974).

280. See Max Weber, "Die protestantische Ethik und der 'Geist' des Kapitalismus," *Archiv für Sozialwissenschaft und Sozialpolitik* 20 (1904): 1–54, and 21 (1905), 1–110, to cite only the text that set off a vast discussion.

281. See, e.g., John A. Hall, *Powers and Liberties: The Causes and Consequences of the Rise of the West* (Berkeley, 1986); Michael Mann, *States, War and Capitalism: Studies in Political Sociology* (Oxford, 1988).

282. See Berman, *Law and Revolution.*

283. I am deliberately avoiding speaking of "interaction" [*Wechselwirkung*], because this would mix the two theoretical figures, and, what is more, compel abstraction from time.

284. See Palmer, "Origins of Property in England" and "Economic and Cultural Impact of the Origin of Property."

285. By no means all advanced civilizations developed this time distinction that was so important for Europe. It is also worth recalling that the Greek word *aiōn* originally meant something like "vitality"—see Enzo Degani, *AIΩN da Omero ad Aristotele* (Padua, 1961). In the Renaissance, this meaning surfaced once more. "Chi ha tempo ha vita," Giovanni Botero writes in *Della ragion di Stato* (1589; Bologna, 1930), 62; here, however, with reference to the necessity of gaining time for disposing wisely over the circumstances. Remaining identical in the succession of events and circumstances therefore does not necessarily have the religious connotation of *aeternitas*.

286. Consider the cosmological, by no means only moral, dimension of this first event, this first, history-making difference between before and after. This incidentally also explains—however incomprehensible it may be for the modern age, with its individual morality—why this original sin was perforce *inherited*, as expressed in the German term *Erbsünde* [*Erbe*, "inheritance" + *Sünde*, "sin"] (cf. Mark Twain's *Letters from the Earth*).

287. See Reinhart Koselleck, "Geschichte," in *Geschichtliche Grundbegriffe*, vol. 2 (Stuttgart, 1975), 593–717.

288. See, e.g., Georg Simmel, *Das individuelle Gesetz*, ed. Michael Landmann (Frankfurt, 1968).

289. The term "reenter" is used here in Spencer-Brown's sense in *Laws*, 56–57.

290. Ibid., 61.

291. On causality see, e.g., Francis Heylighen, "Causality as Distinction Conversation: A Theory of Predictability, Reversibility, and Time Order," *Cybernetics and Systems* 20 (1989): 361–384. I would also point out that Maxwell's demon, which reverses entropy into negentropy, has to have a memory, because it has to remember how it sorted when it continues to sort.

292. This criticism of storage theories also appears to have gained ground in neurobiological and psychological memory research. See the contributions in *Gedächtnis: Probleme und Perspektiven der interdisziplinären Gedächtnisforschung*, ed. Siegfried J. Schmidt (Frankfurt, 1991). In contrast, the social sciences and cultural studies appear to be upholding the storage concept despite Halbwachs [see n. 298 below]. See just Aleida Assmann and Jan Assmann, "Das Gestern im Heute: Medien und soziales Gedächtnis," in *Die Wirklichkeit der Medien: Eine Einführung in die Kommunikationswissenschaft*, ed. Klaus Merten et al. (Opladen, 1994), 114–140.

293. See Heinz Förster, *Das Gedächtnis: Eine quantenphysikalische Untersuchung* (Vienna, 1948). And see also Jonker, *Topography of Remembrance*, 36: "the collective picture of the past can take shape only through a collective forgetting."

Moreover, collective forgetting is even less explicable in terms of individual psychology than collective remembering.

294. See Bernard Ancori, "Temps historique et évolution économique," *Revue internationale de systémique* 7 (1993): 593–612 (602ff.).

295. See Heinz von Foerster, "Gegenstände: Greifbare Symbole für (Eigen-) Verhalten," in id., *Wissen und Gewissen: Versuch einer Brücke* (Frankfurt, 1993), 103–115.

296. See also Heinz von Foerster, "Was ist Gedächtnis, daß es Rückschau *und* Vorschau ermöglicht," in id., *Wissen und Gewissen*, 299–336.

297. Spencer-Brown, *Laws*, 60–61, deals with the "oscillator function" only with reference to the distinction of marked/unmarked in the context of second-order equations. For a semantic theory of memory, we must extend the concept of oscillation to every distinction used for observation, also to those between two marked items, such as nobility and people or castles and churches or cathedral churches and city churches. For their part, the two-sidedly marked distinctions presuppose an unmarked space, since observing is possible only in a world that always remains unmarked.

298. Famous for this is the distinction between individual memory and collective memory in Maurice Halbwachs, *Les cadres sociaux de la mémoire* (1925; 2nd ed., Paris, 1952), and id., *La mémoire collective* (Paris, 1950).

299. See, e.g., James Fentress and Chris Wickham, *Social Memory* (Oxford, 1992). There is naturally no denying that this also exists, but it should be kept in mind that, unlike Fentress and Wickham, I regard communication, not as transmission, but as a special type of autopoietic reproduction.

300. "Every sentence must already have a meaning; affirmation cannot provide it, for what it affirms is the meaning. And the same holds for negation, etc." (Ludwig Wittgenstein, *Tractatus logico-philosophicus* 4.064, in id., *Schriften*, vol. 1 [Frankfurt, 1969], 31).

301. In the sense of Michel Serres, *Genèse* (Paris, 1982), 146ff.—there in opposition to social contract topics requiring consensus.

302. See Mary Douglas, *How Institutions Think* (Syracuse, NY, 1986), 69ff.; Jan Assmann, "Lesende und nichtlesende Gesellschaften," *Almanach (des Deutschen Hochschulverbandes)* 7 (1994): 7–12. See also 162f. above.

303. For the present day, see also *Les lieux de mémoire*, ed. Pierre Nora, 3 vols., with subvolumes (Paris, 1984).

304. For early Mesopotamia, see Jonker, *Topography of Remembrance*.

305. Ibid., 95ff.

306. The historical analysis of memory now also operates with this concept. See esp. Jan Assmann, *Das kulturelle Gedächtnis: Schrift, Erinnerung und politische Identität in frühen Hochkulturen* (Munich, 1992).

307. This has already been dealt with in § 10 of this chapter, on the evolution of ideas, pointing to writing as a condition of this separation.

308. More detail in Niklas Luhmann, "Kultur als historischer Begriff," in id., *Gesellschaftsstruktur*, 4: 31–54.

309. Exceptions must be conceded for the seventeenth century. Vol. 4 of the *Historisches Wörterbuch der Philosophie* (Basel, 1976), s.v. *Kultur*, cols. 1309 –10, mentions Pufendorf. Another example is Baltasar Gracián, *El discreto* (1646; Buenos Aires, 1960), XVIII, "De la cultura y aliño," 56ff.

310. Parsons's proposal to take account of culture as a constitutive condition of action relates to the *concept* of action and serves in the elaboration of a theory that from a methodological point of view makes only analytical claims.

311. See in the first place Pierre Bourdieu and Jean-Claude Passeron, *La reproduction: Eléments pour une théorie du système d'enseignement* (Paris, 1970). The ensuing American discussion has unfortunately been concerned almost only with institutional correlates. See, e.g., Paul DiMaggio, "Social Structure, Institutions and Cultural Goods: The Case of the United States," in *Social Theory for a Changing Society*, ed. Pierre Bourdieu and James S. Coleman (Boulder, CO,1991), 133–155.

312. See Jonker, *Topography of Remembrance*, 105 and passim.

313. Accordingly, the memory theory was to a large extent a revival of antique thought; it thus reminded itself of the once well-known technique of remembering. See Frances A. Yates, *The Art of Memory* (Chicago, 1966).

314. See Patrick H. Hutton, "The Art of Memory Reconceived: From Rhetoric to Psychoanalysis," *Journal of the History of Ideas* 48 (1987): 371–392.

315. This formulation in Matei Călinescu, "From the One to the Many: Pluralism in Today's Thought," in *Zeitgeist in Babel: The Postmodernist Controversy*, ed. Ingeborg Hoesterey (Bloomington, IN, 1991), 156–174 (157).

316. See Niklas Luhmann, "Was ist der Fall, was steckt dahinter? Die zwei Soziologien und die Gesellschaftstheorie," *Zeitschrift für Soziologie* 22 (1993): 245–260.

317. Cf. Mannheim, *Konservatismus*. Asmann and Assmann, "Das Gestern im Heute," 117, also suggests replacing the concept of tradition by the (analytically more flexible) concept of social memory.

318. "Similarity is an institution," Douglas even says in *How Institutions Think*, 55.

319. See, e.g., Dirk Baecker, "Das Gedächtnis der Wirtschaft," in *Theorie als Passion*, ed. id. (Frankfurt, 1987), 519–546; Niklas Luhmann, "Das Gedächtnis der Politik," *Zeitschrift für Politik* 42 (1995): 109–121; id., "Zeit und Gedächtnis" (MS, 1995).

320. See Luhmann, *Gesellschaft*, vol. 2, chap. 5, 9–10.

321. See Jean-François Lyotard's well-known book *La condition postmoderne: Rapport sur le savoir* (Paris, 1979), which has been much discussed.

322. Notably St. Augustine, but only for the *distant* time horizon that in the past as in the future disappears *in occulto*. See Augustine, *Confessions* 11.17–22, where the "being" of nonactual time horizons leads back with remaining doubts to the circumstance that "ex aliquo procedit occulto, cum ex futuro fit praesens,

et in aliquod recedit occultum, cum ex praesenti fit praeteritum [. . . but such as proceeds out of some unknown secret, when out of the future, the present is made, and returns into some secret again, when the past is made out of the present]" (*Saint Augustine's Confessions*, trans. William Watts, Loeb Classical Library [London, 1912], 247), where (implicitly) the hidden status of the origin and disappearance of time (*tempus*) could be seen as a sort of wild card of eternity in time.

323. See Philip G. Herbst, *Alternatives to Hierarchies* (Leiden, 1976), 88.

324. On this lapse of the premises of classical European metaphysics, see further Luhmann, *Gesellschaft*, vol. 2, chap. 5, 4–8.

Index

This index is based on the index to the original German edition, *Die Gesellschaft der Gesellschaft. Band 1* (Frankfurt am Main: Suhrkamp Verlag, 1997).

Cultural Memory in the Present

Alessia Ricciardi, *After* La Dolce Vita*: A Cultural Prehistory of Berlusconi's Italy*

Daniel Innerarity, *The Future and Its Enemies: In Defense of Political Hope*

Patricia Pisters, *The Neuro-Image: A Deleuzian Film-Philosophy of Digital Screen Culture*

François-David Sebbah, *Testing the Limit: Derrida, Henry, Levinas, and the Phenomenological Tradition*

Erik Peterson, *Theological Tractates*, edited by Michael J. Hollerich

Feisal G. Mohamed, *Milton and the Post-Secular Present: Ethics, Politics, Terrorism*

Pierre Hadot, *The Present Alone Is Our Happiness, Second Edition: Conversations with Jeannie Carlier and Arnold I. Davidson*

Yasco Horsman, *Theaters of Justice: Judging, Staging, and Working Through in Arendt, Brecht, and Delbo*

Jacques Derrida, *Parages*, edited by John P. Leavey

Henri Atlan, *The Sparks of Randomness, Volume 1: Spermatic Knowledge*

Rebecca Comay, *Mourning Sickness: Hegel and the French Revolution*

Djelal Kadir, *Memos from the Besieged City: Lifelines for Cultural Sustainability*

Stanley Cavell, *Little Did I Know: Excerpts from Memory*

Jeffrey Mehlman, *Adventures in the French Trade: Fragments Toward a Life*

Jacob Rogozinski, *The Ego and the Flesh: An Introduction to Egoanalysis*

Marcel Hénaff, *The Price of Truth: Gift, Money, and Philosophy*

Paul Patton, *Deleuzian Concepts: Philosophy, Colonialization, Politics*

Michael Fagenblat, *A Covenant of Creatures: Levinas's Philosophy of Judaism*

Stefanos Geroulanos, *An Atheism that Is Not Humanist Emerges in French Thought*

Andrew Herscher, *Violence Taking Place: The Architecture of the Kosovo Conflict*

Hans-Jörg Rheinberger, *On Historicizing Epistemology: An Essay*

Jacob Taubes, *From Cult to Culture*, edited by Charlotte Fonrobert and Amir Engel

Peter Hitchcock, *The Long Space: Transnationalism and Postcolonial Form*

Lambert Wiesing, *Artificial Presence: Philosophical Studies in Image Theory*

Jacob Taubes, *Occidental Eschatology*

Freddie Rokem, *Philosophers and Thespians: Thinking Performance*

Roberto Esposito, *Communitas: The Origin and Destiny of Community*

Vilashini Cooppan, *Worlds Within: National Narratives and Global Connections in Postcolonial Writing*

Josef Früchtl, *The Impertinent Self: A Heroic History of Modernity*

Frank Ankersmit, Ewa Domanska, and Hans Kellner, eds., *Re-Figuring Hayden White*

Michael Rothberg, *Multidirectional Memory: Remembering the Holocaust in the Age of Decolonization*

Jean-François Lyotard, *Enthusiasm: The Kantian Critique of History*

Ernst van Alphen, Mieke Bal, and Carel Smith, eds., *The Rhetoric of Sincerity*

Stéphane Mosès, *The Angel of History: Rosenzweig, Benjamin, Scholem*

Pierre Hadot, *The Present Alone Is Our Happiness: Conversations with Jeannie Carlier and Arnold I. Davidson*

Alexandre Lefebvre, *The Image of the Law: Deleuze, Bergson, Spinoza*

Samira Haj, *Reconfiguring Islamic Tradition: Reform, Rationality, and Modernity*

Diane Perpich, *The Ethics of Emmanuel Levinas*

Marcel Detienne, *Comparing the Incomparable*

François Delaporte, *Anatomy of the Passions*

René Girard, *Mimesis and Theory: Essays on Literature and Criticism, 1959–2005*

Richard Baxstrom, *Houses in Motion: The Experience of Place and the Problem of Belief in Urban Malaysia*

Jennifer L. Culbert, *Dead Certainty: The Death Penalty and the Problem of Judgment*

Samantha Frost, *Lessons from a Materialist Thinker: Hobbesian Reflections on Ethics and Politics*

Regina Mara Schwartz, *Sacramental Poetics at the Dawn of Secularism: When God Left the World*

Gil Anidjar, *Semites: Race, Religion, Literature*

Ranjana Khanna, *Algeria Cuts: Women and Representation, 1830 to the Present*

Esther Peeren, *Intersubjectivities and Popular Culture: Bakhtin and Beyond*

Eyal Peretz, *Becoming Visionary: Brian De Palma's Cinematic Education of the Senses*

Diana Sorensen, *A Turbulent Decade Remembered: Scenes from the Latin American Sixties*

Hubert Damisch, *A Childhood Memory by Piero della Francesca*

José van Dijck, *Mediated Memories in the Digital Age*

Dana Hollander, *Exemplarity and Chosenness: Rosenzweig and Derrida on the Nation of Philosophy*

Asja Szafraniec, *Beckett, Derrida, and the Event of Literature*

Sara Guyer, *Romanticism After Auschwitz*

Alison Ross, *The Aesthetic Paths of Philosophy: Presentation in Kant, Heidegger, Lacoue-Labarthe, and Nancy*

Gerhard Richter, *Thought-Images: Frankfurt School Writers' Reflections from Damaged Life*

Bella Brodzki, *Can These Bones Live? Translation, Survival, and Cultural Memory*

Rodolphe Gasché, *The Honor of Thinking: Critique, Theory, Philosophy*

Brigitte Peucker, *The Material Image: Art and the Real in Film*

Natalie Melas, *All the Difference in the World: Postcoloniality and the Ends of Comparison*

Jonathan Culler, *The Literary in Theory*

Michael G. Levine, *The Belated Witness: Literature, Testimony, and the Question of Holocaust Survival*

Jennifer A. Jordan, *Structures of Memory: Understanding German Change in Berlin and Beyond*

Christoph Menke, *Reflections of Equality*

Marlène Zarader, *The Unthought Debt: Heidegger and the Hebraic Heritage*

Jan Assmann, *Religion and Cultural Memory: Ten Studies*

David Scott and Charles Hirschkind, *Powers of the Secular Modern: Talal Asad and His Interlocutors*

Gyanendra Pandey, *Routine Violence: Nations, Fragments, Histories*

James Siegel, *Naming the Witch*

J. M. Bernstein, *Against Voluptuous Bodies: Late Modernism and the Meaning of Painting*

Theodore W. Jennings, Jr., *Reading Derrida / Thinking Paul: On Justice*

Richard Rorty and Eduardo Mendieta, *Take Care of Freedom and Truth Will Take Care of Itself: Interviews with Richard Rorty*

Jacques Derrida, *Paper Machine*

Renaud Barbaras, *Desire and Distance: Introduction to a Phenomenology of Perception*

Jill Bennett, *Empathic Vision: Affect, Trauma, and Contemporary Art*

Ban Wang, *Illuminations from the Past: Trauma, Memory, and History in Modern China*

James Phillips, *Heidegger's* Volk*: Between National Socialism and Poetry*

Frank Ankersmit, *Sublime Historical Experience*

István Rév, *Retroactive Justice: Prehistory of Post-Communism*

Paola Marrati, *Genesis and Trace: Derrida Reading Husserl and Heidegger*

Krzysztof Ziarek, *The Force of Art*

Marie-José Mondzain, *Image, Icon, Economy: The Byzantine Origins of the Contemporary Imaginary*

Cecilia Sjöholm, *The Antigone Complex: Ethics and the Invention of Feminine Desire*

Jacques Derrida and Elisabeth Roudinesco, *For What Tomorrow . . . : A Dialogue*

Elisabeth Weber, *Questioning Judaism: Interviews by Elisabeth Weber*

Jacques Derrida and Catherine Malabou, *Counterpath: Traveling with Jacques Derrida*

Martin Seel, *Aesthetics of Appearing*

Nanette Salomon, *Shifting Priorities: Gender and Genre in Seventeenth-Century Dutch Painting*

Jacob Taubes, *The Political Theology of Paul*

Jean-Luc Marion, *The Crossing of the Visible*

Eric Michaud, *The Cult of Art in Nazi Germany*

Anne Freadman, *The Machinery of Talk: Charles Peirce and the Sign Hypothesis*

Stanley Cavell, *Emerson's Transcendental Etudes*

Stuart McLean, *The Event and Its Terrors: Ireland, Famine, Modernity*

Beate Rössler, ed., *Privacies: Philosophical Evaluations*

Bernard Faure, *Double Exposure: Cutting Across Buddhist and Western Discourses*

Alessia Ricciardi, *The Ends of Mourning: Psychoanalysis, Literature, Film*

Alain Badiou, *Saint Paul: The Foundation of Universalism*

Gil Anidjar, *The Jew, the Arab: A History of the Enemy*

Jonathan Culler and Kevin Lamb, eds., *Just Being Difficult? Academic Writing in the Public Arena*

Jean-Luc Nancy, *A Finite Thinking*, edited by Simon Sparks

Theodor W. Adorno, *Can One Live after Auschwitz? A Philosophical Reader*, edited by Rolf Tiedemann

Patricia Pisters, *The Matrix of Visual Culture: Working with Deleuze in Film Theory*

Andreas Huyssen, *Present Pasts: Urban Palimpsests and the Politics of Memory*

Talal Asad, *Formations of the Secular: Christianity, Islam, Modernity*

Dorothea von Mücke, *The Rise of the Fantastic Tale*

Marc Redfield, *The Politics of Aesthetics: Nationalism, Gender, Romanticism*

Emmanuel Levinas, *On Escape*

Dan Zahavi, *Husserl's Phenomenology*

Rodolphe Gasché, *The Idea of Form: Rethinking Kant's Aesthetics*

Michael Naas, *Taking on the Tradition: Jacques Derrida and the Legacies of Deconstruction*

Herlinde Pauer-Studer, ed., *Constructions of Practical Reason: Interviews on Moral and Political Philosophy*

Jean-Luc Marion, *Being Given That: Toward a Phenomenology of Givenness*

Theodor W. Adorno and Max Horkheimer, *Dialectic of Enlightenment*

Ian Balfour, *The Rhetoric of Romantic Prophecy*

Martin Stokhof, *World and Life as One: Ethics and Ontology in Wittgenstein's Early Thought*

Gianni Vattimo, *Nietzsche: An Introduction*

Jacques Derrida, *Negotiations: Interventions and Interviews, 1971-1998*, ed. Elizabeth Rottenberg

Brett Levinson, *The Ends of Literature: The Latin American "Boom" in the Neoliberal Marketplace*

Timothy J. Reiss, *Against Autonomy: Cultural Instruments, Mutualities, and the Fictive Imagination*

Hent de Vries and Samuel Weber, eds., *Religion and Media*

Niklas Luhmann, *Theories of Distinction: Re-Describing the Descriptions of Modernity*, ed. and introd. William Rasch

Johannes Fabian, *Anthropology with an Attitude: Critical Essays*

Michel Henry, *I Am the Truth: Toward a Philosophy of Christianity*

Gil Anidjar, *"Our Place in Al-Andalus": Kabbalah, Philosophy, Literature in Arab-Jewish Letters*

Hélène Cixous and Jacques Derrida, *Veils*

F. R. Ankersmit, *Historical Representation*

F. R. Ankersmit, *Political Representation*

Elissa Marder, *Dead Time: Temporal Disorders in the Wake of Modernity (Baudelaire and Flaubert)*

Reinhart Koselleck, *The Practice of Conceptual History: Timing History, Spacing Concepts*

Niklas Luhmann, *The Reality of the Mass Media*

Hubert Damisch, *A Theory of /Cloud/: Toward a History of Painting*

Jean-Luc Nancy, *The Speculative Remark: (One of Hegel's bon mots)*

Jean-François Lyotard, *Soundproof Room: Malraux's Anti-Aesthetics*

Jan Pato ka, *Plato and Europe*

Hubert Damisch, *Skyline: The Narcissistic City*

Isabel Hoving, *In Praise of New Travelers: Reading Caribbean Migrant Women Writers*

Richard Rand, ed., *Futures: Of Jacques Derrida*

William Rasch, *Niklas Luhmann's Modernity: The Paradoxes of Differentiation*

Jacques Derrida and Anne Dufourmantelle, *Of Hospitality*

Jean-François Lyotard, *The Confession of Augustine*

Kaja Silverman, *World Spectators*

Samuel Weber, *Institution and Interpretation: Expanded Edition*

Jeffrey S. Librett, *The Rhetoric of Cultural Dialogue: Jews and Germans in the Epoch of Emancipation*

Ulrich Baer, *Remnants of Song: Trauma and the Experience of Modernity in Charles Baudelaire and Paul Celan*

Samuel C. Wheeler III, *Deconstruction as Analytic Philosophy*

David S. Ferris, *Silent Urns: Romanticism, Hellenism, Modernity*

Rodolphe Gasché, *Of Minimal Things: Studies on the Notion of Relation*

Sarah Winter, *Freud and the Institution of Psychoanalytic Knowledge*

Samuel Weber, *The Legend of Freud: Expanded Edition*

Aris Fioretos, ed., *The Solid Letter: Readings of Friedrich Hölderlin*

J. Hillis Miller / Manuel Asensi, *Black Holes / J. Hillis Miller; or, Boustrophedonic Reading*

Miryam Sas, *Fault Lines: Cultural Memory and Japanese Surrealism*

Peter Schwenger, *Fantasm and Fiction: On Textual Envisioning*

Didier Maleuvre, *Museum Memories: History, Technology, Art*

Jacques Derrida, *Monolingualism of the Other; or, The Prosthesis of Origin*

Andrew Baruch Wachtel, *Making a Nation, Breaking a Nation: Literature and Cultural Politics in Yugoslavia*

Niklas Luhmann, *Love as Passion: The Codification of Intimacy*

Mieke Bal, ed., *The Practice of Cultural Analysis: Exposing Interdisciplinary Interpretation*

Jacques Derrida and Gianni Vattimo, eds., *Religion*